THE

CENTENARY EDITION

OF THE WORKS OF

NATHANIEL HAWTHORNE

Volume XIII

THE ELIXIR OF LIFE
MANUSCRIPTS

EDITORS

General Editors

WILLIAM CHARVAT, 1905-1966

ROY HARVEY PEARCE

CLAUDE M. SIMPSON, 1910-1976

FREDSON BOWERS, *General Textual Editor*

L. NEAL SMITH, *Associate Textual Editor*

JAMES RUBINO, *Assistant Textual Editor*

This volume edited by

EDWARD H. DAVIDSON

CLAUDE M. SIMPSON

L. NEAL SMITH

A PUBLICATION OF
THE OHIO STATE UNIVERSITY CENTER
FOR TEXTUAL STUDIES

NATHANIEL HAWTHORNE

THE ELIXIR OF LIFE MANUSCRIPTS

Septimius Felton
Septimius Norton
The Dolliver Romance

Ohio State University Press

*Editorial expenses for this volume have been supported by
grants from the National Endowment for the Humanities
administered through the
Center for Editions of American Authors of the
Modern Language Association*

*International Standard Book Number 0-8142-0252-7
Library of Congress Catalogue Number 77-00000*

ACKNOWLEDGMENTS

THE EDITORS are grateful for the assistance given by librarians, scholars, and bibliophiles. We are indebted to Jonathan Culler, Selwyn College, Cambridge University; Herbert T. F. Cahoon, the Pierpont Morgan Library; Jeanne Eason, Columbus, Ohio; Elizabeth C. Simpson, Pasadena, California; Lola L. Szladits, the Berg Collection, New York Public Library; and Paul M. Zall, California State University, Los Angeles.

Special acknowledgment is made to James Rubino for his editorial assistance, and our thanks go to Marianne Bailey, Joyce Heter, and Craig Quellhorst for their work also at Ohio State University, and to Carol Hector-Harris.

For permission to edit the manuscript material of *The American Claimant Manuscripts*, we thank the Pierpont Morgan Library, the Henry E. Huntington Library, the Henry W. and Albert A. Berg Collection of the New York Public Library, Astor, Lenox, and Tilden Foundation, the University of California, Berkeley, the Concord Massachusetts Free Public Library, and Mrs. John Gordan, New York City.

We gratefully acknowledge the support of the National Endowment for the Humanities of the National Foundation

• vii •

on the Arts and Humanities, the Henry E. Huntington Library, the Graduate School of the University of Illinois, Urbana, and the following divisions of the Ohio State University: the Department of English, the Graduate School, the University Libraries, and the Research Foundation.

THE EDITORS

CONTENTS

Prefatory Note

Septimius Felton

Septimius Norton

The Dolliver Romance

Ancillary Documents

Editorial Appendixes

  Historical Commentary

  Textual Commentary

  Editorial Emendations in the Copy-Text

  Rejected First-Edition Substantive Variants

  Word-Division

  Alterations in the Manuscripts

  Compositorial Stints in *The Dolliver Romance*,
    Chapter I

THE
ELIXIR OF LIFE
MANUSCRIPTS

At his death in 1864 Hawthorne left unfinished not only the works reproduced as "The American Claimant Manuscripts" in volume XII of the Centenary Edition, but also three pieces of fiction developing the theme of immortality. Along with detached memoranda, a Scenario, and draft fragments relating to these works, they make up the content of volume XIII. In 1872 Una Hawthorne published the first draft of the Septimius story as "Septimus: A Romance" in England and "Septimius Felton" in America. A second draft has remained unpublished until now except for extracts that Julian Hawthorne printed in a series of 1890 "Lippincott" articles. The Centenary editors have chosen to identify the two drafts as "Septimius Felton" and "Septimius Norton" to distinguish their untitled manuscript forms from previously printed texts. Hawthorne's last unfinished work, "The Dolliver Romance," derives its title from the form of his reference to it in letters. Although the first chapter of "Dolliver" was prepared for the printer, the other documents reflect varying degrees of revision and polish, including asides to himself on contemplated changes, here printed in the texts within angle brackets, as well as signals for transpositions that the editors have carried out wherever possible. A historical commentary following the texts discusses the stages in Hawthorne's preoccupation with the Elixir of Life theme, and the posthumuous treatment of the several documents here reproduced.

SEPTIMIUS FELTON

I T WAS A DAY in early Spring; and as that sweet genial time of year and atmosphere calls out tender greenness from the ground, beautiful flowers, or leaves that look beautiful because so long unseen under the snow and decay, so the pleasant air and warmth had called out three young people, who sat on a sunny hill side, enjoying the warm day and one another. For they were all friends; two of them young men and playmates from boyhood; the third a girl, who, two or three years younger than themselves, had been the object of their boy love, their little rustic, childish gallantries, their budding affections; until, growing all towards manhood and womanhood, they had ceased to talk about such matters, perhaps thinking about them the more.

<Septimius must have a weird, half supernatural genealogy, in which the devil is mixed up.>

<Septimius has a gun in the house.>

These three young people were neighboring children, dwelling in houses that stood by the side of the great Lexington road, along a ridge that rose abrupt behind them, its brow covered with wood; and which stretched, with one or two breaks and interruptions, into the heart of the village of Concord, the county town. It was in the side of this hill, that, according to tradition, the first settlers of the village had burrowed in caverns, which they had dug out for their shelter, like swallows, woodchucks; as the slope of the hill was towards the south, and its ridge and crowning woods defended them from the fierce northern blasts and snowdrifts, it was an admirable exposure for the fierce New-England winter; and the temperature was milder by several degrees along this hillside, than on the unprotected plains, or by the river side, or in any other part of Concord; so that here, during the hundred years that had elapsed since the first settlement of the place, dwellings had successively risen, close to the hill's foot, and the meadow that intervened on the other side of the road, a fertile tract, had been cultivated; and these three young people were the children's children's children of persons of respectability who had dwelt there. Rose Garfield in a small house, the site of which is still pointed out by the cavity of a cellar, in which I, this very past summer, planted some sunflowers, to thrust their great discs out from the hollow, and allure the bee and the hummingbird; Robert Hobkinson in a house of somewhat more pretension, a hundred yards or so nearer to the village, standing back from the road in the broader space which the retreating hill cloven by a gap in that place afforded, where some elms intervened between it and the road, offering a site which some person of natural taste for the gently picturesque had seized upon. Those same elms, or their successors, still fling a noble shade over the same old house, which the magic hand of Alcott has improved by the touch with which he throws grace, amiableness, natural beauty over scenes that have little pretension in themselves.

Now, the other young man, Septimius Felton, dwelt in a small wooden house, then, I suppose, of some score of years standing; a two-story, gabled house, but with only two rooms on a floor, crowded upon by the hill, which rose abrupt behind; a house of thick walls, as if the projector had that sturdy feeling of permanence in life which incites people to make strong their earthly habitations, as if deluding themselves with the idea that they could still inhabit them; in short, an ordinary dwelling of a well-to-do New England farmer, such as his race had been for two or three generations past, although there were traditions of ancestors who had led lives of thought and study, and had all the erudition that the old Universities of England could bestow. Whether any natural turn for study had descended to Septimius from these worthies, or how his tendencies came to be different from those of his family, who, within the memory of their neighborhood had been content to sow and reap the rich fields in front of their homestead, so it was that Septimius had early manifested a taste for study. By the kind aid of the good minister of the town, he had been fitted for college, had passed through Cambridge, by aid of what little money his father had left him and by his own exertion in school-keeping, and was now a recently decorated baccalaureate with, as was understood, a purpose to devote himself to the ministry under the auspices of that reverend and good friend whose support and instruction had already stood him in such stead.

Now here were these young people, on that beautiful Spring morning, sitting on the hill side, a pleasant spectacle of youth; pleasant as if they had sprouted out, like green things, under the influence of that warm sun. The girl was very pretty, a little freckled, a little tanned, but with a face that glimmered and gleamed with quick and cheerful expressions, a slender form, not very large, with a quick grace in its movements; sunny hair, that had a tendency to curl which she probably favored in such moments as her household occupations left her; a sociable and pleasant child, as both of the young men evidently thought. Robert Hagburn, one would suppose, would have been the most to her taste;

a ruddy, hardy young fellow, handsome, and free of manner, six feet high, famous through the neighborhood for strength and athletic skill, the young promise of what was to be a man fit for all offices of active rural life, and to be, in mature age, the selectman, the deacon, the representative, the colonel. As for Septimius, let him alone a moment or two, and then you would see him, with his head bent down, brooding, brooding, with his eyes fixed on some chip, some stone, some common plant, any commonest thing, as if it were the clue and index to some mystery; and when, by chance startled out of these meditations, he lifted his eyes, there would be a kind of perplexity, a dissatisfied, wild look in them, as if, of his speculations, he found no end. Such was now the case, while Robert and the girl were running on with a gay talk, about a serious subject, so that gay as it was their talk was interspersed with little thrills of fear on the girl's part, of excitement on Robert's. Their talk was of public trouble.

"My grandfather says," said Rose Garfield, "that we shall never be able to stand against old England, because the men are a weaker men than he remembers in his day—weaker than his father who came from old England; and their women slighter still; so that we are dwindling away, grandfather thinks; only, a little sprightlier, he says, sometimes, looking at me."

"Slighter; to be sure," cried Robert Garfield; "there is the lightness of two English women compressed into little space. I have seen them and know. And as to the men, Rose, if they have lost one spark of courage and strength that the old English forefathers brought from the old land—lost any one good quality, without having made it up by as good or better— then, for my part, I don't want the breed to exist any longer. And this war, that they say is coming on, will be a good opportunity to test the matter. Don't you think so, Septimius?"

· 6 ·

"Think what?" asked Septimius, gravely, lifting up his head. "Think! Why, that your countrymen are worthy to live!" said Robert Hagburn impatiently. "For there is a question on that point."

"It is hardly worth answering or considering," said Septimius, looking at him thoughtfully. "We live so little while, that (always setting aside the effect on a future existence) it is little matter whether we live or no."

"Little matter!" said Rose, at first bewildered; then laughing. "Little matter; when it is such a comfort to live, so pleasant, so sweet."

"Yes; and so many things to do," said Robert Hagburn, "to make fields give produce, to be busy among men, and happy among the women-folk; to play, work, fight, be active in many things."

"Yes; but so soon stilled, before your activity has come to any definite end," responded Septimius, gloomily. "I doubt, if it had been left to my choice, whether I should have taken existence on such terms; so much trouble of preparation to live, and then no life at all; a ponderous beginning, and nothing more."

"Do you find fault with Providence, Septimius?" asked Rose, a feeling of solemnity coming over her cheerful and buoyant nature; then she burst out a laughing—"How grave he looks, Robert;—as if he had lived two or three lives already, and so knew all about the worth of it. But I think it was worth while to be born, if only for the sake of one such pleasant spring morning as this; and God gives us many, and better things when these are past."

"We hope so," said Septimius, who was again looking on the ground. "But who knows?"

"I thought you knew," said Robert Garfield. "You have been to college, and have learned, no doubt, a great many things. You are a student of theology, too, and have looked into these matters. Who should know, if not you?"

"Rose and you have just as good means of ascertaining these points as I," said Septimius. "All the certainty that can be had lies on the surface, as it should, and equally accessible to every man or woman. If we try to grope deeper, we labor for nought, and get less wise while we try to be more so. If life were long enough to enable us to thoroughly sift these matters, then indeed!—But it is so short!"

"Always this same complaint," said Robert. "Septimius, how long do you want to live?"

"Forever," said Septimius. "It is none too long for all I wish to know."

"Forever!" said Rose, and shivering doubtfully; "Ah, there would come many, many thoughts; and after a while we should want a little rest."

"Forever," said Robert Garfield. "And what would the people do, who want to fill our places? You are unfair, Septimius. Live, and let live! Turn about! Give me my seventy years, and let me go—my seventy years of what this life has, toil, enjoyment, suffering, struggle, fight, rest,—only let me have my share of what's going, and I shall be content."

"Content with leaving everything at odd ends; content with being nothing as you were before!"

"No, Septimius—content with Heaven at last!" said Rose, who had come out of her laughing mood into a sweet seriousness. "Oh, dear, think what an iron and ugly thing one of these sweet little blades of grass would seem, if it were not to fade and wither in its time, after being green in its time!"

"Well, well, my pretty Rose," said Septimius, assenting; "an immortal weed is not very lovely to think of, that is true; but I should be content with one thing, and that is yourself, if you were immortal just as you are, at seventeen, so fresh, so dewy, so red-lipped, so golden haired, so gay, so frolicksome, so gentle."

"And I am to grow old, and to be brown and wrinkled, gray haired, ugly," said Rose, rather sadly as she thus enumerated the items of her decay, "and then you would think me all lost and gone. But still there might be youth underneath, for one that really loved me to see. Ah, Septimius Felton, such love as would see with ever new eyes is the true love."

And she ran away and left him suddenly, and Robert Hagburn departing at the same time, this little knot of three was dissolved; and Septimius went along the wayside path, thoughtfully, as was his wont, to his own dwelling.

He had stopt for some moments on the threshold, vaguely enjoying, it is probable, the light and warmth of the new spring day, and the sweet air, which was somewhat unwonted to the young man, because he was accustomed to spend much of his day in thought and study within doors, and, indeed, like most studious young men, was over fond of the fireside, and of making life as artificial as he could, by fireside heat and lamp light, in order to suit it to the artificial intellectual and moral atmosphere which he derived from books, instead of living healthfully in the open air and among his fellow beings. Still he felt the pleasure of being warmed through by this natural heat, and, though blinking a little by its superfluity, could not but confess a pleasure and cheerfulness in this flood of morning light that came aslant along the hill side. While he thus stood, he felt a friendly hand laid upon his shoulder, and looking up, there was the minister of the village, an old friend of Septimius, to whose advice and aid it was owing, that Septimius had followed his instincts by going to college, instead of spending a thwarted and dissatisfied life in the field that fronted the house. He was a man of middle age, or little beyond, of a sagacious, kindly aspect; the experience, the life-time of intimate acquaintance with many concerns of his people being more apparent in him, than the scholarship for which he had early been distinguished; a tanned man, like one who labored in his own grounds, occasionally; a man of homely, plain address, which when occasion called for it, he could readily exchange for the polished manner of one who had seen a more refined world than this about him.

"Well, Septimius," said the Minister kindly, "have you yet come to any conclusion about the subject of which we have been talking?"

"Only so far, Sir," replied Septimius, "that I find myself every day less inclined to take up the profession which I have had in view so many years. I do not think myself fit for the sacred desk."

"Surely not; no one is," replied the clergyman; "but, if I may trust my own judgment, you have at least many of the intellectual qualifications that should adapt you to it. There is something of the Puritan character in you, Septimius, derived from holy men among your ancestors; as for instance a deep brooding turn, such as befits that heavy brow; a disposition to meditate on things hidden; a turn for meditative inquiry;—all these things, with grace to boot, mark you as the germ of a man who might do God service. Your reputation as a scholar stands high at college. You have not a turn for worldly business."

"Ah, but, Sir," said Septimius, casting down his heavy brow, "I lack something within."

"Faith, perhaps," replied the minister; "at least, you think so."

"Cannot I know it?" said Septimius.

"Scarcely, just now," said his friend. "Study for the ministry; bind your thoughts to it; pray; act a belief, and you will soon find you have it. Doubts may occasionally peep in;—

it is so with every clergyman. But your prevailing mood will be faith."

"It has seemed to me," observed Septimius, "that it is not the prevailing mood, the most common one, that is to be trusted; this is habit, formality, the shallow covering which we draw over what is real, and seldom suffer it to be blown aside. But it is the snake-like doubt that thrusts out its head, that gives us a glimpse of reality. Surely such moments are a hundred times as real as the dull quiet moments of faith—or what you call such."

"I am sorry for you," said the Minister; "yet to a youth of your frame of character—of your ability, I will say, and your requisition for something profound in the grounds of your belief, it is not unusual to meet this trouble. Men like you have to fight for their faith—they fight, in the first place, to win it, and forever afterwards to hold it. The devil tilts with them daily, and often seems to win."

"Yes; but," replied Septimius, "he takes deadly weapons now. If he met me with the cold, pure steel of a spiritual argument, I might win or lose, and still not feel that all was lost; but he takes, as it were, a great clod of earth, mingled rocks and mud, soil, dirt, and flings it at me overwhelmingly; so that I am buried under it."

"How is that?" said the minister. "Tell me more plainly."

"May it not be possible," asked Septimius, "to have too profound a sense of the marvellous contrivance and adaptation of this material world, to require or believe in anything spiritual? How wonderful it is, to see it all alive on this spring day, all growing, gushing! Do we exhaust it in our little life? Not so; not in a hundred or thousand lives. The whole race of man, living from the beginning of time, have not, in all their number and multiplicity and in all their duration, come in the least to know the world they live in! And how is this rich world thrown away upon us, because we live in it such a moment. What mortal work has ever been done since the world began! Because we have no time. No lesson is taught. We are snatched away from our study, before we have learned the alphabet. As the world now exists—I confess it to you frankly, my dear pastor and instructor—it seems to me all a failure, because we do not live long enough."

"But the lesson is carried on in another state of being!"

"Not the lesson that we begin here," said Septimius. "We might as well train a child in an American forest, to teach how to live in a European court. No, the fall of man, which Scripture tells us of, seems to me to have its operation in this grievous shortening of earthly life; so that our life here at all is grown ridiculous."

"Well, Septimius," said the minister, sadly—yet not as one shocked by what he had never seen before—"I must leave you to struggle through this form of unbelief as best you may, knowing that it is by your own efforts that you must come to the other side of the slough. We will talk further, another time. You are getting morbid, my young friend, with much study, and anxiety. It were well for you to live more, for the present, in this earthly life that you prize so highly. Can not you interest yourself in the state of the country—in this coming strife, the voice of which now sounds so hoarsely and so near us? Come out of your thoughts, and breathe another air."

"I will try," said Septimius.

"Do," said the minister, extending his hand to him; "and in a little time, you will find the change."

He shook the young man's hand, kindly, and took his leave; while Septimius entered his house, and turning to the right hand, sat down in his study, where before the fireplace stood the table with books, and papers; on shelves, around the low-studded walls, were more books, few in number, but of an erudite appearance, many of them having descended to him from learned ancestors, and having been brought to light by himself, after long lying in dusty closets; good and earnest divines, whose wisdom he had happened, by help of the devil, to turn to mischief; reading them by the light of hell-fire. For, indeed, Septimius had but given the clergyman the merest partial glimpse of his state of mind; he was not a new beginner, in doubt; but, on the contrary, it seemed to him as if he had never been other than a doubter and questioner, even in his boyhood;—believing nothing, although a thin veil of reverence had kept him from questioning some things. And now this new, strange thought of the sufficiency of the world for man, if man were only sufficient for that, kept recurring to him; and with it came a certain sense, which he had felt before, that he, at least, might never die. The feeling was not peculiar to Septimius; it is an instinct, the meaning of which is mistaken. We have strongly within us the sense of an undying principle; and we transfer that true sense to this life, and to the body, instead of interpreting it truly as the promise of spiritual immortality.

So Septimius looked up out of his thoughts, and said proudly:—

"Why should I die! I cannot die, if worthy to live! What if I should say, this moment, I will not die—not till ages hence, not till the world is exhausted. Let other men die if they choose or yield; let him that is strong enough, live!"

After this flash of heroic mood, however, the fire subsided, and poor Septimius spent the rest of the day as was his wont, poring over his books, in which all the meanings seemed dead and mouldy, and like, at best, pressed leaves, some of which dropt out of the books as he opened them, brown, brittle, sapless; so even the thoughts, which when the writer had gathered them seemed to him so beautifully colored and full of life. Then he began to see that there must have been some principle of life left out of the book, so that these gathered thoughts lacked something that had given them their only value. Then he suspected that the way truly to live and answer the purposes of life was not to gather up thoughts into books, where they grow so dry, but to live, and still be going about full of green wisdom, ripening ever, not in maxims cut and dry, but in wisdom ready for daily occasions like a living fountain; and that to be thus, it was necessary to live long on earth, drink in all its lessons, and not to die on the attainment of some smattering of truth, but to live all the more for that, and apply it to mankind, and increase it thereby. Everything partook of the strong, strange eddy into which his mind had been drawn; all his thought set thitherward.

So he sat brooding in his study, until the shrill voiced old woman, an Aunt, who was his housekeeper, and domestic ruler, called him to dinner; a frugal dinner, and chided him for seeming inattentive to some dish of early dandelions which she had gathered for him; but yet tempered her severity with respect for the future clerical rank of her nephew, and for his already being a bachelor of arts. The old woman's voice spoke outside of Septimius, mumbling away, and he paying little heed, till at last it was over, and Septimius drew back his chair, about to leave the table.

"Nephew Septimius," said the old woman, "you begin the meal to day without asking a blessing; you get up from it without giving thanks. And you almost a minister of the word!"

"God bless the meal," said Septimius by way of blessing, "and make it strengthen us for the life he meant us to bear.

Thank God for our food," he added, by way of grace, "and may it become portion in us of an immortal body."

"That sounds good, Septimius," said the old lady. "Ah, you'll be a mighty man in the pulpit yet, and worthy to keep up the name of your great grandfather, who, they say, made the leaves wither on a tree with the fierceness of his blast against a sin. Some say, to be sure, it was an early frost that helped him."

"I never heard that before, Aunt Zeziah," said Septimius.

"I warrant you, no," said his aunt. "A man dies, and his greatness perishes as if it had never been; and people remember nothing of him, only when they see his grave stone over his old dry bones, and say, he was a good man, to day."

"What truth there is in Aunt Zeziah's words," said Septimius. "And how I hate the thought and anticipation of that contemptuous sort of appreciation of a man, after his death. Every living man triumphs over every dead one, as he lies, poor and helpless, under his mound; a pinch of dust, a heap of bones, an evil odor! I hate the thought! I shall not be so!"

It was strange how every little incident thus brought him back to that one subject which was taking so strong hold of his mind; every avenue led thitherward; and he took it for an indication that Nature had intended, by innumerable ways, to indicate to us the great truth that death was an alien misfortune, a prodigy, a monstrosity, into which man had only fallen by defect, and that even now, even if a man had a reasonable portion of his original strength in him, he might live forever, and scorn death.

Our story is an internal one, dealing as little as possible with outward events, and taking hold of these, only where it cannot be helped, in order by means of them to delineate the history of a mind bewildered in certain errors. We would not willingly, if we could, give a lively and picturesque surrounding to this delineation; but it is necessary that we should advert to the circumstances of the time in which this inward history was passing. We will say, therefore, that that night there was a cry of alarm passing all through the succession of country towns, rural communities, that lay around Boston, and dying away towards the coast, and the wilder forest borders. Horsemen galloped past the lone farm-house shouting alarm, alarm!—there were stories of marching troops, coming like dreams through the midnight. Around the little rude meeting-houses, there was here and there the beat of a drum, the assemblage of farmers, neighbors, with their weapons. So, all that night, there was marching, there was mustering, there was trouble; and on the road from Boston, a steady march of soldiers' feet onward, onward, into this land, whose last warlike disturbances had been when the red Indians trod it.

Septimius heard it, and knew, like the rest, that it was the sound of coming war. "Fools that men are!" said he, as he rose from bed and looked out at the misty stars. "They do not live long enough to know the value and purport of life; else they would combine together to live long, instead of throwing away the lives of thousands as they do. And what matters a little tyranny in so short a life. What matters a form of government for such ephemeral creatures!"

As morning brightened, these sounds, this clamor, or something that was in the air and caused the clamor, grew so loud that Septimius seemed to feel it even in his solitude. It was in the atmosphere; storm, wild excitement, a coming deed; men hurried along the usually lonely road in groups, with weapons in their hands, the old fowling piece of seven foot barrel, with which the Puritans had shot ducks on the river and Walden Pond, the heavy harquebuss, which perhaps had levelled one of King Philip's Indians, the old King's Arm that blazed away at the French of Louisburg or Quebec; the hunter, the husbandman, all were hurrying and astir. It was a good time, everybody felt, to be alive in; a nearer kindred, a closer sympathy from man to man, a sense of the goodness of the world, of the sacredness of country, of the excellence of life, and yet its slight account, compared with any truth, any principle; the weighing of the material and ethereal, and the finding the former not worth considering, when nevertheless it had so much to do with the settlement of the crisis. The ennobling of brute force, the feeling that it had its godlike side; the drawing of heroic breath amid the scenes of ordinary life, so that it seemed as if they had all been transfigured since yesterday. Oh, high, heroic, tremulous juncture, when man felt himself almost an angel, on the verge of doing deeds that outwardly look so fiendish; oh strange rapture of the coming battle. We know something of that time now; we that have seen the muster of the village soldiery on meeting-house greens, and at railway stations; and heard the drum and fife, and seen the farewells, seen the familiar faces that we hardly knew, now that we felt them to be heroes, breathed higher breath for their sakes, felt our eyes moistened; thanked them in our souls for teaching us that nature is yet capable of heroic moments; felt how a great impulse lifts up a people, and every cold, passionless, indifferent spectator, lifts him up into religion, and makes him join in what becomes an act of devotion, a prayer, when perhaps he but half approves.

Septimius could not study on a morning like this; he tried to say to himself that he had nothing to do with this excitement, that his studies kept him away from it, that his intended profession was that of peace; say what he might to himself, there was a tremor, a bubbling impulse, a tingling in his being; the page that he opened glimmered and dazzled before him.

"Septimius, Septimius!" cried Aunt Zeziah, looking into the room, "in Heaven's name, are you going to sit here to day, and the red-coats coming to burn the house over our heads? Must I sweep you out with the broomstick? For shame, boy, for shame!"

"Well; I am not a fighting man. Are they coming, then, Aunt Keziah?" asked her nephew.

"Certain they are! They have sacked Lexington, and slain the people, and burnt the meeting-house. That concerns even the parsons, if you reckon yourself among them. Go out; go out, I say, and learn the news."

Whether moved by these exhortations or by his own stifling curiosity, Septimius did at length issue from his door, though with that reluctance which hampers and impedes men whose current of thought and intent runs apart from that of the world in general; but forth he came, feeling strangely, and yet with a strong impulse to fling himself headlong into the emotion of the moment. It was a beautiful morning, spring-like and summer-like at once; if there had been nothing else to do or think of, such a morning was enough for life, only to breathe its air and be conscious of its inspiring influence. Septimius turned along the road towards the village, meaning to mingle with the crowd upon the green, and there learn all he could of the rumors that vaguely filled the air, and doubtless were shaping themselves into various forms of fiction.

As he passed the small dwelling of Rose Garfield, she stood on the door-step, and bounded forth a step or two to meet him, looking frightened, excited, and yet half pleased, but strangely pretty; prettier than ever before, owing to some hasty adornment or other, that she would never have succeeded so well in giving to herself, if she had had more time to do it in.

"Septimius—Mr. Felton—" cried she, asking information of him, who, of all men in the neighborhood, knew nothing of the intelligence afloat; but it showed a certain importance that Septimius had with her. "Do you really think the red-coats are coming? Ah, what shall we do? What shall we do? But you are not going to the village, too, and leave us all alone."

"I know not whether they are coming or not, Rose," said Septimius, stopping to admire the young girl's fresh beauty, which made a double stroke upon him by her excitement, which, moreover, made her twice as free with him as ever she had been before; for there is nothing truer than that any breaking up of ordinary states of things is apt to shake women out of their proprieties, break down barriers, and bring them into perilous proximity with the world. "Are you alone here? Had you not better take shelter in the village?"

"And leave my poor bed-ridden grandmother," cried Rose, angrily. "You know I can't, Septimius. But I suppose I am in no danger. Go to the village if you like."

"Where is Robert Hagburn?" asked Septimius.

"Gone to the village this hour past, with his grandfather's old firelock on his shoulder," said Rose. "He was running bullets before daylight."

"Rose, I will stay with you," said Septimius.

"Oh, gracious, here they come, I'm sure!" cried Rose. "Look yonder at the dust. Mercy, a man at a gallop!"

In fact, along the road, a considerable stretch of which was visible, they heard the clatter of hoofs, and saw a little cloud of dust which approached at the rate of a gallop, and dis-closed, as it drew near, a hatless countryman in his shirt-sleeves, who, bending on his horse's neck, applied a cart-whip lustily to the animal's flanks, so as to incite him to most unwonted speed. At the same time, glaring upon Rose and Septimius, he lifted up his voice and shouted in a strange, high tone, that communicated the tremor and excitement of the shouter to each auditor:—

"Alarum! alarum! alarum! The redcoats! The redcoats! To arms! Alarum!"

And trailing this sound, far wavering behind him, like a pennon, the eager horseman dashed onward to the village.

"Oh, dear, what shall we do!" cried Rose, her eyes full of tears, yet dancing with excitement. "They are coming! they are coming! I hear the drum and fife!"

"I really believe they are," said Septimius, his cheek flushing and growing pale, not with fear, but the inevitable tremor, half painful, half pleasurable, of the moment. "Hark; there was the shrill note of a fife! Yes; they are coming!"

He tried to persuade Rose to hide herself in the house; but that young person would not be persuaded to do so, clinging to Septimius in a way that flattered while it perplexed him. Besides, with all the girl's fright, she had still a good deal of courage, and much curiosity, too, to see what these redcoats were, of whom she heard such terrible stories.

"Well, well, Rose," said Septimius, "I doubt not we may stay here without danger—you—a woman—and I, whose profession is to be that of peace and good will to all men. They cannot, whatever is said of them, be on an errand of massacre. We will stand here quietly; and seeing that we do not fear them, they will understand that we mean them no harm!"

They stood, accordingly, a little in front of the door, by the well-curb, and soon, they saw a heavy cloud of dust, from amidst which shone bayonets; and anon, a military band, which had hitherto been silent, struck up with drum and fife, to which the tramp of a thousand feet fell in regular order;

then came the column, moving massively, and the redcoats, who seemed somewhat wearied by a long night march, dusty, with bedraggled gaiters, covered with sweat, which had run down from their powdered locks. Nevertheless, these ruddy, lusty Englishmen marched stoutly, as men that needed only a half-hour's rest, a good breakfast, and a pot of beer apiece, to make them ready to face the world. Nor did their faces look anywise murderous, but, at most, only heavy, cloddish, good-natured, human.

"Oh, heavens, Mr. Felton," whispered Rose. "Why should we shoot these men, or they us? They look kind of homely and natural! Each of them has a mother and sisters, I suppose, just like our men."

"It is the strangest thing in the world that we can think of killing them," said Septimius. "Human life is so precious!"

Just as they were passing the cottage, a halt was called by the commanding officer, in order that some little rest might get the troops into a better condition, and give them breath, before entering the village, where it was important to make as imposing a show as possible. During the brief stop, some of the soldiers approached the well curb, near which Rose and Septimius were standing, and let down the bucket to satisfy their thirst. A young officer, a petulant boy, extremely handsome, and of gay and buoyant deportment, also approached.

"Get me a cup, pretty one!" said he, patting Rose's cheek with great freedom, though it was somewhat and indefinably short of rudeness; "a mug, or something to drink out of, and you shall have a kiss for your pains."

"Stand off, Sir," said Septimius fiercely. "It is a coward's part to insult our women."

"I intend no insult in this," said the handsome young officer, suddenly snatching a kiss from Rose before she could draw back. "And if you think it so, my good friend, you had better take your weapon and get such satisfaction as you can, shooting at me from behind a hedge!"

Before Septimius could reply or act—and, in truth, the easy presumption of the young Englishman made it difficult for him, inexperienced rustic as he was, to know what to say or do—the drum beat a little tap, recalling the soldiers to their ranks and to order. The young officer hastened back, with a laughing glance at Rose, and a light contemptuous look of defiance at Septimius; the drums rattled out in full beat, and the troops marched on.

"What impertinence!" said Rose, whose indignant color made her look pretty enough almost to excuse the offense.

It is not easy to see how Septimius could have shielded her from the insult; and yet he felt inconceivably outraged and humiliated at the thought that this offense had passed, while Rose was under his protection, and he responsible for her. Besides, somehow or other, he was angry with her for having undergone the wrong; though certainly most unreasonably; for the whole thing was quicker done than said.

"You had better go into the house now, Rose," said he, "and see to your bedridden grandmother."

"And what will you do, Septimius?" asked she.

"Perhaps I will house myself, too," said he. "Perhaps take yonder proud redcoat's counsel—and shoot him behind a hedge."

"But not kill him outright—I suppose he has a mother and a sweetheart, the handsome young officer," said Rose pityingly to herself.

Septimius went into his house, and sat there, in his study, for some hours, in that unpleasant state of feeling, which a man of brooding thought is apt to experience when the world around him is in a state of intense motion, which he finds it impossible to chord with. There seemed to be a stream rushing past him, which, even if he plunged into the midst of it, he could not be wet by it. He felt himself strangely ajar with the human race, and would have given much, either to be in full accord with it, or to be separated from it forever. "I am dissevered from it. It is my doom to be only a spectator of life, to look on as one apart from it. Is it not well therefore, that sharing none of its pleasures and happiness, I should be free of its fatalities, its brevity? How cold I am now, while this whirlpool of public feeling is eddying around me. It is as if I had not been born of woman!"

Thus it was, that drawing wild inferences from phenomena of the mind and heart common to people who, by some morbid action within themselves, are set ajar with the world, Septimius continued still to come round to that strange idea of undyingness, which had recently taken possession of him. And yet he was wrong in thinking himself cold, and that he took no sympathy in the fever of patriotism that was throbbing through his countrymen. He was restless as a flame; he could not fix his thoughts upon his book; he could not sit in his chair; but kept pacing to-and-fro, while through the open window came noises to which his imagination gave diverse interpretation. Now it was a distant drum; now shouts; by and by, there came the rattle of musketry, that seemed to proceed from some point more distant than the village; a regular roll, then a ragged volley; then scattering shots. Unable any longer to keep himself with his unnatural indifference, Septimius snatched his gun, and rushing out of the house, climbed the abrupt hillside behind, whence he could see a long way towards the village, till a slight bend hid the onward road. It was quite vacant; not a passenger upon it. But there seemed to be confusion in that direction; an unseen and inscrutable trouble blowing thence towards him, intimated by vague sounds, by no sounds.

Listening eagerly, however, he at length fancied a mustering sound of the drum; then a march, as if it were coming towards him; while in advance rode another horseman, the same kind of headlong messenger, in appearance, who had passed the house with his ghastly cry of alarum, that morning; then appeared scattered countrymen with guns in their hands straggling across fields. Then he caught sight of the regular array of British soldiers, filling the road with their front, and marching on as firmly as ever; though at a quick pace, while he fancied that the officers looked watchfully around. While he looked, a shot rang sharp from the hillside, towards the village; the smoke curled up; and Septimius saw a man stagger and fall, in the midst of the troops. Septimius shuddered; it was so like murder that he really could not tell the difference; his knees trembled beneath him, his breath grew short, not with terror, but with some new sensation of awe.

Another shot or two came almost simultaneously from the wooded hillside, but without any effect that Septimius could perceive. Almost at the same moment, a company of the British soldiers wheeled from the mainbody, and, dashing out of the road, climbed the hillside that disappeared into the wood and shrubbery that veiled it. There were a few straggling shots, by whom fired, or with what effect was invisible, and meanwhile the mainbody of the enemy pushed its way along the road. They had now advanced so nigh, that Septimius was strangely assailed by the idea that he might, with the gun in his hand, fire right into the midst of them, and select any man of that now hostile band, to be a victim! How strange, how strange it is, this deep, wild passion that nature has implanted in us, to be the death of our fellow-creatures, and which co-exists at the same time with horror. Septimius levelled his weapon, and drew it up again; he

marked a mounted officer, who seemed to be in chief direction, whom he knew that he could kill. But, no! he had really
no such purpose. Only it was such a temptation! And, in a
moment, the horse would leap; the officer would fall, and lie
there in the dust of the road, bleeding, gasping, breathing in
gulps, breathing no more.

While the young man, in those strange circumstances,
stood watching the march of the troops, he heard the noise
of rustling boughs and the curses of men; and soon understood that the party, which he had seen separate itself from
the mainbody and ascend the hill, was now marching along
on the hill-top, the long ridge, which, with a gap or two,
extended as much as a mile from the village. They were
acting as a flank-guard, to prevent the uproused people from
coming so close to the mainbody as to fire upon it. One of
those gaps occurred a little way from where Septimius stood.
He looked, and saw that the detachment of British were
plunging down one descent of this gap, with intent to ascend
the other; so that they would pass directly over the spot where
he stood; a little removal to one side, among the small bushes,
would conceal him. He stept aside, accordingly, and from
his concealment, not without drawing quicker breaths, beheld
the party of British draw near. They were more intent upon
the space between them and the mainbody, than upon the
dense thicket of birch-trees, pitch-pines, sumach, dwarf-oaks,
which, scarcely yet beginning to bud into leaf, lay on the
other side, and in which Septimius lurked. <Describe how
their faces affected him, passing so near; how strange they
seemed.>

They had all passed, except an officer who brought up the
rear, and who had perhaps been attracted by some slight
motion that Septimius made, some rustle in the thicket; for

he stopt, fixed his eyes piercingly towards the spot where he stood, and levelled a light fusil which he carried. "Stand out, or I shoot!" said he.

Not to avoid the shot, but because his manhood felt a call upon it, not to skulk in obscurity from an open enemy, Septimius at once stood forth, and confronted the same handsome young officer with whom those fierce words had passed, on account of his rudeness to Rose Garfield. <Septimius's fierce Indian blood stirs in him, and gives him bloody incitements.>

"Ah, it is you," said the young officer with a haughty smile. "You meant then to take up my hint of shooting at me from hind a hedge. This is better! Come; we have, in the first place, the great quarrel between me a king's soldier, and you a rebel; next our private affair on account of yonder pretty girl. Come; let us take a shot on either score!"

The young officer was so handsome, beautiful in budding youth; there was such a free, gay petulance in his manner; there seemed so little of real evil in him; he put himself on equal ground with the rustic Septimius so generously—that the latter, often so morbid and sullen, never felt a greater kindness to a fellow-man, than at this moment, for this youth.

"I have no enmity towards you," said he. "Go in peace."

"No enmity!" said the officer. "Then why are you here with your gun among the shrubbery? But I have a mind to do my first deed of arms on you; so give up your weapon, and come with me as prisoner."

"As prisoner!" said Septimius, that Indian fierceness that was in him arousing itself, and thrusting up its malign head like a snake. "Never! If you would have me, you must take my dead body."

"Ah, well; you have pluck in you, I see, only it needs a considerable stirring. Come; this is a good quarrel of ours.

Let us fight it out. Stand where you are, and I will give the word of command. Now! Ready, aim! Fire!"

As the young officer spoke the three last words, in rapid succession, he and his antagonist brought their firelocks to the shoulder, aimed, and fired. Septimius felt, as it were, the sting of a gadfly passing across his temple, as the Englishman's bullet grazed it; but, to his surprise and horror (for the whole thing scarcely seemed real to him) he saw the young officer give a great start, drop his fusil, and stagger against a tree, with his hand to his breast. He endeavored to support himself erect, but failing in the effort, beckoned to Septimius.

"Come, my good friend," said he, with that playful, petulant smile flitting over his face again. "It is my first and last fight. Let me down as softly as you can on mother Earth— the mother of both you and me—so we are brothers; and this may be a brotherly act, though it does not look so—nor feel so!—Ah. That was a twinge indeed!"

"Good God!" said Septimius. "I had no thought of this— no malice towards you in the least."

"Nor I towards you," said the young man. "It was boy's play, and the end of it is, that I die a boy, instead of living forever, as perhaps I otherwise might."

"Living forever!" repeated Septimius, his attention arrested, even at that breathless moment, by words that rang so strangely on what had been his brooding thought.

"Yes; but I have lost my chance," said the young officer; then, as Septimius helped him to lie against the little hillock of a decayed and buried stump, "Thank you! thank you! If you could only call back one of my comrades to hear my dying words. But I forgot! You have killed me, and they would take your life."

In truth, Septimius was so moved, and so astonished, that he probably would have called back the young man's comrades had it been possible, but marching at the swift rate of men in peril, they had already passed far on, and their passage among the shrubbery had ceased to rustle behind them.

"Yes, I must die here," said the young man, with a forlorn expression as of a school-boy away from home; "and nobody to see me now but you—who have killed me! Could you bring me a drop of water? I have a great thirst."

Septimius, in a dream of horror and pity, rushed down the hill side; the house was empty; for Aunt Keziah had gone for shelter and sympathy to some of the neighbors. He filled a pitcher with cold water, and hurried back to the hill-top, where he found the young officer looking paler and more deathlike, within those few moments.

"I thank you, my enemy that was, my friend that is," said he, faintly smiling. "Methinks, next to the father and mother that give us birth, the next most intimate relation must be with the man that slays us—that introduces us to the mysterious world to which this is but the portal. You and I are strangely connected, doubt it not, in the scenes of the unknown world."

"Oh, believe me," said Septimius, "I grieve for you like a brother."

"I see it, my dear friend," said the young officer; "and though my blood is on your hands, I forgive you freely, if there is anything to forgive. But I am dying, and have a few words to say, which you must hear. You have slain me in fair fight, and my spoils, according to the rules and customs of warfare, belong to the victor. Hang up my sword and fusil over your chimney-place, and tell your children, twenty years hence, how they were won. My purse; keep it, or give it to the poor. There is something here, next my heart, which I would fain have sent to the direction which I will give you."

Septimius, obeying his directions, took from his breast a miniature that hung round it; but on examination, it proved that the bullet had passed directly through it, shattering the ivory so that a woman's face of the person represented was quite destroyed.

"Ah; that is a pity," said the young man; and yet Septimius thought that there was something light and contemptuous mingled with the pathos in his tone. "Well; but send it— cause it to be transmitted according to this direction."

He gave Septimius, and made him take down on a tablet which he had about him, the name of an English hall, in one of the midland counties of England.

"Ah; that old place," said he, "with its oaks, and its lawn, and its park, and its many Elizabethan gables! I little thought I should die here, so far away, in this barren Yankee-land. Where will you bury me?"

As Septimius hesitated to answer, the young man continued:—

"I would like to have lain in the little old church at Whitnash, which comes up before me now, with its low, gray tower, and the old yew tree in front, hollow with age; and the village clustering about it, with its thatched houses. I would be loth to lie in one of your Yankee grave-yards; for I have a distaste for them, though I love you, my slayer. Bury me here, on this very spot. A soldier lies best where he falls."

"Here, in secret!" said Septimius.

"Yes, there is no consecration in your Puritan burial-grounds," said the dying youth, some of that queer narrowness of English churchdom coming into his mind. "So bury me here, in my soldier dress. Ah; and my watch. I have done with time, and you perhaps have a long lease of it; so take it, not as spoil, but as my parting-gift. And that reminds me of one other thing. Open that pocket-book which you have in your hand."

Septimius did so, and by the officer's directions, took from one of its compartments a folded paper, closely written in a crabbed hand; it seemed considerably worn in the outer folds, but not within.

"I leave it with you," said the officer; "it was given me by an Uncle, a most learned man of science, who intended me great good by what he there wrote. Reap the profit if you can. Sooth to say, I never read beyond the first lines of the paper."

Septimius was surprised, or strangely impressed, to see that through this paper, as well as through the miniature, had gone his fatal bullet—straight through the midst—and some of the young man's blood, saturating his dress, had wet the paper all over. He scarcely thought himself likely to obtain any good from what it had cost in human life, taken (however uncriminally) by his own hands, to obtain. "Is there any thing more that I can do for you?" said he, with genuine sympathy and sorrow, as he knelt by his fallen foe's side.

"Nothing—nothing, I believe!" said he. "There was one thing I might have confessed—if there were a holy man here, I might have confessed and asked his prayers; for though I have lived few years, it has been long enough to do a great wrong. But I will try to pray in my secret soul. Turn my face towards the trunk of this tree, for I have taken my last look at the world. There; let me be now."

Septimius did as the young man requested, and then stood leaning against one of the neighboring trees, watching his victim with a pity and sympathy that made him feel as if the convulsive throes that passed through his frame were felt equally in his own. There was a murmuring from the officer's lips, which seemed to Septimius simple, soft, and melancholy, like the voice of a child when it has some naughtiness to confess to its mother at bedtime; contrite, pleading, yet trusting. So it continued for a few minutes; then there was a sudden start and struggle, as if he were striving to rise; his eyes met those of Septimius with a wild troubled gaze, and as the latter caught him in his arms, he was dead. Septimius laid the body softly down on the leaf-strewn earth, and tried, as he heard was the custom with dead people, to compose the features distorted by the dying struggles. He then flung himself on the ground, at a little distance, and gave himself up to the reflections suggested by the strange occurrences of the last hour.

He had taken a human life; and however the circumstances might excuse him—might make the thing even something praiseworthy and that would be called patriotic, still it is not at once that a fresh country youth sees anything but horror in the blood with which his hand was stained. It seemed so dreadful to have reduced this gay, animated, beautiful being to a lump of dead flesh, for the flies to settle upon, and which in a few hours would begin to decay; which must be put forthwith into the earth, lest it should be a horror to men's eyes; that delicious beauty for women to love, that strength and energy to make him foremost among men—all come to nothing; all probabilities of life in one so gifted, the renown, the position; the pleasures, the profits, the keen ecstatic joy, this never could be made up, all ended quite; for the dark doubt descended upon Septimius, that, for the very fitness that was in this youth to enjoy the world, so much the less chance was there of his being fit for any other world. What good could it do him there, this beautiful grace of form and elegance of feature, where there was no form, nothing tangible nor visible; what good that readiness and aptness for associating with all created things, doing his part, acting, enjoying, when under the changed conditions of another state of being, all this adaptedness would fail? Had he been gifted with permanence on earth, there could not have been a more admirable creature than this young man; but as his fate had turned out, he was a mere feat, an illusion, something that Nature had held out in mockery, and then withdrawn it. A weed might grow out of him now; that little spot on the barren hill top, where he had desired to be buried, would be greener for some years to come, and that was all the difference. Septimius could not get beyond the earthiness; his feeling was, as if, by one act of violence, he had forever cut off a happy human existence. And such was his own love of life—a love of life, and clinging to it, peculiar to dark, sombre natures, and which lighter and gayer ones can never know—that he shuddered at his deed and at himself, and could with difficulty bear to be alone with the corpse of his victim—trembled at the thought of turning his face towards him.

Yet he did so, because he could not bear the imagination that the dead youth was turning his eyes towards him as he lay; so he came and stood beside him, looking down into his white upturned face. But it was wonderful! What a change had come upon it since, only a few moments ago, he looked at that death-contorted face. Now there was a high and sweet expression upon it, of great joy and surprise, and yet a quietude diffused throughout, as if the peace being so very great was what made him surprised. The expression seemed like a light gleaming and glowing within him. Septimius had often, at a certain space after sunset, looking westward, seen a living radiance in the sky—the last light of the dead day— that seemed just the counterpart of this death-light in the young man's face. It was as if the youth were just at the gate of Heaven, which, swinging softly open, let the incon-

ceivable glory of the blessed city shine upon his face, and
kindle it up with gentle undisturbing astonishment and purest joy. It was an expression contrived by God's Providence,
to comfort, to overcome all the dark auguries that the physical ugliness of death inevitably creates, and to say, by this
divine glory on the face, that the ugliness is a delusion; it is
as if the dead man himself showed his face out of the sky,
with heaven's blessing on it, and bade the afflicted be of good
cheer, and believe in immortality.

He remembered the young man's injunctions to bury him
there on the hill-top without uncovering the body, and though
it seemed a sin and shame to cover up that beautiful body
with earth of the grave, and give it to the worm, yet he
resolved to obey. Be it confessed, that, beautiful as the dead
face looked, and guiltless as Septimius must be held in causing his death, still he felt as if he should be easier when he
was under the earth. He hastened down to the house, and
brought up a shovel and a pickaxe, and began his unwonted
task of grave digger, delving earnestly a deep grave—sometimes pausing in his toil, while the sweat drops poured from
him, to look at the beautiful clay that was to occupy it. Sometimes he paused, too, to listen to the shots that pealed in the
far distance towards the east, whither the battle had long
since rolled out of reach, and almost out of hearing. It
seemed to have gathered about itself the whole life of the
land, clustering it about its bloody course in a struggling
throng of shouting, shooting men, so still and solitary was
everything left behind it. It seemed the very midland solitude
of the world where Septimius was delving at the grave; he
and his dead man were alone together, and he was going to
put the dead man under the sod, and be quite alone.

The grave was now deep, and Septimius was stooping
down into its depths among difficult pebbles, levelling off the
bottom, which he considered to be now profound enough to

hide the young man's mystery forever, when a voice spoke above him; a grave, quiet voice, which he knew well.

"Septimius! What are you doing here?"

He looked up, and saw the minister.

"I have slain a man in fair fight," answered Septimius, "and am about to bury him as he requested. I am glad you are come. You, reverend Sir, can fitly say a prayer at his obsequies. I am glad for my own sake; for it is very lonely and terrible to be here."

He climbed out of the grave, and in answer to the minister's inquiries communicated to him the events of the morning, and the young man's strange wish to be buried here without having his remains subjected to the hands of those who would prepare it for the grave. The minister hesitated.

"At an ordinary time," said he, "such a singular request would of course have to be denied. Your own safety—the good and wise rules that make it necessary that all things relating to death and burial should be done publicly and in order would forbid it."

"Yes;" said Septimius; "but, it may be, scores of men will fall to day, and be flung into hasty graves without funeral rites, without its ever being known, perhaps, what mother has lost her son. I cannot but think that I ought to perform the dying request of the youth whom I have slain. He trusted in me, not to uncover his body myself, not to betray it to the hands of others."

"A singular request," said the good minister, gazing with deep interest at the beautiful dead face, and graceful, slender, manly figure.—"What could have been its motive? But, no matter. I think, Septimius, that you are bound to obey his request; indeed, having promised him, nothing short of an impossibility should prevent your keeping your faith. Let us lose no time, then."

With few, but deeply solemn rites, the young stranger was laid, by the minister and the youth who slew him, in his grave. A prayer was made, and then Septimius, gathering some branches and twigs, laid them over the face that was turned upward from the bottom of the pit, into which the sun gleamed downward, throwing its rays so as almost to touch the face; the twigs partially hid it, but still its white gleamed through. Then the minister threw a handful of earth upon it, and accustomed as he was to burials, a tear fell from his eyes along with the earth.

"It is sad," said he, "this poor young man, coming from opulence, no doubt, a dear English home, to die here for no end, one of the first fruits of a bloody war, so much privately sacrificed. But let him rest, Septimius. I am sorry that he fell by your hand; though it involves no shadow of a crime. But death is a thing too serious not to melt into the nature of a man like you."

"It does not weigh upon my conscience, I think," said Septimius; "though I cannot but feel sorrow, and wish my hand were as clean as yesterday. It is, indeed, a dreadful thing to take human life."

"It is a most serious thing," replied the minister; "but perhaps we are apt to overestimate the importance of death, at any particular moment. If the question were, whether to die, or live forever, then indeed, scarcely anything should justify the putting a fellow creature to death. But since it only shortens his earthly life, and brings a little forward a change which, since God permits it, we may conclude as fit to take place then as any other time, it alters the case. I often think, that there are many things that occur to us often in our daily life, many unknown crises, that are more important to us than this mysterious circumstance of death, which we deem the most important of all. All we know of it is—that it takes the dead person away from our knowledge of him, which, while we live with him, is so very scanty."

"You estimate at nothing, it seems, his earthly life, which might have been so happy?"

"At next to nothing," said the minister; "since, as I have observed, it must at any rate have closed so soon."

Septimius thought of what the young man, in his death-moments, had said of his prospect or opportunity of living a life of interminable length, and which prospect he had bequeathed to himself. But of this he said nothing to the minister; being, indeed, ashamed to have it supposed that he would put any serious weight on such a bequest; although it might be that the dark enterprise of his nature had secretly seized upon this idea, and, though yet sane enough to be influenced by a fear of ridicule, was busy incorporating it with his thoughts.

So Septimius smoothed down the young stranger's earthy bed, and returned to his home, where he hung up the young man's sword over the mantel piece in his study, and hung his gold watch too on a nail; the first time he had ever had possession of such a thing; nor did he now feel altogether at ease in his mind about keeping it, the time-measurer of one whose earthly time he had cut off; a splendid watch it was, round as a turnip. There seems to be a natural right, in one who has slain a man, to step into his vacant place in all respects, and from the beginning of man's dealings with man, this right has been practically recognized, whether among warriors or robbers, as paramount to every other. Yet Septimius could not feel easy in availing himself of this right; he therefore resolved to keep the watch, and even the sword and fusil, which was a less questionable spoil of war, only till he should be able to restore them to some representative of the young officer. The contents of the purse, in accordance with the request of the dying youth, he would expend in relieving the necessities of those whom the war (now broken out, and of which none could see the limit) might put in need of it. The miniature, with its broken and shattered face, that had so vainly interposed itself between its wearer and death, had been buried in the grave.

But, as to the mysterious document, the written paper, that he laid carefully aside, without unfolding it, but with a care that betokened more interest in it than in either gold, or weapon, or even in the golden representative of that earthly time, on which he set so high a value. There was something tremulous in his touch of it; it seemed as if he was afraid of it, by the mode in which he hid it away, and secured himself from it, as it were.

This done, the air of the room, the low-ceilinged eastern room, where he studied and thought, became too close for him, and he hastened out; for he was full of the unshaped sense of all that had befallen; and the sense of the great public event of a broken-out war was intermixed with the sense of what he had done personally in the great struggle that was beginning. He longed, too, to know what was the news of the battle that had gone rolling onward, along that hitherto peaceful country-road, converting every where (this Demon of War, we mean) with one blast of its red sulphurous breath, the peaceful husbandman to a soldier thirsting for blood. He turned his steps, therefore, towards the village, thinking it probable that news must have arrived, from messengers or fliers, either of defeat or victory, to cheer or sadden, the old men, the women, and the children, who alone probably remained there.

But Septimius did not get to the village. As he passed along by the cottage that has been already described, Rose Garfield was standing in the door, peering anxiously forth, as is woman's fate to do, to know what was the issue of the conflict—as it has been woman's fate to do from the beginning of the world, and is so still. Seeing Septimius, she forgot the restraints that she had hitherto kept herself under, and flying to him like a bird, she cried out, "Septimius, dear Septimius, where have you been? What news do you bring? You look as if you had seen some strange and dreadful thing!"

"Ah; is it so; does my face tell such stories?" exclaimed the young man. "I did not mean it should. Yes, Rose, I have seen and done such things as change men in a moment."

"Then you have been in this terrible fight," said Rose.

"Yes, Rose, I have had my part in it," said Septimius. He was on the point of relieving his overburthened mind by telling her what had happened, no further off than on the hill-top above them; but seeing her excitement, and recollecting her own momentary interview with the young officer, and the forced intimacy and link that had been established between them by the kiss, he feared to agitate her further by telling her that that gay and beautiful young man had since been slain, and deposited in a bloody grave by his hands. And yet the recollection of that kiss caused a thrill of vengeful joy at the though that the perpetrator had since expiated his offense with his life, and that it was himself that did it; so deeply was Septimius's Indian nature of revenge and blood incorporated with that of more peaceful forefathers, although Septimius had grace enough to chide down that bloody spirit, feeling that it made him not a patriot, but a murderer.

"Ah," said Rose, shuddering; "it is awful when men must kill one another. And who knows where it will end."

"It will end here with me, Rose," said Septimius. "It may be lawful for any man, even if he has devoted himself to God, or however peaceful his pursuits, to fight to the death when the enemy's step is on the soil of his home; but only for that perilous juncture, which passed, he should return to his own way of peace. I have done a terrible thing for once, dear Rose, one that might well leave a dark line with all my future life; but henceforth I cannot think it my duty to pursue any further a course for which my studies and my nature unfit me."

"Oh no, Oh no," said Rose; "never; and you a minister, or soon to be one. There must be some peacemakers left in the world, or everything will turn to blood and confusion; for even women grow almost fierce in these times. My old grandmother laments her bedriddenness, because, she says, she cannot go to cheer on the people against the enemy. But she remembers the old times of the Indian wars, when the women were as much in danger of death as the men, and so were almost as fierce as they, and killed men sometimes with their own hands. But women, now a days, ought to be gentler; let the men be fierce, if they must—except you, and such as you, Septimius."

"Ah, dear Rose," said Septimius, "I have not the kind and sweet impulses that you speak of. I need something to soften and warm my cold, hard life; something to make me feel how dreadful this time of warfare is. I need you, dear Rose, who are all kindness of heart and mercy."

And here Septimius, hurried away by I know not what excitement of the time,—the disturbed state of the country, his own ebullition of passion, the deed he had done, the desire to press one human being close to his life, because he had shed the blood of another, his half-formed purposes, his shapeless impulses, in short, being affected by the whole stir of his nature,—spoke to Rose of love, and with an energy that indeed there was no resisting when once it broke its bounds. And Rose, whose maiden thought, to say the truth, had long dwelt upon this young man—admiring him for a certain dark beauty, knowing him familiarly from childhood, and yet having the sense that is so bewitching of remoteness intermixed with intimacy, because he was so unlike herself, having a woman's respect for scholarship, her imagination the more impressed for all in him that she could not comprehend —Rose yielded to his impetuous suit, and gave him the troth that he requested. And yet it was with a sort of reluctance and drawing back; her whole nature, her secretest heart, her deepest womanhood, perhaps, did not consent; there was something in Septimius, in his wild, mixed nature, the monstrousness that had grown out of his hybrid race, the black infusions, too, that melancholic men had left there, the devilishness that had been symbolized in the popular legend about his family, that made her shiver, even while she came the closer to him for that very dread. And when he gave her the kiss of contract, her lips grew white. If it had not been in that day of turmoil—if he had asked her in any quiet time, when Rose's heart was in its natural mood—it may well be, that, with tears, and pity for him, and half pity for herself, Rose would have told Septimius that she did not think she could love him well enough to be his wife.

And how was it with Septimius? Well; there was a strange correspondence in his feelings to those of Rose Garfield. At first, hurried away by a passion that seized him all unawares, and seemed to develope itself all in a moment, he felt, and so spoke to Rose, so pleaded his suit, as if his whole earthly happiness depended on her consent to be his bride. It seemed to him that her love would be the sunshine in the gloomy dungeon of his life. But when her bashful, downcast, tremulous consent was given, there immediately came a strange misgiving into his mind. He felt as if he had taken to himself some thing, good and beautiful doubtless, in itself, but which might be the exchange for some more suited to himself that he must give up. The intellect, which was the prominent part in Septimius, stirred and heaved, crying out vaguely that its own claims perhaps were ignored in this contract; Septimius had perhaps no right to love at all; that if he did, it should have been a woman of another make, that could be his intellectual companion and helper. And, then, perhaps—perhaps—there was destined for him some high lonely path, in which, to make any progress, to come to any end, he must walk unburthened by the affections. Such thoughts as these depressed and chilled (as many men have found them or similar ones to do) the moment of success that should have been the most exalting in the world. And so, in the kiss that these two lovers had exchanged, there was after all something that repelled; and when they parted, they wondered at their strange states of mind, but would not acknowledge that they had done a thing that ought not to have been done. Nothing is surer, however, than that, if we suffer ourselves to be drawn into too close proximity with people—if we overestimate the degree of our proper tendency towards them, or theirs towards us, a re-action is sure to follow.

Septimius quitted Rose, and resumed his walk towards the village. But now it was near sunset; and there began to be straggling passengers along the road, some of whom came slowly, as if they had received hurts; all seemed wearied. Among these one form appeared, which Rose soon found that she recognized. It was Robert Hagburn, with a shattered firelock in his hand, broken at the butt, and his left arm bound with a fragment of his shirt, and suspended in a handkerchief; and he came along wearily but brightened up at sight of Rose, as if ashamed to let her see how exhausted and dispirited he was. Perhaps he expected a kinder, at least a more earnest reception than he met; for Rose, with the restraint of what had recently passed drawing her back, merely went gravely a few steps to meet him, and said, "Robert, how tired and pale you look! Are you hurt?"

"It is of no consequence," said Robert Hagburn. "A scratch on my left arm from an officer's sword, with whose head my gun stock made instant acquaintance. It is no matter, Rose; you do not care for it—nor I either!"

"How can you say so, Robert?" she replied.

But without more greeting, he passed her, and went into his own house, where, flinging himself into a chair, he remained in that despondency that men generally feel after a fight, even if a successful one.

Septimius, the next day, lost no time in writing a letter to the direction given him by the young officer, conveying a brief account of the latter's death and burial, and a signification that he held in readiness to give up certain articles of property, at any future time, to his representatives;—mentioning also the amount of money contained in the purse, and his intention, in compliance with the verbal will of the deceased, to expend it in alleviating the wants of prisoners. Having so done, he went up on the hill-top, to look at the grave, and satisfy himself that the scene there had not been a dream; a point which he was inclined to question, in spite of the tangible evidence of the sword and watch which still hung over the mantel-piece. There was the little mound, however, looking so incontrovertibly a grave that it seemed to him as if all the world must see it, and wonder at the fact of its being there, and spend their wits in conjecturing who slept within; and, indeed, it seemed to give the affair a questionable character, this secret material, and he wondered and wondered why the young man had been so earnest about it. Well; there was the grave; and moreover, on the leafy earth, where the dying youth had lain, there were traces of blood, which no rain had yet washed away. Septimius wondered at the easiness in which he acquiesced in this deed; in fact, he felt in a slight degree the effects of that taste of blood, which makes the slaying of men, like any other abuse, sometimes become a passion. Perhaps it was his Indian trait stirring in him again; at any rate, it is not delightful to think how readily man becomes a blood-shedding animal.

Looking down from the hill-top, he saw the little dwelling of Rose Garfield, and caught a glimpse of the girl herself, passing the windows or the door, about her household duties; and listened to hear the singing which usually broke out of her. But Rose, for some reason or other, did not warble as usual, that morning; she trode about silently, and, somehow or other, she was translated out of the ideality in which Septimius usually enveloped her, and looked little more than a New England girl, very pretty indeed, but not enough perhaps to engross a man's life and higher purposes into her own narrow circle; so, at least, Septimius thought. Looking a little further, down into the green recess where stood Robert Hagbourn's house, he saw that young man, looking very pale, worn, with his arm in a sling, sitting listlessly on a half-chopt log of wood, which was not likely soon to be severed by Robert's axe. Like other lovers, Septimius had not failed to be aware that Robert Hagburn was sensible to Rose Garfield's attractions; and, now, as he looked down upon them both from his elevated position, he wondered if it would not have been better for Rose's happiness if her thoughts and virgin fancies had settled on that frank, cheerful, able, wholesome young man, instead of on himself, who met her on so few points; and, in relation to whom, there was perhaps a plant that had its root in the grave, that would entwine around his whole life, overshadowing it with dark, rich foliage, and fruit that he could only feast upon alone.

For the sombre imagination of Septimius, though he kept it as much as possible away from the subject, still kept hinting and whispering, still coming back to the point, still secretly suggesting that the event of yesterday was to have most momentous consequences upon his fate. He had not yet looked at the paper which the young man bequeathed to him; he had laid it away unopened, but not that he felt little interest in it; on the contrary, because he looked for some blaze of light, which had been reserved for him alone. The young man had been only the bearer of it to him, and he had come hither to die by his hand, because that was the readiest way by which he could deliver his message. How else, in the infinite chances of human affairs, could the document have found its way to its destined possessor? Thus mused Septimius, pacing to-and-fro on the level edge of his hill-top, apart from the world, looking down occasionally into it and seeing its love and interest away from him; while Rose, it might be, looking upward, saw occasionally his passing figure, and trembled at the nearness and remoteness that existed between them; and Robert Garfield looked, too, and wondered what manner of man it was, that having won Rose Garfield (for his instincts told him that was so) could keep that distance between her and him, thinking remote thoughts.

Yes; there was Septimius treading a path of his own on the hill-top; his feet began only that morning to wear it, in his walkings to and fro, sheltered from the lower world, except in occasional glimpses, by the birches and locusts that threw up their foliage from the hill side. But many a year thereafter he continued to tread that path till it was worn deep with his footsteps, and trodden down hard; and it was be-

lieved by some of his superstitious neighbors that the grass
and little shrubs shrank away from his path, and made it
wider on that account; because there was something in the
broodings that urged him to and fro along this path, alien to
nature and its productions. There was another opinion, too,
that an invisible fiend, one of his relatives by blood, walked
side by side with him, and so made the pathway wider than
his single footsteps could have made it. But all this was idle;
and was indeed only the foolish babble that hovers like a
mist about men who withdraw themselves from the throng,
and involve themselves in unintelligible pursuits and interests
of their own. For the present, the little world, which alone
knew of him, considered Septimius as a studious young man,
who was fitting for the ministry, and was likely enough to do
credit to the ministerial blood that he drew from his ancestors;
in spite of the wild stream that the Indian priest had contributed, & perhaps none the worse, as a clergyman, for having
an instinctive sense of the nature of the devil, from his traditionary claims to partake of his blood. But what strange
interest there is, in tracing out the first steps by which we
enter on a course that influences our life; and this deep-worn
pathway on the hill-top, passing and repassing by a grave,
seemed to symbolize it in Septimius's case.

I suppose the morbidness of Septimius's disposition was excited by the circumstances which had put the paper into his
possession. Had he received it by post, it might not have
impressed him; he might possibly have looked over it with
ridicule, and tossed it aside. But he had received it from a
dying man; and he felt that his fate was in it; and, truly it
turned out to be so. He waited for a fit opportunity to open
it, and read it; he put it off as if he cared nothing about it,
but perhaps it was because he cared so much. Whenever he
had a happy time with Rose (and moody as Septimius was,

such happy moments came,) he felt that then was not the time to look into the paper; it was not to be read in a happy mood. Once, he asked Rose to walk with him on the hill-top.

"Why, what a path you have worn here, Septimius!" said the girl. "You walk miles and miles on this one spot, and get no further on than when you started. That is strange walking."

"I don't know, Rose! I sometimes think I get a little on-ward. But it is sweeter—yes, much sweeter, I find—to have you walking this path here, than to be treading it alone."

"I am glad of that," said Rose; "for, sometimes, when I look up here and see you through the branches, with your head bent down and your hands clasped behind you, tread-ing, treading, treading, always in one way, I wonder whether I am at all in your mind. I don't think, Septimius," added she, looking up in his face and smiling, "that ever a girl had just such a young man for a beau!"

"No young man ever had such a girl, I am sure!" said Septimius; "so sweet, so good for him, so prolific of good influences."

"Ah; it makes me think well of myself to bring such a smile into your face. But, Septimius, what is this little hillock here, so close to our path? Have you heaped it up here for a seat? Shall we sit down upon it for an instant?—for it makes me more tired, I think, to walk backward and forward on one path, than to go straight forward a much longer distance."

"Well; but we will not sit down on this hillock," said Sep-timius, drawing her away from it; "further out this way, if you please, Rose, where we shall have a better view over the wide plain, the valleys, and the long, tame ridges on the other side, shutting it in like human life. It is a landscape that never tires, though it has nothing striking about it; and I am glad that there are no great hills to be thrusting themselves into my thoughts, and crowding out better things. It might be better, in some states of mind, to have a glimpse of water—to have the lake that once must have covered this green valley—because water reflects the sky, and so is like religion in life, the spiritual element."

"There is the brook running through it, though we do not see it," said Rose; "a torpid little brook, to be sure, but, as you say, it has heaven in its bosom, like Walden Pond, or any wider one."

As they sat together on the hill-top, they could look down into Robert Hagburn's enclosure; and they saw him, with his arm now relieved from the sling, walking about, in a very erect manner, with a middle aged man by his side, to whom he seemed to be talking and explaining some matter. Even at that distance, Septimius could see that the rustic stoop and uncouthness had somehow fallen away from Robert, and that he seemed developed.

"What has come to Robert Hagburn?" said he. "He looks like another man than the lout I knew a few weeks ago."

"Nothing;" said Rose Garfield, "except what comes to a good many young men, now a days. He has enlisted, and is going to the war. It is a pity for his mother!"

"A great pity!" said Septimius. "Mothers are greatly to be pitied, all over the country, just now; and there are some even more to be pitied than even the mothers, though many of them do not know or suspect anything about it, their cause of grief at present."

"Of whom do you speak?" asked Rose.

"I mean those many good and sweet young girls," said Septimius, "who would have become happy wives to the thousands of young men who now, like Robert Garfield, are going to the war. Those young men, many of them, at least, will sicken and die in camp, or be shot down or stuck through with bayonets on battle fields, and turn to dust and bones; while the girls, that would have loved them, and made happy firesides for them, will pine and wither, and tread along many sour and discontented years, and at last go out of life without ever having known what life is. So, you see, Rose, every shot that takes effect kills two, at least—kills one, and worse than kills the other."

"No woman will live single on account of poor Robert Garfield's being shot," said Rose, with a change of tone; "for he would never be married, were he to stay at home and plough the field."

"How can you tell that, Rose?" asked Septimius.

Rose did not tell how she came to know so much about Robert Hagburn's matrimonial purposes; but after this little talk, it appeared as if something had risen up between them, a sort of mist, a medium in which their intimacy was not promoted; for the pleasant interchange of sentiment was baulked, and they only took one or two turns in silence along Septimius's trodden path. I don't know exactly what it was; but there are cases where it is inscrutably revealed to persons that they have made a mistake in what is of the highest concern to them, and this truth often comes in the shape of a vague depression of the spirit, like a vapor settling down a landscape; a misgiving, coming and going perhaps, a lack of perfect certainty. Whatever it was, Rose and Septimius had no more tender and playful words that day; and Rose soon went to look after her grandmother, and Septimius went and shut himself up in his study.

<He makes an arrangement to meet Rose the next day.>

Septimius shut himself up, and took forth the document which the young officer, with that singular smile on his dying face, had bequeathed to him as the reward of his death. It was in a covering of folded parchment, right through which, as aforesaid, was a bullet hole, and some stains of blood. Septimius unfolded the parchment cover, and found inside some fold of manuscript, closely written in a crabbed hand; so crabbed, indeed, that Septimius could not at first read a word of it, nor satisfy himself, indeed, in what language it was written. There seemed to be Latin words, and some interspersed ones in Greek characters, and here and there he could doubtfully read an English sentence; but on the whole it was an unintelligible mass, conveying somehow an idea that it was the fruit of vast labor and erudition, emanating from a mind very full of books, and grinding and pressing down the great accumulation of grapes that it had gathered from so many vineyards, and squeezing out rich, viscid juices, potent wine, with which the reader might get drunk. (Take Burton's Anatomy as the thing to be described here.) Some of it, moreover, seemed, for the further mystification of the affair, to be written in cypher; a needless precaution, it might seem, when the writer's natural chirography was so full of puzzle and bewilderment.

Septimius looked at this strange manuscript, and it shook in his hand as he held it before his eyes; so great was his excitement. Probably—doubtless—it was in a great measure owing to the way in which it came into his hands, with such circumstances of tragedy and mystery, as if—so secret and so important was it—it could not be within the knowledge of two persons at once, and therefore it was necessary that one should die, in the act of transmitting to the hand of another, the destined possessor, inheritor, profiter by it. By the bloody hand—as all great possessions in this world have been gained and inherited—he had succeeded to this inheritance, the richest that mortal man could receive. He pored over the inscrutable sentences, and wondered, when he should succeed in reading one, if it might summon up a subject fiend, appearing with thunder and other devilish demonstrations. And by what a strange chance had the document come into the hand of him who alone was fit to receive it? It seemed to Septimius, in his enthusiastic egotism, as if this collection of events had been arranged purposely for this end; a difference had come between two kindred people, a war had broken out, a young officer, with the traditions of an old family represented in him, had marched, and had met with a peaceful student, who had been incited from high and noble motives to take his life; then came a strange brief intimacy, in which his victim made the slayer his heir. All these chances, as they seemed—all these interferences of Providence as they doubt-less were—had been necessary in order to put this manu-script into the hands of Septimius, who now pored over it, and could not with certainty render one word!

But this did not trouble him, except for the momentary delay—because he felt well assured that with strong, con-centrated study as he would bring it, he would remove all difficulties, as the rays of a lens melts stones—as the power of a telescope pierces through the ivory-dense light of stars, and resolves them into their individual brilliancies. He could afford to spend years upon it, if necessary; but earnestness of application should do quickly the work of years.

<(He doubtfully makes out one significant sentence)>

Amid these musings, he was interrupted by his Aunt Keziah, who, though generally observant enough of her nephew's studies, and feeling a sanctity in them, both be-cause of his intending to be a minister, and because she had a great reverence for learning, even if heathenish;—this good old lady summoned Septimius somewhat peremptorily to chop wood for her domestic purposes. How strange it is, the way in which we are continually summoned from all high purposes by these little homely necessities; all symbolizing the great fact, that the earthly part of us, with its demands, takes up the greater portion of all our available force. So Septimius, grumbling, and groaning, went to the woodshed, and exercised himself for an hour as the old lady requested; and it was only by instinct that he worked, hardly conscious what he was doing. The whole of passing life seemed impertinent; or if, for an instant, it seemed otherwise, then his lonely speculations and plans seemed to become impalpable, and to have only the consistency of vapor, which his utmost concentration succeeded no further than to make into the likeness of absurd faces, mopping, mowing, and laughing at him.

But that sentence, of mystic meaning, shone out before him, like a transparency, illuminated in the darkness of his mind; he determined to take it for his motto, until he should be victorious in his quest. When he took his candle, to retire apparently to bed, he again drew forth the manuscript, and sitting down by the dim light, tried vainly to read it; but he could not as yet settle himself to concentrated and regular effort, but kept turning the leaves of the manuscript, in the hope that some other illuminated sentence might gleam out upon him as the first had done, and shed a light on the context around it; and that then another would be discovered, with similar effect, until the whole document would thus be illuminated with separate stars of light, converging and congruing in one radiance that should make the whole visible. But, such was his hard fortune, not one other word of the manuscript was he able to read, that whole evening; and moreover, while he had still an inch of candle left, Aunt Zeziah, in her night-cap, as witch-like a figure as ever went to a wizard meeting in the forest with Septimius's ancestor, appeared at the door of the room, aroused from her bed, and shaking her finger at him.

"Septimius, said she, "you keep me awake, and you will ruin your eyes, and turn your head, if you study till midnight in this way. You'll never live to be a minister, if this is the way you go on."

"Well, well, Aunt Zeziah," said Septimius, covering his manuscript with a book, "I am just going to bed now."

"Good night, then," said the old woman, "and God bless your labor."

Strangely enough, a glance at the manuscript, as he hid it from the old woman, had seemed to Septimius to reveal another sentence, of which he but imperfectly caught the purport; and when she had gone, he in vain sought the place, and vainly, too, endeavored to recall the meaning of what he had read. Doubtless, his fancy exaggerated the importance of the sentence; and he felt as if it might have vanished from the book forever. In fact, the unfortunate young man, excited and tossed to and fro by a variety of strange impulses, was got into a bad way, and was likely enough to go mad, unless the balancing portion of his mind proved to be of greater volume and effect than as yet appeared to be the case.

The next morning, he was up bright and early, poring over the manuscript, with the sharpened wits of the new day; poring into its night, into its old, blurred, forgotten dream; and, indeed, he had been dreaming about it, and was fully possessed with the idea that, in his dream, he had taken up this inscrutable document, and read it off as glibly as he would a page of a modern sermon, in a continual rapture with the deep truths that it made clear to his comprehension, and the lucid way in which it evolved the mode in which man might be restored to his originally undying state. So strong was this impression, that when he unfolded the manuscript, it was with the almost belief that the crabbed old handwriting would be plain to him. Such did not prove to be the case, however; so far from it, that poor Septimius in vain turned over the yellow pages, in quest of the one sentence which he had been able, or fancied himself able, to read yesterday. The illumination, that had brought it out, was now faded, and all was a blur, an inscrutableness, a scrawl of unintelligible characters, alike. So much did this affect him, that he was almost mind to tear it into a thousand fragments, and scatter it out of the window, to the west wind that was then blowing past the house; and if, in that summer season, there had been a fire on the hearth, it is possible that easy realization of a destructive impulse might have caused him to fling the accursed scrawl into the hottest of the flames, and thus return it to the devil who, he suspected, was the original author of it. Had he done so, what strange and gloomy passages would I have been spared the pain of relating. How different would have been the life of Septimius;—a thoughtful preacher of God's word, taking severe, but conscientious views of man's state and relations, a heavy-browed walker and worker on earth, and finally the slumberer in an honored grave, with an epitaph bearing testimony to his great usefulness in his generation.

But, in the meantime, here was this troublesome day passing over him, and pestering, bewildering, and tripping him up with its mean sublunary troubles, as the days will all of us, the moment we try to do anything that, we flatter ourselves, is of a little more importance than others are doing. Aunt Kezia tormented him, a great while, about the rich field, just across the road, in front of the house, which Septimius had neglected the cultivation of, and, unwilling to spare the time to plough, to plant, to hoe it, himself, had hired a lazy lout of the village, when he might just as well have employed and paid wages to the scarecrow which Aunt

Zezia dressed out in ancient habiliments, and set up in the midst of the corn. Then came an old codger from the village, talking to Septimius about the war; a theme of which he was weary; telling rumors of skirmishes that next day would prove to be false, of battles that were immediately to take place, of encounters with the enemy in which our side showed the valor of twenty-fold heroes, but had to retreat; babbling about shells and mortars, battalions, manœuvres, angles, fascines, and other terms of military art; for war had filled the whole brain of the people, and enveloped the whole thought of men in a mist of gunpowder. In this way, sitting on his door step, or in the very study, haunted by such speculations, the wretched old man would waste the better part of a Summer afternoon, while Septimius listened, returning abstracted monosyllables, answering amiss, and wishing his persecutor rammed into one of the cannons he talked about, and fired off to end his interminable babble in one roar. Of great officers coming from France and other countries; of overwhelming forces from England, to put an end to the war at once; of the unlikelihood that it ever should be ended; of its hopelessness; of its certainty of a good and speedy end.

Then came limping along some lame, disabled soldier, begging his way home from the field which, a little while ago, he had sought in the full vigor of rustic health, which he was never to know again, with whom Septimius had to talk, and relieve his wants as far as he could (though not from the poor young officer's deposit of English gold) and send him on his way.

Then came the minister, to talk with his former pupil, about whom he had latterly had much meditation, not understanding what mood had taken possession of him; for the minister was a man of insight, and from conversations with Septimius, as searching as he knew how to make them, he had begun to doubt whether he were sufficiently sound in the faith to adopt the clerical persuasion. Not that he supposed him to be anything like a confirmed unbeliever; but he thought it probable that those doubts, those strange, dark, disheartening suggestions of the devil, that so surely infect certain temperaments and measures of intellect, were tormenting poor Septimius, and pulling him back from the path in which he was capable of doing so much good. So he came, this afternoon, to talk seriously with him, and to advise him, if the case were as he supposed, to get for a time out of the track of the thought in which he had so long been engaged, to enter into active life, and by and by, when the morbid influences should have been overcome by a change of mental and moral religion, he might return, fresh and healthy to his original design.

"What can I do?" asked Septimius gloomily—"What business take up, when the whole land lies waste and idle, except for this war?"

"There is the very business, then," said the minister. "Do you think God's work is not to be done in the field, as well as in the pulpit? You are strong, Septimius, of a bold character, and have a mien and bearing that gives you a natural command among men. Go to the wars, and do a valiant part for your country, and come back to your peaceful mission when the enemy has vanished. Or you might go as chaplain to a regiment, and use the sword in battle—pray for success before a battle, help win it with sword or gun, and give thanks to God, kneeling on the bloody field, at its close. You have already stretched one foe on your native soil."

Septimius could not but smile within himself at this warlike and bloody counsel; and, joining it with some similar exhortations from Aunt Keziah, he was inclined to think that women and clergymen are, in matters of war, the most un-compromising and bloodthirsty of the community. However, he replied coolly, that his moral impulses and his feelings of duty did not exactly impel him in this direction, and that he was of opinion that war was a business in which a man could not engage, with safety to his conscience, unless his conscience actually drove him into it; and that this made all the difference between heroic battle, and murderous strife. The good minister had nothing very effectual to answer to this, and took his leave, with a still stronger sense than before that there was something amiss in his pupil's mind.

By this time, this thwarting day had gone on through its course of little and great impediments to his pursuit—the dis-couragements of trifling and earthly business, of purely im-pertinent interruption, of severe and disheartening opposition from the powerful apposition of different kinds of mind, until the hour had come at which he had arranged to meet Rose Garfield. I am afraid the poor thwarted youth did not go to his love tryst in any very amiable mood; but rather, perhaps, reflecting how all things earthly and immortal, and love among the rest, whichever category of earth or heaven it may belong to, set themselves against man's progress in any pur-suit that he seeks to devote himself to. It is one struggle, the moment he undertakes such a thing, of everything else in the world to impede him.

However, as it turned out, it was a pleasant and happy interview that he had with Rose, that afternoon. The girl herself was in a happy, trustful mood, and met him with such simplicity, threw such a light of sweetness over his soul, that Septimius almost forgot all the wild cares of the day, and walked by her side with a quiet fulness of pleasure that was new to him. She reconciled him, in some secret way, to life as it was, to imperfection, to decay; without any help from her intellect, but through the influence of her character, she seemed, not to solve, but to smooth away problems that troubled him; merely by being, by womanhood, by simplicity, she interpreted God's ways to him; she softened the stoniness that was gathering about his heart. And so they had a delightful time of talking, and laughing, and smelling to flowers; and when they were parting, Septimius said to her, "Rose, you have convinced me that this is a most happy world, and that life has its twin children, Birth and Death, and is bound to prize them equally; and that God is very kind to his earthly children; and that all will go well."

"And have I convinced you of all this?" asked Rose, with a pretty laughter. "It is all true, no doubt; but I should not know how to argue for it. But you are very sweet, and have not frightened me, to-day."

"Do I ever frighten you then, Rose?" asked Septimius, bending his black brow upon her with a look of surprise and displeasure.

"Yes, sometimes," said Rose, facing him with courage, and smiling upon the cloud so as to drive it away, "when you frown at me like that, I am a little afraid you will beat me, all in good time."

"Now," said Septimius, laughing again, "you shall have your choice to be beaten on the spot, or suffer another kind of punishment—which?"

So saying he snatched her to him, and strove to kiss her, while Rose, laughing and struggling, cried out—"The beating! the beating!"—but Septimius relented not, though it was only Rose's cheek that he succeeded in touching. In truth, except for that first one, at the moment of their plighted troths, I doubt whether Septimius ever touched those soft, sweet lips, where the smiles dwelt and the little pouts. He now returned to his study, and questioned with himself whether he should touch that weary, ugly, yellow, blurred, unintelligible, bewitched, mysterious, bullet-penetrated, blood-stained manuscript again. There was an undefinable reluctance to do so, and at the same time an enticement (irresistible, as it proved) drawing him towards it. He yielded, and taking it from his desk, in which the precious, fatal treasure was locked up, he plunged into it again, and, this time, with a certain degree of success. He found the line which had before gleamed out, and vanished again, and which now started out in strong relief; even as when sometimes we see a certain arrangement of stars in the heavens, and again lose it, by not seeing its individual stars in the same relation as before; even so, looking at the manuscript in a different way, Septimius saw this fragment of a sentence, and saw moreover, what was necessary to give it a certain meaning. "Set the root in a Grave, and wait for what shall blossom; it will be very rich and full of juice." This was the purport, he now felt sure, of the sentence he had lighted upon; and he took it to refer to the mode of producing something that was essential to the thing to be concocted. It might have only a moral bearing; or, as is generally the case, the moral and physical truth went hand in hand.

While Septimius was busying himself in this way, the summer advanced, and with it there appeared a new character, making her way into our pages. This was a slender and pale girl, whom Septimius was once startled to find, when he ascended his hill-top, to take his walk to and fro upon the accustomed path, which he had now worn deep. What was stranger, she sat down close beside the grave, which none but he and the minister knew to be a grave; that little hillock, which he had levelled a little, and on which he had planted various flowers and shrubs, which the summer had fostered into richness, to which the poor young man below contributed what he could, and tried to make it as beautiful as he might, in remembrance of his own beauty. Septimius wished to conceal the fact of its being a grave; not that he was tormented with any sense that he had done wrong in shooting the young man, which had been done in fair battle; but still it was not the pleasantest of thoughts, that he had lain a beautiful human creature, so fit for the enjoyment of life, there; when his own dark brow, his own troubled breast, might better, he could not but acknowledge, have been covered up there.

<Perhaps there might sometimes be something fantastically gay in the language & behavior of the girl.>

Well; but there, on this flower and shrub disguised grave, sat this unknown form of a girl, with a slender, pallid, melancholy grace about her, simply dressed in a dark attire, which she drew loosely about her. At first glimpse, Septimius fancied that it might be Rose; but it needed only a glance to undeceive him; her figure was of another character from the vigorous, though slight, and elastic beauty of Rose; this was a drooping grace, and when he came near enough to see her face, he saw that those large, dark, melancholy eyes, with which she had looked at him, had never met his gaze before.

"Good morrow, fair maiden," said Septimius, with such courtesy as he knew how to use (which, to say truth, was of a rustic order; his way of life having brought him little into female society).—"There is a nice air here on the hill top, this sultry morning below the hill."

As he spoke, he continued to look wonderingly at the strange maiden, half fancying that she might be something that had grown up out of the grave; so unexpected she was, so simply unlike anything that had before come there.

The girl did not speak him, but as she sat by the grave, she kept weeding out the little white blades of faded autumn grass and yellow pine-spikes; peering into the soil, as if to see what it was all made of, and everything that was growing there; and in truth, whether by Septimius's care, or no, there seemed to be several plants of flowers, some little asters, that are abundant everywhere, and golden flowers, such as autumn supplies with abundance everywhere. She seemed to be in quest of something; and several times plucked a leaf and examined it, carefully, then laid it down again, and shook her head. At last, she lifted up her pale face, and fixing her eyes quietly on Septimius, spoke.

"It is not here!"

A very sweet voice it was, plaintive, low; and she spoke to Septimius as if she were familiar with him, and had something to do with him. He was greatly interested, not being able to imagine who this strange girl was, or whence she came, or what, of all things, could be her reason for coming and sitting down by this grave, and apparently botanizing upon it in quest of some particular point.

"Are you in search of flowers?" said Septimius; "this is but a barren spot for them, and this not a good season. In the meadows, and along the margin of the water-courses, you might find the fringed gentian, at this season. In the woods, at the proper time, there are several pretty flowers, the side-saddle flower, the anemone. Violets are plentiful in spring, and make the whole hill side blue. But this hill top, with its thin soil, strewn over a heap of pebble-stones, is no place for flowers."

"The soil is fit," said the maiden, "but the flower has not sprung up."

"What flower do you speak of?" asked Septimius.

"One that is not here," said the pale girl; "no matter; I will look for it again, next spring."

"Do you live hereabout?" inquired Septimius.

"Surely," said the maiden, with a look of surprise. "Where else should I dwell? My home is on this hill-top."

It not a little startled Septimius, as may be supposed, to find his paternal inheritance, of which he and his forefathers had been the only owners since the world began (for they held it by an Indian deed) claimed as a home and abiding-place by this fair, pale, strange acting maiden, who spoke as if she had as much right there as if she had grown up out of the soil, like one of the wild indigenous flowers which she had been gazing at and handling. However that might be, the maiden seemed now about to depart, rising, giving a farewell touch or two to the little verdant hillock, which looked much the neater for her ministrations.

"Are you going?" said Septimius, looking at her in wonder.

"For a time!" said she.

"And shall I see you again?" asked he.

"Surely," said the girl; "this is my walk, along the brow of the hill."

It again smote Septimius with strange surprise, to find the walk, which he himself had made, treading it and smoothing it, and beating it down with the pressure of his continual feet, from the time when the tufted grass made the ridge all uneven, until now, when it was such a pathway as you may see through a wood, or over a field, where many feet pass every day;—to find this track and exemplification of his own secret thoughts, and plans, and emotions, this writing of his body, impelled by the struggle and movement of his soul, claimed as her own by a strange girl, with the melancholy eyes and voice, who seemed to have such a secret familiarity with him.

"You are welcome to come here!" said he, endeavoring at least to keep such hold on his own property as was implied in making an hospitable surrender of it to another.

"Yes," said the girl; "a person should always be welcome to his own."

A faint smile seemed to pass over her face, as she said this, vanishing, however, immediately into the melancholy of her usual expression. She went along Septimius's path, while he stood gazing at her till she reached the brow where it descended towards Robert Garfield's house; then she turned and seemed to wave a slight farewell towards the young man, and began to descend. When her figure had entirely sunk behind the brow of the hill, Septimius slowly followed along the ridge, meaning to watch from that elevated station the course she would take; although, indeed, he would not have been surprised if he had seen nothing, no trace of her, in the whole nearness or distance; in short, if she had been a freak, an illusion, of a hard-working mind, that had put itself ajar by deeply brooding on abstruse matters; an illusion of eyes that he had tired too much by poring over the inscrutable manuscript, and of intellect that was mystified and bewildered by trying to grasp things that could not be grasped. A thing of witchcraft; a sort of fungous growth out of the grave, an unsubstantiality altogether; although certainly she had weeded the grave with bodily fingers, at all events. Still, he had so much of the hereditary mysticism of his race in him, that he might have held her supernatural, only that, on reaching the brow of the hill, he saw her just approaching the dwelling of Robert Garfield's mother, who, moreover, appeared at the threshold beckoning her to come, with a motherly, hospitable air, that denoted that she knew the strange girl, and recognized her as human.

It did not lessen Septimius's surprise, however, to think that such a singular being was established in the neighborhood without his knowledge; considered as a real occurrence of this world, it seemed even more unaccountable than if it had been a thing of ghostology and witchcraft. Continually, through that day, the incident kept intruding its recollection among his thoughts and studies; continually, as he paced along his path, that form seemed to sway along by his side, on the track that she had claimed for her own, and he thought of her singular threat or promise, whichever it were to be held, that he should have a companion there in future. In the decline of the day, when he met the Schoolmistress coming home from her little seminary, he snatched the first opportunity to mention the apparition of the morning, and ask Rose if she knew anything of her.

"Very little," said Rose; "but she is of flesh and blood, of that you may be quite sure. She is a girl who has been shut up in Boston by the siege; perhaps a daughter of one of the British officers, and her health being frail, she required better air than they have there, and so permission was got for her, from General Washington, to come and live in the country; as, any one may see, our liberties have nothing to fear from this poor, brain-stricken girl. And Robert Garfield, being to bring a message from camp to the selectmen here, about some military matters, had it in charge to bring this girl, whom his mother has taken to board."

"Then the poor thing is crazy?" asked Septimius.

"A little brain-touched, that is all," replied Rose, "owing to some grief that she has had; but she is quite harmless, Robert was told to say, and needs little or no watching, and will get a kind of fantastic happiness for herself, if only she is allowed to ramble about at her pleasure. If thwarted, she might be very wild and miserable."

"Have you spoken with her?" asked Septimius.

"A word or two, this morning, as I was going to my school," said Rose. "She took me by the hand, and smiled, and said we would be friends, and that I should show her where the flowers grew; for that she had a little spot of her own that she wanted to plant with them. And she asked me if the crepusco herpellana grew hereabout. I should not have taken her to be ailing in her wits, only for a kind of free-spokenness, and familiarity, as if we had been acquainted a long while; or as if she had lived in some country where there are no forms and impediments in people's getting acquainted."

"Did you like her?" inquired Septimius.

"Yes—almost loved her, at first sight," answered Rose; "and I hope may do her some little good, poor thing, being of her own age, and the only companion, hereabouts, whom she is likely to find. But she has been well educated, and is a lady, that is easy to see."

"It is very strange," said Septimius; "but I fear I shall be a good deal interrupted in my thoughts and studies, if she insists on haunting my hill top as much as she tells me. My meditations are perhaps of a little too much importance to be shoved aside for the sake of gratifying a crazy girl's fantasies."

"Ah, that is a hard thing to say!" exclaimed Rose, shocked at her lover's cold egotism, though not giving it that title. "Let the poor thing glide quietly along in the path, though it be yours. Perhaps, after a while, she will help your thoughts."

"My thoughts," said Septimius, "are of a kind that can have no help from any one; if from any, it could only be from some wise, long-studied and experienced scientific man, who could enlighten me as to the bases and foundation of things, as to cryptic writings, as to chymical elements, as to the mysteries of language; as to the principles and system on which we were created. Methinks these are not to be taught me by a girl touched in the wits."

"I fear," replied Rose Garfield with gravity, and drawing imperceptibly apart from him, "that no woman can help you much. You despise woman's thought, and have no need of her affection."

Septimius said something soft and sweet, and measurably true, in regard to the necessity he felt for the affection and sympathy of one woman, at least—the one now by his side— to keep his life warm and to make the empty chambers of his heart comfortable. But, even while he spoke, there was something that dragged upon his tongue; for he felt that the solitary pursuit in which he was engaged carried him apart from the sympathy of which he spoke, and that he was concentrating his efforts and interest entirely upon himself, and that the more he succeeded, the more remotely he should be carried away, and that his final triumph would be the complete seclusion of himself from all that breathed—the converting him, from an interested actor, into a cold and disconnected spectator of all mankind's warm and sympathetic life. So, as it turned out, this interview with Rose, was one of those in which, coming no one knows from whence, a nameless cloud springs up between two lovers, and keeps them apart from one another by a cold, sullen spell. Usually, however, it requires only one word, spoken out of the heart, to break that spell, and compel the invisible, unsympathetic medium which the enemy of love has stretched cunningly between them, to vanish, and let them come closer together than ever; but, in this case, it might be that the love was the illusive state, and the estrangement the real truth, the disenchanted verity. At all events, when the feeling passed away, in Rose's heart, there was no re-action, no warmer love, as is generally the case. As for Septimius, he had other things to think about, and when he next met Rose Garfield, had forgotten that he had been sensible of a little wounded feeling, on her part, at parting.

By dint of continual poring over the manuscript, Septimius now began to comprehend that it was written in a singular mixture of Latin and ancient English, with constantly recurring paragraphs of what he was convinced was a cryptic writing; and these recurring passages of complete unintelligibility seemed to be necessary to the proper understanding of any part of the document. What was discoverable was quaint, curious, but thwarting and perplexing, because it seemed to imply some very great purpose, only to be brought out by what was hidden. Septimius had read, in the old college library, during his pupillage, a work on cyphers and cryptic writing, but being drawn to it only by his curiosity respecting whatever was hidden, and not expecting ever to use his knowledge, he had obtained only the barest idea of what was necessary to the decyphering a secret passage. Judging by what he could pick out, he would have thought the whole essay was upon the moral conduct, all parts of that he could make out seeming to refer to a certain ascetic rule of life; to denial of pleasures; these topics being repeated and insisted on everywhere, although without any discoverable reference to religious or moral motives; and always, when the author seemed verging towards a definite purpose, he took refuge in his cypher. Yet withal, imperfectly (or not at all, rather) as Septimius could comprehend its purpose, this strange writing had a mystic influence, that wrought upon his imagination, and combined with the late singular incidents of his life, his continual thought on this one subject, his walk on the hill-top, lonely, or only interrupted by that pale shadow of a girl, combined to set him outside of the living world. Rose Garfield perceived it—saw and felt that he was gliding away from her —and met him with a reserve which she could not overcome.

It was a pity that his early friend, Robert Garfield, could not at present have any influence over him; having now regularly joined the Continental army, and being engaged in the expedition of Arnold against Quebec. Indeed, this war, in which the country was so earnestly and enthusiastically engaged, had perhaps an influence on Septimius's state of mind; for it put everybody into an unnatural and exaggerated state, raised enthusiasms of all sorts, heightened everybody either into its own heroism, or into the peculiar madness to which each person was inclined; and Septimius walked so much the more wildly on his lonely course, because the people were going enthusiastically on another. In times of Revolution and public disturbance, all absurdities are more unrestrained; the measure of calm sense, the habits, the orderly decency, are in a measure lost. More people become insane, I should suppose; offenses against public morality, female license, are more numerous; suicides, murders, all ungovernable outbreaks of men's thoughts, embodying themselves in wild acts, take place more frequently, and with less horror to the lookers-on. So Septimius;—there was not, as there would have been at an ordinary time, the same calmness and truth in the public observation, scrutinizing everything with its keen criticism, in that time of seething opinions and overturned principles; a new time was coming, and Septimius's phase of novelty attracted less attention so far as it was known.

So he continued to brood over the manuscript in his study, and to hide it under lock and key, in a recess of the wall, as if it were a secret of murder; to walk too, on his hill top, where, at sunset, always came that pale, crazy maiden, who still seemed to watch the little hillock, with a pertinacious care that was strange to Septimius. By and by came the winter and the deep snows; and even then, unwilling to give up his habitual place of exercise, the monotonousness of which promoted his wish to keep before his mind one subject of thought, Septimius wore a path through the snow, and still walked there. Here, however, he lost, for a time, the companionship of the girl; for when the first snow came, she shivered, and looked at its white heap over the hillock, and said to Septimius:—"I will look for it again in spring."

<Septimius is at the point of despair, for want of a guide in his studies.>

The winter swept over, and spring was just beginning to spread its green flush over the most favored exposures of the landscape; although, on the northern side of stone walls, in the northern nooks of hills, there were still the remnants of snow-drifts. Septimius's hill-top, which was of a soil that quickly rid itself of moisture, now began to be again a genial place of resort to him; and he was one morning taking his walk there, meditating upon the still insurmountable difficulties which interposed themselves against the interpretation of the manuscript; yet feeling the new garb of spring bring hope to him, and the energy and spring for new effort. Thus, pacing to-and-fro, he was surprised, as he turned at the extremity of his walk, to see a figure advancing towards him; not that of the pale maiden, whom he was accustomed to see there, but a figure as widely different as possible.

<(He sees a spider dangling from his web, and examines him minutely)>

It was that of a short, broad, somewhat elderly man, dressed in a surtout that had a half military air, the cocked hat of the period, well-worn and having a fresher spot on it, whence perhaps a cockade had been recently taken off; and this personage carried a well-blackened German pipe in his hand, which, as he walked, he applied to his lips and puffed out volumes of smoke, filling the pleasant western breeze with the fragrance of some excellent Virginia. He came slowly along, and Septimius, slackening his pace a little, came as slowly to meet him—feeling a little indignant, to be sure, that anybody should intrude on his sacred hill; until at last they met, as it happened, close by the memorable little hill-ock, on which the grass and flower-leaves were just beginning to sprout. The stranger looked keenly at Septimius, made a careless salute by putting his hand up, and took the pipe from his mouth.

"Mr. Septimius Felton, I suppose," said he.

"That is my name," replied Septimius.

"I am Doctor Jabez Portensoaken," said the stranger, "late surgeon of his majesty's sixteenth regiment, which I quitted when his Majesty's army quitted Boston, being desirous of trying my fortunes in your country; and give there the benefit of my scientific knowledge;—also, to practise some new modes of medical science, which I could not so well do in the army."

"I think you are quite right, Doctor Jabez Portensoaken," said Septimius, a little confused and bewildered; so unused had he become to the society of strangers.

"And as for you, Sir," said the Doctor, who had a very rough, abrupt way of speaking, "I have to thank you, Sir, for a favor done me."

"Done you, Sir?" said Septimius, who was quite sure that he had never seen the Doctor's uncouth figure before.

"Oh, aye, me!" said the Doctor, puffing coolly;—"me, in the person of my niece, a sickly, poor, nervous little thing, who is very fond of walking on your hill-top, and whom you do not send away."

"You are then the uncle of Alice Ford?" said Septimius.

"Even so; her mother's brother," said the Doctor, with a grotesque bow; "so, being on a visit (the first that the siege allowed me to pay) to see how the girl was getting on, I take the opportunity to pay my respects to you, the more, that I understand you to be a young man of some learning; and it is not often that one meets with such in this country."

"No," said Septimius, abruptly; for, indeed, he had half a suspicion that this queer Doctor Portsoaken was not altogether sincere—that, in short, he was making game of him. "You have been misinformed. I know nothing whatever that is worth knowing."

"Oho," said the Doctor, with a long puff of smoke out of his pipe. "If you are convinced of that, you are one of the wisest men I have met with, young as you are. I must have been twice your age before I had got so far; and, even now, I am sometimes fool enough to doubt the only thing I was ever sure of knowing. But, come; you make me only the more earnest to collogue with you. If we put both our shortcomings together, they may make up an item of positive knowledge."

"What use can one make of abortive thoughts?" said Septimius.

"Do your speculations take a scientific turn?" said Doctor Portsoaken. "There I can meet you with as much false knowledge and empiricism as you can bring for the life of you. Have you ever tried to study spiders; there is my strong point, now! I have hung my whole interest in life on a spider's web."

"I know nothing of them, Sir," said Septimius;—"except to crush them, when I see them running across the floor;—or to brush away the festoons of their webs, when they have chanced to escape my Aunt Zeziah's broom."

"Crush them! Brush away their webs?" cried the Doctor, apparently in a rage, and shaking his pipe at Septimius. "Sir, it is sacrilege! Sir; it is worse than murder. Every thread of a spider's web is worth more than a thread of gold, and, before twenty years are passed, a housemaid will be beaten to death with her own broom stick, if she disturbs one of those sacred animals. But, come again. Shall we talk of botany, the virtues of herbs?"

"My Aunt Zezia would meet you there, Doctor," said Septimius. "She has a native and original acquaintance with their virtues, and can cure or kill with any of the faculty. As for myself, my studies have not turned that way."

"They ought! They ought!" said the Doctor, looking mean-ingly at him. "The whole thing lies in the blossom of an herb. Now; you ought to begin with what lies about you; on this little hillock for instance," and looking at the grave, beside which they were standing, he gave it a kick which went to Septimius's heart, there seemed to be such a spite and scorn in it; "on this hillock, I see some specimens of plants which would be worth your looking at."

Bending down towards the grave as he spoke, he seemed to give closer attention to what he saw there; keeping in his stooping position till his face began to get a purple aspect, for the erudite Doctor was of that make of man who has to be kept right side uppermost with care. At length, he raised himself, muttering, "Very curious! Very curious!"

"Do you see anything remarkable there?" asked Septimius, with some interest.

"Yes," said the Doctor bluntly; "no matter what! The time will come when you may like to know it."

"Will you come with me to my residence, at the foot of the hill, Doctor Portsoaken?" asked Septimius. "I am not a learned man, and have little or no title to converse with one, except a sincere desire to be wiser than I am. If you can be moved on such terms to give me your companionship, I shall be thankful."

"Sir, I am with you," said Doctor Portsoaken; "I will tell you what I know, in the sure belief (for I will be frank with you) that it will add to the amount of dangerous folly now in your mind, and help you on the way to ruin. Take your choice, therefore, whether to know me farther or not."

"I neither shrink, nor fear—neither hope much," said Septimius quietly. "Anything that you can communicate, if anything you can, I shall fearlessly receive, and return you such thanks as it may be found to deserve."

So saying, he led the way down the hill, by the steep path that descended abruptly upon the rear of his bare and un-adorned little dwelling; the Doctor following with much foul language (for he had a terrible habit of swearing) at the difficulties of the way, to which his short legs were ill adapted. Aunt Keziah met them at the door, and looked sharply at the Doctor, who returned the gaze with at least as much keenness, muttering between his teeth as he did so; and, to say the truth, Aunt Keziah was as worthy of being sworn at, as any woman could well be; for, whatever she might have been in younger days, she was at this time as strange a mixture of an Indian squaw and herb-doctress, with the civilized old maid, and a mixture of the witch aspect running through all, as could well be imagined; and she had a handkerchief over her head, and she was of hue a dusky yellow, and she looked very cross. As Septimius ushered the Doctor into his study, and was about to follow him, Aunt Keziah drew him back.

"Septimius, who is this you have brought here?" asked she.

"A man I have met on the hill," answered her nephew; "a Doctor Portsoaken, he calls himself, from the old country. He says he has knowledge of herbs and other mysteries;—in your own line, it may be. If you want to talk with him, give the man his dinner, and find out what there is in him."

"And what do you want of him yourself, Septimius?" asked she.

"I? Nothing!—that is to say, I expect nothing," said Septimius. "But I am astray, seeking everywhere, and so I reject no hint, no promise, no faintest possibility of aid, that I may find anywhere. I judge this man to be a quack, but I judge the same of the most learned men of his profession, or any other; and there is a roughness about this man that may indicate a little more knowledge than if he were smoother. So, as he threw himself in my way, I take him in."

"A grim, ugly-looking old wretch, as ever I see," muttered Aunt Keziah. "Well he shall have his dinner; and if he likes to talk about yarb-dishes, I'm with him."

So Septimius followed the Doctor into his study, where he found him with the sword in his hand, which he had taken from over the mantel-piece, and was holding it drawn, examining the hilt and blade with great minuteness; the hilt being wrought in open work with certain heraldic devices, doubtless belonging to the family of its former wearer.

"I have seen this weapon before," said the Doctor.

"It may well be," said Septimius. "It was once worn by a person who served in the army of your king."

"And you took it from him?" said the Doctor.

"If I did, it was in no way that I need be ashamed of, or afraid to tell, though I choose rather not to speak of it," answered Septimius.

"Have you, then, no desire nor interest to know the family, the personal history, the prospects, of him who once wore this sword, and who will never draw sword again?" inquired Doctor Portensoak. "Poor Willie Rogers! There was a singular story attached to that young man, Sir, and a singular mystery he carried about with him; the end of which, perhaps, is not yet."

Septimius would have been, indeed, well enough pleased to learn the mystery which he himself had seen that there was, about the man whom he slew; but he was afraid that some question might be thereby started about the secret document that he had kept possession of; and he therefore would have wished to avoid the whole subject.

"I cannot be supposed to take much interest in English family history. It is a hundred and fifty years, at least, since my own family ceased to be English," he answered. "I care more for the present & future than for the past."

"It is all one," said the Doctor, sitting down, taking out a pouch of tobacco, and refilling his pipe.

It is unnecessary to follow up the description of the visit of the eccentric Doctor through the day. Suffice it to say that there was a sort of charm, or rather fascination, about the un-couth old fellow, in spite of his strange ways; in spite of his constant puffing of tobacco; and in spite, too, of a constant imbibing of strong liquor, which he made inquiries for, and of which the best that could be produced was a certain decoc-tion, infusion, or distillation, pertaining to Aunt Keziah, and of which the basis was rum, be it said, done up with certain bitter herbs of the old lady's own gathering, at proper times of the moon, and which was a well known drink to all who were favored with Aunt Kezia's friendship; though there went a story that it was the very drink which used to be passed round at witch meetings, being brewed from the Devil's own recipe. And, in truth, judging from the taste (for I once took a sip of a draught prepared from the same ingredients, and in the same way) I should think this hellish origin might be the veritable one. "I thought," quoth the Doctor, with an awful oath, "I had swallowed the Devil himself, whom this old woman has been boiling down." But the valiant Doctor sipped, and sipped again, and said with great blasphemy that it was the real stuff, and only needed Henbane to make it perfect. Then taking from his pocket a good sized, leathern covered flask, with a silver cup fastened on the muzzle, he offered it to Septimius, who declined, and to Aunt Zeziah, who preferred her own decoction, and then drank it off himself, with a loud term of satisfaction, declaring it to be infernally good brandy.

Well; after this, Septimius and he talked; and I know not how it was, but there was a great deal of magnetism in this queer man, whether a bodily or a spiritual influence, it might be hard to say. On the other hand, Septimius had for a long while held little intercourse with men; none whatever with men who could comprehend him; the Doctor, too, seemed to bring the discourse singularly in apposition with what his host was continually thinking about, for he conversed on occult matters, on people who had had the art of living long, and had only died at last by accident; on the powers and qualities of common herbs, which he believed to be so great, that all around our feet, growing in the wild forest, afar from man, or following the footsteps of man wherever he fixes his residence, across seas, from the old homesteads whence he migrated, following him everywhere, and offering themselves sedulously and continually to his notice, while he only plucks them away from the comparatively worthless things which he cultivates, and flings them aside, blaspheming at them because Providence has sown them so thickly—grow what we call weeds, only because all the generations from the beginning of time till now have failed to discover their wondrous virtues, potent for the curing of all diseases, potent for procuring length of days.

"Everything good," said the Doctor, drinking another dram of brandy, "lies right at our feet; and all we need is to gather it up."

"That's true," quoth Kezia, taking just a little sup of her hellish perpetration; "these herbs were all gathered within a hundred yards of this very spot; though it took a wise woman to find out their virtues."

The old woman went off, about her household duties; and then it was that Septimius submitted to the Doctor the list of herbs which he had picked out of the old document, asking him, as something apposite to the subject of their discourse, whether he was acquainted with them; for most of them had very queer names, some in Latin, some in English.

The bluff Doctor put on his spectacles, and looked over the slip of yellow and worn paper scrutinizingly, puffing tobacco smoke upon it in great volumes, as if thereby to make its hidden purport come out; he mumbled to himself; he took another sip from his flask; and then, putting it down on the table, appeared to meditate.

"This infernal old document," said he, at length, "is one that I have heard of before, but never seen; yet heard of nevertheless; for it was my folly in youth (and whether I am any wiser now is more than I take upon me to say) but it was my folly then to be in quest of certain kinds of secret knowledge, which the fathers of science thought attainable. Now, in several quarters, amongst persons with whom my pursuits brought me in contact, I heard of a certain recipe which had been lost for a generation or two, but which, if it could be recovered, would prove to have the true life-giving potency in it. It is said that the ancestor of a great old family in England was in possession of this secret— being a man of science, and the friend of Friar Bacon, he was said to have concocted it himself, partly from the precepts of his master, partly from his own improvements; and it is thought he might have been living to this day, if he had not unluckily been killed in the Wars of the Roses; for, you know, no receipt for long life would be proof against an old English arrow, or a leaden bullet from one of our firelocks."

"And what has been the history of the thing after his death?" asked Septimius.

"It was supposed to be preserved in the family," said the Doctor; "and it has always been said, that the heir and eldest son of that family had it at his option to live forever, if he could only make up his mind to it. But seemingly there were difficulties in the way. There was probably a certain diet and regimen to be observed, certain strict rules of life to be kept, a certain asceticism to be imposed on the person, which was not quite agreeable to young men; and after the period of youth was passed, the human frame became incapable of being regenerated from the seeds of decay and death, which, by that time, had become strongly developed in it. In short, while young, the possessor of the secret found the terms of immortal life too hard to be accepted, since it implied the giving up most of the things that made life desirable in his view; and when he came to a more reasonable mind, it was too late. And so, in all the generations since Friar Bacon's time, the D'Aubignys have been born, and enjoyed their young days, and worried through their manhood, and tottered though their old age (unless taken off sooner by sword, arrow, ball, fever, or what not) and died in their beds, like men that had no such option; and so this old yellow paper has done not the least good to any mortal. Neither do I see how it can do any good to you, since you know not the rules, moral or dietic, that are essential to its effect. But how did you come by it?"

"It matters not how," said Septimius gloomily. "Enough that I am its rightful possessor and inheritor. Can you read these old characters?"

"Most of them," said the Doctor. "But let me tell you, my young friend, I have no faith whatever in this trash; and having meddled with such things myself, I ought to know. The old physicians and chymists had strange ideas of the virtues of plants, drugs, and minerals, and equally strange fancies as to the way of getting those virtues into action. They would throw a hundred different potencies into a cauldron together, and put them on the fire, and expect to brew a potency combining all their potencies, and having a different virtue of their own. Whereas, the most likely result would be, that they would counteract one another, and the concoction be of no virtue at all; or else some more powerful ingredient would tincture the whole."

He read the paper again, and continued:—

"I see nothing else so remarkable in this recipe, as that it is chiefly made up of some of the commonest things that grow; plants that you set your foot upon, at your very threshold, in your garden, in your wood-walks, wherever you go. I doubt not old Aunt Zeziah knows them, and very likely she has brewed them up in that hell-drink, the remembrance of which is still rankling in my stomach. It would be curious enough, if the Indians had a decoction that was the same as old Friar Bacon and his acolyte discovered by their science! One ingredient, however—one of those plants, I scarcely think the old lady can have put into her pot of devil's elixir; for it is a rare plant that does not grow in these parts."

"And what is that?" asked Septimius.

"Caudeleucia nigrissimus," said the Doctor; "it has no vulgar name; but it produces a very beautiful flower, which

I have never seen, though some seeds of it were sent me by a learned friend in Siberia. The others, divest them of their Latin names, are as common as plantain, pigweed, and burdock; and it stands to reason, that, if vegetable Nature has any such wonderfully efficacious medicine in store for men, and means them to use it, she would have strewn it plentifully everywhere within their reach."

"But after all, it would be a mockery on the old Dame's part," said the young man, somewhat bitterly. "Since she would thus hold the desired thing seemingly within our reach, but because she never tells us how to prepare and obtain its efficacy, we miss it just as much as if all the ingredients were hidden from sight and knowledge in the centre of the earth. We are the playthings and fools of Nature, which she amuses herself with, during our little lifetime, and then breaks for mere sport, and laughs in our faces as she does so."

"Take care, my good fellow," said the Doctor, with his great coarse laugh. "I rather suspect that you have already got beyond the age when the Great Medicine could do you good; that speech indicates a great toughness, and hardness, and bitterness, about the heart, that does not accumulate in our tender years."

Septimius took little or no notice of the raillery of the grim old Doctor; but employed the rest of the time in getting as much information as he could out of his guest; and though he could not bring himself to show him the precious and sacred manuscript, yet he questioned him as closely as possible without betraying his secret, into the modes of finding out cryptic writings. The shrewd Doctor was not without the perception that his dark-browed, keen-eyed acquaintance had some purpose not openly avowed in all these pertinacious, distant questions; he discovered a central reference in them all, and perhaps knew that Septimius must have in his possession some writing in hieroglyphics, cypher, or other secret mode, that conveyed instructions how to operate with the strange recipe that he had shown him.

"You had better trust me fully, my good Sir," said he. "Not but what I will give you all the aid I can without it; for you have done me a greater benefit than you are aware of, beforehand. No?—you will not? Well; if you ever change your mind, seek me out in Boston, where I have seen fit to settle in the practice of my profession; and I will serve you according to your folly; for folly it is, I warn you!"

Nothing else worthy of record is known to have passed during the Doctor's visit; and, in due time, he disappeared as it were in a whiff of tobacco smoke, leaving an odor of brandy and tobacco behind him, and a traditionary memory of a wizard that had been there. Septimius went to work with what items of knowledge he had gathered from him; but the interview had at least made him aware of one thing—which was, that he must provide himself with all possible quantity of scientific knowledge of botany, and perhaps more extensive knowledge, in order to be able to concoct the recipe. It was the fruit of all the scientific attainment of the age that produced it; (so said the legend, which seemed reasonable enough,) a great philosopher had wrought his learning into it; and this had been attempered, regulated, improved, by the quick, bright intellect of his scholar. Perhaps, thought Septimius, another deep and earnest intelligence added to these two, may bring the precious recipe to still greater perfection. At least, it shall be tried. So thinking, he gathered together all the books that he could find, relating to such studies; he spent one day, moreover, in a walk to Cambridge, where he searched the alcoves of the college library for such works as it contained; and borrowing these from the war-disturbed institution of learning, he betook himself homeward, and applied himself to the study with an earnestness of zealous application, that perhaps has been seldom equalled in a study of so quiet a character. A month or two of study, with practice upon such plants as he found upon his hill top, and along the brook, and in other neighboring localities, sufficed to do a great deal for him. In this pursuit he was assisted by Edith, who proved to have great knowledge in some botanical departments, especially among flowers; and in her cold and quiet way, she met him on this subject, and glided by his side, as she had done so long, a companion, a daily observer and observed of him, mixing herself up with his pursuits, as if she were an attendant sprite upon him.

But this pale girl was not the only associate of his studies, the only instructress whom Septimius found. The observation which Doctor Portsoaken made about the fantastic possibility that Aunt Kezia might have inherited the same receipt from her Indian ancestry, which had been struck out by the science of Friar Bacon and his pupil, had not failed to impress Septimius, and to remain upon his memory. So, not long after the Doctor's departure, the young man took occasion, one evening, to say to his Aunt, that he thought his stomach was a little out of order with too much application, and that perhaps she might give him some herb-drink or other that would be good for him.

"That I can, Seppy, my darling," said the old woman; "and I'm glad you have the sense to ask for it, at last. Here it is in this bottle; and though that foolish, blaspheming Doctor turned up his old brandy nose at it, I'll drink with him any day, and come off better than he."

So saying, she took out of the closet her brown jug, stopped with a cork that had a rag twisted round it to make it tighter, filled a mug half full of the concoction, and set it on the table before Septimius.

"There, child, smell of that; the smell merely will do you good; but drink it down, and you'll live the longer for it."

"Indeed, Aunt Keziah, is that so?" asked Septimius, a little startled by a recommendation which in some measure tallied with what he wanted in a medicine. "That's a good quality."

He looked into the mug, and saw a turbid yellow concoction, not at all attractive to the eye; he smelt of it, and was partly of opinion that Aunt Zeziah had mixed a certain unfragrant vegetable called skunk cabbage with the other ingredients of her witch-drink. He tasted it—not a mere sip, but a good, genuine gulp, being determined to have real proof of what the stuff was in all respects. The draught seemed at first to burn in his mouth, unaccustomed to any drink but water, and to go scorching all the way down into his stomach, making him sensible of the depth of his inwards by a track of fire, far, far down; and then, worse than the fire, came a taste of hideous bitterness and nauseousness, which he had not previously conceived to exist, and which threatened to stir up his bowels into utter revolt; but knowing the touchiness of Aunt Keziah with regard to this concoction, and how sacred she held it, he made an effort of real heroism, squelched down his agony, and kept his face quiet, with the exception of one strong convulsion, which he allowed to twist across it for the sake of saving his life.

"It tastes as if it might have great potency in it, Aunt Keziah," said this unfortunate young man. "I wish you would tell me what it is made of, and how you brew it; for I have observed you are very strict & secret about it."

"Aha! You have seen that, have you!" said Aunt Keziah, taking a sip of her beloved liquid, and grinning at him with a face and eyes as yellow as what she was drinking. In fact, the idea struck him, that in temper and all appreciable qualities, Aunt Keziah was a good deal like this drink of hers, having probably become saturated with the quantities which she drank of it. And then, having drunk, she gloated over it, and tasted, and smelt of the cup of this hellish wine, as a wine-bibber does of his most fragrant and delicate wine. "And you want to know how I make it! But, first, child, tell me honestly, do you love this drink of mine;—otherwise, here, and at once, we stop talking about it."

<The Sagamore was said to have mingled the life-blood of a man with his drink; but Aunt Keziah thought it meant blood-root.>

"I love it for its virtues," said Septimius, tampering with his conscience, "and would prefer it, on that account, to the rarest wines."

"So far good," said Aunt Keziah, who could not well conceive that her liquor could be otherwise than delicious to the palate. "It is the most virtuous liquor that ever was; and therefore one need not fear drinking too much of it. And you want to know what it is made of! Well; I have often thought of telling, Seppy my boy, when you should come to be old enough; for I have no other inheritance to leave you, and you are all of my blood, unless I should happen to have some far off cousin among the cape Indians. But first you must know how this good drink, or the faculty of making it, came down to me from the chiefs, and sachems, and pow-wows, that were your ancestors and mine, Septimius, and from the old wizard, who was my great grandfather and yours, and who, they say, added the firewater to the other ingredients, and so gave it the only one thing that it wanted to make it perfect."

And so, Aunt Keziah, who had now put herself into a most comfortable and jolly state by sipping again, and after pressing Septimius to mend his draught (who declined, on the plea that one dram at a time was enough for a new beginner, its virtues being so strong as well as so admirable) the old woman told him a legend strangely wild and uncouth, and mixed up of savage and civilized life, and of the superstitions of both, but which yet had a certain analogy, that impressed Septimius much, to the story that the Doctor had told him.

She said that, many ages ago, there had been a wise Sachem in the forest, a King among the Indians, and from whom, the old lady said with a look of pride, she and Septimius were lineally descended, and were probably the very last who inherited one drop of that royal, wise, and warlike blood. This Sachem had lived very long—longer than anybody knew, for the Indians kept no record, and could only talk of a great number of moons; and they said he was as old, or older than the eldest trees; as old as the hills almost, and could remember back to the days of godlike men, who had arts then forgotten; he was a wise and good man, and could foretell as far into the future as he could remember into the past; and he continued to live on, till his people were afraid that he would live forever, and so disturb the whole order of nature. So a deputation of the best and bravest of the tribe went to the great Sachem, and told him their thought, and reverently desired his consent to be put out of the world; and the Undying One agreed with them that it was better for his own comfort that he should die, and that he had long been weary of the world, having learned all that it could teach him, and having, chiefly, learned to despair of ever making the red-race much better than they now were; so he cheerfully consented, and told them to kill him if they could; and first they tried the stone hatchet, which was broken against his skull; and then they shot arrows at him, which could not pierce the toughness of his skin; and finally they plastered up his nose and mouth (which kept uttering wisdom to the last) with clay, and set him to bake in the sun; so at last his life burst out of his breast, tearing his body to pieces, and he died. <Make this legend grotesque, and express the weariness of the tribe at the intolerable control the Undying One had of them, his always bringing up precepts from his own experience, never consenting to anything new, so impeding progress, his habits hardening into him, his assuming to himself all wisdom,—his intolerable wisdom— and depriving everybody of his rights to successive command; his endless talk, and dwelling on the past; so that the world could not bear him.>

<Describe his ascetic and severe habits, his rigid calmness &c>

<Perhaps the devil taught him the drink; or else the Great Spirit—doubtful which>

But before the great Sagamore died, he imparted to a chosen one of his tribe, the next wisest to himself, the secret of a potent and delicious drink, the constant imbibing of which, together with his abstinence from luxury and passion, had kept him alive so long, and would doubtless have compelled him to live forever. This drink was compounded of many ingredients, all of which were remembered and handed down in tradition, save one, which either because it was nowhere to be found, or for some other reason, was forgotten; so that the drink ceased to give immortal life, as before. They say, it was a beautiful purple flower. But it still was a most excellent drink, and conducive to health and to the cure of all diseases; and the Indians had it at the time of the settlement by the English; and at one of those wizard meetings in the forest, where the Black Man used to meet his red children and his white ones, and be jolly with them, a great Indian wizard taught the secret to Septimius's great great-grandfather, who was a wizard and died for it; and he, in return, taught the Indians to mix it with rum, thinking that this might be the very ingredient that was missing, and that by adding it he might give endless life to himself and all his Indian friends, among whom he had taken a wife. "But your great grandfather, you know, had not a fair chance to test its virtues; having been hanged for a wizard; and as for the Indians, they probably mixed too much firewater with their liquid, so that it burnt them up, and they all died; and my mother and her mother, who taught the drink to me, and her mother afore her, thought it a sin to try to live longer than the Lord pleased; so they let themselves die. And though the drink is good, Septimius, and toothsome, as you see, yet I sometimes feel as if I were getting old, like other people, and may die in the course of the next half-century; so perhaps the rum is not just the thing that was wanting to make up the recipe. But it is very good! Take a drop more of it, dear!"

"Not at present, I thank you, Aunt Kezeia," said Septimius gravely. "But will you tell me what the ingredients are, and how you make it?"

"Yes, I will, my boy, and you shall write them down," said the old woman. "For it's a good drink, and none the worse, it may be, for not making you live forever. I sometimes think I had as lief go to Heaven, as keep on living here."

Accordingly, making Septimius take pen and ink, she proceeded to tell him a list of plants and herbs, and forest productions, and he was surprised to find that it agreed most wonderfully with the recipe contained in the old manuscript, as he had puzzled it out, and as it had been explained by the Doctor. There were a few variations, it is true; but even here there was a close analogy, plants indigenous to America being substituted for cognate productions, the growth of Europe. Then there was another difference in the mode of preparation; Aunt Kezeiah's nostrum being a concoction; whereas the old manuscript gave a process of distillation. This similarity had a strong effect on Septimius's imagination. Here was, in one case, a drink suggested, as might be supposed, to a primitive people by something similar to that instinct by which the brute creation recognizes the medicaments suited to its needs, so that they mixed up fragrant herbs, for reasons wiser than they knew, and made them into a salutary potion; and here, again, was a drink contrived by the utmost skill of a great civilized philosopher, searching the whole field of science for his purpose; and these two drinks proved to be in all essential particulars, identically the same.

"Oh, Aunt Kezia," said he, with a longing earnestness, "are you sure that you cannot remember that one ingredient?"

"No, Septimius, I cannot possibly do it," said she. "I have tried many things, skunk cabbage, wormwood, and once poison mercury, and a thousand things; for it is truly a pity that the chief benefit of the thing should be lost for so little. But the only effect was, to spoil the good taste of the stuff, and, two or three times, to poison myself, so that I broke out all over blotches, and once lost the use of my left arm, and got a dizziness in the head, and a rheumatiz here in my knee, and a hardness of hearing, and a dimness of sight, and the trembles; all of which I certainly believe to have been caused by my putting something else into this blessed drink, besides the good New England rum. Stick to that, Seppy, my dear!"

So saying, Aunt Keziah took yet another sip of the beloved liquid, after vainly pressing Septimius to do the like; and then lighting her old clay pipe, she sat down in the chimney-corner, meditating, dreaming, muttering pious prayers and ejaculations, and sometimes looking up the wide flue of the chimney, with thoughts, perhaps, how delightful it must have been to fly up there, in old times, on excursions by midnight into the forest, where was the Black Man, and the Puritan deacons and ladies, and those wild Indian ancestors of hers; and where the wildness of the forest was so grim and delightful, and so unlike the commonplaceness in which she spent her life. For then did the savage strain of the woman, mixed up as it was with the other weird and religious parts of her composition, sometimes snatch her back into barbarian life, and its instincts; and in Septimius, though further diluted, and modified likewise by higher cultivation, there was the same.

Septimius escaped from the old woman, and was glad to breathe the free air again; so much had he been wrought upon by her wild legends, and wild character, the more powerful by its analogy with his own; and, perhaps, too, his brain had been a little bewildered by the draught of her diabolical concoction, which she had compelled him to take. At any rate, he was glad to escape to his hill-top, the free air of which had doubtless contributed to keep him in health, through so-long a course of morbid thought and estranged study as he had addicted himself to do. Hereon, as it happened, he found both Rose Garfield and Sybil Dacy, whom the pleasant summer evening had brought out. They had formed a friendship, or at least society; and there could not well be a more unlike pair; the one so natural, so healthy, so fit to live in the world; the other such a morbid, pale thing; so there they were walking arm in arm, with one arm round each other's waist, as girls love to do, and which looks so tempting to the young men. They greeted the young man in their several ways, and began to walk to-and-fro together, looking at the sunset as it came on, and talking of things on earth and in the clouds.

"When has Robert Garfield been heard from?" asked Septimius, who, involved in his own pursuits, was altogether behind hand in the matters of the war, shame to him for it.

"There came news, two days past," said Rose, blushing. "He is on his way home with the remnant of General Arnold's command, and will be here soon."

"He is a brave fellow, Robert," said Septimius, carelessly; "and I know not, since life is so short, that anything better can be done with it than to risk it as he does."

"I truly think not," said Rose Garfield, composedly.

"What a blessing it is to mortals," said Sybil Dacy;—"what a kindness of Providence, that life is made so uncertain; that Death is thrown in among the possibilities of our being; that these awful mysteries are thrown around us, into which we may vanish. For without it, how would it be possible to be heroic, how should we plod along in common-places forever, never dreaming high things, never risking anything. For my part, I think man is more favored than the angels, and made capable of higher heroism, greater virtue, deeds of a more excellent spirit than they, because we have such a mystery of grief and terror around us; whereas they, being in a certainty of God's light, seeing his goodness and his purposes more perfectly than we, cannot be such heroes as often poor weak man, or weaker woman, has the opportunity to be, and sometimes makes use of it. God gave the whole world to man; and, if he is left alone with it, it will make a clod of him at last; but to remedy this, God gave man a grave, and it redeems all, while it seems to destroy all, and makes an immortal spirit of him in the end."

"Dear Sybil, you are inspired!" said Rose, gazing in her face.

"I think you ascribe a great deal too much potency to the grave," said Septimius, pausing involuntarily close by the little hillock, the contents of which he knew so well; "the grave seems to me a vile pitfall put right in our pathway, and catching most of us, all of us, causing us to tumble in at the most inconvenient opportunities; so that all human life is a jest and farce, just for the sake of this inopportune death. For, I have observed, it never waits for us to accomplish anything; we may have the salvation of a country in hand, but we are none the less likely to die for that. So that, being a believer, on the whole, in the wisdom and graciousness of Providence, I am convinced that dying is a mistake, and that by and by we shall overcome it. I say there is no use in the grave."

"I still adhere to what I said," answered Sybil Dark. "And besides there is another use of a grave, which I have often observed in old English churchyards, where the moss grows green and embosses the letters of the grave-stones; and also graves are very good for flower-beds."

Nobody ever could tell when this strange girl was going to say what was laughable, when what was melancholy; and neither of Sybil's auditors knew quite what to make of this speech. Neither could Septimius fail to be a little startled by seeing her, as she spoke of the grave as a flower-bed, stoop down to the little hillock to examine the flowers; which, indeed, seemed to prove her words, by growing there in strange abundance, and of many sorts, so that if they could all have bloomed at once, the spot would have looked like a boquet by itself, or as if the earth were richest in beauty there, or as if seeds had been lavished by some florist. Septimius could not account for it; for though the hillside did produce certain flowers—the aster, the goldenrod, the violet, and other such simple and common things—yet this seemed as if a carpet of bright colors had been thrown down there, and covered the spot.

"This is very strange!" said he.

"Yes," said Sybil Dacy—"there is some strange richness in this little spot of soil."

"Where could the seeds have come from?—that is the greatest wonder," said Rose. "You might almost teach me botany, methinks, on this one spot."

"Do you know this plant?" asked Sybil of Septimius, pointing to one not yet in flower, but of singular leaf, that was thrusting itself up out of the ground, on the very curve of the grave, over where the breast of the sleeper below might seem to be. "I think there is no other here like it."

Septimius stooped down to examine it, and was convinced that it was unlike anything that he had seen of the flower kind; a leaf of a dark green, with purple veins traversing it, it had a sort of questionable aspect, as some plants have, so that you would think it very likely to be poison, and would not like to touch or smell very intimately, without first inquiring who could be its guarantee that it should do no mischief. That it had some richness or other, either baneful or beneficial, you could not doubt.

"I think it poisonous," said Rose Garfield, shuddering; for she was a person so natural that she hated poisonous things or anything speckled especially, and did not indeed love strangeness. "Yet I should not wonder if it bore a beautiful flower by-and-by. Nevertheless, if I were to do just as I feel inclined, I should root it up and fling it away."

"Shall she do so?" said Sybil to Septimius.

"Not for the world!" said he hastily. "Above all things, I desire to see what will come of this plant."

"Be it as you please," said Sybil; "Meanwhile, if you like to sit down here and listen to me, I will tell you a story that happens to come into my mind just now, I cannot tell why. It is a legend of an old hall, that I know well, and have known from my childhood, in one of the northern counties of England, where I was born. Would you like to hear it, Rose?"

"Yes, of all things," said she. "I like all stories of hall and cottage in the old country, though now we must not call it our country any more."

Sybil looked at Septimius as if to inquire whether he, too, chose to listen to her story, and he made answer;—

"Yes; I shall like to hear the legend, if it is a genuine one that has been adopted into the popular belief, and come down in chimney corners, with the smoke and soot that gathers there; and incrusted over with humanity, by passing from one homely mind to another. Then, such stories get to be true, in a certain sense; and indeed, in that sense may be called true, throughout; for the very nucleus, the fiction in them, seems to have come out of the heart of men, in a way that cannot be imitated of malice aforethought. Nobody can make a tradition; it takes a century to make it."

"I know not whether this legend has the character you mean," said Sybil; "but it has lived much more than a century, and here it is."

On the threshold of one of the doors in Smithills Hall there is a Bloody Footstep, impressed into the door-step, and ruddy as if the bloody foot had just trodden there; and it is averred that, on a certain night of the year, and at a certain hour of the night, if you go and look at that door step, you will see the mark wet with fresh blood. Some have pretended to say that this appearance of blood was but dew; but can dew redden a cambric handkerchief?—will it crimson the finger-tips when you touch it?—and that is what the bloody footstep will surely do, when the appointed night and hour come round, this very year, just as it would three hundred years ago.

Well; but how did it come there? I know not precisely in what age it was; but long ago, when light was beginning to shine into what men called the dark ages, there was a lord of Smithills Hall who applied himself deeply to knowledge and science, under the guidance of the wisest man of that age; a man so wise that he was thought to be a wizard; and, indeed, he may have been one, if to be a wizard consists in having command over secret powers of nature, that other men do not even suspect the existence of—and the control of which enables them to do feats that seem as wonderful as raising the dead. It is needless to tell you all the strange stories that have survived, to this day, about the old hall, and how it is believed that the master of it, owing to his ancient science, has still a sort of residence there, and control of the place, and how, in one of the chambers, there is still his antique table, and his chair, and some rude old instruments and machinery, and a book, and everything in readiness, just as if he might still come back to finish some experiment. What it is important to say, is, that one of the chief things to which this old lord applied himself, was, to discover the means of prolonging his own life, so that its duration should be indefinite, if not infinite; and such was his science, that he was believed to have attained this magnificent and awful purpose.

So, as you may suppose, the man of science had great joy in having done this thing, both for the pride of it, and because it was so delightful a thing to have before him the prospect of endless time which he might spend in adding more and more to his science, and so doing good to the world; for the chief obstruction to the improvement of the world, and the growth of knowledge, is, that mankind cannot go straight forward in it; but continually there have to be new beginnings, and it takes every new man half his life, if not the whole of it, to come up to the point where his predecessor left off. And so this noble man—this man of a noble purpose —spent many years in finding out this mighty secret; and, at last, it is said, he succeeded. But on what terms?

Well; it is said that the terms were dreadful and horrible; insomuch that the wise man hesitated whether it were lawful and desirable to take advantage of them, great as was the object in view. You see, the object of the lord of Smithills Hall was, to take a life from the course of Nature, and Nature did not choose to be defrauded; so that, great as was the power of this scientific man over her, she would not consent that he should escape the necessity of dying at his proper time; except upon condition of sacrificing some other life for his; and this was to be done once, for every thirty years that he chose to live, thirty years being the account of a generation of man; and if, in any way, in that time, this lord could be the death of a human being, that satisfied the requisition; and he might live on. There is a form of the legend which says, that one of the ingredients of the drink, which the nobleman brewed by his science, was the heart's blood of a pure young boy or girl; but this I reject as too coarse an idea; and indeed, I think it may be taken to mean symbolically, that the person who desires to engross to himself more than his share of human life, must do it by sacrificing to his selfishness some dearest interest of some other person, who has a good right to life, and may be as useful in it, as he.

Now, this lord was a just man by Nature, and if he had gone astray, it was greatly by reason of his earnest wish to do something for the poor, wicked, struggling, bloody, nasty, uncomfortable race of man, to which he belonged. He bethought himself whether he would have a right to take the life of one of these creatures, without their own consent, in order to prolong his own; and after much arguing to-and-fro, he came to the conclusion that he should not have this right, unless it were a life over which he had control, and which was the next to his own. He looked round him; he was a lonely and abstracted man, secluded by his studies from human affections, and there was but one human being whom he cared for;—that was a beautiful kinswoman, an orphan, whom his father had brought up, and dying, left her to his care. There was great kindness and affection—as great as the abstracted nature of his pursuits would allow—on the part of this lord towards the beautiful young girl; but not what is called love, at least, he never acknowledged to himself. But, looking into his heart, he saw that this, if any one, was to be the person whom the sacrifice demanded, and that he might kill twenty others without effect; but if he took the life of this one, it would make the charm strong and good.

My friends, I have meditated many a time on this ugly feature of my legend, and am unwilling to take it in the literal sense; so I conceive its spiritual meaning (for everything, you know, has its spiritual meaning, which to the literal meaning is what the soul is to the body) its spiritual meaning was, that to the deep pursuit of science we must sacrifice a great part of the joy of life; that nobody can be great, and do great things, without giving up to death, so far as he regards his enjoyment of it, much that he would gladly enjoy; and in that sense, I choose to take it. But the earthly old legend will insist upon it, that this mad, high-minded, heroic, murderous lord, did insist upon it with himself that he must murder this poor, loving and beloved child.

I do not wish to delay upon this horrible matter, and to tell you how he argued the matter with himself; and how the more and more he argued it, the more reasonable it seemed, the more absolutely necessary, the more a duty, that this terrible sacrifice should be made. Here was this great good to be done to mankind, and all that stood in the way of it was one little delicate life, so frail that it was likely enough to be blown out, any day, by the mere rude blast that the rush of life creates, at it streams along, or by any slightest accident; so good and pure, too, that she was quite unfit for the world, and not capable of any happiness in it; and all that was asked of her, was, to allow herself to be transported to a place where she could be happy, and would find companions fit for her— which he, her only present companion, certainly was not. In fine, he resolved to shed the sweet fragrant blood of this little Violet, that loved him so.

<He kills her, and carries her into the wood, & buries her.>

Well; let us hurry over this part of the story, as fast as we can. He did slay this pure young girl; he carried her into the wood near the house, an old wood that is standing yet, and some of its magnificent oaks, and there he plunged a dagger into her heart; after they had had a very tender and loving talk together, in which he had tried to open the matter tenderly to her, and make her understand, that though he was to slay her, it was really for the very reason that he loved her better than anything else in the world, and that he had far rather kill himself, if that would answer the purpose at all. Indeed, he is said to have offered her the alternative of slaying him, and taking upon herself the burthen of indefinite life, and the studies and pursuits by which he meant to benefit mankind. But she, it is said, this noble, pure, loving child, she looked up into his face, and smiled sadly, and then snatching the dagger from him, she plunged it into her own heart. I cannot tell whether this be true, or whether she waited to be killed by him; but this I know, that, in the same circumstances, I think I should have saved my lover or my friend the pain of killing me. There she lay dead, at any rate, and the mad lord buried her there in the wood, and returned to the house; and as it happened, he had set his right foot in her blood, and his shoe was wet in it, and by some miraculous fate, it left a track all along the wood-path, and into the house, and on the stone step of the threshold; and up into his chamber, all along; and the servants saw it the next day, and wondered, and whispered, and missed the fair young girl, and looked askance at their lord's right foot, and turned pale all of them as death.

And next the legend says, that Sir Forrester was struck with horror at what he had done, and could not bear the laboratory where he had toiled so long, and was sick to death of the object that he had pursued, and was most miserable, and fled from his old hall, and was gone full many a day. But all the while he was gone, there was the mark of a bloody footstep impressed upon the stone door-step of the hall. The track had lain all along through the woodpath, and across the lawn, to the old Gothic door of the hall; but the rain, the English rain that is always falling, had come the next day, and washed it all away. The track had lain too across the hall and up the broad stairs, and into the lord's study; but there it had lain on the rushes that were strewn there, and these the servants had gathered carefully up, and thrown them away, and gathered fresh ones. So that it was only on the threshold that the mark remained.

But, the legend says, that wherever Sir Forrester went, in his wanderings about the world, he left a bloody track behind him. It was wonderful, and very inconvenient, this phenomenon. When he went into a church, you would see the track up the broad aisle, and a little red puddle in the place where he sat or knelt; once he went to the king's court, and there being a track up to the very throne, the King frowned upon him, so that he never came there any more. Nobody could tell how it happened; his foot was not seen to bleed, only there was the bloody track behind him, wherever he went; and he was a horror stricken man, always looking behind him to see the track, and then hurrying onward, as if to escape his own tracks, but always they followed him as fast. In the hall of feasting, there was the bloody track to his chair. The learned men, whom he consulted about this strange difficulty, consulted with one another, and with him, who was equal to any of them, and pished and pshawed, and said, "Oh, there is nothing miraculous in this; it is only a natural infirmity, which can easily be put an end to, though perhaps the stoppage of such an evacuation will cause danger to other parts of the frame." Sir Forrester always said, "Stop it, my learned brethren, if you can; no matter what the conse-quences," and they did their best; but without result; so that he was still compelled to leave his bloody track on their college-rooms, and combination rooms, the same as elsewhere; and in street and in wilderness; yes, and in the battle field, they say his track looked freshest and ruddiest of all. So, at last, finding the notice he attracted inconvenient, this unfor-tunate lord deemed it best to go back to his own hall, where, living among faithful old servants born in the family, he could hush the matter up better than elsewhere, and not be stared at continually, or glancing round, see people holding up their hands in horror of seeing a bloody track behind him; and so home he came; and there he saw the bloody track on the door-step, and dolefully went into the hall, and up the stairs, an old servant ushering him into his chamber, and half a dozen others following behind, gazing, shuddering, pointing with quivering fingers, looking horror stricken in one another's pale faces; and the moment he had passed, running to get fresh rushes, and to scour the stairs.

The next day, Sir Forrester went into the wood, and by the aged oak he found a grave; and on the grave, he beheld a beautiful crimson flower; the most gorgeous and beautiful surely that ever grew; so rich it looked, so full of potent juice. That flower he gathered; and the spirit of his scientific pursuit coming upon him, he knew that this was the flower, produced out of a human life, that was essential to the perfection of his recipe for immortal life; and he made the drink, and drank it, and became immortal in woe and agony, still studying, still growing wiser, and more wretched in every age. By and by, he vanished from his old hall, but not by death; for from generation to generation, they say that a bloody track is seen round the house, and sometimes it is tracked up into the chambers, so freshly that you see he must have passed, a short time before; and he grows wiser and wiser, and lonelier and lonelier from age to age; and this is the legend of the bloody footstep, which I myself have seen at the hall-door.

As to the flower, the plant of it continued for several years to grow out of the grave; and after while, perhaps a century ago, it was transplanted into the garden of Smithills Hall, and preserved with great care, and is so still. And as the family attribute a kind of sacredness, or cursedness, to the flower, they can hardly be prevailed upon to give any of the seeds, or allow it to be propagated elsewhere; though the king should send to ask it. It is said, too, that there is still in the family the old lord's recipe for immortality, and that several of his collateral descendants have tried to concoct it, and instil

the flower into it, and so gain indefinite life; but unsuccess-
fully, because the seeds of the flower must be planted in a
fresh grave of bloody death in order to make it effectual.

<(See other sheet)>
So ended Sybil's marvellous legend,—in which Septimius
was struck by a certain analogy in it to Aunt Keziah's Indian
legend, both referring to a flower growing out of a grave; and,
also, he did not fail to be impressed with the wild coincidence
of the disappearance of an ancestor of the family, long ago,
and the appearance, at about the same epoch, of the first
known ancestor of his own family, the man with wizard attributes, with the bloody footstep, and whose sudden disappearance became a myth under the idea that the Devil
carried him away. Yet, on the whole, this wild tradition,
doubtless becoming wilder in Sybil's wayward and morbid
fancy, had the effect to give him a sense of the fantasticalness
of his present pursuit, and that, in adopting it, he had strayed
into a region long abandoned to superstition, and where the
shadows of forgotten dreams go, when men are done with
them; where past worships are; where Great Pan went when
he died to the outer world; a Limbo into which living men
sometimes stray, when they think themselves sensiblest and
wisest, and whence they do not often find their way back
into the real world. Visions of wealth, visions of fame, visions
of philanthropy; all visions find room here, and glide about
without jostling. When Septimius came to look at the matter,
in his present mood, the thought occurred to him that he had
perhaps got into such a limbo, and that Sybil's legend, which
looked so wild, might be all of a piece with his own present life; for Sybil herself seemed an illusion, and so most
strangely, did Aunt Keziah, whom he had known all his life,
with her homely and quaint characteristics; the grim Doctor,

with his brandy and his German pipe, impressed him in the same way; and these, altogether, made his homely cottage by the wayside, seem an unsubstantial edifice, such as castles in the air are built of, and the ground he trod on unreal; and that grave, which he knew to contain the decay of a beautiful young man, but a fictitious swell formed by the fantasy of his eyes. All unreal; all illusion. Was Rose Garfield a deception too, with her daily beauty, and daily cheerfulness, and daily worth? In short, it was a moment, such as I suppose all men feel (at least, I can answer for one) when the real scene and picture of life swims, jars, shakes, seems about to be broken up and dispersed, like the picture in a smooth pond, when we disturb its smooth mirror by throwing in a stone; and though the scene soon settles itself, and looks as real as before, a haunting doubt keeps close at hand, as long as we live, asking—"Is it stable? Am I sure of it? Am I certainly not dreaming? See; it trembles again, ready to dissolve."

Applying himself with earnest diligence to his attempts to decypher and interpret the mysterious manuscript, working with his whole mind and strength, Septimius did not fail of some flattering degree of success. A good deal of the manuscript, as has been said, was in an ancient English script, although so uncouth and shapeless were the characters that it was not easy to resolve them into letters, or to believe that they were anything but arbitrary and casual blots and scrawls upon the yellow paper, without meaning, vague, like the misty and undefined germs of thought, as they exist in our minds before clothing themselves in words; these, however, as he concentrated his mind upon them, took distincter shape, like star dust at the power of the telescope, and became sometimes English, sometimes Latin, strangely patched together, as if, so accustomed was the writer to use that language in which all the science of that age was usually embodied, that he really mixed it unconsciously with the vernacular, or used both indiscriminately. There was a little Greek, too, but not much. Then frequently came in the cypher, to the study of which Septimius had applied himself for some time back, with the aid of the books borrowed from the College Library, and not without success. Indeed, it appeared to him, on closer observation, that it had not been the intention of the writer really to conceal what he had written from any earnest student, but rather to lock it up for safety in a sort of coffer, of which diligence and insight should be the key, and the keen intelligence with which the meaning was sought should be the test of the seeker's being entitled to possess the secret treasure.

Amid a great deal of misty stuff, he found the document to consist chiefly, contrary to his supposition beforehand, of certain rules of life; he would have taken it, at a casual inspection, for an essay of counsel, addressed by some great and sagacious man, to a youth in whom he felt an interest; such excellent maxims there were, so sound and good a doctrine of life propounded, such wisdom in all matter that came within the writer's purview. It was as much like a digested synopsis of some old philosopher's wise rules of conduct, as any thing else. But, on closer inspection, Septimius, in his unsophisticated consideration of this matter, was not so well satisfied. True; everything that was said seemed not discordant with the rules of sound morality; not unwise; it was shrewd, sagacious, it did not appear to infringe upon the rights of mankind; but there was something left out, something unsatisfactory—what was it? There was certainly a cold spell in the document; a magic not of fire, but of ice; and Septimius the more exemplified its fever, in that he soon began to be insensible of it. It affected him as if it had been written by some greatly wise and worldly experienced man, like the writer of Ecclesiastes; for it was full of truth, it was a truth that does not make men better, though perhaps calmer, and beneath which the buds of happiness curl up like tender leaves in a frost. What was the matter with this document, that the young man's youth perished out of him, as he read? What icy hand had written it so that the heart was chilled out of the reader? Not that Septimius was sensible of this character; at least, not long—for as he read, there grew upon him a mood of calm satisfaction, such as he had never felt before; his mind seemed to grow clearer; his perceptions most acute; his sense of the reality of things grew to be such, that he felt as if he could touch and handle all his thoughts, feel round about all their outline and circumference, and know them with a certainty as if they were material things. Not that all this was in the document itself; but by studying it so earnestly, and as it were creating its meaning anew for himself out of such illegible materials, he caught the temper of the old writer's mind, after so many ages as that tract had lain in the mouldy and musty manuscript; he was magnetized with him; a powerful intellect acted powerfully upon him; perhaps even there was a sort of spell and mystic influence imbued into the paper and mingled with the yellow ink, that steamed forth by the effort of this young man's earnest rubbing, as it were, and action of his mind, applied to it as earnestly as he could possibly will; and even his handling the paper, his bending over it, and breathing upon it, had its effect.

It is not in our power, nor in our wish, to preserve the original form, nor yet the spirit, of a production which is better lost to the world; because it was the expression of a human being originally greatly gifted, and capable of high things, but gone utterly astray, partly by its own subtility, partly by yielding to the temptations of the lower part of its nature, by yielding the spiritual to a keen sagacity of lower things, until it was quite fallen; and yet fallen in such a way that it seemed, not only to itself, but to mankind, not fallen at all, but wise and good, and fulfilling all the ends of intellect in such a life as ours, and proving moreover that earthly life was good, and all that the developement of our nature demanded. All this is better forgotten; better burnt; better never thought over again; and all the more, because its aspect was so wise and even praiseworthy. But what we must preserve of it, were certain rules of life and moral diet, not exactly expressed in the document, but which, as it were, on its being duly received into Septimius's mind, were precipitated from the rich solution, and crystallized into diamonds, and which he found to be the moral dietetics, so to speak, by observing which he was to achieve the end of earthly immortality, the physical nostrum for which was given in the recipe which, with the help of Doctor Portsoaken and his Aunt Keziah, he had already pretty satisfactorily made out.

Keep thy heart at seventy throbs in a minute; all more than that wears away life too quickly. If thy respiration be too quick, think with thyself that thou hast sinned against natural order and decorum.

Drink not wine nor strong drink; and observe that this rule is worthiest in its symbolic meaning.

Bask daily in the sunshine, and let it rest on thy heart.

Run not, leap not; walk at a steady pace, and count thy paces per day.

If thou feelest, at any time, a throb of the heart, pause, on the instant, analyze it, fix thy mental eye stedfastly upon it, and inquire why such commotion is.

Hate not any man nor woman; be not angry, unless thy blood seem at any time a little cold and torpid; cast out all rankling feelings; they are poisonous to thee. If, in thy waking moments, or in thy dreams, thou hast thoughts of strife or unpleasantness with any man, strive quietly with thyself to forget him.

Have no intercourse with an imperfect man, with a man in bad health, of violent passions, of any characteristic that evidently disturbs his own life, and so may be of disturbing influence on thine. Shake not any man by the hand, because thereby if there be any evil in the man, it is likely to be communicated to thee.

Kiss no woman if her lips be red; look not upon her, if she be very fair. Touch not her hand, if thy finger-tips be found to thrill with hers ever so little. On the whole, shun woman, for she is apt to be a disturbing influence. If thou love her, all is over, and thy whole past and remaining labor and pains will be in vain.

Do some decent degree of good and kindness in thy daily life; for the result is a slight, pleasurable sense, that will serve to warm and delectate thee with felicitous self-laudings; and all that brings thy thoughts to thyself tends to invigorate that central principle, by the growth of which thou art to give thyself indefinite life.

Do not any act manifestly evil; it may grow upon thee and corrode thee in after years.

Do not any foolishly good act, it may change thy wise habits.

Eat no spiced meat. Young chickens, new fallen lambs, fruits, breads four days old, milk, freshest butter, will make thy fleshy tabernacle youthful.

From sick people, maimed wretches, afflicted people, all of whom show themselves at variance with things as they should be, from people beyond their wits, from people in a melancholic mood, from people in extravagant joy, from teething children, from dead corpses, turn away thine eyes, and depart elsewhere.

If beggars haunt thee, bid thy servants drive them away, thou withdrawing out of ear-shot.

Crying and sickly children, and teething children, as aforesaid, carefully avoid and drink the breath of wholesome infants, as often as thou conveniently canst. It is good for thy purpose. Also, the breath of buxom maidens, if thou mayst without undue disturbance of the flesh, drink in as a morning draught or medicine; also, the breath of cows, as they return from rich pasture at eventide.

If thou seest human poverty or suffering, and it trouble thee, strike moderately to relieve it; seeing that thus thy mood will be changed to a pleasant self-laudation.

Practise thyself in a certain continual smile; for its tendency will be to compose thy frame of being, and keep thee from too much wear.

Search not thy head, thy beard, to see if thou hast a gray hair; scrutinize not thy forehead to find a wrinkle, nor the corners of thy eyes to discover if they be corrugated. Such things, being gazed at, daily take heart and grow.

Desire nothing too fervently, not even life; yet keep thy hold upon it mightily, quietly, unshakeably, for, as long as thou really art resolved to live, Death with all his force shall have no power against thee.

Walk not beneath old tottering ruins, nor houses being put up; nor climb to the top of a mast, nor approach the edge of a precipice, nor stand in the way of the lightning, nor cross a swollen river, nor voyage at sea, nor ride a skittish horse, nor be shot at by an arrow, nor confront a sword, nor put thyself in the way of violent death, for this is hateful, and breaketh through all wise rules.

Say thy prayers at bedtime, if thou deemest it will give thee the quieter sleep; yet let it not trouble thee, if thou forgettest them.

Change thy shirt daily; thereby thou castest off yesterday's decay, and imbibest the freshness of the morning's life, which assist with smelling to roses and other healthy and fragrant flowers, & live the longer for it. Roses are made to that end.

Read not great poets; they stir up thy heart; and the human heart is a soil which, if deeply stirred, is apt to give out noxious vapors.

Such were some of the precepts which Septimius gathered and reduced to definite form out of this wonderful document; and he appreciated their wisdom, and saw clearly that they must be absolutely essential to the success of the medicine with which they were connected. In themselves, almost, they seemed capable of prolonging life to an indefinite period; so wisely were they conceived, so well did they apply to the causes which almost invariably wear away this poor, short life anew, years and years before even the shattered constitutions that they receive from their forefathers need compel· them to die. He deemed himself well rewarded for all his labor and pains, should nothing else follow but his reception and proper appreciation of these wise rules; but, continually, as he read the manuscript, more truths, and for aught I know, profounder and more practical ones developed themselves; and, indeed, small as the manuscript looked, Septimius thought that he should find a volume, as big as the most ponderous folio in the college library, too small to contain all its wisdom. It seemed to drip and distil with precious fragrant drops, whenever he took it out of his desk; it diffused wisdom, like those bits of perfume, which, small as they look, keep diffusing an airy breath of fragrance for years and years together, scattering their virtue in incalculable volumes of invisible vapour, and yet are none the less in bulk for all they give; whenever he turned over the yellow leaves, bits of gold, diamonds of good size, precious pearls seemed to drop out from between them.

<He had not been on the hill for some time.>

And now ensued a surprise that, though of a happy kind, was almost too much for him to bear; for it made his heart beat considerably faster than the wise rules of his manuscript prescribed. Going up on his hill-top, as summer wore away, and walking by the little flowery hillock, as so many a hundred times before—what should he see there? It was a new flower, that, during the time that he had been poring over the manuscript so sedulously, had developed itself, blossomed, put forth its petals, bloomed into full perfection, and now, with the dew of the morning upon it, was waiting to offer itself to Septimius. He trembled as he looked at it. It was too much, almost, to bear;—it was so very beautiful, so very stately, so very rich, so very mysterious and wonderful. It was like a person, like a life! Whence did it come! He stood apart from it, gazing in wonder; tremulously taking in its aspect, and thinking of the legends that he had heard from Aunt Keziah, and from Sybil Dacy; and how that this flower, like the one which their wild traditions told of, had grown out of a grave—out of a grave in which he had lain one slain by himself.

The flower was of the richest crimson, illuminated with a golden centre,—of a perfect and stately beauty. From the best descriptions that I have been able to gain of it, it was more like a Dahlia than any other flower with which I have acquaintance; yet it does not satisfy me to believe it really of that species; for the Dahlia is not a flower of any deep characteristics, either lovely or malignant; and this flower, which

Septimius found so strangely, seems to have had one or the other. If I have rightly understood, it had a fragrance, which the Dahlia lacks, and there was something hidden in its centre, a mystery, even in its fullest bloom, not developing itself so openly as the heartless, yet not dishonest dahlia. I remember, in England, to have seen a flower at Eaton Hall, in Cheshire, in those magnificent gardens, which may have been this; but my remembrance of it is not sufficiently distinct to enable me to describe it better than by saying that it was crimson, with a gleam of gold in its centre, which yet was partly hidden. It had many petals, a great richness and abundance of them.

Septimius, bending eagerly over the plant, saw that this was not to be the only flower that it would produce, that season. On the contrary, there were to be of them, a great abundance, a luxuriant harvest; as if the crimson offspring of this one plant would cover the whole hillock; as if the dead youth beneath had burst into a resurrection of many crimson flowers! And in its veiled heart, moreover, there was a mystery like death; although it seemed to cover something bright and golden.

Day after day, the strange, mysterious crimson flower bloomed more and more abundantly, until it seemed almost to cover the little hillock, which became a mere bed of it; apparently turning all its capacity of production to this flower; for the other plants, Septimius thought, seemed to shrink away and give place to it, as if they were unworthy to compare with the richness, glory, and worth of this their queen. The fervent summer burned into it; the dew and the rain ministered to it; the soil was rich, for it was a human heart contributing its juices, a heart in its fiery youth sodden in its own blood; so that passion, unsatisfied loves and longings, ambition that never won its object, tender dreams and throbs, angers, lusts, hates, all reawakened to life, were sprouting in it; and its mysterious veins and streaks, and shadows had some meaning in each of them.

The two girls, when they next ascended the hill, saw the strange flower, and Rose admired it, and wondered at it, but stood at a distance without showing any attraction towards it; rather an undefined aversion, as if she thought it might be a poison flower; at any rate, would not be inclined to wear it in her bosom. Sybil Dacy examined it closely, touched its leaves, smelt it, looked at it with a botanist's eye, and at last remarked to Rose—"Yes; it grows well in this new soil; methinks it looks like a new human life."

"What is the strange flower?" asked Rose.

"The Sanguinaria Sanguinissima," said Sybil.

<Describe the old woman's dress and appearance minutely, as affected by illness.>

It so happened, about this time, that poor Aunt Keziah, in spite of her constant use of that bitter mixture of hers, was in a very bad state of health. She looked all of an unpleasant yellow, with bloodshot eyes; she complained terribly of her bowels, or inwards. She banged the cat, the old rheumatic cat, sleeping in the chimney-corner, or in the sunshine. She had an ugly rheumatic hitch in her motion from place to place and was heard to mutter many wishes that she had a broomstick to fly about upon; she used to bind up her head with a dishclout, or what looked to be such, and would sit by her kitchen fire, even in the warm days, bent over it, crouching as if she wanted to take the whole fire into her poor cold heart, or gizzard; groaning spitefully whenever she had to move, or sometimes regularly with each breath, a spiteful and resentful groan, as if she fought womanfully with her infirmities; and she continually smoked her pipe, and sent out the breath of her complaint visibly in that evil odour; and sometimes, she murmured a little prayer, but somehow or other, the evil and acidity, bitterness, acridity, pepperiness of her natural disposition overcame the acquired grace which impelled her to pray, insomuch that often you might have thought the poor old woman was cursing with all her rheumatic might. All the time an old broken nosed brown earthen jug, covered with the lid of a black teapot, stood on the edge of the embers, steaming forever, and sometimes bubbling a little and giving a great puff, as if it were sighing or groaning in sympathy with poor Aunt Keziah, and when it sighed, came a great steam of herby fragrance, not particularly pleasant, into the kitchen. And ever and anon, half a dozen times, it might be, of an afternoon, Aunt Keziah took a certain pink bottle from a private receptacle of hers, and also a tea-cup, and likewise a little, old fashioned silver tea spoon, with which she measured three spoonsful of some spirituous liquor into the tea-cup, half filled the cup with the hot decoction, drank it off, gave a grunt of content, and for the space of half an hour appeared to find life tolerable.

<(She gets up to breakfast, but goes to bed again.)>

But one day, poor Aunt Kezia found herself unable, partly from rheumatism, partly from other sickness or weakness, and partly from dolorous ill-spirits, to keep about any longer; so she betook herself to her bed; and betimes in the forenoon, Septimius heard a tremendous knocking on the floor of her bed chamber, which happened to be the room above his own. His sister Rose had long since gone to attend her little school; he was himself the only person in or about the house; so, with vast reluctance, he left his studies, which were upon the recipe, in respect to which he was trying to make out the mode of concoction, which was told in such a mysterious way that he could not well tell either the quantity of the ingredients, the mode of trituration, nor in what way their virtue was to be extracted and combined.

Running hastily up stairs, he found Aunt Kezia lying in bed, and groaning with great spite and bitterness; so that, indeed, it seemed not unprovidential that such an inimical state of mind towards the human race was accompanied with an almost inability of motion; else it would not be safe to be within a considerable distance of her. "Seppy, you good for nothing, are you going to see me lying here dying, without trying to do anything for me?"

"Dying, Aunt Keziah?" repeated the young man. "I hope not! What can I do for you? Shall I go for Rose? Or call in a neighbor? Or the Doctor?"

"No, no, you fool!" said the afflicted person. "Damn the Doctor! You can do all that anybody can for me; and that is to put my mixture on the kitchen fire, till it steams and is just ready to bubble; then measure three teaspoonfuls, or it may be four as I am very badly—three teaspoonsful of spirit into a tea cup—fill it half-full, or it may be quite full, for I am very bad, as I said afore—six tea-spoonfulls of spirit into a cup of mixture, and let me have it as soon as may be—and don't break the cup nor spill the precious mixture; for goodness knows when I can go into the woods to gather any more. Ah me! ah me! It is a wicked, miserable world, and I'm the most miserable creature in it. Be quick, you good-for-nothing, and do as I say!"

Septimius hastened down; but as he went, a thought came into his head which it occurred to him might result in great benefit to Aunt Keziah as well as to the great cause of science and human good, and to the promotion of his own purpose in the first place. A day or two ago, he had gathered several of the beautiful flowers and laid them in the fervid sun to dry; and they now seemed to be in about the state in which the old woman was accustomed to use her herbs, so far as Septimius had observed. Now, if the flowers were really, as there was so much reason for supposing, the one ingredient that had for hundreds of years been missing out of Aunt Keziah's nostrum—if it was this which that strange Indian sagamore had mingled with his drink, with such beneficial effect—why should not Septimius now restore it, and, if it would not make his beloved Aunt young again, at least assuage the violent symptoms, and perhaps prolong her valuable life some years, for the solace and delight of her numerous friends? Septimius, like other people of investigating and active minds, had a great tendency to experiment, and so good an opportunity as the present, where (perhaps he thought) there was so little to be risked at worst, and so much to be gained, was not to be neglected; so without more ado, he shredded three of the great crimson flowers into the earthen jug, set it on the edge of the fire, stirred it well, and when it steamed, threw up little scented bubbles, and was about to boil, he measured out the spirit, as Aunt Keziah had bade him, and then filled the tea-cup.

"Ah; this will do her good; little does she think, poor old thing, what a rare and costly medicine is about to be given her. This will set her on her feet again."

The hue was somewhat changed he thought, from what he had observed of Aunt Keziah's customary decoction; instead of a turbid yellow, the crimson juices of the flower had tinged it, and made it almost red, not a brilliant red, however, nor in the least inviting in appearance. Septimius smelt it, and thought he could distinguish a little of the rich odor of the flower, but was not sure; he considered whether to taste it; but the horrible flavor of Aunt Keziah's decoction recurred strongly to his remembrance, and he concluded that, were he evidently at the point of death, he might possibly be bold to taste it again, but that nothing short of the hope of a century's existence, at least, would repay another trial of that fierce and nauseous bitterness. Aunt Kezia loved it; and as she brewed, so let her drink.

He went up stairs, careful not to spill a drop of the brimming cup, and approached the old woman's bedside, where she lay groaning as before, and breaking out into a spiteful croak, the moment he was within earshot.

"You don't care whether I live or die," said she. "You've been waiting in hopes I shall die, and so save yourself further trouble."

"By no means, Aunt Kezia," said Septimius. "Here is the medicine, which I have warmed, and measured out, and mingled, as well as I knew how; and I think it will do you a great deal of good."

"Won't you taste it, Seppy, my dear!" said Aunt Keziah, mollified by the praise of her beloved nostrum. "Drink first, dear, so that my sick old lips need not taint it. You look pale, Septimius; it will do you good."

"No, Aunt Kezia; I do not need it; and it were a pity to waste your precious drink," said he.

"It does not look quite the right color," said Aunt Keziah, as she took the cup in her hand. "You must have dropt some soot into it." Then as she raised it to her lips, "It does not smell quite right! But, woe's me, how can I expect any body but myself to make this precious drink as it should be!"

She drank it off, at two gulps; for she appeared to hurry it down faster than usual, as if not tempted by the exquisiteness of its flavor to dwell upon it as long as usual.

"You have not made it quite right, Seppy," said she, in a milder tone than before, for she seemed to feel the customary soothing influence of the draught. "But you'll do better the next time. But it had a queer taste, methought; or is it that my mouth is getting out of taste? Hard times it will be for poor Aunt Kezzy, if she's to lose her taste for the medicine that, under Providence, has saved her life for so many years."

She gave back the cup to Septimius, after looking a little curiously at the dregs.

"It looks like blood-root, don't it?" said she. "Perhaps it's my own fault, after all. I gathered a fresh bunch of the yarbs, yesterday afternoon; and put them to steep, and it may be I was a little blind; for it was between daylight and dark, and the moon shone on me before I had finished. I thought how the witches used to gather their poisonous stuff at such times, and what pleasant uses they used to make of it,—but those are sinful thoughts, Seppy, sinful thoughts; so I'll say a prayer, and try to go to sleep! I feel very noddy, all at once."

Septimius drew the bed clothes up about her shoulders, for she complained of being very chilly, and carefully putting her stick within her reach, went down to his own room, and resumed his studies, trying to make out from those aged hieroglyphics to which he was now so well accustomed, what was the precise method of making the elixir of immortality. Sometimes, as men in deep thought do, he arose from his chair, and walked to and fro, the four or five steps or so, that conveyed him from end to end of his little room. At one of these turns, he chanced to look into the little looking-glass, that hung between the windows, and was startled at the paleness of his face. It was quite white, indeed. Septimius was not in the least a foppish young man; careless he was in dress, though often his apparel took on unsought picturesqueness, that set off his slender agile figure, perhaps by some quality of spontaneous arrangement that he had inherited from his Indian ancestry. Yet many women might have found a charm in that dark, thoughtful face, with its hidden fire and energy; although Septimius never thought of its being handsome, and seldom looked at it. Yet now he was drawn to it, by seeing how strangely white it was, and gazing at it, he observed that, since he considered it last, a very deep furrow or corrugation, or fissure, it might almost be called, had indented his brow, rising from the commencement of the nose towards the centre of the forehead. And he knew it, it was his brooding thoughts, his fierce hard determination, his intense concentrativeness, for so many months, that had been digging that furrow; and it must have been indeed a potent specific of the life-water, that could smooth that away, and restore him all the youth and elasticity that he had buried in that profound grave.

But why was he so pale! He could have supposed himself startled by some ghastly thing that he had just seen; by a corpse in the next room, for instance; or else by the foreboding that one would soon be there. And yet he was conscious of no tremor in his frame, no terror in his heart; as why should there be any? Feeling his own pulse, he found the strong, regular beat that should be there. He was not ill; nor affrighted; nor expectant of any pain. Then why so ghastly pale? And why, moreover, Septimius, did you listen so earnestly for any sound in Aunt Keziah's chamber? Why did you creep on tiptoe—once, twice, three times—up to the old woman's chamber, and put your ear to the keyhole, and listen breathlessly? Well; it must have been, that he was subconscious that he was trying a bold experiment, and that he had taken this poor old woman to be the medium of it, in the hope, of course, that it would turn out well; yet with other views than her interest in the matter. What was the harm of that? Medical men, no doubt, are always doing so,—and he was a medical man for the time. Then why was he so pale?

He sat down, and fell into a reverie, which perhaps was partly instigated by that deep furrow which he had seen, and which we have spoken of, in his brow. He wondered whether there was anything in this pursuit of his, that used up life particularly fast, so that perhaps, unless he were successful soon, he should be incapable of renewal; for, looking within himself, and considering his mode of being, he had a singular fancy that his heart was gradually drying up, and that he must contrive to get some moisture for it, or else it would soon be like a withered leaf. Supposing his pursuit were vain, what a waste he was making of that little treasure of golden days, which was his all.—Could this be called life, which he was leading now? How unlike that of other young men! How unlike that of Robert Garfield, for example! There had come news yesterday of his having performed a gallant part in the battle of Monmouth, and being promoted to be a captain for his gallant conduct. Without thinking of long life, he really lived in heroic actions and emotions; he got much life in a little, and did not fear to sacrifice a lifetime of torpid breaths, if necessary, to the heroic ecstasy of a glorious death! And then Robert loved, too, loved his sister Rose, and felt doubtless an immortality in that passion. Why could not Septimius love too? It was forbidden! Well; no matter, whom could he have loved? Who, in all this world, could have been suited to his secret, brooding heart, that he could have led her into its mysterious chambers, and walked with her from one cavernous gloom to another, and said here are my treasures; I make thee mistress of all these;—with all these goods I thee endow; and then revealing to her his great secret and purpose of gaining immortal life, have said, this shall be thine, too. Thou shalt share with me! We will walk along the endless path together, and keep one another's hearts warm, and so be content to live.

Ah, Septimius; but now you are getting beyond those rules of yours, which, cold as they are, have been drawn out of a subtle philosophy, and might, were it possible to follow them out, suffice to do all that you ask of them; but if you break them, you do it at the peril of your earthly immortality. Each warmer and quicker throb of the heart, wears away so much of life. The passions, the affections, are a wine not to be indulged in. Love, above all, being in its essence an immortal thing, cannot be long contained in an earthly body, but would wear it out, with its own sweet power, softly invigorating as it seems. You must be cold, therefore, Septimius; you must not even earnestly and passionately desire this immortality that seems so desirable to you. Else the very wish will prevent the possibility of it. This very divine passion, which no one ever truly felt, without being sensible that his essence must be immortal, because no other substance could conceive such a sentiment; and because it requires eternity to develope itself in, this passion will wear out the body.

By and by, to call him out of these rhapsodies, came Rose home; and finding the kitchen hearth vacant, and Aunt Keziah missing, and no dinner by the fire, which was smouldering, nothing but that portentous earthen jug, which fumed, and sent out long, ill-flavored sighs, she tapped at Septimius's door, and asked him what was the matter.

"Aunt Kezia has had an ill turn," said Septimius, "and has gone to bed!"

"Poor Auntie!" said Rose, with her quick sympathy. "I will this moment run up and see if she needs again!"

"No, Rose," answered Septimius, "she has doubtless gone to sleep, and will awake as well as usual. It would displease her much, were you to miss your afternoon's school; so you had better set the table with whatever there is left cold of yesterday's dinner, and leave me to take care of Auntie."

"Well," said Rose, "she loves you best; but if she be really sick, I shall give up my school, and nurse her."

"No doubt," said Septimius, "she will be about the house again tomorrow."

So she ate her frugal dinner (consisting chiefly of purslain and some other garden herbs which her thrifty aunt had prepared for boiling), and went away as usual to her school; for Aunt Kezia, as aforesaid, had never encouraged the tender ministrations of Rose, whose orderly, womanly character, with its well defined orb of daily and civilized duties, had always appeared to strike her as tame; and she once said to her, "You are no squaw child, and you'll never make a witch." Nor would she ever let Rose so much as put her tea to steep, nor do anything whatever for herself personally; though, certainly, she was not backward in requiring of her a due share of labor for the general housekeeping.

Septimius was sitting in his room, as the afternoon wore away; for some reason or other, or quite as likely for no reason at all, he did not air himself and his thoughts as usual on the hill; so he was sitting, musing, thinking, looking at his mysterious manuscript, when he heard Aunt Keziah stirring in the chamber above. First she seemed to rattle a chair; then she began a slow, regular beat with the stick that Septimius had left by her bedside, and which startled him strangely; so that, indeed, his heart beat faster than the five-and-seventy throbs to which he was restricted by the wise rules that he had digested. So he ran hastily up stairs; and behold, Aunt Keziah was sitting up in bed, looking very wild; so wild that you would have thought that she was going to fly up chimney the next minute; her gray hair all dishevelled, her eyes staring, her hands clutching forward; while she gave a sort of howl, what with pain and agitation.

"Seppy! Seppy!" said she. "Seppy, my darling, are you sure you remember how to make that precious drink!"

"Quite well, Aunt Keziah!" said Septimius, inwardly much alarmed by her aspect, but preserving a true Indian composure of outward mien. "I wrote it down, and could say it by heart besides. Shall I make you a fresh pot of it; for I have thrown away the other."

"That was well, Seppy," said the poor old woman with a groan; "for there is something wrong with it; but I want no more, for, Seppy dear, I am going fast out of this world, where you and that precious drink were my only treasures and comforts. I wanted to know if you remembered the receipt; it's all I have to leave you, and the more you drink of it, Seppy, the better. Only see to make it right!"

"Dear Auntie, what can I do for you?" cried Septimius, in much consternation, but still calm. "Let me run for the Doctor—for the neighbors—something must be done!"

The old woman contorted herself, as if there were a fearful turn in her insides; and grinned, and twisted the yellow ugliness of her face, and groaned, and howled; and yet there was a tough and fierce kind of endurance with which she fought with her anguish, and would not yield to it a jot, though she allowed herself the relief of shrieking fiercely at it, much more like a defiance than a cry for mercy.

"No Doctor! no women!" said she; "if my drink would not save me, what could a Doctor's foolish pills and powders do? And a woman! If old Mother Denton, the witch, were alive, I would be glad to see her. But other women, Pah! Ah! Ai! Oh! Phew! Ah, Seppy, what a mercy it would be now if I could set to and shake my fist at the sky and blaspheme a bit; but I'm a Christian woman, Seppy—a Christian woman!"

"Shall I run for the minister, Aunt Kezia?" asked Septimius. "He is a good man and a wise man!"

"No minister for me, Seppy," said Aunt Kezia, howling as if somebody were griping her guts. "He may be a good man and a wise one, but he's not wise enough to know the way to my heart, and never a woman was! Ah, Seppy, I'm a Christian woman, but I'm not like other Christian women; and I'm glad I'm going away from this stupid world, Seppy. I've not been a bad woman; and I deserve credit for it, for it would have suited me a great deal better to be bad. Oh, what delightful times a witch must have had, starting off up chimney on her broomstick at midnight, and looking down from aloft in the sky on the sleeping village here below, with its steeple pointing up at you, so that you might touch the golden weather cock. You meanwhile, in such an ecstasy; and all below you the dull, innocent, sober humankind, the wife sleeping by her husband, or roused by her child's squall, with wind in its stomach; the goodman dreaming of his cattle and his plough— all so innocent, all so stupid, with their dull days just alike, one after another. And you are up in the air, sweeping away to some nook in the forest! Ha, what is that! A wizard—ha! ha! ha!—known below as a deacon! There is goody Chickering! How quickly she put the young people to bed after prayers. There's an Indian; there's a nigger; they all have equal right and privileges at a witch meeting. Phew! the wind blows cold, up here; why does not the Black Man have the meeting at his own Kitchen Hearth? No, Sir! Oh, dear me; but I'm a Christian and no witch; but those must have been gallant times!"

Doubtless, it was a partial wandering of the mind that took the poor old woman away on this eldritch flight; and it was very curious and pitiful to witness the compunction with which she returned to herself, and took herself to task for the preference which, in her wild nature, she could not help giving to harm-scarm wickedness over tame goodness. Then she seemed to compose herself, and talk reasonably and godly.

"And, Septimius, my dear child, never give way to temptation—never consent to be a wizard, though the Black Man tempt you ever so hard. I know he will tempt you! He has tempted me, but I never yielded; never gave him his will; and never do you, my boy; though you, with your dark complect, and your brooding brow, and your eye veiled, only when it suddenly looks out with a flash of fire in it, are the sort of man he seeks most, and that oftenest serves him. But don't do it, Septimius! But if you could be an Indian, methinks it would be better than this tame life we lead. 'Twould have been better for me, at all events. Oh, how pleasant 'twould have been, to have spent my life wandering in the woods, and smelling the pines, and the hemlock, all day, and fresh things of all kinds, and no kitchen work to do, nor to rake up the fire, nor sweep the room, nor make the beds, but to sleep on fresh boughs in a wigwam, with the leaves still on the branches that made the roof. And then to see the deer brought in by the red hunter, with the blood streaming from the arrow-shot. Ah; and the fight, too; and the scalps, and perhaps a woman might creep into the battle, and stab the wounded enemy of her tribe and scalp him, and be praised for it! But a white woman's life is so dull! Oh, Seppy, how I hate the thought of the dull life that women lead. I'm glad I'm going from it. Thank heaven, I'm done with it. If I'm ever to live again, may I be whole Indian, please my maker!"

After this goodly outbreak, poor Aunt Keziah lay quietly for a few moments, and her skinny claws being clasped together, and her yellow visage assuming as pious an aspect as was attainable by her harsh and pain-distorted features, Septimius perceived that she was in prayer; and so it proved by what followed; for the old woman turned to him with a grim tenderness in her face, and stretched out her hand to be taken by his own. He clasped the bony talon in both of his.

"Seppy, my dear, I feel a great peace; and I don't think there'll be very much to trouble me in the other world. 'Twon't be all house-work, and keeping decent, and doing like other people there! I suppose I needn't expect to ride on a broomstick—that would be wrong in any kind of a world—but there may be woods to wander in and a pipe to smoke, in the air of Heaven, trees to hear the wind in, and to smell of, and all such happy, natural things; and by and by, I shall hope to see you there, Seppy, my darling boy. Come, by and by, Seppy; 'twon't be worth your while to live forever, even if you should find out what's wanting in the drink I've taught you. I can see a little way into the next world now, and I see it to be far better than this heavy and wretched old place. You'll die when your time comes, won't you, Seppy, my darling?"

"Yes, dear Auntie, when my time comes!" answered Septimius. "Very likely, I shall want to live no longer, by that time."

"Likely not," said the old woman. "I'm sure I don't. It is like going to sleep on my mother's breast, to die. So, good night, dear Seppy."

"Good night, and God bless you, Aunty!" said Septimius, with a gush of tears blinding him, spite of his Indian nature.

The old woman composed herself, and lay quite still and decorous for a short time, then rousing herself a little:—

"Septimius," said she, "is there just a little drop of my drink left; not that I want to live any longer; but if I could sip ever so little, I feel as if I should step into the other world quite cheery, and feel it warm in my heart, and not feel shy and bashful at going among strangers."

"Not one drop, Aunty!"

"Ah, well, no matter; it was not quite right, that last cup. It had a queer taste! What could you have put into it, Seppy darling? But, no matter! no matter! It's a precious stuff, if you make it right. Don't forget the herbs, Septimius. Something wrong had sartainly got into it."

These, except for some murmurings, and groanings, and unintelligible whisperings, were the last utterances of poor Aunt Keziah, who did not live a great while longer, and at last passed away in a great sigh, like a gust of wind among the trees; she having just before stretched out her hand again and grasped that of Septimius; and he sat watching her, and gazing at her, and wondering and horrified, touched, shocked by death, of which he had so unusual a horror, and by the death of this creature especially, with whom he felt a sympathy that did not exist with any other creature now living. So long did he sit holding that hand, that at last he was conscious that it was growing cold within his own, and that the stiffening fingers clutched him, as if they were disposed to keep their clutch, and not forego the tie that had been so peculiar.

Then rushing hastily forth, he warned the nearest available neighbor, who was Robert Hagburn's mother; and she summoned some of her gossips, and came to the house, and took poor Aunt Keziah in charge. They talked of her with no great respect, I fear, nor much sorrow, nor sense that the community would suffer any great deprivation in her loss; for in their view, she was a dram-drinking, pipe-smoking, cross-grained, old maid and as some thought a witch, and, at any rate, with too much of the Indian blood in her ever to be of much use; and they hoped that now Rose Garfield would have a pleasanter life, and Septimius study to be a minister, and all things go well, and the place be cheerfuller. They found

Aunt Keziah's bottle in the cupboard, and tasted and smelt of it.

"Good West Indjy, as ever I tasted," said Mrs Hagburn. "And there stands her broken pitcher on the hearth. Ah; empty! I never could bring my mind to taste it; but now I'm sorry I never did; for I suppose nobody in the world can make any more of it."

Septimius, meanwhile, had betaken himself to the hill-top, which was his place of refuge on all occasions when the house seemed too stifled to contain him; and there he walked to-and-fro, with a certain kind of calmness and indifference which he wondered at; for there is hardly anything in this world so strange as the quiet surface that spreads over a man's mind in his greatest emergencies; so that he deems himself perfectly quiet, and upbraids himself with not feeling anything, when indeed he is passion-stirred. As Septimius walked to and fro, he looked at the rich crimson flowers, which seemed to be blooming in greater profusion and luxuriance than ever before. He had made an experiment with these flowers; and he was curious to know whether that experiment had been the cause of Aunt Keziah's death. Not that he felt any remorse therefor, in any case, or believed himself to have committed crime, having really intended and desired nothing but good. I suppose such things (which he must be a lucky physician, methinks, who has no such mishap within his own experience) never weigh with deadly weight on any man's conscience. Something must be risked in the cause of science; and in desperate cases, something must be risked for the patient's self. Septimius, much as he loved life, would not have hesitated to put his own life to the same risk that he had imposed on Aunt Keziah; or if he did hesitate, it would have been only because, if the experiment turned out disastrously in his own person, he would not be in a position to make another and more successful trial; whereas, by trying it on others, the man of science still reserves himself for new efforts, and does not put all the hopes of the world, so far as involved in his success, on one cast of the die.

By and by, he met Sybil Dacy, who had ascended the hill, as usual with her at sun-set, and met him gazing earnestly in his face.

"They tell me poor Aunt Kezia is no more," said she.

"She is dead!" said Septimius.

"The flower is a very famous medicine," said the girl; "but everything depends on its being applied in the proper way."

"Do you know the way then?" asked Septimius.

"No; you should ask Doctor Portsoaken about that," said Sybil.

Doctor Portsoaken! And so he should consult him; that eminent chymist and scientific man had evidently heard of the recipe; and at all events would be acquainted with the best methods of getting out the virtues of flowers and herbs, some of which, Septimius had read enough to know, were poison in one phase and shape of penetration, and possessed of richest virtues in others;—their poison, as one may say, serving as a dark and terrible safeguard, which Providence has set to watch over their preciousness, even as a dragon, or some wild and fiendish spectre, is set to watch and keep hidden gold and heaped up diamonds. A danger always waits on everything that is very good. And what would deserve the watch and ward of danger, of a dragon, or something more fatal than a dragon, than this treasure of which Septimius was in quest, and the discovery and possession of which would enable him to break down one of the strongest barriers of Nature? It ought to be death, he acknowledged it, to attempt such a thing; for how changed would be life, if he should succeed; how necessary it was that mankind should be defended from such attempts in the general case, on the part of all but him. How could Death be spared; then the sire would live forever, and the heir never come to his inheritance, and so he would at once hate his own father from the perception that he would never be out of his way. Then the same class of powerful minds would always rule the state, and there never be a change of policy; <(put in here all the right death does, all the wrong it hinders)> then the same minds would sway in literature, and admit no new ideas, no new tastes and imaginations, but keep new minds down, and never allow anything but the same wearisome old style; then old wrongs would always rule, being administered by the same evil-slanted minds. Then mortals, dusty, encrusted with the mud of life, and the perspiration of life's hot summer, could never bathe themselves in the cold river of Death, and wash off all, and begin anew, pure and refreshed, leaving the worthless ill behind them; then the mind could never take new views of things, by getting rid of deceptions, but would trudge on in the same rut; then there could be no rearrangement of wrongly placed persons, but each would have his fortune, his future, and hope no more—hope; there would be no hope; and of ineffable weariness, men would lie down and die in spite of fate; then the light tenderness of grief would all be gone, and we should hate our dearest, for lack of the possibilities of death; tenderness would be no more, for it feeds upon the possibilities of bereavement. <bring in religion finally>

Here Septimius started; for unawares, he had got into a train of thought so contrary to all his usual reflections, that it was his own mind that suggested it. He had got out of himself, for an instant; it was as if he himself, the hater and defier of Death, had suddenly seen the great Enemy change countenance before him, and assume, instead of hostility, the sweet and gentle aspect of the very friend whom mortals seek through life. But it was only for a moment; or perhaps he acknowledged that all he said or thought was true, in regard to the mass of humanity, but that he himself was exceptional; and that, since he saw the way of winning from Nature an exception of her general law, which imposes Death upon all who are born, that therefore it would be to his own individual advantage. In the upshot, he determined to go to Boston and see Doctor Portensoaken; learn from him what he knew of the recipe, if anything; and at any rate get such enlightenment from his chymical science as should enable him to concoct the drink according to art.

So he waited only a few days, until the mortal remains of poor Aunt Keziah could be committed to the old burial ground in the centre of the village, where they still lie without any monument; producing, it was observed, the same weeds that she used to steep and brew into her panacea; as if, by drinking so much of that horrible compotation, she had become a sort of conglomerated seed of it, so that she grew up again in vervain, dill, monkshood, skunk-cabbage, or whatever were the ingredients, offering to all who passed by her grave the same recipe which had stood her in such good stead; and which, very likely, might have been as wholesome as any medicine, if she had not mingled it with too great a proportion of that fiery ingredient from the pink bottle. So she passed away; and Rose carefully washed her earthen jug, and put it, broken as it was, upon a high shelf, and sometimes looked at it with tearful eyes, from a sense that poor Aunt Keziah had a kind of wild, fierce love and goodness in her, though Rose personally had shared little of it. Her tobacco pipe was laid along two nails, in the jamb of the fire-place, and there it lay for a long, long while, as if

Aunt Keziah were expected to come back, some winter night, and light it again; but we may trust that she had gone where she did not smoke. <(One of the old women of the neighborhood may make this remark about the pipe, in a ludicrous way)>

This being suitably attended to, Septimius, a week or so after Aunt Keziah's demise, took his way along the Lexington road, intending to do the twenty miles between his home and Boston in the course of the day, which was a breezy one of September, warm at midday almost as Summer, but having already a little cool infusion of Autumn into the air. What a potency there is in change of place! It was now many months since Septimius had been away from home, or scarcely out of sight of his own house, except to follow Aunt Keziah to the grave, or had taken any recreation of a walk, except on the eternal level of the hill-top; and now, with every step that he took, it seemed as if he were coming out of a mist; out of an enchanted land, where things had seemed to him not as they really were; where impossibilities looked like things of everyday occurrence; out of some region into which he had wandered unawares, and dreamed a life-like dream, most life-like in its force and vividness, most unlife-like by its inconsistency with all that really is, with men's purposes, fates, business; into such a misty region had he been, and strayed many days, deeming himself at home; but now the mists were thinning away, he was passing the witch-like boundaries, and might never find his way over them again. Then a great depression fell upon him; he had flung himself so earnestly and entirely upon his strange purpose, that when it seemed about to be removed from him, he felt that he must wander vaguely, stagger, go no whither, and finally sit down by the wayside, and remain there, staring at the wayfarers who *had* a purpose, until he died. I know well what his feeling was! I have had it oftentimes myself, when long brooding and busying myself on some idle tale, and keeping my faith in it by estrangement from all intercourse besides, I have chanced to be drawn out of the precincts enchanted by my poor magic; and the look back upon what I have thought, how faded, how monstrous, how apart from all truth it looks, being now seen apart from its own atmosphere, which is entirely essential to its effect. <(Put the above in the third person)>

This is the effect of mood; and every body, it is to be supposed, is liable to lose his point of view in this way. The change was, for the moment, so strong in Septimius, that he was almost of a mind to give up his visit to Doctor Portsoaken, and return to his home, which he had now no reason for leaving;—none, except that it seemed a most forlorn and wretched place, thus deprived of the magic which had made it so interesting. Besides, he could not, somehow, bear the idea of meeting Sybil Dacy again, until he should have attained the object of his journey; he meditated whether it would not be better to go to the wars, which were now drawing into them the energy and courage of every spirited young man. Let him give up all these mystic hopes, and smell the air of the battlefield, put himself on the level on which all humanity stands, be no more lonely, sacrifice himself, give all he had, die if he must, live if he might the full, free, generous life of humanity, the conditions of which are to share all the liabilities of his fellow men. But, thinking these thoughts, Septimius still kept on towards Boston; for, after all, he had that stubbornness of disposition, which still keeps his purpose even in despair. And this was not so much as despair; it was only the temporary revulsion that waits upon a mind too tensely strong, the sinking down of a flame that would quiver up again.

<Insert a description of the town>

It was in the afternoon, that he crossed the ferry, and entered the metropolis of New England; then an inconsiderable town, much injured by the war, by the disturbances of commerce that had preceded it, by the military occupation, during which its interests had been postponed entirely to the needs of the army which held it. So that as Septimius passed through the narrow and crooked streets, he saw many tokens of what had been suffered, and which, during the oppression, syncope, or feverish action, of the war still going on, there was no heart to restore or remedy; here, for instance, were vacancies, over which the grass was beginning to grow, where wooden houses had been torn down for fuel for the soldiers; here was a church that had been a riding-school for dragoons, the hoof-marks still on the door-steps; here were old cannon, with the trunnions broken off, lying idle in the streets; here were maimed persons, limping along the streets; here was a sort of wildness in the look of many of the inhabitants, and elderly citizens, in powder, and ruffles at their sleeves, walked along as men in a dream, unable to realize what great change it was, that had put them into a new, uncomfortable world, since they were young; there seemed to be little business, only, several times, he heard the sound of a drum, and saw the drill of young men preparing for the army. For there seemed to be no other life than this—the purpose to kill one another. In some, and those who seemed the most respectable, he saw a cowed, frightened air; and as these passed by, the people looked suspiciously at them, though formerly, perhaps, these very men had been looked up to and beloved, and worthily;—one poor old man, of this character, became obnoxious to a crowd of boys, who were drilling with sticks, and who stopt in the midst of their exercise to discharge some artillery of mud-balls upon the poor man—shouting, "Tory! tory!—go home to King George, tory!" —and no man rebuked them. On old Faneuil flew a flag of the ten stripes, then but a few months adopted. Grass grew in the streets, and there was a lounge in the gait of people, that seemed to forebode that it would be yet thicker and higher; so that cows might pasture there. In everybody and everything the uncertainty of a transitive state; only, with a dreary stubborness, war was in the ascendant. Women stood in their door-ways looking forlorn, mateless, poor things, knitting stockings for their absent soldier; so the town was sad and strange;—very sad and heavy, the early enthusiasm of the struggle having subsided, and its hard, heavy, dogged, sullen strain being now felt.

Through such scenes, Septimius sought out the direction that Doctor Portsoaken had given him, and came to the door of a house in the older part of the town. The Boston of those days had very much the aspect of provincial towns in England, such as may still be seen there, while our own city has undergone such wonderful changes that little likeness to the aspect which our ancestors gave it can be now found. The streets crooked and narrow, the houses, many gabled, projecting, with latticed windows and diamond-panes; without side walks; with rough pavements.

Septimius knocked loudly at the door, nor had long to wait, before a serving maid appeared, who seemed to be of English nativity; and in reply to his request for Doctor Portsoaken, bade him come in, and led him up a staircase with broad landing-places; then tapt at the door of a room, and was responded to by a gruff voice saying, "Come in!" The woman held the door open, and Septimius saw the veritable Doctor Portsoaken in an old, faded morning gown, and with a night-cap on his head, his German pipe in his mouth, and a brandy-bottle, to the best of our belief, on the table by his side.

"Come in, come in," said the gruff Doctor, nodding to Septimius. "I remember you! Come in, man, and tell me your business!"

Septimius did come in, but was so struck by the aspect of Doctor Portsoaken's apartment, and his own, that he did not immediately tell his business; in the first place, everything looked very dusty and dirty, so that evidently no woman had ever been admitted into this sanctity of a place; a fact made all the more evident by the abundance of spiders, who had spun their webs about the walls and ceiling, in the wildest apparent confusion, though doubtless each individual spider knew the cordage which he had lengthened out of his own miraculous bowels; but it was really strange. They had fastened their cordage on whatever was stationary in the room, and had made a sort of gray, dusky tapestry, that waved portentously in the breeze, and flapped, heavy and dismal, each with its spider in the centre of his own system. And what was most marvellous was a spider over the Doctor's head; a spider, I think, of some South American breed, with a circumference of its many legs as big, unless I am misinformed, as a tea-cup, and with a body in the midst as large as a dollar; giving the spectator horrible qualms as to what would be the consequence if this spider should be crushed, and, at the same time, suggesting the poisonous danger of suffering such a monster to live. The monster, however, sat in the midst of the stalwart cordage of his web, right over the Doctor's head; and he looked, with all those complicated lines, like the symbol of a conjurer or crafty politician in the midst of the complexity of his scheme; and Septimius wondered if he were not the type of Doctor Portsoaken himself, who, fat and bloated as the spider, seemed to be the centre of some dark contrivance. And could it be that poor Septimius was typified by the poor, fascinated fly, doomed to be entangled in the web?

"Good day to you," said the gruff Doctor, taking his pipe from his mouth. "Here I am with my brother-spiders, in the midst of my web. I told you, you remember, the wonderful efficacy which I had discovered in spider's web; and this is my laboratory, where I have hundreds of workmen concocting my panacea for me. Is it not a lovely sight?"

"A wonderful one, at least," said Septimius. "That one above your head, the monster, is calculated to give a very formidable idea of your theory. What a quantity of poison there must be in him!"

"Poison, do you call it," quoth the grim Doctor. "That's entirely as it may be used. Doubtless his bite would send a man to kingdom come; but, on the other hand, no one need want a better life line than that fellow's web. He and I are prime friends, and I believe he would know my enemies by instinct. But come, sit down, and take a drop of brandy. No? Well; I'll drink it for you. And how is the old Aunt yonder, with her infernal nostrum, the bitterness and nauseousness of which my poor stomach has not yet forgotten?"

"My Aunt Keziah is no more," said Septimius.

"No more! Well, I trust in Heaven she has carried her secret with her," said the Doctor. "If anything could comfort you for her loss, it would be that. But what brings you to Boston?"

"Only a dried flower or two," said Septimius, producing some specimens of the strange production of the grave. "I want you to tell me about these."

The naturalist took the flowers in his hand, one of which had the root appended, and examined them with great minuteness, and some surprise; two or three times looking into Septimius's face, with a puzzled and inquiring air; then examined them again.

"Do you tell me," said he, "that the plant has been found indigenous in this country, and in your part of it—and in what locality?"

"Indigenous, so far as I know," answered Septimius; "as to the locality," he hesitated a little, "it is on a small hillock, scarcely bigger than a molehill, on the hill top behind my house."

The naturalist looked steadfastly at him, with red, burning eyes, under his deep, impending, shaggy brow; then again at the flower.

"Flower, do you call it?" said he, after a re-examination. "This is no flower, though it so closely resembles one, and a beautiful one—yes; most beautiful. But it is no flower. It is a certain very rare fungus, so rare as almost to be thought fabulous; and there are the strangest superstitions, coming down from ancient times, as to the mode of reproduction. What sort of manure had been put into that hillock? Was it merely dried leaves, the refuse of the forest, or something else?"

Septimius hesitated a little; but there was no reason why he should not disclose the truth, as much of it as Doctor Portsoaken cared to know.

"The hillock where it grew," answered he, "was a grave."

"A grave! strange, strange," quoth Doctor Portsoaken, "how these old superstitions sometimes prove to have a germ of truth in them, which some philosopher has doubtless long ago—in forgotten ages—discovered and made known; but in process of time, his learned memory passes away, but the truth he discovered survives him, and the people get hold of it, and make it the nucleus of all sorts of folly. So it grew out of a grave! Yes; yes; and probably it would have grown out of any other dead flesh, as well as that of a human being; a dog would have answered the purpose as well as a man. You must know that the seeds of fungi are scattered so universally over the world, that, only comply with the conditions, and you will produce them anywhere. Prepare the bed it likes, and mushrooms will spring up spontaneously, an excellent food, like angels from Heaven. So superstition says, kill your deadliest enemy, and plant him, and he will come up as a certain fungus, which I presume to be this; steep him, or distil him, and he will make an elixir of life for you. I suppose there is some foolish symbolism or other about the matter;— but the fact I affirm to be nonsense. Dead flesh, under some certain conditions of rain and sunshine, not at present ascertained by science, will produce the fungus, whether the manure be friend or foe, or cattle."

"And as to its medical efficacy?" asked Septimius.

"That may be great, for aught I know," said Portsoaken; "but I am content with my cobwebs. You must seek it out for yourself. But if the poor fellow lost his life in the supposition that he might be a useful ingredient in a recipe, you are rather an unscrupulous practitioner."

"The person whose mortal relics fill that grave," said Septimius, "was no enemy of mine (no private enemy, I mean, though he stood among the enemies of my country) nor had I anything to gain by his death. I strove to avoid aiming at his life, but he compelled me."

"Many a chance shot brings down the bird," said Doctor Portsoaken. "You say you had no interest in his death. We shall see that in the end."

Septimius did not try to follow the conversation among the mysterious hints with which the Doctor chose to involve it; but he now sought to gain some information from him as to the mode of preparation of the recipe; and whether he thought it would be most efficacious as a decoction, or as a distillation. The learned chymist supported most decidedly the latter opinion, and showed Septimius how he might make for himself a simple apparatus, with no better aids than Aunt Keziah's teakettle, and one or two trifling things which the Doctor himself supplied, by which all might be done with every necessary scrupulousness.

"Let me look again at the formula," said he. "There are a good many minute directions, that appear trifling; but it is not safe to neglect any minutiae in the preparation of an affair like this, because, as it is all mysterious and unknown ground together, we cannot tell what may be the important and efficacious part. For instance, when all else is done, the recipe is to be exposed seven days to the sun at noon. That does not look very important, but it may be. Then again, 'Steep it in moonlight during the second quarter.' That's all moonlight, one would think; but there's no saying. It is singular, with such preciseness, that no precise directions are given whether to infuse, decoct, distil, or what other way; but my advice is to distil."

"I will do it," said Septimius; "and not a direction shall be neglected."

"I shall be curious to know the result," said Doctor Portsoaken; "and am glad to see the zeal with which you enter into the matter. A very valuable medicine may possibly be recovered to science through your agency, and you may make your fortune by it; though for my part I prefer to tend to my cobwebs. This spider, now, is not he a lovely object? See; he is quite capable of knowledge and affection."

There seemed, in fact, to be some mode of communication between the Doctor and his spider, for on some sign given by the former, imperceptible to Septimius, the many legged monster let himself down by a cord, which he extemporized out of his own bowels, and came dangling his huge bulk down before his master's face; while the latter lavished many epithets of endearment upon him, ludicrous, and not without horror, as applied to such a hideous production of nature.

"I assure you," said Doctor Portsoaken, "I run some risk from my intimacy with this lovely jewel, and if I behave not all the more prudently, your countrymen will hang me for a wizard, and annihilate this precious spider as my familiar. There would be a loss to the world; not small in my own case, but enormous in the case of the spider. Look at him, now, and see if the mere uninstructed observation does not discover a wonderful value in him."

In truth, when looked at closely, the spider really showed that a care and art had been bestowed upon his make, not merely as regards curiosity, but absolute beauty, that seemed to indicate that he must be rather a distinguished creature, in the view of Providence; so variegated was he, with a thousand minute spots, spots of color, glows of radiance, and such a brilliance was attained by many conglomerated brilliancies; and it was very strange that all this care was bestowed on a creature, that, probably, had never been carefully considered except by the two pair of eyes that were now upon it, and that, in spite of its beauty and magnificence, could only be looked at with an effort to overcome the mysterious repulsiveness of its presence; for, all the time that Septimius looked and admired, he still hated the thing, and thought it wrong that it was ever born, and wished that it could be annihilated. Whether the spider was conscious of this or not, we are unable to say; but certainly Septimius felt as if he were hostile to him, and had a mind to sting him; and in fact Doctor Portsoaken seemed of the same opinion.

"Aha, my friend," cried he, "I would advise you not to come too near Orontes! He is a lovely beast, it is true; but in a certain recess of this splendid person of his, he keeps a modest supply of a certain potent and piercing poison, which would produce a wonderful effect on any flesh to which he might choose to apply it. A powerful fellow is Orontes! and he has a great sense of his own dignity and importance, and will not allow it to be infringed on."

Septimius moved from the vicinity of the spider, who, on his part, retreated by climbing up his bowel-spun cord, and ensconced himself in the middle of his web, where he remained waiting for his prey. Septimius wondered whether the Doctor were symbolized by the spider, and were likewise waiting in the middle of his web for his prey. As he saw no way, however, in which the Doctor could make a profit out of himself, or how he could be victimized, the thought did not much disturb his equanimity. He was about to take his leave, but the Doctor, in a decisive kind of a way, bade him sit still; for that he purposed keeping him as a guest, that night, at least.

"I owe you a dinner," said he, "and will pay it with a supper and knowledge; and before we part, I have certain inquiries to make, of which you may not at first see the object, but yet are not quite purposeless. My familiar, up aloft there, has whispered me something about you; and I rely greatly on his intimations."

Septimius, who was sufficiently common-sensible and invulnerable to superstitious influences, on every point except that to which he had surrendered himself, smiled at the Doctor's half serious attempt to impose upon him; nevertheless, he was easily prevailed upon to stay, for he found the singular, charlatanic, mysterious lore of the man curious, and he had enough of real science to, at least, make him an object of interest, to one who knew nothing of the matter; and Septimius's acuteness, too, was piqued in trying to make out what manner of man he really was, and how much in him was genuine science, and self-belief, and how much quackery and pretension, and conscious empiricism. So he stayed, and supt with the Doctor at a table heaped more bountifully, with rarer dishes, than Septimius had before conceived of; and, in his simple cognizance heretofore of eating only to live, he could not but wonder to see a man of thought caring to eat of more than one dish; so that most of the meal, on his part, was spent in seeing the Doctor feed, and hearing him discourse upon his food.

"If man lived only to eat," quoth the Doctor, "one life would not suffice, not merely to exhaust the pleasure of it, but even to get the rudiments of it."

When this important business was over, the Doctor and his guest sat down again in his laboratory, where the former took care to have his usual companion, the black bottle, at his elbow, and filled his pipe, and seemed to feel a certain sullen, genial, fierce, brutal, kindly mood enough; and looked at Septimius with a sort of friendliness, as if he had as lief shake hands with him as knock him down.

"Now for a talk about business," said he.

Septimius thought, however, that the Doctor's talk began, at least, at a sufficient remoteness from any practical business; for he began to question about his remote ancestry what he knew, or what record had been preserved, of the first emigrant from England; whence, from what shire or part of England, that ancestor had come, whether there were any memorial of any kind remaining of him, any letters, or written documents, wills, deeds, or other legal papers; in short, all about him. Septimius could not satisfactorily see whether these inquiries were made with any definite purpose, or from a mere general curiosity, to see how a family of early settlement in America might still be linked with the old country; whether there were any tendrils stretching across the gulf of a hundred and fifty years, by which the American branch of the family was separated from the trunk of the family-tree in England. The Doctor partly explained this. "You must know," said he, "that the name you have, Felton, is one formerly of much eminence and repute in my part of England, and indeed very recently possessed of wealth and station. I should like to know if you are of that race."

Septimius answered with such facts or traditions as had come to his knowledge respecting his family history; a sort of history that is quite as liable to be mythical, in its early and distant stages, as that of Rome, and, indeed, seldom goes three or four generations back, without getting into a mist, really impenetrable, though great gloomy and magnificent shapes of men often seem to loom in it, who, if they could be brought close to the naked eye, would turn out as commonplace as the descendants who wonder at and admire them. He remembered Aunt Keziah's legend, and said that he had reason to believe that his first ancestor came over at a somewhat earlier date than the first Puritan settlers, and dwelt among the Indians where (and here the young man cast down his eyes, having the customary American abhorrence for any mixture of blood) he had intermarried with the daughter of a Sagamore, and succeeded to his rule. This might have happened as early as the end of Elizabeth's reign; perhaps later. It was impossible to decide dates, on such a matter. There had been a son of this connection; perhaps more than one; but certainly one son, <(a grandson, not a son)> who, on the arrival of the Puritans was a youth, his father appearing to have been slain in some outbreak of the tribe,—perhaps owing to the jealousy of prominent chiefs, at seeing their natural authority abrogated or absorbed by a man of different race. He slightly alluded to the supernatural attributes that gathered round this predecessor, but in a way to imply that he put no faith in them; for Septimius's natural keen sense and perception kept him from betraying his weaknesses to the Doctor, by the same instinctive and subtle caution with which a madman can so well conceal his infirmity.

On the arrival of the Puritans, they had found among the Indians a youth partly of their own blood, able, though imperfectly, to speak their language—having, at least, some early recollections of it—inheriting, also, a share of influence over the tribe on which his father had grafted him. It was natural that they should pay especial attention to his youth, consider it their duty to give him religious instruction in the faith of his fathers, and try to exert him as a means of influencing his tribe. They did so; but did not succeed in swaying the tribe by his means; their success having been limited to winning the half-Indian from the wild ways of his mother's people, into a certain partial, but decent accommodation to those of the English. A tendency to civilization was brought out in his character, by their rigid training; at least, his savage wildness was broken. He built a house among them, with a good deal of the wigwam, no doubt, in its style of architecture, but still a permanent house, near which he established a cornfield, a pumpkin garden, a melon patch, <remember that one was hanged as a wizard> and became farmer enough to be entitled to ask the hand of a puritan maiden. He spent his life, with some few instances of temporary relapse into savage wildness, when he fished in the river Misquehannah, or in Walden, a stray in the woods, when he should have been planting or hoeing; but on the whole, the race had been redeemed from barbarism in his person; and in the succeeding generations had been tamed more and more. The second generation had been distinguished in the Indian wars of the provinces, and had intermarried with the stock of a distinguished Puritan divine, by which means Septimius could reckon great and learned men, scholars of old Cambridge, among his ancestry on one side; while on the other it ran up to this early emigrant, who seemed to have been a remarkable man, and to that strange, wild lineage of Indian chiefs, whose blood was like that of persons not quite human intermixed with civilized blood.

"I wonder," said the Doctor, musingly, "whether there are really no documents, to ascertain the epoch at which that old first emigrant came over, and whence he came, and precisely from what English family. Often, the last heir of some respectable name dies in England; and we say that the family is extinct; whereas, very possibly, it may be abundantly flourishing in the new world, revived, and more revived, by the rich infusion of new blood, in a new soil; instead of growing feebler, heavier, stupider, each year, by sticking to an old soil, intermarrying over and over again with the same respectable families, till it has made common stock of all their vices, weaknesses, madnesses. Have you no documents, I say, no muniment chest?"

"None," said Septimius.

"No old furniture, desks, trunks, chests, cabinets?"

"You must remember," said Septimius, "that my Indian ancestor was not very likely to have brought such things out of the forest, with him. A wandering Indian does not carry a chest of papers with him. I do remember, in my childhood, a little old iron bound box or coffer, of which the key was lost, and which my Aunt Kezia used to say came down from her great great grandfather. I don't know what has become of it; and my poor old Aunt kept it among her own treasures."

"Well; my friend, do you look up that old coffer; and just as a matter of curiosity, let me see the contents."

"I have other things to do," said Septimius.

"Perhaps so," quoth the Doctor, "but no other, as it may turn out, of quite so much importance as this. I'll tell you fairly:—the heir of a great English house is lately dead, and the estate lies open to any well-sustained, perhaps to any plausible claimant. If it should appear from the records of that family—as I have some reason to suppose—that a member of it, who would now represent the elder branch—disappeared mysteriously and unaccountably, at a date corresponding with what might be ascertained as that of your ancestor's first appearance in this country; if any reasonable proof can be brought forward, on the part of the representatives of that white Sagamore—that wizard, powwow, or however you call him, that he was the disappearing Englishman—why, a good case is made out. Do you feel no interest in such a prospect?"

"Very little I confess," said Septimius.

"Very little," said the grim Doctor impatiently. "Do not you see, that, if you make good your claim, you establish for yourself a position among the aristocracy of England—and succeed to a noble English estate, an ancient hall, where your forefathers have dwelt since the conquest, splendid gardens, hereditary woods and parks, to which anything that America can show is despicable;—all thoroughly cultivated and adorned, with the care and ingenuity of centuries; and an income, a month of which would be greater wealth than any of your American ancestors, raking and scraping for his lifetime, has ever got together as the accumulated result of the toil and penury by which he has sacrificed body and soul."

"That strain of Indian blood is in me yet," said Septimius, "and it makes me despise—not despise; for I can see their desireableness for other people;—but it makes me reject for myself what you think so valuable. I do not care for these common aims. I have ambition, but it is for prizes such as other men cannot gain, and do not think of aspiring for. I could not live in the habits of English life, as I conceive it to be, and would not, for my part, be burthened with the great estate you speak of. It might answer my purpose for a time. It would suit me well enough to try that mode of life, as well as a hundred others; but only for a time. It is of no permanent importance."

"I'll tell you what it is, young man," said the Doctor testily, "you have something in your brain that makes you talk very foolishly; and I have partly a suspicion what it is—only I can't think that a fellow who is really gifted with respectable sense in other directions, should be such a confounded idiot in this."

Septimius blushed, but held his peace, and the conversation languished after this; the Doctor grimly smoking his pipe, and by no means increasing the milkiness of his mood by frequent applications to the black bottle, until Septimius intimated that he would like to go to bed. The old woman was summoned, and ushered him to his chamber.

At breakfast, the Doctor partially renewed the subject which he seemed to consider most important in yesterday's conversation.

"My young friend," said he, "I advise you to look in cellar and garret, or wherever you consider the most likely place, for that iron-bound coffer. There may be nothing in it;—it may be full of touching love-letters, or old sermons, or receipted bills of a hundred years ago;—but it may contain what will be worth to you an estate of five thousand pounds a year. It is a pity the old woman, with her damnable decoction, is gone off. Look it up, I say."

"Well, well," said Septimius abstractedly, "when I can find time."

So saying he took his leave, and resumed his way back to his home. He had not seemed like himself, during the time that elapsed since he left it, and it seemed an infinite space that he had lived through and traveled over, and he fancied it hardly possible that he could ever get back again. But now, with every step that he took, he found himself getting insensibly back again into the old enchanted land. The mist rose up about him; the pale mist bow of ghostly promise arched before him; and he trod back again, poor boy, out of the clime of real effort into the land of his dreams and shadowy enterprise. "How was it," said he, "that I can have been so untrue to my convictions? Whence came that dark and dull despair that weighed upon me? Why did I let the mocking mood, which I was conscious of in that brutal, brandy-burnt sceptic, have such an influence on me! Let him guzzle. He shall not tempt me from my pursuit with his lure of an estate and name among those heavy English beef-eaters, of whom he is a brother. My destiny is one which Kings might envy, and strive in vain to buy with principalities and kingdoms."

So he trod on air, almost, in the latter parts of his journey, and instead of being wearied, grew more airy with the latter miles that brought him to his wayside home.

So now Septimius sat down, and began in earnest his endeavors and experiments to prepare the medicine; according to the mysterious terms of the recipe. It seemed not possible to do it, so many rebuffs and disappointments did he meet with. No effort could produce a combination answering to the description of the recipe, which propounded a brilliant, gold-colored liquid, clear as the air itself, with a certain fragrance which was peculiar to it, and, also, which was the more individual test of the correctness of the mixture, a certain coldness to the feeling, a chillness, which was described as peculiarly refreshing and invigorating. With all his trials, he produced nothing but turbid results, clouded generally, or lacking something in color, and never that fragrance, and never that coldness, which were to be the test of truth. He studied all the books of chemistry which, at that period, were attainable; a period when, in the world, it was a science far unlike what it has since become; and when Septimius had no instruction in this country, nor could obtain any, beyond the dark, mysterious, charlatanic communications of Doctor Portsoaken. So that, in fact, he seemed to be discovering for himself the science through which he was to work. He seemed to do everything that was stated in the recipe, and yet no results came from it; the liquid that he produced was nauseous to the smell—to taste it he had a horrible repugnance—turbid, nasty, reminding in most respects of poor Aunt Keziah's elixir; it was a body without a soul, and that body dead. And so it went on; and the poor, half-maddened Septimius began to think that his immortal life was preserved by the mere effort of seeking for it, but was to be spent in the quest, and was therefore to be made an eternity of abortive misery. He pored over the document that had so possessed him, turning its crabbed meanings every way, trying to get out of it some new light, often tempted to fling it into the fire which he kept under his retort, and let the whole thing go; but then again, soon rising out of that black depth of despair, into a determination to do what he had so long striven. With such intense action of mind as he brought to bear upon this paper, it is wonderful that it was not spiritually distilled; that its essence did not arise, purified from all alloy of falsehood, from all turbidness of obscurity and ambiguity, and form a pure essence of truth and invigorating motive, if of any it were capable. In this interval, Septimius is said by tradition to have found out many wonderful secrets in Science, that were almost beyond the scope of science; it was said that old Aunt Keziah used to come, with a coal of fire from unknown furnaces, to light his distilling apparatus; it was said, too, that the ghost of the old Archimagus, whose ingenuity had propounded this puzzle for his descendant, used to come at midnight and strive to explain to him this manuscript; that the Black Man too, met him on the hill-top, and promised him an immediate release from his difficulties, provided he would kneel down and worship him, and sign his name in his book—an old, iron-clasped, much worn volume, which he produced from his ample pockets, and showed him in it the names of many a man whose name had become historic, and some whose ashes slept under an inscription testifying to their virtues and devotion—old autographs, for the Black Man was the original autograph collector. But these, no doubt, were foolish stories, conceived and propagated in chimney-corners, while yet there were firesides, and chimney corners, and smokey flues. There was no truth in such stories, I am sure; the Black Man had changed his tactics, and knew better how to lure the human soul than to come to him with his musty autograph-book. So Septimius fought with his difficulty by himself, as many a beginner in science has done before him; and to his efforts in this way are popularly attributed many herb drinks, and some kinds of spruce beer, and nostrums used for rheumatics, sore throat, typhus fever; but I rather think they all come from Aunt Keziah; or perhaps, like jokes to Joe Miller, all sorts of quack-medicines, flowing at large through the community, are assigned to him or her. The people have a little mistaken the character and purpose of poor Septimius, and remember him as a quack doctor, instead of a seeker for a secret, not the less sublime and elevating because it happened to be unattainable.

I know not through what medium, or by what means, but it got voiced abroad that Septimius was engaged in some mysterious work; and, indeed, his seclusion, his absorption, his indifference to all that was going on, in that weary time of war, looked strange enough to indicate that it must be some most important business that engrossed him. On the few occasions when he came out from his immediate haunts, into the village, he had a strange owl-like appearance, un-combed, unbrushed, his hair long and tangled; his face, they said, darkened with smoke; his cheeks pale, the indentation of his brow deeper than ever before; an earnest, haggard, seeking look; and so he went hastily along the village street, feeling as if all eyes might find out what he had in his mind from his appearance; taking by-ways where they were to be found, going long distances through woods and by-fields, rather than short ones, when the way lay through the frequented haunts of men. For he shunned the glances of his fellow-men, probably because he had learnt to consider them not as fellows—because he was seeking to withdraw himself from the common bond and destiny—because he felt, too, that on that account his fellow men would consider him as a traitor-enemy, one who deserted their cause, and tried to withdraw his feeble shoulder from under that great burthen of death which is imposed on all men to bear, and which, if one could escape, each other would feel his load proportionably heavier. With these beings of a moment he had no longer any common cause; they must go their separate ways yet apparently the same; they on the broad, dusty, beaten path, that seemed always full, but from which continually they so strangely vanished into insensibility, no one knowing, nor long inquiring, what had become of them; he, on his lonely path, where he should tread secure, with no trouble but the loneliness which would be none to him. For a little while, he would seem to keep them company; but soon they would all drop away, the minister, his accustomed towns-people, Robert Hagburn, Rose, Sybil Dacy, all, leaving him in blessed unknownness to adopt new temporary relations and take a new course. Sometimes, however, the prospect a little chilled him.

Could he give them all up; the sweet sister, the friend of his childhood, the grave instructor of his youth, the homely life-known faces? Yes; there were such rich possibilities in the future; for he would seek out the noblest minds, the deepest hearts, in every age, and be the friend of human time. Only, it might be sweet, to have one unchangeable companion; for unless he strung the pearls and diamonds of life upon one unbroken affection, he sometimes thought that his life would have nothing to give it unity and identity; and so the longest life would be but an aggregate of insulated fragments, which would have no relation to one another, and so it would not be one life, but many unconnected ones. Unless he could look into the same eyes, through the mornings of future time, opening and blessing him with their fresh gleam of love and joy; unless the same sweet voice could melt his thought together; unless some sympathy of a life side by side with his could melt two into one; looking back upon the same things, looking forward to the same; the long, thin thread of an individual life, stretching onward and onward, would cease to be visible, cease to be felt, cease by and by to have any real bigness in proportion to its breadth, and so be virtually non-existent, except in the mere inconsiderable now. If a group of chosen friends, chosen out of all the world and all time for their adaptedness, could go on in endless life together, keeping themselves mutually warm in their high, desolate way, then none of them need ever sigh to be comforted in the pitiable snugness of the grave. If one especial soul might be his companion, then how complete the fence of mutual arms, the warmth of close pressing breast to breast! Might there be one! Oh Sybil Dacy!

Perhaps it could not be. Who but himself could undergo that great trial and hardship, and self-denial, and firm purpose, never wavering, never sinking for a moment, keeping his grasp on life like one who holds up, by main force, a sinking and drowning friend—how could a woman do it! He must then give up the thoughts. There was a choice—friendship and the love of woman or the lonely life of immortality. There was something heroic and ennobling in choosing the latter. And so he walked with the mysterious girl on the hilltop, and sat down beside her on the grave, which still ceased not to redden, portentously beautiful, with that unnatural flower, and they talked together; and Septimius looked on her weird beauty, and often said to himself, "this too will pass away; she is not capable of what I am; she is a woman; it must be a manly and courageous and forcible spirit, vastly rich in all these particulars, that has force enough to live! Ah; is it surely so? There is such a dark sympathy between us; she knows me so well; she touches my inmost so, at unawares, that I could almost think I had a companion here. Perhaps not so soon. At the end of centuries, I might need one; not now." But once he said to Sybil Dacy—"Ah how sweet it would be—sweet for me, at least—if this intercourse might last forever!"

"That is an awful idea that you present!" said Sybil, with a hardly perceptible involuntary shudder; "always on this hill-top, always passing and repassing this little hillock, always smelling this flower! I always looking at that deep chasm in your brow; you always seeing my bloodless cheek!—doing this, till these trees crumble away, till perhaps a new forest grew up wherever the white race has planted, and a race of savages again possess the soil. I should not like it. My mission here is but for a short time, and will soon be accomplished, and then I go."

"You do not rightly estimate the way in which the long time might be spent;" said Septimius. "We would find out a thousand uses of this world, uses and enjoyments, which now men never dream of, because the world is just held to their mouth and then snatched away again, before they have time hardly to taste it, instead of becoming acquainted with all the deliciousness of this great world-fruit. But you speak of a mission, and as if you were now in performance of it. Will you not tell me what it is?"

"No;" said Sybil Dacy, smiling on him. "But one day you shall know what it is—none sooner nor better than you—so much I promise you."

"Are we friends?" asked Septimius, somewhat puzzled by her look.

"We have an intimate relation to one another!" replied Sybil.

"And what is it?" demanded Septimius.

"That will appear hereafter," answer Sybil, again smiling on him.

He knew not what to make of this, nor whether to be exalted or depressed; but, at all events, there seemed to be an accordance, a striking together, a mutual touch of their two natures, as if somehow or other they were performing the same piece of solemn music; so that he felt his soul thrill, and at the same time shudder. Some sort of sympathy there surely was, but of what nature he could not tell; though often he was impelled to ask himself the same question he asked Sybil—"Are we friends?" Because of a sudden shock and repulsion, that came between them, and passed away in a moment; and there would be Sybil smiling askance on him.

And then he toiled away again at his chymical pursuits; trying to mingle things harmoniously, that apparently were not born to be mingled; discovering a science for himself, and mixing it up with absurdities that other chymists had long ago flung aside; but still there would be that turbid aspect, still that lack of fragrance, still that want of the peculiar temperature that was announced as the test of the matter. Over and over again, he set the crystal vase in the sun, and let it stay there the appointed time, hoping that it would digest in such a manner as to bring about the desired result.

One day, as it happened, his eyes fell upon the silver key which he had taken from the breast of the dead young man; and he thought within himself that this might have something to do with the seemingly unattainable success of his pursuit. He remembered, for the first time, the grim Doctor's emphatic injunctions to search for the little iron-bound box of which he had spoken, and which had come down with such legends attached to it; as for instance, that it held the Devil's bond with his great-great-grandfather, now cancelled by the surrender of the latter's soul; that it held the golden key of Paradise; that it was full of old gold, or of the dry leaves of a hundred years ago; that it had a family fiend in it, who would be exorcised by the turning of the lock, but would otherwise remain a prisoner till the solid oak of the box mouldered, or the iron rusted away; so that between fear, and the loss of the key, this curious old box had remained unopened till itself was lost.

But now Septimius, putting together what Aunt Kezia had said in her dying moments, and what Doctor Portsoaken had insisted upon, suddenly came to the conclusion that the possession of the old iron box might be of the greatest importance to him. So he set himself at work to think where he had last seen it. Aunt Keziah of course had put it away in some safe place or other; either in cellar or garret, no doubt; so Septimius, in the intervals of his other occupations, devoted several days to the search; and not to weary the reader with the particulars of the quest for an old box, suffice it to say that he at last found it, amongst various other antique rubbish, in a corner of the garret.

It was a very rusty old thing, not more than a foot in length, and half as much in height and breadth; but most ponderously iron bound with bars, and corners, and all sorts of fortification; looking very much like an ancient alms-box, which are to be seen in the older rural churches of England, and which seem to indicate a great distrust of those to whom the funds are committed. Indeed, there might be a shrewd suspicion that some ancient church-beadle among Septimius's forefathers, when emigrating to New England, had taken the opportunity of bringing the poor's box along with him. On looking closer, too, there were rude embellishments on the lid and sides of the box, in long rusted steel, designs such as the middle ages were rich in; a representation of Adam and Eve, or of Satan and a soul; nobody could tell which; but at any rate an illustration of great value and interest. Septimius looked at this ugly, rusty, ponderous old box, so worn and battered with time, and recollected with a scornful smile the legends of which it was the object; all of which he despised and discredited just as much, as he did that story of the Arabian Nights, where a demon comes out of a copper vase, in a cloud of smoke that covers the seashore; for he was singularly invulnerable to all modes of superstition, all nonsense except his own. But that one mode was ever in full force and operation with him. He felt strongly convinced that, inside this old box, was something that appertained to his destiny; the key that he had taken from the dead man's breast—had that come down through time, and across the sea, and had a man died to bring and deliver it to him, merely for nothing! It could not be.

He looked at the old, rusty, elaborated lock of the rusty little receptacle; it was much flourished about with what was once polished steel; and evidently when thus polished, and the steel bright with which it was hooped, defended, and inlaid, it must have been a thing fit to appear in any cabinet; though now the oak was worm-eaten as an old coffin, and the rust of the iron came off red on Septimius's fingers, after he had been handling it. He looked at the curious old silver key, too, and fancied that he discovered in its elaborate handle, some analogy to the ornaments about the box; at any rate, this he determined was the key of fate, and he was just about applying it to the lock, when somebody tapped familiarly at the door, having opened the outer one, and stept in with a manly stride. Septimius, inwardly blaspheming, as secluded men are apt to do when an interruption comes, and especially when it comes at some critical moment of projection, left the box as yet unbroached, and said, "Come in."

The door opened, and Roger Hagburn entered; looking so tall and stately that Septimius hardly knew him for the youth with whom he had grown up familiarly. He had on the revolutionary dress of buff and blue, with decorations that to the initiated eye denoted him an officer; and certainly there was a kind of authority in his look and manner, indicating that heavy responsibilities, critical moments, had educated him, and turned the ploughboy into a man.

"Is it you?" exclaimed Septimius. "I scarcely knew you. How war has altered you!"

"And I may say, is it you? For you are much altered, likewise, my old friend. Study wears upon you terribly. You will be an old man, at this rate, before you know you are a young one. You will kill yourself as sure as a gun!"

"Do you think so?" said Septimius, rather startled; for the queer absurdity of the position struck him, if he should so exhaust and so wear himself as to die, just at the moment when he should have found out the secret of everlasting life. "But though I look pale, I am very vigorous. Judging by that scar slanting down from your temple, you have been nearer death than you now think me, though in another way."

"Yes," said Robert, smiling, "but in hot blood, and for a good cause, who cares for death. And yet I love life; none better, while it lasts. I love it in all its looks, and times, and badnesses;—there is so much to be got out of it, in spite of all that people say. Youth is sweet, with its fiery enterprise, and I suppose mature manhood will be just as much so, though in a calmer way, and age, quieter still, will have its own merits;—the thing is only to do with life what we ought, and what is suited to each of its stages; do all, enjoy all;— and I suppose those two rules amount to the same thing. Only catch real, earnest hold of life; not play with it; not defer one part of it for the sake of another; then each part of life will do for us what was intended. People talk of the hardships of military service; of the miseries that we undergo fighting for our country. I have undergone my share I believe—hard toil in the wilderness, hunger, extreme weariness, pinching cold, the torture of a wound, peril of death; and really I have been as happy through it as ever I was at my mother's cosy fireside, of a winter's evening. If I had died, I doubt not my last moments would have been happy. There is no use of life, but just to find out what is fit for us to do, and doing it, it seems to be little matter whether we live or die in it. God does not want our work, but only our willingness to work;—at least, the last seems to answer all his purposes."

"This is a comfortable philosophy of yours," said Septimius, rather contemptuously, and yet enviously. "Where did you get it, Robert?"

"Where? nowhere; it came to me on the march; and though I can't say that I thought it when the bullets pattered into the snow about me, in those narrow streets of Quebec, yet I suppose it was in my mind then; for, as I tell you, I was very cheerful and contented. And you, Septimius, I never saw such a discontented unhappy looking fellow as you are. You have had a harder time in peace, than I in war. You have not found what you seek—whatever that may be. Take my advice. Give yourself to the next work that comes to hand. The war offers place to all of us; we ought to be thankful—the most joyous of all the generations before or after us—since Providence gives us such good work to live for, or such a good opportunity to die. It is worth living for, just to have the chance to die so well as a man may in these days. Come; be a soldier. Be a chaplain, since your education lies that way; and you will find nobody in peace prays so well as we do, we soldiers; and you shall not be debarred from fighting, too. If war is holy work, a priest may lawfully do it, as well as pray for it. Come with us, my old friend

Septimius; be my comrade, and whether you live or die, you will thank me for getting you out of the yellow forlornness in which you go on, neither living nor dying."

Septimius looked at Robert Hagburn in surprise; so much was he altered and improved by the brief experience of war, adventure, responsibility, which he had passed through; not less than the effect produced on his loutish, rustic air and deportment, developing his figure, seeming to make him taller, setting free the manly graces that lurked within his loutish frame—not less was the effect on his mind and moral nature, giving freedom of ideas, a simple perception of great thoughts, a free natural chivalry; so that the knight, the Homeric warrior, the hero, seemed to be here, or possible to be here, in this young New England rustic; and all that history has given, and hearts throbbed, and sighed, and gloried over, of patriotism, and heroic feeling and action, might be repeated, perhaps, in the life and death of this familiar friend and playmate of his, whom he had valued not over highly—Robert Hagburn. He had merely followed out his natural bent, boldly and simply, doing the first good thing that came to hand—and here was a hero.

"You almost make me envy you, Robert," said he sighing.

"Then why not come with me?" asked Robert.

"Because I have another destiny," said Septimius.

"Well; you are mistaken, be sure of that," said Robert. "This is not a generation for study, and the making of books; —that may come by-and-by. This great fight has need of all men to carry it on, in one way or another; and no man will do well, even for himself, who tries to avoid his share in it. But I have said my say. And now, Septimius, the war takes much of man; but it does not take him all—and what it leaves is all the more full of life and health thereby. I have something to say to you about this."

"Say it then, Robert," said Septimius, who having got over the first excitement of the interview, and the sort of exhilaration produced by the healthful glow of Robert's spirit, began secretly to wish that the interview might close, and he be permitted to return to his solitary thoughts again. "What can I do for you?"

"Why, nothing," said Robert, looking rather confused, "since all is settled. The fact is, my old friend, as perhaps you have seen, I have very long had an eye upon your sister Rose; yes from the time we went together to the old school-house, where she now teaches children like what we were then. The war took me away; and in good time, for I doubt if Rose would ever have care enough for me to be my wife, if I had staid at home, a country lout, as I was getting to be, in shirt sleeves, bare feet. But now, you see, I have come back, and this whole great war, to her woman's heart, is represented in me, and makes me heroic, so to speak, and strange, and yet her old familiar lover. So I found her heart tenderer for me than it was; and, in short, Rose has consented to be my wife, and we mean to be married in a week; my furlough permits little delay."

"You surprise me," said Septimius, who, immersed in his own pursuits, had taken no notice of the growing affection between Robert and his sister. "Do you think it well to snatch this little lull that is allowed you in the wild storm of war to try to make a peaceful home? Shall you like to be summoned from it soon? Shall you be as cheerful among dangers afterwards, when one sword may cut down two happinesses?"

"There is something in what you say, and I have thought of it," said Robert sighing. "But I can't tell how it is, but there is something in this uncertainty, this peril, this cloud before us, that makes it sweeter to love and to be loved, than amid all seeming quiet and serenity. Really, I think if there were to be no death, the beauty of life would be all tame. So we take our chance, or our dispensation of Providence, and are going to love and to be married, just as confidently as if we were sure of living forever."

"Well, old fellow," said Septimius, with more heartiness and outgush of heart than he had felt for a long while. "There is no man whom I should be happier to call brother. Take Rose, and all happiness along with her. She is a good girl, and not in the least like me. May you live out your three-score years and ten, and every one of them happy."

Little more passed, and Robert Hagburn took his leave, with a hearty shake of Septimius's hand, too conscious of his own happiness to be quite sensible how much the latter was self-involved, strange, anxious, separated from healthy life and interests; and Septimius as soon as Robert had disappeared, locked the door behind him, and proceeded at once to apply the silver key to the lock of the old strong-box.

The lock resisted somewhat, being rusty, as might well be supposed, after so many years since it was opened; but it finally allowed the key to turn, and Septimius, with a good deal of flutter at his heart, opened the lid. The interior had a very different aspect from that of the exterior; for whereas the latter looked so old, this, having been kept from the air, looked about as new as when shut up from light and air, two centuries ago, less or more. It was lined with ivory, beautifully carved in figures, according to the art which the mediaeval people possessed in great perfection; and probably the box had been a lady's jewel-casket, formerly, and had glowed with rich lustre and bright colors, at former openings of the box. But now, there was nothing in it of that kind; nothing in keeping with those figures carved in the ivory, representing some mythical subjects; nothing but some papers in the bottom of the box, written over in an ancient hand, which Septimius at once fancied that he recognized as that of the manuscript and recipe, which he had found on the breast of the young soldier. He eagerly seized them, but was infinitely disappointed to find that they did not seem to refer at all to the subject treated by the former, but related to pedigrees and genealogies; and were in reference to an English family, and some member of it who, two centuries before, had crossed the sea to America, and who in this way, had sought to preserve his connection with his native stock, so as to be able perhaps to prove it, for himself or his descendants; and there was reference to documents and records in England, in confirmation of the genealogy. Septimius saw that this paper had been drawn up by an ancestor of his own, the unfortunate man who had been hanged for witchcraft; but, so earnest had been his expectation of something different, that he flung the old papers down with bitter indifference.

Then again he snatched them up, and contemptuously read them—those proofs of descent, through generations of esquires, and knights, who had been renowned in war, and there seemed, too, to be running through the family a certain tendency to letters, for some were designated as of the colleges of Oxford or Cambridge; and against one, there was the note, he that sold himself to Sathan, and another seemed to have been a follower of Wickcliffe; and they had murdered kings, and been beheaded, and banished, and what not; so that the age-long life of this ancient family had not been, after all, a happy or very prosperous one, though they had kept their estate in one or another descendant, since the conquest. It was not wholly without interest, that Septimius saw that this ancient descent, this connection with noble families, and intermarriages with names, some of which he recognized as known in English history, all referred to his own family, and seemed to centre in himself, the last of a poverty-stricken line, which had dwindled down into obscurity, and into rustic labor, and humble toil, reviving in him a little; yet how little, unless he fulfilled his strange purpose. Was it not better worth his while to take this English position, here so strangely offered him? He had apparently slain unwittingly the only person who could have contested his rights, the young man, who had so strangely brought him the hope of unlimited life, at the same time that he was making room for him among his forefathers. What a change in his lot would have been here; for there seemed to be some pretensions to a title too, from a barony which was floating about, and occasionally moving out of abeyancy.

"Perhaps," said Septimius to himself, "I may hereafter think it worth while to assert my claim to these possessions, to this position amid an ancient aristocracy, and try that mode of life for one generation. Yet there is something in my destiny incompatible, of course, with the continued possession of an estate. I must be of necessity a wanderer on the face of the earth, changing place at short intervals, disappearing suddenly and utterly; else the foolish, short-lived multitude and mob of mortals, will be enraged with one who seems their brother, yet whose countenance will never be furrowed with his age, nor his knees totter, nor his force be abated; their little brevity will be rebuked by his age-long endurance, above whom the oaken roof-tree of a thousand years would crumble, while still he would be hale and strong. So that this house, or any other would be but a resting-place of a day, and then I must away into another obscurity."

With almost a regret, he continued to look over the documents; until he reached one of the persons recorded in the line of pedigree, a worthy apparently of the reign of Elizabeth, to whom was attributed a title of "Doctor in Utriusque Juris"; and against his name there was a verse of Latin written, for what purpose Septimius knew not; for on reading it, it appeared to have no discoverable appropriateness; but suddenly he remembered the blotted and imperfect hieroglyphical passage in the recipe; he thought, an instant, and was convinced that was the full expression and outwriting of that crabbed little mystery; and that here was part of that secret writing for which, as my poor friend Miss Bacon discovered to her cost, the age of Elizabeth was so famous and so dexterous. His mind had a flash of light upon it; and from that moment, he was enabled to read not only the recipe, but the rules, and all the rest of that mysterious document, in a way which he had never thought of before; to discern that it was not to be taken literally and simply, but had a hidden process involved in it that made the whole thing infinitely deeper than he had hitherto deemed it to be. His brain reeled; he seemed to have taken a draught of some liquor that opened infinite depths before him; he could scarcely refrain from giving a shout of triumphant exaltation; the house could not contain him; he rushed up to his hilltop, and thereon walking swiftly to-and-fro, at length flung himself on the little hillock, and burst forth, as if addressing him who slept beneath.

"Oh, brother, oh, friend," said he, "I thank thee for thy matchless beneficence to me; for all which I rewarded thee with this little spot on my hill-top. Thou wast very good, very kind. It would not have been well for thee, a youth of fiery joys and passions, loving to laugh, loving the lightness and sparkling brilliancy of life, to take this boon to thyself; for, Oh, brother, I see, I see, it requires a strong spirit, capable of much lonely endurance, able to be sufficient to itself, loving not too much, dependent on no sweet ties of affection, to be capable of the mighty trial which now devolves on me. I thank thee, Oh kinsman; yet thou, I feel, hast the better part, who didst so low lie down to rest, who hast done forever with this troublesome world, which it is mine to contemplate, from age to age, and to sum up the meaning of it. Thou art disporting thyself in other spheres; I enjoy the high, severe, painful office of living here, and of being the minister of Providence from one age to many successive ones."

In this manner, he raved, as never before, in a strain of exalted enthusiasm, scarcely treading on air, and sometimes stopping to shout aloud, and feeling as if he should burst if he did not do so; and his voice came back to him afar, from the low hills on the other side of the broad level valley, and out of the woods, afar, imitating his voice; or as if it were airy spirits that knew how it was all to be, confirming his cry, saying, "it shall be so," "thou hast found it at last," "thou art immortal." And it seemed as if Nature were inclined to celebrate his triumph over herself; for above the woods, that crowned the hill to the northward, there were shoots and streams of radiance, a white, a red, a many colored lustre, blazing up high towards the zenith, dancing up, flitting down, dancing up again; so that it seemed as if spirits were keeping a revel there. The leaves of the trees on the hill side, all except the evergreens, had now mostly fallen with the autumn; so that Septimius was seen by the few passers-by, in the decline of the afternoon, passing to and fro along his path, wildly gesticulating, and heard to shout, so that the echoes came from all directions to answer him. After nightfall, too, in the harvest moonlight, a shadow was still seen passing there, waving its arms in shadowy triumph; so, the next day, there were various goodly stories afloat, and astir, coming out of successive mouths, more wondrous at each successive birth;

—the simplest form of the story being that Septimius Norton had at last gone raving mad on the hill top that he was so fond of haunting; and those who listened to his shouts, said that he was calling to the devil; and some said that, by certain exorcisms, he had caused the appearance of a battle in the air, charging squadrons, cannon flashes, champions encountering, all of which foreboded some real battle to be fought with the enemies of the country; and as the battle of Monmouth chanced to occur either the very next day, or about that time, this was supposed to be either caused or foretold by Septimius's eccentricities; and as the battle was not very favourable to our arms, the patriotism of Septimius suffered much in popular estimation.

But he knew nothing, thought nothing, cared nothing about his country, or his country's battles; he was as sane as he had been for a year past, and was wise enough, though merely by instinct, to throw off some of his superfluous excitement by these wild gestures, with wild shouts, and restless activity; and when he had partly accomplished this, he returned to the house, and late as it was, kindled his fire, began anew the processes of chemistry, now enlightened by the late teachings. A new agent seemed to him to mix itself up with his toil, and to forward his purpose; something helped him along; everything became facile to his manipulation; clear to his thought. In this way, he spent the night, and when, at sunrise, he let in the eastern light upon his study, the thing was done.

Septimius had achieved it. That is to say, he had succeeded in amalgamating his materials so that they acted upon one another, and in accordance, and had produced a result that had a subsistence in itself, and a right to be, a something potent and substantial; each ingredient contributing its part to form a new essence, which was as real and individual as anything that it was formed from. But in order to perfect it, there was necessity that the powers of Nature should act gently upon it through a month of sunshine; that the moon, too, should have its part in the production; and so he must wait patiently for this. Wait! Surely he would! Had he not time for waiting? Were he to wait till old age, it would not be too much; for all future time would have it in charge to repay him.

So he poured the inestimable liquor into a glass vase, well secured from the air, and placed it in the sunshine, shifting it from one sunny window to another, in order that it might ripen; moving it gently, lest he should disturb the living spirit that he knew to be in it. And he watched it from day to day, watched the reflections in it; watched its lustre, which seemed to him to grow greater, day by day, as if it imbibed the sunlight into it. Never was there any thing so bright as this. It changed its hue, too, gradually, being now a rich purple, now a crimson, now a violet, now a blue, going through all these prismatic colors, without losing any of its brilliance; and never was there such a hue as the sunlight took in falling through it, and resting on his floor. And strange and beautiful it was, too, to look through this medium at the outer world, and see how it was glorified and made anew, and did not look like the same world, although there were all its familiar marks. And there, past his window, seen through this went the farmer and his wife, on saddle and pillion, jogging to meeting-house or market, and every day the cow coming home from pasture, the old familiar faces of his childhood looked differently. And so, at last, at the end of the month, it settled into a most deep and brilliant crimson, as if it were the essence of the blood of the young man whom he had slain; the flower being now triumphant, it had given its own hue to the whole mass, and had grown brighter every day; so that it seemed to have inherent light, as if it were a planet by itself; a heart of crimson fire, burning within it.

And when this had done, and there was no more change, showing that the digestion was perfect, then he took it and placed it where the changing moon would fall upon it; and there again he watched it; covering it in darkness by day, revealing it to the moon by night; and watching if here too, there were changes. And, by and by, he perceived that the deep crimson hue was departing—not fading; we cannot say that, because of the prodigious lustre which still pervaded it, and was not less strong than ever; but certainly the hue became fainter, now a rose-color, now fainter, fainter, still, till there was only left the purest whiteness of the moon itself; a change that somewhat disappointed and grieved Septimius, though still it seemed fit that the water of life should be of no one richness, because it must combine all. As the absorbed young man gazed through the lonely nights at his beloved liquor, he fancied sometimes that he could see wonderful things in the crystal sphere of the vase; as in Doctor Dee's magic crystal used to be seen, which now lies in the British Museum; representations it might be of things in the far past, or in the farther future, scenes in which he himself was to act, persons yet unborn, the beautiful and wise, with whom he was to be associated, <The witch meetings in which his ancestors used to take part> palaces and towers, modes of hitherto unseen architecture, that old hall in England, to which he had a hereditary right, with its gables and its smooth lawn, <Aunt Kezia, on her death-bed> <and the bloody footstep> and flitting through all the shade of Sybil Dacy, eyeing him from secret nook, or some remoteness, with her peculiar, mischievous smile, beckoning him into the sphere. All such visions would he see, and then become aware that he had been in a dream, superinduced by too much watching, too intent thought; so, that living among so many dreams, he was almost afraid that he should find himself waking out of yet another, and discover that the vase itself, and the liquid it contained, were also dream-stuff. But no; these were real.

There was one change that surprised him, although he accepted it without doubt, as, indeed, it did imply a wonderful efficacy, at least singularity, in the newly concocted liquid. It grew strangely cool in temperature, in the latter part of his watching it. It appeared to imbibe its coldness from the cold, chaste moon, until it seemed to Septimius that it was colder than ice itself; the mist gathered upon the crystal vase, as upon a tumbler of iced water in a warm room; some say it actually gathered thick with frost, crystallized into a thousand fantastic and beautiful shapes; but this I do not know so well. Only it was very cold. Septimius pondered upon it, and thought he saw that life itself was cold, individual in its essence, a high pure essence, chastened from all heats, cold, therefore, and therefore invigorating.

Thus much, inquiring deeply and with painful research into the liquor which Septimius concocted, have I been able to learn about it, its aspect, its properties; and now, I suppose it to be quite perfect, and that nothing remained but to put it to such use as he had so long been laboring for. But this, somehow or other, he found in himself a strange reluctance to do; he paused, as it were, at the point where his pathway separated itself from that of other men, and meditated whether it were worth while to give up everything that Providence had provided; and take instead only this lonely gift of immortal life. Not that he ever really had any doubt about it; no, indeed, but it was his security, his consciousness that he held the bright sphere of all futurity in his hand, that made him dally a little, now that he could quaff immortality as soon as he liked.

Besides, now that he looked forward from the verge of mortal destiny, the path before him seemed so very lonely. Might he not seek one companion—one single heart—before he took the final step. There was Sybil Dacy! Oh what a bliss, if that pale girl might set out with him on his journey; how sweet, how sweet, to wander with her through the places else so desolate; for he could but half see, half know things, without her to help him. And perhaps it might be so. She already must know, or strongly suspect, that he was engaged in some deep, mysterious research; it might be, that, with her sources of mysterious knowledge, among her legendary lore, she knew of this. Then, oh, to think of those dreams which lovers have always had, when their new love makes this old earth seem so happy and glorious a place that not a thousand years, nor an endless succession of life can exhaust it—all those realized for him and her. If this could not be, what should he do! Would he venture onward into such a wintry futurity, symbolized perhaps by the coldness of the crystal goblet? He shivered at the thought.

Now, what had passed between Septimius and Sybil Dacy is not upon record; only that one day they were walking together on the hill-top, or sitting by the little hillock, and talking earnestly together. Sybil's face was a little flushed with some excitement; and really she looked very beautiful; and Septimius's dark face, too, had a solemn triumph in it, that made him also beautiful, so wrapt he was, after all those watchings, and emaciations, and the pure, unworldly, self-denying life that he had spent. They talked, as if there were some foregone conclusion on which they based what they said.

"Will you not be weary, in the time that we shall spend together?" asked he.

"Ah no," said Sybil smiling; "I think that it will be very full of enjoyment."

"Yes," said Septimius. "Though now I must remould my anticipations; for I have only dared hitherto to map out a solitary existence."

"And how did you do that?" asked Sybil.

"Oh; there is nothing that could come amiss," answered Septimius; "for lonely as I have lived apart from men, yet it is really not because I have no taste for whatever humanity includes; but I would fain, if I might, live everybody's life at once—or since that may not be, each in succession. I would try the life of power, ruling men, but that might come later, after I had had long experience of men, and had lived through much history, and had seen as a disinterested observer how men might be best influenced for their own good. I would be a great traveller, at first, and as a man newly coming into possession of an estate, goes over it, and views each separate field, and wood-lot, and whatever features it contains, so will I, whose the world is, because I possess it forever, whereas all others are but transitory guests, so will I wander over this world of mine, and be acquainted with all its shores, seas, rivers, mountains, fields, and the various people who inhabit them, and to whom it is my mission to be their benefactor; for think not, dear Sybil, that I suppose this great lot of mine to have devolved upon me without great duties—heavy, and difficult to fulfil, though glorious in their adequate fulfilment. But for all this there will be time. In a century, I shall partially have seen the earth, and known at least its boundaries—have got for myself the outline, to be filled up hereafter."

"And I, too," said Sybil, "will have my duties and labors; for while you are wandering about among men, I will go among women, and observe and converse with them from the princess to the peasant-girl, and will find out what is the matter that woman gets so large a share of human misery laid on her weak shoulders. I will see why it is, that whether she be a royal princess, she has to be sacrificed to matters of state, or a cottage-girl, still, somehow, the thing not fit for her is done; and whether there is or no, some deadly curse on woman, so that she has nothing to do, and nothing to enjoy, but only to be wronged by man and still to love him, and despise herself for it;—to be snaky in her revenges. And then, if, after all this investigation it turns out—as I suspect— that woman is not capable of being helped, that there is something inherent in herself that makes it hopeless to struggle for her redemption, then, what shall I do? Nay; I know not, unless to preach to the sisterhood that they all kill their female children as fast as they are born; and then let the generations of men manage as they can!—Women, so feeble and crazy in body, fair enough sometimes, but full of infirmities, not strong, with nerves bare to every pain, ailing, full of little weaknesses, more contemptible than great ones."

"That would be a dreary end, Sybil," said Septimius. "But I trust that we shall be able to hush up this weary and perpetual wail of womankind on easier terms than that. Well, dearest Sybil; after we have spent a hundred years in examining into the sad state of mankind, and another century in devising and putting in execution remedies for his chills, until our maturer thought has time to perfect his cure, we shall then have earned a little playtime—a century of pastime, in which we will search out whatever joy can be had by thoughtful people, and what childlike sportiveness comes out of growing wisdom, and enjoyment of every kind. We will gather about us everything beautiful and stately, a great palace, for we shall then be so experienced that all riches will be easy for us to get; with rich furniture, pictures, statues, and all royal environment; and side by side with this life, we will have a little cottage, and see which is the happiest, for this has always been a dispute. For this century, we will neither toil nor spin, nor think of anything beyond the day that is passing over us. There is time enough to do all that we have to do."

"A hundred years of play! Will not that be tiresome?" said Sybil.

"If it is," said Septimius, "the next century shall make up for it; for then we will contrive deep philosophies, take up one theory after another, and find out its hollowness and inadequacy, and fling it aside, the rotten rubbish that they all are; until we have strewn the whole realm of human thought with the broken fragments, all smashed up. And then, on this great mound of broken potsherds (like that great Monte Testaccio which we will go to Rome to see) we will build a system that shall stand, and by which mankind shall look far into the ways of Providence and find practical uses of the deepest in what it has thought merely speculative. And then, when the hundred years are over, and this great work done, we will still be so free in mind that we shall see the emptiness of our theory, though men see only its truth. And so, if we like more of this pastime, then shall another and another century, and as many more as we like, be spent in the same way."

"And after that another playday?" asked Sybil Dacy.

"Yes;" answered Septimius; "only it shall not be called so; for the next century we will get ourselves made rulers of the earth, and knowing men so well, and having so wrought our theories of government and what not, we will proceed to execute them—which will be as easy to us as a child's arrangement of its dolls. We will smile superior, to see what a facile thing it is, to make a people happy. In our reign of a hundred years, we shall have time to extinguish wars, and make the world see the absurdity of them; to substitute other methods of government for the old, bad ones; to fit the people to govern itself, to do with little government, to do with none; and when this is effected, we will vanish from our loving people, and be seen no more, but be reverenced as gods— we, meanwhile, serene, overlooked, and smiling to ourselves, amid the very crowd that is looking for us."

"I intend," said Sybil, making this wild talk wilder by that petulance which she so often showed, "I intend to introduce a new fashion of dress when I am queen, and that shall be my part of the great reform which you are going to make. And for my crown, I intend to have it of flowers, in which that strange crimson shall be the chief; and when I vanish, this flower shall remain behind, and perhaps they shall have a glimpse of me wearing it in the crowd. Well; what next?"

"After this," said Septimius, "having seen so much of affairs, and having lived so many hundred years, I will sit down and write a history, such as histories ought to be, and never have been. And it shall be so wise, and so vivid, and so self evidently true, that people shall be convinced from it that there is some Undying One among them; because only an eye witness could have written it, or could have gained so much wisdom as was needful for it."

"And, for my part in the history," said Sybil, "I will record the various length of women's waists, and the fashion of her sleeves. What next?"

"By this time," said Septimius—"how many hundred years have we now lived?—by this time I shall have pretty well prepared myself for what I have been contemplating from the first. I will become a religious teacher, and promulgate a faith, and prove it by prophecies and miracles; for my long experience will enable me to do the first, and the acquaintance which I will have formed with the mysteries of science will put the latter at my fingers' ends. So I will be a prophet, a greater than Mahomet, and will put all man's hopes into my doctrine, and make him good, holy, happy; and he shall put up his prayers to his Creator, and find them answered, because his prayers shall be wise, and accompanied with effort. This will be a great work, and may earn me another rest and pastime."

<(He would see, in one age, the column raised in memory of some great deed of his, in a former one.)>

"And what shall that be?" asked Sybil Dacy.

"Why," said Septimius, looking askance at her, and speaking with a certain hesitation, "I have learned, Sybil, that it is a weary toil for a man to be always good, holy, and upright. In my life as a Saint and Prophet, I shall have somewhat too much of this; it will be enervating and sickening, and I shall need another kind of diet. So—in the next hundred years, Sybil—in that one little century—methinks I would fain be what men called wicked. How can I know my brethren, unless I do that once? I would experience all. Imagination is only a dream; I can imagine myself a murderer, and all other modes of crime; but it leaves no real impression on the heart. I must live these things. The rampant unrestraint, which is the joy of wickedness."

"Good!" said Sybil quietly; "and I too."

"And thou too!" exclaimed Septimius. "Not so, Sybil! I would reserve thee, good and pure, so that there may be to me the means of redemption; some stable hold, in the moral confusion that I will create around myself, whereby I shall by and by get back into order, virtue, and religion. Else all is lost, and I may become a devil, and make my own hell around me; so, Sybil, do thou be good forever, and not fall, nor slip a moment. Promise me!"

"We will consider about that in some other century," replied Sybil composedly. "There is time enough yet. What next?"

"Nay; this is enough for the present," said Septimius; "new vistas will open themselves before us continually, as we go onward. How idle to think that one little life-time would exhaust the world. After hundreds of centuries, I feel as if we might still be on the threshold. There is the material world, for instance, to perfect; to draw out the powers of nature, so that man shall as it were give life to all shapes of matter, and make them his ministering servants; swift ways of travel, by earth, sea, and air; machinery for doing whatever the hand of man now does, so that we shall do all but put souls into our wheel work and watch-work; the modes of making night into day; of getting control over the weather and the seasons. These are some of the easier things thou shalt help me do."

<The virtues of plants &c &c &c>

"I have no taste for that," said Sybil, "unless I could make an embroidery wonder of steel."

"And so, Sybil," continued Septimius, pursuing his strain of solemn enthusiasm, intermingled as it was with wild excursive vagaries, "we will go on as many centuries as we choose. Perhaps—yet, I think not so—perhaps, however, in the course of lengthened time, we may find that the world is the same always, and mankind the same, and all possibilities of human fortune the same; so that, by and by, we shall discover that the same old scenery serves the world's stage in all ages, and that the story is always the same, yes, and the actors always the same, though none but we may be aware of it; and that the actors and spectators would grow weary of it, were they not bathed in forgetful sleep, and so think themselves new made in each successive lifetime. We may find that the stuff of the world's drama, and the passions which seem to play in it, have a monotony, when once we have tried them; that, in only once trying them and viewing them, we find out their secret, and that afterwards the show is too superficial to arrest our attention. As dramatists and novelists repeat their plots, so does man's life repeat itself, and at length grows stale. This is what in my desponding moments I have sometimes suspected. What to do if this be so?"

"Nay; that is a most serious consideration," replied Sybil, assuming an air of mock alarm, "if you really think we shall be tied to life whether or no."

"I do not think it, Sybil," replied Septimius. "By much musing in this matter, I have convinced myself that man is not capable of debarring himself utterly from death, since it is evidently a remedy for many evils that nothing else would cure. This means that we have discovered of removing death to an indefinite distance is not supernatural; on the contrary it is the most natural thing in the world—the very perfection of the natural, since it consists in applying the powers and processes of Nature to the prolongation of the existence of man, her most perfect handiwork;—and this could only be done by entire accordance and co-effort with Nature. Therefore Nature is not changed, and Death remains as one of her steps, just as heretofore. Therefore, when we have exhausted the world—whether by going through its apparently vast variety, or by satisfying ourself that it is all a repetition of one thing—we will call Death as the friend to introduce us to something new."

<(He would write a poem, or other great work, inappreciable at first, and live to see it famous—himself among his own posterity)>

"Oh, insatiable love of life!" exclaimed Sybil, looking at him with strange pity. "Canst thou not conceive that mortal brain and heart might at length be content to sleep!"

"Never, Sybil," replied Septimius with horror. "My spirit delights in the thought of an infinite activity. Does not thine?"

"One little interval—a few centuries only—of dreamless sleep," said Sybil, pleadingly. "Cannot you allow me that?"

"I fear," said Septimius, "our identity would change in that repose; it would be a Lethe between the two parts of our being, and with such disconnection, a continued life would be equivalent to a new one, and therefore valueless."

In such talk, snatching in the fog at the fragments of philosophy, they conversed fitfully, Septimius wearing down his enthusiasm thus, which otherwise might have burst forth in madness, affrighting the quiet little village with the marvellous things about which they mused. Septimius could not quite satisfy himself whether Sybil Dacy shared in his belief of the success of his experiment, and was confident, as he was, that he held in his control the means of unlimited life; neither was he sure that she loved him—loved him well enough to undertake with him the long march that he propounded to her, making a union an affair of so vastly more importance than it is to the brief lifetimes of other mortals. But he determined, to let her drink the invaluable draft along with him, and to trust to the long future, and the better opportunities that time would give him, and his outliving all rivals, and the loneliness which he undying would throw around her, without him, as the pledges of his success.

It is to be observed that Rose had requested of her friend Sybil Dacy to act as one of her bridesmaids, of whom she had only the modest number of two; but the strange girl declined, saying that her intermeddling would bring ill-fortune to the marriage.

"Why do you talk such nonsense, Sybil?" asked Rose. "You love me, I am sure, and wish me well, and your smile, such as it is, will be the promise of prosperity; and I wish for it on my wedding."

"I am an ill-fate, a sinister demon, Rose; a thing that has sprung out of a grave; and you had better not entreat me to twine my poison tendrils round your destinies. You would repent it."

"Ah, hush, hush!" said Rose, putting her hand over her friend's mouth. "Naughty one, you can bless me, if you will; only you are wayward!"

"Bless you, then, dearest Rose; and all happiness on your marriage."

And now the happy day had come for the celebration of Robert Hagburn's wedding with pretty Rose Garfield; the brave with the fair; and as usual, the ceremony was to take place in the evening, and at the home of the bride; and preparation was made accordingly; the wedding-cake, which the bride's own fair hands had mingled with her tender hopes, and seasoned it with maiden fears; so that its composition was as much ethereal as sensual; and the neighbors and friends were invited, and came with their best wishes and good will. For Rose shared not at all, the distrust, the suspicion, or whatever it was, that had waited on the true branch of Septimius's family, in one shape or another, ever since the memory of man; and all—except it might be some disappointed damsels, who had hoped to win Robert Garfield for themselves—rejoiced at the approaching union of this fit couple, and wished them happiness.

Septimius, too, accorded his gracious consent to the union, and while he thought within himself that such a brief union was not worth the trouble and feeling which his sister and her lover wasted on it, still he wished them happiness. As he compared their brevity with his long duration, he smiled at their little fancies of loves, of which he seemed to see the end, the flower of a brief summer, blooming beautifully enough, and shedding its leaves, the fragrance of which would linger a little while in his memory, and then be gone. He wondered how far, in the coming centuries, he should remember this wedding of his sister Rose; perhaps he would meet, five hundred years hence, some descendant of the marriage, some fair girl, bearing anew the traits of his sister's fresh beauty, some young man, recalling the strength and manly comeliness of Robert Hagburn, and would claim acquaintance and kindred. He would be the guardian, from generation to generation, of this race; their ever re-appearing friend, at time of need, and meeting them, from age to age, would meet with traditions of himself and his intercourse with them, growing poetical in the lapse of time, so that he would smile at seeing his features look so much more majestic in their fancies than in reality. So all along their course, in the history of the family, he would trace himself, and by his traditions, he would make them acquainted with all their ancestors, and so still be warmed by kindred blood.

And Robert Hagburn, full of the life of the moment, warm with generous blood, came in a new uniform, looking fit to be the founder of a race, who should look back to a hero sire; he greeted Septimius as a brother. The minister, too, came, of course, and mingled with the throng, with decorous aspect, and greeted Septimius with more formality than he had formerly been wont; for Septimius had insensibly withdrawn himself from the minister's intimacy, as he got deeper and deeper into the enthusiasm of his own cause. Besides, the minister did not fail to see that his once devoted scholar had contracted habits of study into the secrets of which he himself was not admitted, and that he no longer alluded to studies for the ministry; and he was inclined to suspect that Septimius had unfortunately allowed infidel ideas to assail, at least, if not to overcome, that fortress of firm faith which he had striven to found and strengthen in his mind; a misfortune frequently befalling speculative and imaginative and melancholic persons, like Septimius, whom the Devil is all the time planning to assault, because he feels confident of having a traitor in the garrison. The minister had heard that this was the fashion of Septimius's family, and that even the famed Divine, who in his eyes was the glory of it, had had his season of wild infidelity, in his youth, before grace touched him; and had always thereafter, throughout his long and pious life, been subject to seasons of black and sulphurous despondency, during which he disbelieved the faith which at other times he preached so powerfully.

"Septimius, my young friend," said he, "are you yet ready to be a preacher of the truth?"

"Not yet, reverend pastor," said Septimius, smiling at the thought of the day before that the career of a prophet would be one that he should some time assume. "There will be time enough to preach the truth, when I better know it."

"You do not look as if you knew it so well as formerly, instead of better," said his reverend friend, looking into the deep furrow of his brow, and into his wild and troubled eyes.

"Perhaps not," said Septimius; "there is time yet."

These few words passed amid the bustle and murmur of the evening, while the guests were assembling, and all were awaiting the marriage, with that interest which the event continually brings with it, common as it is, so that nothing but death is commoner. Everybody congratulated the modest Rose, who looked quiet and happy; and so she stood up, at the proper time, and the minister married them with a certain fervor, and individual application, and earnestness, that made them feel that they were married. Then there ensued a salutation of the bride, the first to kiss being the minister, and then some respectable old justices and farmers, each with his friendly smile and joke. Then went round the cake and the wine, and other good cheer; and the hereditary jokes, with which brides used to be assailed in those days. I think, too, there was a dance, though how the couples in the reel found space to foot it in the little room I cannot imagine; at any rate, there was a bright light, out of the windows, gleaming across the road, and such a sound of the babble of women's voices and merriment that travellers passing by, on the lonely Lexington road, wished that they were of the party; and one or two of them stopt and went in, and saw the new made bride, drank to her health, and took a piece of the wedding cake home to dream upon.

Septimius had been duly present at the marriage, and had kissed his sister with moist eyes, it is said, and a solemn smile, as he gave her into the keeping of Robert Hagburn; and there was something in the words he then used, that afterwards dwelt on her mind, as if they had a meaning in them that asked to be sought into, and mused upon.

"There, Rose," he had said; "I have made myself ready for my destiny. I have no ties any more, and may set forth on my path, without scruple."

"Am I not your sister still, Septimius?" said she, shedding a tear or two.

"A married woman is no sister;—nothing but a married woman, till she becomes a mother; and then what shall I have to do with you?"

He spoke with a certain eagerness to prove his case, which Rose could not understand, but which was probably to justify himself in severing, as he was about to do, the link that connected him with his race, and making for himself an exceptional destiny, which, if it did not entirely insulate him, would at least create new relations with all. There he stood, poor fellow, looking on the mirthful throng, not in exaltation, as might have been supposed, but with a strange sadness upon him. It seemed to him, at that final moment, as if it were Death that linked together all; yes, and so gave the warmth to all. Wedlock itself seemed a brother of death; wedlock and its sweetest hopes, its holy companionship, its mysteries, and all that warm mysteriousness that is between men, passing as they do from mystery to mystery in a little gleam of light; that wild, sweet charm of uncertainty, and temporariness, how lovely it made them all, how innocent, even the worst of them; how hard and prosaic was his own situation in comparison to theirs. He felt a gushing tenderness for them, as if he could have flung aside his endless life, and rushed among them, saying, "Embrace me! I am still one of you, and will not leave you! Hold me fast!"

After this, it was not particularly observed that both Septimius and Sybil Dacy had disappeared from the party, which, however, went on none the less merrily without them. In truth, the habits of Sybil Dacy were so wayward and little squared by general rules, that nobody wondered, or tried to account for them; and as for Septimius, he was such a studious man, so little accustomed to mingle with his fellow citizens on any occasion that it was rather wondered at that he should have spent so large a part of a sociable evening with them, than that he should now retire. After they were gone, the party received an unexpected addition; being no other than the excellent Doctor Portsoaken, who came to the door, announcing that he had just arrived on horseback from Boston, and that his object being to have an interview with Sybil Dacy, he had been to Robert Hagbourn's house in quest of her; but learning from the old grandmother that she was here, he had followed. Not finding her, he evinced no alarm; but was easily induced to sit down among the merry company, and partake of some brandy, which, with other liquors, Robert had provided in sufficient abundance; and that being a day when men had not learned to fear the glass, the Doctor found them all in a state of hilarious chat. Taking out his German pipe, he joined the group of smokers in the great chimney, and entered into conversation with them, laughing and joking, and mixing up his jests with that mysterious empiricism which gave so strange a character to his intercourse.

"It is good fortune, Mrs. Hagburn," quoth he, "that brings me here on this auspicious evening. And how has been my learned young friend, Doctor Septimius—for so he should be called—and how have flourished his studies of late? The scientific world may look for great fruits from such devotion as his."

"He'll never equal Aunt Kezia for herb-drinks," said an old woman, smoking her pipe in the corner; "though I think likely he'll make a good doctor enough by-and-by. Poor Kezzy, she took a drop too much of her mixture, after all. I used to tell her how it would be; for Kezzy and I we were pretty good friends, once, before the Indian in her, came out so strongly. The squaw and the witch; for she had them both in her blood, poor yellow Kezzy."

"Yes? Had she, indeed," quoth the Doctor; "now, I have heard an odd story, that if the Feltons chose to go back to the old country, they'd find a home and an estate there ready for them."

The old woman mused, and puffed at her pipe. "Ah, yes;" muttered she at length, "I remember to have heard something about that; and, how, if the Feltons chose to strike into the woods, they'd find a tribe of wild Indians there, ready to take him for their headman, and conquer the whites; and how, if he chose to go to England, there was a great, old house all ready for him, and a fire burning in the hall, and a dinner-table spread, and the tall-posted bed ready, with clean sheets, in the best chamber, and a man waiting at the gate to show him in. Only, there was a spell of a bloody foot-step left on the threshold by the last that came out, so that none of his posterity could ever cross it again. But that was all nonsense."

"Strange old things one dreams in a chimney-corner," quoth the Doctor. "Do you remember any more of this?"

"No; no; I'm so forgetful nowadays," said old Mrs. Hag-burn; only, it seems as if I had my memories into my pipe, and they curl up in smoke. I've known these Feltons, all along, or it seems as if I had; for I'm nigh ninety year old now, and I was two year old in the witch's time, and I've seen a piece of the halter that old Felton was hung with." Some of the company laughed.

"That must have been a curious sight," quoth the Doctor.

"It is not well," said the minister seriously to the Doctor, "to stir up these old remembrances, making the poor old lady appear absurd. I know not that she need to be ashamed of sharing the weaknesses of the generation to which she belonged; but I do not love to see old age put at this disadvantage among the young."

"Nay, my good and reverend Sir," returned the Doctor, "I mean no such disrespect as you seem to think. Forbid it ye upper powers, that I should cast any ridicule on beliefs—superstitions do you call them—that are as worthy of faith, for aught I know, as any that are preached in the pulpit. If the old lady could tell me any secret of the old Felton's science, I should treasure it sacredly; for I interpret these stories about his miraculous gifts, as meaning that he had a great command over natural science, the virtues of plants, the capacities of the human body."

While these things were passing, or before they passed, or sometime in that eventful night, Septimius had withdrawn to his study, when there was a low tap heard at the door, and, opening it, Sybil Dacy stood before him. It seemed as if there had been a previous arrangement between them; for Septimius evinced no surprise; only took her hand and drew her in.

"How cold your hand is!" he exclaimed. "Nothing is so cold, except it be the potent medicine. It makes me shiver."

"Never mind that," said Sybil. "You look frightened at me!"

"Do I!" said Septimius. "No; not that; but this is such a crisis; and methinks it is not you. And your eyes glare on me strangely!"

"Ah, yes! And you are not frightened at me. Well; I will try not to be frightened at myself. Time was, however, when I should have been."

She looked round at Septimius's study, with its few, old books, its implements of science, crucibles, retorts, an electrical machine; all these she noticed little; but on the table, drawn before the fire, there was something that attracted her attention; it was a vase that seemed of crystal, made in that old fashion in which the Venetians made their glasses; a most pure kind of glass, with a long stalk within which was a curious elaboration of fancy work, wreathed and twisted. This old glass was an heirloom with the Feltons, a relic that had come down with many traditions, bringing its frail fabric safely through all the perils of time, that had shattered empires; and if space sufficed, I could tell many traditions of this curious vase, which was said, in its time, to have been the instrument both of the devil's sacrament, in the forest, and of the Christian, in the village-meeting-house. But, at any rate, it had been a part of the choice household gear of one of Septimius's ancestors, and was engraved with his arms, artistically done.

"Is that the drink of immortality?" said Sybil.

"Yes, Sybil," said Septimius. "Do but touch the goblet! See how cold it is!"

She put her slender pallid fingers on the side of the goblet, and shuddered, just as Septimius did when he touched her own.

"Why should it be so cold?" said she, looking at Septimius.

"Nay; I know not, unless because endless life goes round the circle and meets death, and is just the same with it. Oh, Sybil; it is a fearful thing that I have accomplished. Do you not feel it so? What if this shiver should last us through eternity?"

"Have you pursued this object so long," said Sybil, "to have these fears respecting it now! In that case, methinks I could be bold enough to drink it alone, and look down upon you, as I did so, smiling at your fear to take the life offered you."

"I do not fear," said Septimius; "but yet, I acknowledge, there is a strange, powerful abhorrence in me towards this draught, which I know not how to account for, except as the reaction, the revulsion of feeling, consequent upon its being too long overstrained in one direction. I cannot help it. The meannesses, the littlenesses, the perplexities, the general irksomeness of life, weigh upon me strongly. Thou didst refuse to drink with me. That being the case, methinks I could break the jewelled goblet now untasted, and choose the grave as the wiser part."

"The beautiful goblet! What a pity to break it!" said Sybil, with her characteristic, malign and mysterious smile. "You cannot find it in your heart to do it."

"I could—I can—so thou wilt not drink with me!"

"Do you know what you ask?" said Sybil. "I am a being that sprang up, like that flower, out of a grave;—or, at least, I took root in a grave, and growing there, have twined about your life, until you cannot possibly escape from me. Ah, Septimius, you know me not. You know not what is in my heart towards you. Do you remember that broken miniature; would you wish to see the features that were once turned where that bullet passed? Then look at mine."

"Sybil! What do you tell me! Was it you—were they your features, which that young soldier kissed, as he lay dying?"

"They were," said Sybil. "I loved him, and gave him that miniature, and the face it represented. I had given him all; and you slew him."

"Then you hate me!" whispered Septimius.

"Do you call it hatred?" said Sybil smiling. "Have I not aided you, thought with you, encouraged you, heard all your wild ravings which you dared to tell no one else; kept up your hopes; suggested; helped you with my legendary lore to useful hints; helped you along in other ways, which you do not suspect? And now you ask me if I hate you! Does this look like it?"

"No!" said Septimius. "And yet, since first I knew you, there has been something whispering me of harm; as if I sat near some mischief. There is in me the wild natural blood of the Indian, the instinctive, the animal nature, which has ways of warning that civilized life polishes away and eats out; and so, Sybil, never did I approach you but that there were reluctances, drawings-back, and, at the same time, a strong impulse to come closest to you; and to that I yielded. But why then, knowing that in that grave lay the man you loved, laid there by my hand, why did you aid me in an object which you must have seen was the breath of my life?"

"Ah, my friend—my enemy, if you will it so—are you yet to learn that the wish of a man's inmost heart is oftenest that by which he is ruined and made miserable? But, listen to me, Septimius! No matter for my earlier life; there is no reason why I should tell you the story, and confess to you its weakness, its shame. It may be, I had more cause to hate the tenant of that grave, than to hate you, who unconsciously avenged my cause; nevertheless, I came here in hatred, and desire of revenge; meaning to lie in wait, and turn your dearest desires against you, to eat into your life and distil poison into it; I sitting on the grave, and drawing ever fresh hatred from it; and at last, in the hour of your triumph, I meant to make the triumph mine."

"Is this still so," asked Septimius, with pale lips; "or did your fell purpose change?"

"Septimius; I am weak—a weak, weak girl; only a girl, Septimius; only eighteen yet," exclaimed Sybil. "It is young, is it not? I might be forgiven much. You know not how bitter my purpose was to you. But look, Septimius! Could it be worse than this? Hush! Be still! Do not stir!"

She lifted the beautiful goblet from the ground, put it to her lips, and drank a deep draft from it; then smiling, she mockingly held it towards him.

"See; I have made myself immortal before you! Will you drink?"

He eagerly held out his hand to receive the goblet; but Sybil, holding it beyond his reach a moment, looked mockingly in his eyes, and then deliberately let it fall upon the hearth, where it shivered into fragments, and the bright, cold water of immortality was all spilt, shedding its strange fragrance around.

"Sybil; what have you done?" cried Septimius, in rage and horror.

"Be quiet! See what sort of immortality I win by it—then, if you like, distil your drink of eternity again, and quaff it."

"It is too late, Sybil; it was a happiness that may never come again in a lifetime. I shall perish as a dog does. It is too late."

"Septimius," said Sybil, who looked strangely beautiful, as if the drink, giving her immortal life, had likewise the potency to give immortal beauty answering to it. "Listen to me. You have not learnt all the secret that lay in those old legends about which we have talked so much. There were two recipes, discovered, or learned, in the art of studious old Gaspar Felton. One was said to be that secret of immortal life, which so many old sages sought for, and which some were said to have found; though, if that were the case, it is strange that none of them has lived till our day. Its essence lay in a certain rare flower, which mingled properly with other ingredients — of great potency in themselves, though still lacking the crowning virtue till the flower was supplied—produced the drink of immortality."

"Yes; and I had the flower!" said Septimius; "and distilled the drink, which you have spilt."

"You had a flower, or what you called a flower which I sowed on the grave!" said the girl. "But, Septimius, there was yet another drink, in which the same potent ingredients were used; all but the last. In this, instead of the beautiful flower, was mingled the semblance of a flower, but really a sensual growth out of a grave; and this converted the drink into a poison, famous in old time; a poison which the Borgias used, and Mary de Medici; and which has brought to death many a famous person, whose death was desirable to his enemies. This is the drink I helped you to distil. It brings on death with pleasant and delightful thrills of the nerves. Oh, Septimius, Septimius; it is worth while to die, to be so blest, so exhilarated as I am now."

"Good God, Sybil, is this possible!"

"Even so, Septimius! I was helped by that old physician, Doctor Portsoaken, who with some private purpose of his own, taught me what to do; for he was skilled in all the mysteries of those old physicians, and knew that their poisons at least were efficacious, whatever their drinks of immortality might be. But the end has not turned out as I want. A girl's fancy is so shifting. Septimius, I thought I loved that youth in the grave yonder; but it was you I loved;—and I am dying. Forgive me for my evil purposes, for I am dying."

"Why hast thou spilt the drink?" said Septimius bending his dark brow upon her, and frowning over her. "We might have died together!"

"No; live, Septimius," said the girl, whose face appeared to grow bright and joyous, as if the drink of death exhilarated her like an intoxicating fluid. "I could not let you have it; not one drop! But to think," and here she laughed, "what a penance—what months of abortive labor thou hast had—and what thoughts, what dreams, and how I laughed in my sleeve at thee, all the time. Ha, ha! ha! Then thou didst plan out future ages, and talked poetry and prose to me. Did I not take it very demurely, and answer thee in the same style; and so thou didst love me, and kindly didst wish to take me with thee in thy immortality. Oh, Septimius, I should have liked it well—yes latterly, I should have liked it well—only I knew how the case stood. Oh, how I surrounded thee with dreams, and instead of giving thee immortal life, so kneaded up the little life allotted thee with dreams and vapoury stuff, that thou didst not really live even that. Ah, it was a pleasant pastime! and pleasant is now the end of it. Kiss me, thou poor Septimius, one kiss."

<(She gives the ridiculous aspect of his scheme in an airy way)>

But as Septimius, who seemed stunned, instinctively bent forward to obey her, she drew back. "No; there shall be no kiss! There may be a little poison on my lips. Farewell! Dost thou mean still to seek for thy liquor of immortality? ha, ha! It was a good jest. We will laugh at it, when we meet in the other world."

And here poor Sybil Dacy's laugh grew fainter; and dying away, she seemed to die with it; for there she was, with that mirthful, half-malign expression still on her face, but motionless; so that, however long Septimius's life was likely to be, whether a few years or many centuries, he was likely still to have her image in his memory so. And here, among his broken hopes, all shattered, as completely as the goblet which held his draught, and as incapable of being formed again.

The next day, as Septimius did not appear, there was research for him, on the part of Doctor Portsoaken. His room was found empty, the bed untouched. Then they sought him on his favorite hill-top; but neither was he found there, although something was found that added to the wonder and alarm of his disappearance. It was the cold form of Sybil Dacy who was extended on the hillock, so often rummaged, with her arms thrown over it; but looking in the dead face, the beholders were astonished to see a certain malign and mirthful expression, as if some airy jest had been played out—some surprise—some practical joke of a peculiarly airy kind had burst with fairy shoots of fire among the company.

"Ah; she is dead! poor Sybil Dacy," exclaimed Doctor Portsoaken. "Her scheme then has turned out amiss."

This exclamation seemed to imply some knowledge of the mystery; and it so impressed the auditors, among whom was Robert Hagburn, that they thought it not inexpedient to have an investigation; so the learned Doctor was not uncivilly taken into custody and examined. Several interesting particulars, some of which throw a certain degree of light on our narrative, were discovered; for instance, that Sybil Dacy was a niece of the Doctor, who had been beguiled from her home and led over the sea by Cyril Norton, and that the Doctor, arriving in Boston with another regiment, had found her there after her lover's death. Here there was some discrepancy or darkness in the Doctor's narrative. He appeared to have consented to, or promoted or instigated (for it was not quite evident how far his concurrence had gone) this poor girl's scheme of going and brooding over her lover's grave, and living in close contiguity with the man who had slain him. The Doctor had not much to say for himself on this point; but there was found reason to believe, that he was acting in the interests of some English claimant of a great estate that was left without an apparent heir by the death of Cyril Thornton; and there was even a suspicion that he, with his fantastic science and antiquated empiricism, had been at the bottom of the scheme of poisoning, which was so strangely intertwisted with Septimius's fantastic notion, in which he went so nearly mad, of a drink of immortality. It was observable, however, that the Doctor—such a humbug in scientific matters that he had perhaps bewildered himself—seemed to have a sort of faith in the efficacy of the recipe, which had so strangely come to light, provided the true flower could be discovered; but that flower, according to Doctor Portsoaken, had not been seen on earth for many centuries, and was vanished probably forever. The flower, or fungus, which Septimius had mistaken for it, was a sort of earthly or devilish counterpart of it, and was greatly in request, among the old poisoners, for its admirable uses in their art. In fine, no tangible evidence being found against the worthy Doctor, he was permitted to depart, and disappeared from this neighborhood, to the scandal of many people, unhanged; leaving behind him few available effects, beyond the web and empty skin of an enormous spider.

As for Septimius, he returned no more to his cottage by the wayside, and none undertook to tell what had become of him;—crushed and annihilated, as it were, by the failure of his magnificent and most absurd dreams. Rumors there have been, however, at various times, that there had appeared an American claimant, who had made out his right to the great estate of Smithills hall, and had dwelt there, and left posterity, and that, in the subsequent generation, an ancient baron's title had been revived in favor of the son and heir of the American. Whether this were our Septimius, I cannot tell; but should be rather sorry to believe, that, after such magnificent schemes as he had entertained, he should have been content to settle down into the fat substance and reality of an English life, and die in his due time, and be buried like any other man. A few years ago, while in England, I visited Smithills hall, and was entertained there, not knowing, at the time, that I could claim its owner as my countryman by descent; though, as I now remember, I was struck by the thin, sallow American cast of his face, and lithe slenderness of his figure, and seem now (but this may be fancy) to recollect a certain Indian glitter of the eye and cast of feature. As for the Bloody Footstep, I saw it with my own eyes, and will venture to suggest that it was a mere natural reddish stain in the stone, converted by superstition into a bloody footstep.

SEPTIMIUS NORTON

S EPTIMIUS had gone, as was his custom when he
wished to meditate, not pore over books, towards sunset, to the summit of that long ridge, which rose abruptly behind his dwelling, and stretched East and West along the
roadside, affording wide and far views of some of that level
meadowland which was a great feature of his native neighborhood below; a town intersected by a sluggish river, which once
seemed to have overspread many a tract with the surface of
gleaming lake, where now the farmer had long reaped his
richest harvests. Here was his favorite haunt and daily walk,
while he meditated on such subjects as were likely to come
within the scope of a young man who had recently completed such education, as, almost a century ago, was to be
derived from our venerable college, where the traditions of
the great English Universities had lingered on, and had as
yet been invigorated by no fresh life of thought, springing
up in our own soil; <some short remark as to the influence
of puritanism> such meditations, as a youth so instructed,
and, so limited, might be supposed to indulge—while directing
his further studies to that pursuit, which state, as it had
been ever since the Pilgrims came, was deemed the highest
object of earthly ambition, as well as Christian duty, the
ministry; such meditations as might be looked for in a young

man so trained, and so destined. But likewise there were some other meditations, thrusting themselves insidiously or violently through the trim fences and boundaries which the narrow plan of his education had set to his mind, such as were hardly to be expected, nor perhaps to be desired, save that a rich soil is apt to be fruitful in such weeds. But, Septimius, and all his race—though he counted excellent persons among them, were liable to strange vagaries of the intellect and character; principally owing, no doubt, to a wild genealogy, that had infused different strains of powerful blood into their race, and perhaps in part to certain strange traditions that suggested to each generation the exceptional character and fortunes of its ancestors. Of these matters, however, we shall have future occasion to speak with sufficient particularity.

<It was mid-afternoon, not sunset.>

<(Dr. Ormskirk must be preceded by much preparation to make look stately and visionary.)>

<It is a young friend, a student of divinity>

<The minister should have a certain dexterity in his manner, indicating his character.>

Here stood, or walked Septimius, a young man of a slender and alert figure, a dark, brooding brow, and eyes that usually seemed looking inward, except when called especially to outward objects, when they glittered with a quiet gleam like Indian eyes; here he was, enjoying, we may suppose, the fresh verdure with which an unusually early April had overspread the fields, and looking out, through the intricacies, the foliage, the exceeding luxuriance of a young man's thoughts, at the swelling buds of the birch-trees on his hilltop, at the contrast between the freshness of other things <bring in Aunt Nashoba, busy in the house and about it> <—allude to Rose—> and the dusky hues of the pitchpines, which still kept their winter garments (old conservatives there) on, when a companion joined him, ascending the steep hill-side from Septimius's humble abode, at its foot.

"I commend your wisdom, my dear Septimius," said he, "in leaving your dark little room yonder for the better air and wider scope of the hill-top. Two or it might be three hours a day, spent here, and nine hours at your books, in meditating over what you have read in those books, would be a good division of a student's day. It is always good to let the natural sunshine fall into the mind, daily; we thus drain away the mustiness of old learning."

<There is a good deal of familiarity between the minister and the student>

<Some allusions are made in the first speech, to the state of the country>

It was evidently a clerical personage who spoke; a village minister, with somewhat of the Puritan severity of manner, but a kindlier sympathy warming it a little, and probably a wider range of speculation acquired by keeping his faith as a living germ instead of a dead fossil; a man in faded black, as befitted his small stipend, but the rusticity, if such there were, of his garb, was hidden, or, as it were, received a fine gloss, by a certain natural refinement of manner, and the pleasant sound of his voice; so that you would not notice that the country-tailor had made his clothes, and that they had been worn threadbare.

"You say truly, doubtless, Mr. Norton," replied Septimius, after a salutation of deep respect; "—provided the soil be in a good state."

"And I know no soil that has been more faithfully prepared, according to your skill and opportunities," said the minister, "than that of your mind, my young friend—a good soil, too, strong and rich, and promising an abundant harvest, with good seed."

"It is not for me to contradict you, Sir," said Septimius, who, indeed, was at an age, and at a point of cultivation, where young men do not think too lightly of their natural powers. "But I am afraid there are a great many weeds, a wild growth, that springs up, do what I will, from seeds that I have not sown wilfully, yet threatens to choke up the harvest that I would cultivate. Methinks, Reverend Sir, the Papists were wise, who confined their acolytes of divinity to the cloister and the cell; for I find that when I come into the open and free air, many thoughts (that must needs be evil, since they are so unlike what my books and you have taught me) throng about me, to perplex the doctrines that seemed clear enough in my small, dark study down yonder, at the base of the hill."

"I think I have an idea of your meaning," said the Rev. Mr Norton; "in fact, I have seen such matter in your mind, when you did not so frankly allude to it. I believe, however, that you give a substantiality to these things, greater than they really possess. Every thoughtful student must needs see beyond and beside the book he reads, in order fully to comprehend that book; and in proportion to the power with which we receive its meaning, do a hundred things, that look like doubt, or disbelief, or contrary belief, spring up around it, but only to perish in the night, while the strong root of Truth will survive them, and flourish the better for the decay of those rotten things. So, my young friend, be not discouraged. Act as if you had a faith, and it will come,—you will soon find you have it. Ignore your doubts; do not recognize them; and they will quickly take their leave; for they are a sort of gentry that do not long put up with neglect and indifference on the part of their host."

<The talk of the two young men is not exactly in earnest, but rather, in part, a playful exercise of their wits.>

The clergyman smiled encouragingly upon his acolyte, and seemed to hope that he would at once avail himself of the politic process indicated, and declaring battle with his doubts, behave as if a victory were won. But, probably, Septimius's dark forehead, where there were already indications of a perpendicular furrow between the eyebrows, indicated a more stubborn kind of temper than his friend's; a temper that would question earnestly with doubt, and find out what were its claims, and crown it as Belief, if it made its proofs good to his perception. Perhaps, too, he was a little disgusted with something in his friend's mode of getting over the difficulty; and so responded more decidedly than the state of his mind really required him to do.

"No, Norton," said he; "it will never do! I have no right ever to stand in a pulpit."

"Why not, pray?" asked his friend. "If on account of these doubts you speak of, I tell you the best of Christians, have maintained a fight for their faith, throughout life—in this very house, it may be—on the death-bed, and at the last glimpse you catch of them, they are still struggling to hold it, and the dark spirit trying to snatch it away. They fight, in the first place, to get their faith, & ever afterwards to keep it. With you, Septimius,"—and here his friend smiled as he alluded to some of Septimius's family legends—"the devil may be specially in earnest, for he claims a peculiar interest in your family. But turn your back upon him, relative or none."

"Poh, Norton," said Septimius, with a somewhat sullen impatience. "Your mental necessities are not as mine. I cannot away with the thoughts that haunt me, and demand obstreperously to be examined, to be weighed, to be treated according to their worth, to be judged as what they are, and weighed in the balances against each other, and then to be rejected if they deserve it. And if I do so, what if I find that what I took for Belief, is but a slothful mental habit, an early prejudiced impression never faithfully examined, a formality, a surface, a fossil, a dead root that was alive in some other person's mind, but has no principle of life in mine! If the true life is in my Doubt, then let that be my Belief."

"And is it so?" said his friend, really concerned and shocked.

"I know not whether it be so or no," replied Septimius gloomily. "But there is an idea that grows upon me, day by day; and especially upon some studies that I have been trying to make into the physical sciences, chemistry, and the wondrous composition of the earth, and man himself, in his relation to his miraculous frame, and its adaptation to the world in which he lives, so wondrous, so worthy of a godlike creator. Looking at these things, the thought has seized upon me, and I cannot escape from it, that this earth is the great sphere of man, and that the reason we make so little of it, and find it so mean, so barren, so wretched, and our abode on it so short, is because we have really never applied ourselves to develope its possibilities, nor the possibilities of our relation to it. The first man was made, as Scripture bids us believe, with a view to his fulfilling his destinies and being permanently happy—yes, immortal—on this earth. There must therefore be an inherent possibility in the nature of man, that he should be so."

"What can you be driving at, Septimius?" asked his friend, half shocked and half amused. "Are you thinking of Aunt Nashoba's strange legend, of which you told me, and intending to re-discover your ancestor's panacea for earthly immortality?"

"I am not mad, nor a fool," said Septimius, "and I believe Aunt Nashoba's legends as little as you do. Yet, I think that the Creator meant this world, with all its wondrous capabilities, to be something far other than it is, and that he made man, so curiously, so elaborately, so powerfully, to be a creature far different from the weak, puny, sickly, short-lived creature that we find him, just opening his eyes, crawling about a little, and then dying, without really so much as one moment enjoying the earth, for which he was made, and which was made for him, when the elaborateness of the make of each, and the relations between each, would seem to indicate thousands of years for the existence of that relation; if indeed the individual man should not be as permanent as the earth on which he lives."

"What wild stuff is this?" said his friend;—"and impious, too."

"It seems to me neither," replied Septimius; "but the soundest sense, and the truest piety, because it does some degree of justice to the wisdom of the Creator, in making such a world. Else why did he make it? Can a man exhaust it in a little lifetime such as ours? No; nor in a thousand and such. Then what waste, to give us a world, and snatch it away from us, not a thousandth part enjoyed, nor understood; snatch it away, too, before we know enough of it to make it more tolerable for our posterity. The whole race of men, if they had lived from the beginning of time till now, a continuous life, would not have known the world they live in, in all their number and multiplicity, and in all their duration. We find the world propounded to us as a great riddle; and we are to suppose that only seventy years at most—a great portion of which is infancy and decrepit age— was given us to expound it in. Never! It is my belief, that, according to the original scheme of the Creator, each individual man was to inhabit the world until he guessed its riddle; else it is but a mockery to him. That we die so soon, is because we know not how to live, and the first step of human improvement must be, to teach us how, so that we may not be snatched away in the midst of the lesson the world is to teach us. As things at present are, I avow to you, my friend, that the world seems to me all a failure, because we do not live enough to learn its lesson."

"But the lesson is carried on in another state of being," suggested his friend.

"Not the lesson that we begin here," said Septimius. "We might as well train a child in an American forest, with the idea of teaching him how to live in a European court. Another school, another lesson! The effect of Man's Fall, it seems to me, has been to deprive him of all the benefit of his earthly existence by the shortening of his stay here, so that his coming here at all is made ridiculous."

"Well, Septimius," said his friend, smiling, yet a little shocked, "I hardly know what to make of you; for you utter this wild nonsense with almost as sad a brow as if you believed it. I dare not talk with you any further; for, though it is all a play on your part, you disturb and discompose what it is better should remain fixed in my mind; and, if you will take my advice, Septimius, you will quit your books, and that dark room of yours, and this hill-top, with its dismal pitch pines—quit them all, and go amongst living and breathing men a little more, if it were only by way of learning the real make of this world, which you pretend to value so highly. You are getting morbid, old fellow; and that is dangerous, with such blood as yours. We are going to have stirring times! Do you stir in them, and it will be the better for you. Take your part in this coming strife, with which the air is filled."

"Perhaps I may," said Septimius; "but I question whether my vocation is there."

"At any rate," rejoined his friend, "get away from this place. Your house, to speak frankly, is but a dismal place—a kind of dungeon—and Aunt Nashoba, with her legends, and her herb-drink, her pipe, and her queerness, with Witch-blood, Indian blood, Puritan blood, all intermixed and fermenting together, is an unwholesome thing to have before one's eyes. If it were not for your sister Rose, who being but half your sister is good enough, sweet enough, bright enough, to chase away the fiend from any house, I should have little hope of you."

<Aunt Nashoba, witch, church-member, Indian squaw, must be sketched personally, briefly.> <(a grim, witch-like personage, with Indian blood in her veins, and a strange headdress made of feathers)>

"I have my own ways, you yours," replied Septimius; "and to judge from the direction of your eye, your way at present lies down to my sister Rose, who, I see is just coming from orchard-house. And, for myself, I hear the hoarse screech of Aunt Nashoba, bidding me chop some wood for the kitchen-fire."

So the young men parted; and Septimius retired to a room, which ever since he betook himself to studious habits, had been his own domain, and where Aunt Nashoba—who had wonderful instincts of respect for learning, wild as her lineage was—hardly ventured to brush the dust off the little collection of books that had come down to Septimius from his great-grandfather, the Puritan divine. These books Septimius, an early and natural student, had rummaged from the garret, and dusty closets, shabby, aged, with covers torn off, having passed through ignorant generations, and leaves torn out, and had arranged them on shelves, some in Latin, Greek, even Hebrew, and a copy of the Indian bible, and one or two ancient volumes of science, for which Aunt Nashoba had a peculiar respect, having somehow got an idea that they were books of witchcraft,—all these, the young man had long ago read, and so thoroughly, as he deemed, got out all their meaning, that now they seemed like nut-shells, of which the kernel had been eaten. To confess the truth, in some of his moods, Septimius had so read these excellent works, as if Satan were his Professor of Divinity, and his lurid lamp were lighted in the infernal regions; for Septimius was of an order of mind (it may be profound, or shallow) which is born a questioner. Even in his boyhood, it had been so, although a thin veil of reverence had been interposed between some received beliefs and his irreverent speculations. And now, this new, strange thought, of the sufficiency of this world for all the uses and aspirations of man, that of permanent existence among the rest, if man could only be sufficient for the world, kept pressing itself so forcibly upon him that, for the moment, it seemed the one great and only truth that was indisputable. And earthly abode being so perfect for all the purposes of man's creation, was it possible that the purpose of beneficent Nature were merely that he should open his eyes upon it, and then die! It could not be. He fancied that he felt an instinct in him, assuring him of permanent existence. So, indeed, there was an instinct, as in all of us, of an undying soul; but, in Septimius, the earthly energies of unexhausted youth, the strength, the closer intermixture of spirit and body, clothed this spiritual instinct with flesh and blood, and be-wildered him by transferring its sphere from the spiritual world to the material one. Youth always feels itself immortal; only it seldom converts the sense into a thought, as Septimius now happened to do.

"Why should I ever die!" exclaimed he; at the same time, scornfully laughing at his own extravagance; for there was a keen, acrid common sense that kept a balance in Septimius's mind after all. "What if I say, this moment, I will not die!—not till ages hence—not till the world is exhausted;—its uses all wrung out! Death is a weakness! He that is strong enough may live while he will."

Out of this rhapsody he was summoned by the strange, weird shriek of Aunt Nashoba summoning him to split some wood to boil the kettle. After doing Aunt Nashoba's bidding (with the habitual obedience that young men pay to old Aunts and other long accustomed authorities, even while their lawless speculations set them free from all authority), Septimius did little chores, at her bidding, about the house, and came at her bidding to supper, when the old woman set before him a cup of tea, as she called it, but really a horrid decoction made from some sort of abominable shrub that the old woman had gathered in the forest; for these were the times when to drink tea, in New England, was treason against the cause of the people.

<(Here hint at her Christianity)>

"Drink that, Seppy my boy. Ask a blessing over it," said she. "It is made of a herb that your great great-grandfather knew the virtues of; for he was a man much skilled in herbs; and our Indian forefather cured diseases with it" (putting a large spoonful of brown sugar into the cup, as she handed it to him) "and with a few herbs, he knew of, he almost made himself live forever."

"Live forever! That would be a secret worth knowing, Aunt Nashy—a precious drink!" said Septimius, stirring up his cup, and tasting it, then with a long face and a strong internal convulsion, at the abominable taste of the decoction, "I must needs say, though if it required a daily draught of such stuff, it would take away somewhat from the value of life."

His pretty half-sister Rose, a girl of eighteen, who had taken charge of the district school for little children, smiled at his perturbation, at the same time declining a cup of the same mysterious mixture, which Aunt Nashoba somewhat grimly offered her.

"I thank you, dear Auntie," she said, "but I prefer this milk, and all the more, if there is any danger that your excellent tea would make me live forever. Life is very good as long as our friends are about us, but I am not quite brave enough to think of living forever."

"I know it, girl," said Aunt Nashoba, drawing herself up with an odd assumption of superiority, and looking out of her glittering Indian eyes like a sort of wild beast, making itself as humanlike as it could, and sitting down to tea—like the wolf in grandmother's cap, for instance. "You are not of our blood, and are a tame thing. No wonder you don't like my tea. It is a wild drink, and a powerful drink; and nobody knows the herb it's made of, but old Aunt Nashoba."

"Pray Heaven you may never communicate the secret," muttered Septimius to himself.

"Seppy," said Aunt Nashoba, who was rigidly Puritanic, in spite of her heathenish intermixtures, "you are almost a minister. Now that we have finished our meal, thank the Giver for it. You began the meal without asking a blessing, almost a minister though you be. Thank the Giver, now, for decency's sake!"

"God bless the food," said Septimius, putting both ceremonies into one; and with the tincture, of a secret meaning, "and may it strengthen us for the life He meant us to live. Thank God for our repast," he added, "and may it become portion in us of an immortal body!"

Rose gazed at her brother in surprise, imperfectly conscious of some occult meaning in his words, while Aunt Nashoba nodded her head with approbation.

"That sounds good, Septimius," said the old lady. "Ah, you will be a mighty man in the pulpit yet, darling, and worthy to keep up the name of your great-grandfather, who, they say, made the very leaves wither on the trees, and sent them flying over the sky, with the fierce blast of his denunciations against the wicked; though some say there was an early frost that helped him."

"If he could have made them green again with blessings," whispered Rose to her brother, "it would have been the diviner miracle!"

"Aunt Nashy," said Septimius, "this great grandfather must have been a man of might. I never heard of this before."

"A great man he was," said Aunt Nashoba; "and it was the Indian in him that did it. Yes; and the witch-blood helped and the noble English blood that helped him to be a scholar, too. It was said of him, he took up the Tomahawk of Righteousness against sin, and was all the better Christian for a kind of Indian fierceness that somehow was left in him. And you never heard of this? No; people know nothing of him now. They see the grave stone over his old, dry bones, on the burying-hill yonder, and read the inscription, and say he was a good man for his time, and they smile to see how the yellow moss is growing in the letters of epitaphs, and forget him."

"What truth there is in Aunt Nashoba's word," said Septimius to himself. "And how I hate the thought and anticipation of that contemptuous sort of appreciation, whether praise or blame, which the living assign to the dead, over their dust. Every living man thus triumphs over every dead one, as he lies under his little hillock, a pinch of dust, a heap of bones, an evil odor. Truly, a living dog is better than a dead lion. It is strange how every thing I see, hear, think, imagine, dream of, or know with waking senses, confirms my utter antipathy to death. It is the great mistake of the world, which otherwise might be studied. And now, it seems as if my eyes were suddenly opened, and Nature were indicating by innumerable methods the great truth, that Death is an alien misfortune, a prodigy, a monstrosity, a foul and cowardly defeat, into which we have slothfully lapsed, and out of which, even now a man might redeem himself, by exercising only a portion of his natural strength! I will do it!"

After this flash of the heroic mood, however, the fire gloomily subsided; and Septimius passed the evening among his books, as was his custom, poring over them, and finding that their meanings had lost the gloss and green beauty which perhaps they had, when fresh from the author's mind, and now were dead and dry, like some pressed leaves and flowers, which he remembered to have treasured there, three years ago but which now were brown, brittle, sapless. Then he fancied that he could see that this decay of thought was inevitable, when the dead speak to the living; for their thought, in what constitutes its better life, dies with them; so that the principle of life passes out of the wisest and brightest book, and that gathered and plucked off wisdom must ever after lack the very, the mysterious characteristic that gave it its only true value. Thence he inferred, that the way to adapt one's wisdom to the real purposes of men was, not to treasure it up in a book, and die; but to live, and still to be full of green, fresh wisdom, growing on your branches, to day, and for the day, and going about in a perpetual joy of growth, not of dry maxims, like the shells of hickory-nuts, but in fruits ready for daily occasions; such as would be, at once in the lovely blossom and in the rich perfected fruit, after a man had lived long to enrich all the soil of his being with the seeds of wonder, by contemplation of man's nature, the world's principles, the doings and accidents of his fellow creatures. And, for all this, it was necessary to have permanence in life. Amid these wild reflections, he fell asleep, in his chair, but, awaking chill and unrefreshed, forgot to draw the analogy between the day's concluding sleep and the life-time's concluding death. <(Septimius goes out and looks up to the sky, being much disturbed)>

In the depths of that night, there were various sounds unusual in the quiet country neighborhood where Septimius dwelt. Voices of men astir passed along the solitary road; the hoof-tramps of a horse were then once heard; once there was a shout, or a strange kind of shriek, as if it burst out of some strong excitement to which some impressible spirit was wrought up; once there was a drum-beat, that seemed to come from some nook in the woods—again, there was a distinct peal of a solitary musket, set off it might be by accident, or as a signal; and, besides all this, Septimius knew not whether it were a singing in his ears, a murmur in his seething brain that produced it, but he seemed to hear a murmur as of deep troubled breath all through the air, a ghostly stir, a murmur, that made him tremble, without knowing why. The air was full of the shapeless murmur, out of which rumor is made. The Northern lights were probably shining with unusual brilliancy behind the hill, and great, crimson flashes streamed upward, and sank, and rose again towards the zenith. Had there been, as of old, men to see before the Indian wars of this country, a really prophetic spectacle of armies encountering in the air, fighting, slaying, the charge, the shadow rout, the thousands of shadowy slain, the omen would not have overtopped the occasion; for this country was on the eve of a great convulsion which shook the country, and was thence communicated over the world, whence its profound vibrations have not yet ceased to be felt.

Our story has for its central object, to record the dreams, or realities, whichever they might be, of a young man who staked whatever prospects he had in life upon a strange pursuit in which he was encouraged by strange concurrent artifices, or delusions, which he followed with a deep, sombre enthusiasm that led to strange results. If the course of the narrative running along like a vine sometimes leads us amid historic events, and twines its tendrils around some of them, we accept the necessity of alluding to such, only because it is unavoidable; not really caring much for anything that took place outside of Septimius's brains, or merely as helping us to develope and illustrate what passed within it. It is but incidentally, therefore, and with the above end in view, that we glance at a great historic incident, which took place the morning after that conversation between Septimius and his friend, upon the hill-top.

<Describe the mildness, sweetness, balminess, of the April morng. (Rose's school to be alluded to)>

The morning in question, while the sun was yet low towards the horizon, Septimius, and his half-sister Rose, and a young man who dwelt in the neighborhood, had met together, and were talking of rumors of a bloody event that had taken place, and of others that were close at hand; the British, it was said, had attacked a little muster of Americans at Lexington, killing and wounding several, and were now on the march hitherward, preceded far ahead by a mist of rumor, dreadful forebodings, terrible apprehensions, stirring up wrath, dread, and revenge, rolling before the march like a swarm of grisly phantoms. In these circumstances, Robert Garfield had snatched the old Queen Anne's musket which his grandfather had carried in the Indian wars of seventy years before and his father in the Old French war, and was about to join the militia men who were gathering in the neighboring village, a powder-horn slung across his shoulder; but, first, had come to bid farewell to Rose Halleck, for whom, the village gossips said, Robert had a peculiar kindness.

Septimius, too, looking somewhat haggard with his vigils, had shut up his books, and stept out before the door to enquire the news, and felt, indeed, his blood considerably stirred and warmed by the news which Robert told, as men of his nature do; feeling their difference most amid such excitement and yet felt calm, & self enveloped.

"Fifty men, they say," he said, in tones of intense excitement, "lie slain on Lexington Common, and the British are marching hitherward, slaying and burning all before them."

"Oh, Robert," said Rose; "and you are going to leave us!" She was quite white, and trembling.

"Come to the village, dear Rose," said Robert. "You will be safer there."

"No, no," cried Aunt Nashoba, brandishing a broom. "Let her stay here with me. I'm not afraid of the villains, though they spare neither man nor woman. And you, Seppy my boy, what do you mean to do? Where's your old rifle-gun, that came from England, and that was owned by the Norton that lived among the Indians? Some say Satan gave it to him, and that the barrel was forged in Tophet, and so cunningly that it is sure to kill! Where is it I say? It is not in your blood, whether Indian, Norman, or Puritan, to be quiet such a day as this."

"I know not what I have to do with the quarrel," said Septimius coolly, for there was an odd chillness and composure in him, like those places of still water that we see in a rushing stream. "I am almost a clergyman, and bound to be a man of peace. I have no such strong convictions of our right, as would justify me in shedding blood, or taking life; and could the right be unmistakably evident, it is murder—that precious possession, which we should be so much the more careful of, because we know not what it is, nor why it is given, and so cannot justly estimate its value; only, all our instincts assure us that it is incalculably valuable. Ah, what a strength of motive must it be," added he, with a shudder—"that would induce me to take what I myself hold at so high a price, and would keep so tenaciously!"

"Now I wonder," muttered Aunt Nashoba as if to herself, peering askance into his face, "what portion of his blood he gets this strange coldness from. It is not Indian; and his English ancestors were great warriors, and the minister slew an Indian in Phillip's war! Somebody has bewitched him."

"Why, Septimius," cried Robert Garfield, scandalized at a mood which he could not in the least comprehend, "what has got into you, now? These British regulars have killed your countrymen, I say, and are marching hither with bloody hands, to kill us, and burn our houses, and haul away our women by the hair. And you talk of the preciousness of human life! If I get near enough to one of the Englishmen to see the buttons on his waistcoat, he shall find what value I have for his life—just of the powder and bullet that it will take to kill him!"

"Ah, Robert, life is a sacred thing!" exclaimed Rose, growing pale.

"Ah, Rose," said the young man, in a lower voice, "do not say anything to discourage me, or anything to make my hand tremble, and shake my aim, or unnerve, if it comes to wielding the musket-butt, on a day like this! Bid me think what I have to fight for! My country! Your brother's homestead. You, Rose! What is a man's life—an enemy's life or mine— in comparison with these?"

There is an influence in revolution, or any great turmoil of affairs, by the force of which feminine coldness and reserve dissolves like a slight frost-work; so that young girls, if conscious of any weakness at heart, any slightest inclination for a young man, had better not trust themselves with him at such times, for it will be almost certain to display itself; rules of decorum are obliterated, maiden chariness is shaken from its proprieties, the great, restraining orderliness of human life being done away with, for the time, by the interposition of critical circumstances, all the ordinary rules are suspended along with it. I suppose it was owing to this circumstance, that Rose Garfield allowed Robert Hagburn, or rather could not help it, to be aware of a tenderness on her part, that she had never before betrayed, and that, scarcely conscious whether Septimius and Aunt Nashoba were looking on, she suffered him half to enclose her in his arm.

"Look at them!" said Aunt Nashoba, jogging Septimius, and sneering at them like an old witch as she was said to be. "Isn't it a pretty sight, when the people's hearts are stirring up to war, and when in an hour, some of us may be lying dead, and this boy Robert among them, I wonder how a woman feels to be hugged by a man. No man ever hugged me."

No wonder; for to say the truth, there never could have been much feminine charm in poor Aunt Nashoba, even in her freshest days; and now she was surely the ugliest old squaw-like, witch-like figure, so fierce, so wild, so slovenly, that could well be seen or fancied; smoke-dried, too, yellow as the jaundice, wrinkled, and with the Indian look more perceptible than usual under the stir of the morning's alarm. On the other hand, there could not be a chaster, yet tenderer spectacle than that of the young man and girl, whom the flames of mutual affection seemed to envelope in a sort of illuminated veil that gave them privacy, for an instant, before these two spectators; so sweet a sight, so congenial with that soft, sunny morning of early spring, as if that genial sunshine were what had brought it to sudden perfection;

whereas, it was the high atmosphere of danger and trouble in which this alpine flower had bloomed.

"Yes; well," muttered Aunt Nashoba, softening as she looked. "He is a goodly young fellow, six feet and one inch high, at least, and as stalwart a man as shoulders his musket to-day. God bless him, and make his aim sure, say I. And as for Rose, she is a pretty flower—yes a pretty little garden flower, for any common man to wear in his breast. None of the witch blood in her veins—none of the wild blood. She'd never ride on a broom stick, or brandish a tomahawk; but she has her uses for all that. God bless them both."

Septimius, too, out of the cold estrangement into which his morbidly meditative habit had led him, a sort of prisoner, saw these lovers, and felt a sympathy for them that it was like the genial breath of the April morning, about his heart. A smile kindled up his eyes, under that dark, brooding brow, and made his face so delightful that it seemed all its features were softened and made more delicate. Rose saw the smile, and, genial as it was, was startled by it into the maidenly mood of reserve that she had always hitherto maintained; and Robert Garfield likewise, in some confusion, endeavored to resume the talk that had hitherto been flowing on.

"My grandsire tells me, poor old man," said he, "that we never shall be able to stand against old England; for he says we are a slenderer race than those he remembers, who were weaker than the old Englishmen, such as his father, who came from Yorkshire, and was a taller man and a broader man than any of us to-day. And the women are slighter than his mother, or his old wife; so that the race is dwindling away, grandfather thinks, and giving up its strength and sinews for a little sprightliness, which he allows we have. So he thinks we can never stand before them. But I shall be glad to have the matter tried—and to-day as well as any day—for if we have lost any courage, and strength of grip, any one manly quality that our English forefathers had, then, for my part, I say, let the breed die out, the sooner the better. Don't you think so, Septimius?"

"It may be," responded Septimius thoughtfully, "that climates and other influences may change those rough, coarse attributes of men, which many brutes have in as great, or greater perfection, for higher qualities; may gain as more delicate nerves, and finer sensibilities dependent on them, a capacity for deeper insight into things not of sense; so that, ceasing to be so apt for war, we shall become apt for far higher things, and be able to conquer warriors too. In that case, I know not how I could regret that we had lost the brutal strength and brutal hardihood, that are the qualities on which nations have hitherto compared themselves. But hark! What comes here?"

Far along the dirt road, a considerable stretch of which was visible, they heard the rapid clatter of a horse's hoofs, and saw a little cloud of dust, the makers of which, as it approached nearer, proved to be a man on horseback, looking as if he had seen some ghastly sight, at a headlong gallop. He was in his shirt-sleeves, without his hat, and had the appearance of a country man, who had perhaps taken his horse from cart or plough, and in his extremity of haste, was now belaboring his panting sides with a whip of twisted cowhide; putting him to such speed as the poor, clumsy brute had never dreamed of in his friskiest days. Still, as he charged onward, he sent forth his voice—"Alarm! Alarm! Alarm!"— and, as he passed the little group of our acquaintances, his wild, eager, pale face glared upon them with startling effect; out of his cloud of dust, "They're coming! They're coming!" he shouted; "Alarm! Alarm! Alarm!"—trailing the sound behind him like a pennon. And in a minute more, this forerunner of some terrible advance was out of sight towards the village; while the dust was still settling itself along his track, and the hoof-tramps grew fainter and fainter. It seemed as if wars must follow helter-skelter after this messenger of dread.

"Rose," said Robert Hagburn, "I can stay no longer. The company will be gathered on the village-green! Hark; there is their drum! God bless you, Rose! Good-bye! Septimius, take care of your sister."

I know not whether he kissed her or no; nor could Rose, such was the misty confusion of the moment, quite remember what the precise circumstance of their parting had been. At all events, he was gone towards the village, whence they now heard the hasty clang of the bell rung as for fire, and could just distinguish the rub-a-dub of the drum, which, for a generation, had timed the martial theme of the company of militia.

The whole country-side now seemed astir. <Pale-faced women, huddling together, with their skirts over their heads> Young men singly or in squads of three or four, passed along towards the village with arms in their hands; the big, old fowling-pieces of seven foot barrel, with which the Puritan had shot ducks on the river, or loons on Walden Pond, the old King's arm that had blazed away at the French on the ramparts before Louisburg; the old rusty sword, the scythe, or whatever thing had the value (at that moment, the chief one) of being adapted to shed blood; on they went, calling to one another with joke and laughter, that had a strange, small seriousness intermixed with them. We stand afar off, but still may know sorrow best, from the experiences of our own day, of what emotions were in the atmosphere of that April morning, nearly ninety years ago. Ominous as the time was, it was a good time, as everybody felt, to be alive; a time when life was richer and dearer than yesterday, or ever before, and yet could be flung down, as a thing of slightest moment, in lieu of other theories that appealed to the higher nature of those who had hardly been conscious of a nature higher than was concerned with the daily, homely, toil, till now; there was a nearer kindred, a sense of closer sympathy from man to man, of higher love between man and woman; a sense of the sacredness of country. Every ordinary man, with the soil of yesterday's sordid labor still on his garments, was to-day a nobler creature, and drew heroic breath amid the ordinary scenes while besmeared and bemuddled with the toil and petty thoughts of daily life; so that he felt himself another man, and beheld his familiar neighbor transfigured since yesterday. Oh, strange, nervous rapture of the coming battle! Oh high, heroic, tremulous crisis; when, standing on the verge of a struggle that weeded out whatever was feeble in his nature, man felt himself almost an angel, from his set purpose to thrust, to smite, to slay, to take on himself the responsibility of man's life-blood and the tears wrung out of woman's heart. We know something of that time, now; we that have seen the muster of the village company, on the green before the meeting-houses, and heard the drum and fife, drawing the sobs of mother, sister, and sweetheart, watched the farewells, beheld the familiar faces, that we hardly knew, because a moment had transformed them into the faces of heroes; breathed higher breaths for their sakes, and hoped that we, had the summons come earlier, might have been heroes too; thanked them, in our deepest hearts, for showing us that our daily meanness is still capable of being so readily kindled into heroic endeavor and accomplishment; felt how a great impulse lifts up a whole people, and every cold, indifferent spectator, making him religious whether he will or no, and compelling him, however reluctantly, to join in that great act of devotion which we recognize when so many myriads of hearts con-spire together for something beyond their own selfish ends.

Septimius did what he could to keep his cold composure; and persuade himself that he had nothing to do with this excitement, in which the wisest and soberest man could but be observant himself by reason and on principle, and was hurried so much farther than he could be wakened by the wild acts of every man's passion mingling into a whirlwind; but he could not keep his breath from coming quick and irregular;—there was a bubbling impulse of his blood, a tingling in his veins.

"Rose, make haste to the village and shelter yourself," said he. "Join yourself to those women. I can't go."

"Aha, Seppy, you feel it, do you?" cried Aunt Nashoba. "I see the Indian in your eye, now."

"Do not go!" cried Rose, clinging to him. "I hear them. It is too late to fly!"

<they seemed to be mounted officers>

In fact, there now appeared, as far off as they could see, a small party of horsemen, not more than five or six, who seemed to act as scouts, or to be thrown forward like the feelers of some great creeping monster, advancing at a rapid pace, so as to spy out any hidden danger, and then pausing for the column of infantry to come up. It so chanced, that one of these temporary halts took place near Septimius's abode, where the main road was joined by another from the left; and seeing Septimius, with his aunt, and sister, the officers spoke together, and of them, a handsome and gay young man, threw himself from his horse and approached the group.

"How far off is the village, bumpkin," said he, with a kind of insolent good nature, "and which of these two is the way?"

"It is not my business to tell you," said Septimius, haughtily, and incensed at the young man's insolence, though to say the truth, his heart beat quick at finding himself thus immediately confronted with the enemy. "I am no traitor."

"No traitor, only a rebel!" said the young officer, laughing carelessly. "But we will not shoot you for your contumacy, at least, not yet, while we have this very pretty damsel and this respectable old lady to give us the information which you refuse. What say you, my dear," he continued, addressing Rose, "will you tell a poor youth the way, and go astray with him while showing it?"

"Get along with you, villain!" cried Aunt Nashoba, unconsciously clawing into vacancy, as if impelled to clutch the young man's curling locks. "We will show you no way unless it be to the pit. Meddle with me and see what you come by; I have red Indian blood in me, I tell you. My great grand mother took a scalp, & perhaps the hair was as curly as your head."

But Rose, only anxious to get rid of the young man, or perhaps fearing an actual encounter between him and Aunt Nashoba, pointed along the main road. "There, there is your way!" cried she. "Good Englishman, for Heaven's sake do not harm us."

"Harm you! not for the world, my angel! unless you call this harm," said the young man, suddenly throwing his arm round Rose's neck and snatching a kiss; "and as to the excellent and warlike old dame, in case of an encounter, I fear I should come by more harm than I could possibly do her. So another kiss, pretty one, and I am gone!"

"Stop, Sir," said Septimius, who ought, indeed, to have interfered sooner, but being a person of shy habits with no propensity for action, had not readily seen what to do. But he was now in a dark rage. "Coward, do you make war on women?"

Being of a temperament irascible enough, but that kindled gradually, he was by this time in a dark rage; and being of a more stalwart make, then clutching at this insolent young Englishman's throat, might have done him a mischief had they really come to close grips. But the officer, who seemed to keep his physical powers as well as his wits prompt for use, easily escaped from his grasp without laying hand on sword, and as safe as if he were of intangible essence, held up his riding whip, playfully threatening his antagonist.

"Take care, friend, take care, or you will come by a notable disgrace," cried he, "and I would not willingly inflict it in presence of your pretty sweetheart or sister, whichever she be, for the sake of the kiss I snatched from her."

"Come, Norton, no more of this nonsense," cried one of the young officer's companions impatiently. "Here is old Putnam close behind. Mount, and forward, or you will be sharply reprimanded."

The officer made no more delay, but flinging a laughing and kindly glance to Rose, one of gibing defiance at Septimius, and making a mock obeisance to Aunt Nashoba, who uttered a kind of spiteful snort in reply, like a cat just ready for the snatch, he mounted, and rode forward laughing merrily, with his companions.

"I had no heart for this war till now," said Septimius, vengefully. "But they treat us like reptiles, not to say rebels. I will fight, were it only for aiming at that villain's life."

<Rose is a little angry & annoyed>

"It were a pity to kill him for a boy's nonsense," said Rose; "do not kill him outright, hit him in the shoulder—he is a comely young man, and has a mother and sister praying for him in some English house. I wish him no worse, than to be safely back with them, nor no blood of his own to stain his gay uniform, nor any of my countrymen's on his sword!"

Almost immediately afterwards, a great cloud of dust (that had been rolling nearer and nearer, and out of which came the music of drums and fifes, playing a quick step) passed in front of these three spectators, and disclosed the main body of the British soldiers moving massively, with the regular tramp of a thousand feet. Hitherto, they had kept time merely to the tap of drum, but being now in such proximity to the village, the drums and fifes struck up a quick step with all their capacity of warlike sound, by way of heightening the impressiveness of their advance. The men seemed somewhat wearied with a long night-march, their black gaiters bemuddied and bedraggled, and their powdered locks a little in disorder; but each of their red-coated ranks moved as if its component individuals were welded together, their cross belts all aslant in one direction, their bright musket barrels all gleaming in a line; nor could it be doubted that these hearty, ruddy, Englishmen needed only an hour's rest; a good breakfast, and each man his pot of beer, and they would be ready to march, at a somewhat heavy pace, against any peril to which a fat-headed leader could expose them. There was something in their faces, nevertheless, kindly, homely, hearty, honest, obtuse, that made you remember that they had mothers, and homes, much more than if they had been Frenchmen or Spaniards; it seemed a pity to shoot them, at the same time that any spectator was conscious of a heavy, brutal element, which, if it got uppermost, would make these homely Englishmen the most atrocious ruffians, for the time being, that ever murdered men or violated women.

"And these are British soldiers," said Rose. "They are very terrible, melting themselves all into a great body, as they do; but methinks, man by man, they look harmless enough. Somehow or other, I feel sad and pitiful toward them, as I look at them."

"It is the greatest mystery in the world," said Septimius, who perhaps was impressed with the same feeling of a strong, warm human nature, in these Englishmen, which influenced Rose,—"a great mystery how we can think of killing those jolly, lusty bodies, which have so evidently a great power of doing earthly things and enjoying them, but yet are so cloddish that you doubt whether they have souls. This mortal life must be so precious to them and any other life so doubtful."

"If our men are now, Seppy," muttered Aunt Nashoba, "what they were when your great grandfather, the parson, shot an Indian with his great grandfather's gun, not half of these villains will ever see Boston again, not to say their own country. Ha, ho; I wonder how many of these shirts will be bloody before night? I pity the washerwomen."

<(Rose had better go somewhere)>

In spite of the young officer's rudeness to Rose, the awe in which she had stood of the British soldier was considerably lessened by so comparatively harmless an encounter; not worse than she might meet with at a husking, or any other country-merry-making; so, that, instead of fleeing to the woods, as she had previously thought of doing, Rose concluded that there would be no great peril in abiding at home, under the protection of Septimius and Aunt Nashoba. So she went into the house and tried to pacify the nervous anxiety, that was throbbing through her whole system, by helping Aunt Nashoba in her domestic affairs, which the latter carried on with more than her usual vigor, rustling among pots and pans with a sort of frenzy, and often taking a slight potation from a certain earthen jug, the nozzle of which was stopt with a corn-cob, and which seemed much to comfort Aunt Nashoba, although by no means to assuage the fiery ardor of her proceedings; and then poor Rose tried to calm herself by sitting down to write out copies for her school-children, and to study out certain sums, which had a little puzzled her in the arithmetic-class, her head not being of a mathematical turn; but all these methods failing, she sat down in a corner, and looked into vacancy, where she perhaps saw Robert Hagburn doing deeds of heroism, or bleeding to death on his native soil, and gasping out her name with his last breath. And so Rose bore this early woman's part in the long agony that was now come upon the country. <(remarks on the fate of young virgins, in war-time)> And as to Aunt Nashoba she rattled and clattered, like a whirlwind through the house, making still another, and another, and yet other visits, to the brown jug aforesaid, of the contents of which (and they are very important to our story) we shall give the reader such account as we can, in a future page.

As for Septimius, not knowing what else to do, he sat down in his own room, and tried to involve himself in his customary studies; but was disturbed, and kept on the outside of his own thoughts, by that unpleasant state of mind which is apt to vex a man of brooding contemplation, when the world around him is in a state of intense excitement, which he finds it impossible either to sympathize with, or wholly to avoid. He seemed to be strangely ajar with human sympathies, dissevered from them, incapable of being thoroughly stirred by those motives of patriotism, public spirit, or their cunning counterfeits, which were setting other people into such active motion, and thrusting them forward to slay, or be slain, making heroes out of common men by blind impulses which they could nowise translate into reason. There seemed to be a stream turbulent, and full of eddies, flecked with tawny foam, rushing past him, into which, when he tried to plunge, he felt no force from it, nor found his garment moistened with all its volume of water. Conscious of the cold and dreary immunity, he fancied it a token of something innate in himself, or perhaps some decree of fate, signalizing him as marked out for an exceptional destiny; whereas, it was but the necessary consequence of this young man having ill-measured and curiously arranged his own mental powers, and brooded unripely on dark matters, and gone astray by his solitary self over boundaries of thought where the wisest need both staff and guide; it was no more in short, than that, by one of the innumerable paths, he had arrived into that gloomy region of doubt, confused morality, dissolved faith whither all intellects of any depth are apt to tend, at the early periods of life, and whence they are by no means sure to emerge. To be sure, as it turned out, there was a singular destiny in store for Septimius, but, thus far, there were only those morbid symptoms that afflict hundreds of young men whose thoughts gnaw and worry one another, for lack of better employment, and whose sympathies grow to a kind of hatred, at least estrangement, by the tendency of sweetest things left to their own fermentation, to be the sourest.

"Would I could be like other men; or at least, find some recompense for the unlikeness. Why is it my doom to be only a cold spectator in life, standing apart, and gloomily brooding over what really concerns me not? It is as if I were not born of woman! Since I partake of none of life's ordinary interests and common happiness, it were but right that I should be free likewise from its mean and ordinary incommodities, its petty, vexing, sordid races, its brevity too; so that I might have time to create other interests in it, and make a life which I do not find."

Thus Septimius came back again to that absurd idea of earthly immortality, or, at least, long-enduring existence in the flesh, which of late had so singularly obtruded itself among his morbid meditations; as if, the less satisfied he found himself with the conditions of existence, the longer he desired to live for the vain prospect of establishing more satisfactory ones. And, indeed, the hardest necessity connected with life is that of dying wholly unsatisfied; only let life be good, and we might the more willingly give it up; <If I had ever once been happy, methinks I could contentedly be shot to-day> <(Let Septimius say this)> otherwise, we rise from table empty, the windy dainties, that we fancied we had eaten, rumbling in our bowels.

But, after all, he deceived himself, when he imagined that the feverish excitement, which was throbbing through the veins of all his countrymen, had no effect upon his own dreamy composure. There was not a man of them all more stirred from his ordinary state than he. When we are angriest, or most passion-stirred in whatever mode of love or hate, or in highest poetic mood, or in whatever intensest action, there is a certain semblance of quiet, which has a homely symbol in the slumbering and snoring of a child's top, that goes to sleep because it is in such a frantic whirl. Quietly as Septimius seemed to behave, the soul within him was as restless as a flame. He must have been keeping himself down, by a powerful, even if an unconscious effort. Once, he started up, and began slowly to pace the floor, but in a few minutes, was taking the two or three strides that brought him from end to end of the room, with a haste that surprised Aunt Nashoba, who knocked at the door, and sent her unmusical voice through it.

"Seppy, boy, what is the matter with you. Aren't you ashamed to hide yourself in the house, when every young man in the country is astir. Here is the old gun I have brought you, and the powder-horn. You used to shoot ducks well enough. Try if you can hit a man with that Indian eye of yours."

<The ponderous old gun might once have had a matchlock, but now had a clumsy old wheel-lock.>

"Well, Aunt Nashoba," said Septimius, opening the door, "so far as taking the gun in hand, a great bullet-pouch, and going to roam our hill-top, I will do as you bid me. But I will slay nobody. Do not hope it."

"That's as may turn out," said Aunt Nashoba, looking upon him with her wild, cruel eyes all glittering, so that she was transformed into an actual squaw. "You will be the first of your race that did not bloody his hand, when there was good opportunity. But be careful, Seppy dear. Tree yourself, and watch your chance."

Septimius left the house; he heard Rose calling him, but did not turn back. He slung the antique powder horn over his shoulder, carved curiously with Christian devices that looked like an Indian's handiwork; a twining snake a tortoise &c &c.

He climbed the hill-side. The abrupt ascent began directly behind the house and went up abrupt among the small-bushes, the locusts, the sumachs; until it reached the level summit, where Septimius, on a long series of meditative walks, had worn a path along the brow; whence he might catch glimpses through entwining boughs of the dusty road, his own dwelling, and all the montonous little world below. Towards the west the view was intercepted by the direction of the long, ridgy hill, which obtruding itself slightly forward, hid the road that crept along its base, and the village towards which it tended. But Septimius anxiously directed his eyes thitherward, and put his ears upon the stretch, as it were, so as to intercept any sound that might be flung upon the air and indicate what was passing between the soldiers and the little community which they had invaded. There was a mile between Septimius and the centre of the hidden village; so that no doubt, a hundred various noises might have died on the passage, and there might be the shouts of men and the shrieks of women and children, without disturbing the quiet air so far off as this, with the mass of the hill interposed between. If the village were in flames, the smoke would have soared above the hill and rested upon it like a cloud. But the atmosphere was clear and sunny, and windless, except just breeze enough to stir the smoke of Aunt Nashoba's chimney eastward, and moreover as devoid of sound, that it seemed to Septimius a Sabbath stillness, more especially as there were no husbandmen in the wide stretch of fields beneath his foot, and a plough was in a half-done furrow, as if the holy time, the consecrated Saturday night, had surprised the husbandman in the midst of it. The whole spectacle was so full of sunny and slumbrous peace, that the warlike pageant of the morning seemed a dream, such as, for many months past, had been passing through the excited brain of the country with every drumbeat and fantastic gleam of banners and weapons; a vision which the excited imagination of all the people, anticipating war and brooding upon it, had conjured up, and made visible and audible, finishing it off even to the whiteness of the cross-belts and polish of musket-barrels, without its possessing any real existence, although perhaps prophetic, and in the measured tramp, and the ruddy visages &c &c.

But, suddenly, in the midst of this profound repose, Septimius heard one or two musket-shots, so far off that they accorded with the quiet; then immediately what seemed a volley shot off at once; then soon afterwards a muffled, ragged, and irregular report of many discharges, scattered over the space of half a minute—producing a heavy impression by its mass.

"This is war," cried Septimius, with a sudden and sure presentiment of the rattle of musket shot, the thunder of cannon, the clamor of smiting swords, the ghastly armies of slain, that were to ensue from those vollies which he had just heard, sown carelessly in the air, the seeds of a hundred battles.

<The chirp of birds & squirrels, the hum of insects, & other such sounds>

Listening eagerly, however, he heard nothing further to indicate the continuance of a skirmish, but after a considerable interval, there came the roll of drums, faintly heard, from the direction of the village, such a beat as summons scattered soldiers together; and next he perceived that the martial music was approaching along the road, indicating that the troops were in retreat. But as forerunner, there galloped another horseman, the same ghastly messenger, in appearance, who had announced their coming with his ghastly shriek of alarm, and was now preceding them with another cry equally fearful. Then appeared individual countrymen, with guns in their hands, coming along the road, or scattered over the fields or creeping along the fences; and among them, Septimius recognized some of the familiar figures of his townspeople and neighbors, churchgoing-men, peaceful citizens, now seeking opportunities for death-shots at their sudden foes. They seemed other, & the same. To Septimius's morbid way of looking at the spectacle, there was something comical as well as shocking in this sudden transformation of his quiet neighbors, insomuch that he laughed aloud; and perhaps incited by their example, he began to load his ancient weapon, which he had not hitherto thought of doing, and looking down into its immense bore, he poured into it almost a handful of powder, and completed the charge with a bullet that might almost have fitted a small piece of artillery.

"Why do I do this?" said he to himself. "I am a man of peace; neither do I adopt this quarrel. Unless it were in defense of Rose, or Aunt Nashoba, or perchance my own fireside, it were a deadly sin in me, to fire a shot."

Looking down upon the road, as far towards the village as the shouldering hill permitted, he now saw the front ranks of the British column coming into sight, and marching at a brisker pace than that of their advance; though the proud flaunting of their banner in the midst, and stirring, defiant rattle of the drum seemed to forbid its being looked upon as a retreat. Nevertheless, they were evidently in considerable haste, and not without good need to be so; for while Septimius looked, there came a shot from some scattered bushes on the hill side, nearer to the village, and Septimius saw a soldier stagger, drop his firelock, and fall under the feet of his comrades. With some slight confusion, they lifted up the wounded man, and bore him along with them, leaving a track of blood on the road. There were two or three more shots from the same quarter, without apparent effect. Thereupon, one or two platoons of the redcoats wheeled from the mainbody, crossed over the fence, and plunged into the shrubbery; there were shouts, shrieks, and a struggle, as if the concealed marksman on the hill side had been assaulted by an unexpected foe; although he had not perceived that any of the soldiers had left their ranks for this purpose. Septimius shuddered, his knees trembled beneath him, his breath grew short; not that he was afraid, but the whole thing was so like murder that he could not well see the difference, and yet, in the very midst of his awe and repugnance, he felt an almost irresistible impulse to mix himself up with the deed.

Meanwhile, the column was pushing its march, and had now come right beneath Septimius and abreast of his own dwelling; so near that he could distinguish the stern, anxious faces of the officers, and could hear the subalterns, crying, "Steady, Steady!" as if, without such stern word of restraint, there might have been a tendency to hurry onward with broken ranks, it being so difficult for men to keep their hardihood with their backs once turned to their foe. In fact, even Septimius, with his unmilitary life, could detect their irregularity. Septimius marked the commander; a gray headed, stalwart old warrior, on horseback; and thought of the strange fact, that it lay within his will to lift up his great-grandsire's ancient weapon, and in an instant, with hereditary Indian accuracy of aim, that the old man would lie wallowing in the dust, bleeding, gasping, breathing in bloody gulps, breathing no more—and he himself, instead of being hanged, or driven forth with the mark of Cain, would receive great praise among his townspeople. Tampering with the frightful temptation that he felt to realize this abhorred vision, he kindled his weapon, took deliberate aim at the button nearest the officer's heart, and felt that he had his life as much in his power as if he stood over him with a dagger. But he had really no such purpose; only it was such a temptation, and for his country's security, to kill, and yet commit no murder!

While the young man was thus worried with strange thoughts by Satan, or his country's guardian angel, or some good or evil principle in his own moral system, he heard the noise of rustling branches; and the approach of men, talking and blaspheming, and soon understood that this party of soldiers, which he had observed leav'g the main-body, had climbed the hill-top, and were marching along its brow, probably with the purpose of cutting off such strag-gling foemen as might be watching on their flanks for a chance shot. They had descended one side of a gorge, which here cleft the continuity of the long hill, and were now ascending the opposite slope, and as their forward progress would bring them right over the spot where Septimius was now standing, weapon in hand, and to avoid the conse-quences of so questionable a position, he shrank back a few steps among the leafless shrubbery, and concealed himself behind the trunk of a pine or dwarf-oak, on which there was enough dry foliage of last year to hide him, treeing him-self with as instinctive readiness as the canny Indian among his forest ancestry. Scarcely had he done so, when the party of soldiers passed, about a score in number, rustling through the boughs, keeping shoulder to shoulder, as well as the irregularity of the ground would permit, but protruding their bayonets and staring round apprehensively, like men on the watch for a wild beast or poisonous serpent. <As he thrust out his face> The boughs that they shoved aside rustled against Septimius's face, without their detecting him; other-wise, it would have been but the thrust of a bayonet, and Aunt Nashoba and his sister Rose would have wondered much what had become of Septimius. But, in fact, these soldiers were more intent on the space between themselves and the main body, than on the curtain of sumachs, birches, bracken, or ground oak, behind which the young man lurked. The party had now all gone by, except an officer who brought up the rear, and who was perhaps attracted by some slight motion that Septimius made, some rustle in the thicket, sufficient to impress itself on finer organs than those of the common soldier; for he stopt, fixed his eyes piercingly on the cluster of dry foliage that hid Septimius's face, and levelled a light fusil which he bore in his hand.

<make the young officer as fascinating as possible>

"Stand out, or I fire!" cried he.

Not altogether for the sake of avoiding the threatened peril, but because his manhood felt a call upon it, and because his Saxon blood was too strong for his Indian impulses to lurk in obscurity from an open foe, Septimius at once stood forth, and confronted the same young officer whose insolent gallantry towards Rose had already excited his wrath. Septimius felt his blood tingle a little at sight of him, though, to say the truth, he desired nothing better than that the haughty Englishman should go in peace and leave him quietly on his own hill-side.

<(This speech of the young officer is too long. Break it)>

"Ah; it is you, my Yankee friend?" said the young officer, with a mocking smile, which had a kind of spoiled petulance, for he seemed but a boy in years. "So you meant to take your revenge for the kiss I gave your sweetheart by shooting me from behind a bush! This is the better way! Come; we have in the first place, the broad quarrel between me, a King's soldier, and you, a bloody rebel, and next, your own private grudge on account of yonder pretty girl. We will take a shot on either score or both."

The young officer looked so handsome—so beautiful, indeed, in his fresh, budding rosy youth—there was such a free buoyancy in his manner—and, moreover, he so readily put himself on equal ground with the shy and rustic Septimius—that the latter, often morbid and sullen, but capable of generous feeling, had seldom been conscious of a kindlier sentiment towards a fellow-man, than at that moment.

"I have no enmity towards you," said he. "Go in peace!"

"No enmity!" exclaimed the stranger. "Am not I an Englishman and you a Yankee! What would you have more. And if not an enemy, why are you here with that rusty old gun among the shrubbery? Enemy or not, I am resolved to do my first deed of arms upon you; so either fight, or give up your weapon, and surrender yourself my prisoner!"

"A prisoner!" cried Septimius; and the Indian fierceness that was in him bestirred itself, thrusting up its malign head like a snake. "Never! This is my own ground. Assault me on it at your peril."

"Ah; you have pluck, I see, only it needs stirring," rejoined the young officer. "This is a good quarrel between us; for I have not forgotten your gripe upon my throat. We will fight it out like men. Stand where you are, and I will give the word of command. Now, kindle your firelock. Ready!—Aim!—Fire!"

The young Englishman spoke the three last words in rapid succession; and he and Septimius simultaneously raised their muskets to their shoulders, took aim, and fired. Septimius felt something smart and sharp, like the sting of a gadfly, as the officer's bullet grazed across his temple, but was sent into considerably more pain by the kick of his own gun, which, of large caliber, and heavily loaded, came near tumbling him over. Recovering himself, he beheld (to his surprise and horror, for the whole thing was like a dream, and it did not seem possible that the result of it should harden into a reality)—he beheld the young officer drop his fusil and stagger back against a tree, pressing his hand to his breast. He endeavored to support himself erect, but failing in the effort, beckoned to Septimius.

"Come, my good friend," said he, faintly, but with his playful, petulant, half insolent smile flitting over his young face again. "You have vanquished me in my first and last fight. That accursed piece of rusty ordnance of yours must have made a hole through me that you could put your fist in. Set me down as softly as you can on Mother Earth— the Mother of both you and me;—so we are brothers, after all, and this may be a brotherly act, though it does not look so,—nor feel so! Ah, Ah! Ah! Those are sharp twinges! You shot well—and deadly!"

"Good God," cried Septimius, "I had no thought of this— no malice towards you, in the least!"

"Nor I towards you," said his fallen antagonist. "It was boy's play; and the end of it is, that I die a boy, instead of living forever, as perhaps I otherwise might."

"Living forever!" repeated Septimius; for even at that breathless moment, his attention was arrested by words that smote so strongly on the idea that had recently taken possession of him.

"It is nonsense—the ancient, hereditary nonsense that has descended to me. I have no time to waste on it now," said the young man. "At any rate, I have lost my chance." Then, as Septimius, in the hope of giving him greater ease, helped him to rest against the little hillock formed by a buried stump, "Thank you, thank you! If you could only call back one of my comrades, I would fain say a dying word or two, about matters that concern me! But I forget! You have killed me, and they would take your life."

Septimius was so moved with pity and remorse, that he would probably have called back the young man's comrades, had it been possible, at whatever risk to himself; for the encounter had been of such a character, and he himself so little of a partizan, that he could not feel his lot to be included in the great surge of bloody violence which we fling together, and call it war. But the soldiers, marching at the swift pace of men in peril, had passed on, and were completely out of reach. The columns in the road were likewise quite beyond reach, and only the rear ranks were perceptible through the dust which their hasty tread stirred up.

"Yes; I must die here," said the youth, with a forlorn expression as of a homesick schoolboy; "and nobody to watch my last breath save a stranger, who has slain me! Could you give me a drop of water, my slayer? I have a great thirst."

Septimius, in a dream of horror and pity, precipitated himself down the hill, and into Aunt Nashoba's kitchen, where, without stopping to answer the old woman's questions, he snatched an earthen pitcher and hurried to the well. Regaining the hill-top, he found the young officer looking more deathlike within those few moments; but he drank from the pitcher which Septimius held to his lips, and seemed grateful, and still more so, when his enemy—to use a phrase that has little appropriateness—poured some of the cool water into the hollow of his own hand, and bathed his brow.

"You are very kind to me! I thank you!" said he, faintly smiling. "We are friends now. Methinks, next to the father and mother that give him birth, one's most intimate kinship must be with the one that slays him. My parents introduced me to this world; my murderer (nay, forgive me, it was a fair fight, and I fired also upon you, but it is so like murder —old Cain's work) ushers me to the mysterious state of existence to which this is but the portal. You and I will be lastingly connected, doubt it not, in the scenes of that unknown world."

"Oh, believe me," said Septimius, vainly trying to staunch the wound that he inflicted, "I grieve for you like a brother."

"I know it, my dear fellow," said the youth, with a boyish familiarity that brought the tears into Septimius's eyes. "I forgive you freely, if there is anything to forgive. You may erase the thought of guilt from your conscience, as easily as that stain of my blood, and you have done harm to nobody—caused grief only to a single person, who moreover had more cause to rejoice than grieve. My poor mother has gone before me—my father, too, long ago. It was little harm to slay me. There are those who will deem me well out of the way."

These reflections, flitting through the poor dying youth's mind, seemed to recall other thoughts which roused him to a brief energy of which just before he appeared incapable.

"I am dying, and must make my will," said he—"a soldier's will, spoken in the ear of the comrade, or the generous foeman, who bends over him in his last minutes. My spoils belong to the victor. Take them—my silver-mounted gun, with which I shot amiss yet came so near your life; my sword, which my father wore in many a famous battle—hang them up over your mantel-piece, and tell your children, long years hence, how they were won. My watch; I have done with time. My purse—it is a slender one, for I inherited only a claim to a great ancestral property—take my purse, and spend it if you are poor, or else give it to those who need. One word more. There is a picture next my heart—though, truth to tell, the original was never quite so near me—a picture, that I would have sent to the address which I will give you. Pray draw it out, and let me look at it once more."

Septimius, at his desire, drew from the unfortunate young man's neck a miniature, suspended by a golden chain, but on examination, it proved that the bullet had passed directly through the picture, shattering the ivory so that the face was completely obliterated, although the neck and arms of a female figure were partially visible.

"Ah, it is a pity," said the young officer, but Septimius was struck by a shade of scorn that mingled with the pattern of his tones. "Her heart was broken, she told me,— and now her fair face is shattered too. But I repent, I repent! May Heaven forgive me. She was set as a snare for me, and I deemed it but a small crime to entangle her in her own devices. Yet the bullet pierced me through her. On second thoughts, bury her broken image in the grave along with me. And, now, take the tablet from my breast-pocket, and write as I shall tell you."

Septimius complied, and the young officer gave the number of his regiment, the name of the Colonel and also that of another individual—a certain Doctor Zebulon Portsoaken —whose address, he said, would be known by the adjutant of the regiment, and to whom he desired his untimely fate to be communicated. He gave also his own name, which to Septimius's surprise, was Francis Norton, a kinsman, perhaps, at two hundred years remove of the man that had now slain him. But, while the poor lad's breath grew every minute shorter, it was no time to trace out the intricacies of kinship; so Septimius was silent.

"Where will you bury me?" said Francis Norton, opening his eyes suddenly, after a minute or two of deep exhaustion.

As Septimius hesitated to answer, he continued. "I would like well to have lain in the old church at Whitnash, my forefathers' burial-place, which comes up before me now, with its square gray tower, and the hollow ancient yew-tree in front, and the village with its thatched cottages clustering about it, and the gables of the old hall (that should have been my own) rising over the trees. But I hate the thought of sleeping in one of your Yankee-grave-yards; so, if you will grant my dying wish, bury me here on this hill-top, where you have slain me. A soldier sleeps best on the spot where he falls. And, I have another reason for it, a most earnest one, and there may be mischief if you disregard my wish. Bury me here, and tell no-one the spot."

"Here, and in secret," exclaimed Septimius. He was in-clined to think that a feverish delusion had seized upon the poor young man, and indeed the wild, eager brightness of his eyes, as he made this singular request, and pressed it with all the eagerness which his bodily weakness made possible, supported such an idea. But he reflected, that many a fallen soldier, that day, would have no better resting-place, and that blood shed in battle has ever been held to conse-crate such field as the burying place of its victims; so, quickly deciding, for the poor fellow's life was upon his lips, he promised to comply. Norton smiled, and appeared to derive a singular pleasure from the idea.

"A secret shall be buried with me, that has vexed my race too long," said he. "See that you keep your promise, or there may be a penalty even on you. Bury me as I lie. Take nothing from me, save what I have given you. Stay; here is my watch! How could I forget it. I have done with time. Take it! It is my parting gift. Farewell!"

"Shall I pray with you?" asked Septimius, in a faultering voice, remembering that his studies and purposed profes-sion gave him some claim to assume that office; and, more-over, that any man ought to pray beside a dying fellow creature; and so much the more, if his own act had brought him to the verge of the grave.

"I thank you," said Francis Norton, quietly, though speak-ing with difficulty; "but I seem to hear my mother's voice, beseeching me to say the same old familiar words that she used to pray by my bedside, when I was a child. Ah! I have been a wild and naughty child, dear mother; but you are praying for me, and all will be well. Yes; I hear her quiet voice as of old! All will be well. God forgive me. Amen." Seeming to die, Francis Norton uttered no other word; but sank and slid away, as it were, out of life, dying so peacefully that Septimius, who was kneeling by him with measureless compassion, really did not know whether his parting breath was not already drawn. <Septimius stood leaning against a tree.> But, a few moments later, he gave faint signs of life, uttering some half-shaped words, if words they were, and not rather a breathing of content, intermingled with a slight reluctance, so that Septimius doubted whether he were quite willing to die, or, being so young, would fain have lived a little longer. He lay quite still awhile; then started and struggled as if to rise—and met the eyes of Septimius with a wild, troubled gaze, which changed to a smile as he appeared to recognize his face.

"I had a dream," said he. "I thought a hand was groping in my breast. And I know not whether I am awake now; for life is a dream. I am going now. Goodbye!"

He closed his eyes, and died with the smile lingering on his lips. Septimius flung himself on the ground, at a little distance, and gave himself up to the reflections suggested by the occurrences of the last hour. What was it? He had taken a human life; and however the circumstances might excuse him, or even convert his act of homicide into a patriotic and praiseworthy deed, still it was not at once that a fresh country youth could feel any thing but horror at the blood with which his hand was stained. Yesterday it would have been murder; nor was the change of position so evident, to-day, that he could help shuddering at himself, for reducing that gay, beautiful boy to a lump of dead flesh, which a fly was already settling upon, and which must speedily be put into the earth else it would grow a sensible horror, that beauty for women to love, that strength and courage for men to fear, all annihilated, all the probabilities which life offered to one so gifted come to naught; the joys of earthly life, only of the soil, and that could be recompensed in no other sphere, all blighted; and a gloomy doubt descended upon Septimius whether any possible conditions of life, hereafter, could make up to the dead youth for that which had been ravished from him. What a waste it was! This beauty of form, and bright intelligence of feature, to be exchanged for some mode of being intangible, invisible; that readiness and aptness for impressing himself delightfully on all his fellow creatures, doing his part among them, helping, enjoying, all to be exchanged for altered conditions, or else to perish. Was not the latter the more probable event? Would it not be the easier work for the Creator to make an entirely new being, than to change this one into anything so excellent and beautiful as he had already been, and had ceased to be. Had he been gifted with permanence on earth, there could not have been a more admirable creature than this young man. There might have been everything in his future; but, in his past, nothing worth preserving. It would have been worth the trouble of making a world, and all the concomitant sorrow that it cost to thousands, only to have made it possible for him to exist; but as it had been his fate to perish so untimely, therefore it was all a jest, he was an illusion, a thing that Nature had held out in mockery, and then withdrew it into nothingness; serving human life, and all that inherited it, by showing how little account she made of the best of it, giving it for manure for a crop of weeds to grow out of; and while he might have been enjoying a happy life for long years—how long, why not centuries, or forever—a small spot of earth would be made greener by him on the hill side, where Septimius was to bury him, and that be all that the earth got by his having existed. Thus Septimius could not rise beyond this earthliness; his mind came back to the thoughts which we found haunting it, when we first found him on the hill side; and his feeling was, not as if he had introduced a mortal creature to the spiritual world, but had cut off an existence that might have been happy, and long. What a thing for him to do; for him, whose own love of life was so intense—a strength of life-tenacity peculiar to dark and sombre natures which lighter and gayer ones can never know, and which, if sometimes it impels the dark man to self-violence, it is because he cannot any longer bear the anticipation of losing it, and rushes to the reality. These thoughts came so darkly & fearfully upon Septimius, that he could scarcely bear to be alone with the corpse of his victim, shuddered at the idea of performing the act of burial which he had promised, dreaded even to turn his face towards the bloody form that was lying on the yellow leaves.

But now he heard steps, and next a screeching voice; as ugly a voice as ever came from the human throat, if it were not rather a screech-owl's, for it was fierce, and all the worse because it was a woman that made it; and Septimius knew whose it was, in spite of a fierceness & horror that he had never heard in it before.

"Seppy! Scalp him, Seppy!"

He turned slowly round, and there, just peeping over the brow of the hill, was Aunt Nashoba, with whatever of witch and Indian squaw there was in her, & triumphing over what civilization & christianity had been trying for a century and a half to do towards taming her; a strange, truculent figure, with her Indian eyes glittering, stretching out her claws towards the poor victim; as if she would herself do what she bade Septimius do. As he made no response, the old woman came stealthily creeping towards the corpse, appearing to be drawn by it, as such things have a singular attraction for wild beasts, or like a crow snuffing carrion, still she stood over it looking down upon it with an insatiable curiosity and a kind of greediness.

"Ah the villain!" muttered she. "That was a shot worthy of old Wampenoag, our red grandsire. Scalp him, Seppy, scalp him!"

"Hush, witch! are you woman at all! Look at the boy, and think that he had a mother!" said Septimius, in utter loathing of poor Aunt Nashoba.

Whether it were that Septimius's harsh rebuke produced the effect, or that her milder womanhood—the English womanhood, capable of tender love, sweet and mild affections, and household woes & joys awoke in her, awoke the fireside influences and overcame the savage strain, whose instinct it was to be like the she-wolf—so it was that as Aunt Nashoba looked down on the dead youth, a strange change came over her face, and as well as its ugliness might be capable, it began to show symptoms of compassion.

"Well; he is a beauty, and such a boy too, with his mother's milk hardly out of him. Oh, Seppy, Seppy, it was a cruel thing to kill him, when the Indian has been tamed out of you so long. But; is he quite dead? If there's any life in him, a taste of my drink might raise him back from the dead. Your great-great grandsire could all but raise the dead with it."

This drink, to which Aunt Nashoba referred with so much confidence, and to which she herself had recourse on all

occasions, and, indeed, without occasion, as her constant refreshment, her Nepenthe, had by no means an equal reputation with the world at large, nor with Septimius, who remembered having once been made to sip a spoonful, in some
sickness of his infancy.

"Your drink will not help him," said he. "Nothing will
help him. He is dead! and I must bury him here."

"Here! On our hill-top? Without a funeral? Without a
coffin?" cried Aunt Nashoba. "Why, Seppy, 'twill be Heathenish! I shall lose my church-membership if I consent
to it."

"He chose it himself, poor fellow," answered Septimius;
"and I have promised to gratify him. And it is not for you
or me, Aunt Nashoba, with the blood that we inherit, to
be horror stricken at the thought of putting a man to his
last rest where he chanced to fall and die. Many of our ancestry have lain unburied in their native forest, except as
the leaves fell, autumn after autumn, and covered them."

"You say true, Seppy," said Aunt Nashoba. "And him
such a fresh blossom, that it would be a pity not to let him
lie in fresh earth; for in our burial-ground, it has been turned
over much, and is made up of deacons, good housewifes,
heavy farmers, and such tame clay, that I should hate to have
fat earth, clinging round my own old bones. So I'll help you
bury the poor lad according to his own notion."

Feeling an uneasiness as long as the dead youth lay there,
Septimius hurried to the house, and returning with a pickaxe and shovel, he marked out a six foot space, and began
his unwonted office of grave-digger; and delving and burrowing vigorously, he threw out yellow earth, and small
pebbles, which seemed to form the composition of the site,
and was soon half hidden in the hollow that he made. Aunt
Nashoba, meanwhile, with tender care, laid the dead youth's

limbs straight, and arranged the clustering curls over his brow; and taking off his crimson silk sash (which was very wide and voluminous, when unfolded, and might have served to bear him off in, wounded, from a battle field) she decided that this would be a fitting shroud to envelope him in. When this was done, she sat down quietly by side of the corpse, waiting till Septimius should finish his toil; nor, such was the earnestness with which the young man wrought, did an hour elapse by the officer's watch (which lay on the dry leaves, ticking as busily as ever, while its owner's inner mechanism had come to an untimely pause) before the new grave, though a somewhat ragged-sided and unshapely specimen of the narrow house, was ready for its tenant.

"Look at him," said Aunt Nashoba, as Septimius climbed out into the sunshine. "He's smiling at me, as if he were pleased with what we're doing for him."

<(Septimius makes the grave, afterwards, look as much like a mossy seat as possible, but never sits down on it)>

The old woman was right. A wonderful change had been wrought upon the face, since Septimius last looked at it, and it was impossible to imagine a more gentle and peaceful expression of perfect repose, and consummate well-being, than was presented in those marble pale features of one who had come to a sudden, a violent, and an untimely end; so that you would have thought it the very thing, and at the very moment, that was needed to complete his felicity. His beauty, which, while he lived, was so striking, had now suddenly been transfigured to nothing less than angelic. It seemed as if a light were gleaming and glowing within him, and making its way through his mortal substance, and etherealizing it in its passage. A high and sweet expression was brightening forth, and appeared to grow more vivid from one moment to another, an expression of great joy, mingled with great surprise, and yet a quietude diffused through it all, as if the quiet joy was what remade the vast emotion of surprise. It was as if the youth were just at the gate of Heaven, which, swinging softly open, let a portion, as much as he could yet bear, of the inconceivable glory of the blessed city shine upon his soul, and kindled it up with gentle, undisturbing astonishment and serenest rapture. Septimius had often, at a certain brief time after sunset, gazing westward, beheld a living radiance in the sky—the last lingering light of the dead day, that seemed just the counterpart of the death-radiance in this young man's face. Doubtless, this expression, the likeness of which is seen so often on dead faces, has been decreed by God's Providence, to comfort those who stand round their departed friends, and have seen the agonies and physical ugliness of death, and, by this glow of immortality, this divine glory on the countenance, to assure them that the ugliness is a delusion, a shape or horror, that vanishes at the first step beyond the grave; and coming when all is over, it is as if the dead man showed his face out of the sky, with heaven's blessing on it, and bade the mourners be of good cheer, and keep firm faith in immortality.

Septimius struggled so to interpret it; but, sad doubter and questioner that he was, another view of the matter obtruded itself, and would not be shut out. What claim had this young man, having led a wild and evil life, and dying with a wrong upon his conscience, as Septimius inferred from some of his implied confession, and lost the purity of childhood, and contracted early the vices of a man, what claim had he to receive the hallowed radiance of bliss at once upon his brow? How could it be the sign and seal of Heaven's approval, dying, as he did, in attempting a bloody act, and having scanty time for the beginning of repentance, none for the genuine change of heart that could have transformed the dissolute boy into the purified spirit! Was this bliss upon the features, therefore, anything more than a token of that contemptuous kindness (it was Septimius's expression, not ours) which Nature shows, in innumerable ways, for our physical comfort, never giving us a needless anguish; and so, when death is inevitable, then she has contrived that the bitterness of it should be past, and that the last effect of life, and the last sensation of the body, before feeling quite deserts it, should be a thrill of the very highest rapture that the body has ever experienced; and the glow resulting from it is what we see upon the features. This idea was of a piece with the earthliness that haunted all Septimius's unending meditations, at this period; he valued mortal life so much, chiefly because doubts, an evil ingenuity in this idea, had got possession of his mind, whether the end of all our being was not to be consummated here. Therefore none the more joyfully for this sweet and high expression, did he proceed to lay his slain antagonist in the hasty grave prepared for him.

At Aunt Nashoba's suggestion, they spread the crimson sash upon the ground, where it proved to be a six feet square, and very strong, though of so delicate a texture as not to have been cumbersome to the wearer; then lifted the corpse and laid it upon the silk, and gathered up the corners for a shroud.

"Lift you his head," said Aunt Nashoba.

"Are you strong enough to lift his feet?" said Septimius.

"I think so," said Aunt Nashoba; "I am a vigorous woman of my age; but, to tell you the truth, Seppy, I am a good deal taken down with the thought of this poor boy being killed here on our hill. I thought the Indian blood would have helped me better than it does. Seppy, I must go down the hill and take just a sip of your great-grandsire's chief drink; it will strengthen me for anything. Meantime, do you be thinking of a prayer to say over him; else there will be nothing to keep him quiet in the new grave!" With these words, poor rheumatic Aunt Nashoba went down the hill, but speedily returned, looking much invigorated, refreshed, and comforted.

"Now say your prayer, Seppy, and we lift him into the grave. You are almost a minister, you know."

"Would you have me lift hands like these to Heaven?" asked Septimius, holding them out before her eyes. "I will make no prayer to-day. Pray you, if you like."

<They lay the broken miniature on his breast.>

"I have no gift of prayer, Seppy," said Aunt Nashoba, "and I have heard it told of our great grandmother, that she was mumbling a prayer, one day—she had lost her teeth, and spoke very indistinctly, and perhaps she did not quite know in her heart which of the two she heard—in the wood, and the Black Man showed himself and said he was her God. At any rate, they hung the poor thing for it. Now, Seppy, I have sometimes, in my trouble, and when my drink was low in the bottle, had a temptation to try what would happen if I were to mumble a prayer, and whether the Black Man would do as much for me. So I will not pray at this grave, lest the wrong one hear it, lest the young man's soul fare the worse for it."

"He will sleep as well without it," said Septimius.

"It's a pity to bury up this good silk," said Aunt Nashoba, feeling of the sash, "but it serves him instead of all other decorations."

<The green verdure lies lightly within the grave and some of the branches show themselves out of it>

Before carrying the dead youth to his grave, however, Aunt Nashoba gathered sprigs of winter-green, twigs of ground hemlock, and branches of the white pine, and made a thick layer of them into the bottom of the pit, so that, as the old woman said, it would be a soft and springy couch for him. Then taking hold of the corners of the sash, they easily lowered the slender form of the young stranger into the grave, and then threw in branches of white pine, twigs of winter green, and of ground hemlock; so that he was enclosed in a sort of green coffin, through which no glimpse of the marble face was visible, on which it would have been dreadful to throw earth. Then they each threw a handful of earth into the grave; after which Septimius set to work with minuscule vigor and rapidity, shovelling the earth and pebbles into the pit; for he had a repugnance to the lingering way in which Aunt Nashoba seemed inclined to perform their strange rites, as if she derived a dismal sort of enjoyment from the thing; something like that of a mother putting her child to bed; and finally she smoothed down the little hillock, that rounded itself over what just now was a pit, as the mother, aforesaid, smooths the pillow and bedclothes. <(The same strange beauty of face they still see thro' the branches that they threw in.)>

All this while, the battle had been rolling far away eastward, and the ear might track by the report of musketry, in single shots, vollies, and rattling discharges, growing more and more indistinct, as the rapid retreat of the British troops carried along with it the atmosphere of smoke and strife of which the column was the nucleus; and, as they were filling up the grave, a distant boom of cannon smote upon the air, indicating that the enemy's disastrous rout was staid by a junction with reinforcements from Boston. All these sounds served for the young soldier for the volley which his comrades should have shot over him.

"Let it alone, now, Aunt Nashoba," said Septimius, as the old woman kept smoothing down the heap. "You make it look too much like a grave already. People will wonder what it can be."

"Let them wonder, or let them know—what do you care, Seppy," said Aunt Nashoba. "A score of our townsmen will boast all the rest of their lives of having done just such a deed as you have done to day. To be sure, it is not quite the thing for a minister to do! Bloody fingers should not break the communion bread; and yet I don't know; your great-grandfather preached and prayed, and broke the communion-bread too, twenty years after he slew and scalped the Indian."

"Scalped him!" exclaimed Septimius. "Did he scalp him, Aunt Nashoba?"

"That he did! and got the reward for it—twenty pounds currency," answered the old lady.

"Then it's my belief he's had a fitter reward since," said the young man. "But, come, we have done all we can for poor Francis Norton. Let us leave him now!"

"Francis Norton, do you call him," said Aunt Nashoba, staring. "Dear me, I thought I loved the boy strangely. Then he was one of your own English relations; and nobody had a better right to bury him than we, though mayhap some other hand might more fitly have slain him. Here, Seppy, here's something that may tell you something about him, and what his kinship to us was. It's well we did not bury it."

She put into his hand, a parchment case, or envelope, tied up with a string and sealed with black wax, and apparently containing papers; and as Septimius took it, he perceived that his bullet had gone directly through it, and that it was besmeared with blood from the young officer's wound. The truth was, that, in arranging the body for its extempore burial, Aunt Nashoba's hand had touched this parchment package and having a reverence for all written documents the greater that she could not read them, she had taken possession of them, thinking that they might be of use above ground, and could be of none beneath it. In so doing, however, she had probably defeated the whole object which Francis Norton had in view, in prescribing the secret burial, and had kept still on earth some secret which he apparently had wished to be buried from the knowledge of men, and had kept a mischief alive and active, which otherwise would have gone to decay, like a pestilence hidden among the bones and ashes of its last victim.

"Aunt Nashoba, you have done wrong," said Septimius sternly; for it is to be noted, that, since he had slain a man, he insensibly took more state and authority on him than before. "You made me violate this poor youth's dying wishes, and break my own promise to bury along with him everything save the articles which he mentioned, and which he freely bequeathed to me, his slayer. It is impressed on my mind, that there is deadly mischief within this parchment, besmeared with blood as it is, and bored with the deadly bullet. You are responsible to me and to the world for it."

"No, no, Seppy," said Aunt Nashoba. "I'll not be answerable for any witchcraft that there may be in that package. You need never break the seal, unless you like; and if you choose to bury it again, there is the spade, and there's the earth, lying loose as yet; so 'twill be easy digging. But if you'll take my advice, you'll keep the package, and open it, and puzzle it out at your leisure. Who knows what it may be? I've often heard that, if ever we had our rights, there are great estates coming to us in England; and these papers may tell us all about it. But, bury them if you like. 'Tis at your own choice to keep them or no!"

If there had been no other inducement to keep the package than the one suggested by Aunt Nashoba—the chance, namely, that it might contain documents enabling him to trace out and establish his claim to an English inheritance—it is probable that Septimius would again have betaken himself to the grave digger's toil, and not have rested till he had deposited the mysterious parchment on the dead breast of its former possessor, thus hiding forever the secret that it contained. But the young officer had uttered a few words, which sank into Septimius's memory, and were more strongly felt and appreciated by him now, than when he heard them. When uttered, they had seemed to partake of the mocking, mystifying, playful, boyish mood, in which, so far as Septimius had opportunity to observe, the young officer indulged, and which even his deadly wound had not wholly done away with; therefore, it might have been all a jest, perhaps an old, hereditary jest, handed down from generation to generation, and laughed at by each with a mirth that was but an echo, and could not be appreciated by strangers. But, now, with that untimely hillock before him, and the blood-stained corpse that he knew was beneath it, the words took the solemnity of a dying man's almost latest utterance; the assertion (for so Septimius interpreted it) that his fatal bullet had cut off the prospect of an existence capable of being prolonged indefinitely beyond the common lot of mortals; and what was more natural than to suppose the secret of such existence contained in the package, so strangely treasured in the young man's breast; or what likelier, than that, disappointed of his hope of such long life, he should choose, in a natural resentment, to keep the benefit of it from his slayer.

"At all events," thought he, "it was a mad wish of his to seek to bury the secret with him, be it what it may. I am his executor, at least, if not his heir; and can better judge what is fit to be done, than he, in the surprise and agony of his dying moments. I will examine the papers, and bury them afterwards, should that appear the best mode of dealing with them."

They now descended the hill, Septimius bearing along with them the spoils of the poor youth; the sword, the gun, and the rest of the property which he had rescued out of the grave, and which he resolved to keep in trust for the heirs of the young man, whenever they should appear. On reaching the house, Aunt Nashoba betook herself to the chimney-corner, where she squatted (a favorite attitude of hers derived from the Indians) over the little remnant of embers, looking much like a very old and withered frog; and first of all taking a cup full of her favorite herb drink, she lighted a pipe, and smoked, and mused over the occurrences of the day, uttering no distinct word, though mumbling a good deal of indistinct matter, which seemed to be of much the same substance as the puffs of strongly odorous smoke which came from her lips. Probably it was this habit of muttering to herself, together perhaps with the deep rumblings of wind in the chimney that seemed to answer, that led to the odd stories about Aunt Nashoba's holding conversations with demons; a scandal for which it was once moved to bring her before the church, and to unite with this investigation an inquiry into the composition of the herb drink, of which she made such a mystery. Fortunately, the minister discouraged the idea, and Aunt Nashoba still continued to mumble in her chimney, puff her rank tobacco, and sip her herb-drink, in peace. In reference to this very drink, moreover, there was an awful statement, that it was concocted after a recipe handed down to Aunt Nashoba from that famous ancestress who had been hanged for witchcraft, and that it was the liquor brewed in the infernal regions, which used to be handed round for the refreshment and delectation of the company, at the merrymakings of witches, wizards, Indian sorcerers, and demons, in the primitive forest. And, furthermore, those who had been favored by Aunt Nashoba with an opportunity to taste this exquisite nostrum, ever afterwards believed the legend, deeming that such a brewage could have had no less diabolical origin.

Septimius entered his study, where the first thing that he did was to put away the sealed package in a drawer of his desk, lock it, and take out the key; after which he sat down among his books of divinity, his Greek and Latin, the tasks which even yesterday had here seemed dry and lifeless to him, but which to-day were not any more than the slight trammel of a book to keep his wildly excessive spirit. It is difficult to tell what it was that so inspired him, and made him feel stronger over his circumstances than ever before, strong to combat with time and fate, and make out for himself that bright peculiarity of destiny which young men, with any force of character, so earnestly desire; the situation of the country, the disturbances, the struggles, the beginning moral earthquake, and the mephitic vapors which it evolved were such as to intoxicate him and tend to thrust him aside from the calm, equal course of life, which, had his lot been cast in another generation, he might have fallen into; then, it might well be, that the fact of his taking a human life had served to create a brief insanity, as it has often been observed to do, in one way or another, the influence of the spirit untimely and irreverently freed being breathed in, as it were, by the slayer, and setting him aside from his propriety forever after; there being few, and those naturally hard and cold, who can settle down again to be precisely what they were, after having fed the fierceness of their nature on a human life. Add these, and other considerations which might easily be evolved, to the influence of a character, morbidly imaginative, prone to dark speculations, afire with wisdom, which he had derived from the peculiar and mixed nature of his ancestry—being of an anomalous and mixed brood, which Nature might not seem to have reckoned upon or purposed—and we need not wonder that poor Septimius in his desires, his purposes, his ambition, went somewhat astray from common sense, and shall be seen to have turned his little knowledge won from books, his small smattering of natural science, the boundaries and capabilities of which were then far less accurately defined than now, his crude dreaming about philosophy, a sphere in which all assume a right to be dreamers, to this day; his discontent with life, and his own part in it, his vague ambition; if out of all this chaos, set into wilder seething by the strange event of the day, and the strange circumstances of Francis Norton's death, and the pacquet which should have been buried with him, and, as if by the force of fate, was kept out of the grave which was dug, we may say, for the very purpose of receiving it—a secret, therefore, which the grave itself could not receive nor hide—there evolved out of all this a course of conduct which minds of another order might call madness. After all, it would be difficult, it appears to us, from the incidents of this narrative, to show that Septimius did anything that a wise man, on similar grounds, and with the same phenomena before him, would not have felt impelled to do; and it is a point which we are not aware that human science has yet attained, if his idea can be said, on absolute proof, to be an absurdity. Besides, we do not yet know whether or no he attained it.

But while he was sitting among these phantom-like meditations, which might be said to arise out of Francis Norton's grave, or to be conjured up by some written spell in that poor youth's fold of manuscript, a low tap sounded at his door, and his half-sister Rose entered. She looked at the sword, the watch, the purse, which lay on the table, and then questioningly at Septimius.

"What are these things, Septimius?" said she.

"Trophies that I fairly won," he replied, meeting her eyes in a shy kind of way, however.

"Not by entering into this fight, I hope," said Rose. "I would not have you do that!"

"Why not, Rose?" said Septimius. "Is not the country mine—am not I its child—bound to fight for it, as well as another of its children. You let Robert Hagburn go to the fight—you almost sent him—at least, followed him with your approbation and prayers for his success. And why not me as well."

"What you say is true, brother," replied Rose; "but, for all that, I wish you had not done it. I remember the sword-hilt. Ah; that poor boy!"

"Silence, Rose," harshly cried Septimius. "Do you feel his kiss on your lips still, that you so bewail him! If I killed him, I repent it not—neither rejoice. He wrested his fate from me by main force, as I may say. Let us talk no more of it. What news from Robert Hagdorn?"

This, indeed, was the very point on which Rose had come to Septimius, seeking consolation; for Robert Hagdorn, with all the able-bodied men of the village, had followed on the track of the retreating foe, and had not yet returned; and Rose's fancy figured doleful visions of her lover slain, or wounded; and lying in some lonely spot, bleeding and help-less. Partly moved by her anxiety, and partly from the fever-ishness that this strange day had left in him, Septimius proposed to go in quest of him; and, indeed, there was a quiet, sober influence in Rose, a sort of domestic influence, that he had often felt, that made him wish to escape her, when he had anything wild in his mind. So he set forth, and travelled in the dusk of the even'g on the road over which the battle had rolled; espying now and then a dead man lying in the dust, now the smoking ruin of a house; till in the twilight he beheld Robert Hagdorn approaching, weary, with blood on his face; and an English tower-musket and a bayonet on his shoulder. Both of these young men had taken a human life.

"An English grenadier levelled this bayonet against me, Septimius," said Robert—"a stalwart fellow, but I settled him with a blow of the butt of my father's old fire-arm."

Robert Hagdorn was anything but a bloodthirsty fellow, but he did not seem at all disturbed, nor feel anything but triumph. There are some natures that blood rolls off of, without staining it; healthy, wholesome natures; others into which it sinks, as it were, and makes an indelible stain. Warriors should be of the former variety, and then their trade does them no moral injury.

<The mixture of race a crime against nature, therefore pernicious.>

It may contribute to the better understanding of our story, if we give some slight sketch of Septimius's ancestry; although it must be done with a large intermixture of legendary matter, such gossip as clusters round old truths, like gray lichens, or moss; having their roots and nourishment in what is true; and if ruthlessly separated, there remains only some thing very unpicturesque, sapless; and indeed it is these fanciful things, these lichens, and natural growth over dull truth, that after all constitute its value, as springing from whatever is rich and racy in it, and being a distillation from its heart, oozing out, & clustering in a sort of beauty on the outside.

The first ancestor of the family of Norton, on this side of the ocean, was a personage enveloped to a singular degree in the picturesque vapors which gather over the region of the long past, and give heroic proportions to the objects and figures over which they spread, and of which they become the medium of sight. He was believed by his descendants—and those who had searched deepest into the obscurity of the epoch just before the arrival of the pilgrims, found some ground for the belief—to have been the very earliest Englishman that settled on these shores. They claimed (if claim it can be called, when there was quite as much to blanch at as to be proud of in the pretension) that when the first settlers came to this region, they found here a certain powerful Sachem, ruling over a wide extent of primitive forest, and governing his wild subjects with such an intelligent sway, that it seemed as if a cultivated intellect had adapted itself to their primitive laws and modes of life, and had breathed through these a wisdom and polity that must have been acquired amid far different institutions. This remarkable chief appeared to have no desire to civilize his people, to adopt European customs, but only to improve what we call savage life on its own plane, and make it, if a civilization, still a civilization of the woods, of hunters and fishers, with few and simple arts, not husbandmen, not artizans, owning individually no land, children of the woods, children of Nature, but all this made sweet and soft, made beautiful, idealized, by improving such life within its own laws. This appeared, according to the observation of the most impartial witnesses, and according to the best testimony which could be gained on such a point, in after years, to have been the design of the great Sagamore. On the other hand, however, there were rumors rife during his lifetime, and subsisting long afterwards, and shrouding his memory in dread among the superstitious Puritans, that this wise Sagamore had terrible attributes, supernatural gifts; that he was a magician, powerful to raise tempests on the sea (with one of which he had sought to overwhelm a barque of the early emigrants,) and to drive tornadoes through the forest, hurling down great branches or whole trees to crush the intrusive emigrants, as they journied painfully and aghast among the untrodden depths. There are dells, still shown, vallies and hollows, once awful with shaggy trees, though now thrown open to the sunshine, where this mighty conjurer was supposed to have held conclaves of demons, and of other dark priests like himself, frightful things, the creatures of old idolatry, Dagon, Baal, made grosser than of old and uglier, by the large growth of their devilish nature, and intermingled there, after the settlers came, the witches and wizards that used to affright English homesteads, now teaching their homely horrors a wilder character, by joining in the demon worship that they found here established. There in highest place among them, sat that dread personage known in the blackest portion of our sombre annals, as the Black Man; there attended on him, the chiefest subject and high priest of that portentous deity, this wise and wicked Sagamore; and so well credited were these tales among the first settlers, that they never heard the roar of the blast, at midnight, among the pine-trees, without shuddering at the thought that here were Wachusett and his weird followers sweeping through the air to their place of meeting.

<And a century afterwards, the same sound still &c>

It is probable that this dark Puritan portrait of the great Sagamore Wachusett was drawn with much more hideous exaggeration of outline, and painted in far more hideous colors, because he was undeniably an inveterate enemy of the English settlers; fierce, irreconcilable, bloody. He appeared to hate them with more than an Indian hatred, and directed such forces as he had with a view to thwarting their designs, and defending his forest kingdom against them, and annihilate their settlements by their own extermination; he directed these measures with an art or skill, which the English leaders, new trained in European warfare, affirmed, must either have been taught him by the Devil, or by some such general as Grave Maurice, or Alba. As regarded the Red Men, his policy was peaceful; wars almost entirely ceased among them; by his eloquence, his wisdom, his deep art of proposing measures, and making them acceptable to the people, touching the simple springs of their nature, with wonderful effect, this great Prophet—for so, as readily as by the word conjurer might his Indian character be translated— he seemed not unlikely to convert the many broken, hostile, mutually destructive tribes into one great and mutually supporting people. Looked at from that side, at which it seems just to look, from the influence which his rule was calculated to have over his people he might be said to deserve the title of a Benefactor, of a wise, beneficent, heroic man, a Law Giver, a Prophet, inspired by wise thought and grand beneficence with the faculty of seeing what is to be done, and the practical skill to execute it—such a being as, when a nation, among her long, dreary, troubled centuries, is fortunate enough to possess him, she embalms, and deifies him in her love and reverence, and attributes all good to this godlike being. Among other attributes, he was said to have possessed a divine gift of healing, a knowledge of the roots and herbs of the forest, of the virtues of each thing that grows, by means of which he could extract from them at his pleasure, the deadliest and most instantaneous poison, or a medicine that could add years to the life of frail humanity. There was reason to believe, that, by this medicinal knowledge, he had stayed a pestilence that threatened the absolute annihilation of the Indian race; and it was furthermore said, that, by a yet more wonderful exercise of skill, he had endowed himself with miraculous length of days, and had dwelt among them for unknown years, never changing, never wrinkling, never a hair growing white. But there was a contrary story, that he had suddenly appeared among the Indians, none knew whence; but so recommending himself by his good gifts and beneficence, his majesty of mien, his wisdom, that he was considered a direct messenger from the Great Spirit. Nor were the Puritans utterly inclined to repudiate this idea; always provided that the Great Spirit of Indian worship was to be identified with Satan, who was generally understood to be their deity.

It will not surprise those who have impartially considered the character of our forefathers, to learn that they were utterly unable to appreciate any favorable side of a character like this; that saw in him nothing but the enemy of the white race, the obstacle to the success of their great enterprise of turning the wilderness into a cultivated land, the prophet of a diabolical superstition, the enemy of the true religion. They would probably have converted the Sagamore if they could. Desperate of effecting this, and perhaps considering it not quite so desirable as the severer method, they resolved, with their usual energy, to exterminate him. It is not our purpose to tell a story of Indian warfare, the meanest kind of contest in which blood has ever been shed, nor to illustrate another incident of the Red Man's struggle with the Whites; a struggle in which there is such a character of fate, that it almost precludes the ideas of wrong and pity. Let the bare feat suffice; the wigwam of the Great Sagamore and Prophet was surprised by a party of armed Puritans, their hearts as true steel as their breastplates and head pieces; the Prophet himself was slain, by over a score of bullets, and cut and pierced by as many swords, before he could muster his weapons; his wife, his children, his household, shared his fate; his wigwam and village were plundered. And when all was over, examining the mangled body of the slain Prophet, it was pronounced that here were the lineaments, the hair, the skin, the noble features, of a man of European race. Among the spoil, moreover, there were certain articles evidently brought from beyond the sea, and indicating that their possessor must, at some former period of his life, have been acquainted with state and luxury; and why he had given these up, and betaken himself to the forest, was a matter upon which there were no grounds for conjecture.

In the wigwam of the slain chief, it is said that some articles were found, which appeared to be hereditary heirlooms of an English family; such as several pieces of plate, with coats of arms upon them, inscribed with the name of Norton; also, a box or coffer, of small size, curiously ornamented and strengthened with steel. Some of these were said to have been retained by the descendants of the race, for many years afterwards; but if this were so, they had all vanished before the epoch of our story, unless, as was averred, a certain beautiful crystal goblet were one; but this article was so fragile that it seems almost impossible to believe that it could have escaped through the rough vicissitudes of life in an Indian wigwam. Such a goblet there was, however, and with a legend appended to it (which we cannot now stop to relate) about its having been the sacramental cup at a witch communion, and being supernaturally fortified against fracture. <Vague talk in the family of the glories of their ancestors>

We have said that the dusky wife and the wild progeny of this mysterious man were slaughtered along with him—all but one, an infant of two or three years old, for whom perhaps it would have been well if he had been laid to sleep in the bloody breast of his Red mother. But, the next morning, he crept forth from the heap of the slain, and it is even said, out of the smouldering flames, rubbing his eyes, as if just awake, and setting up a squall that sounded sufficiently like a Christian child's cry to awaken some compassion in the breasts of the Puritans. Their pity, to be sure, was considerably impeded by a story (which grew to be a legend, in due time, and always clung to the race) that his breed was partly diabolic, his mother having been the offspring of a family that traced its origin, not remotely, to the Principle of Evil; and this story was held to be confirmed, or nearly so, by the way in which the infant had come out, unharmed and unsinged, as the byestanders averred, from a perfect mass of fire; and it was earnestly suggested, that the way to test the fact was to toss him back into the flames, where, if he was really a little devil, Satan would take care of him; or if mortal, and partly Christian, it were better that he should be baptized in fire and die before the heathen part of him grew more powerful. But the gentler opinion prevailed, and the child was given to a christian mother to be nourished, cared for, and educated in the faith of his father's slayers.

The boy did no credit to either of the races of which he was a representative. He grew up, idle, incapable of steady exertion, addicted to his gun and to fishing, inapt to cultivate the land, although a lot had been assigned him comprising some of the most fertile acres in the township beneath the hill, on which his father's wigwam had stood, but which under his mode of cultivation, in his unthrifty hands, produced the poorest crops. Instead of building himself a house, he continued, for years after the other inhabitants were sheltered under a comfortable roof, to burrow into the sandy hill side, like a certain species of swallow which builds its nest in some yielding earth, and there he made his darksome home, and would have continued to do for life, if some of his neighbors, scandalized at his thriftlessness and inefficiency, had not hewn out the frame of a house and compelled him to assist in building it. Sparks of devilish qualities appeared in his drunken fits. Among his other Indian traits, of which his incorrigible idleness and uselessness were some, he had a propensity for strong drink, the true, fatal, helpless love of it, which drew him to that brief, wild, passionate enjoyment, and kept him sometimes in a state of drunken insensibility for whole days together. In short, he was a specimen of what the Indian has generally been, when in contact with the whites, all saving virtues blighted by civilized air, all civilized ones failing to root themselves, a poor miserable creature, with blunted instincts, the jest, the by-word, of the settlement, living half on charity, partly by his rod and gun, partly, unless he were belied, by petty theft. Where all trace of his race had gone, in his wretched composition, it was hard to say. <sometimes a devilish rage>Finally, he was missing, after the great snow-storm of the season, and after being sought for in vain, was found when a great snow drift melted away in the early spring; he having buried himself there in a drunken fit.

Wretched creature as he turned out to be, the half Indian Norton had been comely in his youth, and somehow or other, against the remonstrances of everybody, had contrived to win the affections and the hand of a pretty white girl, and carry her off from several apparently more eligible suitors;—a fact which was attributed to some devilish art inherited by him from his evil ancestry. From this union sprung two children, a son and a daughter; and this further dilution of the wild blood produced a generation of singular force in each of the two children, though of very strongly marked differences. The son grew up with an earnest, searching, most vigorous intellect; he took to study as it were by instinct, and with such excellent results as to attract the attention of those who were able to help him. He was sent to school; all the advantages of early culture that the times supplied were afforded him; he became the pupil of that school of the Prophets which the Puritans so early founded, and a scholar of productive acquirements, and, of course, entered the ministry, which then absorbed all the promising talent of the times. The ecclesiastical biography of that day still remembers him; a minister of great learning and wonderful power; a fierce, rather than a tender preacher, insomuch that, in allusion to his Indian origin, he was said to wield the Tomahawk of Righteousness, and preach the religion of peace as if he were battling to the death in savage fashion with an enemy. Mighty as this clergyman was, however, and in a day when a clergyman was the most powerful member of society, there were some who held him in ill will as his decided character rendered almost inevitable; and these persons were wont to circulate certain malign whispers about him, to the purport that the devilish strain of his forefathers was not as yet purged out of him, holy as he pretended to be; and that he had been overheard to curse and swear to that horrible extent, that a tree, under which he was standing at the time, was blasted and never put forth leaf again, in consequence of the anathemas that nestled among its branches; and that all the seeming fervor of his preaching was only a diabolical covering which his ancestor Satan taught him to wear under this crafty pretense. These foes, moreover, censured him for having gone to war, in King Phillip's time, and slaughtered and scalped an Indian with his own hands, as a chaplain. <In the latter part of his life, he tries to found a new sect, & is excommunicated> There were stories, too, about his having inherited his father's propensity for strong

drink and that he—a sly, crafty man—composed his most
powerful sermons under its influence, and always indulged
himself after preaching them; but these were probably
slanders that spring up under the shadow of great excellence,
miserable and poisonous fungi, ugly echoes of praise; only,
there was this to be said, that the great minister's wife, who
was beautiful and bright when he married her, did not look
like a happy woman;—forlorn, defeated, subdued, nervous,
early withering from her beauty into yellow ill-health, she
died in what should have been her prime, and was said to
have shrunk as if afraid from her husband's parting kiss, in
her last moments. But her funeral sermon, preached by himself, is still extant, in venerable print, and bears powerful
testimony to her virtues, and to her husband's passionate
affection, and to the happiness, almost too great for the lot of
fallen beings, which subsisted between them; so that this
testimony must needs be accepted as tantamount to every
other. His own funeral sermon, by an eminent brother, speaks
of the happiness of the relation; so does the grave-stone that
serves for both.

We have said that there was a daughter of the same marriage that produced this light of the church; and in her, it must
be allowed, the enemies and slanderers of the family of Norton had some grounds for affirming that the race was of the
Devil, bone of his bone, and of his own flesh and blood, and
that he would have them one and all, in his own good time.
We shall speak of her no further than to say, that, during
the prevalence of the witchcraft delusion, she was accused,
found guilty, and executed; and that her brother preached
her sermon in commemoration of her death, in which he
fully approved of it, and related incidents from his own
personal knowledge, confirmatory of the dreadful guilt of this
beloved sister. Yet such traits of her character, as can be

learned of her from traditionary old people, do not indicate anything worse than that the wild traits of her heathen ancestry overpowered those of the civilized race with which her blood was mingled; she was said, too, to have had a very dark skin, the straight black hair, and that Indian form of the face, and Indian eye, lineaments which are said to be harder to eradicate, longer in disappearing from a line, than those of the negro race. Something, also, perhaps of the fierce and cruel Indian temper; and generally, a cast of character that made her disliked by her neighbors, and prepared them to believe any fatal mischief of her, when the contagion of terrible suspicions was in the atmosphere.

<Aunt Nashoba has great fame and practice as an Indian doctress. Hinted that she had killed several.>

With her sad fate, and the close of the eminent career of her gifted brother, which occurred not many years afterwards, the noteworthy history of the family had ceased; but, during the period already spoken of, it might be thought to have shown symptoms of genius, at all events great ability, mixed with somewhat of morbid, something at odds with the ordinary sympathies of men, something that developed itself in strange pursuits, ill-temper, passionateness, secret grudges. Something in the mixture of bloods, first of Indian and civilized blood, then of this with the hostile blood of the Puritans, had not amalgamated well; it occasionally showed itself a powerful mixture, but on the whole, there was something amiss. Whenever there was ability, it aimed at strange things, was not content with ordinary, was rebellious, unhappy, went astray out of very vigor. But, for the last two generations, these characteristics did not show themselves, and the peculiar ability, as well as the singularity of the family, seemed to have died out. It had been a common saying now, for above half a century, that the Devil of the

Nortons was washed out in tame blood. The men of the family had subsided into the middle class of yeomanry, had cultivated their little farms, built a decent house, just at the foot of the hill where their great-great grandsire, the terrible Sagamore, had lived and died, and beside the road, and, though without much energy of any kind, had cultivated the field till it justified its character as the best soil in town. They were people of but moderate intellect, which they never attempted to cultivate further than by puzzling over the Bible or the Almanac, newspapers not being a feature of their days. Some people pretended to trace the Indian in them by a peculiar knack, which they were said to possess, of hitting the turkey on Thanksgiving day; but one must have determined to find such traits, or else it was difficult to imagine anything wild in these tame creatures. Aunt Nashoba, to be sure, the only woman who had appeared in the family for above a century, had some faint smack of the Indian in her, or it might be little more, perhaps, than the wayward singularity, the uncouthness, a propensity to laugh at the tavern, or store, the asperity, the solitary self-indulgence of oddity, which is often seen in a female, whose rich juices of the heart have fermented and soured in old maidenhood.

And thus our hasty sketch has brought this family down to the time of Septimius, whose early exhibition of ability and studious propensities we have noticed. Those who had known him from childhood hoped that he would rival the fame of the great Divine; whose eminence in the former part of his life had won him such high place; and whose singular backsliding, as it was termed, in later life, had created a trouble in the church, the tokens of which were not yet entirely obliterated in the religious aspect of the country.

One thing we must not forget to mention, although we should hardly venture to put forth as of prominent importance.

The Nortons, all the way downward from their first Indian ancestor, the devilish Sagamore, were supposed to have a certain instinctive knowledge of medicine, something like what are called natural doctors, to have a peculiar acquaintance with roots and herbs, and their virtues. Even the great clergyman had possessed this gift, though he was very reluctant to exercise it, and was supposed to pray earnestly for forgiveness after it. His witch sister had exercised the gift with far less scruple, and was said to have cured several people of terrible diseases, and, unless she were belied, to have killed several others in slight ones, in the course of her adventurous practice. The fact was, probably, that there had been handed down among them some modes of cure derived from the Indians, perhaps amended by scientific knowledge, very probably possessed by their white ancestor, who seems to have been an educated Englishman, who, on some disappointment, distaste, or misanthropy somehow contracted, had abjured civilized life, and betaken himself a savage. Instances of this sort have not been rare; nor is the step so long as might be supposed, from the highest refinement and most extensive knowledge, from the most artificial life, into the simplest. It is not worth while to repeat certain idle legends about a draught of immortaility, which was said to have been known in the family as late as the clergyman's time, and which, according to one story, his wife had killed herself by drinking of, in an immature state of concoction, while he was preparing it for his own drinking. If the gift of medicine, or any of their recipes, existed at the epoch to which we have now come, it was only in poor Aunt Nashoba's herb-drink, to which she was so devoted herself, but of which the very few others who had tasted it gave such awful reports, both as to its flavor and its effect on the stomach, that she had not had a patient for the last twenty years, at least. <(Aunt Nashoba used to go round peddling herbs and medicines.)>

We have given this perhaps too long account, in order to suggest some natural causes why, being the representative of such a peculiar family, the only heir of all their oddities, and crudities, and morbidities, their talents and their weaknesses— being perhaps not yet entirely turned from Indian superstitions, having such wild elements in him, some smack of the devil yet lurking in his blood, Septimius, with all his good sense, and education, should still be liable to devote himself to the pursuant of an object which we choose to pronounce impossible. But if it were so, the state of natural science, in that age, had not proceeded so far, at least in this country, as to be able to say so. Moreover, electricity had been discovered, and at a comparatively recent date, by an American. It had seemed to open a new epoch, from which no one could tell how much might be expected, or what effect this mysterious agency was destined to have; so subtle as it was, so like spirit, so pervading; and there were many who deemed themselves philosophers, at that day, who had projects at least as absurd as that of our poor Septimius, who, after all, was not so very absurd in so far as he supposed that human life had been shortened, by men's own neglect of natural laws, to a period very far briefer than his Creator originally intended. The difference might be ten years, or ten centuries—still he was right as to his fact.

<Rose had shared Septimius's studies, had read his books, and was a very informed person—a pattern of the New England girl.>

One thing more—the father of Septimius had made a second marriage, and had thereby acquired a step-daughter, Rose Garfield, who was like a flower transplanted into the family from a softer and sweeter soil. Septimius loved her; but, though brought thither an infant, she never quite amalgamated with him or Aunt Nashoba. There was no great intimacy between herself and her half-brother, though great love on her side as well as his; but Septimius was seldom, if ever, inclined to talk of anything that he imagined, purposed, or deeply wished, to Rose. I think it was because she lacked that element of wildness, extravagance, incompatibleness, which ran in his blood, and instinctively brought a standard of ordinary judgment to bear upon all his plans. Rose, however, had been the partner of some of his studies, and had thus obtained a much larger share of education than was common with the girls of that period; so deeply tinctured was she, indeed, with grammar and arithmetic, and even with more than the rudiments of Latin, that she might have been capable of instructing a considerably higher seminary than the litttle school, where she presided over twenty male and female readers, and (contrary to Septimius's wishes) earned the bread which she ate at their frugal board. Septimius was glad to have her there, and yet was shy of her, and reserved towards her; he felt that she connected him with the great sphere of true daylight, of healthy effort, of warm love, and that a full communication with her would be like opening a window in his breast, and letting the air and sunshine into dark and musty chambers, and making the air fit to breathe, chambers haunted by ancestral ghosts, by weird ideas, notions, thoughts akin to madness, things that vanish at a healthy touch, though having a strange and portentous semblance of reality, as long as nothing true and wholesome is at hand to compare them with. Methinks a sensible woman is more terrible to a man of insane projects than a sensible man; for the latter comes to his conclusions by comparison of your notions with his observations and experience, by inferences from them, by logic and argument, all of which can be resisted, and often with apparent success; but the female judge arraigns you at the bar of her instinctive knowledge of what is true, and speaks the truth from seeing it face to face, without any remove, or veil between; and so her judgments upon you have an authority of inspiration, and, however you may pooh-pooh them, they sink into your deeper consciousness, and lurk there, disturbing you with remonstrances that are like twinges of conscience, so subtle and profound. Septimius had therefore concealed many of his cherished thoughts from Rose, and determined to conceal this matter also. It is singular, this judgment which we evidently form within ourselves, respecting our schemes and thoughts, and which tells whom we may trust with them, hoping for sympathy in wrong and error, and what pure, upright, clear minds they must be hidden from, as mystic plants from the light of day.

Septimius, the day after the battle, considered with himself how to dispose of the property left by Francis Norton; for not feeling that he, a non-combatant, had a right to profit by any laws of war, in such a cause, he could not feel at ease to keep possession of it, as the last words of the deceased left him at liberty to do—at least, without a reference to elder and more pacific heirs. He wrote, as the young officer had requested, a letter to the Lieutenant Colonel of the regiment, mentioning in a general way his death and burial, and giving an inventory of the property, including money and valuables, found in his possession, all of which he declared himself ready, at any time, to account for to the legal heirs of the deceased, or their authorized agents. In this formal and business-like letter, however, Septimius made no mention of the parchment envelope, with its as yet unknown contents;

and, considering that the poor young officer had intended that to be no part whatever of his legacy to the world, but to be buried in his untimely grave, there was certainly no claim of conscience upon him to deliver them up. But, on the other hand, his sister Rose would probably have counselled him, that, as the dying man had so plainly claimed them for himself, he was bound in honor and conscience to commit them to the keeping of the dead body, and to mention the secret to none. It is quite possible that Septimius himself felt this; for he still kept the package with its seal unbroken, and had not even trusted himself with handling it, since depositing it in the drawer; but he felt a dark, gnawing curiosity to know what the secret could be which, in this young man's judgment, was to be hidden from the world in such awful guardianship, and wondered upon whom, if the sanction were violated, the evil consequences would come, or what remote, unsuspecting person, or group of persons, or how widely the evil would be diffused—what age-long misfortune, that had vexed generations, and which here there was a possibility of being, would be let loose by his breach of faith. And would the burial hide it? Would it not be still lying in the pit, if he were to deposit it there, and when years hence, the hill-side might have been dug up, the husbandman would let forth this secret, like the pestilence that has sometimes been let out of ancient graves, to commit ravages anew. No; it would be better to burn it, to commit to the faithful guardianship of flame, and if the secret had anything devilish in it, perhaps the same portent would happen as in the case of an ancestor of his, who used to communicate with Satan by tossing little scraps of writing into his household fire—and a great dusky hand would snatch the missives, be withdrawn and vanish with them into the intensest heat. But Septimius only played with the idea either of burning or burying them;

his insatiable thirst to know—especially for hidden knowl-edge—made it certain, that, one time or another, he would break the seal.

After concluding the letter—which, by the by, the usual intercourse with the metropolis being interrupted by the breaking out of hostilities—he was at a loss how to send—Septimius stept out of his study, and went up to his favorite haunt on the hill-top; for, in spite of the evidence of the sword that he had hung up over the mantel piece, and the gold watch that lay ticking on the table, he could not quite think that the occurrence of yesterday was real; it seemed so ir-reconcilable with all the other events of his quiet and studi-ous life, that he should have slain a man, and laid him in the earth, within his own familiar precincts. If it were indeed true, there would still be the grave; if a dream, the grass, the sweet fern, and the huckleberry bushes would be clustering over the sod, guiltless of an untimely corpse beneath. But it had been no delusion; there was not only the tell-tale hillock of the grave, so evidently a grave, that it seemed as if all the world must see it, and consider how it came to be there, and per-haps, some idly curious person might burrow into it to seek out the mystery; but likewise the pressure on the sweet fern bushes, where Francis Norton had lain and died, and drops of blood, too, on the yellow leaves, and on the twigs, which no rain of heaven had as yet fallen to wash away. Septimius wondered whether it would trouble poor Francis Norton now, when the uncomfortable secret had already evaporated out of the earthy prison in which he had sought to confine it, whether it would trouble him, for the sake of his poor clay, to have this spot known for his grave. At all events, he tried to take away this appearance of a grave, levelling the soil, and scattering it over a wider space of ground, but still to his own eyes, it seemed evident, to the most careless inspection, what was laid beneath. Not that his conscience troubled him for it in the least. It is very singular how ready man is to satisfy himself with the excuse of war, for having slain his fellow-creatures. I have talked familiarly with many men who have shed blood—with one who had slain no less than twenty-three of his fellow-creatures—and it struck me with wonder, searching for horror in him, to see how little they were disturbed by this ugly stain of blood upon them, this noisome scent of it, year after year, steaming up in their nostrils. It seems to become a common-place affair, when once it has happened.—The fingers that have dabbled in blood lose their daintiness; its scent, a sort of fragrance. Duellists find this. Perhaps, too, Septimius's Indian blood might have something to do with a feeling of triumph that he felt, yet crushed down, and made him yearn for more battle, more bloodshed, more of that desperate game in which life is staked against life. Oh, dark heart of man, tremendous is the responsibility of those who stir thee up to the dread things of which thou art capable.

So Septimius had no horror of the grave which he himself had dug, and for which he had slain the victim; but it is very possible that its existence there, so near his dwelling, had an influence upon his feelings and on his sombre imagination, and helped and strengthened the impression which was made upon him, by the manner in which the packet had come into his possession. The unfortunate young man, here taking his last rest, had been the bearer of some high message to him, and had died by his hand, merely because that was the readiest way of delivering his message, and of impressing the receiver with a sense of its gravity and importance. How else, in the infinite difficulties interposed between, could this document have found its way out of the possession of an English family of rank, dwelling in their hereditary hall, into that of the New England student, fixed by his destined profession to a narrow circle of business and intercourse with the world, and confined within the circuit of a country village. Thus musing, he paced to-and-fro on the level brow of his hill-top, gathering himself up into that enthusiasm which comes to lonely thinkers, that selfish enthusiasm, when they keep themselves too much apart from their fellow-men, and become the centre of their own world, and, by and by, adopt some object of pursuit, which they are ashamed and afraid to acknowledge, and so lose the rectifying influence of criticism, the wisdom that is to be gathered like flowers from other men's common-place judgments, and distilled into wisdom in our own mind like a rich essence from common herbs. As he walked, he looked down through the pines, the birches, the locusts, that clothed the hill side, and saw Rose, whose little school had been broken up, for the time, by the disturbance caused by the terrible battle that had rolled through the peaceful town; he saw her at the foot of the hill, where she seemed to be busying herself in the garden-patch that lay to the westward of the house, examining the few rose-bushes and other homely flower-shrubs, that the meager and uncultivated taste of that day had set round its borders. But, by and by, came Robert Hagburn skirting along the foot of the hill, the short distance that lay between his house and that of Rose and Septimius, and joined the girl, helping her to train up a struggling rose-bush upon sticks, apparently without asking her whether she needed his help. But the frankness with which she turned to him, and a tenderness and trust that was somehow expressed in her very attitude towards him, told full surely that she did not reject it.

The relation between Septimius and Rose was peculiar; she was sister, and yet not his sister; bred up with him, since he was four years old, and she but two; playing together on the hill, quarreling, and being reconciled, remembering the same things, looking up to the same people, they were so far like brother and sister; and, yet, the unity of blood being wanting, it might be that there was not the intimate sympathy that this tie would have given. Yet its place was supplied by a kind of intimate strangeness, that had thrills of a more poignant delight in it. It was a kind of affection, not unsusceptible of a degree of jealousy; and therefore Septimius had seen, not wholly with acquiescence, the growing interest between Rose and Robert Hagburn, though the latter was the nearest friend he had, and being brought a little closer to him by Rose, would have been nothing short of a brother. But now Septimius felt a cold, shivering sense, that the two would not be brought nearer to him, but both estranged, and that he should be left solitary, given up to his own wild schemes, wandering away farther and farther into the remote wilderness of schemes and speculations, desolate and horrible if they failed, perhaps only the more so if they succeeded. He felt an intense reluctance to have another person thrust himself between him and Rose, into whose sphere he came for protection, as it were, against wild thoughts and dreams, as a child, in the dark, creeps close to some known friend, presses against her warm skirts, and feels itself then safe from the shadows that affright it. To express it less fancifully, he was secretly conscious of something to be guarded in himself, and felt as if this sister—yet no sister—had been assigned him as a safeguard.

Therefore, seeing in her a softened manner, feeling thus far off that she was passing from him, and from the unreal nature of this connection, would be no more his sister when she had once left his roof, he called out:—

"Rose! Rose! I want you, Rose!"

They both looked up, perhaps fancying that Septimius was suddenly taken ill; for there was something lamentable and awful in the cry—at least, they fancied so—though when they saw Septimius standing on the sunny hill-top, well and vigorous, they dismissed the idea, especially as he beckoned to them and smiled. Indeed, he was ashamed of his appealing cry, as soon as it was uttered. They both climbed the hill, however, and greeted him, having something to communicate which might as well be said then as at any time.

"Robert," said Septimius, looking at him when they stood on the level summit, "how changed you are since yesterday! How came you by this soldierlike air?"

In truth, Robert Hagburn, heretofore a well-built, comely young man, but with an air of rusticity, seemed developed, free, erect, martial. His eye had a fire in it, unknown before. <his arm in a sling, but he carried it with a sort of grace.>

"I don't know how it is, Septimius," he replied, laughing, "except that I am determined to be a soldier, and having already fought my first battle, I suppose I begin to look like a veteran. But, seriously, we are in for a civil war, which, sooner or later, will make soldiers of all of us who have any fighting quality in our nature, and perhaps some others. Till yesterday, I was rather at a loss about my vocation; to day, I begin to know it a little better. An army is gathering before Cambridge, and I am going as a soldier."

"And what says my sister Rose to this?" asked Septimius; for, looking into her face, he was confirmed in the idea that the long unuttered word between her and Robert Hagburn had been spoken, and that they were betrothed lovers. He went on, still trying to look into her downcast eyes:—"How dangerous they are, these times of commotion, revolution, upturning of old ideas, how dangerous to the hearts of the most retired and equable maidens. It might have been years, before a tumultuous throb would have disturbed the breast of my sage sister Rose; but the tumult of yesterday, the bloodshed, your danger, Robert, your purpose of encountering war—the great ocean of tumultuous emotion, outside of us in short, spreads its swell and toss into the little quiet bay of her breast. I know it is so. You have more to tell me! Say it at once, then!"

"I did not think you had so much knowledge of women's hearts, Septimius," said Rose, with a blush, and a fresh smile, "of a woman's heart, and the effect of a great tumult upon it."

"I am right then," he continued. "And what do you say to Robert Hagburn's purpose of going for a soldier?"

"He takes a manly part," replied Rose, "and I try to take the womanly one, though that is the hardest. I bid him go."

"And so does my mother," said Robert.

"I pity these mothers, and these sweethearts," cried Septimius, "at a time like this. And there are some all over our country even more to be pitied than either, though they know nothing and suspect nothing of their cause of grief, at present."

"Who are they?" asked Rose.

"I mean the thousands of good and sweet young girls, who have never had a word of love spoken to them, and will never know even so much of the life they were born for, as to have been in love, and been wretched. In due time, they would have met the thousands of young men, who, like Robert Hagburn, are going to the war. But these poor fellows—how many of them will sicken and die in camp, or be shot down with bullets, shattered by cannon-balls, pierced through with bayonets, and turn to dust and dry bones on the spot where they fall. The girls, meanwhile, that would have loved them for the asking, and made happy firesides for them, will yearn vaguely, and wither and grow yellow, not knowing what has blighted them, and loiter along many sour and discontented years, and at last go out of life without ever tasting the reality of a definite disappointment and grief. These poor girls are the real martyrs of the war; more so than are the wives and mothers of slain men."

"Rose will escape that worst luck, at least," said Robert Hagburn, taking her hand and drawing her towards him. "We are engaged, Septimius, and we have come to tell you so; and there is good hope in me, that I shall come safe back from the wars, and live happily in my old homestead yonder, and come often to see you, who will be happy in this dismal old house of yours, for it will be dismal and dungeon-like when I have stolen Rose away. But, Septimius, as you do not mean to enlist, you must save one, at least, of those poor damsels, whom you talk so pathetically about, from the ill-fate you jested for them. You will have a better chance to make your choice, while the rest of us are away; and I advise you to take advantage of it. When we come back with our laurels, you will stand a poor chance."

"Why should not I gather laurels, too?" inquired Septimius, a little jealously; for to say the truth, the freer, bold nature of Robert had its effect upon him, as such natures often have on those of men who lack the impulse to practical action, and he felt it a shame to do anything but fight. "I might shoulder a musket, too."

"And so you might," said Robert, "and you have the old fighting blood in you—that of the pastor, to say nothing of the Indian chiefs. You would fight well enough, no doubt; but there are thousands of heads, with less brains in them, that would do just as well to be hit by a bullet; and I hope you will find something better to do with yours. Besides, you are to be a minister."

Septimius accepted this speech of Robert's as an omen that there were higher toils for himself, and that he was dispensed from the duties which other young men felt so strongly.

"What is this, Septimius?" said Robert, looking at poor Francis Norton's hillock, near which they were standing. "It looks strangely like one of the beds where a good many poor fellows have been laid to their last sleep since yesterday. Was there a skirmish here?"

"No matter what it is, Robert," answered Septimius, looking away with an ambiguous smile. "I have planted something precious there, from which I expect to gather rich fruit, after a season."

"Come, Robert," said Rose, "you are robbing your mother of too much of the little time you have to give her. Do not waste any more time on our hill-top."

Robert Hagburn shook hands, and said farewell to Septimius, and drawing Rose along with him, they descended the hill. Robert appeared to muse as they went, and at last spoke:—

"This brother of yours—nay he is not your brother, and I am glad of it—he is, however, as old a friend as I have in the world, and yet I don't know what to make of him. Why don't he tell us frankly, that he was stirred up out of his studies and foolish fancies by the uproar, yesterday—that the breath of the battle made him drunk, as it did all of us— and that he took his great-grandfather's long gun, and shot an Englishman here on his own ground? It would have been an honor to him, and we should all have been glad to see such a flash of manly spirit, in a shy, moody lad. But here he buries him secretly, and says nothing of it to his best friends, and makes it a kind of secret, personal matter, hiding it away in his heart, as if that were a proper place for a grave. It is not wholesome to do so. I saw the blood stains on the leaves, and it made me feel sick because it looked so like murder. Now, I killed a man yesterday, and more than one, for aught I can tell, but I make no secret of it, and should go mad if I did; it is relief to tell of it, and somehow shifts part of the responsibility from my conscience upon the conscience of the community."

"He seems not particularly anxious to conceal it," said Rose;—"as why should he try, when the terrible state of things, has made the most religious and humane men among us aim at the life of those who were their fellow-subjects, till yesterday. But he is in a strangely absorbed mood, and gleams out of it, when he speaks, like fire in a dark place. There is something in his mind. Ah, Robert, I am troubled for his sake. He has such noble qualities, such great gifts, it seems to me—such penetrating sense. How wise and feeling he was, for example, in what he said about those poor girls, who will never know their mates. Who taught him that, I wonder. And yet, in spite of all, I feel as if he might do some wild, mad thing!"

"There is something wrong in his blood. That Indian blood has fermented with his forefathers, these two hundred years," said Robert. "And, you know what stories the old women tell in the chimney-corner, about his descent from Satan. But how strange it is, Rose, to see you, such a sweet, wholesome flower, growing among those strange, questionable plants, that have poison in them, that draw poison and blackness out of the soil, and you draw nothing but beauty and wholesomeness out of the same. I think Septimius will go mad, and Aunt Nashoba will turn witch outright, (if she is not one already,) when I take you from them."

"In that case," said Rose quietly, "I shall certainly not leave my poor brother and Aunt to such a fate."

Meanwhile, after his sister and his friend had quitted him, Septimius walked to and fro along the brow of the hill; passing and repassing that ominous little hillock, where, as he told Robert Hagburn, he had planted something precious, but out of which he had left the one thing that ought to have been buried there; to and fro he strode, and the people casually passing along the road, saw him there amid the branches of locust and birch, and their ideas being all military just then, wondered why he was keeping a centinel's walk on that hill-side, when the enemy had retreated forever. On that day, Septimius began a walk which, under the influence of an inward stimulus, which excited his mind to intensest action in that particular locality, he kept, from day to day, for a long, long time, until he had worn a pathway with his own individual feet, that looked as if it might have been trodden daily, as a common way, by many people; but it was only he, only his feet, made heavy by thought, quickened sometimes to a flying pace by excited hopes, moving slowly sometimes amid thickly tangled meditations, that thrust themselves in his way, embarrassing him, refusing to let him out;—then would suddenly open themselves, as if by magic, and show him the long sought, clear passage through. On one side of his narrow walk were the pitch-pines, and a depth of sombre wood, where the squirrel, the partridge, the woodchuck, and even a wild cat, might be found; an old Indian hunting ground, where the great, weird Sagamore, his ancestor, had dwelt, and made his incantations, and walked in friendly converse with the Black Man, and died. On the other side, was a placid view of a meadow, bordered at a distance by low ridges, like this on which Septimius walked; the calm, quietest landscape anywhere to be seen, not worth looking at once, yet good to have before one's eyes, day after day, and year after year, because it never thrusts itself forcibly in amongst the thoughts of a meditative man, asserting its claims to a place there, but always is ready for him, with a calm, mild sweetness, like the face of a placid, sympathizing friend, when he turns to it for sympathy. But it was seldom, now a days, and seldomer as the days went on, that Septimius turned to the wide, simple countenance of Nature for pleasure or for sympathy. A dense shrubbery of meditations, of which he scattered the seeds more and more as he walked, grew up along that often-trodden pathway, and shut out the view of external things, and arched over him, and made a cloistered walk, as sombre as those where monks used to tread,—keeping out the sun, allowing only a damp, unwholesome atmosphere. There Septimius walked, and brooded on strange matters.

In course of time it came to be said, and half-believed, by some of his superstitious neighbors, that the grass and little tender shrubs shrank away from this path of Septimius's, in a way not to be accounted for by his mere tread; and some thought that it was on account of unnaturalness that seized upon himself, or was caused by the nature of his meditations, having for their gist to change a law of nature, and so all forms of nature shrank from him, and the herbage withered, and the branches turned their tender twigs away, and the long pitch pine branches looked brown, on that side. Others whispered, that the sooty shape of that strange, old legendary Sagamore, him of doubtful race, walked there with his descendant, and taught him secrets that had better never have been known, and that Francis Norton got up out his grave, and demanded back the papers which, he said, had been fraudulently kept above ground. But this was only the idle babble that men must expect to be the subject of, when they choose to withdraw ever so little from the common pathway—even no farther than the brow of Septimius's hill was from the Lexington road below—and involve themselves in pursuits and interests unintelligible to the wayfarer there. In due time, the reader shall know all that need to be told of what Septimius thought of, while treading out that path, and of the apparitions that encountered him there.

But we have got considerably in advance of our story.

Many weeks passed; Spring brightened, blossomed, and deepened into Summer; the first convulsive spasms of the outbreak of the war, which disturbed everybody out of the settled movements of their life, subsided into the gradual heavy tug, and pressure, which were to last for years,— before Septimius opened the package, which had been rescued out of the young officer's grave.

<Old yellow & musty papers, from their mere dinginess, give a dreary idea of the times & circumstances to which they relate—so do portraits &c>

I know not how long it was that Septimius left the parchment covered packet untouched in the drawer to which he had first consigned it; only now and then taking a peep at it, to satisfy himself that it was still there. Probably, if the truth were known, he was afraid to look at it; afraid that the discovery of some common place documents, interesting only to the poor dead youth himself, might at once dissipate all his claims of a mystic secret, brought by so many strange chances to his hand, as the only one able to receive it; and to convey it to whom, a chain of events had been arranged providentially to this end, of which this was to be one of the incidental consequences, and in view of which, to say the truth, what other people considered the main end was of slight importance;—a long series of irritating disputes between two kindred people, a war, in the first conflict of which had fallen a young man, entrusted with the charge, and surrendering it to the hands of a retired student who—the last man in the world to commit such an act—had been strangely led on to take his life, and so receive the trust. <(his strange, hostile intimacy in his last moments)> I trust that our poor friend Septimius did not stray so far beyond decency and modesty, as to conceive that all this embroilment of motives, and the fierce tumult of war that shook the spheres, and the commotion of which did not subside for a half century, was arranged with a principal view to this object; but such is the characteristic egotism of men like Septimius, and their idea (and a veil of modesty and self abnegation) of their own importance to the universe, that it is questionable whether he had not a secret belief that the war would hardly have a more important result than the vivifying of his thought by the secret which the young officer's document would communicate. And, indeed, he was so far right, that a war is well ended, and performs its purpose, if any grand truth of morals or religion be but established by it; and many a war has raged without, so far as mere human intellect can discern, half effecting anything of the kind. But, deeming the matter of so much importance, on the one hand, and, on the other, secretly fearing (for there was a quality of keen sense in Septimius, which continually criticised his extravagances) fearing that it might prove all a ridiculous dream, it is not strange that he hesitated, and put himself off, on one pretence or another, from opening the packet.

Another reason also there might have been; the feeling that he was violating the sanctity of the grave, and his own contract with the man whom he had slain, by prying into the secret which he had so evidently intended should be buried with him. It perhaps requires no remarkable powers of sophistry to make out a plausible case against this idea; but still conscience is apt to be a stubborn entity, in our early years, as when we stifle it ever so slowly, keeps struggling and lifting up its voice, throbbing, giving inconvenient signs of life, long after it ought to be dead. Possibly, Septimius was conscious of some such convulsive remonstrances, and was waiting for his conscience to be quite benumbed, before he violated its dictates.

<Aunt Nashoba was going to gather herbs for drying, & to make Indian medicines of &c &c.>

When, at last, he took an irrevocable step in the business, it was quite unexpected to himself, and in such a quiet, matter of course way, that it was done before he had any time for any emotions. He had promised to go into the woods with Aunt Nashoba and Rose, in quest of some shrubs, twigs, and all such matters, with which the old lady was to brew some drink;—not her own peculiar concoction, the ingredients of which she gathered herself, with much mystery, at a peculiar time of the moon, and never imparted to anyone, but a light foaming drink for summer with the fragrance and flavor of the wild woods in it. There being a few spare minutes, while Aunt Nashoba was setting her kitchen in order, or Rose was putting on her bonnet, Septimius, all of a sudden, went to his drawer, unlocked it, took in hand the blood-stained package and broke the seal, before he consciously thought of what he was doing. It often happens, that, by much musing on expected events, looking at them on all sides, steeping them in our emotions of wonder, hope, fear, beforehand, we expand our interest in advance, and come to the moment of crisis with a veteran-like composure. So it was with Septimius; and he unfolded the stiff envelope, and took out perhaps a dozen folds of yellow, age-worn paper, written over with a strangely obscure handwriting, with as few throbs of the heart as he would have opened a letter from Robert Hagburn, now in camp. Something dropt out of the envelope and fell rattling upon the floor; he picked it up, and found it to be a small, antique key, curiously wrought, and with intricate wards, and seeming to be of silver. In the handle of the key, there was a sort of open-work tracery, which made the cypher H. N. in old English letters. Septimius looked at this key, with great minuteness, before proceeding further, wondering where on earth could be the key-hole that suited it, and to what sort of a treasure it was the passport. Then laying it carefully away in the drawer, he proceeded to inspect the manuscripts.

They appeared to be a collection of deeds, chiefly, or some documents of legal weight and operation, so far as Septimius could judge by the formal signatures and seals on more than one of them; but they seemed of very considerable antiquity, and as chirography was very different, two or three centuries ago, from what it is now, and as Septimius had no practice in reading it, he did not readily make out what these papers were, nor, indeed, did he feel much interest in decyphering a parcel of family documents, relating, probably, to property in England, with which he could have nothing to do, or pedigrees and descents, which had probably ended with the poor youth lying on the hill top. He tossed them one after another into the desk, after a careless glance or two, and finally came to a fold or two of manuscript, written with exceeding closeness, and in a character which appeared at first glance to be wholly illegible. In fact, ancient handwriting is apt to be without form, singularly individual, only to be read by faith; and I know not whether it was by faith or revelation that Septimius, turning over these old yellow pages (which, old as they were, were crisp, and had a kind of newness, as if nobody had ever fingered them before till this day) read, or fancied that he read, a single sentence, the purport of which stamped itself into his mind. more from the mere inappositeness and absurdity of it than from any other cause. To say the truth, he was by no means certain whether he read that one sentence, or only imagined it; and at all events, it grew more distinct to his mind, after he had laid away the manuscript, than while he was actually trying to read it.

<(Make out Aunt Nashoba's wildness more strongly)>

He had but glanced at it, indeed, when Aunt Nashoba's shrill screech called his name, and the old lady herself came to his door, hurrying him; for she was an unquiet old thing, and it appeared as if the races of which she was mixed kept a war in her blood, and would never let her be at rest. So, in fine, he locked up the manuscript, just as he was beginning to be interested—just as a light seemed to be kindling on the dark, mysterious page, that promised to enlighten it all, and make the faded letters that once were black, shine like burnished gold.

<Rose has some knowledge of botany.>

They went over the hill and into the woods, these three together; and in the shadows of the pines, and among the tangled undergrowth, it was singular to see the delight with which Aunt Nashoba snuffed in the fragrance of the wild growing things; how the rugged, rough old pitch-pines seemed to have a charm for her, and be old acquaintances; what a natural motion she had, in making her way through the under-brush; in fact, she was like a half-domesticated animal, a wild cat, that has been taught life-long to sit by the kitchen fire, a fox or a wolf that has done duty like a household dog, that, coming to the wild haunts of its race, feels the powerful, blind, imperfect stirrings of its nature, and snuffs a delight, which yet it cannot wholly know—without any sense of beauty, she loved the beautiful things of the woods, the violets, the anemones, the skunk cabbage, the choke-berries, studding the ground with red beads; she stood, and snuffed, and snuffed, with an animal delight.

A strange look of wildness came over the old woman; yes and of possible agility, too, spite of her rheumatism, and the manifold decrepitude of which she was always moaning and complaining; insomuch that it would have seemed almost a natural transformation, had the stooping, slow-moving old thing suddenly taken the shape of a wild cat, or perhaps a strange, ugly fowl, and gone scrambling or flapping away; a sort of change, very customary with witches.

"Ah, Seppy," said she, "it is but two or three times a year that I can get out of my kitchen into the woods; but when I do it, methinks I'm another woman, or rather no woman at all; but something that belongs here, and that ought to be wandering here, all the while, and never thinking of kitchen chimneys nor meeting-houses. Rose, now, I dare to say, has no such feelings."

"Oh, yes, Aunt Nashoba, I love dearly to come into the woods, and gather these delicate little flowers, so much more delicate than those of the garden, and with such a sweet, faint smell," said Rose. "It is strange, how gentle and delicate the things are, that grow in this deep, solemn shade. They seem to have no kindred with it. They are sad, never gay; their beauty is melancholy; and being rightfully children of the sun, they live and die without having a glimpse of him, and so never come to what they should be, on account of this black sternness, and these tangled things, that brood over them."

"Delicate, do you call them?" said Aunt Nashoba, "tender, of no account? I tell you girl, there are herbs here, that in hands that know how to use them, would do wonderful things. Here is where the Indian doctors used to come for their medicines; and if Septimius had inherited the gift that belongs to his race, he would be able to come out hither, if he had never been before, nor ever saw a forest and the leafy things that grow in it—he would be able to come here and lay his hand on leaf and root, that would be worth all the medicines doctors ever brewed. Even I—wretched old thing, that have steamed my life out over the kitchen fire— I have an instinct of things, and feel as if I could fill my bucket with herbs that would make me a young woman again. Ah, Seppy, I know more than I ever told you; and some day I'll give you the recipe of my drink. As for you, wench, it's not your inheritance."

They went burrowing into the wood; and whatever Aunt Nashoba pointed out to Septimius, that he gathered, and stowed into a great fragrant green mass of woodland spoil; the sweet-smelling twigs, spruce, sweet-fern, sassafras, white pine burls, making up the bulk of it, while, in her bucket, the old witch, with an air and look of mystery, put other things; and whenever she gathered any of them, she winked and nodded at Septimius, thereby most needlessly adding to the ugliness of her visage; so that you would have thought that they two had laid a plot to poison the innocent and sweet Rose, and that this was the old woman's hideous exultation, as she got together, one after another, the ingredients. But to the best of my belief, these mysterious herbs were merely intended to brew a fresh quantity of that valuable drink, for which Aunt Nashoba was so famous, and of which nobody, as yet, had ever tasted twice, and few people once; its smell being enough. And so Septimius's burden grew, until it would have been a pretty thing to paint; and as for Rose, she gathered flowers and pretty things that had been growing in the wild woods, never hoping to be appreciated, but thinking to shed their delicate beauty, after their little day, upon the spikes of the pine, and the withered leaves, and have them decay into the soil, and add their mite to its fertility against the time when it should be ploughed up.—Aunt Nashoba refused to let her add anything to the contents of her own bucket.

"No, no, girl," said she. "Your touch would take the virtue out of the stuff. You're not born to it. Let me gather my own herbs, I tell you," saying which, she poked into little recesses of shade and under heaps of rocks, and sometimes into hollow nooks of trees; and brought out vegetables, as if she had put them away there, long years ago, and knew just where they were to be found.

"Let her go on," said Aunt Nashoba; "and do you stay by me, Seppy, for I have something particular to tell you."

When Rose, still looking for buds of beauty, had passed on; and the whispering which the woods kept up among themselves, which high over head was like the sound of a sea, was loud enough to drown Aunt Nashoba's words at a little distance, she drew Septimius nearer to her; and looking so intelligent and so full of meaning, that the young man was half afraid of her, there in the lonely wood, she said,

"Septimius, my dear lad, I am getting old; and it is time I told you a secret that I would not have die with me; for I am afraid I should have to come back to tell it to you."

"Dear me, Aunt Nashoba," said Septimius. "Have you such a terrible secret on your conscience!"

"On my conscience? Fie, Seppy! I'm a church-member, and have nothing on my conscience that it can't very well bear. D'ye think I've a murder to confess; no; and though they say my medicines hurried some people off sooner than they would otherwise have gone, I don't believe it; and if I did, I meant their good, and any regular Doctor, as they call themselves, has filled ten graves to my one. No; what I want to tell you (and 'tis time, for it's all the inheritance I have to leave you) is the secret of my drink. Here are all the herbs and mysteries within reach of us now, and I can show you where they grow, and how to gather them."

"Where would be the use, Aunt Nashoba? I never should taste, nor would any body else."

"The use!" cried Aunt Nashoba, in vast indignation. "The use. Why to make you live forever;—a thousand years, certain, and forever for aught I know."

Septimius was considerably startled by an idea which thus hit right against the subject which he was brooding upon, and stared aghast at the old woman, before he answered:—

"Forever, Aunt Nashoba?"—or a thousand years? And yet you talk of dying already. If the secret has done so little for you, why should it serve me any better?"

"Ah, Seppy, there is something lost out of the secret," said Aunt Nashoba, "and so it has not its correct virtue. But with your book-learning, and your natural brightness, and your being a natural Indian doctor by descent, you'll find it out, though I never could. You must give yourself up to it, and think of nothing else till you find it out. And if it takes you a year—or ten years, twenty years, thirty years—or your whole lifetime, so you find it out at your last day, what matter? The end pays for all; and besides these you have the comfort and delight of the drink as I tell it to you, meanwhile. It's kept me alive this many a day, and made it worth the trouble to live."

"Excuse me, now, Aunt Nashoba," said Septimius. "My mind is very busy on a certain matter. Let me finish that, and I'll take up this. But not now."

"Well, Seppy, you'll live to repent it!" said Aunt Nashoba, shaking her head, and looking so darkly intelligent that Septimius was half afraid of her again. "This is not my secret, but your grandfather's and your great grandfather's, and his father's; and as to whom he had it from, there are different stories. But take your own way; and if the thing dies with me, it's not my fault."

And now, having gathered enough of her pharmacopeia to make up a yearly stock of medicines, even if the war should greatly increase her practice, the old woman signified her intention of returning home, and after calling Rose, Septimius followed thoughtfully in her steps.

Various interruptions kept him from further examination of the manuscript, during the day; for it may be observed, that a man no sooner sets his heart on any object, great or small, be it the lengthening out of his life interminably, or merely writing a romance about it, than his fellow beings, and fate and circumstance to back them, seem to conspire to hinder, to prevent, to throw in each his obstacle, great or small according to his power. In the original composition and organic purpose of the world, there is certainly some principle to obviate great success; some provision that nothing particularly worth doing shall ever get done; so inevitably does a mistiness settle between us and any such object, and harden into granite when we attempt to pass through it; so strongly do mocking voices call us back, or encouraging ones cease to be heard, when our sinking hearts need them most; so unaccountably, at last, when we feel as if we might grasp our life-long object by merely stretching out our hand, does it all at once put on an aspect of not being worth our grasp; by such apparently feeble impediments are our hands subtly bound; so hard is it to stir to-day, while it looks as if it would be easy to stir to purpose tomorrow; so strongly do petty necessities insist upon being compared with immortal desirablenesses, and almost always succeed practically in making us feel that they are of the most account. This being the case, Septimius had no such individual cause of grumbling against his stars as he supposed, on the score of the little tormenting incidents that assailed him, that day.

<(This is an educated old gentleman; and Septimius asks him about old age, and he discusses it.)>

One of the incidents was a visit from a lank and bony old patriarch who came to get a remedy from Aunt Nashoba for his rheumatism, which lasted longer into the summer than had been its wont; and his errand being done, he hobbled familiarly into Septimius's study to talk of the war (a theme of which the young man was heartily weary,) and to tell stories of other wars in which the old man had been personally engaged, Indian and French, and where he had contracted this self-same rheumatism by sleeping, as he said, in the beds of running streams. Then, going farther and farther back along the line of times gone by, the old man talked of Septimius's forefathers, telling of their peculiarities and oddnesses, with hard Yankee shrewdness; and how they were a people that never mixed up kindly with others, either because the Indian or the Devil was in them, and how the old man said that there was something strange in them, some singular property, so that if the witch woman had not been hanged, it was said, she would have lived forever; and that there did go a story, that the great preacher (whom the old man had heard preach, when he was a little child) only escaped the same doom by killing himself. For, somehow, he had toughened himself, so that time and disease never would have sufficed to kill him. And staring Septimius in the face, with his bleared eyes, he said that he had a look of him, he being a dark, cloudy-browed man wrapt up in himself; and he told traits of him, which he had heard babbled round the fire in his age-long distant infancy, in which Septimius fancied that he could see his own characteristics. And he was depressed and appalled by the idea that he had really been extant, nobody knows how long; repeated identically from generation to generation, and that this was the sort of interminable life which he should find, and the other only a dream. And still the old man was going on, wandering and stumbling among traditions, and wild, dreary, sordid stories, and would probably have found no end; when luckily there came along the road a neighbor in a wagon, beholding whom, the old gentleman feebly hailed him from the window, and (all to save his rheumatism from farther pedestrianism) obtained a lift to the village.

Septimius, finding that the old gentleman was not reluctant to speak of his age, but, on the contrary, seemed to find a positive pleasure in making it the subject of conversation, as valetudinarians do their diseases, ventured to ask him how it felt to be old—what it was that made the difference between age and youth, to the person most concerned. "Why," said the old gentleman, "I suppose I seem to you a very old codger, as old as the hills, and as if I had never been anything else but old—don't I?"

Septimius admitted, that, as he had known his visitor from childhood, and as he had always looked to him just as old as now, he did have an impression that he had never been other; though, of course, the moment he began to think and reason about it, he knew that he must once have been a young man, once a child.

"Just so," quoth the old gentleman, "but I assure you, my son, that it is a new and strange thing to myself to be old, & I have not yet convinced myself of it; and that, for my part, I have to think and reason to convince myself that I am not young any longer. I was so yesterday, why not to-day?

But this, I suppose, is a sort of instinct; there is something still young in me, and nearest to me—the kernel of me, as I may say—and, for most purposes, it warms me through and through."

"But don't you know at all that you are old?" said Septimius. "How when you look in the glass?"

"Why, unless I look of set purpose," replied the old man, "I don't see the white hair and the furrows, but only a look that I have seen all my life—an expression—the real me, I suppose, and that is altered little or none. When I look for the marks of age, then, to be sure, I see them. And so, too, when I seek through my physical life for the signs of age, there they are, plenty of them, and easily to be found, and not very delightful. These twenty years, I have had a rheumatism in my left shoulder, that never quite goes away, though it uses me pretty tolerably. Then I have a dread of hills, and high staircases, my knees being weak; and yet I think I would rather climb up than come down, because my eyesight makes me uncertain where my foot will step. I used to be a great climber, but now my old head is off its balance. I can't run a step, nor walk fast nor far. I am short of breath. The tears come into my eyes without my being greatly grieved, and I think it takes but a little matter to set me a laughing, and I get angry sooner than I used to. I don't sleep very sound, but make it up by catching a little bit of a nap at all sorts of odd times. I am terribly irresolute, and sit thinking an hour about anything I want to do, and then don't do it. I think over all the objections to a thing, and see the dark side, and so, if a person comes to me for advice, and listens to me, he seldom gets what's good for him; and yet I do speak truth and wisdom; but this world makes progress by folly, not by wisdom. I see these patriots, for instance, to be fools; but I should not wonder if their acts came out right, though I can't see the possibility of it. I always have a tired feeling; if anything, I wake up more tired than I go to bed—I suppose it is the weariness of my whole life, that only a church-yard nap can help. And speaking of that, I don't think I like to think of churchyards, and coffins, and other melancholy things, as young men often do for mere whim's sake, and because they think them so far off from themselves; though I don't know that they really seem near to me, for all I am seventy-nine. <always frost-nipt> I love to get on the sunny, south side of things and bask there; because there is always a sort of chillness in me, even when I am warm. Dear me, I wish fire or sunshine could warm me, and that our winters were not so long and cold. I hate to have the sun get to the south'ard. Do you know the first feeling of having a cold?"

"Yes," said Septimius.

"A sort of stuffiness all through you, a sleepiness," continued the old man, "a subdued ache, an incommodity that is very subtle, and don't quite declare itself, but still is there. Well; I think old age is something like that feeling, as if you had a cold for the rest of your life. Then, to go on, my eyes ache, and my eyelids, without any cause, that I know of. I have no great appetite, and have to be very careful to restrain what I have. I used to like a cheerful glass, and should still, only it is as likely as not to swamp my brain. My pipe was a great comfort to me, but it has got too much for me, and makes me nervous.

"They call us old people money-lovers; but, you see, 'tis the only thing we can hold on to; for our strength goes, our enterprise and energy, and if we lose what we have, we can get no more; and for my part, though I am in pretty warm circumstances, I don't know but I shall die in the poor-house yet, there are so many chances and changes in the world, especially in revolutionary times—and that's a true old man's terror. I think, leaving out money, that other things have not so strong a hold of me as they had. A friend of all my life died the other day, but I did not mind it as I should thirty years ago. My children are dead before me—one of them not long ago—but it's strange how well I bear it. I sometimes think the saddest thing about my griefs is, that I cannot be even sensible of them. I should have been young a good while longer, if you and the other young fellows would have let me; but you get behind in a great crowd, and shove us out of our places, for the sake of filling them yourselves."

"Do you think," said Septimius, "that, as you approach the verge of life, you can see any better or any farther what is beyond?"

"Not a bit," said the old gentleman, "my faith is good, but my sight is dim."

"Would you like to have back your youth and strength, if you might?" asked the young man.

"Well, yes," said the old man, "if it were not for that tired feeling that I told you of. It seems as if I could not begin life again without a sleep, better and sounder than I can now get."

"Would you be content to begin your sleep now?" asked Septimius.

"Not quite yet," said the old man, shaking his white head. "Well, well, my boy; 'tis getting late, and the mists on the meadows here are bad for my rheumatism; and as for old age, if you wish to hear any more about it, come and see me any day; though, for that matter, you might as well wait for your own old age. It will seem only like the space between now and yesterday morning."

"Longer than that, please God," said Septimius to himself. "And yet this old man is happier than I. But how Nature tries to keep us comfortable by a succession of delusions. She shall not cheat me, whatever comes of it; and I never will be old—I will fight her with her own weapons.

"My ears stuffed with cotton, so that I hear nothing distinctly; my fingers muffled in mittens, so that I feel nothing; my eyes with a fog before them, my palate obtuse to taste; my sense of smell—I don't know that I have any, but that can be spared. Things slip strangely out of my memory— especially words and names—all of a sudden, when I seem to have firm hold upon them. I am tired of old things, and don't like new ones. When I was younger I should have told you these things in some sort of order and classification, but now, as you see, I turn them out like emptying the contents of a rag-bag (—I have a great many nameless aches all over me, that come and go, and no questions asked; for I have found out that they mean nothing, except that my machine is pretty near worn out). To tell you the truth, I have only to open the flood gate of my mouth, and out flows a stream of talk, just as now, and sometimes I have half a suspicion that people wish it were shorter.—I have a strange desire to build a new house, though my own will last, no doubt, a hundred years longer than I shall, and I have no child to live in it after me."

The legendary patriarch had scarcely gone, when the village-pastor made his appearance, to discover what had become of his pupil; for he had great share in directing Septimius, in the first place, to a college education, having been struck by his ability, and its turn towards thoughtful and studious pursuits, insomuch that it was under him that the youth acquired his preliminary education. He had kept an eye upon him through his collegiate course, and when that was completed it was under his care and auspices that Septimius had begun the study of theology. But, ever since the battle-day, what with the blood upon his hand, what with the other interest that absorbed his thoughts, the young man had not felt impelled to near his reverend instructor, and the latter had now come to look after his truant pupil. After suitable greetings, good Mr Porter sat on the other side of the table, with the piles of books between, looking at Septimius with a grave, friendly earnestness, paternal in its character; for he had given almost a father's care to the training of this young intelligence, and felt an interest in it because he had thought it somewhat shaped by himself. He spoke of the length of the interval that had occurred, since they had last talked together on the subject of Septimius's studies, and probably, without seeming to do so, got some insight into a discontented state of mind, an absorption in some other direction than the right one, a condition of doubt, carelessness, where he ought to have been certain and earnest, and at last spoke.

"Septimius," said he, "there is something in your face that troubles me."

"What is that, Sir?" asked Septimius.

"It is something signifying a mind ill at ease," said the minister. "Moreover, do you remember the look of that dark, hand engraving of your ancestor done in copper-plate, during his visit to London, and prefixed to the same volume of his sermons, which I have in my library. Considering that the portrait represents a man of fifty, and you are nearly thirty years younger, there is a wonderful resemblance. I am sorry to see it."

"Why so, Sir?" asked Septimius. "My ancestor was reckoned a good man, and a bright one."

"He was a remarkable man, at all events," said the minister. "But what I have to say is, that there are some races of strongly characterized men, who are liable to get into ruts, as

I may say, and run to and fro from one generation to another in the same lines of thought, and consequently, in the same lines of action; and by and by this becomes exaggerated into madness. I know some traits of your ancestor, and some legends of a still earlier ancestor, that make me hesitate whether it would be better to cultivate those seeds of uncommon ability, which I discerned in you, and thereby bring to light perhaps qualities combined with those peculiar talents; or to leave your race, so far as in me lay, to go through the process of a yet longer obscurity than the two or three immediately past generations. It is such obscurity, I assure you, that preserves the sanity of races, interposing intervals of repose in lines distinguished for ability; inaction or extinction, or else mental disease, is the way Nature cares for them."

"I do not well understand, Reverend Sir, what you dread on my behalf," said Septimius; "but, whatever the consequence, I can scarcely regret that I am not the clod, the uninstructed, undeveloped mind, which my poor father was. I remember, in my boyish petulance, thinking that it were as well never to have existed, and fearing that a native so little cultivated here would die in the transplantation to another state."

"That was a mistake," said the minister drily. "I doubt whether the intellect is accounted of great worth as the selection of plants for Heaven from this nursery of the world. But, my dear Septimius, will you receive from an old friend, who takes a great interest in you, some advice?"

"Certainly, Sir, and with gratitude," answered his pupil; "and with a desire to find it possible for me to follow it."

"I would advise, then," said the minister, "to plunge for a time into a life of action. There is a danger for you, which I do not wish to state more explicitly, in this little, quiet room.

Moreover, if I put rightly together many indications which I have noticed in you, there are doubts, speculations, questionings, which scarcely leave you a right to devote yourself to the Christian ministry. The time may come, but is not now. Meantime, adopt some life that will sweep all the accustomed thoughts out of your mind."

"What can I do," said Septimius "—what pursuit turn myself to, when the whole land, and the whole intelligence of it, lies waste and idle, except for this war?"

"There, providentially, is the very calling to which you may turn yourself," said the minister. "Put your whole heart into it; for it is God's call. Let it absorb you while it lasts; and come out of it, at its close, your mind cleared of all rubbish, made simpler, by simple and high emotions, religious; by trust in God. It is a great thing for a young man, wandering, erring, straying though darkness, and among visions of the evil one, to have the opportunity to live a life of devotion to your country, when religion may be put even into outward acts, when, too, the darkness, wildness, destructiveness in his nature (instead of lying morbid in his hope, and leading him to dark private acts) may be acted out in the service of God and of his country,—when to slay a fellow-man may be an act of worship."

Septimius was removed, by the peculiarity of the thing that absorbed him, apart from other men, and contemplated their passions from an insulated point of view; and, in consequence, the ardor of the patriotic struggle, in which his countrymen were involved, though not wholly unfelt by him, was felt in a far less degree than by almost any other man of his age. He replied, respectfully, but cooly, that he thought that a person capable of reasoning ought not to engage in war unless upon the very strongest command of conscience; else any life he took would be reckoned against him—a murder; that he had no such clear feeling with regard to this war, and, moreover had a peculiar value for human life; and that as for any moral disease, which his revered friend seemed to think was threatening him, he could not perceive the symptoms of it; but that it must be a direful disease, indeed, for which the remedy was to make himself a portion of the great fever-fit of his country. In short, as people sometimes can, who plant themselves stedfastly upon an individual folly, he spoke from this stand-point very wise words against the reverend gentleman, who, certainly, was shaken a little from the propriety of his office by the zeal with which he entered into the cause of his country. The good man took his leave of Septimius, with a strong impression of something wrong about his pupil, and with an understanding that, for the present, at least, the relation between them was at an end.

When again left alone, Septimius took forth the envelope, and held it a moment in his hand, looking at the hole through which the deadly bullet had gone, and at the life-blood which besmeared the package; as if a life had been the seal, and had been destroyed in the opening it. He unfolded the package, and though the twilight was now darkening into the low-browed room, pored into it; into its strange old mystery, so bewildering even to look at; and, indeed, the darkening twilight was precisely the fit medium in which to study that bewitched, mysterious, bullet-penetrated, blood-stained manuscript, the secrets of which might be expected to fade under the light of noon, or any glimpse of the natural sun, and only to shine out in lurid light, phosphorescent, glimmering, when other means of seeing and interpretation were withdrawn. Soon, however, it grew so dark that the light of the summer moon, which was nearly at the full, succeeded to the twilight, and Septimius held the old pages in it, straining his young eyes, to distinguish one of the scraggly, untraceable, crabbed letters from another, but in vain, the whole hue of the page being so dark a yellow, and of the letters so reddish a brown, and sometimes faded quite out, that the moonshine which often had served well enough to read a printed page at hours which Aunt Nashoba deemed him sung in bed, now saw little more than an indistinguishable confusion. He, having neither lamp nor candle, of which the strict economy of the house was very sparing, lighted with flint and steel one of a heap of pitch-pine knots, which he had heaped up in the chimney with a view to any of those thoughtful illuminations, which students often feel, impelling them to rise at midnight, and take a sip out of their books, as people of an unhealthy thirst cannot wait till day to sip wine or brandy. With a succession of these flaming, bickering, smoking, brilliant, yet obscure torches, he pored over the manuscript holding the torch in one hand, and sometimes dropping its hot melted pitch over the page, burning his own fingers, trying to make his way through the mysterious old Gothic record, like one who should wander through old intricate vaults of a ruined building, with the same kind of smoky and bewildering light. It seemed to have more efficacy, indeed, than a steadier light; for just as the last of his torches expired, he caught a glimpse of the same sentence, which he now saw, did not follow in regular succesion of words, but was sprinkled about, as it were, over one of the pages, so as only to be legible, like a constellation in the sky, when you chanced to bring those words into the proper relation with each other. It was to this effect. "Plant the seed in a grave, and wait patiently for what shall spring up"; and then again —"wondrous rich, and full of juice." Then the pine-torch flickered and went out, and Septimius, not well-satisfied with what he had achieved but willing to rest upon it, and see if the mysterious fragment would develope any meaning, put the manuscript in his desk and went to bed.

It would be wearisome to trace step by step Septimius's slow progress (if any progress, indeed, he made, which he was himself sometimes inclined to doubt, deeming his interpretation all moonshine and fancywork) into the mysteries of the manuscript; and leaving it aside, we shall here record the appearance of a new character upon our scene.

<Septimius & the girl first pass each other without speaking, then they mutually turn back, & she pauses by the grave—she glancing askance>

<(The girl should throw out uncertain hints, as if she knew what had happened)>

Septimius was on the hill-top, one afternoon, towards sunset, treading to and fro along his now well-worn path, and letting the wind breathe in among his thoughts, and blow the more unsubstantial of them away; when, as he reached the eastern extremity of centinel-walk, and turned to retread his steps westward, he saw a feminine figure approaching him. At first he thought it might be Rose, and was, to say the truth, a little inclined to be offended that she should venture to intrude, without invitation, on a spot which he had appropriated himself for the cloister of his most secret meditations, and where no other person could set a foot without treading, as it were, on a pavement of rejected thoughts, or pass along, without brushing and disturbing the unseen buds and blossoms of thoughts not yet gathered and flung aside. It would not be like Rose, however, knowing his peculiarities, his subtle egotism, the sort of sanctity that he ascribed to this haunt, above all his resorts, so well, to have intruded here; for, with all the familiarity of sisterhood, and that arising from the mixed up life of those who have grown up in one household, there still was a quality in poor Septimius that kept him in the middle of a circle, which delicate natures could not step into, and which duller ones, if they attempted it, found it vacant of him who seemed to be there; so this figure turned out not to be Rose, but that of a girl slighter and slenderer than she, and, as Septimius thought on a nearer view, not by any means so pretty or so pleasing. Such as she was, however, she continued to advance, and so did Septimius, until, as chance ordered it, they met close by that little spot of ground where poor Francis Norton lay under the sods, with Septimius's poor attempt to set a flower-patch over him. The strange girl stooped down, apparently attracted by their flowers. After examining them a little, she began to pull them up, one after another, and fling them away.

"You seem not to like my flowers," said Septimius; "yet I have taken some pains to set them out, and make them grow on this thirsty hill-top."

In fact, he was inclined to be offended that this strange girl should take such liberties with a spot of ground, that six feet of earth, which he considered to be more peculiarly his own than any other spot ever could be, until he, like poor Francis Norton, should lie beneath the sods. Francis Norton, to be sure, might have contested his title, but until he appeared as a claimant, he could hold it against all others, having enriched so dearly with what was mortal of a beautiful human being, and having chosen these flowers to grow and be beautiful, so that people might wonder whence they got the sustenance that made them so rich. His sombre fancy had indulged itself much here, in thinking that Francis Norton would reappear in these flowers, putting his own characteristics into them, giving a partly human life to them, deepening their colors, living again in them, and betokening by some rich and delicate odor forgiveness of the deed that laid him there, holding forth a flower, perhaps, for him to give to the woman he should love; for Septimius had no enmity nor ill-will against the young man he slew, and had indeed come to think (such again was his egotism) that it was not amiss that, having done his errand so well, he had here lain down to rest; as Septimius had no kindlier feelings towards any than him.

"Nay, do not pull up any more!" he exclaimed, as the girl still weeded up the flowers.

"Poh! what do you know of the flowers that ought to grow here," answered she, in a pettish kind of way. "They are not the right ones!"

"They are the prettiest to be found on our woods and fields," said Septimius; "and, besides, with your leave, fair lady, if I choose to set violets, wood anemones, asters, golden-rod, or even butter-cups on the spot, I fancy it concerns only myself."

The girl looked up and laughed in rather a flighty way; insomuch that Septimius began to suspect that the oddities of her behavior were to be accounted for by a touch of insanity; a pitiful thing, if it were so; for, on a closer view, he saw that her face, though pale and lacking fullness, was pretty, and had a singular capacity of vivid expression; her intelligence seeming to glow not merely through her eyes, but her whole face. And yet, full of meaning as her face looked, he could not in the least tell what it meant.

"Concern only you," she exclaimed still laughing. "Why, I have come on purpose to find the place. And, I tell you the right flower is not here!"

And again she bent down, and having by this time weeded up all the flowers, she closely examined some other little plants, that had sprung up spontaneously among the grass that covered, with tolerable luxuriance, the ominous spot, making it, in spite of Septimius's care, look liker a grave than he wished. She plucked a leaf or two, looked closely at their shape, and rubbed them between her fingers to express any odorous juice that might be in them; but again said, in a discontented sort of way, like a pouting child—"It is not here! I wonder whether it will spring up!—and when!"

<(She looks up at him, askance, and with snakelike malignancy)>

"What flower are you looking for?" asked Septimius.

"It has no name," answered the girl; "or if it has one, it is a very long, learned name, and I have forgotten it."

"Is it, the flower, so beautiful?" asked Septimius.

"That's as you happen to fancy it," said the girl. "Well it is not here; but I will seek for it again. Perhaps it is not time yet."

She sat a little while without speaking, but drooping over the flowers, flaccid, looking faint, as if she were going to sink down, and Septimius, stooping down to see what was the matter, found that the tears were flowing out of her eyes. Then there came sobs; and suddenly she burst into a passionate fit of sorrow and weeping, a sort of flurry and hurricane, which astonished poor Septimius, who could make nothing of its purport, nor knew how to proceed to allay it. It was fortunately of very short duration, however, and before it was well over, the strange girl began to laugh, or rather giggle, turning her mobile face upon him with such an expression that he knew less than ever what to make of her; though I suppose that those accustomed to the freaks of nervous and hysterical women would have seen nothing very odd in it.

"I was thinking how to comfort you," said Septimius, "but there seems little need."

"Oh, not a bit," said the girl, "I am in excellent spirits, as you see, and was only crying a little by way of watering the spot where the flower is to grow. Different things require different modes of cultivation."

"And I suppose these smiles and this bright expression are to serve by way of sunshine," said Septimius, trying to enter into her mood, though he knew not what to make of it. "It will be a rare flower when it grows. What will it be like?"

Without answering, the girl arose, and seemed preparing to go away, when Septimius, not willing to lose sight of her without gaining some hold upon her, and thinking, too, that she might be one of those strange anomalous vagrants, who often turn up at a country house, and appear to be wandering wide and wild, without any hold upon the community anywhere; beggars, insane people, idiots, adventurers, castaways of all kinds, people from the most outlandish and remote places, East Indians, religion crazed preachers, missionaries, jugglers, outlaws of themselves, wildly running away from the recollection of murder, mind readers, sharpers—all such people, who have somehow broken the chain with which circumstances strive to confine almost all individuals to one place, and one circle of associates—break it, and drift wildly at large—yet serving, in their wild airy way, to tie together by slender ligaments distant parts of the world, and places that have no other connection;—thinking this, Septimius did not want the connection to cease, without knowing more about her than now. It was partly humanity and compassion, and partly curiosity (which seldom stirred in him, but was now awake,) and aimless and inconsequent as the girl seemed, there was a certain magnetism, perhaps, in her action upon him. If he let her go, so uncertain seemed her mood, so incalculable her emotions, she might go no farther than the quiet brook which flowed across the cross-road, dividing Septimius's fertile field from that of a neighbor; and then she might be found in the shallow pool that it formed, drowned;—a death that forlorn maidens seem to affect, especially when the water has its summer warmth in it.

"Are you going far?" said he, putting out his hand to detain her; but she avoided it with a shudder.

"Far?—no! Home, to be sure," said the girl. "What strange questions you ask!"

"Your home is nigh, then," said Septimius.

"You may stand on the brow of the hill, if you like," answered she, "and see my house; but do not try to touch me again, please. Perhaps you may find me not a thing of flesh and blood."

"If so," remarked Septimius, "you may as well vanish into thin air, here, before my eyes. Otherwise, I give you fair warning, I shall follow you, be it far or near, till I see you in charge of your friends."

"You are perfectly welcome," said the girl pettishly, "only I fear you will have a long ramble, like a person who chases Puck, or a will-of the whisp. But you have no such things here. But I am of the same substance."

"Will you ever come back?" asked Septimius.

"Often!—always," said the girl, looking back and laughing. "I shall haunt that hill-top."

<(Perhaps he loses sight of her over the brow of the hill, and does not see where she goes)>

Septimius looked at her down the hill; and such an unsubstantial impression had she made upon him, that he almost expected to see her dissolve, and lose her out of sight, in some unaccountable way. However, no such marvel occurred, but, on the contrary, she went to the door of Robert Hagburn's respectable house, and entered it without knocking, as if she had the gift of making herself at home there, as well as elsewhere. Septimius remained behind, and walked to-and-fro, meditating on the adventure, on the sudden appearance of this phantom of the vacant space, and especially on her usurping his hill top, and preparing, in her caprice, to haunt his especial walk which he had worn—which the struggle and movement of his spirit had made, by the handwriting of his whole body, and where he had strewn thoughts so thickly, that surely a sensitive and impressible person, such as this seemed to be, would know them all, by treading it. He had a feeling that he was not alone any longer, but that a being was somehow, for an inscrutable purpose, and inscrutable means, connected with him. That is, if there had indeed been any such real person, talking with him, weeping and laughing so without cause, and behaving so fantastically; if she had not rather been the freak and illusion of an over-wrought mind, brooding so much on its own thoughts that it was getting unsound, and sought a natural relief in the wild sport of creating toys; or a sort of fungus from the buried secret, buried in his heart, of Francis Norton's death; an evidence of the need of communion with his kind, lacking which, his imagination created shapes, for the purpose of talking with them; a crazy offspring of a mind getting unhinged by wild speculations; a day-dream. He almost convinced himself of this, and was chiefly kept in doubt of it by the flowers that still seemed to have been plucked up from Francis Norton's grave, and to be withering in the sun beside it—or a dream of some girl in England who had been in love with Francis Norton, and now wandered hither in sleep.

The doubt, perhaps, indicated a secret consciousness of something unsound in his mental life, and a secret qualm as to his own sanity; at all events, so phantom-like was the impression that the girl had left behind her, that, though intensely desiring to know whether such a person had been seen in the neighborhood, he said nothing of his adventure either to Aunt Nashoba or Rose; determining to await further developments, and if, as she promised, the phantom came again, to apply such tests as his ingenuity should suggest to know her nature, her purposes, whence she came, and how long her home was to be here. However, at supper, Rose made a remark that threw so much light upon the matter that it quite lost its imaginative aspect.

"Have you heard of our new neighbor, Septimius?"

"No," said he. "Who is it?"

"It is a poor young lady," said Rose, "a daughter or connection of some English gentleman, not a combatant, now in Boston; and her health being very delicate, means have been used for her to come into the country, and Robert Hagburn, being to bring a message from the camp to some of the selectmen here, about some military matters, had it in charge to bring her, and his mother (needing somebody to bestow her care upon, now her son is gone) has taken her to board."

"Have you seen her?" asked Septimius.

"Yes," said Rose, "I met her on my way to school and found her a very pleasant little body, with sweet familiar ways. If she is brain-touched, poor thing, the only way she seemed to show it was by disregarding some stiff and formal ceremonies which impede people from coming together. She seemed to have known me before; at least, I should have thought so, for she spoke about my little school, and about you, who were walking on the hill-top at the time, and about Aunt Nashoba; but all this, I suppose she got out of good Mrs Hagburn, with whom she had already some hours' acquaintance."

"And that's enough for the silly old goose to have told all that was in her," grumbled Aunt Nashoba.

"What might she say of me?" asked Septimius.

Rose appeared a little confused, and declined to answer, but being pressed, she said that the girl had made some remarks about his strange solitary habits, his walks alone; adding, "But he is a crazy, and I am beside myself; so, there will be a great sympathy"; and then she had laughed, in a singular flighty way, as she was continually doing, without much reference to the matter in hand. "She talked something wildly about a flower—I could not understand it. And then she had talked about the name of Norton, and said that she had grown up in England near the residence of a grand old family of Nortons, at Poulton Hall, and knew ever so many stories about them; and she might have told me of some of them; but by this time, we had come to the door of my school-house, and there she bade me good bye. But she said, with a good deal of pathos (which kept coming in, in the strangest way) that she hoped I would take pity on her, a poor, crazed young woman, among strangers and enemies, with a weakness in her brain, and a rent in her heart—and then she burst into tears, and giggled in the midst of them. I was a good deal moved, as anybody must have been, and put out my lips to kiss her; but then she took a cold, forbidding look on her pale face, and I saw that I must never do that. So that, I suppose, was going to take too great a liberty; or else kissing between girls is not so common a thing in England as here. Yet such was her sweet free-spokenness and familiarity, that I had a feeling as if we had known each other a long while, and at the same time a perception that she was very strange."

"I wish she had not come here," said Septimius, bending down his heavy brow. "I fear I shall be a good deal interrupted in my meditations by her haunting the hill-top, as she threatens; and my thoughts and studies, methinks, are of a little too much importance to be put aside for the fantasies of a brain-sick girl."

"Fie, Septimius," said his sister Rose. "I don't believe 'twill be good to keep your thoughts so much apart from any other person's thought. Let the poor thing glide quietly along your path, though it be yours. Perhaps, when you get accustomed to her presence, it will help your thoughts. You must be careful, my dear brother, not to pull up your thought out of the broad soil of our common humanity, in which it ought to be rooted, and try to make it grow in a flower-pot. Cultivate your thought for yourself, but yet let it grow among common sympathies."

"You speak as wisely as a Sybil, Rose," said Septimius, smiling rather scornfully; "but knowing nothing about the matter in hand, your arrow hits I know not where. Nobody can do good to my thoughts—nobody could help me or—unless, indeed, it were some long-studied man, who could enlighten me as to the methods of cryptic writings, and other mysteries of language. Or does she know anything of chemical elements?"

"Probably not," said Rose; "but the poor thing has had an experience of some kind, as I think, has a kind of sybillic wisdom, and a sort of sacredness of sorrow. If she will let me be her friend, I gladly will be."

Thus it was that the strange maiden became connected with Septimius Norton's neighborhood, and with our story, gliding in, as it were, with a gentle, stealthy step, and though an odd kind of a creature, making sure of her place by a kind of inevitableness; so that there she was, among them, without anybody's well knowing how to resist it, even if he desired. And Septimius, whatever had been the apprehensions that he expressed to Rose, did not find the sort of annoyance from her that he had seemed to anticipate, but accustomed himself to meet her again and again, in his study on the hill-top, and in all kinds of moods, sometimes gliding by him like a shadow without a word, sometimes prattling lightly—sometimes giving out deep, sybillic utterances, which seemed to have no meaning at the time, but sometimes acquired one afterwards, when he had put them away in the obscurity of his own mind, where they showed their hidden light.

By dint of continual poring over the musty manuscript, Septimius began after a while to see some reasonable prospect of attaining to the interpretation of it, from beginning to end; except, indeed, where the ink had quite faded out, or the paper had apparently been burnt or corroded by its chemical effect, or, as the young man half-fancied, by the fervent and potent meaning of what had been there written, and of which earthly paper was not fit to be the recipient. As we have before said, moreover, the characters were not easy to resolve into letters, nor the letters into words, so uncouth and shapeless did they appear, resembling the undefined germs of thought as they exist in the mind, before clothing themselves in the appropriate terms which make them definite; and yet Septimius sometimes fancied himself sensible of a splendor in these undecyphered sentences, like that of the dim star dust in the remote sky, which a telescope of sufficient power would resolve into vast globes of light. He was not a little perplexed and surprised by the nature of the contents, so far as it had as yet dawned upon him. The document, or essay, as it might more properly be termed, proved to be written in a singular mixture of Latin, not of the purest style, and ancient English, with an occasional scrap of Greek, but rarely, and not with the spontaneous freedom of the Latin utterances. These last, indeed, whether quotations or original sentences, made a constant patchwork with the vernacular; as if the author found readier expression in that language for any idea in the least elevated or abstruse, than in the vernacular, which at that early period, having been little used by poets, or philosophers, had hardly begun to be the medium of communication except for the purposes of daily life. Invariably, too, when the author seemed on the verge of some utterance that would illuminate his whole subject, and make all its obscurities, the seeming absurdities that Septimius had hitherto puzzled out, blaze out into vivid meaning, and wreathe them together, from beginning to end, by a chain of light, its golden links all a-flame, there came in an interval of cryptic writing, a tract of dense, impenetrable darkness, on the other side of which appeared a disconnected radiance, which could not be brought into relation with what had gone before. Yet, so far as Septimius could judge, this secret cypher was intended not so much ultimately to conceal the mystic meaning from a genuine and persevering search, as to be the test of earnestness in the seeker, by locking up golden truths, and diamonds of intelligence in a sort of coffer, of which diligence, natural insight, and practical sense, should be the keys, and the keen intelligence, with which the meaning should be sought, should be the test of the seeker's title to possess the inestimable treasure.

<(He finds a method prescribed for cultivating a bit of ground, so as to produce a flower)>

Leaving, for the present, the cryptic passages apart and unattempted, the young student applied himself to the mixture of Latin and English, which we have already spoken of, and wrote out fair in the stiff and formal chirography of his own day, as much as he found it possible to decypher. The result, he was fain to confess to himself, was not in the least what he had expected, while holding the yellow, blood-stained,

bullet-perforated manuscript in his hand, and musing on the
mystic truths which he imagined it to comprise; nor, had he
been in a natural state of mind, could he have thought that
those things, however true many of them were, were either so
novel or so momentous, that the passage of them from one
possessor to another need have required so much machinery,
or have been accompanied by the precious sacrifice of a human life. But Septimius's mind, we readily say, was not in a
healthy state. His sombre imagination, excited by the late
singular incidents, brooded over all his daily life, and made
false things and true look alike in its shadow. Then the great
war, in which the whole country was so desperately engaged,
had an influence on poor Septimius, modified by the morbidness and extravagance of his character; for he, like all others,
drank of the prevalent passion and excitement, drained the
cup that was offered to everybody's lips, but was intoxicated
in his own peculiar mode. He walked so much the more wildly
on his own course, because the people were rushing enthusiastically on another. In times of Revolution, or whatever public disturbance, even the calmest person is, to some degree, in
an exaggerated and unnatural state, most probably without
suspecting it; there is enthusiasm, there is madness in the
atmosphere. The decorous rule of common life is suspended;
absurdities come in, and stalk unnoticed. Madmen walk
abroad unrecognized. Heroic virtue marches among us, with
majestic step; vices, too, and great crimes, creep darkly, or
stalk abroad. Woman, likewise, catches the wild influence, and
sometimes, flinging aside her fireside virtues as of little worth,
is capable of crimes that man shudders at, of virtues and valor
that he can never imitate, of deeds and thoughts that she
would, a little time ago, have died to anticipate; the disen-
franchised soul exults at losing its standpoint; old laws are
annulled; anything may come to pass; miracles are on the

same ground as the commonest occurrence. So, in respect to Septimius, his common sense, of which he had no small portion, had no such fair play with his wilder characteristics as it might have in quiet and ordinary times; when besides, there were the throes attending the birth of a new epoch in the world; and among seething opinions and systems, and overturned and deposed principles, Septimius had nothing fixed and recognized with which to compare his own pursuit, and recognize its absurdity. Thus must we say, that this young wild thinker may not look too ridiculous in the errors to which a solitary pursuit led him.

So he continued to brood over his musty manuscript, to hide it under lock and key as if it were a murder secret, and to pick out, from its heap of moss-grown ideas, such nuggets of what he fancied to be gold, as he could contrive to shape into an aspect of definite meaning. We have in our possession a few portions of it, as transcribed by Septimius, and mean to present them to the reader, whom, doubtless, after all that we have said about the manuscript, they will surprise as much as they did Septimius; though we can hardly hope that they will be received, as by him, as golden nuggets from a mine of thought, further digging into which would reveal inestimable treasures. He gathered them from various portions of the document, writing them down as he succeeded in puzzling them out; and being thus brought together, they took the aspect of certain rules of life, precipitated from the rich solution of the essay, and crystallized into diamonds; and, whereas, many of these rules had but a mean aspect in themselves, and seemed to concern low matters of dietetic, Septimius took it for granted that this more obvious meaning was of comparatively no importance, and that they doubtless had a symbolic value, which he should by and by discover, and also what tendency and force they had towards his great object of earthly immortality. These were but golden beads, strung on something more valuable than themselves; and what that precious string might be, the discovery of the cypher would reveal. "Precious Maxims from an Unknown Intelligence."

Bask daily for a convenient time in whatsoever sunshine thou shalt find, and lay in it the garment which thou art about to put on; for this kind of light and warmth has more virtues than are seen. In dark, wintry days, worship fire, but with the lattice of thy chamber ajar, lest thou shut up an evil demon along with thee, and he steal away the centuries of thy life.

Hate not any man nor woman. Be not angry with mankind nor brute kind, thy neighbor, thy servant, or thy horse or thy dog; save it be that thy blood seem at any time some whit cold and torpid, and thou require anger as a medicament, a little dose thereof not to be exceeded. Cast out from thy heart all passions that seek to rankle there; for such are a poison, and, moreover, work in deadly fashion against thy purpose. If, in thy waking moments, or in thy dreams, there be fancies, thoughts, or visions of enmity and contention with any man whatsoever, strive quietly with thyself, first of all, to forget him.

If thy enemy may not be thus put aside, and yet nevertheless the sacredness of thy repose be utterly set at naught by him, take due counsel with thyself what is right and reasonable to be done; bethinking thee in whatsoever case that it is better there should live one man for the advancement of peace, than two men at strife, that thine own sore trouble is thy nearest concern, and &c. The matter being ended to thy liking, sweep the remembrance thereof from mind and heart, enjoying the rest thou hast earned.

Keep thy heart at some five and seventy throbs in the minute; else will thy life wear away more speedily than thy art can supply the waste. Think not over much of high matters; it will make thy respiration deep and irregular.

Drink not wine nor strong drink, nor obfuscate thyself with ale; taking heed, that this rule is worthy in itself, and worthiest taken symbolically.

Kiss no wench, if her lips be red and full; look not upon her, if she be very fair; touch not her hand against thine, if thou perceive thy finger-tips to thrill with hers. If thou love her, all is over, and thy whole past labor and pains have been in vain. Wherefore, on this whole matter, flee from woman, and better cast stones at her from a distance, than salute her close at hand. She shortened Adam's days, and will shorten thine.

Have no friendship nor intercourse with a melancholy man, a passionate man, a great lover of his country, a madly benevolent man, a misanthrope, or any man whatsoever who has lost his balance, and, according to the degree of his influence, will tend to throw thee from thine. For, in this world, we are as those who dance upon a rope, and find a feather casts us on one side or the other. This rule is only for the first stages in thy progress; for, passing onward, thou wilt forget that so slight a thing as friendship ever was a toy for thee.

Walk at a steady pace, and count thy paces per diem. Nevertheless run and leap, and frisk as joyously as a young kid, but always of set purpose, and keep thy bodily life from stagnating in a pool.

Interweave some decent and moderate degree of human kindness and benevolent acts in thy daily life; for the result, there is reason to believe, will be a slightly pleasurable titillation of thine own heart, and thy nature will be wholesomely warmed and delectated with felicitous self-laudation; and most beneficial is an admixture of such; but all that concentrates thy thoughts cheerfully upon thyself tends to invigorate that central principle, by the growth and nourishment whereof thou art to attain indefinite life. Do not, without special need, any act that human prejudices set down as evil, because such evil acts, so called, are apt to have a corrosive quality, and are unwholesome. Neither do any act extravagantly good, because one such act might be the seed of others like it, and so cover the whole field of thy life with a waste harvest.

From sick people, maimed wretches, from madmen, from persons in heavy affliction or extravagant joy, (both being a disease, and of the same class) from teething and sickly children, turn away thine eyes and thine ears, especially if there be reason to think that thou canst do aught for their easement; for wherein thou dost them good, there is much reason to fear that by just so much thou dost thyself harm. Come not near a corpse; for in the neighborhood of death, life oozes insensibly through the pores of thy skin. But, at convenient times, taking wholesome infants into thine arms as if to kiss and embrace (thereby gaining their foolish mothers' good will,) drink in their breath, which is special good to renew thy flagging life. Howbeit, beget not children for such purpose; it is buying the drug at too costly a rate. Likewise, take a morning draught of the breath of buxom maidens, so it can be done without unsuitable commotion, and solely as a medicinal drug; also, if the above drug be not convenient, the breath of cows, as they return from rich pasture, is very good, and pleasant to take.

Eat no spiced meat.

Practise thyself in a certain continual smile; for the outward aspect of benignity shall tend to compose thy entire frame of being, and keep thee from much wear.

Search not thy head or thy beard to see if there be gray hairs lurking among the brown ones; scrutinize not thy forehead in quest of wrinkles, nor the corners of thine eyes for crowsfeet. Such marks of time, being overlooked, are the more likely to disappear; being gazed at and made much of, they take heart and increase.

Desire nothing too fervently, not even life itself; yet keep thy gripe upon the possession of life mightily, quietly, unshakeably; for so long as thou art really in the mind to live, Death nor all his force shall have power against thee. Men die, finally, because they choose not the toil and torment of struggling longer with Time, for mere handsfull of moments. But, to thee, under wise guidance, the struggle shall be as of a strong man with a child.

Walk not beneath old tottering walls nor stand underneath a great stone, as the builders crane it aloft, nor approach a precipice's edge, nor voyage at sea, nor confront the lightning, nor cross a swollen river, nor ride an ill-broken steed, nor offer thy bosom to the stroke of sword, the stab of dagger, nor the shot of arrow, nor thy head to be beaten by a bludgeon; for these things are apt to be deadly, and are hateful and horrible, as making all good rules of no effect. By them, the wise man may die even as the fool dieth.

Say thy prayers at bedtime, so thou deemest thereby to gain the quieter sleep. Yet forget them, or devize them, at thy convenience; they are superfluous, because thy whole life is a prayer in deed and in thought for life, and still more life.

Change thy shirt daily, or hourly, if need be; thereby thou flingest off yesterday's decay, and imbibest the freshness of the morning's life, which, moreover, thou shalt assist with smelling to roses, and all manner of fragrant flowers, with the dew yet on them. To no other end were flowers created, than, with their sweet breath, to eke out man's life a little longer.

Such were some of the golden rules which Septimius gathered from the old manuscript. He meditated long upon them, making each the theme of as much interpretation, enlargement, symbolical reading, and practical development, as his acquaintance with the world of thought or action enabled. It must not be supposed that the moral tone of the precepts altogether satisfied him, or that he failed to be shocked by the intense and utter selfishness from which they must have emanated, and which made it the whole purpose of life to prolong itself, instead of desiring earthly life to be immortal for the sake of making it divine with benevolence, good works, sweetness, righteousness, the sweet savor of which might be enough of themselves, to keep off the ugliness of death. The young man had made such the conditions, in all his aspirations of his living long;—the attainment of wisdom, and the use of it for benign, majestic, unselfish purposes; and he deemed, too, that these would come inevitably from the removal of the miserable fear and low and grovelling necessity of death, and the consciousness of possessing a longer tenure in the world—knowing which, we should endeavor to improve it, morally and materially, just as a tenant with a long lease seeks to improve his land, while a tenant at will, or for a brief period, looks only to get the most he can out of it at once. He saw, however, or thought he saw that the good of these precepts might be separated from the evil, without depriving them of their real efficacy, and that, whereas they counselled a selfish withdrawal from all sympathy with poor suffering mankind, a making use of men without contributing to their good, the real meaning was, to keep one's self in an awful and holy reserve from the passion of life, its violent struggle, its dust, its heat, as the angels do, who live long, and do good, and probably are stronger and livelier with all the good they do. When once he had gained the rare secret, which was as yet concealed in the cryptic writing, this should be his course. As for the rules, he deemed them to have been the production of some man of cold intelligence, and worldly

experience, and self-concentrated heart, who had perhaps succeeded in finding the secret, but using it in a wrong spirit, had
had the heart die out of him in the course of his long life,
wasting its forces drop by drop, till doubtless he had thus lost
all human moistures, and so escaping death in one direction,
had finally fallen upon extinction in another.

<(Insert, at the end of this chapter, how Septimius
gathered the autumnal acorns and planted them, thinking how
he would live to see them in perfection and decay &c)>

So absorbed as Septimius was in delving into the inscrutable
manuscript, and in various studies into which it led him,
the summer and the autumn passed over, and the New England winter came sternly down out of the farthest North;
bending down the pitch-pines on the hill with the weight of
snow that it laid upon them, so that they bent, as if doing
reverence, and sometimes kept their reverent attitude long
after the snow had melted away. A drift was heaped over
Francis Norton's grave, almost as high as the cairn of a slain
warrior; Nature not thinking it fit, apparently, that he should
sleep there without some kind of distinction of the spot from
ordinary soil; so she heaped it up with all this mass of her
frozen tears, and Septimius could not but look with a kind of
jealousy upon the spot, as thinking it strange it should be
thus shown by the very snow that ought to have hidden it.
Still, however, he continued to walk there daily, breasting
the storm that blew its cold stinging particles into his face,
treading out his path anew, following the old track as nearly
as might be, but made to swerve aside, because the boughs,
heavily weighted with ice and snow, here hung so low that
he could not pass beneath them, and here was the drifted
heap; but to-and fro he still passed, and where there had been
foliage of green, there was now white, or perhaps silvered

stems. And hither, too, came Sybil Dacy, haunting the spot, and haunting him, with a strange peculiarity, the causes of which however, he soon ceased to inquire into, setting it down as due to the partial insanity which was thought to afflict her. Nor, in truth, was Septimius disturbed by the girl, as he would undoubtedly have been by another person, had he been liable to the same interruption of his private walks and thoughts, as by her; whether it were because he deemed that in her the keen, curious, investigating, criticizing intellect was wanting, or because, the sphere of thought in which he was himself wandering being so wild, he felt a pleasure that this half-crazed girl had the privilege of meeting him there, as one of the denizens of the realm which he invaded. And so a kind of strange familiarity, even intimacy, grew up between them; they discoursed of many things, sometimes earnestly; sometimes the girl gave the tone to a mood of wild, fantastic merriment, which Septimius joined in with the more zest because it was such a relief from the stern, heavy, pressure of his solitary meditation, so long wearing into his brain, and wild were the colloquies thus held between the pair. Then again, the girl had fits of deep, sombre, unexplorable sadness, in which Septimius could elicit no word from her, no response to any question, in which she seemed separated from him and all other living beings by a medium of darkness and coldness, by death, as it were, and as if she had been a creature of another kind. And, again, there was a mood in which Septimius had an instinct as if there were something dangerous and deadly in this poor girl, something malevolent; he had caught her eye upon him like that of a malignant thing, and, little noticing it at the time, had thought of it again and again, wondering what it might be—whether there might not be moments and phases, of her mental disease, when she would be capable of coming behind him with a deadly weapon, and stabbing him, and then exulting with that wild laugh which, in her merry moods, had sometimes made the woods echo with questionable mirth. Yet, it seemed to Septimius, that this latter state of mind was not so frequent as when the girl first came; and when it did occur, it was often followed by tears, and long depression, low sobs, moans, as of a child wanting its mother for some unspeakable grief. This was different from the stern mood of gloom, already mentioned. All the moods, and their rapid change and succession, the cloud, the tempest, the gleams of sunshine, were to be accounted for by a shattered state of nerves, perhaps born with her, perhaps aroused by the cause assigned when Sybil first appeared in our story (the death of a person dear to her,) or by some sorrow of the heart, which women are so apt to lay up for themselves betimes. Such as she was, Septimius tolerated her, pitied her, but scarcely wondered at her, or speculated about her, nor among the interminable unaccountable things and circumstances of life, thought it worth while to insist upon accounting for this poor girl.

His sister Rose had been from the first attracted towards this girl, had tried to sympathize with her, and to make her life tolerable, if not pleasant, in a strange country; lonely, among enemies, if she chose so to consider those whose countrymen had slain one dear to her; and Sybil accepted Rose as a friend, without an intermixture of those vagaries, and gusts of morbid feeling, which agitated her intercourse with Septimius. The quietude and womanly reasonableness, as well as the natural refinements of Rose's character seemed to produce a corresponding effect on her; though still a fanciful creature, she was a reasonable one under Rose's eye, and gave evidence of qualities of mind and heart which made it the more sad that anything should have occurred to give them that slight mind's adjustment, that swerve aside from the true balance, that makes eccentricity, or, in greater degree, insanity. Even to Rose, however, she still preserved a degree of mystery, while seeming to talk much; although she told, that, at present, she was under the guardianship of an elderly man of science, Doctor Jabez Portsoaken, her nearest relative, an English physician of great skill, who had come to Boston shortly before the breaking out of the war, meaning to make his residence in Boston, and though not connected with the army, was inevitably shut up there, and, though of peaceful purposes, towards the Americans, so far shared the predicament of their enemies. This was all that Sybil told of herself; but it, from time to time, appeared, in the course of communication with her, that she had received a good, though desultory education, <she knows music> was well read in poetry, and spoke more than one continental language with an idiomatic freedom as if she had learned them where they were vernacular; and it often happened that she brought up little reminiscences of sunnier climes than England. On the whole, a malign observation might have seen something that was questionable; but the simpler life of New England, at that period, was not of a nature to lead the people to imagine evil in this poor, lonely child; and even the gossips of the village, though they babbled much about Sybil Dacy, surmised little harm of her, and Aunt Nashoba kept a grim smile for Sybil.

(Sometimes Septimius came out of his den when he heard her wild musical laughter, sounding in the house, and sat down by the fire with them.)

She seemed naturally a sociable creature, as well as a solitary one. When sufficiently familiar with Rose, she used to come of a winter evening, and sit down by the fireside, where Rose sat at her work, and Aunt Nashoba smoking her pipe in the deep chimney-corner; for this latter personage lacked some of those feminine and civilized instincts that impel women to keep the hands always busy with knitting, darning, sewing, and, with ineluctable necessity, make the higher classes embroider; but Aunt Nashoba was one of the few women in whom a native indolence indulged itself, whenever she sat down; though she busied herself about the house, like a restless and relentless fate, during the day. Sybil, likewise, manifested the same tendency; being an impressible creature, and growing fond of Rose, she tried to imitate her pursuits, and began a course of study of Latin under her, but never got through the first declension of nouns. She likewise tried needlework, and knitting, but with as little success, and holding out her litttle hand, said that there was nothing in the world that her fingers were ever fit for, except to play on the keys of a harpsichord.

"Do you call this a hand?" quoth Aunt Nashoba, taking it in her own brown claw—"what a wee little thing it is. You need a dose of my medicine, child, to put some warmth of life into you. This will make you live forever, if I could only find one other herb."

So saying, she pointed to a large earthen jug, which stood among the ashes, shoved up close to the embers, covered with the lid of a black tea-pot; beneath which it kept sputtering and snorting, and sending out puffs of vapor, as it slowly half-boiled and steamed, as it was generally doing from morning till night, sending its little incense up the chimney. Aunt Nashoba had a grim kindness and fervor for this strange girl, it was difficult to say why; except that she was as wayward as a breeze, and, like Aunt Nashoba herself, was somehow ajar with the world.

"No, no, Aunt Nashoba," said Sybil; "I must take no drugs save what my guardian Doctor Portsoaken gives me. He is a wizard, almost, such as you have had in your family, and knows the virtues of all herbs. He knows a drug that will make one live forever, if any Doctor knows it; and perhaps he can tell you what is wanting."

"I should like to talk with him about it," said Aunt Nashoba, drawing in a long whiff of tobacco and letting it come out of her nose (and some people said she could also send it from her ears; so that she appeared like a portent, smouldering within, and letting out the smoke from all possible vents). "What sort of a guardian is he, I wonder, to send you into a strange place, and never inquire whether you live or die."

"You will see him one of these days," said the girl, subsiding out of her cheerful mood into a silent fit.

<(In her first mention of Dr. Portsoaken, his characteristics must be mentioned in a wild, fantastic, mirthful way; so as to give the idea of a strange being.)>

"I shall be glad to talk with him," said Septimius. "I am in a perplexity for just such a man."

"I suppose," observed Rose, sensibly, "that Doctor Portsoaken is not to blame for not visiting his dear little Sybil, since he is closely cooped up in Boston, and could not probably obtain permission to ramble about our country, even for so important a purpose. But, in that case, we may soon look for him; for Robert writes that the enemy cannot hold the town a great while longer, and must either take to their fleet, or the fleet be sunk."

<(Like one removed to another land, or another state of being, who asks news of his old acquaintance)>

"Then you have news of Robert?" said Septimius, who, buried in his own pursuits and aspirations, did not keep up with the passage of events, and was only conscious of a rumor of war, coming as it were, through the thick walls, and narrow, latticed windows of a cell; who had broken off his connection with mankind by a strange pursuit, and heard news of them only at intervals, as of what intimately concerned him not; like a person in a strange land, who looks askance at the earnestness, the fears, the enthusiasm, the patriotism, of those deeply stirred, and feels it all to be an unnatural state. "How has he been doing, these months past? He has shown himself a brave man, doubtless?"

"So those who should know say of him," answered Rose, with restrained pride.

"Robert Hagburn must be brave," said Septimius, speaking like one who gives praise, which he does not think greatly valuable. "It strikes me that he was made especially for the life he has chosen; and to say the truth, if life is to be at all events brief, I don't see that there can be a better use made of it than to fight."

"For one's country—yes," said Rose trembling, however, at the heroic sentiment that came into her mind to be expressed; "and then the briefest life is well spent, and rewarded by Death so encountered."

"Ah, Death!" said Septimius gloomily; "it is an ugly obstacle in the way of these soldiers, and of all other people, in the present condition of our race. The Grave! What a vile pitfall it sets right athwart our pathway, and engulphing all of us, sooner or later, and oftenest, just as we are about to do something worth coming into the world for. It is as if two powerful Divinities had the control of us miserable mortals—one giving us opportunities of accomplishing great deeds; the other, with a touch of his fore finger, turning us into heaps of insensible dust, before we can do anything;—so that all existence is a mockery, merely because it is so wretchedly brief. Life, which seems such a priceless blessing, is made a jest, emptiness, delusion, a flout, a farce, by this inopportune Death, who never waits a moment for us to accomplish the work of a thousand years. If we have the salvation of a country, of the whole race, in hand, methinks we are all the likelier to die then. So that, being a strenuous believer in the wisdom, graciousness, and good faith of Providence, I am convinced that Death is a weakness, the grave a wretched mistake which by and by we shall overcome, a liability into which we have lapsed by deterioration, and that we shall finally rise above it."

"Then do not tremble at it so dreadfully," said Rose, "but rise up and go further."

They all looked at Septimius, perhaps wondering at the earnestness and passion with which he objected to a circumstance of our existence, generally considered as essential to permit a hope of evading it.

"Your great, great, great grandfather made nothing of it," quoth Aunt Nashoba, knocking the ashes out of her pipe, "but filled his pipe afresh, and went on again; and some think he's alive yet."

"Poor lad!" said Sybil Dacy—"he abuses his best friend, the best friend of all of us; and, for one, I will say a word in defense of this poor slandered skeleton death, this meagre atomy, this ill-fed fellow. As to other blessings, that they say are given to mortals here below, I have reason to doubt, for none of them can fall to my share; but I can see the kindness of a heavenly Father when he made Life so uncertain, and threw Death in among the continual probabilities of our being, and surrounded him with those awful mysteries, into which we vanish. Without them, we should plod along in common-places forever, never dreaming of high things, never risking anything, never drawing a deep breath, never conscious of a soul. But, now, for my part, I deem that mortal man, and mortal woman too, are more favored than the angels of Heaven, and capable of higher heroism, greater virtue, deeds of a more excellent kind than they, because we have such a cloud of grief and terror, interposed by thy

shadowy Death, between us and the things we strive to do;
and the very best wreath can only be snatched out of Death's
hands; whereas the angels live in the certainty, the utter
blessedness of God's light, and see his good purposes too
perfectly to doubt them, and therefore cannot be such heroes
as poor weak man, and weaker woman, have sometimes been.
And not acting it, being it, suffering it, they cannot realize it.
God gave the whole world to man, but were he left alone
with such a great, perilous plaything, it would make a beast
of him at last; but to remedy this danger, God gave him the
final gift of Death, and it redeems all, while it seems to
destroy all and bury all. You put a dead into the grave, and
behold a spirit comes from it, as I have seen Doctor Portsoaken put lead into a crucible, and pour out gold."

"Dear Sybil, you have spoken heavenly breath!" said Rose,
with tears in her eyes, for the girl's tones were full of a sentiment that seemed loftier than her words.

"Poh. I was in jest," said Sybil, changing her manner in a
moment, so that she seemed another creature, laughing like
a sprite, and throwing a mocking eye round the circle. "Do
you think I believe this nonsense?"

"Come here, child, and let me feel if you are flesh and
blood," quoth Aunt Nashoba, protruding her brown claw.
"You tell us of old English fields, but I think you are an imp
that people used to be haunted by in the woods."

Sybil tapped with her finger on the bowl of Aunt Nashoba's pipe, knocking the live coal out. "You see I am flesh
and blood;" said she. "A sprite could not do that."

"I don't know," muttered the old woman, "there was an
imp they say used to bring a live coal from parts unknown
to light my great-great Aunt's <imp used to light her> pipe.
As easy shake it out as put it in."

"Well; sprite or no," continued Sybil, "I know but one pleasant use of a grave; and that is, to raise flowers upon it. I can tell you a story, to that purpose. It is a legend connected with an old English Hall, which I used to be well acquainted with in my childhood; would you like to hear it, all of you?"

Rose assented eagerly, and Aunt Nashoba granted her acquiescence.

"I, too, shall like to hear the legend," said Septimius, "if it is a genuine one that has come down in chimney corners from time immemorial, and has got imbued with the smoke and incrusted with the soot that gathers there, and so, by passing from one homely mind to another, has gained a truth that it did not begin with. No single man can make a fireside legend; it takes a century, at least, of successive narrators to make it, and it is only good when its originator is long dead buried."

"So then," said Sybil, "it grows out of a grave like the very flower I am going to tell you about; and it shows another of the uses of Death, for, as you confess, stories would never get moss-grown as long as the lips that first spoke them were alive. This old tale has been told by grandams in the chimney corner more than a century, or two centuries, and, for my part, I uphold it to be gospel truth."

The Bloody Footstep

At Smithills Hall, on the stone-threshold of a door by which you emerge into the shrubbery, at the rear of the house, there is an appearance known far and wide as the Bloody Footstep, being a mark, or stain upon the door-step, as if a foot had trodden there, and slipt in blood. I have seen it, a hundred times, with my own eyes, and know that much of my story to be true. What I never saw, and should be afraid to make experiment of, is the marvel they tell of this bloody footprint on a certain night of the year, and hour of the night, and minute of the hour, when, if you go and look at the door-step, you will see the stain gleaming with fresh blood. Some have protested that this moisture was but the dew, that might be seen any night of the year, or the rain that drizzles night and day, in England, from one year's end to another. But will the innocent dew stain a cambric handkerchief?—or the rain from heaven crimson your finger-tips?—yet that is what will happen, as my grandmother used to tell me, if you try to wipe up the Bloody Footstep, on that fated night of the year. For three hundred years, the successive inhabitants of Smithills Hall have sought to wipe out this stain and still, as they step forth into their rich domain, they see it as fresh as ever.

Smithills Hall is one of the oldest houses in England. It is not of stone, like other English houses, but a timber framework, filled in with brick and plaster. If you go up into one of the gables, you can see the ancient framework of the house; it is of oak, and the center wall beams and rafters are awfully ponderous, insomuch that it is a wonder how their own weight has not crushed them; for architects say that it is above a thousand years since this ponderous old skeleton was put together, and that the wood, stalwart and solid as it looks, has not really its strength, and would snap short off if any additional weight were put upon it. It is impossible to ascertain the exact date of the original foundation of the house; but it was an old house, five or six centuries ago, and was then extensively repaired and restored, and the newness of that latter day now seems as venerable as what then was in decay. The house formerly stood around all the four sides of a quadrangle, enclosing a court-yard, into which there was an entrance through an archway; but the front side has been removed, or fallen of itself, and now there are but three sides left, looking more ancient and venerable than anything that you can conceive, with their ranges of ivy grown gables, and lesser peaks. On one side, is a chapel, where the proud old family used to have their own priest, and their own worship, from time immemorial; on the opposite side of the quadrangle, are state apartments, panelled with magnificent old oak, highly polished, carved in quaint devices, imitations of foliage, intricate puzzles of intersecting lines, sacred devices of Catholic times, anagrams of family names, portrait figures, all relics of a skill that the world has lost forever; a kind of magnificence that never will be equalled, because its richness is sombre, stately, and has a glow in it, being intended to last from age to age; whereas, in our times, to day is ashamed of the magnificence of yesterday. In the central side of the quadrangle, you pass into the entrance-hall, a large, low room furnished in a Gothic style, and hung round with old armor, and ornamented with a stuffed fox, that looks like life, and the great antlers of a deer, and other things that intimate that the business of the inhabitants has been hunting and fighting; and in a great old chimney-place, there burns a coal-fire, summer and winter alike, giving a bright and hospitable smile to all that enter, and beholding it, the dreariness that so old a house would cast upon a new-comer, the chill that he would feel in coming into this haunt of people where coffins have been borne out of that same door, in long, long succession, is quite closed away; and you feel as if it might be still possible for the heir of the old house to bring a young bride here, and lead a happy life among the musty remnants of former christian lives. But when you wander through the old house, and hear the ghost-stories that there are, in the dismal chambers—one called the Dead Man's Chamber—and think how many graves there are, whose tenants have a right to haunt this place, methinks it would be pleasanter to live in the frailest hut that ever was built on the hill side, or to burrow into the earthen bank, like the swallows, as Aunt Nashoba's great-grandfather did, than to live in the musty old Smithills Hall. <Ghosts glimmering along the galleries, drawing the curtains of the beds (Heap up all sorts of ghastly images)>

Such was the old house, which bore, on one of its thresholds, the mark of the Bloody Footstep; and whatever was the interpretation put upon the sign, nobody could doubt that it was a memorial of some most dismal crime that had been perpetrated within these aged walls, and still, as it was thought, unexpiated; else, surely, the murderous stain would have faded away, or been washed out by penitential tears, wherever shed; but remaining still as deep and red as rose, it could not but strike any thoughtful observer with the conviction, that, from century to century, his blood, refusing to sink into the ground, was crying out for vengeance. There is, to say the truth, more than one legend pretending to explain how the stain came, and why it can never be washed away, several stories, assigning different dates, and different circumstances; but the one which I am about to tell, seems to me as probable as any, especially as regards the persistency of the stain.

There lived (I know not how long ago, but it must have been in what they call the Dark Ages, or just when the first daylight was beginning to glimmer in among them) a certain Baron, then the lord of Smithills Hall, who tried to enlighten his own mind, and perhaps the minds of his contemporaries, with scientific knowledge. Some say that he was a contemporary of Friar Bacon, and a partner in his studies, and that, if the truth were known, the greater part of the wonderful things that are attributed to the monk were really achieved by the nobleman, who, deeming such credit beneath his rank, allowed Friar Bacon to reap the whole fame; the more especially as a reputation of that kind was not wholly un-attended with danger, when a man of science was reckoned a wizard, and perhaps consigned to as hot a fire as that into which he put his crucibles. The Baron did not succeed so far in hiding his wisdom, as to escape this imputation, and to this day he is remembered in tradition, and, I believe, recorded in the pedigree of the family, and even put down by Heralds, as the Wizard Lord; and if it be wizard lore, to be acquainted with some of the secret powers of Nature, which are innumerable, compared with what few we know—to be acquainted with these, and thereby perform what to the vulgar might seem miraculous things—then, unquestionably, the Baron was a sorcerer. In those days, a man might thus perform feats that seemed to the people as wonderful, as now a days to raise the dead. One feat the Baron is believed to have attempted, which, certainly, if mortal man can con-trive or win the power to achieve it, then he may surely be said to have conquered Nature with her own weapons. The thing was thus; he had not proceeded far in his studies, when he took a view of the whole field of science, estimated all the millions of things that it seemed possible to know and do, if a man had only time, and came to the conclusion, that either, when a lifetime of seventy years at most afforded time to know only a few inconsequental fragments of things, it was not worth while to try to know anything; so that, if knowledge were worth having, then the first thing to be sought was to lengthen out interminably the life of the stu-dent, that he might reach some worthy end of knowledge. With this idea, and feeling such courage, such potency of mind, such rightful heirdom over all creation that everything seemed possible, then in the enlivening dawn of knowledge, he set himself to find out the way to be, if not immortal, yet of age-long endurance; meaning, too, (for he was a man of loving and noble nature) to employ all the years he should thus gain, in contriving new and never known benefits for his race, so that his wisdom should bear fruit for all, and his long life should be brightened not with his own happiness, but one reflected from millions of happy firesides.

"I must do this," said he to himself, "first of all, and will study only to that end; for if I fail in it, then I see that this dream of knowledge is only a delusion which a fiend hangs out before me, and before all men that have a noble thirst to know things, as I have. For without it, the pursuit of knowledge means an endless series of beginnings, cut off untimely by that grinning Death, whom I hate, because he will let nothing really be accomplished, and laughs, with his fleshless chops, at all heroic purposes and stunts, ends all things with a sweep of his scythe. I will lay a fall with the ugly skeleton; and laugh he that wins!"

<(The study of the recipe leads him to apply himself to all sorts of cognate subjects)>

With this resolution (and on such grounds, surely, it was no ignoble one) he devoted himself for many years to the study of science, searching into the mysteries of life and death, and tracking a path for himself into the dim wilderness of things to be known, and gathering whatever he deemed suited to his purpose; until, at length, when he was wrinkled and worn, and old moreover with the sternness of resolve to be forever young, he found out the spell by which Death was to be kept at bay. He would wrest from reluctant Nature the means counteracting her own decree; which assigns to all a little life of ceaseless effort, failure, and then a sleep, as children sleep, by way of forgetting all their little troubles and disappointments; he would gain for himself a loftier destiny than this but on dreadful and horrible terms.

So fearful, it seems, was the condition, that this wise and upright man (for upright he was, unless zeal to be more than mortal had depraved him) at first resolved to die like the meanest man ever born, like the dog that licked his hand and loved him, and that was as worthy of immortality by his faithful affection as he himself could ever be by his potent intellect. The whole case may be put into a very few words. It was the object, you understand, of the lord of Smithills Hall to wrest from the control of Nature his own life, and as Nature (who is gentle with her children, in some respects, but still will have her way) did not choose to be utterly defrauded, it was necessary to pay with another life for his own, since he would not let Nature have his body, to turn to grass and flowers, which she holds it her right to do. According to some accounts, this sacrifice was to be repeated once for every thirty years that he might think fit to live; thirty years being the accounted term of a generation of men, and therefore to be bought with a new life; and if, in any way, once in thirty years, the possessor of the secret should cause the death of a fellow creature, that death would satisfy the condition, and he might live on. But other, and methinks more reasonable versions of the legend, speak only of one sacrifice as being required, after which the worker of the spell might live interminably, unless slain by violence. Even in this last mentioned version, there are one or two discrepancies; for an old woman, whom I remember dwelling by the front gate at Smithills hall, insisted upon it that some drops of the heart's blood of a pure young boy or girl (a drop for each year that he chose to live) was to be mingled with a certain potent drink that the Baron had taught himself how to brew from potent herbs. But this seems to me too horribly repugnant an idea—Death was better than such a beverage—and I think the fiction must have been framed symbolically, purporting that the person who seeks to engross to himself more of life, its advantages, comforts, pleasures, than rightfully belong to an individual, can only do so by depriving some other human being, with the same rights as himself, of his due share, and so, in fine, immolating that victim to his selfishness.

Now, the Baron, as I have already said, was a man naturally upright, and tender and pitiful towards all mankind; and if he had gone astray, and was impious in his desires and purposes, it was greatly by reason of his earnest wish to confer some effectual benefit on the poor, wicked, bloody, nasty, hungry, contemptible race, to which, nobleman as he was, it was his misfortune to belong. He was weighed down with all their misery, humbled with all their shame, defiled with all their sin, and persuaded himself that he desired long life, only for the sake of studying out some way to make it a better world. He bethought himself moreover (being of such equity in his way of thinking) whether he could have the right to take the life of one of his fellow creatures, for the sake of prolonging his own, without the victim's free consent; and, after a year's deep consideration of this one point, he came finally to the conclusion that it were a deadly wrong, unless it should be a life freely flung down for his sake, and one at least as dear to him as his own. The poor Baron looked all around him; he was a lonely and abstracted man, secluded by the nature and intensity of his studies from the usual interchange of human affections; he looked on every side for some beloved victim, but, for a long while, averting his glance with instinctive cunning, he forbore to cast his eyes at an object that was close beside his knee. This was a beautiful young kinswoman, an orphan child, of whom, when a baby, he, still a youth, had become the active guardian, as being the head of that old family. All along, there had been great kindness between the budding child, the blossoming maid, and this earnest, abstracted, lofty-purposed scholar, as great kindness, on his part, as the thoughtful depth of his inward life left him the power to bestow, and, on hers, a rich, abundant affection, that twined around him, and everything into which he put his life, like a luxuriant vine clinging with its tendrils to the broad chair in which he sate, to the table on which he wrote, or spread the folio volumes, spreading its green lines, as it were, on the musty page, and filling all the old Gothic chamber with the fragrance of its bloom; so that perhaps he already lived upon her bloom and freshness, and knew it not. On neither side, however, was there that flower, of the which the perfume is rapture and the expressed juice a deadly poison, the flower of Love; or if it existed, whatever the beautiful girl might have done, the Baron, at least, had never owned it to himself. But looking into his heart (as well as he could, through the learning and the science, and the matters of thought rubbing against one another, that had settled down like dust upon it) he came to the conclusion that Sybil, if anyone, was the person required by the spell. He might kill twenty others without effect; but mixing Sybil's pure and fragrant life with the other ingredients of the medicine, it would be the draught of immortality.

Dear Rose, and you Septimius, and Aunt Nashoba, bear with me, though the legend has this very hideous aspect. Either of you, beyond a question, would have been wiser and less wicked than this poor Baron. I am shocked at the thing I tell, as much as you, who listen. To say the truth, I have meditated deeply on this ugliest feature of my story, and am very loth to take it in its most obvious sense; and looking for a spiritual meaning (every fact, you know, has its spiritual truth, which, to the outer one, is what the soul is to the body) I am resolved to believe, that spiritually, the interpretation of the legend is, that the scholar to earnestly seek knowledge, must give up to it the warm joy of life—that no man can be great, or do great things without sacrificing to Death and Nothingness inconceivable things that other men enjoy, and especially the one thing that his heart craves; for the Mind and the Heart struggle together, and one must triumph. In this sense I interpret this demand for a victim. But the earthly old tradition, which I endeavor faithfully to recount to you, strenuously insists that the lord of Smithills Hall did actually resolve to murder this loving and beloved maiden.

I will not linger upon this horrible matter, nor tell you how he argued the matter with himself, and how, the more he thought of it, the more reasonable it seemed, and the more necessary, the more an absolute duty, that this terrible sacrifice should be made. Here on the one hand, was this vast good to be done to mankind; for you must know, he hid his mighty selfishness quite out of sight, or transformed into another thing, by persuading himself that the progress of the world depended upon his success in this scheme—his having time to develope and execute the plans for human good, that he would set to work upon, as soon as he had done this thing. But, on the other hand, no doubt, there was a natural instinct, struggling in the deep, deep dungeon to which he had confined it; crying out ever and amain, and sometimes making its voice come up, stifled, hollow-sounding, to his consciousness; and this was oftenest when Sybil, the poor doomed maiden, hovered about him with her little ministrations, warming his furred slippers, for example, in cold weather, or bringing him summer flowers, putting her hand upon his knee, with the pretty familiarity that was her innocent wont; beckoning as if she were some angel, who was given to this poor man to keep his heart from utterly dying out in the stern and cold intellectual life which it was his tendency to live. But, if he thought her an angel, it only confirmed him in his purpose; for then her fitting place was heaven, whither he resolved to send her. Her texture, at best, was so delicate and frail that it was likely to be blown out, any day, by the mere rude blast that the rush and whirl of life creates; she was quite unfit for such an evil world, and incapable of breathing its hard necessities; and, for her sake, as well as for other considerations, it was well that she should vanish, fade out, and brighten into another state of being. In fine, to make short of it—for I find it almost as difficult to tell as if I myself were to plunge the knife into her—the poor wicked Baron stabbed her; he had the heart (no, not the heart, for he had stifled that) to be the death of this one thing that loved him.

There are heart-breaking stories touching the manner in which this dreadful deed was done; how he sat moodily in his old Gothic study, buried in his own terrible meditations, and sometimes throwing a glance at the poor girl, where she sat, busy with making him a ruff, such as the gentlemen wore in those days, and glancing at him with innocent smiles, which by degrees faded away as she became conscious that some deep trouble and terror was in his breast; how the gloom and terror spread into her heart, likewise, but, in the strength of her innocent affection, how she pressed close to his side, and tried to win him, with her innocent caresses, to tell her what was his grief, and why he threw such dark and terrible, and sorrowful looks at her, who heretofore had met none but gentle and loving looks from him, beaming out from amid the shadow of his thoughts; how, at last, in his madness, he told her his dreadful purpose, having his dagger drawn as he spoke, and how the poor child—partly, I suppose, in despair, partly to save him a portion of his crime by taking what she could of it upon herself—flung herself upon the deadly blade, received it into her heart, and died; and how, when the sweet breath had left her, there was a tender smile upon her lips, as if—in the very agony of death—it had still been sweet to give her life for his sake. For you never can think, Rose, unless you have gone through that experience, what a foolish delight a woman has in letting herself be the victim of the man she loves; and, as they both found out, in that last moment, she loved him as a woman loves, and he loved her as well as a man could—that is to say, next to those things that were closest to him.

<(He pauses, & sets his foot on the door-step, thinking a moment how lonely the house into which he is entering now is; but &c he thinks of what he has gained.)>

He sat there in the Gothic room several hours, with the manuscript out, the instruments of science about him, and the dead girl at his feet, looking down upon her, and wondering that he was not more moved than he found himself to be; for such men as he, by means of their intellect, build a wall of stone between themselves and their emotions, and stand looking coldly over, on their own worst sorrow. At midnight, he took the body in his arms, (for he had studied the whole matter, and well knew what to do,) and bore it down the winding stair, and out by the door in the rear of the house, and so into the ancient wood, more ancient than any memories and traditions, where the Druids were wont to sacrifice their victims. Thither he brought this new victim, and dug a grave for her among the oaks and left her there, to be changed into violets and daisies, and into one other flower which he had learnt (either from his books or his own scientific researches, or from some whisper of the Evil One in his ear) would grow up out of her very heart. And there the matter of the poor maid's death and burial was ended; and nothing remains to be said of it, for the present, save that the Baron had the hap to set his left foot in a pool of her blood (which had welled out while he was digging in the grave) and his foot left a bloody track all along the wood path and a very marked one on the threshold of the hall, and a fainter one up the winding stair into his study-chamber. Then he warmed himself by the wood-fire in the deep chimney, and drank a goblet of a certain potent and fiery liquor that he himself was wont to distil, ten times hotter and stronger than the strongest wines of Spain (though some say the Devil taught it to him, for mankind's future bane) and earnestly resumed his studies. The next morning, having slept none that night, nor thrown off his clothes, he descended into the hall, where there was ale, and canary wine, and cold beef, and a venison-pasty, and an omelet or two, spread at the upper end of the board, for the Baron's breakfast; but whether his appetite was good, the legend does not say. The servants, at all events, ate little or nothing, but swilled ale enormously; being disturbed and greatly frightened at two things—the first, that the sweet mistress Sybil was nowhere to be found; the second, that there was a bloody track across the rushes that strewed the floor of the hall to the Baron's chair, and also a pool of blood where his left foot rested, as he sat at the breakfast board. Moreover, the chamber maid found a similar track up the turret stair, and so onward to the very threshold of the Baron's chamber, but what lay beyond, could only be surmised, as no servants ever dared to enter those awful precincts. All that day, there was whispering, and shudders, and ghastly looks of dread and perturbation, among the serving men and maidens of Smithills hall; they scrubbed amain; and washed out the bloody tracks on the turret-stair, and across the pavement of the hall; the rain, moreover, drizzled down, as it always does in England, and washed away a bloody track that was seen passing into the depths of the old wood; but there was one foot mark on the threshold of the door, that opened to the shrubbery—one crimson foot mark there, which no rain could wash away, no scrubbing could efface, though it wore out the solid rock into which the stain had sunk. They soon gave up the effort.

<Intersperse ludicrous things>

<(Read next paragraph through before beginning.)>

But from that time forward, the most toilsome office at Smithills Hall was that of the washerwoman who washed the Baron's stockings (which he changed twenty times a day, and always one of them was bloody,) the man who strewed rushes on the hall-pavement, and of the chamber-maid, or whatever the poor creature was called, whose business it was to keep the hall-floor and the staircase in decent trim. Blood, blood, blood! Wherever the poor Baron went, he left his track behind him; and when he had passed, people shuddered and turned pale. If he himself chanced to turn round, he threw up his hands, always as if a new horror had smitten him, and then hurried on the faster, and thus faster reddened his own awful footstep behind him. At last, he fled away from his ancestral hall, and could not be tracked (though here, one would think, his bloody footprint might have served a good purpose) until, exactly a year from the date of the dreadful crime, the Baron came again. And as he approached his door-step, there was the crimson-stain upon it, as fresh as ever, and wet, as if the poor maiden's blood had just gushed forth. The foot print on the threshold struck him with new horror; but he set his foot in the same place and passed, leaving the mark wet afresh. It was said, that, during his absence, he had made a pilgrimage to the holiest shrines, and had knelt at the confessionals, but went away unshriven, and leaving an ugly little puddle where his left foot had rested; he had been once to the royal court; but the ushers and pages, with white staffs and golden rods, pointed and whispered, behind him, and the King himself, catching a glimpse of his track, frowned, saying, "My Lord, your ancestors have fought knee deep in blood for mine; but I think never one of them left his bloody footprint so near our throne. We like it not. Let our court-surgeon look to it, Sir Baron, and so farewell!" But though the court surgeon was a man renowned throughout the realm, the Baron never troubled him for his professional advice. And wherever he traveled, there were rumors, terrors, whisperings, behind him, even in crowded cities, where there would be a bloody track along the street, raising rumors that a murder had just been committed in the town & settle the constables to follow it; the dogs, too, would go snuffing after it, yet not as if it were a scent that they liked, but lifting up their muzzles into the air, with evident anger and disgust, drooping their tails, bristling their backs, looking fierce, and yet cowering, snuffing along after the track, as if they would rather turn tail and run away; sometimes, the constables, the dogs, the crowd would throng behind this pale, noble, stately-looking, yet horror struck man, wondering at him, shuddering at him; so that, finally, the Baron found it convenient to take his walks only at night, or during heavy rains, and was compelled to forswear the blessed sunshine. After a year of such experiences, the Baron returned to the old hall, and was received by the menials with low reverence, for they had been born in the old hall, and had known him from his innocent babyhood; but they looked curiously after him, as he trode up the stairs, and nodded ominously to one another as they beheld the fatal mark still reddening behind him. The old butler whispered to the old housekeeper, and several of the under-servants were sent to gather fresh rushes to strew the hall-floor, and to bring hot water to wash the turret stairs.

The next day, the Baron arose betimes, and went into the wood, and was gone the space of half an hour; and when he came back, the servants took notice that he held in his hand a plant of the most beautiful flower that had ever been seen; a splendid crimson flower, shedding a rich fragrance all up the turret staircase, so that you could have tracked him by that alone, had not the bloody track still followed him close behind; beautiful flowers they were, as if he had been to the garden of Paradise to gather them, or as if an angel had met him, and in requital of the virtuous and religious life he lived, had given him these flowers as a foretaste of the joys that awaited him hereafter; or as if the vanished lady Sybil had sent them to him, as a token of her dear love, and gratitude for all his kindness to her. However that might be, the servants noticed that the Baron immediately betook him to his former pursuits of science, or witchcraft and alchemy, distilling, and doing other strange things, sitting up whole nights for these purposes; for they could see the light always burning in his chamber, and his shadow coming between it and the window as he busied himself pouring out liquids; and sometimes they fancied they saw him bending down and scrubbing the floor, as if he himself could not bear the bloody track always bleeding out, wherever he trod; but one would think he might have become accustomed to it by this time. At last, one morning, there was no trace of the Baron; except, of course, the red one down the stairs, and out of the door, and into the rain, that had poured heavily all night. In his study, there was a dying fire, some empty retorts and crucibles, and a goblet that contained a few drops of some fragrant liquid, exhilarating to the smell, but which no one dared to taste, and which soon effervesced away. And it was believed, that the Baron had distilled the rich flower, with other ingredients indicated by his science or wizard skill, into a liquid, and had drunk it off, and made himself immortal, and had wandered away to enjoy his immortality as he best might; but whither he went was never certainly known, from that long past day to this.

<(Some ignore this tradition of endless life, and think him a spectre, haunting the spot where he did the murder— a spectre ominous of ill to the family)>

It was the belief of many, that he never had the good fortune to taste of death, but was doomed to wander to and fro about the earth, leaving everywhere the track of his terrible guilt behind him; and from generation to generation, with perhaps many years between, the superstitious peasantry pretended to have seen a crimson footstep near the hall, and under the old oak, and the servants used to whisper (but this was sternly hushed up) that it was necessary, even yet, occasionally to scour the turret stairs, and strew fresh rushes on the hall-pavement. And, at long intervals—intervals of a century perhaps—there were stories whispered about that a stately, dark, melancholy figure in a cloak, having the hereditary mien and air of that ancient family, had been seen near Smithills Hall, or following, like a dusky shadow, the funeral of some departed member of the race, and stooping to gaze into the funeral vault, with a longing, weary, hopeless mien, like a tired traveller who can find no lodging. But, when observed, he would hurry away, leaving, some said, a crimson stain behind him. I put little or no faith in such stories. Another story was, that he was tracked to the seaport of Bristol, and that his crimson foot print was last seen on the edge of the quay, where a vessel had just sailed for parts beyond the seas, whence she never returned. But certain it is, that the Baron never came back to occupy his ancient inheritance; although the faithful old servants kept a fire always burning, the great logs crumbling into massive brands and coals, in the enormous fire-place of the hall, where (as I told you early in my story) it has been burning ever since; the custom having originated in the idea, that some dreary night or other, the lost Baron might return, chill and damp with the rain in which, as already hinted, he found it most convenient to pursue his travels. But he never came. After a certain term of years, the nearest heir took possession of the estate, and his lineage kept it for two hundred years, and then became extinct; other claimants of the estate sprang up, and are still contending who shall be the heir; but the lawyers say, that if Old Bloody Foot himself (for by that ugly title he is known in the traditions of the family) or any of his lineal male descendants should now appear and prove his descent, he would inherit a Baron's title and the property of Smithills Hall.

After the Baron had disappeared, some rich crimson flowers were found growing in the neighboring wood, on a little hillock that looked wonderfully like a grave; and being of unknown species, and of tropical richness of hue and fragrance, such flowers, in short, as were never known to be indigenous in sober and homely England, they were transplanted to the flower-garden of the hall, where they flourished less abundantly than in their native bed; but when, in the improvements of horticulture, a hot-house was instituted at Smithhills Hall, these flowers were cultivated there, and have been perpetuated to the present day. Scientific botanists make great account of them, and have tried to cultivate them elsewhere, though with little or no success; but they sneer at the traditions respecting this flower, which linger near its native site, that the flower grew out of the heart of the poor maiden, and had in it the essence of a pure human life, sacrificed to prolong another life; and that the Baron drank of the liquor distilled from it, and grew immortal in woe and agony, becoming wiser and more wretched in every age. Other people, nevertheless, have tried to distil the immortal liquid from the same flower, but always without success, because, to give it potency, the seeds should be planted in a new grave of bloody **Death.**

<—telling a story with the voice, you can run off into any wildness that comes into the head; whereas the pen petrifies all such flights—>

When Sybil's marvellous legend (which the girl had told with a singular mixture of fun and earnestness, almost affrighted at the extravagant horror of her own tale, and at the same time a wild inclination to laugh in the most tragic or melodramatic passages of it) was concluded, Aunt Nashoba gave her opinion of it. The old woman had got into a most comfortable and jolly state, in the chimney corner, toasting and stewing herself in the generous heat of the great logs, smoking pipe after pipe of strong tobacco, and sipping her nostrum with extreme satisfaction, which manifested itself in a strange sort of guttural, wordless exclamation, at its excellent flavour; for, in truth, Aunt Nashoba was of opinion that, in all her brewages of this admirable drink, she had never been quite so successful as in this very jug. Taking the pipe from her lips, she spoke:—

"That's what I call a real pleasant story, and I believe it every word; and I only wish the girl Sybil here could get me some seed of that crimson flower; for I reckon it's the very herb I've always been wanting, to make my drink perfect.

There is nothing else can improve the stuff, but that flower might. Can you get me some of the seed, child?"

"Perhaps I might, Aunt Nashoba, if I were in England now," said Sybil.

"Well; remember it when you go back again," said the old woman; "for I am mighty curious in herb-drink, and perhaps I might have taught Old Bloody-Foot himself a thing or two. And now, as you've told us such pretty things about him, I'll see if I can't remember a story that was told me, when I was a little child, by my grandmother, who was sister-in-law of her that was hanged for witchcraft, and had the facts from her. I'm more forgetful than I was (though the drink keeps me pretty bright, too) and may not tell it quite regular; but the main drift of the thing was pretty much as I shall tell it. And it shows, too, that there must be some kind of truth in this notion of a drink that makes people live forever; because my story hangs upon it, too." (I change Aunt Nashoba's language a little; for except as Lowell uses it, I hate the Yankee dialect, for literary purposes.)

"Let us hear it, by all means, Aunt Nashoba," said Septimius.

Sybil and Rose both added their entreaties; and in the flue of the chimney, over Aunt Nashoba's head, there was a great roaring voice of the wind, roaring and laughing, like some obstreperous fellow who had taken up his position there, and was calling with impatient glee for the next story; while applauding the last. "Just so the Indian powows used to bellow down chimney to my great Aunt, calling her to come out and dance with them," said Aunt Nashoba, winking to her auditors. "I've often heard them; but I'm a Christian woman and a church member, and never take any notice. Hush, old fellow," she called up the chimney, "and I'll tell my story as soon as I can fill my pipe. I'm afraid it won't be much of a story, after all."

All prepared to listen with attention, especially Septimius; for, to say the truth, Sybil's wild traditionary tale, perhaps made wilder by her morbid & wayward fancy, had had the effect to give him an uncomfortable sense of the fantasticalness of his present pursuit, so almost identical with that of the Baron of the legend, and by linking such evident absurdities with it, had given the whole the aspect of absurdity. His keen New England sense assuming a temporary control, he began to suspect that he had strayed into a region frightfully abandoned to superstition, and at best to the defeated dreams of early science; a Limbo to which all exploded things are assigned; and among them, the childish dreams of mankind, and the visions of one's own youth, and religions which the world has outgrown, and which Great Pan has haunted, since he died on earth; a Limbo into which mortal men are most apt to stray, when they fancy themselves brightest and wisest, most godlike, and if they find their way back into the real world, are careful to conceal that they once stept across those haunted borders, yet often loiter through life despondently, longing to find the dim path that leads thither again. Was Sybil's legend wilder than the purposes and hopes he entertained, and the things on which he was expending his most earnest faculties! And then, the frame-work of his mental life being thus shaken, the solid substance of what he knew to be actual seemed to grow fragile along with it; and he almost believed Sybil herself to be an illusion, and doubted if Aunt Nashoba, whom he had known all his lifetime, whether she had more substance than the curling fumes of her pipe; and Rose Garfield, too, with her homely beauty and decorousness, whether he had not dreamed such a sisterly presence, and what, too, was the substance of the timber-work of the cottage, nestling under the hill, which he had inherited from his father, and even what was the steadfastness of the hill itself, and the reality of the path that he had trodden there, with so many walkings to-and-fro, and whether that was a real grave, and did it hold the decay of a beautiful young man whom he had slain. If part of his life, and that which seemed as solid as any other, was an illusion, then why not all. It was, in short, a moment with Septimius such as many men have experienced, when something that they deemed true and permanent appearing suddenly questionable, the whole scenery of life shakes, jars, grows tremulous, almost disappears in mingled and confused colors, as when a stone is thrown into the smooth mirror of Walden Lake, and seems to put in jeopardy the surrounding hills, woods, and the sky itself. True; the scene soon settles itself again, and looks as substantial as before; but a haunting doubt is apt to keep close at hand, persecuting us forever with that troublesome query—"Is it real! Can I be sure of it? Did I not once behold it on the point of dissolving?" And he is either a very wise man, or a very dull one, who can answer one way or the other for the reality of the very breath he draws, and steadfastly say "Yes!" or "No!"

Aunt Nashoba's everlasting pipe (it was an iron pipe by the way, and had belonged to her great-aunt, the witch, who, they say, used to summon an imp to bring her a red hot coal from subterranean hearths) being by this time replenished, she related a family tradition that seemed little qualified to settle Septimius's disturbed imagination.

Now, touching the legend, it may be pertinent to remark that Aunt Nashoba was of Yankee blood (one of the Yankees, extant indeed, considering how long before the epoch of the pilgrims she dated her New England ancestry,) and it is a characteristic of theirs, to tell very strange stories with a grim face, and yet, as I think, without the purpose or expectation of being seriously believed. As regards stories, it seems to me that my countrypeople give their imaginations a license, which they do not assume to so great an extent among themselves; just as some savage tribes, while practising scrupulous integrity in their home relations, have no conscience about thieving and robbing, to any practicable extent, on their foreign visitors; and so, perhaps, Aunt Nashoba fabled chiefly for Sybil's benefit. But she was a queer old woman, and in her witch-haunted mind, may have believed the greater part of what she told, and, no doubt, had at least some nucleus of family traditions, a part of them made up of Indian as well as English superstition—around which she gathered the uncouth figments of the legend.

<He was acquainted with unknown or forgotten arts, derived from vanished races>

This hill, right above our heads (which Septimius inherited from his forefathers, and which he has such a queer habit of walking, as if he had made an appointment to meet the Black Man there, and had mistaken their hour), this hill, bleak and barren as it looks, was once the dwelling place of a great Sagamore, who might have had his choice of the fruitfullest spot within a score of miles. There was his great wigwam, under the pine-trees, and there, too, was an Indian village, stretching back towards the great meadows, that lie between the hill and the slow creeping river; and, if you know how to look for them, you may still pick up arrowheads with the mossy soil, and among the roots of the pines and birches, and may see the traces of the corn-fields, where the red people used to exercise what little skill they seemed to have, in husbandry. But let the red people go; the great Sagamore, if all stories told of him are true, was not of the red race, though he wore their dress, and lived in their way of life, and had married a Squaw among them, and his children and their children were of a paler red than their mothers. Nobody knew what place he came from, though the Powwows said it was from Tophet (or whatever they call the place, in the Indian tongue) and were very proud of their Sagamore, for coming of such good stock; nobody knew how old he was, only that there were traditions that thus he had appeared among them in the times of their great-grandfathers, looking just the same age as now, and helped them in war, and cured them of their wounds and diseases (knowing all about herb-drinks, mind you,) and had come to be their chief, by a kind of natural necessity, because he was the strongest, bravest, wisest man, and as the powows said, had more of the devil in him than all the rest of the tribe together. For, you see, they worshipped the Devil, those red folks, and glorified their great men, as was reasonable, for such qualities as the Devil may be supposed to have. But, above all, nobody knew when the great Sagamore was going to die, if ever.

To tell you the truth, this last uncertainty perplexed and troubled the Red Race more than any of the preceding doubts, and especially it troubled the powwows, or prophets, the middle-aged chiefs, and medicine-men; and other such people, who by bravery in war, or wisdom in peace, might have hopes of rising to be the chief warrior in the tribe. In the first place, it was tedious and wearisome beyond all idea (though few people have ever had the chance to try the wearisomeness of it) to be always governed wisely, and always be compelled to submit to good laws, and never take any the least recreation into foolish courses; but always to live in plenty, never any risk of starving, to make plenty sweet, never any defeat, to make them know the joy of victory; and all this they owed to the tedious old Sagamore, who seemed an elder brother of the hills, and had so gathered up experience that life, under his guidance, seemed an old story, and a very flat one. It was truly a terrible thing, to look forward, and see themselves always under the rule of one man, with his one way of thinking, though it might be the wisest; and they say the whole tribe began to grow more stupid, and less able to take care of themselves than Indians usually are, on account of this queer tryranny of the wizard, & their minds losing energy for lack of use. What a wretched thing it was, too, for eloquent counsellors, as there happened to be many in the tribe who esteemed themselves such, to be tongue tied, because there was one among them who could make their eloquence seem childish babble, and their wisdom nonsense! Who could be brave either, when here was a warrior, who had drunk, they say, such quantities of the blood of his enemies, that it oozed continually out of one of his feet, and soaked his moccason, and made a red track wherever he went. If there were a prospect of his dying in any reasonable—say, in a dozen more generations—they would wait patiently, and live out their own lives, in the hope that their great-great-grandchildren might have a chance to call their souls their own; but, it was known that the Great Sagamore had a certain drink, which he brewed from herbs, and it was thought that every five hundred moons (to reckon as the red folks do) he drank a sip of this stuff, and so renewed his strength, and went on living. So that there was no hope in that way; he was absolutely deathless.

Well; they plotted against him; but the Great Sagamore, with his wisdom and long experience, saw through their simple, babyish schemes of murder, by knife or by poison, and defeated them, and laughed at them; and sent them away ashamed, to be the laughing stock of all the tribe. The priests and powwows tried to kill the terrible old fellow by witchcraft; but he, you know, was hand and glove with the Black Man, and came down upon their incantations with a whole legion of imps, and put them to such shame that they almost gave up devil-worship in despair. And, at last, being fully convinced of the reasonableness of their own side of the question, (and, to say the truth, I really think they had the rights of the matter) they determined humbly to state the case to the everlasting Sagamore, and throw themselves entirely on his mercy. So a deputation of the wisest and bravest of the tribe (if any one of them could be called wise or brave, when there was one who so much excelled) went to the royal wigwam, and tremblingly requested an audience. The great Sagamore happened to be changing his bloody moccasson, but looked at them in a stern and solemn way (for naturally he had the aspect of a man that carried an awful doom within him) and bade them be seated, or squat on their hams, after the Indian fashion, and gave them a pipe to smoke, and asked them gruffly what was their business. And they first filled the wigwam with tobacco smoke, and under the veil of it, they found such freedom as to lay the whole case before him, stating the hardship that one man should live, while all other men had to die, and suggesting whether it were not agreeable to the general propriety of things, that so great a warrior and hunter should depart to the happy hunting-grounds, or that so wise a counsellor should go and tell his experience of life to the Great Father, giving him an account of matters on earth, and perhaps suggesting some ideas that would operate for the benefit of the red men, or that so mighty a wizard, since the great

Sagamore so far outdid the awfullest of the Powwows, might go to their other Deity, the Devil, where he evidently belonged. And at any rate, they besought him to depart, since they confessed themselves unworthy to be any longer honored by his presence.

The great Sagamore scowled at them, and laughed at them. At his scowl they fell on their faces, and at his laugh, they shook with convulsions, and tried to roll themselves out of the wigwam; but the terrible old wretch bellowed after them, and told them he consented to die, and that they should summon all the warriors of the tribe, and kill him in any way that they liked best. So, with great force and rejoicing, they all took their weapons, and first they shot their arrows at him from a distance; but the flint arrow-points made no impression on his skin, because it was tough with living so many centuries; and, I suppose, if I have found one, I have found fifty of those very arrow-points, blunted with the toughness of his skin. Then growing bolder with despair, and because the great Sagamore made no sort of resistance, they gathered round him and battered fiercely upon his bare, shaven head, with their tomahawks and war-clubs; but the war-clubs splintered like pipe-stems, and the stone tomahawks struck fire against his skull, and crumbled into fine dust, because his skull was hardened with such long life. Then, as a last resort, they built a great pile of wood about him, felling an acre of pitch-pine trees and heaping straw upon him, and set it on fire, and it burned three days and nights, while they danced about it in the cremation's blaze and smoke, and feasted, and rejoiced, because now they had got rid of the man that would never die, and that was too wise for any set of mere mortal men to hold their own with. The white ashes lay thick upon him, as he sat, and the charred brands had blackened him; but there he sat, visible through the glow and whirl of the subsiding flames; and they thought how quietly and majestically he had died, as an Indian warrior ought, leaving his incombustible body as a memorial of the great soul that had breathed out in a whirlwind of fire. But as the fury of the furnace subsided, they saw clearer; and behold, there he sat in the middle of the most glowing embers, sitting upon the mighty trunk of a pine, which was all one live coal, and calmly smoking his pipe, as if that furnace heat were just the atmosphere he liked best to breathe. At that sight they fell into utter despair, and re-solved to build another pile of pitch pine trees, larger than the first, and fling in their squaws, their children, and them-selves, and all perish together, and leave the Undying One alone, since they could neither get rid of him, nor live with such an awfully wise man any longer.

<A ground-hemlock grows in a circle, on the hill-top, where the middle of the pile was>

But as the stately figure of the great Sagamore sat there, on his throne of an enormous coal, and with the flames quivering about his garments, he beckoned to them, with a commanding gesture; and they were all constrained to come and gather round the edge of the furnace, although its heat was still powerful enough to blister all the faces. He was smoking this very iron pipe which was white hot. And out of that realm of fire, it seemed as if he were speaking to them from another state of being. He told them that he knew he had lived too long, and that he was a-weary of the world, and would look upon that man as his greatest bene-factor who should help him out of it. He said, nevertheless, that they, of all people in the world, had least reason to com-plain of him, because, by his wisdom, he had made them mightiest among the tribes, and had taught them what arts were good for them to know, and had withheld a thousand other arts that he knew of, and other ways of living that he had tried, because he hoped to keep them simply virtuous and happy. But, old as he was, and wise as he was, the old Sagamore told them, there was a thing or two that he had never fully learned till they taught him, foolish as they were. And truly, if I may speak my mind, it was hardly worth the trouble of living so long, to learn such a poor, dreary, little bit of wisdom as this; for it was nothing else than that the human race is only to be taught by its own follies, and blunders, and crimes, and that, in order to do them the little good anybody can, a man must stay among them, fooling, blundering, and sinning, and squeezing a bitter wholesome juice out of these ugly herbs; but if he gets apart from them, in any way, he can do nothing. And that now he was going to try to make away with himself, and at any rate, would leave them forever, bequeathing them all to the Black Man, whom they worshipped. And before he went, it is funny to think how he could not overcome the tediousness, and authoritativeness which these poor Indians complained of; for he made them a regular sermon, out of the midst of the fire, and gave them ever so much good advice, and directions how to act in all sorts of cases, and instructions for war and for peace, for hunting and planting, and how to build their wigwams in a better fashion, and how to make an excellent drink of herbs; every one of which instructions these foolish red men forgot the moment his old back was turned —except the herb-drink, the recipe of which was preserved, as you shall hear in a moment.

And all this said, he strode through the dying embers, kicking them impatiently aside, and coming to the outer verge of the furnace, he beckoned to his great, great, great, great grandson (for the great Sagamore had taken to himself a squaw, in some past generation, and had a family, who were dead and forgotten long ago, save this one descendant) and said something to this young warrior in a low voice, which nobody could overhear. And then, stepping quickly out of the fiery circle, and shaking off the ashes from his feet (as he did it, it was observed that bloody foot of his was still crimson and wet, though it should seem as if the fire might have dried it up, but he had drunk a vast deal of the blood of his enemies) he departed through the forest, never looking behind him, but leaving a bloody track, which they did not dare to follow, nor, to say the truth, even wished it. But, had they had the sense to know it, it was a dark day for the tribe when the great Sagamore departed. Their enemies soon heard that they had lost their mighty chief, and set upon them on all sides, and took vengeance for past defeats. They lost the useful and comfortable arts that he had taught them, and grew more ignorant and helpless than other Indians, because they were unused to take care of themselves. Then came a terrible pestilence, that swept off the poor disheartened creatures, as a wind in November sets a great crowd of red and brown leaves flying before it, nobody knows whither. Lastly came the English, who killed some of the few that were left, and poisoned them with fire-water, and teazed them to death with catechisms, <scenes in Walden, and Flint Pond &c, and the Concord> and took their land, and are still ploughing and planting it—and poor enough it is.

The great, great, great, great grandson of the great Sagamore was still living, a middle-aged man, when the English settlers came; and he remembered the advice of his forefather, and went to the chief among the white men, and told them that he was of their blood, and that he chose to keep his Indian fashions himself, being too old to change, yet he besought them to bring up his son in the English way. And so they did; for they taught him to drink rum, and set him in the stocks for being drunk, and made him caper round the whipping-post to warm his blood of a frosty morning, and when he grew old, they put him in the poor-house and finally starved him to death. But, somehow or other, when he was a fine, straight young fellow, he had persuaded a white girl to marry him (the women always liked our men-folks, though they were a silent, stern, melan-choly race,) and had a son and daughter by her; and the son grew up to be a mighty minister, and the daughter was hanged for a witch. There are one or two things still in the family, that, they say, came to us from the Great Sagamore; such as an old iron-box, that I have not seen this many a day, and never saw the inside of, and an old-fashioned cup, that I should think was silver, only, if it were, it would have been stolen long ago. But the only really valuable inheritance the great Sagamore left to his posterity was the recipe for my herb-drink, which I verily believe was the drink that made him live such a tedious while, only he left out just one herb, for fear any that came after him should be tempted to do the same thing. And when I die, I have nothing else to leave Septimius but the secret of that same drink; and it is right he should have it, and no other, for he and I are the only mortals that inherit a drop of the great Sagamore's blood, unless there should be some unknown relatives of ours among the Cape Indians.

"When I was a young woman, I went to look for the great Sagamore's bloody track, thinking he might be still alive, and strolling on the hill where he used to have his wigwam; and once I saw a line of bloody footsteps, but it seemed that Abner Garfield had cut his foot with an axe, as he was felling a tree, and went bleeding home; but I've always had a fancy it might have been the great Sagamore's track, nevertheless, and it kind of startled me, I tell you. But hear that old fellow laughing up there in the chimney. I should not wonder—since he stood the fire and smoke so well, if it were the great Sagamore himself, holding his ear over the flue and listening to his own true history."

And Aunt Nashoba laughed back again, up the chimney, and again the blast responded, so that it seemed really as if she were keeping up a kind of cachinnatory intercourse with the powers of the air. As to her legend, nobody could tell how much ground this queer old woman had for it, a genuine tradition, and what liberties she had taken in piecing it out from her own quaint fancy; but there were points in it which set Septimius to meditating profoundly, and determined him, at some convenient opportunity, to have a set and serious talk with Aunt Nashoba about herb-drinks and family matters. And, for the present, he even went so far as to ask the old woman to let him taste her nostrum.

"With all my heart, Seppy dear," said she, getting a clean tea-cup and filling it from a brown earthen jug, corked with a bit of corn cob, round which a rag was twisted. "Drink the whole, and you'll find yourself the better for it, this fortnight to come! Just smell of it, and 'twill do you good; but drink it down, and you'll live the longer for it. If it only had one other herb in it (and I've been trying to find that herb all my days, and at last have substituted a little good rum, as the next best thing) 'twould make you live forever."

"Indeed, Aunt Nashoba, that would be a potent medicine," said Septimius, his head throbbing tumultuously at a recommendation that so assimilated to what he was seeking for.

<(Perhaps, as in temper, and other moral qualities, there was an appreciable similarity between Aunt Nashoba and her drink, and she herself but a moving jug of it.)>

"I am afraid the herb does not grow in earthly soil," said Rose, laughing.

"Poh!" said Sybil, flightily. "I've seen it growing myself, in the garden of Smithills Hall, but there they have lost the other ingredients."

Septimius looked into the cup, and saw a half-opaque yellow liquid, by no means delightful to the eye; in truth, it was the precise hue of Aunt Nashoba's own jaundiced complexion, and the young man had a fantasy that the good lady had so constantly replenished her veins with this concoction that it now served her instead of natural blood, and therein contributing to the growth of her tissues, she was now but an incarnation of her own favorite drink. He smelt delicately and at a respectful distance, of the cup, sniffing daintily at the undelightful fragrance, in which he fancied there was a sickening odor of a certain vegetable, probably unknown in the garden of Paradise, called skunk-cabbage; although the smell seemed rather a composite affair, miraculously produced by an unhappily contrived union of discordant elements, than any of which Nature was separately guilty. Nevertheless, having sternly resolved to make proof, so far as one draft might go, of the virtues and delights of Aunt Nashoba's vaunted beverage, he drank,—not a mere sip, but an heroic gulp, which caused the turbid element to subside halfway down the interior of the cup, and show the painted crimson sprig at bottom, looking like the bloody flower which Sybil fabled of. The draught seemed at first to burn in his mouth, unaccustomed to any drink save water, and to go scorching all the way down into his stomach, making poor Septimius fully sensible of the depth of the descent by a track of fire, terminating in a place there below, in which a familiar fiend might have taken his ease. This was its first effect. Next, worse than the fire, came a hideous sense of mingled bitterness and nauseousness, which the poor young man had not previously conceived to exist, and which he remembered afterwards as an ugly dream; for there are certain combinations of mercy and heart-sickness in dreams, which real, waking life is too beneficently over-tender ever to present. However, knowing the sensitiveness of Aunt Nashoba as regarded this horrible beverage, and the hereditary sanctity in which she held it, and, furthermore, the hopelessness of obtaining any of her herb-secrets, if he should suffer his disgust to be visible, he crushed down his agony, and kept his face heroically quiet; except for one brief convulsion, which (because otherwise his heart must have burst) he allowed to twist across it, and vanish.

"Isn't it good, darling?" inquired Aunt Nashoba, smacking her lips; for she had quaffed off what was left in the cup.

"It tastes as if it might have great potency, Aunt Nashoba," said the miserable youth; "and I doubt not, by your example, that the drink may become very agreeable, on better acquaintance."

"And so it does, Seppy," said the old woman, "and you shall drink a cup of my bitters every morning before breakfast, by way of improving the acquaintance. And, my dear lad, I have often thought of telling you how to make it, and it is time to do it, for I'm getting to be an old woman, and if I delay too long the blessed secret may be utterly lost to the world. You're the only one left of my blood, unless it be some fourteenth cousin, of those Darkies, as they call them, among the Squaddick Indians; and I have no other inheritance to leave you, and could not leave you a better one. Ask me, some day, Seppy, when I'm at leisure, and these silly girls are not by, and you shall know all about it."

"And perhaps he may find the missing herb, Aunt Na-shoba!" said Sybil with her sharp, sprightlike, jeering glance as she rose to go, "and so brew the drink of immortality!" But up in the chimney, laughed the hollow wind-spirit &c.

<apply all this paragraph to Septimius, and to him alone>
<Begin—Months went by, and at last (most unusual) Septimius had a visitor>

It has often seemed to me that winter is the active time, in New England, to the intellectual laborer; whether because the outward world presents so few inducements to tempt him beyond the fireside, the woodland walks being choked up, the lake and river frozen, the garden calling him to no gentle toil, all being waste and white; so that, as in a bottle of generous wine in those zeroic times, all the watery parts are congealed, but the strength and richness of the wine still remains liquid and potent, in a small quantity in the centre of the bottle; so with the mind, it becomes a fiery power, and is capable of better things in the hard frost, because it has fewer things to enjoy, and so gets a stern and manful enjoyment out of its own action. The quality of the air, too, the sparkling north-west, puts the intellect upon its mettle, by its brisk hostility; deferring any sybaritic mood, and making friends with you only when you face it, and then, in a few deep draughts, giving you life and courage on the hill-top for many hours thereafter; and then the snowy atmo-sphere, when all the air is full of flakes, and the sun shrouded, and the whole universe turned to snow, covering deeply the earth, lying on the roofs, the window sills, the boughs of the trees, clinging half-way up the window panes; slowly melting on the great logs that he had heaped on the hearth, and hissing on the hot bricks; compassed here, in this little space of warmth, he became full of activity. That crumbly, yellow, scrawly manuscript, with its infirm old texture, that could scarcely bear to be handled, lest it should turn to so much dust, and little scraps, with one or two illegible scratches of an ancient pen on each. What voluminous thought, what intense mental life, it was the cause of, so many ages after the hand that wrote it was (or at least ought to have been, for the fact was a matter of doubt with Septimius) crumbled into dust. It is not essential, just now, to explain what discoveries he deduced himself; but, by bringing the focus of all his powers to bear upon the manuscript, as upon a stubbornly resisting substance in the focus of a lens, he had unquestionably succeeded in getting a meaning out of most of those mystic pages; although, so well skilled were ancient writers in the sublime art of hiding meanings under a veil of words, while seeming to reveal them—weaving only a thicker garment out of the very light which they throw around a subject—that he was not perhaps fully satisfied with his achievement. He began to think, indeed, that it would require all science, all learning, fully to comprehend what was written in this little space; so impossible was it to grasp this flower, and pull it up out of the remainder of human knowledge, its roots being so deep in the soil, and so intertwined with the heart-strings of the Universe. It is, I presume, in this way that a man's peculiar branch of study often seems to him of such paramount importance to all others; because, when he gives a tug at it, hoping to pull it up, he feels the whole soil quake around him, and so convinces himself (and with a certain correctness) to have grappled with the whole universe in that one thing. So it is ever with what seems an idle tale, that, too, slight as it is, wreathes its tendrils about human knowledge, belief, superstitions, hopes, efforts, and, being taken only for a flower growing wild on a hill-side, with a fragrance of its own, we find that we have life and death, and burdens, and all the questions that men ever argued about, twining with its tendrils, so that here, too, we have hold of the moral universe. <I find myself dealing with solemn and awful subjects, which I but partly succeed in putting aside.>

It has been mentioned that a considerable part of the manuscript was written in what appeared to be a cypher; and that whenever the old author appeared to be verging towards a crisis in his thought, he took refuge in this apparently impenetrable character, and, under its protection, wrote freely, no doubt, what he feared to communicate otherwise, or perhaps thought that the world was not yet worthy of. It was a whimsical and pucklike way of writing, no doubt, thus to give the reader the shells and husks of his real thought, and to keep free the golden grains, to communicate which was the only rational object of writing at all; but perhaps the author considered, that when the world arose to that stage of improvement that it could advantageously read his hidden meanings, the cryptic characters would shine out in legible light, potent to a comprehension that would embrace all particulars in its universal lore; or that if, before that epoch came, the earnest desire of an individual for knowledge made him worthy to possess it, the test of his worthiness would be shown by his being able to find the cryptic key, and turn it, in the mysterious lock. Septimius, as it happened, did find a key which suited it passably well, but the discovery was made under favorable circumstances, thereby detracting somewhat from the credit of subtle ingenuity that would otherwise have been his due. The uproar and confusion of war, it must be remembered, had invaded the precincts of our ancient seat of learning; soldiers were quartered in scholastic bowers;

and the learners, (as they said in their day, meaning President ——— with two or three tutors, his coadjutors, and about forty students,) had been driven for refuge to Septimius's native town, bringing along with them such literary materials as the college possessed, and among them a few cart loads of volumes, comprising the college library. In this small collection, which has since extended to such respectable a size, there chanced to be some treatises on cryptic writing, expounding the curious art by which any system of characters, provided there be enough of it, and consistent with itself, is as capable of being read as a child's primer. Among his other winter studies, all connected with his main object, Septimius had read these volumes, and by dint of this, had succeeded in bringing out many paragraphs of the ancient manuscript. He was not likely to undervalue the results which he had obtained with so much toil; he deemed himself well rewarded; he considered himself on the eve of great results; but it is very remarkable, in these mysticisms, how the real, definite meaning dodges many of us, offers itself to our grasp, but yet cannot really be grasped, so that, after all, it is doubtful whether all the truth that can be caught at all is not actually our own, before we think of seeking for it. But Septimius, at all events, fancied himself within a single step of a practical result.

<(He uses some peculiar method of cultivation, so as to produce the flower.)>

Meanwhile, Spring had opened. If Septimius had drawn the right moral from the winter, he might have seen in that dead sleep of nature, that a repose, so profound, so cold, so dry and juiceless, that it looks like death, when the heart does not weary us with beating any longer, is necessary to the life of man, in Nature, and of the whole that we call Nature, and that endless life and endless summer will come together, when they come at all; he might have learned, too, that no uninterrupted life could have the exaltation, the joy, the activity, the exhilaration, which the earth exhibits, awaking out of its death, and beginning again as if just made; whereas, how weary would it have been, if last summer had dragged itself out till now; and just so weary, the Man of Ages, if his crumbling particles should have no rest embracing each of them separately. There is surely something strangely comfortable, in that interpretation of the doctrine of immortal life, which promises the dying a new, a sound sleep from his death moment till the resurrection morn; it seems so hard, so hopeless, to go immediately from the weariness which the toils, sorrows, sicknesses, loves, joys, even studious aspirations, of this life have brought us, to the far intenser activity and sensibility of a spiritual sphere. There should be an interval between the acts. With all eternity to come, the most ravenous of life can afford to wait. Then, after that rigid, stirless winter, delightfully will come the Spring, and we plants of immortality sprout up, all juicy, from the places where we were hidden under the snow, just as herbage, grass, came up on Septimius's hill; just as the twigs of the birches swelled; nothing being lost in the dead, hopeless winter; not even the weeds, any more than the herbs of grace, the violets, the sweet fern, the wood anemones. Even Septimius unconsciously bore testimony to the benefit, the wholesomeness, the necessity of Death and resurrection, by the exhilaration of spirit with which he breathed the new warmness of the air, and looked over the new green that was blushing over the wide, far meadows that lay between hill and hill, while yet some strip of the world's winding-sheet, a rag or two of the white sheet that had enveloped her, when she lay seemingly dead, lay along the stone walls, and on the northern slopes of the declivities, and in hollows. Rags of the world's winding-sheet were there, where she lay in illusion of death; and now, as they dissolved, they would make her summer dress the greener. And so, without knowing why, Septimius trod that weary path over the hill-top, as if these were his first footsteps there, and he just wanted to tread them, when, to his infinite surprise, he beheld a stranger just ascending over the brow of the hill. And yet it was not exactly surprise, because, like all men in perplexity, seeking they know not what, yearning for light, he had felt as if somebody would come to enlighten him.

The apparent figure, it is true, was not in the least that of an angelic messenger, nor even that of one whom he should expect to be the bearer of deep earthly wisdom; not the kind of apparition, in short, from whom a young man looks for the word, the magic sentence, the sign, the hint that is to begin for him the explanation of all this bewilderment of life, and reduce its chaos to order. This was a short, broad figure of a somewhat elderly man with a red, rough face on which, conforming to the general fashion of the period, he wore a bristly and grizzled beard; he had on a kind of foraging cap, a blue surtout, and horseman's boots, all of which served to give him a half-military air, while yet a pair of green spectacles made him seem of the owlish or student genus. He had a German pipe in his hand (a strange implement to Septimius, who had hitherto seen no pipes but ordinary clay ones, and that iron pipe which Aunt Nashoba inherited from the famous lips of the Great Sagamore) applying which to his mouth, he sent out huge puffs of smoke, which the west wind brought to Septimius's nostrils and made him sensible of a rich and delicate fragrance. The stranger came slowly along, on short legs, a squat, bluff figure, with protuberant paunch, making himself, as Septimius thought, wonderfully at his ease on the hill-top, and the young man, slackening his ordinary pace, came as slowly to meet him; and when they were pretty near, the stranger planted himself astride of the path as well as his short legs permitted, blew out a puff of smoke, and nodded in a gracious and familiar kind of way.

"Mr. Septimius Norton, I presume," said he.

"That is my name," said Septimius, in his shy, distant manner.

<Speak of his profanity very decidedly.>

"And I am Doctor Jabez Ormskirk," said the stranger, holding out his hand, "late connected with the chemical department of his majesty's army, (a chemist or apothecary, to tell you the truth, rather than a surgeon,) which employment I quitted, when his majesty's troops (on the gentle suggestion of Mr. Washington's forces) quitted Boston. I saw no reason for accompanying them, Sir, and some very good ones for staying behind."

"I am glad, Doctor Ormskirk," said Septimius, civilly, still distant, and shy, so unaccustomed had he grown to strangers, "that you have thought favorably enough of my country to adopt it for your own, even temporarily."

"Why," answered the Doctor, with a careless puff of smoke, "I am a philosopher, in more ways than one; and a man that labors for the good of his race, belongs to no country, or to all. True, I am sincerely desirous of giving your countrymen the benefit of my scientific acquirements, (which several learned societies, in the old world, have acknowledged to be not inconsiderable) and there seems to be room for their beneficial employment here. Then I have other objects;—as, for example, to examine the botany of your region, and more particularly to make some investigations about your native spiders."

"Spiders, Sir?" answered Septimius, not knowing what to make of the Doctor.

"Yes, spiders," said Doctor Ormskirk nodding. "But that is a subject we need not enter upon, at present. I have ventured to encroach upon what I understand is your favorite walk, principally for a favor done me, on the part of your family, and I believe yourself, in the kindness shown to a ward of mine."

"You mean Miss Sybil Dacy," said Septimius. "I have heard her speak of you. She is very welcome to anything we can do for her; and her society, in this lonely place, is more than an equivalent to my sister. As for myself I am absorbed in my studies, and cannot suppose that my society has done anything for her; except that she has given me some assistance in botanizing along this hill top."

By this time, the Doctor had taken Septimius's arm, with a familiarity not quite agreeable to the shyness of his companion, but which he had not tact and readiness enough to avoid, unless he had frankly told his new acquaintance that he preferred not to be touched; and turning back with Septimius, Dr. Ormskirk began to talk very fast, and very freely, in a rough, loud tone, making remarks about Sybil Dacy and her peculiarities with a freedom that rather surprised Septimius and, indeed, for some reason or other, a little shocked him.

"She was my sister's child," said he—"an orphan, and needed a mother; but a man in my position has no facilities for acting a mother's part, or even a father's, knocking about the world, with his head on science. And there is a science in young girls' hearts, they say, as well worth learning as any other; but that is a study which men addict themselves to, at your age, with better results than at mine. Sybil, you see, was sickening, cooped up in yonder town, for she was a country-born child, and so I was very glad to get her off my hands for a time."

As the Doctor thus talked, they had proceeded so far along the path, that they came abreast of poor Charles Norton's grave, and Doctor Ormskirk, being on that side, had nearly stumbled over it, with his short legs, in dudgeon at which almost mischance, apparently, he gave the ground a sudden kick, exclaiming, "What's this, boy! A pretty stumbling block in a man's path!" and drew his companion onward. Septimius knew not till that moment what a sympathy existed between his own corporeal frame and poor Norton's dust; for Doctor Ormskirk's kick seemed to take effect on his own person; especially as he fancied that there was a kind of spite and malice in it, which the mere obstruction ought not to have excited even in such a choleric little man. Probably the Doctor perceived a sort of convulsive start in the young man, for he apologized, saying, "I beg pardon, but the wicked mole-hill nearly threw me down." And so they kept on, the stranger talking with great volubility, smoking voluminously, and perplexing the shy Septimius to know why such a visitor had befallen him. He seemed the most communicative man, talking with the utmost freedom of his pursuits, his scientific discoveries (of which, it seems, he had made several of acknowledged importance) his correspondence with learned bodies; so that Septimius could not but suppose that he had a man of eminence by his side, although he smiled internally to think of the contrast between this singular individual and the awful, wizard-like attributes which Sybil's account of him had portrayed. The Doctor had a way, too, of pausing, and causing his companion to pause, speaking with great emphasis, and much gesticulation of his fore-finger, pointed uncomfortably at Septimius, and laid occasionally on his breast; then nodding, with great emphasis, and renewing his walk. In this way, they were some time in reaching the end of this path, by which time Septimius had come to the conclusion that Doctor Ormskirk was a very eminent man, but could not guess why he wasted his time upon such an ignorant young rustic as himself. In the same way, and with the same volubility on the good Doctor's part, they returned along the pathway, till, reaching the little hillock over which he had so nearly stumbled, the Doctor paused.

"What have we here?" said he; "some very curious specimens of the botany of this region, the more curious as growing together within so small a space; some herbs that I have known in Old England, the wild worthless flowers of which I have more than once observed cultivated as garden flowers. Hum, hum! The plot seems to have been richly manured, too. Are you learned in flowers and herbs of grace, my young friend?"

"Very little, Sir," said Septimius. "My sister Rose takes an interest in such things, and your ward, Miss Sybil Dacy, appears to have a certain acquaintance with them, and my Aunt Nashoba, without being what you would call scientific, has Solomon's kind of acquaintance with every vegetable, I believe, from the cedar to the hyssop upon the walk; so that some little knowledge of the matter has remained upon me, by brushing my garments against those about me. Besides, I have felt an interest in the subject, lately, from certain private reasons."

"Aha!" said Doctor Ormskirk, looking up sideways, as, with great insouciance, he continued to bend his squat frame over the hillock; then, rising, red in the face, he continued, "If I were now where I was twenty years ago, and had not more important matters at hand,—more important discoveries before me, as well as behind—I should beseech it of your courtesy to let me remember your neighborhood, and watch the progress of certain things that I see in this curious little spot. But my spiders need me! I cannot be spared from that great interest of humanity and science. The web holds me, though like a fly, I struggle the harder to escape it. But you are young, and at your studies, which I understand, tend towards divinity—a direction, I may say, very different from the one I squat over, so it is useless speaking of it."

Septimius greatly desired to know what was in the Doctor's mind; but there had come upon his shy and sensitive character, in the presence of this demonstrative, yet inscrutable personage, a sudden doubt and shame of his pursuit, and all connected with it, and he reasonably feared, moreover, that a man of such apparent science as Dr. Ormskirk would perceive, at his very first attempts to talk upon such a subject, precisely what he was aiming at, and what his hopes were. And, indeed, just at that instant,—he knew not why, it took slight causes or none to bring about these moods —he had a clear perception that he was an exceeding fool, and would rather have shared poor Francis Norton's earthy bed with him, than have stood up in the sunshine and avowed to it to Dr. Ormskirk. So, although the Doctor seemed to linger and hover (a strange image for the squat solidity of his person) about the subject, making remarks about occult properties in vegetable nature, and what stores and powers of both life and death there are, in the homeliest little bit of garden ground, or even in the flowerpot that a city seamstress puts in her window, he responded not, or next to nothing. The Doctor, however, appeared to have taken a great fancy to his companion, though why, or on the score of what unknown social endowment on his part, Septimius could not conceive; having scarcely opened his lips during the interview, except to make an occasional necessary response to the Doctor's own abundant talk.

<(Septimius makes some remark which draws out Dr. O's speech about the faith of young men)>

"It is meat and drink to me," said the Doctor, "old student as I am, doubting of most things, because it is so hard actually to teach anything—it is meat and drink, I say, to meet with a young man of fresh powers and fresh faith, confident that he can get anything out of the hands of his mother Nature that he chooses to ask her for, just as a spoilt child can successfully teaze his kind mother to give him the scissors, the needle, anything for a plaything, though in her private opinion it may be dangerous for him. And it is very wonderful, how much the young enthusiasm and faith will really win from Nature, through natural causes, when such an old doubter as I am would to a certainty fail. No; I must still hang in my spider's web. But it's meat and drink with me to see a young man who has still power through faith. And, speaking of meat and drink, I must be on the lookout for a dinner. I smelt a cabbage—a vegetable I hate—in good Mrs Hagburn's house, and declined her invitation."

"Well, Sir," said Septimius, rather reluctantly, "my own dinner hour is at hand; and if you like to take the chance of what a table, never very sumptuously provided, will present, you shall be welcome."

"Oh, with pleasure," said the Doctor, "with pleasure; and, my dear young friend, your society would more than make amends, were the food nothing more than bread and cheese. I have gone through the ordinary vicissitudes of a philosopher's life, and have occasionally lacked so much. I shall be delighted to sit at your board."

And, after another look at the hillock, which certainly did appear to interest him almost as strongly as if his green spectacles had a magical power, and showed him what ghastly object lay beneath, (and at every fixed look which the Doctor cast it, a nervous thrill ran through Septimius's frame) he turned away, with a kind of smile just fading from his rubicund visage, as Septimius's eyes fell upon it. The hill-side proved too steep for the Doctor, with his short legs, to descend it with convenience, or even safety; for his foot slipping, the rotundity of his form was exemplified by his rolling till brought up by the interposing trunk of a tree; and as Septimius hastened to his assistance, he overheard him, under his breath, muttering curses upon the hill, and all belonging to it, dead or alive.

"That is a very comprehensive anathema, Doctor Ormskirk," said Septimius, whose ecclesiastical training made him rather sensitive on such points; besides that, he did not relish curses, which, if at all effectual, must fall upon himself, his friends, and poor Francis Norton.

"Oh, I beg your pardon, my dear friend," said the Doctor, getting up and adjusting himself as well as he could. "It's an old, bad habit of mine, this cursing and swearing. A bad habit, and yet I think it does one good, as a breaking out of disagreeable humors sometimes does a patient from internal disorders; and at worst, you know, a curse is like a stone flung into the air—it is likelier to fall on your own head than anywhere else. Now, you, if you ever feel inclined to curse anybody, will stifle it in your own breast, where it will do you a good deal of mischief. I am a free, open hearted old fellow, you see."

But this was what Septimius did not precisely see, though some of the Doctor's demonstrations certainly indicated it; although Septimius, with that keen, subtle, ineluctable instinct of character, which shy men are so often gifted withal, had more than once already raised the question.

As they reached Septimius's door, Aunt Nashoba met them and looked sharply at Dr Ormskirk, who returned the gaze and bowed, but seemed surprised, at least, if not alarmed, by the good lady's aspect; for to say the truth, whatever she might have been in her younger days, Aunt Nashoba had now come to be an awful mixture of the Indian squaw and herb-doctress, with the dry old maid of New England pattern, and a sort of wild witch-aspect running through the whole, and a skin as yellow as gold, being either the hue of her Indian intermixed blood or else the effect of her herb-drink; and she looked, moreover, as forbidding as if she were a dragon guarding the threshold. When Septimius had ushered the learned man into his study and was about to follow him, Aunt Nashoba beckoned him back.

"Who is that you have brought home?" asked she, motioning Septimius to close the study-door.

"A stranger who met me on the hill," said the young man —"a Doctor Ormskirk, who calls himself the guardian of Sybil Dacy, and pretends to great knowledge of botany, and science, especially as regards spiders. He has skill in the virtues of herbs; and if you will give the man his dinner, it may be worth your trouble to talk with him about old English hedge-growths and garden-herbs."

"And what do you want of him yourself, Seppy?" said Aunt Nashoba.

"Nothing—at least, I expect to gain nothing by him," said Septimius, with an expression of bitterness. "I don't believe in men of science, even if this Dr. Ormskirk is really one. As he threw himself in my way, I take him in—that's all."

"That's well," said Aunt Nashoba; "though a beastly, bearded old wretch he is, as ever I saw," muttered she. "But he shall have his dinner, and, if he likes to talk about herbs, I'll put an old Indian doctress's science against his, any day. As for dinner, he may take pot-luck."

When Septimius entered the study, he found the squat Doctor standing on tiptoe to take down poor Francis Norton's sword, from the mantel-piece, where it had been hanging untouched, and gathering the dust, ever since the day of Lexington fight. A spider, moreover, had taken occasion to weave his web along the hilt and guard, and thence appended silken threads to the scabbard, and thence to the wall, as if to do all in its power to prevent the weapon's ever being drawn again. The Doctor examined this web with some attention, and looked round for the insect whose handiwork it was, and espied it on the wall.

"A spider, if you have ever observed it, is the most peaceful creature in the world," said he. "What pains, now, to keep the sword in its sheath; and, whenever they have an opportunity, they make a web right across a cannon's mouth. But, my young friend, I have seen this sword before."

"Very likely," replied Septimius, not shrinking from the subject, although he would rather it should not have been broached; "it was the sword of a British officer, and it came into my possession fairly."

"Poor Francis Norton," said the Doctor; and yet Septimius's ear did not detect any real grief in the melancholy tone with which he said it. He drew the sword from the scabbard, and cast his eye along it, the hilt being of silver, apparently, wrought in open work, with an heraldic device, and the blade having a motto engraved on it, in old English letters. "It is an old family weapon, Sir, that the young fellow's father and grandfather had done their part towards maiming and murdering their race with. His family would value it much, if it might be restored to them."

· 381 ·

<(Herbs, so needful to man, that they follow his footsteps wherever he goes.)>

Septimius replied, that he had long since written to inform the representatives of the young officer, whoever they might be, that the weapon and other articles were in his keeping, and that he should be prepared to give them up to any person duly authorized to receive them. The Doctor appeared inclined to pursue the subject further, notwithstanding his host's evident unwillingness to enter upon it; but by this time they were summoned to dinner, which consisted of a stew of veal, made savory with some of Aunt Nashoba's spicy herbs; and a dish of boiled weeds, very fresh and tender; for this good lady found food scattered by bold Nature's double handsfull, everywhere, whether in the wood and fields, or in her familiar path about the barn-door, and had a peculiar name, among her neighbors, as for many other evil things, so for feeding her household on poisons; whereas, it was only that she had the instinct of bird or beast for what was good for her. Before sitting down to table, Aunt Nashoba offered the man of science a preliminary drop of her bitters, and eyed him with a warm glance almost malign in its keenness, as he applied it to his squab nose, snuffed, and finally shook his head and set down the tempting goblet. "Pray excuse me, Madam," said he. "It is good, I doubt not, but I took the precaution to provide myself with a restorative to which an inward complaint forces me often to have recourse."

<During dinner Aunt Nashoba plies him with shrewd questions, at which he sometimes seems embarrassed>

So saying, he took a leathern flask, with a silver cup screwed on, from his ample pocket, and offering it to Aunt Nashoba, Rose, and Septimius, all of whom declined, poured out a bumper of what seemed to be right Nantz, and drank it off with evident relish. He fought rather shy of Aunt

Nashoba's vegetable dishes, but ate boldly and abundantly of whatever else was on the table, such as ample drafts of potent old cider, which he enriched with fiery life from his own flask, and, to all appearance made an excellent drink out of these homely materials. While this was going on, he was by no means silent, but talked much with all three of his table-companions, not forgetting Rose Garfield, to whose beauty and grace he paid strong homage, and who talked with him a little about Sybil Dacy, but was not enough impressed with liking for the burly guest to encourage much intercourse. With Aunt Nashoba he talked about natural medicine, and the powers of herbs, assenting to her view that the concoctions of Doctors are worth nothing, and that the knowledge of physic should be sought among natural and unsophisticated races, and that here, in New England, it had died out with the destruction of the Indians, or their vile degradation in the white men's society; or whatever relics of it lingered were in such an old, half-squaw as herself, who, likewise, had lost what was most efficacious. She propounded it as her theory, that the Great Spirit had given to man, naturally, as he does to the brute creatures, the instinctive knowledge of what remedies were sovereign for all the diseases of which he was susceptible, and if his instincts were not blunted, he will still see these precious things scattered all about his feet, springing up, offering themselves, sending up their odors, attracting him by their prettiness, growing in spite of him among the meaner things that he prizes so much more; and that the husbandman roots up & flings aside as worthless a thousand things more valuable than all he raises. This view the old lady supported with a spicy eloquence, that seemed to have the rich fragrance of the herbs she talked of in it, and was no doubt made more earnest by sips from her famous jug, the frequency of which vied with those which Doctor Ormskirk drew from his leathern-covered flask. The Doctor seemed much impressed with Aunt Nashoba's vigor and shrewdness, and native strength of idea, and had not much to say for the regular system of physic; only he uttered a word or two about spiders, but was put down at once by Aunt Nashoba, who brushed his theory away like so many cobwebs, and, fierce and shrill, seemed to threaten to crush the squat Doctor himself, like the spider in the midst of it. Septimius, meanwhile, said little or nothing, but let the subject be bandied to and fro between these disputants, each pretending to be so skilled in their several ways.

After dinner, the Doctor, who professed himself a man of homely breeding, and still loving to recur to his native habits, whenever he might, asked liberty to sit down in the chimney corner, and smoke his pipe; which license Aunt Nashoba not only freely accorded, but volunteered to share in his enjoyment, and accordingly this queer pair sat down under the great jaws of the chimney, talking together voluminously, the Doctor occasionally swallowing great gulps of smoke, which, after a few moments, seemed to break out from his mouth, his nose, his ears, even his eyelids, as if he were a thing of smoke and fumes, pervaded with it; this feat he performed two or three times, while Rose wondered, Septimius started, and Aunt Nashoba maintained an Indian indifference; merely nodding and smiling grimly, and saying once "The Old Harry himself could not beat that,—only he would make a flash or two of fire and brimstone come out with the smoke. You can't do that, can you?"

"Not quite, my good lady," said the Doctor.

<He talks of occult matters, elixirs, instances of long life &c &c>

But the after dinner conversation took a different tone from that which preceded it. The Doctor made some observation, referring to the peopling of the British colonies in America, and the kinship that must needs exist, though often unsuspected, between families of distinction in England, and offshoots in America; and that doubtless, in many cases, here was the lawful hereditary branch of houses that had gone into the female line in England, or were deemed extinct; and that cottages, log-houses, held the heads that might be held up proudly in ancestral halls, and that sunburnt husbandmen tilled their scraggy and meagre fields, who were rightfully the owners of park and domain, where a hundred tenants held vastly better properties than these wretched & barren New England hills. He said that there were doubtless proofs of such descent existing in galleries, old desks, & such receptacles, perhaps used to kindle fires, old family papers, the value of which was utterly unsuspected by the possessors, but which, in the right hands, would serve as magic spells to bring wealth and honors to the unsuspecting possessors. And he observed, what good might be done to the old, worn out, aristocratic races of England, if a infusion of fresh life could be poured into them from such sources. For he said, England was decaying, and needed new blood; that they had dwelt too long in that climate, which made them thick and soggy, and that the welfare of the English race demanded that, every thousand years or so, there should be new infusions; and that till another conquest could be made, which he foresaw would be from America, the best thing was to do it partially, and among families. By some easy transition, he passed from this subject to the name of Norton, which he said was an old and honorable family name in England, and inquired what traditions or records there might be, respecting the emigration of the family, the part of England they came from. In answer to these queries, Aunt Nashoba emitted several wilder legends than that which we have already recorded about the Great Sagamore; it seemed indeed, as if a lying spirit had got into the queer old woman, and, as if besides, she were tipsier than usual with her bitters; such strange pictures did she give of the characteristics of the family, their doings from age to age, piling up and laying on trait after trait, which, if from her own imagination, yet had a strange sort of propriety and characteristicalness, so that you could not help taking them as true. The Doctor stared, and smoked, and stared again, and puffed, ejaculating, "Very strange! Singular truth!"—but in the meanwhile seemed wandering in a mist, and floundering to get out. Meantime Sybil Dacy, who was as familiar about the house as a bird, had come in, and sat aprt listening to Aunt Nashoba's queer stories, till at last she broke into a peal of shrill laughter, that seemed to operate as breaking a spell.

"You are a very queer family, Madam!" growled the Doctor, partly suspecting that Aunt Nashoba had made a fool of him.

"Ah, Doctor Ormskirk," said Sybil &c &c &c.

<(The Doctor's parting remarks should indicate a suspicion that Septimius had the recipe for the elixir in his possession.)>

The guest fell into a reverie, either at Sybil's words, or some reflection of his own, and again betook himself to swallowing tobacco-smoke, and letting himself be permeated by it, and then giving it out again; and to such an extent did he carry this, that it seemed to the observers as if he were dissolving and going up chimney. However, that was not really the mode of his departure; for finally knocking the ashes out of his German pipe, he made his farewells to the family, in a suitable manner, thanking Aunt Nashoba for her communications, from which he had learned so much, and civilly making overtures towards a salute to Rose, which she declined. As for Septimius, he congratulated himself upon having made the acquaintance of a young student of so much promise, and expressed the hope and purpose of meeting him again. <(Before the Dr. goes away he must say some one thing that dwells on Septimius's mind, and makes him follow him to Boston.)>

"Seppy," said Aunt Nashoba, as soon as the door had closed behind the Doctor and Sybil, "that man is a humbug. Take care of him; he means you a mischief."

"What do you mean, Aunt Nashoba?" said the young man. "Very likely he is a humbug; my own impressions about him rather make me think so; but what harm can he do me, if he be?"

"Well, Seppy, I am a witch you know, and I know he comes here with some mischief in his mind; and so, if you observed, I did not tell him a word of truth in answer to any question that he asked. His mind is full of humbug in this talk about spiders, and I don't believe he has any real knowledge about anything."

The next morning, they learned that the Doctor had departed on horseback, as he came; so that, on this occasion, at least, no harm happened to Septimius. <(Look at page 43 of first sketch)> The Doctor vanished as it were, in a cloud of tobacco-smoke from his pipe, leaving a flavor of brandy and tobacco behind him in Septimius's study; who mused much on his parting words, but felt an indefinite doubt of the man which made him reject the frequently recurring idea of trying to make use of his assistance. <(Something about the grave having been disturbed)>

In all these months that had passed, and were passing, an acquaintance, approaching to intimacy and not unworthy to be called friendship, had sprung up between Rose Garfield and Sybil Dacy; for the characters of the two young women, unlike as they were, had many points which adapted them to one another. The gentle, equable, quiet, New England girl, with her calm sweet reasonableness, being well qualified to be the friend of the impulsive, wayward Sybil, while at the same time, by her cultivation and thought, she could appreciate the value of a nature much unlike her own. At first, Sybil did not seem well inclined to be friends with Rose, held herself in a somewhat haughty, or sullen and petulant reserve; but when the latter persevered in kindness, and availed herself of the simple habits of intercourse, common to the time and place, to cheer the queer stranger, to show her the wood walks, the pleasant places of the river and the ponds, Sybil by and by yielded at once not gradually, and manifested warmer affection for Rose than the quiet, undemonstrative habits of a New England girl were quite prepared to respond to. And so they walked together, and talked together, and the sweet, wild character of Sybil came out to Rose with gush and effusion, in songs, in laughter, in tears; but it was all without anything of what is called confidence on Sybil's part; although she talked to her of her life in England, in an English village, which she dwelt on, with long descriptions of its quiet scenery, its old church and the graves about it. She had been of rank little elevated, not connected with the aristocracy, the old family of which she said much in her girlish talk. Sometimes she mentioned

Doctor Ormskirk, whom Rose conjectured to be sole remaining protector, for Sybil was an orphan. Rose sometimes thought that there were portions of her life which Sybil concealed from her, or which she buried from herself, and never alluded to some chamber in her heart that was shut up in darkness; there seemed to be some purpose, she half fancied, with which she was residing there; some recollection that made her knit her brow, and brought flashes into her eyes, some madness, perhaps, lurking in her system, which flashed out at unawares; but these demonstrations decreased, as time went on, though perhaps there was a certain gentler sorrow which took its place.

Early in the acquaintance, Rose's female acuteness had led her to think that Septimius was viewed with a certain strange interest, the nature of which she could not satisfactorily determine. Sybil had been accustomed to watch him in a certain way, letting nothing of his demonstrations escape her, looking at him under her brows with a sort of furtive glance, that had more the aspect of insanity than any of her other demonstrations. There was always a perceptible change of tone, whenever their conversation turned upon him; and yet she seemed curious to know more and more about him. Sometimes, a fit of trembling took her, when they came suddenly upon him; once, early after her coming, she saw Sybil make a strange gesture of menace at him, which caused her to look absolutely murderous, as if she could have plunged a dagger into his heart, or given him poison to drink, so strange a gesture that Rose could never after get it quite out of her memory, but often revolved it in her mind, wondering what it could mean. But, after a time, the demonstrations were of a somewhat different character, though still such as to perplex Rose with wonder as to what they could signify. A close acquaintance, as has been said, grew up between the girl and Septimius; she was, as it were, the privileged intruder on his walk on the hill-top, where Rose herself did not feel altogether privileged to intrude; but thereto Sybil went, with the freedom of a child, whenever the fancy took her, and spoke to Septimius when she pleased, or if the mood bade, was silent, watching him as he walked, in his reverie and wilderness of thought; watching him in his trances, sometimes smiling, moving her lips as if talking to herself, sometimes frowning, sometimes bursting into tears —then again, for days together, keeping out of his sight;— then suddenly re-appearing. Rose did not well know what to make of it, but was apprehensive that this poor brain-shattered girl, was contracting a sort of interest in her brother which could not turn out well for either of them; although this idea, too, was counteracted, as we have said, by many symptoms, and perhaps most of all by that fierce, murderous gesture which she remembered. If it were love, Rose could not wonder at it; for Septimius, with that Indian grace of his figure, that dark, expressive face of his, with a certain natural courtesy towards woman, which distinguished him, was not ill-calculated to make an impression on an imaginative girl's heart; and, besides, there was always somewhat peculiar in his deportment towards Sybil.

Rose could not satisfy herself what was the nature of Septimius's feeling, any more than what was Sybil's. She sometimes felt inclined to talk with him upon the subject, to tell him her suspicions as to Sybil's sanity, and all the proofs that she noted of it; to warn him of the necessity of being careful not to take upon himself the responsibility of engaging the affections of a being so situated; to caution him, too, with sisterly care, about his own heart, and to set before him the inevitable misery of an attachment (should such spring up between them) where marriage ought not to be thought of as its result. But Septimius was one of the most unapproachable persons, so far as his inner life was concerned, that ever lived; and, loving him as a sister, and being loved by him equally, Rose felt no more at liberty to open such a conversation as she thought of, than if they had never spoken a word together in the world. It was an impossibility; it seemed as if there were no language provided in which she could do it. And besides, as far as Sepitimius was concerned, there seemed little danger; he cared only for the subject, whatever it was, the study, that so absorbed him; those smiles that came out like sunlight from behind a cloud, and fell upon Sybil—they meant nothing. He did not love her. It was absurd to think that this dark nature loved anything. And as for Sybil, whenever Rose's apprehension about an ill-omened attachment on her part was at its height, there most frequently came one of those symptoms of passionate aversion that so perplexed the kind and quiet observer. Nevertheless, much revolving all these things, Rose could not but wish, much as she loved Sybil, that this strange connection with her were at an end, and that she would vanish into the mystery out of which she had come; and be remembered kindly, and with regret, but never come again with that train of dreary griefs and fears.

The intimacy and habits of daily intercourse between Rose and Sybil Dacy being such as we have described, the two friends had been one day on an excursion of a mile or more to where the slow river wound lazily among its meadows, a dark stream, and were returning through a tract of wood which, by a very gradual ascent, led them to the more abrupt brow of Septimius's hill. It was a wood of pitch pine-trees, with tufts of small birches intermixed, and a few shrub-oaks; this growth of a meagre soil, all of them, little worth clearing for the sake of the timber, and not more so for any crops that it might promise. This was a region known to them both, and having an imaginative interest, by means of Aunt Nashoba's legends of Indian life, and witchcraft, and as having been the home of the Great Sagamore, of wondrous memory. The shrubbery was so dense and entangled, in the interior part of the wood, that the girls with some difficulty forced their way through it, but the trees and bushes scattered, as they approached the brow of the hill, and, by and by, Sybil laid her hand on Rose's dress, and drew her back a little, pointing with her finger at Septimius, who was present at his customary haunt.

"He has found a prize now," said Sybil, with a strange, little laugh.

It was so strange a laugh, that, instead of looking at Septimius, Rose looked first at her, and saw such an expression of mischief in her eyes, and smiling out of her lips, all so brightening up the face with malign intelligence, that she half-believed Sybil to be such a being as Aunt Nashoba talked about as haunting the spot of old. And yet, in the very moment when this sprightish, puck-like, elfish, impish merriment was at its height, an acute look of distress assumed its place, her eyes filled with tears, she wrung her hands—"Woe! woe!" murmured she.

"What is the matter, Sybil?" exclaimed Rose, in much alarm at what she thought nothing less than a sudden access of madness.

"He has found it!" repeated she. "Look at him!"

And, this time, Rose turned her eyes towards Septimius, whose appearance, however, did by no means account for the singular and violent agitation, of a double nature, into which it seemed to have thrown Sybil. He was bending down over that little mound, which Rose had so often seen without conjecturing the secret which it covered, and appeared to be closely examining what grew there—examining the spot with a searching, earnest, absorbed interest that indicated, certainly, a very great scientific interest in some specimen that he found there. But, soon, he threw up his hands with a gesture of wonder, Rose thought too it might be thankfulness, then he rose to his feet and clasped his hands; then knelt down again, and examined the spot closer than ever.

"Come," said Sybil, taking Rose's arm and drawing her along. "Let us go and see what he has found. It must needs be something very curious to have thrown so staid and immoveable a person as your brother into such a wonder and such a rapture. I really did not guess, before, what an enthusiastic lover of botany he is."

Had Rose been alone, she would have hardly ventured to come within Septimius's sphere at such a moment, but Sybil's irresistible impulse, and something more respectable in herself than female curiosity—a desire, on Septimius's account, to know what it was that so interested him, and thereby, perhaps, to gain some light on the subject of those dark and absorbing pursuits that had insulated Septimius, now in the freshness of his youth, from all the business, the interests, the hopes of men around him, from all consciousness of or sympathy with the civil war that was going on, from consciousness that an old system of things had gone to wrack, and a new one had come to existence, since, as it were, he had last opened his eyes upon the world, or given token that he felt himself as belonging to it;—feeling as if, at this juncture, points so important to one so affectionately cared for might be illustrated, she overcame her repugnance, and went along with Sybil. The latter, as they drew nearer the young man, sent her voice before her among the trees, in a light, airy tone, in which, however, Rose fancied that she could detect a little of that malign quality which had gleamed from her eyes; though, if she had heard it at another time, she might have thought it as cheerful as the note of a bird.

"What blossom has some angel dropt there, that attracts you so much? Soho, Sir Florist."

Septimius turned towards them, and, Indian-like, was at once as composed as if he had been looking at the commonest weed that ever grew by his door-step—plantain, pig-weed, or one of the mullens that denoted the barren soil of his hill.

"Come," said he, quietly—"perhaps you can help me. I find here a flower which I cannot account for, either by my experience of flowers growing hereabout, or by anything that I have read in books. You, who have seen what wonders the gardeners of the old world produce, can perhaps throw some light upon it."

<A bloody toad stool>

"Oh, no;—not I," said Sybil, laughing as she drew near. "You must ask Aunt Nashoba, who knows all the plants of the soil and the virtues of them, and brews them all up into her bitters;—turning all sweets to bitterness, as I sometimes think. But why should you not think it altogether a new production? Is Nature so old, that new conditions should not produce new things, and out of a soil strangely prepared something as strange should not come? I think, for my part, the earth corresponds with the state of the dwellers on it; and flowers of paradise or poisonous herbs spring out of it, according to what sort of light comes from the eyes that look upon it;—that light has more effect than sunshine."

"Then look here," said Septimius, quietly, yet with a sort of meaning in his tone that came there in spite of himself;— "look at these buds, just opening, and tell me what sort of soil, or what sort of light from what eyes, could have caused them to spring up on this barren New England hill-side.

When was their seed planted? How is it, in the long course of ages since the creation, that violets, white-weed, fox-glove, asters, have grown out of this barrenness, but never these. Speak, learned professor!" His inward excitement could not be quite restrained, but flashed forth a little in these words.

<It must be heart-shaped.>

The girls both approached, and stooping down, beheld a crimson flower growing on the turfy seat (for into such form, as we have said, Septimius had shaped the grave) close to the ground, out of which it might be supposed just to have sprung, right over the breast of the corpse. It had not been there yesterday; here it was now, quite in bloom, but closing its red petals over its heart. There seemed to be no stem to elevate it from the soil, no leaves, nothing but the flower, deep set in soil, like a gem more than anything else, such rich color it had, such a glow, such a shine upon its petals. On such of its petals as were spread abroad, there were spots of glistening jet, else it was all crimson. It seemed not a flexible flower, but there was a kind of fleshiness, apparently, in the texture of its petals, and something singular in the way that it clasped them, as it were, over its heart; as if that, at all events, must not be disclosed, and as if it would wither without full bloom, rather than open to the sun whatever mystery was beneath it. The sun was now shining full down upon it, as if to woo it out of its mystery, but it was still closely folded, and, what looked more singular, there were two or three drops of dew, or else some peculiar moisture of the flower, that appeared to have oozed from among the closed petals, out of its heart, and did not exhale; the rich color of the flower itself, either seen through the transparency of these dew-drops, or reflected in them, made them resemble drops of blood; and, indeed, to one who knew the mystery of that little mound, it might have seemed that the entire flower was a drop of crimson agony in which the secret of death had burst forth from the virgin and innocent earth. Or, on the other hand, so brilliant, and in a certain sense beautiful it was, it might have been taken for the spontaneous outgush of a certain richness in the soil, and happy adaptation of sun, shower, and earth, to develope a seed that perhaps had lain dormant till now, when it gushed forth for joy. The heart of the beholder might interpret it in either fashion, accordingly as it itself was fertile of joyous or sombre fantasies. For myself I once saw what I suppose to be the same flower—if flower it were, or not rather a knob of fleshy richness and splendor—in the magnificent garden grounds of Eaton Hall, in England, and felt, I never yet know why, a sort of fascination and repugnance, both in one.

"What a strange flower!" said Rose. "Has it any fragrance?"

<(There should be hesitation, doubt, and varying emotions before she destroys the flower)>

"Yes; such as it is," said Sybil, bending towards it, and expanding her delicate nostrils, then shrinking back. "But I like it not—Ah! it makes me faint! Come, Rose, let us leave him with the beautiful flower he has brought to light. It should be called after his name, and make him live forever— in scientific fame, I mean. The 'spreading Nortoniensis.' Pah, it is an ugly smell, now I think of it."

With one of those freaks of petulance to which she was so liable, she plucked the flower from the soil, whence it seemed to be drawn without difficulty, and flung it away with her whole force. Then, flitting away with sprite-like laughter, she called to Rose to follow her, and made her escape down the hill; looking back however, and clapping her hands as she saw Septimius standing stupified with horror at this sudden destruction of the gem which Nature had just offered him, and which he could not but suppose to have had a purport and potency, which the act of this wild girl had annihilated forever. We should be loth to set down the anathemas with which poor Septimius filled the air, and which, as it were, he sowed into the grave, caring not what dark harvest might spring up from them; for when fully aroused, there was a terrible fellness and blackness in his passion, nor was it at once to be quelled or modified by the consideration that poor Sybil was an unaccountable being, and even had she been in full health of mind, neither she nor any other could have suspected all the hopes, the immortal projects, that he connected with this strange flower; what study, what pains, what art, had been lavished there, what rich science; and now, in the moment of success, all was brought to naught by the freak of this girl. What was singular, too, it seemed to add to his passion and despair and wrath, that it was Sybil who had thus destroyed his hopes, had stood up his enemy; had torn the bloody flower out of his heart. Had it been Rose, he could have borne it better; it was enough in keeping with her quiet strength to reject, repel, destroy, if she could, a certain monstrousness that he could not but acknowledge in this production; but from Sybil he had rather looked, out of his loneliness, for sympathy. Yet she had done it. Amid thoughts and wild passions like these, there is reason to think that Septimius spent the whole summer-night upon the hill-top, pacing to and fro, or flinging himself on the ground, pillowing his head on Francis Norton's grave, and wildly gesticulating beneath the stars, and howling to the roar of the blast among the pines. In all his history, he never came quite so near to madness—if, indeed, he did not touch it, as on this occasion.

And, after all, there was the slightest possible occasion for it. Nature—or the power, whatever it might be, aside of Nature—that produced the flower, was not so poor or so niggardly as he supposed. As morning brightened upon him, spreading crimson and gold for the new day to tread upon, Septimius threw his dull eye upon the grave, which all night long, had lain a black heap, and there he was surprised by an appearance as of gems now flashing and shining, and a fragrance that grew heavily, ascending into the morning air. The hillock had burst forth with these strange flowers—these sanguine blossoms—each on the same precise pattern as the first, with what seemed petals folded over its heart; in some of them Septimius fancied that he caught glimpses of a golden centre, gleaming out, but still it was a mystery. It made him tremble as if they were apparitions; as if the buried one were reappearing in this form of a new flower, as he remembered in some of the antique myths dead youths had been transformed into flowers, which, to this day, pass as love-tokens, and are worn in reminder by some. He grew faint; perhaps it might be the perfume, sweet, but heavy, that came up in the morning air. The grave looked studded with drops of fire over it, or blood. He plucked one of the flowers and, tearing open the heart, pulled it to pieces with his fingers. There was no flexibility in the petals; they broke off abruptly, and he filled his hand with the red fragments, staining his finger tips with the juice. He could not overcome a certain antipathy; yet he knew not why. There was no discoverable secret in the heart.

"It is not a flower," said he to himself. "Methinks it is a sort of scarlet toad-stool!"

Whatever it was, there was and continued to be a most abundant growth of it on the hillock, sanguine hearts breaking out continually, and no root perceptible; for those which Septimius pulled up had a thick fleshy stem, and a sort of broad, round foot, but no fibres clinging to the ground. They lasted but a day in perfection, and the next morning were decayed, and their pleasant, though heavy fragrance changed to something disagreeable; so that, every morning, Septimius's first care was to weed up the whole crop of yesterday, and fling them away; a task which he performed with infinite disgust and repugnance, shuddering as if he were touching the decaying mortality of Francis Norton. Still it was to be done; and every morning, as we said, there was the splendid show of sanguine hearts growing all over the mound, radiating from the centre, spreading, and appearing in more abundant number every morning. How long would this luxuriant production continue? Was it the rich growth of the heart of his slain foeman? How rich a heart must it be, if it could long supply such a daily crop. He must make haste to avail himself of it, if it were indeed available, since any day, the production might cease, and he find only the ghastly heap of yesterday.

Thus spurred and excited, he applied himself with more force and assiduity than ever to evolving the intricacies of the old manuscript, and ravelling out, from the apparently studied and purposed ambiguities and labyrinthine methods it inculcated, some definite method of proceeding. But, still, there was that chasm, not to be supplied, that torn leaf, that revoked the very life out of the essence of mortality. In his earnestness, he soon deemed himself competent to read every line and letter of what was in his possession; though there was a fantastic character in its instructions, that sometimes made him fancy it the work of a dreamer, and possessing a bewildering power of making whosoever should read it a dreamer too. Once, to say the truth, in moments of despondency, he took an entirely different view of the whole thing, and was inclined to believe that some mystic, under the guise of inventing a drink of immortality, had been prescribing the methods (in the language of parables and symbol, under which the wise hid their wisdom, in days of darkness) by which a nation, not an individual being, might attain enduring existence on earth; and perhaps the mystic writing had still another purport, teaching how the soul might attain a better immortality; and all the talk of herbs, of processes, alchymic or other, were but a symbolic mystery, purporting what were the virtues, and how to enrich the human nature, or the national character with them, by which this great result was to be claimed. Perhaps it was the spirit of mysticism, which he inherited from his great grandfather the Tomahawk of Righteousness, that led Septimius to this idea; for it certainly did not belong to the time in which he lived, nor had the present dynasty of New England mystics then begun to be; and he himself coming out from it as from a dream, resumed again his former and literal interpretation of what he read. Another idea pressed sometimes upon him; it was, that, after all, the possibility of living forever depended upon the will of the individual concerned, and that the formula of a rich prepared drink, to be taken at intervals, was but a material assistance to the will, strengthening and encouraging it with the semblance of help; whereas, at last, it could be only the power of the spirit over and throughout the body, remorselessly exerted, never faultering, that could do anything. In this view, what a labor must it be to live forever.

But these were only the struggles of a powerful, and naturally profound and sagacious intellect, to escape an unworthy thraldom to which it had once yielded itself. Septimius still clung to his delusion—if such it were.

<(binds her head with a dish-clout, or what looked like it)>

Aunt Nashoba, as it happened, in spite of her hereditary doctor-ship, her acquaintance with the medicinal virtues of all herbs, and her constant use of her famous bitters, fell, about this time, into a very bad state of health. The poor woman (if woman she really were, which many people questioned,) had never, in her best days, been lovely, either in person or character, and now, in this morbid condition of her being, she developed uglier aspects than her oldest acquaintances remembered. She grew as yellow as old brass, and, indeed, was said to have a dull metallic gleam from her sun-wizened, wrinkled face, as she sat cowering in her chimney-corner, even in the summer days, spreading herself over the smouldering embers, as if grudging the least spark of warmth to escape up the flue. She seemed deadly chill, never warm enough, although, in the torrid noon, she used to creep to the door-step and sit there, with the white blaze of the sunshine on her; an odd figure as you could see, with her handkerchief hat tied down over her ears, and a few of her gray locks straggling beneath; a blanket on her shoulders; and all the skirts and petticoats she had, girded about her; a forlorn, neglected, wretched looking thing, shivering and quaking, and groaning always when she shifted her position, and sometimes when she sat still, as if a pain gnawed her inwardly, or it hurt her to breathe. There was a spitefulness in her groans, that made people, passing by the house, somewhat loth about stopping, in a friendly way, to ask how she did; and they said, so yellow and unwholesome she looked, she seemed as if she had been gathering poison and mischief all the days of her life, and that now she was as full of it as a toad; but, not to belie poor Aunt Nashoba, there was probably no harm in her, beyond what old age, disease, and a disposition naturally energetic and ambitious, now compusively inert, would account for and extenuate. She was not so malign an old woman as people supposed her; sometimes, if they had listened with charitable ears, they might hear her muttering a prayer; but such was their notion of the acridity, bitterness, pepperiness, of the old thing's disposition, and so little of the angel was there in her looks, that they probably mistook these utterances under her breath for curses on them and herself. If her groans were spiteful and resentful, it was because she fought with her own infirmities. She kept her pipe alight, from morning till night, and it was pitiful to see what a rusty, henlike motion she had, as if her joints were rusty iron, when she got up from the door-step to hobble to the kitchen hearth, and rake the ashes for a coal to light it afresh; and sitting there for the smoking of one pipe, would refill it, light again, and come back to the sunny door-step, after taking a sip of her bitters. For. all day long, the brown earthen pitcher stood among the hot ashes, at the edge of the fire, covered with the lid of a black teapot, steaming forever out of its broken nose, and sometimes bubbling, so that the lid was lifted up, and a cloud of questionable fragrance puffed out into the kitchen, with the noise of a sigh, as if that jug were the one thing that sympathized with poor Aunt Nashoba.

Not that this was the truth; there might have been sympathy enough to keep poor Aunt Nashoba's heart warmer than either the fireside or the sunshine could keep her chilled frame. Rose saw her state with pitying affection, and besought that she might nurse her, and even make that precious brewage which had so long kept her alive, and light her pipe; but Aunt Nashoba shook her head, and gave a kind of snort, at these suggestions, and demeaned herself so ungraciously that Rose felt that the best thing she could do for the poor old soul, would be to keep out of her way. Septimius might have done something for her, perhaps, if he could have emerged so far from the shadow, obstruction, the underbrush and growth of thought, in which his obstructed studies and pursuits involved him, as to take note how much she needed it. In fact, he sometimes, when they met at table, or when he saw her sitting so forlornly on the door-step, as he passed her to go up the hill, was struck by the infirmity, the yellowness, the inertness that had fallen on her, and would say—"Aunt Nashoba, I'm afraid you are not well." "Ah, never fear, Seppy, never fear," she would reply, with a pitiful sort of briskness, which there was just life enough in her to supply. "I'm well enough; only I happen to have taken a sip too little of my bitters, so I'll just try it again." Then, leaning on his arm (but so that he thought it rather for affection than need) she would hobble to the fireplace, and pour the salutary draft out of the earthen jug, and drink it hot. "It's my life blood," she would say, "excellent stuff, Septimius, and, before I die, I'll teach you how to make it. Only use it right, and you'll live forever!" Then blessing him for being so attentive to her, (poor soul, when he had done everything mechanically, and not once really lifted his mind off its constant theme, as young people never think the aged are worth the least of their delusions) she bade him go his ways, and someday she would tell him what would repay him for all his kindness. This tenderness of old, acrid Aunt Nashoba ought to have warned him that all was not right; but, at this phase of his life, it was hard to get at his sensibilities, through all that cold and hard exterior covering of thought.

But, one morning, when she had come down stairs as usual, and made some infirm effort to go on with her household business (there being the more need of it, because Hannah Lord had quarreled with her the day before, and taken her departure) poor Aunt Nashoba found herself actually too ill to be out of her bed. So she tried, once and again, to get up stairs to her chamber, but being unable to surmount the very lowest step, she finally (and it was the first time in her life) bent down her dry, stiff, shrivelled, old heart to ask human assistance. She went to Septimius's study door, tried to open it, and finding it locked, rapped with her bony-knuckles; so dry they were, that it sounded as if a skeleton were knocking. "Who's there?" called Septimius, with a short, stern voice, feeling mightily wronged at the interruption, because he fancied himself, at that instant, just on the point of touching some invaluable mysteries of the manuscript.

"It is your Aunt Nashoba, Seppy," croaked the old woman. "I'm not very well, Seppy; and the rheumatize, or something, hinders me from getting up stairs. Couldn't you just come and help me? But if you're busy, just now, I can squat here on the floor, Indian fashion!"

At this pitiable appeal—just such a humble one as the proudest people make—Septimius opened the door at once, and was greatly shocked to see the yellow paleness of poor Aunt Nashoba, and the desolate, dry eyes with which she gazed up into his face, from her squatting posture, like some half wild thing, out of the forest, that, in its great necessity, had crept to a human's door for aid. He lifted her tenderly in his arms (wondering to find what a weightless heap of dry bones she was) and bore her up the stairs and laid her on her own bed, and inquired what he should do next. Septimius was of that order of shy, veiled natures (never like Aunt Nashoba herself) who are ashamed of their own tenderness, and rap it on the head, as if it were a snake, when it peeps forth; but Aunt Nashoba saw that he was really moved, and turned her yellow eyes on him gratefully.

"Thank you, Seppy," said she. "You're very kind to a poor old creature. Yes, dear, there is one thing you might do for me, and perhaps be doing yourself a service at the same time. I've felt so sick for a day or two back, that (which never happened to me afore this forty years) I've drained my pitcher of bitters without setting any more to brew. Now, Hilly dear, take paper and pen and ink, and sit down by my bedside, and I'll tell you what you may study a lifetime and never find it out."

Hilliard did as she bade him, a little grudging the time that would be wasted in humoring the old woman's whim, yet glad, on the whole, to do the poor soul this little kindness. Seeing him with his pen suspended over the paper, she said, with a faint laugh—"I've wondered if you were going to write down my will for me; and in fact, it is all I have to leave you, and it's a rich legacy, and you're welcome to it. It's a list of the things that go to the making of my wonderful bitters, Hilly."

Hilliard made a wry face, but hid it with his hand, and wrote faithfully, while Aunt Nashoba dictated a list of herbs, some of them common enough, others of much more rare occurrence, though all, as his tincture of botanical science made him aware, to be found, either of old transplantation from Europe, or of indigenous varieties, in New England soil; roots, as well as herbs, buds, blossoms, in a certain state of growth, full flowers, leaves, twigs, barks; it gave him a great deal of practical knowledge. He at first wrote carelessly, but as the name of one shrub, weed, or plant after another, fell from the old woman's lips, he became interested, inscribed the more hastily, and waited for the next with an eager empathy that seemed as if his intelligence was trying to snatch it from hers, before her slow speech could utter it. At last, she seemed to have come to an end;

yet Hilliard still kept his pen over the paper (where the ink fell and made a great blot in the place of the period that should have been,) and seemed to expect her to continue.

"That's all, Hilly dear," said Aunt Nashoba.

"No; not all, dear Aunty," said Hilliard. "Surely there was one more!"

"I never knew any more, Hilly," said she. "That's the recipe, as it came down to me."

"One other precious herb there surely was, Aunt Nashoba," persisted Hilliard, as if his life depended on it.

"I don't say but there might have been, in the great Sagamore's days," said Aunt Nashoba; "for this was the drink that he made by his wisdom and witchcraft, and toughened himself to be proof against death by it. They do say—the old tradition always said—that there was something that ought to have gone into this precious drink, and that tied the knot, as I may say, of all its other virtues. I suppose it must have been so; for though the drink has made me tough, it's going to let me die at least. These are all the herbs that have ever been put into the drink since the Great Sagamore's time; and so, because I knew something was lacking, I've always put in the next best thing I knew of—and that was a half-pint of good spirits to each jug-ful, Hilly. And it answers a good purpose, though the real thing might be better."

Hilliard was ready to tear his sable locks with unutterable vexation; for, strange to say, he recognized in Aunt Nashoba's receipt that very list of vegetable ingredients which he had been so many months employed in making out from the old manuscript, where some ancient sage had reposited the secret, as the concentrated richness distilled from years of study. Here it had been, all the while, within the knowledge of the old herb-woman, and not only that, but its steaming fragrance had been all his life in his nostrils, a remembered smell, from his earliest infancy, so that the whole idea of his poor, yellow, acrid relative, was bathed and permeated with it. But, what was equally strange, the one all-potent ingredient, which had dropt out of the manuscript, or which he still vainly hunted there, had likewise vanished from Aunt Nashoba's concoction.

<She directs him to a closet, but does not look closely at the bundle he takes.>

As his nature was, he grew dark and stern; the emergency being so unusual of seeing the possibility of bringing the draught of immortality to perfection forever pass away, by the death of the only human being who might or ought to have possessed it.

"I abjure you, woman, search your memory; look far back to things that you may have heard, before your intelligence took note of them. Remember the one other ingredient, and you may rise up from this bed of death, new, made over, refreshed for another lease of life."

"I shouldn't care about it, Hilly," said the old woman, quietly and wearily; "my heart's old, and the drink couldn't reach it; but, for your sake, if I knew the thing, I'd gladly tell it. But it was lost a hundred years, at least, before I was born; so now, Hilly, for the sake of the old Aunt that loves you, and loves nothing else, take that bundle of herbs in the paper bag, that hangs yonder—yes, that's it, and the herbs are all right—and fill the old earthen jug with them, and put them to simmer on the kitchen hearth. In two hours it will be done; then put in a half pint of spirit, you know, Hilly dear; and it will put me on my legs again for a month or two more. I don't want to die while there's any green thing left on the hill, or in meadow, field or wood. I must gather another harvest of herbs and roots, Hilly, and teach you the virtues of them. Make haste, Hilly, but let them simmer moderately."

Without more delay, Septimius took the fragrant bundle (for unlike the consummated drink to be distilled from them, the herbs, roots, twigs, bark, and flowers, combined into a genuine and natural perfume, like that of the woods), and hastening to the kitchen, put them into the earthen jug, which was just of sufficient capacity to receive them; then, as Aunt Nashoba had directed, he filled it within two inches of the brim with water fresh from the well, and placed it within the influence of the smouldering embers. He then covered the jug with the lid of the broken teapot, and sat down in Aunt Nashoba's old, short-legged, lath-bottomed chair, to watch the tedious process, often removing the lid, to see whether there were yet any tokens that the magic influence of the heat was at work upon the mysterious herbs of grace gathered within the compass of this earthen jug. The strangeness of the coincidence between Aunt Nashoba's despised mixture which he might have tasted, any day, and nourished himself upon from boyhood, and that rare medicine which the old manuscript had revealed to him, out of a remote antiquity, struck him more and more. There must be a potent virtue in it, stronger than death; else why should it have survived? Why else should Providence, or fate, have provided for its transmission; on one hand, in the hereditary hall, and among the archives of an ancient and noble family, by a leap, as it were, from a far generation to the present; on the other, by transmission from one old woman's hand to another, in a humble chimney corner—in two separate methods. Who could tell what far antiquity it came down from? With some changes, losing ingredients of power by the way, here might be the spell, the concoction of natural drugs, which Medea brewed into her cauldron, and so renewed her from age to rosy youth. Myths have their truth, and why not this, since the heart of man (ever dying just as he begins to live) so imperatively demands that it should be true, reaching old age and decrepitude with the burning spark of youth torturing him still, when it can no longer vivify him. Ah, but one ingredient—the precious one, that had the spell in it, the mighty herb of Paradise, that married all the rest, and made it possible for their varying virtues to combine, the medicine, this condition of their efficacy—that, alas! had vanished forever. Without it, as Aunt Nashoba's experience had proved, this draught was a mere wretched stew of quackery, virtueless, perhaps a slow poison, filling the veins with yellow ichor instead of blood, as had been the case with her, making her acrid, jaundiced, a thing with a shrivelled skin over rheumatic bones, and kept in infirm motion by an acrid spirit. Was the ingredient indeed gone out of the list forever! Must it always be a slow poison!

While thus Hilliard sat brooding, the earthen jug, having gathered a good deal of heat into itself, and the herbs, roots, twigs, flowers, buds, bark swelling with it, and the water now beginning to turn to medicine, it thrust up the lid of the teapot a little, and sent forth, as it were, a long sigh, and a visible puff of steam. Septimius started, as if somebody had spoken to him; he had got so estranged from actual things, so fancy involved, so much off his feet, that he felt as if the devil might be in the earthen pot. He turned pale; no matter why; he was in a strange, scarcely an accountable state of mind. Then, quietly and softly removing the jug just a little farther from the embers, so that it might not boil over while he was away, he stole out on tip-toe, and climbed the Hill, concealing his course as well as he could by the clumps of white birches that grew on the hill side. Why he trode so softly, why he was so instinctively anxious to be unseen, we cannot analyze the obscure phases of his temperament sufficiently to explain. Enough, that he went up the hill, and in the space of a few minutes returned to the kitchen hearth. We will not overlook what he did there. Let the earthen jug puff and steam as it had done thousands of times before. Aunt Nashoba's draught will be ready in due season.

At last the jug forced up its lid, and sent forth a long sigh, embodied and visible in a blast of steam, emitted so forcibly that Hilliard felt its warm moisture on his face, as he bent towards the hearth, and was sensible of (or else he fancied) a certain heavy richness in the odor, differing from the acrid pungency characteristic of Aunt Nashoba's concoction. He uncovered it, and saw the surface studded with little beads, which bursting, proved to be scented bubbles. The process was finished; the fire had combined all those vegetable potencies into one; and there needed now only that one other ingredient which the old herb-woman had been wont to add, on her own responsibility, in order to give a fiery life to this draught. So Hilliard, who had often observed where Aunt Nashoba kept this precious liquor, brought forth a friendly demijohn, and measuring out the prescribed quantity, poured it into the steaming pitcher. Before it could mix with the concoction, it apparently was kindled by the contiguity to the fire, and burned for a moment with a quivering blue flame, which Hilliard permitted to dance upon the surface till it expired. It looked very ghastly, and so did Hilliard's face as he sat eyeing it.

"I am in doubt as respects this last unauthorized ingredient," thought he. "Not unlikely, its weaker potency may, however, have adulterated the whole draught, weakening the fine strength of the celestial medicine of which Aunt Nashoba unawares held the secret. But beyond all question, she will refuse to taste it unless she smell the well-known spirituous steam."

He poured out a tea-cupfull of the liquid, and was half tempted to taste it, but remembering his horrible experience of a former sip, refrained, with a convulsive shudder of repugnance. He might drink deep of it hereafter; not now. At the point of death, he might drink; prolonged existence might be worth its nauseous bitterness. He was not yet ready for such mighty consequences as might result; it required, after all, a series of thoughtful considerations on which he had not yet entered, to satisfy him whether it were wise to accept a longer than the ordinary duration of human life. Aunt Nashoba, with her slighter woman's glance at the conditions of existence, would have no such scruples. Let her, therefore, take all the advantages of the new experiment, if so it could be called, when she had been trying it upon herself almost identically, through a course of two score years. Yet there seemed to be a certain reluctance, a strange hesitation, hanging about Hilliard, considering what a state of suffering poor Aunt Nashoba was in, and that the concoction of the beverage had already taken up more than an hour, during which he had sometimes heard a groan from above stairs, indicating unabated pangs on her part.

"Poor soul!" thought he, as one of these painful utterances again reached him, "I will keep her in agony no longer. We men are not fit to be nurses. We lack the empirical courage of women."

He went up stairs, treading carefully, lest he should spill a drop from the brimming and steaming cup, but yet left a little slop on every stair, owing to an unwonted tremulousness of his hand. Aunt Nashoba lay moaning, as before, and broke out into a much sharper and more spiteful croak, though feeble and weary, the moment she found Hilliard within earshot. "So, you've come at last. I might have died twenty times over, and I have, reckoning by death pangs. Have you made the bitters!"

"Here is the drink, Aunt Nashoba," he replied in an encouraging tone, "with all the virtues of forest and meadow in it."

"And the good stuff, too—the spirit, I mean," said the old woman eagerly. "Sometimes I lose my faith in the roots and herbs, and think the big-bellied demijohn holds the soul of my drink, after all."

"Then the soul is not wanting to it," replied Hilliard, "in full measure."

"Won't you taste it yourself, Hilly dear?" said Aunt Nashoba, mollified by the kindness which the usually self involved young man had shown her. "You look pale, and you little know what good it may do you."

"I need it not, dear Aunt," said he. "Do you drink it off, and tomorrow, maybe you will be quite well."

"You are a kind soul, after all, Hilly," said Aunt Nashoba, sitting up in bed, and taking the cup. "People that don't like us, often say of our family that it's full of bad blood and cold blood; but, I say, if you go deep enough, you find it rich and warm—just as I've found this drink, these forty years."

So saying, she gave an enormous gulp, and swallowed half the contents of the tea-cup at once; then paused an instant and looked Hilliard in the face, with a puzzled expression, but immediately put the cup again to her lips, and finished the draught, as a patient gobbles down a potion of doctor's stuff with all the greater haste, the less dulcet it is to his palate.

"You meant well, Hilly," said she, screwing up her mouth, "but it is too much to expect you to make this precious stuff, at the first trial, as well as an old herb-woman, that has put her whole skill into it for twice the time you've lived. You'll do better next time. But it has a queer taste, that's a fact, or else my wretched old mouth is getting out of taste—a sad thing that would be. I did think, my last pleasure in this world (and to tell you the truth, Hilly, I've had few others first as last) would be the trickling of these bitters down my throat. But my pains are easier already. 'Tis a good drink still."

She gave back the cup to Hilliard, after looking a little curiously at the dregs.

"It looks like the piece of blood-root, don't it," she remarked. "Perhaps it is my fault, after all. I gathered that bunch of herbs, a night or two ago, in the moonlight, as my great-aunt Kezzy taught my mother, as I've often done, and as the witches (Lord bless us) always used to do for their herb-drinks; but my eyesight isn't what it was, specially in the dark, and it may well be I slipt in an herb or two that did not belong there. As with other precious and delightful things, so with this one, it takes but little to spoil it. Well, Hilly, I feel awful drowsy now the pain's left me; cover me up, and I'll try to get a wink of sleep."

< (Perhaps an Indian cloak of dressed skin) >

< He leaves her a broomstick to knock with >

As she still complained of being very chill, Hilliard drew the bed clothes up about her shoulders, and withdrew after throwing an old red riding cloak over her shoulders, and carefully putting her stick within reach, in order that she might summon him by knocking upon the floor, in case of need. Returning to his study, he sat down to the old manuscript upon which he had poured out so much of his young life in the effort to make it intelligible, and tried whether Aunt Nashoba's communications would not cause its imperfectly read instructions to be seen in a new light. It might well have been so, perhaps, had he ever been able to fix his thoughts so intensely and exclusively as on other occasions, when bringing the whole light of his mind to bear upon it, as a great burning-glass concentrates the light of the sun, he had solved mysterious passages that looked hard as adamant. But, now, there was a portentous inquietude—portentous, we term it, because it seemed to watch and wait feverishly for something to take place, but whether in the sphere of reality, of thought, or dreams, he could not define—a feverish inquietude, however, which snatched away his thoughts from any point on which he strove to fix them. He started from his chair and paced to-and-fro, impetuously, as if he had the whole range of his hill-top before him, though five or six paces brought him, at each turn, to the wall of the room. In one of these brief tramps and rapid turns, he chanced to cast his eyes into the small looking-glass, that hung between the two front windows, and was startled at the paleness of his face. Dark face people have an especially ghastly aspect, when they turn pale, and Hilliard (who never gave himself credit for personal beauty though, in many a woman's eyes, he might have been thought to possess it) fancied that he had never seen a more ill-conceived countenance than his own. Moreover, it was a long time since he had consciously seen his own face in the glass—so absorbed had he been by the inner world in which he lived, and he was absolutely frightened to observe how much older he had apparently grown, since he last stood face to face with his double-ganger of the mirror. It was so long since, and he found himself so changed, that he positively enjoyed the rare privilege of contemplating himself as if he were another person. The most obvious mark that the past months of intense mental action had left upon him, was a deep furrow, or corrugation, or fissure, as it might almost be called, which was cut perpendicularly between his eyebrows, from the central point of his forehead to the root of his nose; but besides this deeply engraved word, there were various smaller and slighter scribblings, in which he could read the cares that had consumed his bloom, quite as distinctly as any portion of the old manuscript. He sighed, as he asked himself what had become of his youth, and had he lost it forever unenjoyed, undeveloped, even, but only blighted and dried up, for want of the dew of natural feeling that should have kept it fresh. Potent, indeed, must be the life-water that could smooth way that furrow from his brow, and wash his visage clean of the duskiness that brooding thoughts had left upon it; potent, indeed, since his heart must first be steeped in it.

He sat down and fell into a reverie, which, spreading itself abroad over a wide compass, as is the way with such misty atmospheres of thought, still kept recurring and settling itself down heavily upon that furrow in his brow. The sight of it had taken him entirely by surprise. He had gone seeking for immortal youth, and here, in his first footsteps, he was already in the clutch of age. He wondered whether there was any quality in the pursuit which he had adopted, which, of necessity, wore out life preternaturally fast; whether some dreary spell might not have been wrought into the old manuscript whereby the age, the incessant toils, the sorrows, and the crimes, of the original author, were charmed within its blurred characters, and would be evolved, and settle in sombre misery upon the heart and brain of him whose disastrous toil should succeed in decyphering them; and so he might be taking up the burthen of years and life-experience which some craftier man, in a long past age, had succeeded in flinging down. Or, acknowledging this supposition for the wild fantasy which it surely was, might it not be, that, for the attainment of permanence in earthly life, it was necessary to sacrifice whatever in life was most precious, burning its standards in potent fire, melting its precious things, doing what was equivalent to his fossilizing a green tree, with its tender leaves, and flexible boughs, its capacities for enjoying shower and sunshine, in order to make it indestructible, and no longer responsive to any impulse of delight. Was it not evident to reason, that life could only be preserved permanently by depriving it of its natural juices, all that was soft, tender, flexible, all that evanescent charm, continually perishing and reviving, in which alone lies its value as an enjoyable possession. Was he not already conscious of such a process within him! Did not his heart, even while it throbbed, strike cold and hard against the very breast that held it! And then came that terrible thought which often, though we have seldom spoken of it, thrust itself into his mind; often knocked for admittance when the poor student, knowing its rap, as he would that of an importunate creditor, hastily barred the door to keep it out. It was a thought that assails most men who aim at objects ever so little out of the common path, whether it be to write a poem, or found or subvert an empire, or to render possible a better life for mankind, as reformers strive to do, or to make his own life endless, as Hilliard purposed—to all, in some ugly moment, comes this terrible doubt, under the aspect of sturdiest truth and reality. "You are a dreamer."—that is what it says. "You are deluding yourself. You are toiling for no end." And supposing his object illusion, what a waste was Hilliard making, and had already made, of that little treasure of golden days which Providence gave him to spend, and to buy withal whatever the world had to give, as fully, it might be, in one lifetime as in a hundred. How much wiser was Robert Garfield, for example. News had come, yesterday, of his performing a gallant feat of arms at the Battle of Monmouth, and being promoted to a captaincy for valor in the field. In his ordinary mood, Hilliard would have thought little of such a reward, nor greatly estimated the quality of courage that had won it. But now it seemed to him that Robert Garfield had found, without even seeking it, the true, golden mystery of life, and, should it prove but short, was yet making it equivalent to any length of days, by filling its term full of high action, and emotion cramping much into little, nor chaffering to give an unknown repetition of torpid breath, for the few great throbs that might prelude a heroic death. But leaving heroic deeds and death apart, Hilliard descended to a yet lower plane, and asked himself where was his happiness! Love was to be forbidden him, by the jealous nature of his purpose, which required the whole ardor and energy of personal character to be concentrated upon itself, with stern determination to keep his foothold among shifting and gliding things, dying empires, wrecked republics, falling stars, and decaying firmaments, or else he would pass away with the other shadows. But, love, as Hilliard had imagination enough to know, though never a beloved shape of woman had taught him the experience of it, had the spark of immortality within itself, and, though it should endure but for an hour, and then be hidden in a grave, yet in that one hour would have had a portion of Heaven, the quality of which is to be eternal in the briefest space. Thus every mortal man, if but true to his instincts, might have a taste of immortality on earth; only Hilliard, the one mortal creature that sought it, would miss the reality, even if he gained a delusion of interminable days. What would he be the better, if his heart lay like a pebble in the stream of time forever; all life was in the heart, and his must be as sensible!

Ah Hilliard, unhappy youth, you are getting beyond the permitted precincts of that code of philosophy, some of the cold and subtle advices of which you elicited with such pains from the old manuscript, and thought them such Golden Rules for human conduct. Obey them strictly, and (always with the help of the great elixir, just now on the verge of consummation) they may yet guide you to all that you have dreamed of. Fling them aside, and you toss the possibilities of a thousand years to the winds, in the same reckless handfull. Love, most of all, must be eschewed. Every warmer and quicker throb of the heart wears away so much of life. The passions, any of them, are a wine too potent to be indulged in by one who is bound to keep his finger on the pulse, counting its throbs, lest they exceed five and seventy in amount. But love, above all, being in its essence an immortal thing, an ethereal, not an earthly immortality, cannot be long entertained within a material body, but must wear it out even by its own sweet potency, softly invigorating as it seems. Yes; this passion—which he that truly feels of an infidel purpose, becomes sensible that he has a deathless soul, because it must require character to develope fully the germ now planted—this very divinest passion assists Time and Death to make us Old, to lay us in the grave.

Ever, the feeling kept recurring to Hillard Veren, that he was growing old immeasurably fast, and that unless he might quickly avail himself of the drink of immortality, it would serve no better purpose than to preserve him like a dry leaf pressed in a book, continued forever, with the decayed hopes of declining life, its distress, its weariness, wilted into him; so that he should never accomplish anything with his length of days, after obtaining them, because the path of the interminable would strike with horror and despair any man who had not the vivacity and fresh courage of youth, wherewith to tread it. He again went to the looking-glass, to peruse that fatal furrow in his forehead, and measuring its depth, to decide whether it indicated so deep a mark in his soul, that it was not worth while to strive any longer for a life that would already have lost its better substance. There, to be sure, was the furrow, portentously deep, with poor Hilliard's youth buried in its open grave. But what impressed him still more, at this time, was the preternatural paleness that still overspread his face. Why should he look so pale? Had he seen that hue on the visage of another, Hilliard would have supposed him startled by some ghastly object or scene, that he had just witnessed, a murder, for instance; or that, going into some familiar chamber of his home, he had seen there on the bed where he was wont to sleep, the corpse of some-one whom he knew and loved, untimely dead. The complexion suggested death, inevitably, for if mortality proved too strong for him, and finally conquered Hilliard Veren himself, he never could look paler than now. Why was it? He was conscious of no tremor in his frame, no terror in his heart, such as ought to have manifested itself in that blood-less face. He felt his pulse, and found its steady throbs limit-ing themselves fairly within the prescribed number per minute. But I know not. Some men have a strange faculty of shutting off one part of their mind from another, by let-ting fall a deep dense curtain of tapestry, through which no sight nor sound of what is going on in the next chamber may penetrate. After all, it is possible, that, in a region be-yond his immediate consciousness, Hilliard was in a state of infinite alarm and perplexity, expectation, hope, dread. All that we know is, that, once, when he had sat down to the manuscript in apparent quiet, he rose, crept softly up stairs on tiptoe to Aunt Nashoba's chamber-door and put his ear to the keyhole, until he heard a long breath drawn within! Had he, then, detected such dismal prognostics in the sick woman's case, as to be apprehensive but she should die in her sleep? No;—no such fear as that! Aunt Nashoba was as much a part of his life-long recollections, as the hill behind his dwelling, and it takes more than one death to make the young sensibly aware that their near kindred are mortal;—but actually the poor old woman seemed very ill, and it was an anxious position, in one so unaccustomed to such cares as Hilliard was, an absorbed student, to be alone with her in the house, watching her long-drawn, painful breaths.

By and by, his heavy sense of solitude was relieved, as it should seem, by the return of Rose, who came home to get her dinner in the recess of her little school. Finding the kitchen hearth vacant, the fire dead, Aunt Nashoba missing, and even the brown jug empty, (for Hilliard had thrown away the contents) she was impressed with a grievous feeling of desolation, and going to Hilliard's study-door, tapped softly with the ends of her fingers. Bidden to come in, she found her brother sitting with a pen in his hand, bending down his head to his work, a quire of paper before him (beneath which peeped out the loose, tattered edges of some antique document or other). He scarcely glanced aside at her in his grim abstracted way, without lifting his head and looking her in the face.

"Well, Rose," said he, "you find nobody at home, I suppose. Aunt Nashoba has had an ill turn, and is gone to bed."

"Ill in bed! It is no slight thing that would bring poor Auntie to that!" exclaimed Rose, with quick sympathy. "And nobody to attend to her but you, Hilliard. My scholars must have a half-holiday then, for I will be her nurse, and will creep up stairs this very moment, to see if she needs anything."

"No, Rose; not for the world!" cried Hilliard, starting up with singular energy, and stopping the girl as she was hurrying away. "Aunt Nashoba has taken a medicine of her own choosing, and has quickly gone to sleep. If left undisturbed, she will probably wake in her usual state of health, or perhaps much better. And you know, Rose, she—she has certain prejudices against you, and, being in a nervous state, might not feel quite comfortable to find you at her bedside."

"It is true, and a great pity," said Rose, sighing, "for I love Aunt Nashoba, and would nurse the poor, lonely thing as tenderly a daughter could. Then, Hilliard, I will run into Mrs. Hagburn's, and ask her to come."

"You know they are no cronies," objected Hilliard, "for Mother Hagburn, to her knowledge, has sneered at her Indian blood (and mine, too, the old wretch) and turned up her nose at her bitters. The truth is, Rose, you must leave Aunt Nashoba with me, and I will do my best for her, if it should turn that there is anything to be done. It is her nature, like that of other wild creatures, to creep away and hide herself when she is ill at ease; and none but I, who am akin to her in blood and spirit, can have any effectual sympathy with her, or do her the slightest good."

"What a sad case it is, Hilliard!" said Rose, looking him in the face with a sort of kindly horror, as of this ever chill, impenetrable atmosphere about him. "Do not let it grow upon you, this moodiness, or whatever it be, that has snatched Aunt Nashoba away from those who would fain cherish her, and that seems to be stealing you away likewise. And I think you have caught Aunt Nashoba's illness, too. Let me be your nurse, then! Your face is deadly pale."

"Nonsense, Rose," answered Hilliard, with a short and angry laugh. "Did you never hear of a man's face being 'sicklied o'er with the pale cast of thought'? That is all my malady. Begone, you foolish girl, and teach children the alphabet, instead of talking about moods which you cannot comprehend. You do not know Aunt Nashoba and me."

"I did not mean to offend you, Hilliard. We used to know each other better," said Rose submissively and sadly, and then smiling again. "But I will be your sister, whether you choose or no; so remember it, when you need me."

Thus rebuffed by that bitter mood of which this was far from her first experience in Hilliard Veren, and conscious, too, that Aunt Nashoba would probably repel her from her bedside, Rose ate a morsel of food and went back to her school, drooping under a kind of gloom that seemed suddenly to have enveloped the house, like the mists that sometimes rose from the adjacent meadow. As for Hilliard, after his petulance had hurried her away, he longed to call her back again, because a certain shapeless, intangible dread, which her presence had kept somewhat at a distance, now immediately closed in upon him, and made him absolutely afraid to look about the room. His ears were on the alert, however; and after what seemed an endless time (it was half past four by Francis Veren's watch, which ticked above the mantel-piece) he heard a slight movement overhead, in Aunt Nashoba's chamber. First, she appeared to be rattling a chair that stood by the bedside; then, she had clutched the staff which Hilliard put there for the purpose, and was giving a succession of hurried knocks, heavy and yet tremulous. Septimius (I know not how he could think of it, at such a juncture) snatched an indivisible point of time to glance at the looking-glass, in order to see if that awful paleness were still on his face, and were likely to frighten poor Aunt Nasho-ba; then hurrying up stairs, he opened her chamber-door.

Aunt Nashoba was sitting up in bed, with dishevelled hair, and looking very wild; so wild, indeed, that in connection with the broomstick which she still held in her hand, the gossips of that day or an earlier one might have supposed her just re-turned from one of those aerial jaunts, for which she was said to have a hereditary predilection. But it is a time to desist from any such unkind gibes at the harmless old woman, (if harmless we may safely call such an inveterate dealer in nos-trum,) for she was evidently in great distress, and greeted Hil-liard with a peculiar howl, in which, however, there was no anger, but an unknown amount of pain and nervous agitation.

"Ah, Hilly, Hilly," cried she, "I knew it! There was some-thing wrong! Darling, what have you given to your poor old Auntie? Are you certain that you steeped the right bundle of herbs for my drink? I thought you took the right one, but my eyes were dim, and bleared, and bloodshot, and my head dizzy."

"I took it from the place you bade me, dear Auntie," said Hilliard, inwardly much alarmed, but preserving a true Indian composure of deportment; "and of my own little knowledge of botany, I could tell that all, or most of the herbs, were those you named to me. Some of the barks and roots I could not so well tell. But is there anything amiss? Dear Aunt Nashoba, let me run for the Doctor."

"The Doctor!" cried Aunt Nashoba, with the intense bitter-ness of professional rivalry. "Do you talk to the old herb-woman of a Doctor, on her death-bed? No; if my own bitters have killed me at last, let me die of them, and not of the Doctor. Is there anything amiss, did you ask, Hilly? Nothing in the world, dear. Only, I have been a poor, evil, bitter, venomous thing, all my life, out of place, lonely, one whose race, and blood, was gone, a poor yellow creature, whom nobody loved (unless you loved me a little, Hilly, dear), with wishes, and movements that were for another sort of life—and so the world hated me, and I hated the world. But this is the last day of it, darling. I don't know whether I'm going to the Christian Heaven, Hilliard, or to the happy hunting-grounds whither the squaws, my great grandmothers, have gone. But I've done with this. You'll never see me creeping out of the woods again, with the green bundle on my shoulders, as when you used to run to me, Hilly, and put your little hand in mine."

This reminiscence of his childhood, and how, through all his life, there had been a peculiar tie between him and this old woman—something in the depths of character and idiosyncrasy that made them continually understand many of one another's peculiarities, when all others set them down as merely odd and unaccountable—these feelings of deep kindred smote upon Hilliard Veren's heart, and drew down a blinding flood of tears. Not a smoothly flowing flood, but convulsive, agonizing, the more so, as in that extremity, his proud, dark nature was ashamed of being thus overcome, and he turned away from the dying woman to hide his tears, but could not hide his convulsive sobs.

"Dear Hilly," said she, in a tone of surprise, commiseration, and yet joy that there was yet something belonging to her, in the world she was leaving. "Did you love the poor old creature a little bit? Did you love me so much? Be comforted; though I cannot help being glad of a little sorrow, I would not have it so much."

"Do not leave me, dear Auntie!" exclaimed the young man, even more utterly taken by surprise than she at the passionate emotion which the crisis had so suddenly aroused in him. "I shall be so lonely! We are the last of our race. The world is very desolate."

"Yes; darling," said Aunt Nashoba, "it is a dismal world enough for those that are out of place in it, and who can never find their like, such as we of the Indian blood, or of a strange new blood made out of two races, and so that we are a kind of monster in the world. But it is no great matter what sort of world it is, seeing we have so little time to live in it. And speaking of that, Hilly, what a mercy it is that the one herb was wanting out of the Great Sagamore's drink and that I had to put spirit into my bitters instead. Only for that—just think of it—with the quantities I've steeped in that brown jug and drunk, I would no more have died than Satan can. I see just how it is now. I used to think the Great Sagamore had won the blessing of endless life; now I see that he had got the curse of never dying. I used to long for it myself, sometimes; and almost thought I had it. Do not you aim at it, Hilliard; for being bright, and full of learning, perhaps you might find it."

"Do you then find it good and pleasant to die, Auntie?" said the young man, whose keen, investigating nature, always especially alive in such subjects, suggested this question, seeing that Aunt Nashoba was just at the point of time and position of circumstances to answer it.

"Pleasant? Not just that, Hilly dear;—for methinks that monstrous fire, in which the Indian folk tried to burn old Bloody Foot, is burning now inside of me," answered Aunt Nashoba, with a groan. "But, is it good? I think it is, my darling; because in this world, everybody seems out of sorts and out of place, and I more so than most folks; and we go about seeking for our place, and for the folks that belong to us, and never find them, if we live to Methuselah's age, and if we think so, we live long enough to see our mistake. Now, in my judgment, the good of the other world will be, that we settle into our right place at once, and find our real kinfolk round about us. Now I'm a Christian woman, and believe my Bible, and I've always defied Satan (or the Black Man, as they used to call him,) though, if he'd happened to tempt me at the right time, I can't say but I might have yielded, as well as my great-aunt Tituba. But, I never did, and I'm a Christian woman; and yet, Hilly, I don't expect to be with other Christian people in the next world (at least, I hope not,) but to talk with great-aunt Tituba, and perhaps with Old Bloody Foot, if he is there, and with the Indian folk that are kin to me, and all other sour and discontented people. I'll try to make matters easier with them, and persuade them not to think so hard of the Lord—that is, as soon as I understand his ways a little better, myself. And I've no ear for sermons. And I shouldn't care to be in their garden of Paradise, with its straight gravel-walks, and the flowers all growing in rows, and the ground so well-weeded, and all the trees pruned according to the gardener's fancy, but in a wild, rough forest, with its old mosses, and creeping, clambering vines, and its pale, frightened-looking flowers, its intricacy, its clustering shade, and here and there a streak of sunshine coming down into it like an angel, or like a good thought in my own heart. And though it'll be of no use there, I'll search all through that forest, till I find the one herb that was wanting to make my bitters the drink of immortality. Thank God, I never found it here. And, Hilliard, by the time you die, I will be the first to welcome you; so that it shan't be like coming to a strange place!"

The old herb-woman had not made this long utterance in any smooth and well-connected way, but with many interruptions, when breath failed her, and sometimes her words rose almost into a scream, when her inward pain writhed her, or sometimes sank into a whisper, when the weakness of exhaustion seemed to take away her voice, so that Hilliard Veren rather guessed at than absolutely knew, the strange, distracted, yet characteristic purport of her speech. Now, the young man, it is to be remembered, had been educated with a view to the ministry, and of course could not have escaped being tortured with certain ideas which made him feel that Aunt Nashoba's death-bed ought to be smoothed down with religious rites, such as he felt himself unfit to administer, and words of holy comfort, which he had not the wherewithal to offer. She seemed to be departing in strange fashion, and (having within him half, if not all the hereditary instincts of a Puritan) he was loth to take upon himself the responsibility of letting her cross the borders of eternity in her Indian herb-woman's garb, as it were. And yet, since she had so decidedly expressed her sense of being a Christian woman, it might not have been amiss to let her wander on, with her bundle of forest-products on her back, still stooping down and plucking a root, a leaf, a flower, till, looking up, she would find that she had overstept the mortal boundary, and that the foliage on the huge trees around her was of the kind that does not wither; that the leaves she plucked had a sweeter fragrance, the roots she pulled up the rich spiciness of a better soil. But, Hilliard, wild speculator as he might be in the depths of his own mind, now felt a yearning desire, to light, as it were, a lamp from the old altar fires, and hold it above Aunt Nashoba's head, or put it into her hand, that she might not go all astray in what was to him the darkness of her onward way.

"Dear Aunt Nashoba," he said, bending over her pillow, "let me go for the minister. It is not well to die thus without a prayer, with not a word of guidance from one who has stood by many death-beds, and looked with the eyes of the many dying into the world to come; so that, it may be, he knows more of it than we. The minister is a good man, and a wise one, holy and benign. Let me make haste to bring him."

<She howls too>

"Pshaw, Hilly, I did not think you were half such a fool!" exclaimed Aunt Nashoba, with a good deal of the acridity of her old character and giving a violent contortion of inward pain; so that it was partly a spasm and partly Hilliard's proposal that so vexed her. "The Minister! Yes; he is a good man, as you say; but what have I to do with good men, or bad, or any man, but yourself, who ought to know me better than all others? It keeps my heart a little warm to have you near me; so I let you stay, Hilly dear, but without you I should scowl and scold at all people, till they fled away, and then, turning my face to the wall, I would die peaceably enough. What could the minister do for me? I can find my own way better, and I won't go to the singing-seats, where he would try to send me; for I never had any ear for music, and don't want to sit among the Saints, harping forever, and singing a psalm tune—I'm afraid I should find our great-great grandfather, the Tomahawk of Righteousness, there, and I'm afraid of his dark stern face, Hilly, and that's much for old Aunt Nashoba to say, and more than she'd say of Satan. I've just been telling you, that in the other world you find your place and your like; and, judge for yourself what sort of a figure should I cut in the singing seats, up among Saints, so neatly dressed as they'll be. For I tell you, Hilly, come what will, and heed when I say, I'll wear the clothes I like in Heaven, and follow my own ways, and perhaps smoke my pipe; or else I'll go where there'll be liberty allowed. It would suit me just as well, for aught I know; only, if I'd looked forward to it, I'd led a little different life here, on earth. I'd have been a witch, Hilly, like great-aunt Tituba. Ah, dear me, what pleasant times I've missed, flying up out of the chimney with the smoke and the sparks, on the very broomstick that you gave me to knock with, and shooting right up into a flight of witches and wizards from all the country round, flying along over the land asleep below, sometimes up among the clouds, sometimes so low that you brush the golden weathercock on the village-steeple. That would have been sport, Hilly; and think how frightened the good people would have been, if any of them heard us laughing and chattering up aloft, in the height of a frolic. Ah; that would be sport. And I've missed it all, and had a dull life, Hilly, going about seeking for herbs, till my poor old back is bent into a bow. I wonder if it'll come straight again in the other world."

Aunt Nashoba's voice here seemed to mumble itself quite away, and Hilliard hoped that she might be falling asleep, and would perhaps get ease, and awake refreshed. But, after a while, she spoke placidly and softly to him, and feebly put out her hand to grasp his own.

"My darling," she said, "I think I've been wandering in my mind, and saying strange things, for which I'm no more answerable, I hope, than for what we think and do in dreams, when it always seems to me that the righteous part of us is asleep. I seemed to know what I was saying, and yet I could not help it, and didn't quite want to help. Now, darling, you mustn't think that I'm a heathen, though I don't want the minister at my bedside (he's a good man, too) and choose to say my own prayers in my own mind, it being all between the Lord and myself, and He knows me pretty well. He thinks me a Christian, I'm pretty sure. I feel a great peace."

"Are your pains gone?" asked Hilliard.

"All gone," said Aunt Nashoba, "and I don't believe I shall have any more in this world—no, nor in the next. Only that I'm so weak and spent, I've never felt so comfortable in fifty years. Well; after all, a human creature wouldn't like to miss dying-off, Hilly. It makes me feel so contented. Still, I smell a pleasant breeze of wind fanning me from the other world, and if I could only draw in a full breath of it, 'twould do me good. I wish I could; for there's a thing or two I want to say to you, darling, and I am wasting my breath talking nonsense, and never said one of them. One of the things was about that girl there, Sybil Dacy; for she haunts me, Hilly, and I seem to see her, all the time I'm lying here, peeping in at the door, and nodding to me, staring up between the bedside and the wall and pointing to you, and laughing in her strange way, but without any giggle. There, don't you see her? She is looking into that empty cup, and smiling! Ah; I see! I'm wandering again! But sometimes I've thought there's mischief in that girl, Hilly—and sometimes not."

"You said there were other things to tell me, dear Aunt Nashoba," said Hilliard. "If there's aught you would bid me do, speak!"

There was something about an iron box," said the old woman, "that I've had on my mind a great while, and began to speak of, once or twice before. But I'm so dreamy just now, that the iron-box shifts away from me like a shadow, like the sun glimmering on the water, and I can't catch it with my mind. It's no great matter, I dare say."

"Aught else?" asked the young man; for he had a singular feeling as if there were some word, some knowledge, some spell, trembling on the tip of Aunt Nashoba's tongue, that if it were once spoken, would light up the obscuring mist in which he wandered, like one of those meteors that so suddenly blaze out in the midnight darkness.

"Yes; something," said Aunt Nashoba dreamily, "—no, nothing that I know on; only, be ready to die when your time comes, for it's no such terrible business as we think. The girl's gone out of the chamber now, Hilly."

"Can I do nothing for you, Aunt Nashoba?" said Hilliard, passionately grasping her hand—forgetting everything, for the moment, except the desire, the needing, of making the dying woman feel his affection and his sorrow; for, indeed that deep likeness that was between this lonely pair, pulled at his heart-strings with most painful force, as he felt her going.

"Nothing; and it's no matter; I know you love me, Hilly, and for what's ugliest in me, too, as I do you," she gasped out.

"Yes; one thing. If there's a drop more of my bitters, I'd like to take a sip. But it might make me a little more sprightly to climb over the wall, between this world and the next, and not be downcast at going among strangers."

"Not a drop, Aunt Nashoba. I have flung it all away."

"Never mind," said she. "It had a queer taste—not quite right, Hilly. Well; I'm going to sleep; and when I awake, I shall remember what I want to say. It's getting dark, and time to sleep. Tomorrow at sunrise, I shall go gathering some sweet-smelling herbs. But now, goodnight, my darling."

Thus murmuring, the old herb-woman fell asleep as quietly as ever did an infant on its mother's breast; but as Hilliard Veren looked upon her face, he knew that she would never wake again, or perhaps was already broad awake, or it might be only half awake, from the dream of life, and looking back at himself and at earlier things, the woods, the shrubbery, the chimney, and steaming herb-pot, just as we lie with shut eyes and see the objects of a dream fade and whiten speedily out of our waking consciousness. Hilliard wondered at the strong, yearning agony which, as it were, wrenched at his heart, as if a part of himself had gone with her; so much is there in sympathy, so little has it to do with beauty, goodness, desires, and magic, amiable, or loveable qualities of any kind, and so tenacious are the affections of those who have but one or two, and finally, so little can we tell about the strength of them, till they are tried. We know not what other emotions may have melted themselves into the hot tide of Hilliard Veren's grief, and added venom to its proper bitterness. Perhaps remorse was among those feelings, though we have no authority for saying so, and, indeed, have never quite been satisfied that there was occasion for it. But supposing that one or two of those sensuous flowers had been put to steep with Aunt Nashoba's customary herbs, and had made the draught fatal by some quality of their mysterious juice, which, if rightly concocted, might have renewed her youth. Hilliard had administered it, if at all, with no deadly purpose, but the contrary; and I have observed that men may seldom burthen their consciences with remorse for results, however calamitous, which they did not directly and absolutely intend. How could Doctors, the least perspicacious of them, ever rest upon their pillows, if they took to heart so much as one of the many deaths which the mistakes of the witch must have caused or hastened? And, moreover, if any man could trace, and not very remotely, the consequences of his own actions, as he passes carelessly along the narrow bridge of life, he would see that the mere swing of his arms, as it were, and sway of his body, has thrust people into the black gulf on either side. Not only soldiers (who have a dispensation for drinking blood) but statesmen, quiet, elderly people, who have never hurt a fly, bring about the deaths of myriads, by blunders, mistakes, or even of fell purpose, and never dream of immorality. Even the child unborn, so innocent as it proverbially is, is often a fratricide. We are all linked together in a chain of Death, and feel no remorse for those we cause, nor enmity for that we suffer. And the Purpose? what is Purpose? Who can tell when he has actually formed one? Or how little it may have to do with the very deeds that follow upon and seem entirely in accordance with it? And speaking of remorse, it has sometimes occurred to me to doubt whether there really is such an emotion, independently existent in the criminal's own breast, or whether it be not—as men are generally constituted—a pang and agony caused by the condemnation of the world or some influential part of it, an arrow shot by alien opinion, and rankling in the guilty breast, that otherwise would well enough have digested its secret guilt. People have so often been known to live comfortably and even fat under great hidden crimes, and all at once to wither away and die, in unmistakeable agony, when exposed to the public eye. I know not what to make of this.

While Hilliard Veren sat by the bedside, possibly perplexing his mind with questions and dark surmises like these here suggested, he suddenly became conscious that his hand, which Aunt Nashoba had grasped so long ago as when she lived, was still held in the hand that had been hers, and that the fingers of the latter were growing cold and stiff round his own; even as if she had clutched him, and been drawing him along with her into the new woods where she purposed to wander, and gather herbs. Hilliard quickly released himself, and was seized with a lothful shuddering at the presence of death, and at his contact with it; it being (as perhaps we have said before) most repugnant to his dark, melancholic temperament, whence, no doubt, had partly arisen all those dreams and studies and long, long, perplexed contrivings to escape it, raking up anew the folly and insanity of past ages, wasted youth, trying to petrify the flower of life, so that he might wear it the longer without its dewy leaves falling. "Oh what a misery it is," he thought, "that the dead do not vanish from us into thin air, instead of leaving this ugly, cold, distorted mass of their mortality behind them, for us to bury, with absurd formalities, and ceremonies, and markings of the place; each one that dies flinging his mortality upon our heavenly hopes, till they are quite crushed down, as mine are now, by this one corpse of poor Aunt Nashoba. Who would not cling to earth, as I do, when this is all we know of the departed? But if, while I was gazing at her, she had faded away into thin air, and left the memory of a smile, growing fainter and fainter till it was no longer there, I could have believed that she was still living, and in a blessed state."

Aunt Nashoba's hand, from which the young man had released his own, slid down by her side, and Hilliard was startled by the movement, thinking that it was meant for a token to him, but how to be interpreted he could not decide; poor bewildered youth, who sought auguries from this dead lump of clay, in the shape of an old woman, as if the fact of the spirit being departed made it the fitter to reveal the mysteries of spirit.

Then rushing hastily forth, Hilliard summoned Robert Hagburn's mother, who was the nearest neighbor; and this good old woman communicated the news to several of her gossips, and they all came to the house, discussing among themselves poor Aunt Nashoba's sudden death, and the character that she had left behind her. They talked of her, it is to be feared, with no great respect, shed few tears, and estimated the public loss by her decease at a low figure; for, in their view, she had been a dram-drinking, pipe-smoking, cross-grained old maid, no church member or hardly a Christian, and too much Indian blood and witch-blood in her veins ever to be on good terms with her neighbors or the minister or the rest of the world, or, they suspected, the world to come. As to her herb-drinks, some of them might be good for cold or rheumatism; but the Doctor, when asked about them, had turned up his nose at them all, and said that Aunt Nashoba's patients might thank their stars, if they did not find themselves poisoned some day. It would be no wonder, indeed, if she had at last made an end of herself with continually sipping those dreadful bitters, of which she made such amount; but it was all right enough, whether or no, and the house would be cheerfuller, now that she was gone out of the the chimney-corner, and they were glad that Rose Garfield had no more to suffer with her ugly temper, and they hoped that Hilliard (who latterly seemed to be getting into the queer ways of his forefathers, half-blooded people) would now study in good earnest to be a minister, or do anything else that was useful. Entering the kitchen, they saw the earthen jug standing uncovered and empty on the hearth.

"There's the last drop of the stuff that will ever be made in the world," said Mother Hagbourn, turning the jug upside down to let it drip off, and looking curiously at it. "She's carried the secret with her, and much good may it do them that she goes amongst. Dear me, how red it is! Red as a drop of blood!"

Meanwhile, Hilliard Veren had betaken himself to the hill-top, which was always his refuge when troubled with more expansive thoughts or more riotous emotions, or when the chimney smoked, or the heat stifled him, than he could fairly manage within doors.

Hilliard Veren was not, however, conscious of any such extreme emotion, at this time, as made it indispensable that he should have the whole height of the sky and the expanse of the vast landscape around his hill, to bear it in; on the contrary, though he had been sensible of more than one ebullition of passionate grief during Aunt Nashoba's death scene, he appeared to himself to be in a state of preternatural calmness. In truth, he upbraided himself with indifference to the fate of this poor creature, who had loved him so well, and to whom he was linked by the ties of hereditary peculiarities, such as existed between himself and no other human being, since the herb-woman was the last of that wild and evil blood from which they sprang; and therefore he wondered that he could tread so calmly, now, in the path which his footsteps had worn, or in any of his old paths, seeing that the world and its ways must needs be incalculably changed for him, now that this familiar creature, who had scented his life with strong-smelling herbs, and influenced his mind and feelings, with a certain bitter astringency of character, was forever gone. But, in truth, Hilliard was probably mistaken in supposing himself calm; or, at least, it was that kind of calmness and repose into which the turbulence of emotion apparently subsides, when its cycle is completed; but which yet has within it all the passion, which, in a less degree, would seek to assuage itself by tears; such showers lying far beneath the region into which a great emotion exalts the sufferer. He was only conscious, now, of a singular expansion, whether of intellect or spirit, as if he had unexpectedly emerged from an obscure and tangled, and narrow and difficult way, upon a height, whence he could look far round about him, and see, to-day, where the half-blinded youth of yesterday had been wandering; but then again, it is to be observed, this feeling must have been a delusion because it produced no change either in his purposes or his mode of pursuing them; it was only as certain kindling up of the atmosphere, by lurid light, gives wonted objects a certain aspect less common place than the ordinary one and therefore nobler and more striking. And great emotion seems thus to calm the turbulence of life, and dignify its sordid course.

Hilliard had climbed the hill presently for space to expand, but partly to be alone; a necessity, the inward perception of which, of itself, indicated that he was most deeply moved, instinctively repelled by his own unlikeness for other spheres. When he came, however, to that little mound, in which the root of his destiny seemed to have been planted, <(see below)> and out of which it was growing with such dark and rich luxuriance with blossoms that promised fruit, he saw that Sybil Dacy was there, sitting on the grave, with her head on her hand, drooping like a flower; or as if she had fallen asleep. He stood a moment, expecting that, with her ordinary quick and irritable sensibility to the presence of those near her, she would start up and address him; but she remained motionless. She had plucked and scattered many of the flowers, as if in wantonness, about the ground.

"Sybil," said he, at last.

"Well! What have you to say?" answered she, in a low, dejected, weary voice.

"Why do you scatter these precious flowers?" said Hilliard.

"Are they precious, then?" said the girl. "I have used them for playthings;—flowers of immortality, some people call them. I wonder what seed they sprout from. Death is the seed of immortality; so I have heard the parson say; it is a strange crop to grow from such a seed. How came it to be planted here?"

"Sit up, Sybil," said Hilliard Veren, laying his hand on the girl to raise her. "I would speak with you."

She writhed nervously at the touch of his hand; it being perhaps the first time, after so many months of a kind of familiarity, that he had ever touched her, and now only her garment. She rose from the ground, however, and stood gazing into his face, with her large eyes fixed upon him, oddly intelligent, and, as it were, menacing.

"You have no right to touch me!" said she. "Do not dare to do it again."

"Pardon me, Sybil," said he. "I meant no harm or rudeness. Why do you make such account of a touch? We have known each other a great while."

"No, you have never known me, but you will know me one day," said she—"that is, perhaps you will, or it may be I shall vanish off your path, as I came into it; for whatever they say of me—however they may account for my being here, with a reasonable story—the truth is I grew up out of this— this strange-looking little hillock. This is a rich bit of soil for you. Out of it grows, unseen to you, a vine. I was the first flower that grew after what you planted here—and then this crop, which are my sisters, though they do not resemble me. And we are all mischievous."

Hilliard could not but see that Sybil was in one of those fits of disordered mind, which he had been given to understand that she was liable to, and which, indeed, slightly tinctured her whole life, and sorrow heighted into what might be called fits of insanity; yet it seemed to him that there were causes, that there was something underneath, some knowledge of which he might avail himself, some acquaintance—though he could not imagine how—with the secret things that influenced his life.

"What seed is it you speak of," said he, looking steadily into her eyes, but perhaps growing pale as he did so, "that you say is planted here, and that produces all these things?"

"Poh!" said Sybil, suddenly altering her manner, and laughing, "you must not question me in that way. I am in my tantrums now, as good Mrs. Hagburn says; and yet I had a mind to be very sad; for they tell me poor Aunt Nashoba is dead. Is that true?"

"Too true—yet not so true," said Hilliard, "since life, so good in itself, had ceased to be good for her. She's gone."

"So suddenly," said Sybil, gazing curiously at him, and with a freaking expression of mirth in her face in spite, too, of a horror and tremulousness with which she seemed affected. "Poor old thing! I wish I had seen her die! I never did see anybody die. I wonder whether it is true, that sometimes, just before a person dies, there comes upon them a resurrection, and renewal of their youth, so that it shines through their age and their wrinkles, and though these remain, yet you cannot see them, because the spirit makes them so beautiful. Do you believe it?"

Hilliard Veren was thunderstruck by these words of Sybil, bringing up, as they so forcibly did, that brief interval, just before Aunt Nashoba's last breath, when she had sat up, and suddenly seemed so changed, and with such a youthfulness, such a grace, only for a flitting moment; as if her youth had come back, or rather, since Aunt Nashoba's mortal youth could not have been so very beautiful, as if it were a smoky shadow of what she might be, when glorified, in a future state of being. And now, from what Sybil said, he could almost have supposed that she had stood with him by the bedside, and seen that strange transfiguration; so beautiful, and with such an awe in it. How else could she have alluded to that smile, unless she had seen it? And yet, for aught he knew, it might be a common phenomenon of death-beds.

"Sybil," said he, "what smile, what kindling of the spirit, is this you spoke of?"

"Will you tell me," said she, with that kind of childish simplicity she sometimes put on, or which really came out of a simple and childish heart, "all about Aunt Nashoba's dying, and how she behaved, and what she said, and how she looked? Perhaps it will comfort you to tell me!"

Now, there was a need in Hilliard's breast, a fullness,— and he felt, as Sybil spoke—a longing, as he found, to share with somebody the knowledge of the scene which he had just gone through; and these many reasons, as it seemed to him, why Sybil should be the chosen confidant, in preference to any other; being a stranger, and not a village-gossip, from whom what he said would run into the common village talk; being an inconsequential sort of person, too, of flighty mind, incapable, probably, of drawing any inferences; and though so bright in occasional glimpses of the truth, yet having no broad comprehension of it; so that, with her, of all persons in the world, he might talk around and around anything that he did not wish wholly to reveal, and come close to it, brush against it, almost produce it, without actually betraying it; she so like a child. And, indeed, something of the kind, he felt in his tumultuous heart-throb at the thought, was nothing less than needful to him, so lonely, so overburthened, so shut up, as he had long been. Who else was there? Rose? Oh no, with her calm sense, her equable affection; he would never choose her as his confidant.

So, at this wild creature's request, Hilliard set himself to telling the scene of Aunt Nashoba's death-bed, as one would tell a story to a child; or as one child would tell a story to another; he told all the incidents of the beginning of the sickness, of how tenderly he nursed her, how he put down her old earthen jug to steep; and here, (whatever were the cause) his voice changed a little, and his eye sank beneath Sybil's, but he recovered himself and went on; and gave an account of the manner of Aunt Nashoba's calling, but when he came to speak of the singular phenomena of her last moments, and especially of the peculiar light in her face, Sybil suddenly arose, and clasping her hands above her head, uttered a cry;—so that Hillard Veren broke off.

"What is the matter?" asked he. "Why do you do so?"

"Nothing—go on!" said Sybil.

"I have no more to say," said Hilliard Veren, drawing back within himself.

And, in truth, that cry of Sybil's had frightened back his shy confidence within his own breast, whence he looked out askance at her, wondering what it meant, what she knew; whether she knew anything; whether it were more than a freak of her partial insanity. All this he could not determine upon; only it seemed wonderful to him, how he could just now have been talking so freely to this strange girl, and yet, he could not regret it; he was glad of the link that he had thus formed with her, and felt a strange wild reeling of himself towards her.

"How would you have felt," said Sybil, "if poor Aunt Nashoba had risen from her bed, straight, young, beautiful, to lead a sweeter life than ever—instead of dying?"

"Such things are impossible!" said Hilliard.

"I suppose so," said Sybil, looking down. "Yet they had strange legends round that Old Hall in England, and, I have heard, my uncle, Dr. Portsoaken, in his youth, studied upon the matter, a long while; but he missed something; could not find some document; and so failed."

"That was very strange, Sybil," said Hilliard; and said no more.

But two things were effected by this meeting of Sybil and himself. One was, that there had been a closer meeting between Hilliard and the girl than ever before, and he had felt the strange enchantment of a woman's intercourse, had felt the touch of her to him; something had taken place, which could not be gone back from. True; he did not know in what spirit she had admitted it; it might be hate, but it stirred and thrilled the melancholy secluded young man, that touch of her hand, and he lingered, longed, shivered with anticipation of future intercourse. Ever afterwards it might, it must, be different from what it had been before. Another thing was, the suggestion of Dr. Portsoaken, and his former experience in the study on which Hilliard was now engaged. How foolish, how idle it would be, it was, to go over all the ground which had been traversed by a person, now within his reach, without obtaining the benefit of the errors or partial successes which that person had achieved. This idea wrought so strongly upon Hilliard Veren, that, within a short time after the herb-woman's funeral (when, it may be observed, the neighbors almost filled her grave with fragrant herbs, and Sybil threw in a scarlet flower, as appropriate to her character) he set out on a journey to Boston, to pay a visit to the scientific Doctor.

So Hilliard waited only a few days, until the mortal remains of poor Aunt Nashoba were committed to the burial-ground, on the brow and slope of the hill that fences in the village from the north aspect; among many generations of her townspeople, the herb-woman still sleeps without a monument, unless a singular abundance and variety of herbs may be thought to serve as such. For it was really noteworthy, that in the course of the next summer, the grave sprouted with vervain, dill, apple, pear, wormwood, monkshood, catnip, and I know not what besides, which, as those who pretended knowledge on the subject solemnly affirmed, were the herbs of which she had been wont to compound those famous bitters, which, since her departure for a better world, were no more quaffed on earth; so that, being for so many years imbued with that valuable nostrum, it seemed as if she had acquired its composite nature, and even became a bed of all, and grew up again in this mode, offering to the world, after her death, that which she had most valued during her life, and becoming that, in the concocted state, which she had most delighted to concoct. Learning, not long

since, that her resting-place was still distinguishable, or supposed to be so, I went thither, one afternoon, and easily
found the range of family graves, among which was that of
the famous divine, the Tomahawk of Righteousness, and
likewise that of a certain Kezhba Veren, the name being
engraved on a very rude stone, much moss-grown, and
scarcely decypherable, which I presumed to be that of the
great aunt, celebrated as a witch; more especially as some
unkind person (who had probably long since accounted for
it to the poor witch face to face) had taken upon himself
to scratch a rude representation of a gallows on the stone.
She lies with these two, and other graves of the family; it
was a questionable sort of mound, which rather disappointed
me in not being so luxuriant of herbs as my authority had
led me to expect. However, I managed to get a leaf or two
of vervain and dill, which I have pressed in Barlow's Colum-
biad, which I keep for such purposes, and please myself
with thinking that these are a veritable portion of poor
Aunt Nashoba's mortal substance; her immortal part, I hope,
delighting itself among sweeter and better herbage. But you
cannot expect the fertility of her poor withered substance to
endure forever.

But, from the house where she dwelt, Aunt Nashoba had
forever passed away; nor do I know that she haunts it even
as a ghost, although it would seem natural enough, at midnight, to see a stooping, antiquated figure, laden with a
burthen of herbs and twigs, climbing the stairs to spread
them on the garret floor to dry. She was gone, and Rose shed
some kindly tears from a sense that the poor herb-woman
had a kind of wild capacity for love, and some spicy, pungent
virtues, like some of her own bitter herbs, though, towards
Rose herself, there was little but the bitterness and pungency,
the wormwood without the fragrance. Moreover, Rose set

the brown jug on a shelf, and covered it with the broken teapot lid, where it remained year after year, still imbued with old fragrance; and she laid Aunt Nashoba's pipe over two nails, on the jamb of the fire-place, with Aunt Nashoba's smoke varnished seat close by, as if she expected to come, perhaps at midnight, creeping in, shivering from her cold bed, and fill the pipe with tobacco and strong herbs, and light it from among the smouldering embers and smoke, and get her gone again; only leaving a somewhat disagreeable and doubtful perfume in the kitchen, the next morning. Septimius, in fact, recollecting some of the passages of her death-bed conversation, had an idea that, constrained and irked with some formality of the better life, and tried with the primness, neatness, orderliness of Saints and Angels, poor Aunt Nashoba might sometimes like such a little excursion, and return to her objectionable earthly habits; but, for my part, I think she would not have taken many steps over the border, before she became, in all desirable respects, a new woman.

Aunt Nashoba thus disposed of, Hilliard Veren, a week afterwards, took his way, on foot, along the Lexington road, intending to accomplish the twenty miles between his home and Boston in the course of the September day. It was a sunny and breezy morning, promising a mid-summer warmth at noon, but possessing in these early hours a slightly autumnal coolness, akin to the hoar frosts that would soon decorate each blade of herbage with silvery rime. A natural regret at the departure of summer affected Hilliard's mind, although he drove it away with the thought that it was not for him, with an interminable vista of future years before him, to mourn for the flighting of one summer, as those must do naturally who, before many layers of autumn leaves are strewn, will begin to be covered up forever by their fall.

It was for him to rejoice in decay, as well as in new growth; one was but the preparation for the other, and he himself the undying witness of the show of changing seasons with which Nature defrocked or rearrayed all her other children.

But what a potency there is in change of place! How do our follies and delusion intrude themselves upon the circles which we inhabit, and make an enchanted room of our familiar chambers, and indeed the atmosphere that we breathe too constantly, so that, by and by, it is but an enchanted room, where we get nothing but slightly varied proportions of our old illusion. It was now many months since he had been away from home, or scarcely out of sight of his own house, except when he followed Aunt Nashoba to the burial ground; all his other pacings to and fro having been on that eternal brow of his hill-top, passing and repassing that hillock, out of which, as if some seed of mysterious potency had been planted there, had grown a fatality that entwined him with its branching luxuriance, so that he himself almost seemed to have taken root there. But now, in the very first mile or two of his journey, the mere change of his material position seemed to give him a new standpoint, and showed him, as it were, the outside view of all his purposes and speculations, his plans, his beliefs looking like clouds in the sky; like dreams, to him who has wandered in them through the night, but feels a shock at the suddenness with which they dissolve, grow thin, show the surrounding relations through their poor substance, as wakefulness rushes upon him. It was as if he had come out of an Enchanted Land, where he had dwelt so long that his proper life and consciousness was in it, and his nature so much acclimated there that it had become his home; and now, by his sudden step out of that fantastic sphere upon the firm earth, all stable things seemed to whirl round, and made him dizzy. So he sate down upon a stone by the wayside, bewildered, fearing that he had lost his right of citizenship among men, a stranger on this solid earth, a companion of fictitious beings, and creatures of fable, a sham that ought to vanish with the morning mists; because, by such long energy and concentration of thought as he had applied to what had no existence, though he had done nothing towards making that real, he had at least exhaled this substance out of his own being. So there he sat; and when a wayfarer passed him by, and stared curiously at him, Hilliard wondered whether the beggar saw more than a wreath of vapor such as had not yet passed away from the meadows into the morning air; and so unreal did he feel, that it seemed as if the warm, genuine sun would exhale him soon.

It is not necessary to have been bewildered in precisely such a dream as Hilliard Veren's, in order to feel a similar, cold, disheartening, miserable shiver at the sudden contact with realities. All have felt, or are doomed to feel it, whose schemes, even though far more akin to truth than his, and even if in a measure practicable, rise up about them, with the aspect of marble pillars, an overarching roof, a solid pavement, and all such magnificence of a palace, before the foundation has entirely been laid. Inevitably, sometimes, the airy architect steps out of this magnificent edifice by some side-portal, and sees what a vaporous material he has builded with. Every man, however prosaic his pursuit, however plodding himself, knows something of this despair; the merchant sees heaps of gold as unreal as the yellow of sunset; empires, that were to be, and based on the wisest calculations of statesmen, and statesmen, would vanish into nothing, beneath the feet of those who plowed, leaving statesmen, homes, people, that were to be, to sink into perdition, if once they could slip out of the magic influence and see the sober truth. Perhaps none are more subject to it than Romance writers;

they make themselves at home among their characters and scenery, and know them better than they know anything actual, and feel a blessed warmth that the air of this world does not supply, and discern a fitness of events that the course of human life has not elsewhere; so that all seems a truer world than that they were born in; but sometimes, if they step beyond the limits of the spell, ah! the sad destruction, disturbance, incongruity, that meets the eye; distortion, impossibility, everything that seemed so true and beautiful in its proper atmosphere, and nicely adjusted relations, now a hideous absurdity. Thus he that writes the strange story of Hilliard Veren may well sympathize with the emotion of that moment.

Hilliard would perhaps have turned back, in this mood of cold despair; but that his home seemed a more forlorn and wretched place than he could endure; a dismal dungeon, and his hillside, a growth of gloomy pines, among which he would gaze around seeking one on which to hang himself, and the place of a grave out of which issued a subtle gloom, which pervaded all his life. The ghost of Aunt Nashoba pervaded his recollection of the house with an odor of unfragrant herbs. Sybil Dacy, too, frightened him now that he was apart from her, with a sense of something questionable, if not malign; and Rose, for a different reason, repelled him by that pure atmosphere of truth, reason, and right feeling, which was not the medium in which his sick spirit could find fitting breath. No; it were better for him to go on; perhaps he would never see his home again; nor, once knowing the delusion under which he had lived, again trust himself where the enchantment might have power. His dream of everlasting life had failed him. Then what was the next choice? Was it not, to seek the readiest passage out of an existence that, so miserably brief, in comparison with the long measure which his thoughts, for many months past, had made him familiar with, seemed not worth returning to for the little time that would bring old age. And how easy, at that time, to find a battle field to die on; and, perhaps, in the sweet, exhilarating sense of living, with his fellow men— the free life of humanity, risking all, sacrificing all for the triumph of his country, and dying in the attainment of victory for her, there might be an intensity of life, into the few moments of which would be compressed all that heat, vigor, earnestness, which would have been thinly scattered over such an interminableness as he had dreamed of.

THE DOLLIVER ROMANCE

FRAGMENTS OF A ROMANCE

CHAPTER I: THE BRAZEN SERPENT

DOCTOR DOLLIVER, a worthy personage of extreme antiquity, was aroused rather prematurely, one summer morning, by the shouts of the child Pansie, in an adjoining chamber, summoning Old Martha (who performed the duties of nurse, housekeeper, and kitchen-maid, in the Doctor's establishment) to take up her little ladyship and dress her. The old gentleman woke with more than his customary alacrity, and, after taking a moment to gather his wits about him, pulled aside the faded moreen curtains of his ancient bed, and thrust his head into a beam of sunshine that caused him to wink and withdraw it again. This transitory glimpse of good Dr. Dolliver showed a flannel nightcap, fringed round with stray locks of silvery white hair, and surmounting a meagre and duskily yellow visage, which was crossed and criss-crossed with a record of his long life in wrinkles, faithfully written, no doubt, but with such cramped chirography of Father Time that the purport was illegible. It seemed hardly worth while for the patriarch to get out of bed any more, and bring his forlorn shadow into the summer day that was made for younger folks. The Doctor, however, was by no means of that opinion, being considerably encouraged towards the toil of living twenty-four hours longer by the comparative ease with which he found himself going through the usually painful process of bestirring his rusty joints, (stiffened by the very rest and sleep that should have made them pliable) and putting them in a condition to bear his weight upon the floor. Nor was he absolutely disheartened by the idea of those tonsorial, ablutionary, and personally decorative labors, which are apt to become so intolerably irksome to an old gentleman, after performing them daily and duly for fifty, sixty, or seventy years, and finding them still as immitigably recurrent as at first. Dr. Dolliver could nowise account for this happy condition of his spirits and physical energies, until he remembered taking an experimental sip of a certain cordial, which was long ago prepared by his grandson, and carefully sealed up in a bottle, and had been reposited in a dark closet among a parcel of effete medicines, ever since that gifted young man's death.

"It may have wrought effect upon me," thought the doctor, shaking his head, as he lifted it again from the pillow. "It may be so; for poor Cornelius oftentimes instilled a strange efficacy into his perilous drugs. But I will rather believe it to be the operation of God's mercy, which may have temporarily invigorated my feeble age for little Pansie's sake."

A twinge of his familiar rheumatism as he put his foot out of bed, taught him that he must not reckon too confidently upon even a day's respite from the intrusive family of aches and infirmities, which, with their proverbial fidelity to attachments once formed, had long been the closest acquaintances that the poor old gentleman had in the world. Nevertheless, he fancied the twinge a little less poignant than those of yesterday; and, moreover, after stinging him pretty smartly, it passed gradually off with a thrill, which, in its latter stages, grew to be almost agreeable. Pain is but pleasure too strongly emphasized. With cautious movements, and only a groan or two, the good doctor transferred himself from the bed to the floor, where he stood awhile, gazing from one piece of quaint furniture to another (such as stiff-backed Mayflower chairs, an oaken chest of drawers, carved cunningly with shapes of animals and wreaths of foliage, a table with multitudinous legs, a family-record in faded embroidery, a shelf of black-bound books, a dusty heap of gallipots and phials in a dim corner,)—gazing at these things and steadying himself by the bed-post, while his inert brain, still partially benumbed with sleep, came slowly into accordance with the realities about him. The object which most helped to bring Dr. Dolliver completely to his waking perceptions was one that common observers might suppose to have been snatched bodily out of his dreams. The same sunbeam that had dazzled the doctor between the bed-curtains, glimmered on the weather-beaten gilding which had once adorned this mysterious symbol, and showed it to be an enormous serpent, twining round a wooden post, and reaching quite from the floor of the chamber to its ceiling.

It was evidently a thing that could boast of considerable antiquity, the dry-rot having eaten out its eyes and gnawed away the tip of its tail; and it must have stood long exposed to the atmosphere, for a kind of grey moss had partially overspread its tarnished gilt surface, and a swallow, or other familiar little bird, in some by-gone summer, seemed to have built its nest in the yawning and exaggerated mouth. It looked like a kind of manichean idol, which might have been elevated on a pedestal for a century or so, enjoying the worship of its votaries in the open air, until the impious sect perished from among men—all save old Dr. Dolliver, who had set up the monster in his bed-chamber for the convenience of private devotion. But we are unpardonable in suggesting such a fantasy to the prejudice of our venerable friend, knowing him to have been as pious and upright a Christian, and with as little of the serpent in his character, as ever came of Puritan lineage. Not to make a further mystery about a very simple matter, this bedimmed and rotten reptile was once the medical emblem or apothecary's sign of the famous Dr. Swinnerton, who practised physic in the earlier days of New England, when a head of Æsculapius or Hippocrates, would have vexed the souls of the righteous as savoring of Heathendom. The ancient dispenser of drugs had therefore set up an image of the Brazen Serpent, and followed his business for many years, with great credit, under this Scriptural device; and Dr. Dolliver, being the apprentice, pupil, and humble friend of the learned Swinnerton's old age, had inherited the symbolic snake, and much other valuable property, by his bequest.

While the patriarch was putting on his small-clothes, he took care to stand in the parallelogram of bright sunshine that fell upon the uncarpeted floor. The summer warmth was very genial to his system and yet made him shiver; his wintry veins rejoiced at it, though the reviving blood tingled through them with a half-painful and only half-pleasurable titillation. For the first few moments after creeping out of bed, he kept his back to the sunny window and seemed mysteriously shy of glancing thitherward; but as the June fervor pervaded him more and more thoroughly, he turned bravely about, and looked forth at a burial ground on the corner of which he dwelt. There lay many an old acquaintance, who had gone to sleep with the flavor of Dr. Dolliver's tinctures and powders upon his tongue; it was the patient's final bitter taste of this world, and perhaps doomed to be a recollected nauseousness in the next. Yesterday, in the chill of his forlorn old age, the doctor expected soon to stretch out his weary bones among that quiet community, and might scarcely have shrunk from the prospect on his own account; except, indeed, that he dreamily mixed up the infirmities of his present condition with the repose of the approaching one, being haunted by a notion that the damp earth, under the grass and dandelions, must needs be pernicious for his cough and his rheumatism. But, this morning, the cheerful sunbeams, or the mere taste of his grandson's cordial that he had taken at bedtime, or the fitful vigor that often sports irreverently with aged people, had caused an unfrozen drop of youthfulness, somewhere within him, to expand.

"Hem!—ahem!" quoth the doctor, hoping with one effort to clear his throat of the dregs of a ten-years' cough. "Matters are not so far gone with me as I thought. I have known mighty sensible men, when only a little age-stricken or otherwise out of sorts, to die of mere faint-heartedness, a great deal sooner than they need."

He shook his silvery head at his own image in the looking-glass, as if to impress the apothegm on that shadowy representative of himself; and for his part, he determined to pluck up a spirit and live as long as he possibly could, if it were only for the sake of little Pansie, who stood as close to one extremity of human life as her great-grandfather to the other. This child of three years old occupied all the unfossilized portion of good Dr. Dolliver's heart. Every other interest that he formerly had, and the entire confraternity of persons whom he once loved, had long ago departed, and the poor doctor could not follow them, because the grasp of Pansie's baby-fingers held him back.

So he crammed a great silver watch into his fob, and drew on a patchwork morning-gown of an ancient fashion. Its original material was said to have been the embroidered front of his own wedding waistcoat and the silken skirt of his wife's bridal attire, which his eldest grand-daughter had taken from the carved chest of drawers after poor Bessy, the beloved of his youth, had been half-a-century in the grave. Throughout many of the intervening years, as the garment got ragged, the spinsters of the old man's family had quilted their duty and affection into it in the shape of patches upon patches, rose-color, crimson, blue, violet, and green, and then (as their hopes faded, and their life kept growing shadier and their attire took a sombre hue) sober gray and great fragments of funereal black; until the doctor could revive the memory of most things that had befallen him by looking at his patchwork-gown as it hung upon a chair. And now it was ragged again, and all the fingers that should have mended it were cold. It had an eastern fragrance, too, a smell of drugs, strong-scented herbs, and spicy gums, gathered from the many potent infusions that had from time to time been spilt over it; so that, snuffing him afar off, you might have taken Dr. Dolliver for a mummy, and would hardly have been undeceived by his shrunken and torpid aspect, as he crept nearer.

Wrapt in this odorous and many-colored robe, he took staff in hand and moved pretty vigorously to the head of the staircase. As it was somewhat steep, and but dimly lighted, he began cautiously to descend, putting his left hand on the banister, and poking down his long stick to assist him in making sure of the successive steps; and thus he became a living illustration of the accuracy of Scripture, where it describes the aged as being "afraid of that which is high"—a truth that is often found to have a sadder purport than its external one. Halfway to the bottom, however, the doctor heard the impatient and authoritative tones of little Pansie— Queen Pansie, as she might fairly have been styled, in reference to her position in the household—calling amain for grandpapa and breakfast. He was startled into such perilous activity by the summons, that his heels slid on the stairs, the slippers were shuffled off his feet, and he saved himself from a tumble only by quickening his pace and coming down at almost a run.

"Mercy on my poor old bones!" mentally exclaimed the doctor, fancying himself fractured in fifty places. "Some of them are broken, surely, and methinks my heart has leaped out of my mouth! What! All right? Well, well; but Providence is kinder to me than I deserve, prancing down this steep staircase like a kid of three months old!"

He bent stiffly to gather up his slippers and fallen staff; and meanwhile Pansie had heard the tumult of her great-grandfather's descent, and was pounding against the door of the breakfast-room in her haste to come at him. The doctor opened it, and there she stood, a rather pale and large-eyed little thing, quaint in her aspect, as might well be the case with a motherless child, dwelling in an uncheerful house, with no other playmates than a decrepit old man and a kitten, and no better atmosphere within doors than the odor of decayed apothecary's stuff, nor gayer neighborhood than that of the adjacent burial-ground, where all her relatives, from her great-grandmother downward, lay calling to her—"Pansie, Pansie, it is bedtime!"—even in the prime of the summer-morning. For those dead women-folks, especially her mother and the whole row of maiden-aunts and grand-aunts, could not but be anxious about the child, knowing that little Pansie would be far safer under a tuft of dandelions than if left alone, as she soon must be, in this difficult and deceitful world.

Yet, in spite of the lack of damask roses in her cheeks, she seemed a healthy child, and certainly showed great capacity of energetic movement in the impulsive capers with which she welcomed her venerable progenitor. She shouted out her satisfaction, moreover, (as her custom was, having never had any over-sensitive auditors about her to tame down her voice,) till even the doctor's dull ears were full of the clamor.

"Pansie, darling," said Dr. Dolliver cheerily, patting her brown hair with his tremulous fingers, "thou hast put some of thine own friskiness into poor old grandfather, this fine morning! Dost know, child, that he came near breaking his neck down-stairs at the sound of thy voice? What wouldst thou have done then, little Pansie?"

"Kiss poor grandpapa and make him well!" answered the child, remembering the doctor's own mode of cure in similar mishaps to herself—"It shall do poor grandpapa good!" she added, putting up her mouth to apply the remedy.

"Ah, little one, thou hast greater faith in thy medicines than ever I had in my drugs," replied the patriarch with a giggle, surprised and delighted at his own readiness of response. "But the kiss is good for my feeble old heart, Pansie, though it might do little to mend a broken neck; so give grandpapa another dose, and let us to breakfast!"

In this merry humor, they sat down to the table, great-grandpapa and Pansie side by side, and the kitten, as soon appeared, making a third in the party. First, she showed her mottled head out of Pansie's lap, delicately sipping milk from the child's basin without rebuke; then she took post on the old gentleman's shoulder, purring like a spinning-wheel, trying her claws in the wadding of his dressing-gown, and still more impressively reminding him of her presence by putting out a paw to intercept a warmed-over morsel of yesterday's chicken on its way to the doctor's mouth. After skilfully achieving this feat, she scrambled down upon the breakfast table and began to wash her face and hands. Evidently, these companions were all three on intimate terms, as was natural enough, since a great many childish impulses were softly creeping back on the simple-minded old man; insomuch that, if no worldly necessities nor painful infirmity had disturbed him, his remnant of life might have been as cheaply and cheerily enjoyed as the early playtime of the kitten and the child. Old Dr. Dolliver and his great-grand-daughter (a ponderous title, which seemed quite to overwhelm the tiny figure of Pansie) had met one another at the two extremities of the life-circle; her sunrise served him for a sunset, illuminating his locks of silver and hers of golden brown with a homogeneous shimmer of twinkling light.

Little Pansie was the one earthly creature that inherited a drop of the Dolliver blood. The doctor's only child, poor Bessy's offspring, had died, the better part of a hundred years before, and his grand-children, a numerous and dimly-remembered brood, had vanished along his weary track in their youth, maturity, or incipient age, till, hardly knowing how it had all happened, he found himself tottering onward with an infant's small fingers in his nerveless grasp. So mistily did his dead progeny come and go in the patriarch's decayed recollection, that this solitary child represented for him the successive babyhoods of the many that had gone before. The emotions of his early paternity came back to him. She seemed the baby of a past age oftener than she seemed Pansie. A whole family of grand-aunts (one of whom had perished in her cradle, never so mature as Pansie now, another in her virgin bloom, another in autumnal maidenhood, yellow and shrivelled, with vinegar in her blood, and still another, a forlorn widow, whose grief outlasted even its vitality, and grew to be merely a torpid habit, and was saddest then)— all their hitherto forgotten features peeped through the face of the great-grandchild, and their long inaudible voices sobbed, shouted, or laughed, in her familiar tones. But it often happened to Dr. Dolliver—while frolicking amid this throng of ghosts where the one reality looked no more vivid than its shadowy sisters—it often happened that his eyes filled with tears at a sudden perception of what a sad and poverty-stricken old man he was, already remote from his own generation, and bound to stray farther onward as the sole playmate and protector of a child!

As Dr. Dolliver, in spite of his advanced epoch of life, is likely to remain a considerable time longer upon our hands, we deem it expedient to give a brief sketch of his position, in order that the story may get onward with the greater freedom when he rises from the breakfast table. Deeming it a matter of courtesy, we have allowed him the honorary title of Doctor, as did all his townspeople and contemporaries, except, perhaps, one or two formal old physicians, stingy of civil phrases and over-jealous of their own professional dignity. Nevertheless, these crusty graduates were technically right in excluding Dr. Dolliver from their fraternity. He had never received the degree of any medical school, nor (save it might be for the cure of a toothache, or a child's rash, or a whitlow on a seamstress's finger, or some such trifling malady) had he ever been even a practitioner of the awful science with which his popular designation connected him. Our old friend, in short, even at his highest social elevation, claimed to be nothing more than an apothecary, nor, in these latter and far less prosperous days, scarcely so much. Since the death of his last surviving grandson, (Pansie's father, whom he had instructed in all the mysteries of his science, and who, being distinguished by an experimental and inventive tendency, was generally believed to have poisoned himself with an infallible panacea of his own distillation)—since that final bereavement, Dr. Dolliver's once pretty flourishing business had lamentably declined. After a few months of unavailing struggle, he found it expedient to take down the Brazen Serpent from the position to which Dr. Swinnerton had originally elevated it, in front of his shop in the Main-street, and to retire to his private dwelling, situated in a by-lane and on the edge of a burial-ground.

This house, as well as the Brazen Serpent, some old medical books, and a drawer full of manuscripts, had come to him by the legacy of Dr. Swinnerton. The dreariness of the locality had been of small importance to our friend in his young manhood, when he first led his fair wife over the threshold, and so long as neither of them had any kinship with the human dust that rose into little hillocks, and still kept accumulating beneath their window. But, too soon afterwards, when poor Bessie herself had gone early to rest there, it is probable that an influence from her grave may have prematurely calmed and depressed her widowed husband, taking away much of the energy from what should have been the most active portion of his life. Thus, he never grew rich. His thrifty townsmen used to tell him, that, in any other man's hands, Dr. Swinnerton's Brazen Serpent (meaning, I presume, the inherited credit and good-will of that old worthy's trade) would need but ten years' time to transmute its brass into gold. In Dr. Dolliver's keeping, as we have seen, the inauspicious symbol lost the greater part of what superficial gilding it originally had. Matters had not mended with him in more advanced life, after he had deposited a further and further portion of his heart and its affections in each successive one of a long row of kindred graves; and as he stood over the last of them, holding Pansie by the hand and looking down upon the coffin of his grandson, it is no wonder that the old man wept, partly for those gone before, but not so bitterly as for the little one that stayed behind. Why had not God taken her with the rest? And then—so hopeless as he was, so destitute of possibilities of good—his weary frame, his decrepit bones, his dried-up heart, might have crumbled into dust at once, and have been scattered by the next wind over all the heaps of earth that were akin to him.

This intensity of desolation, however, was of too positive a character to be long sustained by a person of Dr. Dolliver's original gentleness and simplicty, and now so completely tamed by age and misfortune. Even before he turned away from the grave, he grew conscious of a slightly cheering and invigorating effect from the tight grasp of the child's warm little hand. Feeble as he was, she seemed to adopt him willingly for her protector. And the doctor never afterwards shrank from his duty nor quailed beneath it, but bore himself like a man, striving, amid the sloth of age and the breaking-up of intellect, to earn the competency which he had failed to accumulate even in his most vigorous days.

To the extent of securing a present subsistence for Pansie and himself, he was successful. After his grandson's death, when the Brazen Serpent fell into popular disrepute, a small share of tenacious patronage followed the old man into his retirement. In his prime, he had been allowed to possess more skill than usually fell to the share of a colonial apothecary, having been regularly apprenticed to Dr. Swinnerton, who, throughout his long practice, was accustomed personally to concoct the medicines which he prescribed and dispensed. It was believed, indeed, that the ancient physician had learned the art at the world-famous drug-manufactory of Apothecary's Hall, in London, and, as some people half-malignly whispered, had perfected himself under masters more subtle than were to be found even there. Unquestionably, in many critical cases, he was known to have employed remedies of mysterious composition and dangerous potency, which, in less skilful hands, would have been more likely to kill than cure. He would willingly, it is said, have taught his apprentice the secrets of these prescriptions, but the latter, being of a timid character and delicate conscience, had shrunk from acquaintance with them. It was probably as the result of the same scrupulosity, that Dr. Dolliver had always declined to enter the medical profession, in which his old instructor had set him such heroic examples of adventurous dealing with matters of life and death. Nevertheless, the aromatic fragrance, so to speak, of the learned Swinnerton's reputation had clung to our friend through life; and there were elaborate preparations in the pharmacopœia of that day, requiring such minute skill and conscientious fidelity in the concoctor, that the physicians were still glad to confide them to one in whom these qualities were so evident.

Moreover, the grandmothers of the community were kind to him, and mindful of his perfumes, his rose-water, his cosmetics, tooth-powders, pomanders, and pomades, the scented memory of which lingered about their toilet-tables or came faintly back from the days when they were beautiful. Among this class of customers there was still a demand for certain comfortable little nostrums, (delicately sweet and pungent to the taste, cheering to the spirits, and fragrant in the breath,) the proper distillation of which was the airiest secret that the mystic Swinnerton had left behind him. And, besides, these old ladies had always liked the manners of Dr. Dolliver, and used to speak of his gentle courtesy behind the counter as having positively been something to admire; though of later years, an unrefined, an almost rustic simplicity, such as belonged to his humble ancestors, appeared to have taken possession of him, as it often does of prettily-mannered men in their late decay.

But it resulted from all these favorable circumstances that the doctor's marble mortar, though worn with long service and considerably damaged by a crack that pervaded it, continued to keep up an occasional intimacy with the pestle; and he still weighed drachms and scruples in his delicate scales, though it seemed impossible, dealing with such minute quantities, that his tremulous fingers should not put in too little or too much, leaving out life with the deficiency or spilling in death with the surplus. To say the truth, his staunchest friends were beginning to think that Dr. Dolliver's fits of absence (when his mind appeared absolutely to depart from him, while his frail old body worked on mechanically) rendered him not quite trustworthy without a close supervision of his proceedings. It was impossible, however, to convince the aged apothecary of the necessity for such vigilance; and if anything could stir up his gentle temper to wrath, or, as oftener happened, to tears, it was the attempt (which he was marvellously quick to detect) thus to interfere with his long-familiar business.

The public, meanwhile, ceasing to regard Dr. Dolliver in his professional aspect, had begun to take an interest in him as perhaps their oldest fellow-citizen. It was he that remembered the Great Fire and the Great Snow, and that had been a grown-up stripling at the terrible epoch of Witch Times, and a child just breeched at the breaking out of King Philip's Indian War. He, too, in his school-boy days, had received a benediction from the patriarchal Governor Bradstreet, and thus could boast (somewhat as Bishops do of their unbroken succession from the Apostles) of a transmitted blessing from the whole company of sainted Pilgrims, among whom the venerable magistrate had been an honored companion. Viewing their townsman in this aspect, the people revoked the courteous Doctorate with which they had heretofore decorated him, and now knew him most familiarly as Grandsir Dolliver. His white head, his puritan band, his threadbare garb, (the

fashion of which he had ceased to change, half-a-century ago)
his gold-headed staff that had been Dr. Swinnerton's, his
shrunken, frosty figure, and its feeble movement, all these
characteristics had a wholeness and permanence in the public
recognition, like the meeting-house steeple or the town-pump.
All the younger portion of the inhabitants unconsciously
ascribed a sort of aged immortality to Grandsir Dolliver's infirm and reverend presence. They fancied that he had been
born old, (at least, I remember entertaining some such notions about age-stricken people when I myself was young,)
and that he could the better tolerate his aches and incommodities, his dull ears and dim eyes, his remoteness from
human intercourse within the crust of indurated years, the
cold temperature that kept him always shivering and sad,
the heavy burthen that invisibly bent down his shoulders—
that all these intolerable things might bring a kind of enjoyment to Grandsir Dolliver, as the life-long conditions of his
peculiar existence.

But, alas, it was a terrible mistake. This weight of years
had a perennial novelty for the poor sufferer. He never grew
accustomed to it, but long as he had now borne the fretful
torpor of his waning life, and patient as he seemed, he still
retained an inward consciousness that these stiffened shoulders, these quailing knees, this cloudiness of sight and brain,
this confused forgetfulness of men and affairs, were troublesome accidents that did not really belong to him. He possibly
cherished a half-recognized idea that they might pass away.
Youth, however eclipsed for a season, is undoubtedly the
proper, permanent, and genuine condition of man; and if
we look closely into this dreary delusion of growing old, we
shall find that it never absolutely succeeds in laying hold of
our innermost convictions. A sombre garment, woven of life's
unrealities, has muffled us from our true self, but within it

smiles the young man whom we knew; the ashes of many perishable things have fallen upon our youthful fire, but beneath them lurk the seeds of inextinguishable flame. So powerful is this instinctive faith, that men of simple modes of character are prone to antedate its consummation. And thus it happened with poor Grandsir Dolliver, who often awoke from an old man's fitful sleep with a sense that his senile predicament was but a dream of the past night; and hobbling hastily across the cold floor to the looking-glass, he would be grievously disappointed at beholding the white hair, wrinkles, and furrows, the ashen visage and bent form, the melancholy mask of Age, in which, as he now remembered, some strange and sad enchantment had involved him for years gone by!

To other eyes than his own, however, the shrivelled old gentleman looked as if there were little hope of his throwing off this too artfully wrought disguise, until, at no distant day, his stooping figure should be straightened out, his hoary locks be smoothed over his brow, and his much enduring bones be laid safely away, with a green coverlet spread over them, beside his Bessie, who doubtless would recognize her youthful companion in spite of his ugly garniture of decay. He longed to be gazed at by the loving eyes now closed; he shrank from the hard stare of them that loved him not. Walking the streets seldom and reluctantly, he felt a dreary impulse to elude the people's observation, as if with a sense that he had gone irrevocably out of fashion, and broken his connecting links with the network of human life; or else it was that nightmare feeling which we sometimes have in dreams, when we seem to find ourselves wandering through a crowded avenue, with the noonday-sun upon us, in some wild extravagance of dress or nudity. He was conscious of estrangement from his townspeople, but did not always know how nor wherefore, nor why he should be thus groping through the twilight mist in solitude. If they spoke loudly to him, with cheery voices, the greeting translated itself faintly and mournfully to his ears; if they shook him by the hand, it was as if a thick, insensible glove absorbed the kindly pressure and the warmth. When little Pansie was the companion of his walk, her childish gaiety and freedom did not avail to bring him into closer relationship with men, but seemed to follow him into that region of indefinable remoteness, that dismal Fairy Land of aged fancy, into which old Grandsir Dolliver had so strangely crept away.

Yet there were moments, as many persons had noticed, when the great-grandpapa would suddenly take stronger hues of life. It was as if his faded figure had been colored over anew, or at least, as he and Pansie moved along the street, as if a sunbeam had fallen across him instead of the gray gloom of an instant before. His chilled sensibilities had probably been touched and quickened by the warm contiguity of his little companion through the medium of her hand, as it stirred within his own, or some inflection of her voice that set his memory ringing and chiming with forgotten sounds. While that music lasted, the old man was alive and happy. And there were seasons, it might be, happier than even these, when Pansie had been kissed and put to bed, and Grandsir Dolliver sat by his fireside gazing in among the massive coals, and absorbing their glow into those cavernous abysses with which all men communicate. Thence come angels or fiends into our twilight musings, according as we may have peopled them in by-gone years. Over our friend's face, in the rosy flicker of the fire-gleam, stole an expression of repose and perfect trust that made him as beautiful to look at, in his high-backed chair, as the child Pansie on her pillow; and sometimes the spirits that were watching him beheld a calm surprise dawn slowly over his features and brighten into joy, yet not so vividly as to break his evening quietude. The gate of Heaven had been kindly left ajar, that this forlorn old creature might catch a glimpse within. All the night afterwards, he would be semi-conscious of an intangible bliss diffused through the fitful lapses of an old man's slumber, and would awake, at early dawn, with a faint thrilling of the heart-strings as if there had been music just now wandering over them.

But such enjoyment, whether spiritual or physical, was altogether distinct from the kind of alacrity with which Dr. Dolliver had bestirred himself on the morning of our story.

CHAPTER II

WE MAY NOW SUPPOSE Grandsir Dolliver to have finished his breakfast, (with a better appetite, and pleasanter perception of the qualities of his food than he has generally felt, of late years, whether it were due to old Martha's cookery, or the cordial of the night before). Pansie had finished her bread, hasty-pudding, and milk with an excellent appetite, and afterwards nibbled a crust, greatly enjoying its resistance to her little white teeth. How this child came by the odd name of Pansie, and whether it was really her baptismal name, I have not ascertained. More probably, it was one of those pet appellations that grow out of a child's character, or out of some keener thrill of affection in the parents, an unsought-for and unconscious felicity, a kind of revelation teaching them, as it would seem in some instances, the true

name by which the child's guardian angel would know it—a
name with playfulness and love in it—that we often observe
to supersede, in the use of those who love the child best, the
name that they carefully selected and caused the clergyman
to plaister indelibly on the poor little forehead at the font—
the love name, whereby, if the child lives, the parents know
it in their hearts, or by which, if it die, God seems to have
called it away, leaving the sound echoing faintly & sweetly
through the house. If it signified anything in Pansie's case, it
must have been a certain pensiveness, which was often seen
under her childish frolick, and so translated itself into French,
her mother having been of Acadian kin; or, quite as probably,
it alluded merely to the color of her eyes, which in some
lights, were very like the dark petals of a tuft of pansies in the
Doctor's garden. It might well be; for the child's gaiety had
no example to sustain it, no sympathy of other children, or
grown people, and her melancholy, had it been so dark a
feeling, was but the shadow of the house and the old man.
If brighter sunshine came, she would brighten with it. This
morning, surely, as the three companions, Pansie, puss, and
Grandsir Dolliver, emerged from the shadow of the house
into the small adjoining garden which had stolen a corner of
the burial ground, they seemed all frolicksome alike.

The doctor, however, was intent over something that had
reference to his life-long business of drugs. This little spot of
garden was the place where he was accustomed to cultivate
a variety of herbs supposed to be endowed with medicinal
virtue, some of which had been long known in the pharmacopeia of the old world, and others, in the early days of the
country, had been adopted by the early settlers from the
Indian medicine-men; though not without fear and even
contrition, because these wild doctors were supposed to draw

their professional knowledge from no gracious source; the Black Man himself being the principal professor in their medical school. From his own experience, however, Dr. Dolliver had long since doubted, though not bold enough quite to come to the conclusion that Indian shrubs, and the remedies prepared from them, were considerably less perilous than those so freely used in European practice, and singularly apt to be followed by results quite as propitious. Into such heterodoxy our friend was the more liable to fall, because it had been taught him early in life, by his old master Dr. Swinnerton, who, at those not infrequent times when he indulged a certain unhappy predilection for strong waters, had been accustomed to inveigh in terms of the most cynical contempt and coarsest ridicule against the profession by which he lived, and to which, in either case, he was held an ornament, and, as he affirmed, inflicted death on his fellow-men. Our old apothecary, though too loyal to the learned profession with which he was connected, fully to believe this bitter judgment, even when pronounced by his revered master, was still so far influenced that his conscience was, possibly, a little easier when making a preparation from forest-herbs and roots, than in the concoction of half a score of nauseous poisons into a single elaborate drug, as the fashion of that day was.

<(he rather neglects the culture of the plants)>

But there were shrubs in the little garden of which he had never ventured to make a medical use, and indeed, knew not the process or the virtue; although, from year to year, he had tended and fertilized them, weeded them, pruned them, with something like religious care. They were of the rarest character, planted by the learned and famous Dr. Swinnerton, who, on his death-bed, when he left his dwelling and all his abstruse manuscripts to his favorite pupil, had particularly directed his attention to this row of shrubs, and told him that, properly used, they would be worth all the rest of the legacy a hundred fold. They had been collected by himself from remote countries, and had the fragrancy of torrid climes in them. As the apothecary, however, found the manuscripts, in which he conjectured a treatise on the subject of these shrubs, mostly illegible, and quite beyond his comprehension in such passages as he succeeded in puzzling out, (partly, perhaps, owing to his very imperfect knowledge of Latin, in which they were written,) he had never derived from them any of the promised benefit; and, to say the truth, remembering that Dr. Swinnerton himself never appeared to infuse, or triturate, or decoct, or do anything else with the mysterious herbs unless he did it in secret, our old friend was inclined to imagine the weighty commendation of their virtues was the idly solemn utterance of mental aberration, at the hour of death. So, with the integrity that belonged to his character, he had nurtured them as tenderly as was possible, in the languid climate and soil of New England, putting some of them in pots in the winter, where they had rather dwindled than flourished, but he had reaped no harvest, nor observed them with any degree of scientific interest. <(Here introduce the tragic reminiscence about his wife having worn one of the flowers)>

His grandson, however, while yet a school-boy, had listened to the old man's legend of the miraculous virtues of these shrubs, and it took so firm a hold of his mind that the row of outlandish vegetables seemed rooted, and certainly flourished with richer luxuriance than in the soil where they actually grew. The story, acting thus early upon his imagination, may be said to have influenced his brief career in life, and perhaps bro't about its early close. The young man, in the opinion of competent judges, was endowed with remarkable abilities, and according to the rumor of the people, had wonderful gifts, which they instanced by stories of cures which he had wrought by remedies of his own invention. His talents were employed in the direction of scientific research analysis and inventive combination of chemical powers. While under the pupilage of his grandfather, his progress had rapidly gone quite beyond his instructor's hope, leaving him to tremble at the audacity with which he overturned and invented theories, and to wonder at the depth at which he wrought beneath the superficialness and mock-mystery of the medical science of those days, like a miner sinking his shaft, and running a hideous peril of the earth caving in above him. Especially did he devote himself to these plants, and with such exhaustive research that he was thus led into extensive study of botany, to such degree as means for the pursuit then existed in the country, and embracing many varieties of plants which had never before been brought within the scope of science. Under his care, they had thriven beyond all former precedent, bursting into luxuriance of bloom, and most of them into bearing beautiful flowers, which, however, in two or three instances, had the sort of natural repulsiveness that the serpent has in its beauty, compelled against its will, as it were, to warn the beholder of an un-revealed peril. He long ago, it must be added, demanded of his Grandfather the manuscripts included in the legacy of Professor Swinnerton, and had spent days and nights upon them, growing pale over their mystic lore, which seemed not merely the fruit of the Professor's own labors, but those of more ancient sages than he, and often a whole volume seemed to be compressed within the limits of a few lines of crabbed manuscript, judging from the time which it cost even this quick-minded student to decypher it.

Meantime, these abstruse investigations had not wrought such disastrous effects as might have been feared, in causing Edward Dolliver to neglect the humble trade, the conduct of which his grandfather had now relinquished almost entirely into his hands. On the contrary, with the mere side results of his study, or what may be called the chips and shavings of his real work, he created a prosperity quite beyond anything that his simple-minded predecessor had ever hoped for, even at the most sanguine epoch of his life. The young man's adventurous and imaginative endowments were miraculously alert, and connecting themselves with his remarkable abilities for solid research, and perhaps his conscience being as yet imperfectly developed (as it is a quality which sometimes lies dormant in the young) he spared not to produce compounds which, if their names were anywise to be trusted, would supersede all other medicines, and speedily render any medicine a needless thing, and regenerate the world—making the trade of phisique an untenable one, and the title of Doctor obsolete. Whether there was real efficacy in these nostrums, and whether their author himself had faith in them, is more than can safely be said, but at all events the public believed in them, and thronged to the old and dim sign of the Brazen Serpent, which, familiar to them and their forefathers, now seemed to shine with auspicious lustre, as if its old Scriptural virtues were renewed. If any faith were to be put in human testimony, many marvellous cures were really performed, the fame of which spread far and wide, and caused demands for these medicines to come in from places far beyond the precincts of the little town. Our old apothecary, now degraded by the overshadowing influence of his grandson's character to a position little above that of shop-boy, stood behind the counter, with a face sad and distrustful, and yet with an odd kind of fitful excitement in it, as if he would have liked to enjoy this new prosperity, had he dared; then his venerable figure was to be seen, dispensing these questionable compounds by the single bottle and the dozen, wronging his simple conscience as he took in silver for what he feared was trash or worse—shrinking from the reproachful eye of any ancient physician who might chance to be passing by, but, withal, examining closely the silver or the New England coarsely-printed bills which he took in exchange, as if his faith in all things were shaken, as if apprehensive that the emptiness and delusive character of the commodity which he sold might be balanced by equal counter-feitings in the price received. Is it not possible that this gifted young man had indeed delved down to the earth, and found out those remedies which Nature has provided and laid away for every ill?

The disastrous termination of this most brilliant epoch that ever came to the Brazen Serpent must be told in a few words. One night, Edward Dolliver's young wife awoke and, seeing the gray drawn creeping into the chamber while her husband, it should seem, was still engaged in his laboratory, arose in her night clothes and crept to the door of the laboratory to put in her gentle remonstrance against such labor. There she found him dead, sunk down out of his chair upon the hearth, where were some ashes apparently of burnt manuscripts, which appeared to comprise most of those included in Dr. Swinnerton's legacy, and it seemed as if, in a great hurry, he had thrown them into the fire, on a sudden impulse, and in a passion, though one or two had fallen beside the heap and lay merely scorched beside it. It may be that he came to the perception of something fatally false and deceptive in the successes which he had appeared to win, and was too proud and too conscientious to survive it. Doctors were called in, but had no power to revive him. An inquest was held, at which the jury (under the instruction, perhaps, of those same revengeful doctors) expressed their opinion, that the poor young man, being given to strange contrivances with poisonous drugs, had died by incautiously tasting them himself. This verdict, and the terrible event itself, at once deprived the medicines of all their popularity, and the poor old apothecary was no longer under any necessity of violating his conscience by selling them. The medicines at once lost their repute and ceased to be in any demand; in the few instances where they were tried, the experiment was followed by no good results, and even those individuals who had fancied themselves cured, and had been loudest in spreading the praises of these beneficent compounds, now, as if for the utter demolition of the poor youth's credit, suffered under a recurrence of their worst symptoms, and, in more than one case, perished miserably; insomuch (for the days of witchcraft were still within the memory of living men and women) it was the general opinion that Satan had been personally concerned in this effusion, and that the Brazen Serpent, so long recognized and honored among them, was really the type of his subtle malevolence and perfect iniquity. It was rumored, even, that all preparations that came from this shop were harmful; that teeth decayed that had been made pearly white by his dentifrice, that cheeks were bleached that had been made to look like damask roses by his cosmetics, that hair turned gray or fell off, that had been made black, glossy and luxuriant by his cosmetics, that breath, which his drugs had sweetened, now had a sulphurous smell. Moreover, all the money heretofore amassed by the sale of them had been exhausted by Edward Dolliver in his lavish expenditure for the processes of his study, and nothing was left for Pansie, except a few valueless and unsalable bottles of medicine, and one or two others, perhaps more recondite than their inventor had seen fit to offer to the public. Little Posie's mother lived but a short time after the shock of the terrible event; and, as we began our story with saying, she was left with no better guardianship or support, than might be found in the efforts of a long superannuated man.

Nothing short of the simplicity and integrity and piety of Grandsir Dolliver's character, known and acknowledged as far back as the oldest inhabitant remembered any thing, and inevitably discernible by the dullest and most prejudiced observer in all his natural manifestations, could have protected him in still creeping about the streets. So far as he was personally concerned, however, all bitterness, all suspicion, had speedily passed away, and there remained still the careless and neglectful good-will, the prescriptive reverence, not altogether reverential, which the world carelessly awards to the unfortunate individual who outlives his generation. And now that we have shown the reader sufficiently, or at least, to the best of our knowledge, and perhaps at tedious length, what was the present position of Grandsir Dolliver, we may let our story creep onward, though at such a pace as suits the feeble gait of an old man and an infant.

The peculiarly brisk sensations of this morning, to which we have more than once alluded, enabled the old man to toil pretty vigorously at his medical herbs, his catnip, his vervain &c &c &c, but, he did not turn his attention to the row of mystic plants, with which so much of trouble and sorrow either was, or appeared to be, connected. In truth, his old soul was sick of them, and their very frangrance, which the warm sunshine made strongly perceptible, was odious to his nostrils. But the simple, spicy, homelike scent of his other herbs, the old English simples, was grateful to him, and so was the earth-smell, as he turned up the soil about their roots, and eagerly snuffed it in. Little Pansie, on the other hand, perhaps scandalized at great-grandpapa's neglect of the prettiest plants in his garden, resolved to do her small utmost towards balancing his injustice; so, with an old shingle fallen from the roof, which she had appropriated as her agricultural tool, she began to dig about them, pulling up the weeds, as she saw grandpapa doing. The kitten, too, with a look of elvish sagacity, lent her assistance, plying her paws with vast haste and efficiency at the roots of one of the shrubs. This particular one was much smaller than the rest, perhaps because it was a native of a torrid climate, and required greater care than the rest to make it flourish; so thus shrivelled, cankered, scarcely showing a green leaf, both Pansie and the kitten probably mistook it for a weed. After their joint efforts had made a pretty big trench about it, the little girl seized the shrub with both hands, bestriding it with her plump little legs, and giving so vigorous a pull that the plant, long accustomed to be transplanted annually, came up by the roots, and little Pansie came down in a sitting posture, making a round impress in the soft earth.

"See, see, Doctor!" cried Pansie, comically enough giving him his title of courtesy. "Look grandpapa, the big naughty weed!"

Now the Doctor had, at once, a peculiar dread and a peculiar value for this identical shrub, both because his grandson's investigations had been applied more ardently to it than to all the rest, and because it was associated in his mind with an ancient and sad recollection; for he had never forgotten that his wife, the early lost, had once taken a fancy to wear its flowers, day after day, through the whole season of their bloom, in her bosom, and one glowed like a gem, and deepened her somewhat pallid beauty with a richness never before seen in it; at least, such was the effect which this tropical flower imparted to the beloved form in his memory, and thus it, somehow, both brightened her and wronged her. This had happened not long before her death, and whenever, in the subsequent years, this plant had brought forth its annual flower, it had proved a kind of talisman to bring up the image of Phoebe, radiant with this glow that did not really belong to her naturally passive beauty, quickly interchanging with another image of her form with the snow of death on cheek and forehead. This reminiscence had remained among the things that the Doctor always was conscious of, but never breathed a word, thoughout the whole of his long life, a sprig of sensibility that perhaps helped to keep him tenderer and purer, than other men who entertain no such follies. And with the sight of the shrub, it often brought the faint golden gleam of her hair, and her form in the sun gleams of the garden, quivering into sight and out of it. And therefore, when he saw what Pansie had done, he sent forth a strange, inarticulate, hoarse, tremulous exclamation, a sort of agued and decrepit cry of mingled emotion.

"Naughty Pansy, to pull up grandfather's flower," said the Doctor, as soon as he could speak; then, remembering the doubtful character of the shrub, "Poison, Pansie, poison. Fling it away, child!"

And dropping his spade, the old gentleman scrambled towards the little girl as quickly as his rusty joints would let him, while Pansie, as apprehensive and quick of motion as a fawn, started up with a shriek of mirth and fear, to escape him. It so happened that the garden-gate was ajar, and a puff of wind blowing it wide open, she escaped through this fortuitous avenue, followed by great-grandpapa and the kitten.

"Stop, naughty Pansie, stop!" shouted our old friend. "You will tumble into the grave!" The kitten, with the singular sensitiveness that seems to stir it at every kind of excitement, was on his back.

And indeed, this portentous warning was better grounded and had a more literal meaning than might be supposed; for the swinging gate communicated with the burial-ground, and almost directly in little Pansie's track there was a newly dug grave, ready to receive its tenant that afternoon. Pansie, however, fled onward with outstretched arms, half in fear, half in fun, running as if to escape Time or death in the person of Grandsir Dolliver, plying her round little legs with wonderful promptitude, and happily avoiding the ominous pitfall that lies in every person's path, till, hearing a groan from her pursuer, she looked over her shoulder and saw that poor grandpapa had stumbled over one of the many hillocks. Then she suddenly wrinkled up her little visage and sent forth a full-breathed roar of sympathy and alarm.

"Grandfather has broken his neck now!" cried little Pansie amid her sobs.

"Kiss Grandpapa, and make it well then," said the old gentleman, recollecting her remedy, scrambling up more readily than could be expected; then he murmured to himself. "A hair's breadth more, and I should have tumbled into yonder grave. Poor little Pansie! What wouldst thou have done then?"

"Make the grass grow over grandpapa," answered Pansie, laughing up in his face.

"Poh, poh, child! That's not a pretty thing to say," cried grandther pettishly, and disappointed, as people are apt to be when they try to calculate on the fitful sensibilities of childhood. "Come, you must go in to old Martha, now."

The poor old gentleman was in the more haste to leave the spot, because he found himself standing right in front of his own peculiar row of gravestones, consisting of eight or nine slabs of slate, adorned with carved borders, rather rudely done, and the earliest, that of his Phoebe, bending aslant, because the frost of so many winters had slowly undermined it; and over one grave in the row, that of his gifted grandson, there was no memorial. He felt a strange repugnance, stronger than he had ever felt before, to linger by these graves, and felt none of the tender sorrow, mingled with high and tender hopes, that had sometimes made him feel it good to be there. Such moods perhaps often come to the aged, as the hardened earth-crust over their souls shuts them out from spiritual influences.

Taking the child by the hand, her little effervescence of infantile fun having passed into a downcast mood, though not well knowing, as yet, what a duskey cloud of disheartening influence arose from these green hillocks, he went heavily towards the garden-gate. Close to its threshold, so that anyone issuing forth or entering must needs step upon it or over it, lay a small flat stone, deeply imbedded in the ground, and partly covered with grass, and inscribed with the name of Doctor John Swinnerton, Physitian.

"Aye," said the old man, as the well-remembered figure of his ancient instructor seemed to rise before him in his grave apparel, with band, and gold headed cane black velvet doublet, and cloak, "here lies a man, who, people have thought, has it in his power to avoid the grave! He had no little grandchild to teaze him. He had the choice to die, and chose it."

<(Here the Colonel calls from the window)>

So the old gentleman led Pansie over and carefully closed the gate; and as it happened, he forgot the uprooted shrub, which Pansie, as she ran, had flung away and it fell into the open grave, and when the funeral came, that afternoon, the coffin was let down upon it, so that its bright, inauspicious flower never bloomed again.

CHAPTER III

" . . . see you again on yonder subject. Be secret!" and kept his stern eye fixed on him as the coach began to move.

"Be secret!" repeated the apothecary. "I know not any secret that he has confided to me thus far, and as for his nonsense—as I will be bold to style it now he is gone— about a medicine of long life, it is a thing I forget in spite of myself, so very empty and trashy is it. I wonder, by the by, it never came into my head to give the Colonel a dose of that cordial whereof I partook last night. I have no faith that it is a valuable medicine—little or none—and yet there has been an unwonted briskness in me, all the morning."

Then a simple joy rushed over his face, a flickering sunbeam among his wrinkles, as he heard the laughter of the little girl, who was running rampant with a kitten in the kitchen.

"Posie, Posie!" cackled he, "grandpapa has sent away the ugly old man now. Come let us have a romp in the garden. Te hee, te hee, te hee." And then whispered to himself again, "That is a cordial yonder, and I will take it according to the prescription, knowing all the ingredients." Then after a moment's thought, he added—"All, save one." <Sight, hearing; both improved; his feet not so cold. &c &c &c>

<(He does not take the cordial till after some time.)>

So, as he had declared to himself his intention, that night, when little Posie had long been asleep, and his small household was in bed, and most of the quiet, old fashioned town likewise, this good old apothecary went into his laboratory (if it be not too high flown to style the little place so) and took out of a cupboard in the wall a certain ancient-looking bottle, which was cased over with a network of what seemed to be woven silver, imitating the wicker-woven bottles of our days. He had previously provided a goblet of pure water. Before opening the bottle, however, he seemed to hesitate, and pondered, and babbled to himself, being long since come to that period of life when, our bodily frames having lost much of their value, we become a great deal more careful of them, than when they were a perfect and inestimable machine.

"I triturated, I infused, I distilled it myself in these very rooms, and know it all—all the ingredients save one," thought he. "They are common things enough, comfortable things, some of them a little queer, one or two that folks have a prejudice against,—and then that one thing that I don't know. It is a foolish thing in me to be dallying with such a mess, which I knew was a piece of quackery while that strange visitor bade me to it—and yet what a thing has come from it. He said it was a rare cordial; and methought it has brightened up my weary old life all day, so that Posie has found me the fitter playmate. And then the dose; it is so absurdly small. I will try it."

He took the silver stopper from the bottle, and with a practised hand, tremulous as it was with age, so that you would have thought it must have shaken the liquor in a perfect shower of misapplied drops, he dropt—I have heard it said only one single drop—into the tumbler of water. It dropped into it with a dazzling brightness as it fell, like a spark of ruby flame, and subtly diffusing itself through the

whole body of water turned it to a rosey hue of great brilliancy, which he held up between him and the light, and
seemed to admire and wonder at it.

"It is a very odd thing," said he, "that such a pure, bright
liquor should have come out of a parcel of weeds that mingled their juices here. The thing is a folly; one of those
compositions in which the physicians and chemists—the alchemists, perhaps—used to combine what they thought the
virtues of many plants, thinking that something would result
in the whole which was not in either of them, and a new
virtue be created—whereas, it has seemed to be the teaching
of my experience, that one virtue counteracts another and
is the enemy of it. I never believed this theory, even when
that strange madman bade me do it—and what a thick turbid
material it was, until that last ingredient, that powder which
he put in with his own hand. Had he let me see it, I would
first have analyzed it and discovered its composition. The
man was mad, methinks, and this may have been poison.
But its effect was good. Poh. I will taste again, in this weak,
agued, miserable state of mine, so decrepit as I am, though
it is a shame in me, a man of decent skill in my way, to
believe in a quack's nostrum. It is a comfortable kind of
thing!"

Meanwhile, that single drop, as it might seem, (for good
old Dr. Dorsey had immediately put a stopper into the bottle) had diffused a sweet smell through the chamber, so
that all the ordinary fragrances and scents of apothecary's
stuff seemed to be controlled and influenced by it, and take
a certain dimness out of it; so potent was it, for the Doctor,
at the pressure of a great need, had given incredible pains
to the manufacture of this medicine, so that, reckoning the
pains more than the ingredients (all except one, of which
he was not able to estimate the cost or value) it was really

worth its weight in gold; and as it happened, he had bestowed the hard labor of his poor old life, and the time that
was necessary for the support of his family, without return;
for the customer, after playing off this cruel joke upon the
old man, had never returned, and, now for seven years, this
bottle had stood in a corner of the cupboard. To be sure,
the silver-cased bottle was worth a trifle for its silver, and
still more, perhaps, as an antiquarian knick-knack. But all
things considered, the honest and simple apothecary thought
that he might make free with this liquid, to such small extent
as was necessary; and there had been some things in the
concoction that struck him, and he had been breaking fast,
lately, and so, one night, in the dreary fantasy and lonely
recklessness of his old days, he had suddenly bethought
himself of this medicine (cordial, as the strange man said,
that had come to him by long inheritance in his family)
and determined to try it. And again, as the night before, he
took out the receipt—a fold of antique parchment, out of
which, provokingly, a fold had been cut—and put on his
spectacles to puzzle out the passage—one drop—guttam uni-
cam, in aquam puram, 2 gills.

"If the old Colonel hears of this," said Dr. Dorsey, "he
might fancy it his nostrum of long life, and insist on having
the bottle for his own use. The foolish, fierce old gentleman!
He has grown very earthly, else he would not desire such a
thing. And a strong desire it must be, to make him feel it
desirable. For my part, I only want something that, for a
little while, may clear my eyes, so that I may see little
Posie's beauty, and quicken my ears that I may hear her
sweet voice, and give me a little nerve, while God keeps me
here, so that I may have longer to earn bread for dear little
Posie—and she provided for, I would glady lie down yonder
with Alice and our children. Ah this vanity of desiring

lengthened days! There, I have drunk it, and methinks its faint subtle savor hath a potency in it."

The old man shivered a little, as I have seen those do who like good liquor, when just swallowed, and while it is permeating their vitals. Yet he seemed to be in a good state of feeling, and, as was generally the case with this good and simple old man, in a devout frame of mind; he put on his spectacles, read a chapter in the bible, and said his prayers for Posie and himself before he went to bed, and had a much better sleep than usually comes to people of his advanced age; for at that period, sleep is diffused through all one's wakefulness, and a dim and weary half-perception through all one's sleep, so that nothing comes out of the mixture but weariness.

So far as I know, nothing very extraordinary happened to Dr. Dorsey, or in his small household, for some days afterwards. The old gentleman was favored with a comfortable winter, for a man of his age, and thanked Heaven for it, and put it to a good use (at least, he intended it so) by concocting drugs, which perhaps did a little towards further peopling the grave yard into which his windows looked; but that was neither his intention nor his fault. None of the sleepers, at all events, interrupted their slumber to upbraid him; he had done according to his own simple conscience and the recipes of licensed physicians, and he looked no further, but pounded, triturated, infused, made electuaries, bolusses, juleps, or whatever he termed his productions, with skill and diligence, thanking Heaven that he was spared to do so when his contemporaries were generally getting incapable of similar efforts. It struck him with some surprise, but much gratitude to Providence, that his sight seemed to be growing rather better than worse; he certainly could read the crabbed handwriting and hieroglyphics of the physicians with more readiness than he could a year earlier. But he had been originally near-sighted, with large, projecting eyes; and such organs always seem to get a new lease of light when other men's are decaying, and in his case, they were perhaps coming to their perfection in this his latter age. One thing was perceptible about those eyes, not only to himself in the glass but to everybody else, namely, that they had an unaccustomed gleaming brightness in them; not so very bright, either, but yet so much so that little Posie noticed it, and sometimes, in her playful, roguish way, climbed up into his lap and put both her little palms over them; telling Grandfather that he had stolen somebody's else eyes instead of his own, and that she liked his old ones best. The poor old Doctor did his best to smile through his eyes, and so reconcile Posie to their brightness; but still she continually made the same silly remonstrance, so that he was fain always to put on a pair of green spectacles when he was going to have a romp with Posie, or took her upon his knee. Nay, if he looked at Posie, as had always been his custom, after she was asleep, in order to see that all was well with her, the little thing would put up her hands, as if he held a light that was gleaming on her eye-balls, and unless he turned away his gaze all the quicker, would wake up in a fit of crying.

<He accustomed himself to sit in the sunshine as much as possible.>

But, on the whole, the apothecary had as comfortable a time as a man of his age could expect. The air of the house and the old grave yard seemed to suit him. What so seldom happens, in man's advancing age, his night's rest seemed to do him good; whereas, generally, an old man wakes up ten times as weary, and rheumatic, and achy, and nervous, and dispirited, as he went to bed, just as if, during his sleep, he had been working ten times as hard as ever he did in the day-time. It had been so with the Doctor himself until within a few months. To be sure, he had latterly begun to practise various rules of diet and exercise, which commended themselves to his approbation; he used to saw some of his own firewood, and fancied, that, as was reasonable, it fatigued him less, day by day; he used to take walks with Posie, and though, of course, her little footsteps, treading on the elastic air of childhood, far outdid his, still the old man saw that he was not beyond the recuperative time of life, and that air, exercise, and proper food, can do somewhat towards retarding the approach of age. And then he was inclined to impute much good effect to a daily dose of Santa Cruz rum (a liquor much in vogue in that day) which he was lately in the habit of quaffing daily in the meridian hour; all thro' his earlier life, he had eschewed strong liquors, but "after seventy," quoth old Doctor Dorsey, "a man is all the better in head and stomach, for a little stimulus";—and it certainly seemed so in his case. He likewise took (I know not precisely how often, but complying punctiliously with the recipe, as an old apothecary naturally would) his drop of the mysterious cordial; but he was inclined, on due thought, to impute little or no efficacy to this, and to laugh at himself for having ever thought otherwise. The dose was so very minute. Then, too, he had never been sensible of any remarkable effect on taking it; a genial warmth, he sometimes fancied, diffused throughout him, and perhaps continuing through the next day; a quiet and refreshing night's rest, as already said, and alacritous awaking the next day; but all this was far more probably owing, as was already hinted, to excellent and well-considered habits of diet and exercise. Nevertheless, he still continued the cordial with tolerable regularity, the more because, happening, on one or two occasions to omit it, it so chanced that he slept wretchedly, and awoke in strange aches and pains, torpors, nervousness, shakings of the hand, blear-edness of sight, backaches, tremors, lowness of spirit, and all other ills of age, as is, indeed, the misfortune of old men, who are often threatened with a thousand evil symptoms that come to nothing, foreboding no particular disorder, and pass-ing away as unsatisfactorily as they came. Another time, he took two or three drops at once, and was alarmingly feverish. Nevertheless, it was very true, that these perverse symptoms were pretty sure to disappear on his renewal of the drops. "Still it could not be they," thought the old man, a hater of empiricism (in which, however, is contained all hope for men,) and disinclined to believe in anything that was not according to rule and art. And, then, as aforesaid, the dose was so ridicously small.

Sometimes, however, he took, half laughingly, another view of it, and felt disposed to think that chance might really have thrown in his way a very remarkable medicine, by which, if it had happened to him earlier in life, he might have amassed a large fortune, and might even now rake together such a competency as would prevent his feeling much uneasiness about the future of little Posie. Feeling so strong as he did, he might reasonably count upon ten years more of life, and, in that time, the precious liquor might be exchanged for much gold. "Let us see!" quoth he. "What taking name shall it be advertised by! 'The Old Man's Cor-dial'?—that promises too little. 'Life-drops'? 'Youth in a bottle'! Poh, poh! I would stain my honesty, my fair reputa-tion, the accumulation of a lifetime, and befool my neighbors and the public by one thing that might make them imagine I had found that ridiculous charm, that the alchemists have sought. 'The old man's cordial'!—that is best. And five shill-ings sterling a bottle! That surely were not too costly, and would give the medicine a better reputation and higher vogue (so foolish is the world) than if I were to put it lower. I will think further of this! But pshaw, pshaw!"

"What is the matter, grandpapa!" said little Posie, who had stood by him, wanting to speak to him, at least a moment, but was deterred by his absorption. "Why do you say 'Pshaw'!"

"Pshaw!" repeated grandfather. "There is one ingredient that I don't know."

So this very hopeful design was necessarily given up; but its having occurred to good old Dr. Dorsey was perhaps a token that his mind was in a very vigorous state, for so old a man; for it had been noted of him, through life, that he had little enterprise, little activity, and that, for the want of it, his very considerable skill in his art had been almost thrown away as regarded his private affairs, when it might easily have led him to fortune; whereas here, in his extreme age, he had bethought himself of a way to grow rich. Sometimes this latter spring, indeed, comes, as blossoms come on the autumnal tree, a spirt of vigor, or untimely greenness, when Nature laughs at her old child, half in kindness, and half in scorn, although it is observable, I fancy, that after such a spirt, age comes on with redoubled speed, and it is found that the old man has only run forward with a show of vigor in order to tumble into his pit the sooner.

Several times, as he was walking briskly along the street, to church meeting with little Posie clutching his hand, or to muster, or taking his walk with her for exercise—and perhaps frisking a little more than becomes a person of his venerable years, he had met the grim old wreck of Colonel Dabney, moving goutily along, and gathering wrath anew with every touch of his painful foot to the ground; or driving by in his carriage, showing an ashen, stern, wrathful, wrinkled face at the window, and frowning, the apothecary thought, at him, with a peculiar wrath, as if he took umbrage at his audacity in being less broken by age than a gentleman like himself. The apothecary could not help feeling as if there were some unsettled quarrel or dispute between himself and the Colonel; he could not tell why or what. The Colonel always gave him a haughty kind of nod or half recognition; and the people in the street, to whom he was a familiar object, would say, "The worshipful Colonel begins to find himself mortal, like the rest of us. He feels his years. He'd be glad, I warrant, to change with you, Doctor. It shows what difference a good life makes in men, to look at him and you. You are half a score of years his elder, methinks, and yet look what temperance can do for a man. By my credit, neighbor, seeing how brisk you have been lately, I told my wife you seemed to be growing younger. It does me good to see it. We are about of an age, I think, and I like to see how we old men keep young, and keep one another in heart. I myself—ahem, ahem—feel younger, this season, than these five years before."

"It rejoices me that you feel so," quoth the apothecary, who had just been thinking that this old neighbor had lost a great deal, both in mind and body, within a short period, and felt a kind of scorn at him for it. "Indeed, I find old age less uncomfortable than I thought it. Little Posie here, and I, make excellent companions for one another."

And then, dragged along by Posie's little hand, and also impelled by a certain alacrity that rose with him in the morning, and lasted till his healthy rest at night, he bade farewell to his contemporary and hastened on, while the latter left behind, was a little irritated as he looked at the vigorous movement of the apothecary's legs.

"He need not make such a show of briskness, neither," muttered he to himself. "This touch of rheumatism troubles me a bit, just now, but try it on a good day, and I'd walk with him for a shilling. Pshaw, I'll be one of his pall-bearers."

One day, while the old man, with the activity that bestirred itself in him, now a days, was mixing and manufacturing certain medicaments that were in frequent demand, a carriage stopt at his door; and he heard the voice of Colonel Dabney talking, in his customary stern tone, to the old woman who served him. And a moment afterwards, the coach drove away, and he actually heard the old dignitary lumbering up stairs, and bestowing a curse upon each particular step, as if that were the method to make them softer and easier when he came down again.

"Pray, your worship," said the doctor from above, "let me attend you below stairs!"

"No," growled the Colonel, "I'll meet you on your own ground. I can climb a stair yet, and be hanged to you!"

So saying, he painfully finished the ascent, and came into the laboratory, where he let himself fall, with an anathema on the chair, the doctor, and himself, into the doctor's own easy-chair, and, staring round through the dusk, met the wide open, startled eyes of little Posie, who had been reading a gilt picture-book in the corner.

"Send away that child, Dorsey," cried the Colonel angrily. "Confound her, she makes my bones ache. I hate everything young."

"Lord, Colonel," the poor apothecary ventured to say, "there must be young people in the world, as well as old ones. To my mind, a man's grandchildren keep him warm roundabout him."

"I have none, and want none," growled the Colonel. "And as for young people, let me be one of them, and they may exist—otherwise not. It's a cursed bad arrangement of the world, that there are young and old here together."

When Posie had gone away, which she did with anything but reluctance, having a natural antipathy to this old monster of a Colonel, the latter personage tapped with his crutch-handled cane on a chair that stood near, and nodded, in an authoritative way, to the apothecary to sit down there. Dr. Dorsey complied submissively, and the Colonel, with dull unkindly eyes, looked at him sternly, and with a kind of intelligence amid the aged stolidity of his aspect that somewhat puzzled the Doctor. In this way he surveyed him all over, like a judge when he means to hang a man, and, for some reason or none, the apothecary felt his nerves shaken beneath this steadfast look.

"Aha, Doctor," said the Colonel at last, with a kind of a dull sneer, "you bear your years well!"

"Decently well, Colonel, I thank Providence for it," answered the meek apothecary.

"I should say," quoth the Colonel, "you are younger at this moment than when we spoke together, two or three years ago. I noted then that your eyebrows were a handsome snow white, such as befits a man who survived fairly beyond his threescore & ten, & five years more. Why, they are getting dark again, Mr Apothecary."

"Nay, your worship must needs be mistaken there," said the apothecary, with a timorous chuckle. "It is many a year since I have taken deliberate note of my wrinkled old visage in a glass; but I remember they were white when I looked last."

"Aha, Doctor, I know a thing or two," said the Colonel, with a bitter sneer. "And what's this, you old rogue? Why, you've rubbed away a wrinkle since we met. Take off those infernal spectacles and look me in the face. Ha! I see the devil in your eye. How dare you let it shine upon me so?"

"On my conscience, Colonel," said the apothecary, strangely struck with the coincidence of this accusation with little Posie's complaint, "I know not what you mean. My sight is pretty well for a man of my age. We near-sighted people begin to have their best eyesight when other people have lost it."

<(The recipe is in Latin, so that the Colonel speaks only on hearsay knowledge of it)>

"Ah, ah, ah, old rogue!" said the insufferable Colonel, gnashing his ruined teeth at him, as if, for some incomprehensible reason, he wanted to tear him to pieces and devour him. "I know you. You are taking the life away from me, villain. And I told you it was my inheritance. And I told you there was a Bloody Footstep bearing its track down through my race!"

"I remember nothing of it," said the Doctor in a quake, nothing doubting that the Colonel was in one of his mad fits. "And, on the word of an honest man, I never wronged you in my life, Colonel."

"You shall see," said the Colonel, whose old wrinkled visage absolutely grew terrible with its hardness, and his dull eyes, without losing their dullness, seemed to look through him. "Listen to me, Sir. Some ten years ago, there came to you a man on a secret business. He had an old musty bit of parchment, hardly legible, on which was written some words in an antique hand, an old deed it might have been, some family document; and here and there the letters were faded away, but this man had spent his life poring over it, and he had made out the meaning by putting his life upon it, and he interpreted it to you, and left it with you. Only there was one gap, one torn or obliterated place. Well, Sir, and he bade you, with your poor little skill with the mortar and the still that you have, and for a certain sum, ample repayment for such a service, manufacture this medicine, this cordial. It was an affair of months. And just when you thought it finished, the man came again, and stood over your cursed brewage, and shook a powder, or dropt a lump into it, or put in some new ingredient, in which was all the hidden virtue, or, at least, it drew out and concocted all the hidden virtue of the other mean and common herbs, and married them into a wondrous efficacy. This done, the man bade you do certain other things with the potation, and went away, and"—the Colonel hesitated a moment—"and never came again!"

"Surely, Colonel, you are correct," said the apothecary, much startled, however, at the Colonel's showing himself so well acquainted with an incident which he had supposed a secret with himself alone. Yet he had a little reluctance in owning it, although he did not exactly understand why, since the Colonel had apparently no rightful claim to it, at all events.

"That medicine, that receipt," continued his visitor, "is my hereditary property, and I charge you on your peril to give it up."

"But what if the original owner should call upon me for it?" objected Dr. Dorsey.

"I'll warrant you against that," said the Colonel, and the apothecary thought that there was something ghastly in his look and tone. "Why 'tis ten years, you old fool; and do you think a man, with a treasure like that in his possession, would have waited so long?"

"Seven years it was ago," said the apothecary, "septem annis passatis, so says the Latin."

"Curse your Latin," says the Colonel. "Produce the stuff, you vile apothecary. You have been violating the first rule of your trade—taking your own drugs—your own in one sense;

mine by the right of three hundred years! Bring it forth, I say!"

"Pray excuse me, worthy Colonel," said the apothecary; for though convinced that the old man was only in one of his insane notions, when he talked of the value of this concoction, yet he really did not like to give up the cordial, which perhaps had done him some benefit; besides he had at least a claim upon it for much trouble and skill expended in its composition. He suggested this to the colonel, who scornfully took out a net-work purse, with more golden guineas in it than the apothecary had seen in the whole seven years, and was rude enough to fling it in his face.

"Take that," thundered he, "and give it up, or I'll have you in prison before you're an hour older. Nay," continued the old man, growing pale (which was his mode of showing terrible wrath, since, all through life, till extreme age quenched it, his ordinary face had been as red as blazes), "I'll put you to death, you villain, as I've a right!" and putting his hand in his great waistcoat pocket, lo! the old madman had a small pistol in it, which he cocked and presented at the poor apothecary. The old fellow quaked, and cowered in his chair, and would indeed have given his whole shopfull of better concocted medicines than this to be out of the scrape. Besides, there were the guineas; the Colonel had paid him a princely price for what was probably worth nothing.

"Hold! hold! answered he, as the Colonel with stern eye pointed the pistol at his head. "You shall have it."

So he got up, all trembling, poor old man, and crept to that secret cupboard where the precious bottle—since precious it seemed to be—was reposited. In all his life, long as it had been, the poor apothecary had never before been threatened, or seen any other man threatened, by a deadly weapon; though many as deadly a thing had he seen poured into a glass without winking. And now it seemed to take his heart and life away, and he brought it forth feebly, and stood before the Colonel tremulously, ashy pale, and looking ten years older than his real age, instead of five years younger, as he had seemed just before this disastrous interview with the Colonel.

"You look as if you needed a drop of it," said the Colonel with grim scorn. "But not a drop shall you have. Already have you stolen too much," said he, lifting up the bottle, and marking the space to which the liquor had subsided in it by the minute doses with which the poor apothecary had made free. "Fool, had you taken your glass like a man, you might have been young. Now creep on, the few months you have left, poor torpid knave, and die. Come, a goblet, quick."

He clutched the bottle, meanwhile, voraciously, miserly, eagerly, furiously, as if it were his life that he held in his grasp, angry, unguessing, as if something long sought were within his grasp, and not yet secure, with longing thirst and desire, hateful, suspicious of the world and of fate, feeling as if an iron hand were over him, a hundred violent robbers roundabout him, struggling for it. At last, unable to wait longer, just as the apothecary was tottering away in quest of a drinking-glass, the Colonel took out the glass stopper, and lifted the bottle itself to his lips.

"For Heaven's sake, no," cried the old man. "The dose is a single drop!—one drop, Colonel, one drop!"

"Not a drop, to save your wretched old soul," responded the Colonel, probably thinking that the apothecary was pleading for a small share of the precious liquor. He put it to his lips, and as if quenching his life long thirst, gulped deep draughts, sucking it in with desperation, till void of breath, he set it down upon the table. The rich intense fragrance spread itself through the air. The apothecary, with an instinctive carefulness that was rather ludicrous in the circumstances, caught up the stopper, which the Colonel had let fall, and forced it into the bottle, to prevent any further escape of virtue. He then fearfully watched the result of the madman's potation.

The Colonel sate a moment in his chair, panting for breath; then started to his feet with a prompt vigor that contrasted widely with the infirm and rheumatic movements that had heretofore characterized him; he struck his forehead violently with one hand, and smote his chest with the other; he stamped his foot thunderously on the ground; then he leaped up to the ceiling, and came down with an elastic bound. Then he laughed, a wild, exulting ha, ha, ha, with a strange, exulting roar that filled the house and reechoed through it, a sound full of fierce, animal rapture, enjoyment of sensual life, mixed up with strangeness and a certain horror. After all, real as it was, it was like the sounds a man makes in a dream. And all this while, the potent draught seemed still to be making its way through his system, though the frightened apothecary fancied that the Colonel's eye was seeking the bottle for another draught. The apothecary thought that he intended a revengeful onslaught on himself. Then, finally, he gave a loud, unearthly screech, in the midst of which his voice broke as if some unseen hand were throttling him, and starting forward he fought frantically, as if he would clutch the life that was being rent away from him, and fell forward with a dead thump on the floor.

"Colonel! Colonel!" cried the frightened apothecary.

<(He sets him up on end, and corpse looks at him with fierce reproach—a revengeful look.)>

There was no answer; not even a groan. The feeble old man with difficulty turned over the heavy frame, and saw at once, with practised eye, that the Colonel was dead. He was so startled, that his subsequent recollections of the moment were neither distinct nor steadfast; but he fancied, though he told the strange impression to no one, that on his first glimpse of the face, with a dark flush of what looked like rage still on it, it was a young man's face that he saw, a face with all the passionate energy of early manhood, the capacity for rage which the old man had lost half a century ago; rammed to the brim with vigor, till it became agony. But the next moment, if it were so (which it could not have been) the face grew ashen, withered, shrunken, more aged than in life, though still the murderous fierceness remained, and seemed to be petrified forever upon it.

After a moment's bewilderment Dorsey ran to the window looking to the street, threw it open and called loudly for assistance; he opened also another window and the air blew through; for methought he was almost stifled with the rich fragrance of the cordial which filled the room, and was now exuded from the corpse. He heard the voice of Posie crying at the door, which was locked, and turning the key, he caught her in his arms, and ran with her below stairs, and gave her into the charge of the old woman, who seemed half stupefied with the sense of something awful that had occurred. Meanwhile, there was a rattling and banging at the street-door, to which several people had been attracted both by the Doctor's outcry from the window, and by the startling and awful screech in which the Colonel's spirit (if, indeed, he had that divine part) had just previously taken its flight. He let them in, and pale and shivering ushered them up to the death-chamber, where one or two, endowed with a more delicate sense of smelling, snuffed the atmosphere as if sensible of an unknown fragrance, yet appeared afraid to breathe when they saw the fierce face, leaning back against the chair, and eyeing them so truculently.

I would fain quit this scene, and be done with the old Colonel, who I am glad has happened to die and take himself off my hands at so early a period of the narrative. I therefore hasten to say, that a Coroner's inquest was held on the spot (though everybody felt that it was merely ceremonial, and that the testimony of their good and ancient townsman, Dr. Dorsey, was amply sufficient to settle the matter,) and the verdict was, "Death by the visitation of God." The apothecary gave evidence that the Colonel, without asking leave, and positively against his advice, had drunk off a quantity of distilled spirits; and one or two servants or members of the Colonel's family, testified that he had been in a very uncomfortable state of mind, for some days past, so that they fancied he was possessed. So nobody thought of blaming Dr. Dorsey for what had happened; and if the plain truth must be told, everybody that saw the old wretch was too well content, I imagine, to be rid of him, to trouble themselves more than was quite necessary about the mode in which the incumbrance had been removed. The corpse was taken to his own mansion house, in order to receive a magnificent funeral; and Dr. Dorsey was left in quiet outwardly, but much disturbed, and, indeed, almost overturned inwardly by what happened. Yet it is to be observed, that he had accounted for the death with a singular dexterity of expression, when he attributed it to a dose of distilled spirits. What kind of distilled spirits were those, Doctor, and will you venture to take any more of them?

ANCILLARY DOCUMENTS

I N THE COURSE OF PLANNING the Septimius
and Dolliver stories Hawthorne followed his practice
with the earlier unfinished romances and wrote a series
of detached memoranda, sketching elements of character and
plot or grappling with problems of motivation. These Studies
cannot be definitively ordered, but such sequential development as the evidence suggests lies behind the editors' arrangement here.

The first section comprises "Septimius" Studies 1 through
8, followed by a Scenario which recapitulates the "Felton"
draft and anticipates the "Norton" revision. The second section presents Dolliver Studies 1 through 11; Study 5 is reproduced from a transcript by Sophia Hawthorne, the original having apparently not survived. The third section contains three *Dolliver* draft fragments that add no new text but
represent earlier stages of composition; fragment C derives
from a printed transcript in the absence of the original.

I. "Septimius" Studies and Scenario

Study 1

It is strange how these familiar places are haunted. We
think that it is only by old memories; but my belief is that

it is by ghosts of those who once dwelt here, and whose spirits took such hold of the spots, the dwellings, that they cannot easily be disjoined with them, when they would fain be so. I could almost swear, for instance, that there is such a haunting spirit, gliding about, sitting at my fireside, peeping through the twilight windows, shrinking into dusky corners, of the house where I have taken up my abode. If a man ever lingered about the house of his earthly abode, this man might be expected to do so, from the strong hold which he took of this house, this hill side, during his life-time.

Thoreau first told me about this predecessor of mine; though, I think he knew nothing of his character and history, nor anything but the singular fact, that here, in this simple old house, at the foot of the hill, and so close to the Lexington road that I call it the Wayside (partly for that, and partly because I never feel as if I were more permanently located than the traveller who sits down to rest by the road which he is plodding along) here dwelt, in some long-past time, this man who was resolved never to die. He, at all events, did not mean to make of his earthly abode a mere wayside rest, where he should sit while the sun threw his shadow a little further on the soil; he would sit there while oaks grew up and decayed; he would be always here.

This was all that Thoreau communicated; and that was many years ago, when I first came to live at the old cottage, which Alcott had relinquished, after terracing the hillside, and building fragile summer-houses, and giving it beauty, as if his genius had a magic to change common scenes into rare ones. I staid here but a little while; but often times, afar off, this singular idea occurred to me, in foreign lands, when my thoughts returned to this place which seemed to be the point by which I was attached to my native land. It gave me a stronger interest in this spot; and according to my custom,

I mused and meditated, and thought within myself, and tried to make out what manner of man this might be, that deemed it within his power to subvert the usual conditions of humanity. How did he mean to do it? Had he discovered, as he might suppose, the great secret which philosophers used to seek for? Did he think himself born with a frame unlike that of other mortals?

Much time had now passed; and the contemporaries of Septimius were beginning to show a little the wear of life; shrunken, dried, they were becoming, after the manner of New England men, when they begin to grow old—as if they had lain out drying through a succession of hot summer sunshines; as if they had stood up facing easterly winds and gales, beating right into their faces for years and years together. Anxious, struggling, the struggle had wrought itself into their manner of being. They were accustomed to look at Septimius, and tell him, "you wear well; you have not grown older these ten years!"—and so, indeed, it seemed. Seemed, on a casual notice; but if you looked closer at Septimius, you began to doubt whether he was really younger than his companions. There was a singular wrinkle, or fold, that had established itself between his eyebrows, strong, stern, and it gave him the expression as if he were holding on with a firm gripe, and as if, should he let go his hold, his very life might be the sacrifice. This look, whenas you once observed it, went far towards counteracting all the effect of his youthful appearance. It was as if age lurked in those stern folds, and if he should once allow his brow to unfold itself, forthwith age would spread itself over his features. But it never happened; there was this mark, through toil, through pleasure, through sleep itself; there was good evidence; for once, Septimius had fallen asleep in the room, beside his field, and there was this stern restraint upon his brow, unrelaxed just as if he were abroad awake. Thus it was, too, on the day of rest, when he sat in his pew at the meeting-house, looking up into the pastor's face; scowling back upon him the kindly or awful words that he addressed to the congregation, with a cold indifference, as if they were nothing to him. It was probably much in consequence of this air of indifference, that a rumor got abroad that Septimius Flint was an infidel.

It might have been so; but more probably not. He had merely taken himself out of the category of the rest of the human race. He might not question that the Bible, its promises, its threats, were true for the rest of mankind; with him they had nothing to do. His lot was not with theirs. It was with the rich beautiful earth where they all dwelt, in which they would lie, but never he.

"Septimius, Septimius, where are you going from me? What is taking you away from us? Is it true then, that we have never belonged to one another?"—and Septimius shook his head, as not knowing whether it were true or no. For, certainly, something there was, that daily and continually separated him more and more from his kind; from father, from mother, from minister, from man, from woman, from Alice, from all—flinging him back upon himself; so that he lugged himself along with weary shoulders; whereas always there had been a hitherto unestimated portion of himself borne on the kindly shoulders of his fellow-men. Oh this weary weight! Was it never to be got rid of? "Perhaps not," quoth Septimius somewhat hopefully. "But I shall get used to it!—there will be time enough!" And at that thought, he laughed in the kitchen where he was sitting alone—and went out laughing, laughing still as he climbed the hill. So here now were these two brothers, living on in their little inheritance, and agreeing so ill, and loving so well:—one content to share with his fellow men whatever came to them—the other aiming at something removed from them, unexampled; and yet pretending to seek it in no remote way, but only to take the birthright which any other might have as well, if the force were in him to claim it and make it good. Jairus was his only confidant, the free, joyous fellow, the love of men and maidens. "Oh, Septimius," said he, "don't you see how you are losing all this youthful time of life, by your projects for prolonging it? This is not worth while, at all events; for if life stretches out ever so far, youth cannot come back again. You will have but one youth—not renewable. Take hold now and enjoy it. Don't you see, you are giving up all the good of life? You are turning it into a thing of stone, without the juice of growth; for all that is dependent on change, the coming of decay, which is sweet in its place." "There's something in what you say," quoth Septimius. "Then will not you give up this mad notion?" said Jairus. "Not a bit," coolly returned his brother. "I tell you I have made my choice so firmly, that it is impossible for me to change it. My will is petrified, and is no longer in my own power." "Then, Septimius," quoth his brother, "you are a madman, and should be confined."

Septimius, as he felt that he was freeing himself from all other ties in taking a lonely lot—yet clung the closer to this brother who so much differed from him; he could not bear to leave him behind. Therefore, though the pull of their different dispositions had removed them to a little greater distance from one another, still the cord was not broken. Septimius felt it the more sensibly for the tug, the strain, the painful pull, because their mutual life lived so vividly along that cord. He felt as if, should that be broken, there would be nothing to keep him human; he should go off into unknown, infinite space, that moment. Oh, why would Jairus persist in keeping himself down to that horrid death, that cold, heavy, leaden, solid phantom? But sometimes, on the other hand, Septimius had a perception that it was death, after all, that gave the warmth to life—that kept the sap running, which would otherwise petrify; kept things green and vegetable, which else were stone; it was what made sentiments high and holy; the dark shadow that brought into high relief the beautiful things of this life; the promise of better; without it, how hard and prosaic. Such were the representations which the young clergyman made to his brother; and their earnestness showed how much the stern emphasis and faith in himself of Septimius had done towards convincing him that his brother had really this power of self-continuance which he claimed. In fact, whenever they talked together on this subject, Jairus usually did believe it; he argued against his brother's determination in the full belief that unless his argument were potent and prevailed, the unfortunate Septimius would really make his awful choice to be earthly immortal; and the choice once made, every succeeding hour would produce such baleful changes, that there would be continually less and less chance of his being redeemed. I think the brothers never loved each other so much, as at this time of direst difference between them.

Jairus, however, had something to keep his thoughts from dwelling too continually upon his brother. In the next house to the Wayside, as I have said, a little farther along towards the village, between the hill and the Lexington road, dwelt Cyrus Maine, his wife, and one young daughter; a pretty, rustic belle, with the somewhat petite-appearing frame that our women were already getting; but which often is capable of exertion and endurance greater than those who have more flesh to bear.

Study 2

Begin, with a reference to a certain room in my house, which I hint to be haunted; or to be remarkable and interesting to me for certain occult reasons.—Leave the matter thus, for the present, and diverge to a description of the hill and ground generally, the distant village, where the clock is heard to strike, the Academy bell to ring &c.—give an idea of the quiet of the places—mention Alcott, &c & Mr. Bull with his grapes; refer to the battle long ago, how the feet of soldiers trod over the hill.

Then come to the annals of the house, and introduce Thoreau's legend of the man who would not die. Make the impressions about the room, or chamber, more striking, and begin to connect this legend with this particular locality of the house. In the process of making repairs and additions to the old house, I may fable that a manuscript was found, containing records of this man, and allusions to his purpose to live forever. It might be a journal, extending over a long series of years. This should help me out, as regards Thoreau's legend, and also seem to account, on further perusal, for some of the strange phenomena of the east-room. Terribly stained and almost illegible shall this old record be, only decypherable here and there. I shall also have stories about him from old people, some of whom may have personally known him, and recognized certain queernesses.

The records introduce him as longing for an immortality on earth, and as convinced that he is to have it. He shall perhaps have strong affinities for earth, a love of the soil, of this particular spot, of the house which he himself has built on it; of eatables and drinkables—taking strongly hold of earth. He gets into a delusion—which shall likewise be communicated to the reader—that he can and will live forever. It shall appear as if he had given up all his spiritual life for this eternity of earth. He shall be a very narrow man, but of great strength of purpose; he shall keep himself young and vigorous by the force of his will, his determination, his faith that he can resist death. So his hair shall be dark, his limbs vigorous, longer than usual; but a settled frown of a determined purpose shall gather on his brow. He shall grow apart from the world, hard, selfish, isolated, estranged from his nearest and dearest. Perhaps he shall lose the first love of his youth for this passion; the woman for whom he built his house—the building of which shall be described, and how he thought it would be but like a hut of boughs, so transitory as compared with his long duration. All these anticipations shall be mixed up with trivial details of a husbandman's daily life. He shall discover that any engagement of the affections draws off his mind from its intentness, and makes him grow progressively older; so he gives up all that, for he is determined to live.

His figure must not stand alone in the story; perhaps his beloved may be still alive, a woman of very decrepit age; or, at least, something living to link the imagination more closely with him, after all these strange attributes shall have been imparted to the reader's idea of him. She may have been a child when he lived; but still there might be some testimony she would give that would add to the weirdness of this.

Study 3

Septimius has a share of some kind in the fight of Lexington; he shoots a man, and brings him into his house, and views the corpse, and is affected with strange remorse at it.

It seems not fair for him, a deathless one, thus to give death to another. His horror of death must be expressed over this corpse, and all the shuddering and shrinking of his nature therefrom. He brings him into the room and lays the body down. Some few words pass between him and the corpse, who perhaps shall be a young British officer, and shall say something mysterious and soul-stirring to him before he dies. In truth, perhaps the story might open here; and Septimius first conceive his notion of earthly immortality on this occasion. But I think not. At any rate, this interview with the dying soldier, whom he has shot, has an influence on all this story; and often his grave is referred to, for probably Septimius buries him on his own ground, claiming the corpse for his own, and saying nothing to anybody. A root springs out of this grave, as it were. Perhaps the young stranger gives him his own secret of immortality; which of course is good against natural death, by disease or old age, only. It cannot turn aside a bullet or ward off a sword. Perhaps the secret is contained in a written paper which Septimius finds on his body, or which the dying man confides to him. Septimius has been deeply thinking on this subject of death, already. The paper might be a recipe for immortality, which an uncle of the dying man, a recluse student and natural philosopher, had given him; but which the young man had despised, never believed it, or desired to profit by, from generous motives of sympathy, and English love of fair-play. It falls in so with Septimius's previous state of mind, that it gets full possession of him. "You have given me death; I give you life!" Certain conditions are required by this recipe, the general tendency of which is, to contract a man within himself, estrange him from his fellows and all the earnest struggle of humanity, cut off the foliage of his affections &c. Perhaps the recipe shall be given in a letter to the young man from his uncle, written in a quaint style, with moral precepts inculcating egotism under the guise of a philosophy of restrained passions. The old gentleman himself had made some attempts towards immortalizing himself, but had failed partly by a love of wine and good English cheer. Septimius buries the body on his hillside, and with it all the property he finds on him, his purse, his silver-hilted sword, &c. all in his regimentals he buries him, and plants a tree over his grave; and keeps back nothing but the paper. After this epoch, a change is perceptible in Septimius's life, conduct, character; so great a one, that his position in society is changed by it. The minister comes to see him about it; having been his [sincere?] friend heretofore.

Study 4

Express strongly the idea that the shortness &c of life shows that human action is a humbug.

The story opens, discovering Septimius a young man of some education—possibly a student of theology with the clergyman. A young girl, living next door, must also be brought soon into sight. Septimius muses much on life and death, and is dissatisfied with death, on noble grounds, because it so breaks off and brings to naught all human effort; so as to make a man a laughing stock to whoever created him. Then his sense of life and love of life must be strongly expressed in this first part of the story, the beautiful, young, vivacious girl being the medium of bringing out this characteristic. He, I suppose, is of a melancholic temperament, and therefore the fonder of life—the more horrified at death. He conceives the idea, from an instinctive sense, that he may possibly live forever. In this first chapter, the house, the hill, the village, must all be sketched more or less distinctly, and the time, at the commencement of the revolution. There must be a conversation between the clergyman & Septimius; perhaps the story might open with one.

Next chapter; begins with the tumult of the April morning when the British marched to Concord. Everybody is astir, except Septimius, whose brooding spirit does not heartily share in any action; besides he is a theological student. As the troops pass by, there is a little scene between a young British officer and the girl; he steals or forces a kiss from her, and Septimius interferes fiercely; but the order to march is given, and so they are separated for the time. Septimius remains at the house, or on the hill, listening to the sounds and signs of the morns—the reports of musketry &c. By and by, come the troops in retreat; and Septimius again meets the gay young officer; a rencounter ensues, and Septimius shoots him;—the troops and the Americans meanwhile passing on, leaving Septimius, who supports the dying officer into his cottage. A scene ensues, in which the young man and he become friends, though of such different characters. The Briton dies, after giving Septimius the letter of the old philosopher, his uncle. Septimius, for some reason, to be sufficiently specified, buries the body on his hill; perhaps the young man desires it;—on the spot where he was shot. Possibly, too, the clergyman happens to come, and performs services over his grave, and has another talk with Septimius, who does not mention the secret of immortality. Here Septimius's state of mind on the idea that he has the means of living forever. The composition of the recipe; it is partly moral, partly material.

Study 5

These preliminary incidents having taken place, Septimius remains with his recipe for immortality. It is a very abstruse matter, requiring great study to comprehend it, and after all appearing to be partly incomprehensible. There are various ingredients of a recipe, some of which can be found, others are unknown to Septimius; these lead him to chemical and botanical studies, in which he abstrusely employs himself; he finally becomes sure of all the ingredients except one, which he takes to be the rarest on earth. The conditions of the receipt require, too, a great moral circumspectness, a government of the passions, a restraint, a supervision over the food; all of which Septimius endeavors to practise, and so gets his whole way of life within rule. The effect is perceptible to everybody who comes in contact with him. Through it all, however, there is nothing spiritual, nothing affectional. He is thus gradually estranged from the girl, between whom and him, there has never been any declared love, but only the possibility of such a developement; he now sometimes gazes at her as from another sphere, sadly, perhaps, wishing that he could get at her, but feeling the impossibility. She probably falls in love with another man, yet not without a sighing instinct that she might have better loved Septimius.— These things, on his side and hers, may perhaps be developed in an interview. The clergyman has also an interview, and is astonished at the improvements, the deterioration, the changes, that he finds in Septimius; how whatever was best in him seems blighted, at the same time that his intellect has acquired wonderful force and expansion.

The old man is not revealed till the end.

Years pass; the war is over; and Septimius is still pursuing his studies, which by this time have led him to a profound depth, though, at the same time, so estranging him from the world that nobody is aware what eminence he has attained. One day, there comes along a coach, or it may be a man on horseback, or else on foot, a stranger, an old man, inquiring for Septimius, and finding his way to his door, where he enters with a certain freedom and establishes himself in the house and study. He is a severe, unprepossessing old man, but with a certain grandeur about him, and state; a roughness, which yet is anything but boorishness. He looks at Septimius with a scarcely concealed hatred, yet engages in discussion with him. For the first time in his life, Septimius feels that he has met a man who understands his object; he is terrified at the idea, but still will not let go of the man. He receives him as a guest; they converse together. The old man shows his knowledge of Septimius's recipe, and points out the wanting ingredient growing abundantly on his own ground. The conversation sometimes turns on the war, and the old man seems interested in the sword & watch of the slain officer, which Septimius has hanging up in his study. At last, it turns out that the old man is the very Uncle who gave the young officer the receipt of immortality. He has come for vengeance, doubtless, but this Septimius does not know; nor does he, till the old man's purposes are accomplished, suspect who he is. Neither should the reader more than suspect him.

The old man, having thus instructed Septimius, goes away. Septimius remains, pursuing his studies, concentrating himself more and more within himself, acquiring a mighty force, but at the expense of whatever makes life beautiful, benevolent, holy; giving up the great aims for which he had desired earthly immortality, despising mankind, relinquishing love, friendship, brewing his secret, which still requires great research and elaboration. There should be a friend introduced very early, who sticks by him long—a natural man, loving, hating, shunning none of the ties that connect him with his kind. He shall have had an early and secret affection for the girl, which he stifles and represses, because he saw that Septimius was inclined to fall in love with her. But, at last, seeing how Septimius has allowed this impulse to wither, he indulges it, and perhaps gives him notice that he shall press his suit. Septimius is at first shocked at this, and has a glimpse of how lonely he has made himself—the fearful strait that he has arrived; but, at last, he gives her up, and becomes still more egotistic. His friend should have fought through the Revolution, and come back an officer; and the story must be relieved with his character and that of the girl throughout. His suit to her is successful, although she has some reminiscence of her early, virginal, tender feeling towards Septimius.

Thus things go on. The reader is made to see how all that is highest and holiest in this life depend on death and the expectation of it; how it immortalizes the love that, at first sight, it seems to blight and make a dream; how, without, man would be but an intellectual brute. At last, Septimius's recipe is fully concocted, ripened by the years that are necessary for that purpose. A beautiful, clear, golden liquid, with a strange perfume; but with an unearthly coldness; and he is prepared to drink it, one evening. His friend, meanwhile, is married to the girl, and they are living at one of the neighboring houses. Perhaps he makes a festival, on the christening of his little son; or for thanksgiving; or some such thing, and invites Septimius, who (feeling that the drinking of his draught will separate him forever and finally from mankind) accepts the invitation, by way of taking leave of humanity. The old man, too, reappears on this occasion. Septimius has a reflux of the natural feelings of humanity, but returns to his house, taking the old man with him.

Study 6

Perhaps the young man had some personal defect that made him earnestly desirous that he should be buried without being undressed; and therefore he makes this request to

Septimius. And perhaps afterwards, in the story, it comes out what this defect was.

Septimius has a wild genealogy, being descended from an old witch on one side, who was said to have had connection with the devil; and on the other from an Indian prophet and powow. This mixture of bloods had given him a strange and exceptional nature; and he had brooded upon the legends that clung around his race, following his ancestry, not only to the English universities, but into the wild forest, and into hell itself. The mixed race had probably made him morbid, in reality, besides giving his dark imagination this unwonted scope & lawlessness. His mind and character had a savage and fiendish strain, intermixed with its Puritan characteristics; so that he was particularly liable to unbridled thoughts.

By shooting this young man, Septimius has influenced the fortunes of an old family in England.

When he goes to see the old Doctor, he recognizes something that he buried with the young man.

Rose is a schoolmistress of a district school, and so may have a decent degree of cultivation.

It shall be observed that the requisitions of the scheme for prolonging life deprive a man of the glow and gush of life, of generous impulses, of youth, and all that makes life desirable.

Septimius thinks that he shall live to see the glory and the final event of the American Republic, which his contemporaries, perishing people, are fighting to establish.

Study 7

The old man and Septimius discourse about the recipe and other matters; & Septimius asks him whether he has ever drunk it himself?—and why not?—to which the old man makes some mysterious response. Septimius, at this latest stage, falls into a vein of reflection (and perhaps addresses it to the old man) on the benign influence of the usual course of time, in its action on the human being, on age, on death. The sweetness of old age, how it softens hard and weary manhood, making it our nature and happiness to be affectionately helped, taking down our pride; the sweet prospect of rest before us; the doing away of all that is hard and bad; the putting all action on a higher plane. So a sweeter, lovelier flower springs out of our descent and decay, than we can anywise produce from our richness and vigor. The dreariness of the prospect of living forever amid these small and mean necessities of life—feeding, getting up, going to bed, dressing ourselves in an interminable series;—seeing the wretched old sun rise forever; especially when, as in Septimius's case, the highest and tenderest interests would be sublimated from it. Were he to marry, his wife could be but a concubine, because she would soon be divorced from him forever by death; his children mere playthings of a moment. And then he begins to feel that his own choice has confined him eternally in a wretched prison house, dark, so that you cannot see whither you are going, sordid, grimy, when, on the other side of the low door, is bright sunshine, and all sweet and noble things. He remembered the sweet and triumphant expression that he had seen on the countenance of the young officer after his death; it was his joy at seeing the glories of the other world, through the open door —opened for his admittance. From all, the cold, bright liquid, which he has been so long brewing, and preparing himself to drink, is to debar him.

The old man sits by, and watches this struggle. But how is it to terminate; that is to be left to further developement.

By the by, the toil of preparation for availing one's self of this recipe, besides the concoction of the recipe itself, is such that not one in a million would undergo it. It may be, too, that Septimius had quite broken down his constitution by study, vigil, poisonous fumes, carking care &c &c &c; so that, so far from seeming likely to live forever, he would appear to need instant medical advice to enable him to last even a little while longer. His deathly appearance, in the eyes of outward observers, to be contrasted with his prospects of illimitable life, in his own idea.

Perhaps the curtain shall drop on this conflict within himself, and rise the next morns. The friend and his wife shall come into the cottage, sent there by the old man, and shall discover Septimius dead in his chair; the fragment of a broken vase; a strange perfume in the room.

The old man shall have disclosed himself in the last scene; and boast of his revenge for his slaughtered nephew, whether Septimius shall choose to live or die. In one case, only lengthened misery; in the other, untimely death, without having lived, or done anything good in the world.

Septimius felt that the drinking of this potion would sever him from the whole human race—would make him cease to be a man, in fact.

It may be, that Septimius becomes concerned to use up some other human being in the process of preparing himself for earthly immortality. He at first fixes on the girl of his first love, but afterwards takes another female, who turns out to have been the paramour or beloved of the young officer; she must be introduced very impressively. She might have dwelt either in Boston or in old England.

The diamonds, emeralds, rubies &c. seen on the surface of the snow, in the early morning sunshine.

Study 8

The clergyman is the more terribly earnest in his religion, because he is conscious of the devil in his blood.

Traditions of the temptations the Divine used to have to go into the Forest and meet the Devil, and his wizard ancestor, and how his whole life was a struggle thereby, and his death troubled.

The secret of the elixir of immortality is said to be in the family, in a fragmentary way; but there is something missing, & persons have since tried to put it together, but in vain.

As regards the inheritance:—The ancestor of Septimius had left England, on account of some dark domestic tragedy, before the Pilgrims came; perhaps ten or twenty years before. He throws off civilized uses, and betakes himself to the wilderness, where he becomes chief of a tribe of Indians, a great medicine man, or prophet and priest; and when the Puritans come, they find him in this position, and consider him a wizard. Possibly they slay him. He leaves a son, whom they adopt and bring up in the christian faith, though many think his father was the Devil himself. The son lives and dies among the Puritans, a reputable person enough, though with some wild traits; he transmits to his posterity some heirlooms, singularly preserved, among them the goblet, and the iron-bound box; and also traditions of his father's home in England, of the bloody footstep, of the family being entitled to rank and wealth; and these come down, mingled with wilder legends. In the next generation, the grandson of the old wizard is a clergyman, eloquent, dark, mighty, a son of thunder; with something of the devil in him still. He marries a beautiful and tender maiden, who softens the race a little. Then there are two generations of husbandmen, in whom the talent of the race, and their dark characteristics seem dormant; to awake again in Septimius. His mother, after his father's death, had married a second time, and had a daughter Rose, who was free from the morbid taint of all the rest.

The place where Septimius now lives was that where his ancestor, the wizard, had his wigwam; and now, perhaps, he finds a spear or arrow head, which may have been his. It was on that hill-top, overlooking the wide scene of meadow land; and his ghost might be sometimes fancied as meeting Septimius there. Bloody footstep.

The Puritan Divine has great share in Septimius's speculative turn, his gloomy, soberly enthusiastic character; all his ancestry is represented in him.

Aunt Keziah's story embodies these traditions, made as wild as possible. The bloody footstep is seen on the forest-leaves.

In England, it was an old family, long occupying an ancient Hall, on the model of Smithills. In the reign of Elizabeth or James (leave it uncertain which) there was an ancestor who partook in the great intellectual movement of the time, and became a philosopher, as Bacon did. Many alchemists lived in those days, and searchers for immortality; he was thought to have discovered secrets beyond human nature. He is jealous of his wife, or his mistress, and tries some magic out upon her, or poisons her. It is said that he possessed the secret of immortality and of poison; and that once a mistress of his drank of one by mistake for the other, wishing to share his immortality, and so died; or perhaps he tried the experiment on her, and killed her, having mistaken one kind of flower for another. A brother of his, who likewise loved the girl, had caused this catastrophe by wilfully changing the flowers; the wizard slays him on the threshold, and takes flight, stepping in his blood. Thus comes the bloody footstep, by which he was tracked everywhere, and even to the last verge of English ground. She is admired for her golden hair; and long afterwards, an ancient chest being opened, it was found full of golden hair, to which this maiden had turned.

The person, who had contrived this crime, was in love with the girl, and also heir presumptive of the estate; and so he was acting through jealously, and also from cupidity, and meant to be the death of them both. The alchymist bids her drink first, which she does; but when he lifts it to his own lips, he grows pale, finding by the smell that the poisonous flower has been distilled into it, instead of the other. Perhaps, the heir is his dearest friend, and assists him in his process.

The other member of the family succeeds to the estate; but his descendants die after a generation or two; and thus there is a disputed succession. Some important documents are missing, that should prove the claim, and also entitle the representative of the name to an ancient baronial title long in abeyance. The estate goes into chancery, where it is at the present day, waiting for the true heir to come.

Sybil's story must not refer to the alchymist having migrated to America; this the reader is to infer from Aunt K's story. Perhaps Septimius may make that inference, and follow it out in his thoughts, but without speaking of it to Sybil.

Aunt K has some strange story about a bloody footstep's being seen round the door of the wigwam. The sufferer must have been his brother.

The drink is fabled always to bring fatal and accursed consequences with it; however fine the motives of those who manufacture it.

There has always been a tradition in England, that the missing heir went to America, and that the family is still extant there; so that, at least, the documents necessary to prove the claim to the estate and title are there, or may be there. So Doctor Portsoaken, a quackish adventurer, has been sent over by the claimant, to possess himself if he can, of the papers in the possession of the young officer;—that might be the main purpose. He discovers this American claim, to his own surprise, and seeks to get hold of the iron-box, and is at least willing that Septimius should poison himself. When he first comes to Concord, it is with the purpose of getting hold of the papers left by the young officer, he having no suspicion of any others; but what he hears from Aunt K. & Septimius convinces him that these are the true heirs. Sybil had been used by him to get the papers from the young officer, but she fell in love with him and was seduced.

Of course, the Doctor contributes all he can to the mystification of Septimius.

Aunt Nashoba mixes some strong, intoxicating herb with the tobacco she smokes.

Scenario

First Scene:—Three young people sitting on the hillside, in a cheerful & bright April morn'g. Their characters must be slightly developed. No; I think that Septimius's must first be shown in a conversation with the minister, the afternoon previous; in which is developed this peculiar trait of Septimius, in desiring to live always on earth; his hereditary traits must be hinted at, or slightly sketched, to be brought out more strongly hereafter. Their talk is about Septimius's studying for the ministry, which has been an understood thing hitherto; but latterly he has relented, and has seemed more inclined for physic; he clings strongly to the earthly and material, yet in an intellectual way. The minister is somewhat dissatisfied and alarmed at the state in which he finds him. This conversation takes place on the hill-top; and there is a glimpse of Robert Hagburn & Rose Garfield; a peaceful, Arcadian spectacle of two rural lovers. <Allusions to the troubled state of public affairs. Aunt Kezia is seen.>

Second Scene:—the next morning, after a night troubled by the preliminaries of Lexington battle, horses are galloping; muskets discharged, dreams troubled &c &c. Septimius, his sister, and Robert meet on the roadside, and talk together, and Aunt Keziah bursts forth upon them in a savage characteristic way. While they talk, a horseman, at full speed, ghastly with terror and excitement, dashes by. There must have been previous, half-jesting allusion to an ancestor of Septimius, a wizard, and another among the Indians; all predisposing him to wild speculative ideas. On the passage of the ghastly horseman, Robert rushes into his house, and snatches an old gun of his father's, used in the old French War, and goes to the village. Septimius, partly because he is studying for the ministry, and partly that he is merely speculative, remains behind; yet in a strange state of cold, quiet excitement. He hears the town-bells, he sees the march of the British troops, and witnesses the treatment of Rose by the young British officer. Then he listens to the sounds from the village, the beat of drum, rattle of musketry &c. Finally, overcome by the warlike impulses of the moment, he takes an old gun, said to have belonged to his great-grandfather, and to have been bewitched, and goes up on the hill-top. I think here will be an opportunity to introduce more of Septimius's characteristic modes of thoughts, and wild aims, founded on the superstitious legends about his ancestors. Something, too, should very early be said, and decidedly, about the claims of the family to rank and wealth in England; this might come from the minister, in the first scene.

Third Scene:—Septimius meets and slays the young officer on the hill-top. The officer was a collateral relative of Septimius, and perhaps was a claimant of the estate of England; it being now in possession of a man not rightfully entitled to it. He is poor, having little except his commission in a cavalry regiment. He wishes to have the papers buried with him; so that they should not fall into this man's hands; also, perhaps, because he wishes this receipt for a deadly poison to be hid from men. He has been much persecuted and wronged by this man, and feels that he escapes a struggle in dying, which has lasted in his family for two or three generations. Perhaps he learns that his name is the same as that of his slayer, and therefore warns him of mischief, if he does not bury him & all that belongs to him—at least the papers. Aunt Keziah comes, & shows the savageness of her nature, mixed with Christian characteristics; also, the minister, and they three are the funeral;—possibly Rose, but I think not. He finds a silver key &c.

Fourth Scene:—Robert Hagburn, having fought through the day, is going to Cambridge to enlist, and there is a parting scene between him, Rose, and Septimius, who also feels some motions towards going, but gives up the idea, under pretence of his studies. After the parting, he shuts himself up in his study, and examines the papers. Here must be introduced, more fully, the ancestral traditions of the family, about wizard and powwow, and certain heirlooms must be alluded to; for instance the splendid old goblet used in witch sacraments; also an iron-bound box, once set with precious stones, now fallen out, that had not been seen for a great many years. The legend about the long-lived Indian must be dimly alluded to, to be brought out more fully by Aunt Keziah; also, Aunt Kezia's herb-drink, said to have been of witch brewage. All these things considered and conglomerated, the reader will see a propriety in Septimius's giving a sort of credence to the idea of an immortal drink; also, the English alliance must be covertly insisted upon. Thus, he is prepared to be greatly bewitched by the young officer's old papers; and broods over them continually and unavailingly. Meanwhile, he has written to Boston to give an account of the event, as the young officer requested; and his request was made with some allusion to the circumstances of his claim to the estate, mysteriously couched.

Fifth Scene:—one day, during Septimius's much walking on the hill-top, he sees a pale young woman there, who seems attracted by the grave; indeed, she appears so suddenly, that he could almost have thought she springs up out of it. She looks at him, he thinks, in a careless sort of way; but they enter into conversation, and her talk strangely chimes in with the tenor of his thoughts. On descending afterwards to the house, he learns from Rose that this girl is living with Robert Hagburn's mother and grandmother; Robert, who is now with the army, having been commissioned by a high officer to find her a boarding-place; she being out of health and needing country air. She is understood to be an English girl, whose protector has fallen in the war. She remains so long, that at last she becomes an accustomed thing. Sometimes, in her conversations with Septimius, it shall appear as if she wanted to find out something about the dead man, or what was buried with him; for, probably, she is an agent of the person in England, and was employed as a spy upon the young officer, but fell in love with him and was seduced by him. Her relative is Doctor Portsoaken, who had used her for various purposes of his; he being a quack, adventurer, humbug, astrologist, &c &c &c. Thus the winter passes, Septimius puzzling over his paper, and talking with the girl, who prepares the way for the appearance of Doctor Portsoaken by frequent allusions to him, his scientific knowledge &c so that Septimius almost expects to see a picturesque ancient magician.

Sixth Scene:—After the siege of Boston is over, the Doctor appears in person, the queer moody old fellow already described. He is wicked, a humbug, yet partly believing in his humbuggery. He shows a desire to find out what was discovered in the grave; but Septimius, being of a secret nature, is careful not to disclose it to him; yet from his covert inquiries, the Doctor suspects that he has found something. He chimes in with Septimius's thought, and half-believingly, talks of the possibility of discovering the secret of endless life, and how, hand in hand with this secret, are said to run those of deadly poison so that the ingredients of each are almost identically the same. The herb-drink of Aunt Keziah gives occasion and illustration to much of this talk. During his stay, or after it, Septimius is visited by a transitory idea that the grave has been opened; and this recurs to him afterwards, when he sees something, that was buried with the young officer, in the Doctor's study. The Doctor, during his visit, may discover that there is a new, and the rightful, claimant to the estate in the person of Septimius; and so, he is ready to see him concoct a poison, instead of the immortal drink, and forwards this mistake as much as he well can. He professes himself a believer in the virtues of spider's web, and so prepares the reader to see his laboratory, by and by. He goes away, after private colloquies with Sybil, and inviting Septimius to come to Boston to see him. There must be a mixture of love of science with his villainy. The estate is in chancery; and the Doctor is to have half its value if he gets it for the claimant. Perhaps he writes a letter to the claimant in England, after his return to Boston.

<The ancestors of the barons were greatly interested about death, as well as life, & sought easy modes of it.>

Seventh Scene:—Septimius digs away at his manuscript, and begins to see glimmerings of light; he also holds colloquies with the girl, and gets into a sort of intimacy with her, fitful on her part; she being influenced by a revengeful feeling on her own part, by Doctor Portsoaken's instigations likewise, to subtly impel him onward to concoct a deadly poison and drink it instead of the draught of immortality; and on the other hand, her own woman's nature is moved with pity for him, and perhaps she has a struggle not to love him; so that there may be very queer and picturesque phenomena in her behavior towards him. His sister Rose instinctively shrinks from Sybil, and warns Septimius against her. In this conversation, there may arise a discussion of the question of endless earthly life, Rose taking a tender woman's view of it. All through the book, Rose must peep, with natural sweetness.

<Iron-box. Aunt K. keeps the secret so long that she dies, it untold.>

Eighth Scene. The flower grows out of the grave. This flower had figured in a legend told by Sybil; and also in one told by Aunt Keziah; and likewise Septimius had found reference to it in the recipe which he has puzzled out of the manuscript; but could not make out what earthly flower it was. It must be described with great elaboration. On some slight disorder of Aunt Keziah, he puts it into her herb-drink, and she dies in great torment. Sybil seems a good deal interested in this event, and behaves and talks so that Septimius is struck, but not made suspicious.

Ninth Scene. By this time, Septimius has been much acted on, morally and intellectually, by his strange pursuit. A description given of him. He is estranged from everything but himself, his studies, and Sybil. Bethinking himself, at some crisis, of Doctor Portsoaken's assistance, he makes a journey to Boston, and spends a day and night with him. Again the Doctor endeavors to ascertain what papers he possesses, either of his own or the young officer's; he talks of his English ancestors, and hears that there was formerly an iron-bound and ornamented box, one of the family heirlooms; of which perhaps the secret has died with Aunt Keziah. Indeed, Aunt Keziah has treasured this up, and meant to tell the place of deposit at the last moment to Septimius; but defers it till she is unable to speak. The Doctor, on scientific grounds, as he pretends, expressess a great wish to have the contents of this box. Septimius determines to find it, not to give up the contents to the Doctor, but to use them himself. He finds the box, which is to be described as made with a great deal of antique art, and opens it with the silver key, found in the young man's bosom.

<(Before this, & after his return from Boston, he makes renewed efforts to distil the drink & fails.)>

<There is a lock of golden hair, bright as ever, in the strong box.>

Tenth Scene. The opening of the iron-bound box. Its contents are some ancient documents, on parchment and paper. Some of them appear to be certified proofs of descent, being papers which have long been sought for in England, to prove claims to a title and estate; for lack of which the title has long lain dormant, and the estate has been many years in chancery. All these, Septimius looks at carelessly, and with disappointment, although he knows that they give him an undeniable claim to the estate; he connecting them with stories that he has always heard, and with Aunt K's traditions. But, while throwing these aside, indignant with Providence for offering him such a paltry boon, instead of earthly eternity, an old wasted writing falls out from among them. This he snatches up, & finds that it supplies vacancies in former papers, makes out the receipt, and gives an interpretation to whatever he was in darkness about before.

Eleventh Scene. The distillation of the drink; and description of the process, and how aetherial the liquid looks; then, he sets it in the sun by day & the moon by night, for a certain time; and all the beautiful changes that take place in it; and in one stage of the process he seems to see past features in the crystal goblet, among others the face of the old progenitor, in his scholar's garb, or his Indian one, and perhaps the dead young soldier's face &c &c. The old English hall, too, with its quiet ancient beauty, contrasted with an Indian wigwam. At another stage, he sees future personages and events. All this may be accounted for by his watchings, and fastings, his perturbations of mind and disturbed fancy. At last, it settles down into a pure, cold, bright crystal fluid, cold, cold as death; whereas, in its previous changes, there has been a good deal of caloric elicited, indicating chemical action. No images whatever can be seen in the fluid now.

Twelfth Scene. An interview between Septimius & Sybil on the hill-top. His heart is flowing out with success, and he feels a love and pity for the world. In this new warmth, too, a latent passion for Sybil, which he has long been cherishing unconsicously, bursts forth, and hurries him into a declaration, and a solicitation to her to share his endless life. She treats his proposal with a kind of scorn, and ridicule, but with coquetry, or somehow does not yield, nor yet discourage him; they have a playful, half earnest discussion of what they would do with their earthly immortality. In this scene, Sybil should struggle with her enmity; perhaps she finds, and is surprised to find, that it is converted into love; for, after all, in Septimius's dark and wild nature, there is something that suits her own better than that of the young soldier. All through the book, there should be tokens of pity, remorse, and finally love, contending with her evil purpose. Finally, Sybil gives a sort of consent to drink the liquid with him, on the eves of his sister's wedding.

Thirteenth Scene. The Wedding of Rose Garfield and Robert Hagburn, who has come back with military rank (a major perhaps) and distinguished honor. A good deal of rustic pomp and magnificence to be displayed. Septimius throws off a good deal of his reserve, and astonishes people by his gaiety, which has a tincture of extravagance. Sybil, too, appears to be under a similar influence, and between them they make the company wildly merry. The talk of old women and men, about the family, to be told. Towards the last, a strain of pathos comes over Septimius, because he feels that he is taking leave of his sister Rose, and indeed of all mankind, and is stepping forth into a dim future, shelterless and lonely. He disappears quietly from the company and so does Sybil; and soon after Doctor P. makes his appearance, and sociably sits down among the company. He makes himself appear gay; yet symptoms of disquietude might be seen by a keen eye; for he has been informed, perhaps by letter from Septimius, that he has succeeded in concocting the drink, and means to quaff it.

Fourteenth Scene. Septimius and Sybil in the study, with the vase of immortality before them. They talk; and by and by Septimius pours out the liquid into the antique goblet. Sybil is in a strange, fitful mood; she seems to love him, and yet hate breaks through. Covert allusion is made to her having been seduced by the young soldier; perhaps she says so herself. Septimius wishes to kiss her; she resists decidedly. At last, she gives him a hint of the trick that she has played on him, drinks off the liquor herself, and throws down the goblet with the remainder on the hearth. The sensations of this sort of dying are a delightful intoxication, in which she becomes sweet, amiable, delightful, most fascinating, and Septimius cannot believe that she is dying. It is the peculiarity of this poison to give a euthanasia. Perhaps she acknowledges her affection here; and she lets him kiss her lips, because she knows she is dying. At last, she tells him, "Septimius, it was poison;" and dies.

Fifteenth Scene. Sybil Dacy is discovered dead in Septimius's study; on the hearth, the fragments of the crystal goblet, with gilding on them. Also, cinders of burnt old papers. Also a shattered apparatus for chemistry &c. The iron box is there, empty. Septimius has vanished. Doctor Portsoaken comes, and gives vague hints. He returns to Boston, and is found dead, with his great spider hanging over him, who is supposed to be a devil who has got his soul. On examining the spider, it is found to be only the cast off skin of one. Nothing is certainly known about Septimius subsequently; but there are rumors that he went to England, proved his claim to the estate and title, and got them; and my own English reminiscences are here brought in. It might have happened, while, for so many years, the intercourse with England was broken off, during the Revolution.

In the last interview, Sybil sports with Septimius, laughing at his rage, under the influence of the intoxication of the draught; at first drinking it, its cold made her shudder; then it deliciously intoxicates; and he thinks this is the natural effect of his elixir. She seems to look forward to a heavenly prospect of life on earth. She is tender, bewitching, this girl heretofore so elusive and unattainable; she lets him kiss her lips; then asks him "Do you know why I wiped my lips? No? The draught was poison."

Then explain that there were two flowers, which made all the difference in the liquor;—one (which was an extinct flower now) producing immortality, and probably a painful one; the other, death.

Septimius must be endowed with grand and heroic qualities; and must desire long life, not meanly, but for noble ends. No mean dread of death, but an abhorrence of it, as being cloddish, inactive, unsuitable. Make his nobility of character grow upon the reader, in spite of all his defects. It shall be on this account, too, that Sybil finally loves him, and spares him, and sacrifices herself instead; punishing herself with death for having plotted his.

Sybil must be introduced with very little display of beauty; a girl nearly colorless in her first appearances, as to character. She is very young. Perhaps Septimius at first is inclined to treat her almost as a child, so simple and helpless she seems; but gradually she comes out with stronger traits.

One of Septimius's grand objects is to reform the world, which he thinks he can do; if he can only live long to study and understand the nature of men, and get at the proper methods of acting on them. The reason why the world has remained dark, ignorant, and miserable is, because the benefactors of the race have been cut off before they more than partially understood their task, and the methods of it. This must be broached in his first conversation with the minister; perhaps in reference to the troubles of the country, and the war, then about to begin. When he shall have completed the reformation of the world, seen war, intemperance, slavery, all manner of crime, brought to an end; then he will die. His love for Sybil shall be a falling off from his high aims; and, in truth, he naturally grows more selfish as he goes on. Some satire on man's philanthropic aims might be introduced by this view of Septimius; their short sighted aims, their absurd hope of success in a single lifetime, the fragmentary way in which the strife against evil is necessarily carried on.

Septimius, if he might otherwise have felt any remorse for Aunt K's death, shall console himself with the thought that she dies for a great end. So does the young soldier; their graves are the footmarks, in which he plants his giant steps, on the way to a mighty and magnificent result.

Perhaps the moral will turn out to be, the folly of man in thinking that he can ever be of any importance to the welfare of the world; or that any settled plan of his, to be carried on through a length of time, could be successful. God wants short lives, because such carry on his purpose inevitably and involuntarily; while longer ones would thwart and interfere with his purpose, by carrying on their own.

Medea's cauldron, in reference to Aunt Nashoba's brewing people. There may be a young man about the village, whom she is supposed to have stewed, and recreated from an old one; so like he is to his grandfather. And he has that queer flavor and aspect of old age, which we sometimes see in youth.

All through, represent Septimius as visited by frequent fits of despondency as to the pursuit he is engaged in, perception of its utter folly and impracticability; but after an interval, without any apparent reason why, he finds himself in full faith again—just as in writing a poem or romance.

<(It was whispered that Aunt Nashoba brewed herself in the jug, to make her drink; so much did it look like her.)>

<(Dwell upon Aunt Nashoba's Indian love of the woods.)>

II. "Dolliver Romance" Studies

Study 1

A husband & wife in their old age, after a long and happy wedded life.

The husband has been addicted to occult studies with reference to the principle of physical life, and, by natural means, has attained to a secret of feeding that principle, so that, at last, not only has he become able to keep decay from going farther, but can make life go back upon its steps. He communicates to his wife that he possesses this power, and proposes that, hand in hand, they shall go back, and gradually be young again. But the wife is submissive to the common law; she has had children, and lost them long ago; she has religion; she shrinks from the thought of going back; she has an instinctive sense of what would be best for them both; she prefers to live out her life, and die. Perhaps the agitation of his proposal (for, with her reliance on his intellect and power, she little doubts that he can make good what he says) contributes to hasten her end. She dies and leaves him alone.

He lives on, and gradually it begins to be noticed that he does not decay—that he seems to grow younger—but this is attributed to such things as a wig, false teeth &c.; so that it is long before it strikes his acquaintances that it is marvellous; he is considered as a well-preserved old man, aping a younger age than his real one. And this might last till his contemporaries have passed on and been buried. He becomes more and more a wonder, growing younger, year by year, but, being alone and a recluse, it very gradually grows miraculous. This effect may be given in a grotesque way, which should be the tone of the whole narrative.

There should be some particular reason for which he wishes to live back—for instance, in order to discover some secret, left unravelled on his previous path—to study out some particular subject, of an earthly nature—to effect something, that shall give a substance to all his life. What? Something which, once effected, he feels as if he could die willingly, and with a sense of completeness. The gist of the thing lies in this idea. There must be some clear connection with human sympathies in the particular object of this desire. He shall seem just to have missed something in his onward course, which he now goes back to finish and perfect.

Study 2

He must have been a man of high purposes, which he hates to leave unaccomplished. This nostrum to bring back his youth is a thing to which he otherwise attaches no importance. He knows that it is inconsistent with the plan of the world, and, if generally adopted, would throw everything into confusion; he therefore considers it justifiable only in his own exceptional case. It is but a side-thing, in which he takes no pride, nor considers it of much importance; indeed, being rather ashamed of it than otherwise.

It might be a metaphysical discovery that he wishes to complete. Perhaps physical. He might have imagined a way to clean disease out of the world; some great beneficence, at all events. Perhaps the object for which he wants renewed youth may appear to the reader ridiculously trifling compared with the means used, as for example, to find out the solution of an algebraic sum. No; better, to confer a material benefit on the world, how to get rid of poverty, or slavery, or war—and, the gist of the story might be, that while he was trying to accomplish this by so much toil and disturbance of the order of nature, the real tendency and progress of mankind accomplishes it without any agency of his; whereas his method would have destroyed the whole economy of the world.

As he returns down the road of life, he meets all mankind full in the face coming towards him. A most earnest desire to finish a poem; to ascertain some historical facts; to find out the whereabouts of a lost daughter, or a son, who was left he is uncertain whether dead or alive, for many years past. Well; he is reluctant to leave a baby, entrusted to him, friendless in the world, and therefore avails himself of this secret, which he had discovered in the course of his researches, but would not, on his own account, have thought of using it. No; there must be some mystery, which perhaps, missing it all through maturity, he discovers when he is a little boy again; and as the story ends, you shall see it in his childish eyes. The cordial might be taken at intervals of five years.

Study 3

He lives over again in order to correct some great error;— he has done something in his past life, which he fears will be of very bad influence on mankind, & therefore he lives again to grub up this evil by the root. He attaches himself to the family to whom he did the wrong, trying to influence their fortunes to good, but finds that the evil is ineradicable, unless he will pull up a great deal more good with it. But some definite thing. He is a poor, simple old scholar, and has incurred an obligation in long past years—a debt—which weighs upon his mind as he approaches the limit of his life. He has this invaluable secret of prolonging or renewing life; he might sell it, if he chose, for incalculable lucre; but this is against his conscience; so he determines to live back again and get the money in some other way. Yes; this debt, due to a poor widow, troubles him. It might have been incurred by his father, and have grown by interest up to its present amount. The widow has perhaps an infant son; he lives to take charge of him. So they live on towards some central event.

He brings up this boy, and gives him good instruction, and himself goes on growing younger and younger, while the boy comes up to meet him. He establishes him in life. Perhaps, when the hero's age begins to attract too much attention (he having been mobbed on that account) he and the young man emigrate together; and still the strange on-growing youthfulness attends him. At last, the young man asks an explanation. It might appear to him, such were opinions of his father's excellence, that it was a heroic attribute.

He may begin at 75—when the young man was 23, or so, the hero would be 55; and at that period the explanation and separation might come about—their ages would pretty nearly coalesce, when the hero was about 40. Then they should meet again by chance; and the protege would not recognize him 50—30—60—20—70—10. At last the young should die old, and an infant be found on his door-step.

Study 4

He lives for the sake of an infant boy, not his own descendant, but that of a friend, who sacrificed his own life for him. There should also be some other motive: perhaps to study the new order of things that seems to be opening on the world. That would open too wide a vein. Well then, leave his motives to be determined after the incidents have been settled. He leaves his wife, and immediately begins to grow young. He has been heretofore a loving and sympathizing old gentleman; and everybody is sorry for him & comes to condole with him on the loss of his wife. But there makes itself apparent, by and by, a certain briskness which rather shocks them; they think perhaps that he recreates himself with strong liquors to make his trouble the more tolerable. And so there is a great deal of wonderment. An old contemporary comes to see him, and they have a long talk, in which the other expresses a vague suspicion, perhaps, and a wish that he might share this advantage. What if he should see the bottle, and secretly put it to his lips and drink a great gulp, and go home and be found dead in the morning? Yes. The scene to be described with grotesque horror; he dances, he sings, he falls dead. This old person should, if possible, be somehow connected with the course of the story. After this event, there are some sinister rumors, as if it were the chemist's fault that his old friend had died; at least, something vague survives from it, and then the rumors spread, and curiosity is awakened by his youthful aspect, and he becomes a marked man, vulgarly thought to deal with the devil. He lives in an old house, alone, with only this child (a girl whom he has taken to bring up,) and in her he satisfies himself for solitude. So, pass ten years till Alice comes to be a young maid (perhaps 15 or more) and she does not see that anything is amiss with his age; because one old man looks as old as another to the young &c &c. But outside the scandal waxes great, and at last the people raise a riot, intending to take him out of his house and hang him.

He flies with Alice and a few valuables, and his bottle of medicine, away into the country, afar, and finds shelter with an Indian Doctress, an herb woman, who herself pretends to know great secrets of herbs. The figure and character of this crooked old thing to be detailed picturesquely. She shall be the representative of the New England witches, being hereditarily descended from them. The herb woman and the doctor carry on trade together; she having some wily and evil purpose or other, which the Doctor foils, whereupon she poisons herself. In the meanwhile, Alice has fallen in love with a young man in the neighborhood, and the Doctor find-ing it out, promotes the marriage, though feeling in terrible

despair, and solitude, and goes away; indeed, Alice has begun to wonder at his continued and increasing youth; and
it is time for him to do so. The young man may be a college graduate, just beginning the study of law—perhaps a
minister.

He sets forth again on his quest (?) which has been somewhat remitted during these events; and he has now gone
back to about his 55ᵗʰ year. He finds it possible to remain
two or three years in a place without attracting much attention to his youthful tendency. Sometimes he meets a man
whom he had known when he was about the age he now
pretends to be. His true contemporaries are by this time
dead.

Being put into this singular position with regard to mankind, he contracts a most intense scorn of all human pursuits and things, which must be developed; at the same time,
has a failing belief in spiritual things, in high objects. It must
be so handled as to show the necessity of Death in order to
keep us tender and loving. His tendency is to make matter
of observation of everything, and sport of many things, he
finds himself growing to be a devil by force of solitude and
long life. It should have been a benevolent object for which
he desires to live, and when the time comes for accomplishing it, he has ceased to desire it, or thinks it not worth the
price he would have to pay. This happens when he is 35
years old. But not doing it, it becomes a curse to him thence-
forward.

The difficulty is to know what he wants to live for; it
should appear to be a great object when he adopts it, but
should gradually lose its importance in his view. Can it be,
that he wants to find some particular person, or is it something that affects a great landed property; or does he, being
a very conscientious man, wish to live in order to discharge
a heavy debt, which, if recovered, would be the dowry of

little Alice. He may have discovered this medicine accidentally, seeking merely to concoct a restorative; and so he is himself taken by surprise at his effects, and only slowly comes to the idea that he has discovered the elixir of life. The receipt should be ancient, a mouldy old document which existed among the papers of an ancient man of science. He might be a simple minded kind of person himself. Thus he is rather betrayed into living, than designs it, though he finally becomes attached to it. A simple old chemist or apothecary, of some skill, but no widely extended reputation. He comes slowly to the idea of his gradual youthfulness. The old woman shall have been a sister of the person who found out the secret. It shall have been a physician's recipe, left with him long ago for concoction; but which was never called for; and he shall not know the reason till he meets with the old herb woman, who, by and by, confides in him about its having been left with her family. Her brother perished by some accident. When he knows he has this power, a thousand reasons immediately impel him to exercise it; but there must be one particular wish, in order to give an interest and animation to the story. Perhaps I had better look to the end to suggest the beginning.

Study 5

NOTE: The original having apparently not survived, the following study is here reproduced from a transcript in the hand of Sophia Hawthorne headed "another scrap." Where she was uncertain of a word she underlined a blank space; most of these she later filled in and such insertions are here italicized. Except for the parenthetical reference to Joseph Dorr, all parentheses and square brackets can be assumed to be her signal that she has supplied elements wanting in Hawthorne's text but necessary to the sense.

The elixir which he has made prize of might be the object of the story, somebody else is in quest of it. The old herbwoman, for instance, knows that it is in existence somewhere. It is traditionary in her family; they have long been trying to get it made up. The old woman begins to pry about his chattels in a suspicious way. He, in the earlier part of his career, had some scruples of conscinece about availing himself of this mighty medicine, of which he was not the rightful owner; but now, finding reason to think that the old herbwoman is the heiress of it, he is intent on nothing so much as keeping it to himself. Perhaps the old woman gets him into such a position that there is no way for him except to murder her, or else give up his bottle; and so he gives her a potation of it, sufficient in his judgment to cook her gruel. The young lover of Alice is her nephew. I think the old man and the herb-woman might have a downright contest about this matter in the woods, and perhaps her death might come about there. All along, the sweet, simple, innocent character of Alice must be brought into striking contrast with that of the old-people (man), who shall have a real love for her, and for her only. The moral of the story may turn out to be, the necessity of death for any high *view* of life—that without, we should be mean, grovelling, guilty, selfish; that in the obscurity of death are hidden the high motives that make life good and noble. It might come to a ———— *and* struggle with the old woman, in which a little violence on his part terminates her slender thread of life.

Something that filled his whole mind at the moment; and attention shall be called to its trifling nature at the time; so small, when there (were) so many persons, statesmen, poets, philosophers &c, who had so many stronger motives for desiring length of days. To try some experiments in his garden; to watch the growth and eat the fruit of an apple-tree which he had planted in his back yard, then a young sapling. There may be something in this. He must be a simple character, harmless, with a vein of genius and humor in him. His life up to that time may have been very peaceful; but from that time all sorts of trouble besets him. There should, I think, be something peculiar about the *two*? He should go about the world, doing involuntary mischief all his new life. This should have been one of his motives, but perhaps not of sufficient weight if no other motives had come in to determine him. He wanted [to] witness the completion of some building that had just begun to rise? He wanted to see how the American Union was going to succeed. He wanted to *witness* the happiness of a daughter of his, just married. In consideration of a good many things, he had determined not to live, when something happened that determined him otherwise, and gives a *zest* and aim to the story. Some charge is bequeathed to him. (Joseph Dorr, Esqr. —————————.)Here I come back to the same difficulty with which I began. Might it be that beginning with almost a distaste to longer life, he gradually contracts a great tenacity of life, becomes earthly, losing sight of hea-[ven] because his back is now turned upon it? His face being turned from the light.

Study 6

Points thus far. The hero an old apothecary. Years before, a prescription for an invigorating medicine had been left with him to make up, by a strange old man; he had made it up, some of the ingredients having been left by the old man, but it was never called for; and he has a suspicion that the old man had come to a violent death. But ever since, the medicine has remained in his possession, 50 years perhaps;

he had sometimes looked at it, and seen a strange brightness in it gleaming forth from it. Ten drops at a draught. In this last stage of life, apparently, having something to do which he deems of greatest moment, he deems it well to take a dose of this medicine; it seems to produce an invigorating effect, and he follows it up till he begins to suspect that he is growing young again.

Then follows the death of his old acquaintance; which brings some discredit and suspicion upon him. Then, the popular odium settles upon him as dealing with the black art; and he takes flight and comes across the old herb-woman. After he & Alice have dwelt there some time, it turns out this was an old family recipe. A great deal of wild Indian traditions shall be introduced here as told by the old herb-woman.

Alice falls in love with the young lawyer, and besides the youthful briskness of the old man is again attracting attention from her and others, and perhaps the old woman tries to poison him, & so he sets forth again.

There is need of some great central event.

He is to seek for the evidencies of a great estate coming to Alice?

After leaving Alice he returns at intervals of years, being veiled from her by his youthful aspect, and hovers round her, for longer or shorter spells; and then goes away again on his quest. She shall always appear to have some dim recognition, perhaps to be on the point of knowing him. The approaches of age which are to be described; and they affect him very sadly indeed. The central thought! the central thought.

The title to an estate in England? To find whether a child were alive that he had lost long ago? He has been long regretting some error in middle life, or earlier, which, he thinks, has caused a long ill success through subsequent years; he wishes now to return and retrieve that error, in the hope of living to some purpose thereafter? It need not have been a very high motive, but perhaps ridiculously homely in consonance with the simplicity of the man's character. To recover an antique gold coin, belonging to a friend, which he had lost, and thus a discredit had fallen on his character? To get an ancient sarcophagus to be buried in? Something not startlingly strange, but homely and familiar, I think, should be the motive; and he might gradually get drawn into living on, forgetful of the first motive, until, at some unexpected moment (for instance, when he is a little boy playing in the street) he shall find the ring, or whatever it was, which first inclined him to live. Might it be some crime, committed long ago, which he felt himself bound to live to bring down justice upon? The ring, or ornament, or coin, should be the material symbol of some spiritual matter. Old Dr. Harris of Dorchester, whose ghost I saw. This thing that he is in search of should guide him into all sorts of trouble, change, and devilish turmoil of circumstances. Something connected with the witch craft of New England. It might seem to be some light and trivial thing that he is in quest of; but by and by he finds that fishing at random he has got hold of something as impossible to pull up as the bottom out of the sea. Alas! What a bother!

Study 7

He tries to make out the missing ingredient by engaging in scientific studies, in which he spends precious years of manhood, making discoveries which he flings aside as useless, because they do not tend to lengthen his life. Delusive stories spring up, suggestions, dreams, which lead him to-and-fro, and everywhere he seems on the point of gratifying his desires—but always comes the disappointment.

All through the book, the prettiness, sauciness, cheerfulness of Alice, & her humor, expressions—as child, girl, woman, grandmother, must redeem the gloom, selfishness, morbidness, unnaturalness of the rest.

Perhaps the old man, who dies, may have evinced a certain knowledge about this thing, which may cause the chemist afterwards to regret his death. It may have been a flower, which was to be put in at a certain stage of the concoction; or some rare natural production. Both the English & American branches of the family have retained some incomplete tradition of the secret. The first old man, who brings the receipt to be made up, has a rustic appearance, like a county schoolmaster, or minister, dark, severe, disagreeable, acute, intelligent, but homely & unrefined. He shall be the elder brother of the old herb-woman.

The drug which is wanting—what is it? A mysterious and rare flower that grows out of a grave?—a jewel? a mystery—a powder—a distillation of various rich ingredients—a charm—some herb known to the old woman, and transmitted down to her from her witch ancestors. Gracious mercy me!

The little bright-eyed old man—perhaps his eyes should not be so bright at the beginning of the story, but should have a mild look, gentle, slumbrous, aged; but they grow brighter and brighter through life, with the intensity of his search. He grows into an intensity of selfishness from all the bad and unnatural influences acting on him.

Begin with the old man first taking the cordial because he does not wish to leave this little girl; and because he wants to see a tree grow up which he has just planted, &c &c. Have the man seem tender, grotesque, natural. His wife shall have died long ago, his daughter more recently; the child has no guardian but himself. The moral ruin of this character must be exemplified in the book. Great affection, at first, between the old man and the child. The decline of this to be distinctly marked. Make him in the first place a picture of happy old age. Let the means by which he has the elixir be a secret until revealed, I think, when he meets the old herbwoman. She knows what he lacks of the secret, and he what she lacks.

Study 8

At the last advices, the old herbwoman has come to her death; it seems as if he bought his own prolonged life at the expense of periodically sacrificing another. After this, he finds it is necessary to leave the place, Alice having perhaps evinced a kind of suspicion of him; and so he determines to go to Europe; and there, too, he finds somebody in quest of his secret, the descendant of the original family whose ancestor had discovered it; so that it seems to him as if the whole world were in league against him. He comes upon the traces of the Bloody Footstep. Everywhere, if he stays awhile, somebody starts up, who seems to know his secret, and is sure to be in close relation with him. Perhaps there is some mark by which the initiates know him; a peculiar expression of the eye, it might be, a look of age, or possibly a gray lock of hair, or a withered hand, with the prominent veins of age—some one little mark, which, once seen, gives the lie to all the appearance of youthfulness, and throws the aspect of age over his entire person. This keeps him continually uneasy. It often makes people turn to look after him in the street. It throws a mystery, terror, and hatefulness around him, which spreads far wider than the knowledge of its cause. People of insight see it; people of innocence and delicacy. Children see it. The insight, however, should not be frequent.

The Englishman shall be a quiet and respectable old English squire, who talks to him with English ideas and prejudices; and has himself an objection to living too long, because he feels that he is bound to leave his estate in due time to his son, and not to contravene the laws and conventionalities of old establishment. Nevertheless, he throws himself upon his rights, and demands that the stranger shall surrender to him his hereditary secret. There is a struggle, perhaps; or somehow the old Englishman dies, but the Young Old's foot treads in the Bloody Footstep and renews it. There should be something which he hopes to find at Smithills hall;—perhaps the original receipt, in order to help him to concoct another bottle-full of the medicine when the first shall be exhausted, which he sees prophetically, because time seems comparatively so short to him now.

At first, the simple old man thinks he will only live till a certain tree bears fruit; then, his ideas growing larger, he thinks he will live to see and to help on certain great affairs, political changes, public properties, all, however, of an earthly realm, because he is now so conservative; then, the risks that he runs of losing the secret, and his new measurement of time, lead him to care for nothing but getting the power of renewing his life to any extent, so that he is wholly absorbed in this new pursuit, wasting life to get the means of living, and growing, through the years, more and more hard, cruel, selfish, ready to commit any crime to gain his ends.

Study 9

Still another bit.

He has now escaped from Smithell's Hall; whither does he go?—what happens next?—what is added to the story by this incident? Perhaps with all the murders and wrongs that he commits, some new peculiarity attaches to him; as here, for example, the leaving a bloody track behind him. When he went to the Hall, he was in quest of some important part of the recipe, which he gets, at the expense of the old gentleman's life. There is a curse upon this secret from the beginning, leading him into all sorts of mischief, each variety of which leaves its mark upon him. Of course, there is a curse on everything that God did not mean us to have; and on a wrong track, a man meets nothing but wrong.

He finds the medicine. A neighbor, having some knowledge or hint of it, tries to share in it; and he lets him drink too much & thus poison himself. Not long afterwards, he has to flee from the town & finds out the old herb-woman, who is the rightful possessor of the secret from her ancestors; he is the death of her too. But he has learned from her, that a part of the secret exists in England, so he goes thither to seek it. The mischief, as may be obscurely intimated, lies in the utter selfishness that necessarily grows out of a peculiar privilege. That must be it; and it grows more and more powerful—this in addition to the loss of all the tender *reflections* of Death, making life holy, its clouds, resting on life and keeping it green and moist. Alice, I think, must be his own granddaughter. After the adventure at Smithell's Hall, he might disappear for some years; and the story should take up Alice in America, still in her young married life, say fifteen years after, and describe her domestic happiness and prosperity. Then the old-young man might appear as a middle-aged man, whom, of course, she does not recognize. The curse must follow him here, too, in some way. He gets intimate with them; though there are always instinctive shudderings and repugnance on the part of these innocent people.

The great moral of the story, against the spirit that desires exclusive privilege, instead of to share our good with all. And in favor of that poor maligned individual, Death.

His long experience and selfish view of life would enable him to make money at will, in any way he chose; so that he would have now an immense estate, chiefly in English funds, and would advance into youth with all these advantages. He must be described at this period with the craft, cruelty and coldness of a wicked old man, passionless, still pursued by his curse and doing evil among his young companions. And still there ought to be a strange strain of his former self, from the very beginning of the story running through.

Scene 1st The old man with his grandchild playing on his knees; he feeling himself with but little life in him, & loth to leave her alone in the world. He remembers the medicine & resolves to try it. The gradual invigorating effects.

Scene last—A little boy of 3 or 4 years old, just able to toddle alone, found on the doorstep of a house where dwells the little girl, now a grandmother, after a happy life. Their good old age described and the introduction of this weird ———— among them, in whom they feel an indefinable interest. He has a vial; or small vase, in his possession, to which he clings as if it were a favorite plaything, but there is nothing left in it—but still he could not bear it taken away from him. The scene must be grotesque, yet with tenderness and pathos, as must the whole work. The infantile ways of the little stranger must be funnily contrasted with his aged look, so often seen in babies and young children. Yet he shall have infantile beauty.

Study 10

Begin here

First, the old chemist to be introduced in his shop, in the very act, in the very first sentence, of taking a single drop of liquid in a tumbler of water; and in this first sentence, too, must be introduced the little girl, reaching up, attracted by the old bottle, to get hold of it. He seems doubtful and fearful what it may do to him; regretful, hopeful, but seems a little moved by it. Possibly he dropt it into a glass of wine—which is made to foam by it?—no, yes, doubtful.

Then comes a description of the chemist, his present aspect, his origin, his fortunes &c, all in a grotesque way, yet with a certain earnestness. All this time, the child is playing about, interesting the reader, and amusing suggestions as to the old man's character and purposes. Refer to some mysterious way in which he had got possession of the receipt.

Then a few years pass, and the old man continues to take his drop a day, and it produces its effect as a powerful cordial; and it must be described in its inevitable evidences, in various physical ways. People begin to wonder about him, but think it is only false teeth and perhaps false hair. He, by his dress &c, makes himself look as young as he can. Besides, being an emigrant, nobody knows exactly how old he is. The women say, the old man is looking out for another wife, &c &c. Nevertheless, a certain rumor and wonderment spreads abroad concerning him.

Then comes in another old man—perhaps an old gentleman of eminence in this place, who had never condescended to notice the chemist before, being entirely above him. Powdered, finely dressed, but old, old—aristocratic, puffed up, but wanting something very particular of the chemist. He talks about his age, and about the chemist's and the two old men discuss old age together—the chemist being the freest in talking about infirmities, though in his case they get lighter every day. But he wants to conceal that fact. At last it appears that his visitor has, in some mysterious way, a knowledge of the recipe, and even of the way in which it came into the chemist's possession. A great mystery should be made on this point. And he demands that the bottle be given up to him—then, that he at least share in it. To this the chemist strenuously objects, being now in love with life, and determined not to give up a drop of it. Finally, the chemist being called hastily into his outer shop, the old gentleman rummages for the bottle, and drinks a wine glass full of it, which operates in some strange way, to be hereafter considered—ending in his death.

This old gentleman may be of the same family as that of the Smithills Hall, and a brother or a nephew of the man who brought it there, and whom he may have murdered, or played foully with, in order to get possession of the secret.

His whole life is a quest for the means of living longer—utterly neglectful of all the high opportunities which long life and indestructible vigour would seem to offer him. He has no scruple in violating any law for the purpose of attaining his object; and at last fate seems to point out that the thing which he has sought all over the world, is really in the keeping of his own granddaughter and her family. So he comes back thither.

The utter, utter loneliness of the poor monster must be brought out. I think that this should be exemplified by a love affair after he has grown to be a young man again.

Long ago, a stranger came, and got him to make up this recipe, leaving it behind him for that purpose. The ingredients were chiefly poisonous, some of them rare, others common herbs enough; there was one thing left blank or written in indecypherable characters, and this the stranger supplied by giving it to the chemist in a small lump, to be put in with the rest. While the preparation is concocting, he goes away, promising to be back at such & such a time, but never returns. Or possibly, he dies on the spot, or in the chemist's presence, in some mysterious way, so as to suggest the idea that there is something fearful and awful about the matter. The process of preparation demands very nice skill, which none but an expert chemist could possess.

The heavy years and days could only be recalled one by one; if you tried to do it faster, you perished. If more slowly, you might slip back along down the whole height which you had regained.

Study 11

The Apothecary and the Colonel must be specimens of two different modes of growing old; the latter fossilized, harshly defined, narrow, hard, selfish, with the humanity petrified out of him, his communications with mankind getting dammed and stored up, the good humor, which belonged to him in health and well being, yielding to the fierceness that characterizes an old brute—so selfish that he would eat child broth, and have a daily child slaughtered to make it with, if he thought it would do him any good &c &c &c; the Doctor mild, gentle, getting worn away and defined by age, readily melting into tears, fading out, cackling into mild laughter &c &c &c &c.

The Colonel is famous in the town, for desiring to continue young, and there are strange and absurd stories about his contrivances to keep so, such as his kissing children, his counterfeiting a love for them in order to inhale their breath &c &c.

When he gets back to young manhood, he shows a remnant of fidelity by falling in love with a young woman who reminds him of his long dead wife. She seems to have her excellent traits, but perceives something wrong in him, and so avoids him. Perhaps she has a glimpse of his age.

He questions with himself whether he would share his beloved liquid with the girl with whom he falls in love; but finds himself incapable of that sacrifice. She tries to convert him, speaking just as his wife would.

After the old Colonel dies, there is a look of youthfulness in his face—perhaps it is quite the face of a wild, passionate, excited young man; but as the old Doctor stands gazing at him, it suddenly withers, wrinkles, and changes into the face of an old man again.

Love, which he feels for the above girl, brings him back his real youth, and makes him feel what a dry, dusty, miserable mockery he has been in. All the hopes, the generosity, the magnanimity, the hope on the world's behalf, are reawakened for a time.

III. "Dolliver" Draft Passages

Notes: The following texts represent (A) an earlier draft of the four paragraphs concluding Chapter I (Centenary 463.19–466.12), and (B) an earlier version of the third- and second-last paragraphs of the second *Dolliver* segment (478.13–28). For a physical description of the manuscript containing both fragments, see the Textual Commentary. An additional section (C) describes another version of the end of Chapter I written on a sheet not now known to be extant.

A

warmer condition of life; whereas, long as he had borne its burthen, he probably had not yet grown accustomed to it, feeling its fret even now as a new torment, constantly remembered his prime, and felt these aches, this weakness of the knees, this cloudiness of brain, this confused struggle of memory with names, ideas, & things, this inability to struggle into consciousness of life, were something that did not belong to him, and might yet pass away; and, perhaps, even yet, he awoke in the morning with an idea that all these aches and infirmities were but an ugly dream of the past night, and he hobbled hastily to the looking-glass, half-hoping. He was very surprised by the sight of the white hair and wrinkles, the melancholy furrows, the bowed form, the masque of hoary age in which some sad enchantment had invested him. Youth is unquestionably the proper, permanent, and genuine condition of man, and if we look closely into this delusion of being old, we shall find that we really believe in nothing else, and that it still survives, a coal of fire under the ashes of what was perishable, and within the chill torpor, that garment woven of life's unrealities, which so strangely muffles us as we grow old. Be that as it may, Grandsir Dolliver, it must be owned, looked, in those latter days, very much as if it might now be time for his form to be straightened, his white hair smoothed over his brow, and his poor old bones to be laid away, with a green coverlet spread over him, beside the young wife who, unlike himself, had never worn this ugly garniture of decay. The poor shrivelled old gentleman, so forlorn amid the bustle of the street, yellow as his own old-fashioned ruffles, was remote from his townspeople. Even when they spoke loudly to him the cheery voice came faintly through his deafness, or when they shook him by the hand, or jostled against him, it was a thick glove kept him from the warm touch. When bright little Pansie was his companion in these walks, his aspect was still stranger by the contrast and they two moved within a sort of sphere of their own, out of which the child looked cheerily, and seemed not to feel any chill in the aged hand that enclosed her own, but though sometimes the children would call—Pansie, come and play with us—or a lady stopped to kiss her—Pansie smiled graciously, but kept fast hold of Grandsir Dolliver's hand, and walked on with him. Somehow or other, his remoteness from the present generation of men enveloped her likewise, and made her quaint. Now and then, great-grandpapa would be conscious of her little clasp and his face would brighten, as when a great gush of warm sunshine breaks out over the desolate world, towards an evening of a December day, and his whole manner would brighten all through love and sympathy with this little person. There were other moments happier for the old man than these; as when Pansie was kissed and put to bed, and he sat lonely by his fireside, gazing into the glow of the coals, a look of peace and trustful happiness mingled with a look of calm surprise, and an earthly sadness through all, would sometimes shine out from within, and mingle with the ruddy comfortable glow from his hearth; and then, I hope, the forlorn old creature had a consolatory glimpse into Heaven, the gate of which was kindly left ajar for the purpose; or perhaps that woman, whom he had known and loved in her brief earthly pilgrimage, stole through the opening, was permitted to show herself dimly, in that dim light, to his dim eyes. And the happy influence of these visions, or trances, or dreamy meditations by the fireside, call them what you will, would be felt all through the fitful slumbers of an old man's night and cause him to awake next morning with a happy anticipation like that of a healthy young man awaking to a summer day. But this was not just the kind of alacrity with which he had awaked on the morning of our story.

B

trod over a tombstone lying horizontally on the ground, to the memory of Doctor John Swinnerton, the old physician whom Grandsir Dolliver remembered as his patron, and who had been lying there at least sixty years in the ground, at his own gate.

"And yet," thought Grandsir Dolliver, "I remember it used to be said of him that he need not die until he liked."

C

The catalogue of the Huntington-Bixby-Church sale, Anderson Galleries, March 29-31, 1916, Lot 575, describes a manuscript leaf containing twenty-two lines of *The Dolliver Romance* "written by Hawthorne on blank spaces of a letter addressed to him requesting his autograph," dated conjecturally "[Novr. 1863?]". The present whereabouts of the leaf is unknown, but the catalogue quotes enough of the text to identify it as a version of the final paragraph of Chapter I, closer to Hawthorne's final text (Centenary 465.23–27) than to the earlier state represented by fragment A (552.13–16). The first words of the quoted passage may have been altered to accommodate the syntax of the catalogue description:

those seasons, happier than even these, when Pansie had been kissed and put to bed, and Grandsire Dolliver sat by his fireside gazing in among the massive coals

EDITORIAL APPENDIXES

HISTORICAL COMMENTARY

I

SOMETIME TOWARD the middle of 1861 Hawthorne abandoned his efforts to write an English romance on the American claimant theme and turned to another subject. Its initial focus was "The Wayside," the house on the eastern edge of Concord that he had acquired in 1852. Soon after taking possession, he had written his friend G. W. Curtis, "I know nothing of the history of the house; except Thoreau's telling me that it was inhabited a generation or two ago by a man who believed he should never die." [1]

The theme of immortality had long interested Hawthorne. As a youth he had read William Godwin's *St. Leon*, in which the secrets of the philosopher's stone and the elixir of life were opened to the protagonist, but, far from bringing him happiness, estranged him from humankind. [2] Twice in 1836 during his months as magazine editor he scoffed at the idea of living forever, writing that "We have no yearnings for the grossness of this earthly immortality" and insisting that the advances of science would not lead to the arrest of time or the perpetuation of youth, "because the Creator has abso-

[1] July 14, 1852, MS, Fruitlands Museums, Harvard, Massachusetts.
[2] Hawthorne named this novel among his current reading in a letter to "Dear Sister," October 31, 1820, MS, Essex Institute.

lutely debarred mankind from all inventions and discoveries, the results of which would counteract the general laws, that He has established over human affairs." [3]

A story hint, recorded probably in the same year, suggests that Hawthorne would have emphasized the paradoxes of transcending the limitations of mortality: "Curious to imagine what murmurings and discontent would be excited, if any of the great so-called calamities of human beings were to be abolished,—as, for instance, death." [4] In 1840 he noted: "The love of posterity is a consequence of the necessity of death. If a man were sure of living forever here, he would not care about his offspring." [5] And during the Old Manse years he envisioned another fictional idea that might apply to creative individuals: "The advantages of a longer life than is allotted to mortals—the many things that might then be accomplished." A nearby notebook entry gave concrete emphasis to "the advantages, or otherwise, of having life assured to us, till we could finish important tasks on which we were engaged"; Hawthorne was thinking specifically of the painter Washington Allston, who had recently died before he could complete the monumental "Belshazzar's Feast." [6]

No tales or sketches grew specifically out of these germinal ideas,[7] but Hawthorne's men of science (including alchemists, herbalists, charlatans, wizards) repeatedly focused attention on transcending the limits of knowledge, and he saw in them more of the sinister or diabolical than the benevolent.

[3] *American Magazine of Useful and Entertaining Knowledge*, II (April, 1836), 315; ibid. (August, 1836), 520.

[4] *The American Notebooks*, ed. Claude M. Simpson (Centenary Edition, 1973), p. 23.

[5] Ibid., p. 186.

[6] Ibid., pp. 241, 242.

[7] Minor parallels in thought occur, such as Hawthorne's remarks in "The Artist of the Beautiful" on untimely death foreclosing "any task

In Aylmer and Rappaccini he portrayed experimenters whose zeal so warped them that they could sacrifice beloved human beings. Hawthorne's own skepticism is clear, but he also saw as an abiding theme mankind's yearning for more than his allotted term of life and recognized the ambiguities that he could exploit, even in the grotesque-pathetic mode of "Doctor Heidegger's Experiment." It is not surprising, therefore, that he should take up the subject once again after he had abandoned his English romance.

The documents developing the Elixir of Life theme consist of two independent sequences, one of which clusters around a young student Septimius, the other an old apothecary named Dolliver. The Septimius tale exists in two substantial drafts, the first here labeled "Septimius Felton," the second "Septimius Norton," after the predominant form of the protagonist's name in each. Associated with the "Septimius" drafts are eight Studies—memoranda detailing aspects of plot and character, and probably composed as the "Felton" draft progressed—together with a Scenario written between the "Felton" and "Norton" drafts. Hawthorne abandoned the "Norton" revision well before the end of the story and thereafter conceived a wholly new approach to the Elixir theme. *The Dolliver Romance,* as he called it, exists only in fragments: three chapter-length segments of narrative plus a handful of memoranda—eleven Studies that offer fitful insight into the story as it might have unfolded had he not

___

that seems assigned by Providence"—which include an allusion to Allston (*Mosses from an Old Manse* [Centenary Edition, 1974], pp. 466–67); or the narrator's rejection of the Elixir Vitae in "A Virtuoso's Collection" on the ground that "Were man to live longer on the earth, the spiritual would die out of him" (ibid., p. 489), echoed by Aylmer's hint in "The Birth-mark" that "a liquid that should prolong life . . . would produce a discord in nature" (ibid., p. 46).

become too enfeebled to continue. These several drafts and notes, then, are the subject of the discussion that follows.

The outbreak of the Civil War at the time Hawthorne was beginning to plan the new romance had a bearing on the opening episodes, set in the Concord of 1775 that had suddenly become a theater of warfare. Especially significant is the initial exhilaration of the populace, which in the "Felton" draft he likened to the mood of 1861: "We know something of that time now; we have seen the muster of the village soldiery on meeting-house greens, and at railway stations; . . . seen the familiar faces that we hardly knew . . . ; thanked them in our souls for teaching us that nature is yet capable of heroic moments." But even in the midst of such euphoria Hawthorne's ambivalence imposed itself as he noted that "a great impulse" caused even an "indifferent spectator" to "join in what becomes an act of devotion, a prayer, when perhaps he but half approves" (p. 17.18–29). And this dialectic he dramatizes in the contrast between the aloof Septimius and the activist Robert Hagburn.

With the battle of Concord as an important episode for defining characters, setting and plot direction, Hawthorne sketched out the action in a succession of detached memoranda. In Study 3, "Septimius has a share of some kind in the fight . . . ; he shoots a man, and brings him into his house, and views the corpse, and is affected with strange remorse at it. It seems not fair for him, a deathless one, thus to give death to another." Before dying, the British officer becomes friendly toward Septimius and gives him a document containing a recipe for an elixir of life. Study 4 goes over much the same ground, and it remains for Studies 5–8 to introduce new characters and sketch subsequent action, albeit tentatively.

These Studies, which cannot be precisely dated, are here arranged and labeled for identification in as nearly a developmental sequence as the evidence allows. Thus, the Studies called 1 and 2 are the most general; both start from the Thoreau legend and appear to be following out its implications in an exploratory sense. Study 2 is the only one in which Septimius is not named, and therefore might seem appropriate to head the sequence, but since Study 1 reflects a more introductory tone and suggests directions of plot development largely abandoned, it is placed first in this edition. Studies 3 and 4, which carry the story through the Concord battle and the soldier's burial, form another pair, the order determined by Hawthorne's initial reference to *a* written paper from *an* uncle in the one, whereas the other assumes familiarity with "the letter of the old philosopher." In the same way, Study 5 introduces an old man whose presence is presumed in Studies 6 and 7, and who is finally given a name in Study 8. The ordering of the last two Studies recognizes that only after he had written half the "Septimius Felton" draft did Hawthorne alter the relationship of Rose and Septimius, thus paving the way for Sybil Dacy to appear in later scenes. Studies 5 and 6, though they project some of this later action, do not mention such a figure; her role is hinted at in Study 7, but only in Study 8 is she named and characterized. Finally, Study 5 might appear to be the last drawn up because in it the closing scene of the story is partially outlined; but many of the intermediate plot details are unformulated here, and it is therefore placed before Studies 6–8, in which they are developed.

Although the stages of Hawthorne's progress in planning and drafting his new romance cannot be calendared, it is clear that by mid-September, 1861, he had sketched the story for his publisher James T. Fields, who was also editor of the *Atlantic Monthly*. With his usual enthusiasm Fields wrote Hawthorne, "I wish very much to begin your new story (about the house) in our *January* number. Now dip your pen steadily and briskly to that end. . . . I shall depend upon seeing the early chapters of yr. story 'right away.'" [8]

But Hawthorne was not to be unduly pressured. In early October he reported that his plans were taking shape but that he had not begun a draft. "I shall *not* be ready by the first of December; for I don't mean to let you have the first chapters till I have written the final sentence of the story." [9] A week later, however, he wrote his old friend Horatio Bridge, "I find myself sitting down to my desk and blotting successive sheets of paper, as of yore. Very likely I may have something ready for the public long before the public is ready to receive it." [10] Although we cannot be sure, this remark suggests that Hawthorne was referring to a sustained work on which he was making progress, and not to the English essays he was contributing occasionally to the *Atlantic*.[11]

On November 5, Fields asked again for the serial, which he wanted to announce in the *Atlantic* prospectus for 1862.

[8] Wednesday [i.e., September 18, 1861], MS, Huntington Library. The date is established by Fields's reference to Anthony Trollope, whom Hawthorne had met on Monday, September 16. In his *Yesterdays with Authors* (Boston, 1872), p. 96, Fields recalled a visit to Concord during which Hawthorne outlined the story to him. Fields's memory seems only partially accurate, however, since he placed their interview before Hawthorne's reply to the letter just quoted, but identified the work as *The Dolliver Romance*, which Hawthorne would not begin until 1863.

[9] To Fields, October 6, 1861, MS transcription, Hawthorne-Fields Letter Book, Houghton Library, Harvard University.

[10] October 12, 1861, MS, Bowdoin College.

[11] After "Pilgrimage to Old Boston," published in the issue of January, 1862, his next essay was "Leamington Spa," finished in July for October, 1862, publication.

Hawthorne's answer was the same as before, but with more concrete indication that it was under way. "The story certainly will not be ready for the first months of the year, and I don't know precisely how soon it will be. Judging from appearances, it will be a pretty long story, though I cannot answer for two volumes." He disliked serial publication because he felt that "harping on one string . . . when prolonged from month to month" would fatigue his readers; in any case, he wouldn't deliver the manuscript until it was finished. He broached the possibility of an English sale and of his crossing the Atlantic to protect the English copyright. Meantime, he asked Fields, "Can't you announce it conditionally, or hypothetically?" [12]

A further interest attaches to Fields's letter in that Hawthorne used its blank spaces to jot down Study 8, thus establishing that wherever he stood with his draft, he was still shaping the last—and perhaps earlier—stages of the "Septimius" plot at a date later than November 5. This process of simultaneous planning and execution could explain the almost contradictory and noncommittal language of a letter Hawthorne addressed to his young English friend Henry Bright on November 14: "latterly," he said, "I am meditating a Romance, and hope to have it finished by the time the public shall be ready for any other literature than the daily bulletins, or treatises on warlike strategy." [13]

It is equally difficult to estimate his progress when, three months later, he gave several reasons for being reluctant to accept Horatio Bridge's invitation to visit him in Washington. He was not well, he said. "Also, I am pretending to write a

[12] Fields to Hawthorne, November 5, 1861, MS, Morgan Library; Hawthorne to Fields, November 6, 1861, MS, Massachusetts Historical Society.
[13] MS, Marquess of Crewe.

book, and though I am nowise diligent about it, still each week finds it a little more advanced; and I am now at a point where I do not like to leave it entirely." [14] Nevertheless, in March he did leave it for a month's sojourn in and around Washington, one immediate result of which was an *Atlantic* essay, "Chiefly about War-matters," finished in May and published in the July issue. We have no further word on the romance except for a comment by a British journalist Edward Dicey who had met Hawthorne in Washington and had visited him at the Wayside in June, 1862. He noted that "Hawthorne was going to write—or, rather, was thinking of writing—a novel, to be brought out in England simultaneously with its production in America; and it was arranged, at Hawthorne's request, that Ticknor was to accompany him over to England to make the arrangements for the sale of his copyright. I can recall now the plans we made for meeting and dining together in London." [15]

Dicey's language is curiously at variance with the substance of Hawthorne's hints at progress; it may reflect the author's natural diffidence and common self-disparagement, or it may be an indirect cue that Hawthorne was then about to embark on his revised, or "Septimius Norton" draft. What is significant, however, is that during the twelve months ending in June, 1863, he wrote nine of the English essays that were collected as *Our Old Home*, but before that volume was published in September he had started afresh on a quite different treatment of the elixir theme, which he would call *The Dolliver Romance*. His major attention to the "Septimius" drafts was more than likely concentrated in

[14] February 13, 1862, MS, Bowdoin College.
[15] Edward Dicey, "Nathaniel Hawthorne," *Macmillan's Magazine*, X (July, 1864), 245.

the closing months of 1861 and well on through 1862, but we cannot know how long he continued to work alternately at "Septimius" and the English essays.

The story Hawthorne told—completely plotted only in the "Septimius Felton" draft—began with the battle of Concord at the outset of the American Revolution. Septimius, a young ministerial student who had brooded much on the limitations of the human lifespan, killed a young British officer and found on his body a manuscript containing a recipe for an elixir reputed to confer immortality. In his efforts to decipher the manuscript Septimius became increasingly alienated from family and friends, except for an old part-Indian aunt who preserved traditions of her mixed ancestry, and an elfin figure Sybil Dacy who materialized after the soldier's death. Septimius eventually concocted his elixir and persuaded Sybil to join him in drinking, whereupon she drained the glass herself and fell dying from poison, for the elixir contained one wrong ingredient. Septimius disappeared from Concord and was rumored to have established his claim to an English estate through his distant relationship to the slain British officer.

The "Septimius Felton" draft is generally straightforward and proceeds with fair consistency to a logical conclusion of the plot. As with his other unfinished work, however, this manuscript reflects Hawthorne's experimentation with character names. Septimius's neighbor Robert Hagburn (initially Hobkinson) is often called Garfield, a form Hawthorne sometimes caught and corrected. Once he is named Roger. Hawthorne vacillates in naming the Indian herb-woman Kezia(h) or Zezia(h), all four forms being found along with further spelling variants. Dr. Jabez Portsoaken is called "Portensoak" and "Portensoaken" in what may have been moments of authorial levity.[16] The doctor's niece appears as Alice Ford and as Edith before the name is permanently established as Sybil Dacy.[17] The young English officer remains nameless throughout the Studies, and also in the draft until after his death. The doctor calls him Willie Rogers, and in the closing pages he is referred to as Cyril Norton and Cyril Thornton. As for Septimius, he is given no surname in the Studies, and only occasionally in the draft is the family name of Felton invoked, notably in seven instances clustered near the end, preceding which Hawthorne had once referred to his protagonist as Septimius Norton, as if trying out a name which he would adopt in the revised draft. Following standard Gothic technique, Hawthorne waited until the end to reveal that Sybil had been the British soldier's lover and that after setting out to avenge his death had fallen in love with Septimius. More crucial to story management, near the middle of the draft Hawthorne abruptly changed Rose Garfield's relationship to Septimius from fiancée to sister, but preserved her name intact. The Scenario and the revised draft explain the different surname by making her Septimius's half-sister. The change was scarcely necessary, for Hawthorne had earlier emphasized Septimius's growing estrangement from all normal human relationships, and in Study 5 had suggested that Rose might in consequence fall in love with another man. Robert

[16] The doctor's name derives from Hawthorne's acquaintance with Sir Francis Moon, with whom he dined July 1, 1859 (Pocket Diary, MS, Berg Collection, New York Public Library). Moon, a London printseller and publisher, was Lord Mayor 1854–55 and Alderman of Portsoken Ward, 1844–71. Ironically it was an English critic who objected to Hawthorne's use of the name as "one of the crudities which after-thought would have removed" (*Spectator*, No. 2307 [September 14, 1872], 1179).

[17] The sybilline nature of this English girl's role is clear. One can only speculate whether her surname is a refraction from "Dicey"; if so, Hawthorne's acquaintance with the British journalist would help to date Sybil Dacy's appearance in the manuscripts as no earlier than April, 1862.

Hagburn was already available as a fellow-townsman whose very normality contrasted with Septimius's visionary indulgences and whose bravery under fire made him a worthy suitor. The "Septimius Felton" manuscript was far from being a fair copy and even without the Rose Garfield change would have required another draft to incorporate such proposed alterations as "Put the above in the third person" or "Make this legend grotesque . . . " or "Describe his ascetic and severe habits . . . " Moreover, numerous passages contained directions for rearrangement, not always completely worked out, but in any case needing the author's clarifying mind and hand. Before beginning his revision, however, Hawthorne set down a précis of the "Septimius Felton" draft, organizing it into fifteen scenes and concluding with further notes on details. That this Scenario, as its structure justifies us in calling it, was a transitional document between the two drafts is suggested by the fact that it summarizes the action of the first draft (taking account of Rose's half-sister relationship to Septimius) and occasionally foreshadows changes found in the revision. The old aunt appears as Keziah until near the end of the Scenario, when she is rechristened Nashoba, the name she would bear thereafter.[18] Evidence from other

---

[18] The same transition from Keziah to Nashoba is evident also at the end of Study 8, presumptively written—or at least concluded—about the same time as the Scenario.

The old aunt belongs to the succession of eccentric females going back at least as far as Hepzibah Pyncheon. Keziah is a direct continuation of Crusty Hannah in "Grimshawe," with further individualizing traits attributable to the Indian strain in her ancestry. Rose Hawthorne Lathrop (*Memories of Hawthorne* [Boston, 1897], p. 161) said that Mrs. Peters, the Hawthornes' Negro servant in Lenox, "no doubt stood for a suggestion of Aunt Keziah." The name itself recalls a family figure of Hawthorne's Maine adolescence, Kezia Dingley, who was a sister of his aunt, Mrs. Richard Manning. Hawthorne appropriated Nashoba from the name of an early settlement of Christian or "praying" Indians near Concord, as if to stress further the mixed inheritance.

characters' names in the Scenario is neutral: Robert Hagburn, Dr. Portsoaken, and Sybil Dacy retain their original names, while the English officer and the minister are not otherwise identified, and Septimius appears without surname. What is remarkable about the document is that it offers evidence of planning and story management more carefully detailed than in individual Studies, and structurally as precise as in the completed romances. The contrast is striking between the motivational uncertainties besetting the American Claimant manuscripts and the generally confident, tidy unfolding of the Elixir drama.

One would therefore have expected that Hawthorne's revision, the "Septimius Norton" draft, would smooth out the few wrinkles and bring rough spots to a state of polish usual in his finished work. But this is not quite what happened. From the outset he expanded the narrative, amplifying both conversation and psychological analysis to such an extent that although a third longer than its "Felton" predecessor, the "Norton" draft breaks off soon after Aunt Nashoba's death, with fewer than two-thirds of the Scenario's fifteen scenes accounted for. Hawthorne followed the structure of the first draft and Scenario without great changes, except that he reversed the order of Sybil's and the Aunt's legends of the bloody footstep and inserted them both before the Doctor's first appearance. The Rules of Life too he moved up to a position well before the Doctor's arrival on the scene.

Characters' names also underwent change, as they had in the course of the Claimant manuscripts. In addition to Septimius Norton and Aunt Nashoba, the revision altered the Doctor's name to Jabez Ormskirk (borrowing the surname from the opening pages of "Grimshawe") but later reverted to Portsoaken with a new forename of Zebulon. The minister unaccountably became Mr. Norton, though no relation to Septimius's family; subsequently he was referred to as Mr. Porter. The otherwise stable name of Rose Garfield appears once as Halleck, and Robert Hagburn is sometimes styled Garfield and in two instances Hagdorn. The young British officer is called either Francis or Charles Norton. Late in the revision Hawthorne changed Septimius's name yet again, this time to Hilliard Veren (derived from a prominent Salem court and customs official of the seventeenth century), called Hillard once in the narrative. The original conception remained vivid enough in Hawthorne's mind for the name of Septimius to recur occasionally in the final pages, sometimes uncorrected. The dead soldier became Francis Veren to preserve the distant kinship with his American slayer.

As Hawthorne proceeded with the "Norton" revision, it is clear that he had the "Felton" draft before him on his writing desk. A representative passage of each ("Felton" page 67, "Norton" pages 317–18) short enough not to require analysis, sheds light on his compositional habits; it concerns the initial wave of patriotic spirit that swept over the Concord populace in 1775—and the not dissimilar feelings in 1861. Hawthorne reordered the parts of the "Felton" passage, and rephrased language constantly; but he also copied bits of verbiage literally and followed the original sequence of parts closely enough to produce a carefully revised paragraph. This indeed is his usual way of working from an earlier draft. He does not mechanically or slavishly copy his original language: one is keenly aware that fresh detail is constantly being added, phraseology refined, conversation and soliloquy amplified. All in all, though plot development remains steady, the "Norton" draft contains more fresh language than it retains from the "Felton" draft.[19]

The most striking difference between the two drafts is the physical state of the manuscripts. Where the "Felton" draft contains from forty to sixty lines in a medium-sized generally legible hand on a 9¾ inch page, the "Norton" text on the same paper stock varies from about eighty to nearly one hundred lines of minute and tightly squeezed inscription. Further, "Norton" far exceeds "Felton" in number of revisions Hawthorne characteristically made: cancellations, new wording over wiped-out original text, interlined additions, numerous transpositions, along with suggestions for yet further development possible only in another draft. The evidence points to his intense absorption in nuance, whether of tone or of narrative technique. In expanding the proportions of his story he added crisp circumstantial detail; he also elaborated Septimius's ruminations so considerably as to produce a drag in story movement largely offsetting the gain in concrete observation and shrewd insight. Early in the "Felton" manuscript he had announced that he was writing an "internal" story (anticipating almost the word Melville would use to describe *Billy Budd* a generation later); but this emphasis, which continues in the "Norton" draft, is characteristic of all Hawthorne's major fiction. Here, perhaps more than in other contexts, Hawthorne's own judgment emerges transparently in his reports of Septimius's reveries which leave no doubt that he considered them misguided.

Although the "Septimius" story was independent of the

---

[19] Such comparisons could be made at a hundred points. To cite but one other example, the scene in which the Doctor first appears ("Felton," pp. 68–80, "Norton," pp. 372–87) illustrates still greater freedom in revision, but a few literal echoes show that here too the "Felton" text was at hand.

earlier American Claimant plot line, Hawthorne freely re-
introduced such motifs as the legend of an English inheritance. The bloody footstep legend he used too, but changed
it fundamentally and offered a pair of full-blown English and
American analogues. Again Hawthorne introduced a quackish
spider-loving doctor, resembling Grimshawe in his brandy-
drinking and tobacco-smoking; Portsoaken is once even called
"the grim old doctor," echoing the earlier manuscript. The
old Aunt is a variation on Crusty Hannah, whose "East
Indian part" has become a North American Indian intermixture. And along with mysterious family papers an iron
coffer and a silver key reappear,[20] as well as incidental references to Whitnash church, thatched cottages, a tree blasted
by a mighty swearer.

Other details floated up out of Hawthorne's memory. In
Liverpool an old Kentuckian named Philip Richardson had
told of killing a British officer at the battle of New Orleans,
and when he turned him on his back "there was the sweetest
and happiest smile over his face that could be conceived." [21]
Hawthorne elaborated the image in describing a look of
beatific serenity on the face of the British soldier whom
Septimius killed. Years earlier James Russell Lowell had
given Hawthorne an account of a woodchopping youth who
left his chores behind the Old Manse to investigate the fight
at the nearby Concord river bridge on the April day in

[20] In the "Etherege" manuscript the iron chest when opened was
found to be full of golden hair. The detail reappeared in Study 8 and
Scene 9 of the Scenario but was not used in either "Septimius" draft.

[21] *English Notebooks*, ed. Randall Stewart (New York, 1941), p. 438.
Richardson said that he "fired twenty-four times" during the battle, always
at a definite target, " 'and I was a good rifle-shot.' " Perhaps it was
Richardson to whom Hawthorne referred when in an authorial aside in
"Septimius Norton" (p. 274.4–11) he said that he had talked with a
man who had killed twenty-three people.

1775, was surprised by a sudden movement of a wounded British soldier, and as if by reflex action brained the soldier with his ax. In recording the story in "The Old Manse" Hawthorne wondered how the experience might have affected the young boy in later life—whether he would have been haunted by guilt—and in some sense explored the problem when he drew the character of Septimius.[22]

Also worked into the narrative was a village character who frequently regaled Hawthorne with rumors and gossip in the early stages of the Civil War.[23] His translation to 1775 occupied half a paragraph in the "Felton" draft, and was much expanded in the "Norton" revision. Later Hawthorne took up a fresh sheet, labeled it "25 (additional)", and filled both sides with a quirky conversation focusing on problems of old age and death.

Thus the manuscript grew: from the tentative memoranda we call Studies to a relatively stable but unfinished "Felton" draft, followed by a Scenario that organized the external aspects of the story as a reflection of the "Felton" draft in content and order; then the "Norton" revision, which added factual detail and amplified every aspect of the story up to the point of abandonment about two-thirds of the way through.

[22] Although the youth's name is unknown, the story is substantiated by documents assembled in Harold Murdock, *The Nineteenth of April*, 1775 (Boston, 1923), pp. 71–77. When Edward Dicey visited Concord in 1862, Hawthorne told him the story, and was evidently Dicey's authority for saying that the youth had only recently died and that the memory of killing a "wounded man in cold blood haunted him to his grave."—*Six Months in the Federal States* (London and Cambridge, 1863), II, 227–28.

[23] Julian Hawthorne identified him as "a real old codger who used to pester Hawthorne" with his frequent visits to the Wayside—"Nathaniel Hawthorne's 'Elixir of Life,' " *Lippincott's Magazine*, XLV (March, 1890), 419.

II

But Hawthorne did not abandon his attempts to write a romance of immortality. During the last half of 1863, probably beginning soon after he had finished work on *Our Old Home* in July, he took up a new approach to the theme and before the end of the year had sent Fields the first chapter of a work that he elsewhere called *The Dolliver Romance*.[24] His progress to that point can be amply traced, though not always definitely dated. For instance, of the eleven detached memoranda we call Studies, six were inscribed on letters written to Hawthorne or Sophia between mid-June and mid-September, 1863; but the dates are only a *terminus a quo* and tell us neither when nor in what order Hawthorne took them up for his jottings. It is clear, however, that within a few days after July 18, when he had put in final form his controversial preface dedicating *Our Old Home to* Franklin Pierce, he was beginning to focus his thoughts in another direction, for he remarked to W. D. Ticknor that "I must try to get my poor blunted pen at work again pretty soon; especially as Fields threatens me that nobody will buy the new book on account of the dedication."[25] By the end of August Fields was making overtures, perhaps more optimistic than his conversations with Hawthorne justified, for his proposal by no means confirms an agreement: "In the event of your sending that story, of which we spoke this morning, for publication in the 'Atlantic,' let it be understood between us

[24] The title appears in letters of Hawthorne to Fields, December 9, 15, 1863, MSS, Huntington Library. The manuscript of the first chapter is headed simply "Fragments of a Romance," as he had earlier proposed.
[25] July 27, 1863, MS, Berg Collection, New York Public Library.

that we shall pay you $200. for each monthly instalment."[26]
Fields's offer was an advance over the $150 Hawthorne re-
ceived for the last handful of *Our Old Home* papers in the
Atlantic, and he needed the money.

Six weeks later Hawthorne's commitment was still uncertain. He told Fields that he could not say when, if ever,
the first chapter would be ready. "There is something preternatural in my reluctance to begin." He continued in a
gloomy strain, saying, "I linger at the threshold, and have
a perception of very disagreeable phantoms to be encountered,
if I enter."[27] But the implication that he had nonetheless
been planning was borne out within a week's time, when he
told Fields, "There are two or three chapters ready to be
written." And despite his hesitancy and uncertainty, his
grasp of the new story idea was firm enough for him to say
that Thoreau's tradition of the deathless man (the germinal
impetus for the "Septimius" drafts) "is now taking a shape
very different from the original one." Fields had been pressing Hawthorne for permission to announce the *Atlantic*
serial, but Hawthorne as usual had no title in mind at this
early stage. Parrying the question he invited Fields or his
wife Annie to offer suggestions.[28]

The response was not very satisfactory: "The New
Tithonus," "The Deathless Man," "The Modern Tithonus."
Fields advanced these possibilities self-deprecatingly, saying
that Hawthorne would himself "prefix a title that will sound
on long after it is spoken." Again he expressed his wish to
announce that serialization of the new romance would begin
early in 1864. And in his postscript he praised Hawthorne's
plans to prefix a sketch expressing his indebtedness to

[26] August 31, 1863, MS, Huntington Library.
[27] October 18, 1863, MS, Huntington Library.
[28] October 24, 1863, MS, Huntington Library.

Thoreau.[29] On November 8 Hawthorne wrote that he couldn't meet a deadline of November 15, but declared that the first chapter would be ready by the end of the month, in time for the February *Atlantic*. The title must wait "till the book is fully written"; meantime, he said, "I see nothing better than to call the series of articles 'Fragments of a Romance.' " He was concerned lest the untried form of serial publication constrict his freedom, for evidently he had not worked out details of story management sufficiently to be confident of its salient emphases. Thoreau was still on his mind, but he planned to "mix him up with the life of the Wayside and produce an autobiographical preface for the finished Romance."[30]

Fields replied the very next day, delighted at the prospect for February and postponing a decision on the title until they could "muse together" when the first installment was in hand.[31] A few days later Hawthorne confirmed that he felt "pretty certain" of having "a chapter or two of absurdities ready" for the February issue.[32] But his health was not good, his spirits were low, and after Thanksgiving day Sophia Hawthorne reported to Annie Fields that "Tomorrow he says he shall go into his study and write, for he wishes to be ready with his chapter for Mr Fields. I am afraid the coming book will be sad, under the Circumstances—but I hope not."[33] Two diary entries of Mrs. Fields in early December record that Hawthorne had brought to Boston "the first part of a story which he says he shall never finish. J. T. F. says it is very fine, yet sad." She noted that Hawthorne "thought so

[29] October 28, 1863, MS, Huntington Library.
[30] MS, Huntington Library.
[31] November 9, 1863, MS, Huntington Library.
[32] November 14, 1863, MS transcription, Hawthorne-Fields Letter Book, Houghton Library, Harvard University.
[33] November 29, 1863, MS, Boston Public Library.

little of the work himself as to make it impossible for him to continue until Mr. Fields had read it and expressed his sincere admiration for the work. This has given him better heart to go on with it."[34]

As usual, Fields paid promptly upon receipt of manuscript. But Hawthorne, acknowledging the $200 check, said that "there must still be a further consideration forthcoming on my part, because the first instalment of the Dolliver Romance is not completed." He asked that the chapter be returned to him in proof "in order that I may write the rest in a similar strain, and so conclude this preliminary phase of Dr. Dolliver," adding that February publication must be postponed.[35] Fields amiably proposed a month's delay and was consciously supportive in remarking, "Your pleasure is mine & I trust you know me well enough by this time to feel this is so in every enterprize." [36] A few days later Hawthorne asked for half a ream of paper, "which will probably be as much as I shall want for the Dolliver Romance." Ominously he confessed that he had "not yet had courage to read the proof-sheet, but will set about it soon, though with terrible reluctance—such as I never felt before." [37]

For the next several weeks he was able to do nothing, and a letter to Longfellow summed up his almost fatalistic state of mind:

> I have been much out of sorts of late, and do not well know what is the matter with me, but am inclined to draw the conclusion that I shall have little more to do with pen and ink. One more book I should like well enough to write,

[34] December 4 and 6, 1863, quoted in M. A. DeWolfe Howe, *Memories of a Hostess* (Boston, 1922), pp. 57–58.
[35] December 9, 1863, MS, Huntington Library.
[36] December 10, 1863, MS, Huntington Library.
[37] December 15, 1863, MS, Huntington Library.

and have indeed begun it, but with no assurance of ever bringing it to an end. As is always the case, I have a notion that this last book would be my best; and full of wisdom about matters of life and death—and yet it will be no deadly disappointment if I am compelled to drop it.[38]

Lassitude was upon him, as his wife Sophia implied when she noted that "He thought of trying to write when the New Year came in; but I observed that he did not try yesterday. But he has no positive malady now, and is only negative." [39] He told Ticknor on January 7, "I have felt considerably better of late, and begin to be conscious of an inclination to resume the pen." On the same day Fields visited him in Concord and found him "sitting alone gazing into the fire . . . He said he had done nothing for three weeks." [40] Ten days later Hawthorne confessed, "I am not quite up to writing yet, but shall make an effort as soon as I see any hope of success." The uneasiness he had expressed to Longfellow clearly showed beneath his calm appraisal that "my mind has, for the present, lost its temper and its fine edge, and I have an instinct that I had better keep quiet. Perhaps I shall have a new spirit of vigor, if I wait quietly for it—perhaps not—"[41]

We do not know whether Hawthorne returned proof of the first chapter (though he probably did), nor when he wrote rough drafts of two additional sections—whether before or after the mid-winter impasse. What we do know is that late in February—three months before his death—he an-

[38] January 2, 1864, MS, Houghton Library, Harvard University.

[39] Sophia Hawthorne to Annie Fields, January 2, 1864, MS, Boston Public Library.

[40] Hawthorne to Ticknor, MS, Berg Collection, New York Public Library; *Memories of a Hostess*, p. 61.

[41] January 17, 1864, MS transcription, Hawthorne-Fields Letter Book, Houghton Library, Harvard University.

nounced poignantly but with an almost desperate bravado that *Dolliver* was a lost cause.

> I hardly know what to say to the Public about this abortive Romance, though I know pretty well what the case will be. I shall never finish it. Yet it is not quite pleasant for an author to announce himself, or to be announced, as finally broken down as to his literary faculty. It is a pity that I let you put this work in your programme for the year, for I had alway a presentiment that it would fail us at the pinch.

And he went on to suggest what Fields could tell *Atlantic* readers—that ill-health had interrupted the author's labors, or that "Mr. Hawthorne's brain is addled at last . . . We consider him finally shelved, . . . " or that the romance would be published when received: "We are quite at a loss how to account for this delay . . . especially as he has already been most liberally paid for the first number." If Fields chose, he might "publish the first chapter as an insulated fragment, and charge me with $100 of overpayment." Facing his worsened state realistically, he concluded, "I cannot finish it, unless a great change comes over me; and if I make too great an effort to do so, it will be my death." [42]

It is doubtful that Hawthorne pursued *Dolliver* significantly after this poignant confessional letter to Fields. The surviving manuscripts, especially the eleven known Studies, reflect some of the difficulties besetting Hawthorne's last attempt to write a romance, and perhaps serve to explain the anxiousness that his letters express by such terms as "reluctance," "presentiment," "disagreeable phantoms." For, try as he might, he was never able to establish a firm plot skeleton. His principal new approach was to reverse the

[42] February 25, 1864, MS, Huntington Library.

aging process, and a projected final scene would complete the return of a patriarch to babyhood.[43]

He was preoccupied also with the wish to prolong life for some ruling purpose and devoted much effort to hit upon a plausible motive, in which he was no more successful than when he tried to define the ancient family crime in the American Claimant manuscripts. He vacillated between motives of altruism and curiosity, benignity and scorn for mankind. In Study 7 his central notion was the eventual "moral ruin" of his protagonist, who was prepared to commit crimes (Study 8) and did so (Study 9), but Study 11 described the apothecary's gentleness as contrasted with the stock autocratic airs of the Colonel, directly foreshadowing the third *Dolliver* segment and perhaps indicating that the "Septimius" alienation theme was to be only gradually developed here.

Mixed into the Studies are remnants of the earlier unfinished romances—Smithills Hall, riotous citizens, the bloody footstep, the old herb-woman—which Hawthorne did not exploit in the *Dolliver* chapters but which suggest that he expected somehow to integrate the matter of his abortive drafts into a single grand structure and therefore kept such motifs in the foreground of his mind.

The only character given a name in the Studies appeared there first as a baby, then as a young boy entrusted to the apothecary's care; within Study 4 the boy became the girl Alice, and in Study 7 the apothecary's ward Alice became

[43] An undated paragraph entered in his journal during the winter of 1848–49 (*American Notebooks*, p. 285) contains the germ of this idea: "A man, arriving at the extreme point of old age, grows young again, at the same pace at which he has grown old; returning upon his path, throughout the whole of life, and thus taking the reverse view of matters. Methinks it would give rise to some odd concatenations."

his granddaughter. In his opening chapter Hawthorne further changed the relationship to great-granddaughter and her name to Pansie, invoking the flower and implying also Acadian influence in the word "pensée." Later it gave way to Posie, easy enough to accept as a generalized "floral" name but more probably drawn from a nickname of Dr. George B. Loring's five-year-old daughter Mary, whom Hawthorne and Una saw on a visit in September, 1863.[44]

Hawthorne's penchant for shifting character names continued with the protagonist Dolliver (perhaps suggested by Charles Dolliver, a blind piano-tuner whose advertisements Hawthorne would have seen in the Salem Gazette in the 1840s), rechristened Dorsey in the third segment, and his wife named successively Bessie, Bessy, Phoebe (an echo of Hawthorne's pet name for Sophia), and Alice. Other reminiscences include the memory of a Florentine trio made up of the English painter Seymour Kirkup, a reputed spiritualist and necromancer; a young child Imogen; and her kitten.[45] For his setting he drew, as he had done earlier in the American Claimant manuscripts, upon the Peabody home adjoining the Charter Street cemetery in Salem. The apothecary's great age is validated by linking him with the seventeenth-century Salem physician Dr. John Swinnerton, who is said to have trained him and bequeathed to him his effects including a Brazen Serpent sign; the latter recalls also Hawthorne's early sketch "Dr. Bullivant," where a similar caduceus emblem appeared.

[44] Julian Hawthorne, *Nathaniel Hawthorne and His Wife* (Boston, 1884), II, 331; Moncure Conway, *Life of Nathaniel Hawthorne* (London, 1890), p. 209; Charles H. Pope, *Loring Genealogy* (Cambridge, 1917), pp. 193–94. Mrs. Loring was a cousin of Sophia Hawthorne.

[45] Hawthorne recorded his visit to Kirkup's studio in an Italian notebook entry of August 12, 1858, as G. P. Lathrop noted in *A Study of Hawthorne* (Boston, 1876), pp. 278–79.

In the introductory chapter Grandsir Dolliver and Pansie sit for an amiable portrait in Hawthorne's felicitous familiar-essay style. The apothecary is unusually spry for his years, thanks to a cordial his dead grandson had concocted. In the second segment we see more of the domestic life of old man, child, and kitten, including a near-farcial cemetery scene that ends soberly when Pansie pulls up a flower Dolliver recalls as one his wife had often worn and we are made conscious of its dark relationship to the elixir. The third scene, which follows after a gap in the manuscript, features a boisterous encounter between the apothecary and Colonel Dabney, who knows that a customer had ordered the elixir some years before and had never returned to claim it. Ignoring the minute dosages by which the apothecary's eyes have brightened and his step quickened, he seizes the bottle and drinks a fatal draught. At the close of the scene Hawthorne expressed a sardonic satisfaction at finishing off the arrogant aristocrat thus early in the story. At this point he himself seems to have lifted his pen for good.

Had he continued he might have followed hints in the Studies and developed the increasing conspicuousness of the apothecary as he grows more youthful amid his aging contemporaries; the relationship with the herb-woman (drawing doubtless on the Crusty Hannah–Aunt Keziah/Nashoba figures from the abandoned manuscripts); the "involuntary mischief" following from the apothecary's desire to prolong life unnaturally; and, as a foil to the generally somber tone, the little girl's growth to womanhood and marriage. Whether he could have fused these or other suggested themes into a single fiction is beyond speculation, but the very wealth of gambits in the Studies indicates that he had not found a unifying approach. His point of view toward immortality remained clear, however, for in three Studies he declared that the moral of his tale should be the necessity of death as a relief from the delusions of an elixir of life, a conclusion consistent with the implications of the "Septimius" plot.

Death struck close to Hawthorne in April, 1864, when W. D. Ticknor suddenly expired in Philadelphia while the two were traveling together primarily for Hawthorne's health. And in the following month he himself died in his sleep soon after he and his old friend Franklin Pierce had reached Plymouth, New Hampshire, on a similar tour designed to restore Hawthorne's ebbing strength. The funeral on May 23 was attended by a notable gathering that included Longfellow, Emerson, Holmes, Lowell, Whittier, Pierce, and Fields, and the manuscript of the first *Dolliver* chapter lay on the coffin during the service.[46]

This initial episode, which Hawthorne had seen in proof, was published in the July *Atlantic*, along with a note by Holmes, who had briefly examined Hawthorne and prescribed for him before he set out with Pierce on his last journey. A pirated edition prefaced by the Holmes piece appeared soon afterward in England as a sixpenny booklet *Pansie: A Fragment*.[47] The other two segments, which exist only in rough draft, did not follow immediately. The first of these appeared in the *Atlantic* of January, 1865, while the remaining fragment, perhaps because its opening pages were missing, was not offered for publication during Sophia's life-

[46] Fields confirmed the fact of its having lain on the coffin in a note accompanying his presentation of the manuscript to the Concord Free Public Library. Nonetheless it was sometimes said to have been buried with the author.

[47] (London: J. C. Hotten [1864]). First American book publication of Hawthorne's chapter was in a Ticknor & Fields holiday volume, *Good Company for Every Day in the Year* (Boston, 1866), pp. 288–304.

time. She did, however, prepare a transcription far more faithful to Hawthorne's manuscript than was the text finally published in 1876, when the three sections were brought together to lead off a volume titled *The Dolliver Romance and Other Pieces*.[48]

III

During the years following Hawthorne's death the Septimius story had not been neglected. Among her multifarious labors with her husband's manuscripts Sophia Hawthorne undertook to transcribe the "Septimius Felton" draft and her version of the first one-third has survived.[49] The title *Septimius A Romance* is in Una Hawthorne's hand, as is all of MS p. 7, and so too are occasional additions and corrections; printers' marks show that the English edition of 1872 was set from this transcript.[50] Whether Sophia's work

[48] Sophia Hawthorne's transcript of "Another Fragment" is in the Berg Collection, New York Public Library. In 1872, the year after her death, *Publishers' Weekly*, I (June 13, 1872), 558, announced that the *Dolliver* chapters (presumably all the surviving manuscript) along with *Fanshawe* would be issued in the autumn by Osgood, but nothing came of the plan. Another note in ibid., II (August 15, 1872), 151, cast no further light on the abortive intention.

[49] MS, Berg Collection, New York Public Library. Sophia's fragment of 63 leaves reached 83.2 in the 1872 English edition. Her son-in-law George P. Lathrop, in his Introductory Note to the Riverside edition of *Septimius Felton* (Boston, 1883), XI, 221, said that she took up the romance in 1870 and that after her death in February, 1871, the transcript was "completed by her daughters." The part played by Rose is unknown; Una signed the preface and has received editorial credit to the exclusion of her mother.

[50] Compositors' names and stint markings are related to "takes" of so many manuscript pages and could apply to either magazine serialization or book publication. Signature indications in the transcript, however, key exactly to the book.

went beyond the extant pages is not certain, but the fact may be significant that her alterations of Hawthorne's holograph cease just where the surviving transcript stops. Here or at some later point Una evidently took over as copyist. Whatever her share in preparing the work for publication, her preface acknowledged Robert Browning's assistance in "interpreting the manuscript, otherwise so difficult to me," implying that her own responsibilities were not negligible. Browning modestly spoke of his "insignificant help" in a note to Una,[51] but there is no evidence to show just what he did in Una's behalf.

The romance was serialized in *Saint Pauls Magazine* and the *Atlantic Monthly* beginning in January, 1872, and book publication followed during the summer. The English edition was issued by Henry S. King & Co. in June as *Septimius: A Romance*, but the opening page bears the subtitle "A Romance of Immortality," following that of the *Saint Pauls* serial. The first American edition, published by J. R. Osgood in July, was (like the *Atlantic* serial) titled *Septimius Felton; or The Elixir of Life*. It subsequently became part of the Little Classic, the Riverside, and the Autograph editions, as well as other editions derived from their plates. The published text reflects Hawthorne's "Septimius Felton" draft with far fewer liberties than Julian took in his recklessly conflated edition of *Doctor Grimshawe's Secret*. Most of Hawthorne's interpolated notes on story management were parenthetically inserted and a gap resulting from a then-missing manuscript leaf was acknowledged. Rough spots were smoothed, names regularized, transpositions usually made as Hawthorne's signals directed. But there was no way to escape the inconsistency of Rose Garfield's relationship to Septimius, and a forthright editorial note at the point where she became

[51] June 26, 1872, MS, Berg Collection, New York Public Library.

his half-sister acknowledged that Hawthorne had changed his original plan in mid-draft, and that for publication he would have modified the early pages accordingly. It was evident that Hawthorne had left other problems unsolved, as the internal memoranda suggest, and the volume was presented to the public as an unfinished work.

"Septimius Norton," the revised draft, has not heretofore been published except for an extensive and apparently conscientious mixture of summary, paraphrase, and quotation embodied in Julian Hawthorne's 1890 series of *Lippincott* articles.[52] Although Julian gave a generally accurate account of this revision, he was uncertain whether it preceded or followed the "Felton" text, and he inaccurately assumed that Hawthorne wrote "with no definite scenario of a plot before him"—overlooking the one instance where just such a document has survived. He correctly placed the "Septimius" drafts after "Etherege" and "Grimshawe,"[53] but he ignored the change of the protagonist's name to Hilliard Veren, and less pardonably he did not warn his readers that the "Norton" draft was incomplete; instead, his summary silently appropriated the last stages of the plot from the "Felton" version. The Centenary edition presents a complete text of the "Septimius Norton" draft for the first time.

When *Septimius Felton* was published in book form in 1872 it was cordially received, but critics were by no means

[52] "Nathaniel Hawthorne's 'Elixir of Life,'" *Lippincott's Magazine*, XLV (January–April, 1890), 66–76, 224–35, 412–25, 548–61.

[53] In *Nathaniel Hawthorne and His Wife*, II, 301–2, Julian reckoned the "Septimius" manuscripts the earlier; moreover, he garbled the relation of the "Septimius" drafts to each other (II, 300), stating that the revised version was the one published, although correctly describing the first draft (i.e., the "Felton" text actually published in 1872) as filling more manuscript pages.

unanimous in their appraisal.[54] They often conceded that it would not be a popular work but would appeal strongly to a select audience. As an example of the artist in his workshop it was valuable, and several critics agreed with Higginson that the "fragments of scaffolding" were properly retained. The *Eclectic* took a common easy view in saying that though *Septimius Felton* could not rank with Hawthorne's finished romances, it was a work no one else could have written. The *Times* of London said that it would "do no injustice" to Hawthorne's reputation, but *Appleton's* deplored its publication, as did the *Southern Magazine*, which felt that Hawthorne must have abandoned it as "hopeless and worthless." The *Literary World*, on the other hand, in a curiously mixed view, considered it perhaps Hawthorne's "greatest" but "least attractive" work. The *Saturday Review* voiced a recurrent objection to its grotesqueness and detected an unhealthy cast in its otherwise admirable art. *Lippincott's*

[54] This account of the contemporary reception of *Septimius Felton* draws on the following reviews and notices: H. Lawrenny [i.e., Edith Simcox], *Academy*, III (November 1, 1872), 404–5; *Albion*, L (August 24, 1872), 537; *Appleton's Journal*, VIII (August 17, 1872), 192; *Athenæum*, No. 2330 (June 22, 1872), 775–76; G. P. Lathrop, "History of Hawthorne's Last Romance," *Atlantic Monthly*, XXX (October, 1872), 452–60; *Boston Daily Advertiser*, July 18, 1872, 2:3–4; *Boston Transcript*, July 17, 1872, 2:2, and July 27, 6:2; *British Quarterly Review*, LVI (October, 1872), 540; [Leslie Stephen], *Cornhill Magazine*, XXVI (December, 1872), 732–33; *Eclectic Magazine*, n.s. XVI (October, 1872), 505; *Examiner*, No. 3366 (August 3, 1872), 770–71; *Galaxy*, XIV (October, 1872), 569–70; *Harper's*, XLV (October, 1872), 784; *Independent*, XXIV (August 8, 1872), 6; *Lippincott's Magazine*, X (September, 1872), 367; *Literary World*, III (August 1, 1872), 35–36; *London Quarterly Review*, XXXIX (October, 1872), 261–62; *New Englander*, XXXI (October, 1872), 785–86; *New York World*, July 22, 1872, 3:1; *Overland Monthly*, IX (December, 1872), 573–75; *Saturday Review*, XXXIV (July 20, 1872), 89–90; Thomas Wentworth Higginson, *Scribner's Monthly*, V (November, 1872), 100–105; E[dward?] S[pencer?], *Southern Magazine*, XI (September, 1872), 378–79; *Spectator*, No. 2307 (September 14, 1872), 1179–80; *Times* (London), October 11, 1872, 5:3–5; *Westminster Review*, n.s. XLII (October, 1872), 544.

found Hawthorne "far gloomier . . . and more resourceless" than in any of his other romances. The *Harper's* reviewer ridiculed Septimius's speculations as unheard of outside an asylum. But to *Albion* the "mingled beauty and wildness" were attractive, and the *Westminster Review* praised the romance for showing "with what care a really great novelist works."

Comparisons with other unfinished pieces of artistry were inevitable: Allston's "Belshazzar's Feast" was invoked by Higginson, Dickens's *Edwin Drood* by the *Independent*, and Thackeray's *Denis Duval* by the *Westminster Review*. A thematic relationship with the *Faust* of Goethe or of Rembrandt's etching interested several critics, including Higginson, who also contrasted the gradual shifts in Septimius's character to the absence of gradations in Mary Shelley's *Frankenstein*. Although only the *Athenæum* reviewer immediately noted the relationship of the *Septimius* theme to that of the *Dolliver* fragments, Lathrop later established the linkages in convincing detail. At least three English reviewers found reason to compare *Septimius* with *The Marble Faun*. Edith Simcox in the *Academy*, for instance, saw common ground in the mingling of the actual and the imaginary. *Septimius* ended more satisfactorily but its melodrama "rather interferes with the tranquil manifestation of the spiritual truths of the conclusion."

Leslie Stephen called Septimius a "rather disagreeable hero"; to the *Overland* he was "a rhapsodic madcap," a "visionary fanatic or lunatic—or perhaps a cross between the two"; and both the *Galaxy* and the *Independent* stressed his unattractiveness. The *Albion*, on the contrary, considered him as skillfully drawn as Hester Prynne. And both Lathrop and the *Literary World* praised Hawthorne for telling the story through Septimius's sensibility. Rose inspired little comment except for a general understanding that the change of her relationship to Septimius was excusable in an unfinished work. The *Southern Magazine* described Sybil Dacy as "one of Hawthorne's own psyche-moths," while she seemed to the *Academy* too slightly developed to be effective. Aunt Keziah inspired the most vigorous reactions: she was "the best character in the book" (*Athenæum*), the "greatest failure of all" (*Southern Magazine*), an unusual mixture successfully presented (*Albion*), "not at all weird, but altogether grotesque, and rather vulgarly so at that" (*Southern Magazine*). Her death scene the *Times* considered memorable, but to the *Literary World* it was "one of the most repulsive episodes." In reactions that may not be wholly antithetical, the *Overland* described Aunt Keziah and Dr. Portsoaken as "two other full-fledged lunatics" while they seemed to the *Galaxy* more distinctly drawn than Hawthorne's major characters.

Two other comments must suffice. The *Saturday Review* recognized in the figure of Septimius a possible reflection "of Hawthorne himself, and of the consequences of the revolt of a fine but ill-balanced nature against the prosaic realism of modern life." And Higginson suggested that Hawthorne abandoned the romance because he could not instill in Septimius "a more unselfish ambition," a "generous impulse," to animate his wish for immortality. Whether or not the failure was of moral vision, it seemed to Higginson "a defect of art." Neither critique penetrated sufficiently to carry much weight; the two views were, however, characteristic of the common strains of biographical and moral-aesthetic interpretation.

By comparison, the *Dolliver* fragments received virtually

no critical attention.[55] The first chapter when separately published in England as *Pansie* was greeted cordially by the *Athenæum*. "All the signs, and therewith the warrant, of a great master may be found in this sketch," not of Pansie herself but of "Dr. Dolliver, who stands . . . like a rich, dark, mellow, mystic, and yet real, figure before a grand but gloomy background of a picture by Rembrandt." The *Examiner* described the chapter as "A charming little bit of Hawthorne," and the *Reader* conjectured that had it been completed, it "would certainly . . . have been the chief work of one of the most finished of American prose-writers"; both notices thereupon filled the bulk of their space with quotation. When *The Dolliver Romance and Other Pieces* appeared in 1876, it competed for attention with *Fanshawe and Other Pieces*, and since the contents of the simultaneously issued volumes were largely reprints, they were usually given summary treatment at best. *Appleton's* and the *Boston Daily Advertiser* merely cited the titles; the *Literary World* was content to summarize the third *Dolliver* fragment, published for the first time. The *Boston Evening Transcript* described the chapters as "powerful" but said little else. The *New York Tribune* review, written probably by the sympathetic Bayard Taylor, recognized *Dolliver* as "another form of the same conception which we find in 'Septimius Felton' " and declared that if Hawthorne had been able to complete

[55] This discussion draws on reviews and notices of *Pansie* in *Athenæum*, No. 1924 (September 10, 1864), 338; *Examiner*, No. 2953 (September 3, 1864), 569; *Reader*, IV (September 10, 1864), 325; and of *The Dolliver Romance and Other Pieces* in *Appleton's Journal*, n.s. I (August, 1876), 190; *Boston Daily Advertiser*, June 30, 1876, 2:2; *Boston Evening Transcript*, June 21, 1876, 6:1; *Independent*, XXVIII (July 13, 1876), 11; *Literary World*, VII (July, 1876), 18–19; *New York Tribune*, July 7, 1876, 6:1.

it, *Dolliver* would have surpassed *Septimius*. The *Independent* went even further to predict that it would "have proved his greatest work." Subsequent criticism has dealt sparsely with these unfinished efforts, and even Davidson's descriptions of the manuscripts Hawthorne produced in his poignant attempts to find an effective vehicle for his "elixir" theme do not seem to have prompted systematic return to the evidence. Now, however, scholars and critics have before them the complete textual evidence on which to base judgments affecting Hawthorne's last manuscripts as they compare in thought and manner with his other work, finished and unfinished.

C. M. S.

E. H. D.

TEXTUAL COMMENTARY

MANUSCRIPT COPY-TEXTS FOR THE
CENTENARY EDITION

"Septimius" Manuscripts

HAWTHORNE WROTE two untitled drafts of the "Septimius" story, the second and longer of which is incomplete. They are here reproduced in full, with supplied titles drawn from the form of the protagonist's name dominant in each draft—Septimius Felton in the first, Septimius Norton in the second. Duplication in pagination of the first draft is indicated below (but not in Hawthorne's manuscript) by superscripts preceding the page number.

First Draft ("Septimius Felton"): Written in a small hand on 47 leaves of white laid paper, 9¾ by 7¾ inches, with oval blindstamp of a locomotive and tender above "P & P"; chain lines are approximately 1³⁄₁₆ inch apart. Paginated by Hawthorne 2–94, with page 38 numbered 37. A leaf comprising pages 67–68 was lost when the 1872 edition of *Septimius* (U.S. title *Septimius Felton*) was being prepared from this draft, and its text ('ideas. . . . suspiciously', Centenary 127.10–131.28) is here published for the first time. A sheet accompanying this draft contains a note by Stephen H. Wakeman stating that four additional pages were missing when he acquired the manuscript from Julian Hawthorne but that he secured them later from another owner. Wakeman did not identify the pages, but a further note in a librarian's hand gives them as pages 9–12, and differences in guards bear out that statement. The division of the draft between libraries is as follows: pages 1–¹37, ²37, 39–66, 69–94 (Morgan); pages 67–68 (Berg).

On an additional leaf following page 94, Sophia Hawthorne has pencilled "Septimius From 1 to page 96/Rose and I have read to 108 p." These terminal page numbers could not apply to Hawthorne's manuscript, and one is tempted to associate them with a transcript, of which there is an extant fragment. Pages 1–63 of this transcript (Centenary 3.1—53.33), in Sophia's hand save for a few insertions by Una, have survived (Berg), and signature markings show that it was used as printer's copy for English book publication of *Septimius*; stint marks could have been made by compositors of the book or of the antecedent serialization in *Saint Pauls*. Additions and corrections written into Hawthorne's draft in Sophia's hand appear only among the pages represented by the extant Sophia transcript, but whether her copying was limited to these surviving pages cannot be determined. In any case, the page numbers in Sophia's pencilled note reflect an undefined relationship with a larger proportion of the work. Her son-in-law George Parsons Lathrop, in his Introductory Note to the Riverside edition of *Septimius Felton* (Boston, 1883), XI, 221, said that she took up the romance in 1870 and that after her death in February, 1871, the transcript "was completed by her daughters." Una has usually received credit for the enterprise because the preface bears her signature. But from Sophia's pencilled notation and from Lathrop's testimony, it appears that Rose should not be overlooked even though her precise contribution may never be known. The same is true of Robert Browning, whom Una thanked in her preface for his assistance in "interpreting the manuscript, otherwise so difficult for me," but who described his help as "insignificant" in a note to Una. Documentary evidence is lacking to show just what he did in Una's behalf.

Second Draft ("Septimius Norton"): Written closely in a very small hand—often ten manuscript lines to the inch—on 29 leaves, 9¾ by 7¾ inches, of the same white laid stock as used for the "Septimius Felton" draft. Paginated by Hawthorne 1–57; [58] blank except for Sophia Hawthorne's pencilled note: "Septimius/from 1/To page 57", which may mean no more than that she had read the manuscript (Morgan).

A supplement to the draft is represented by a single leaf of white laid paper, 8 by 4¹⁵⁄₁₆ inches, with blindstamp of a griffon, marked by Hawthorne "25 (additional)". It contains a conversation between Septimius and an old man of Concord amplifying a summary paragraph on MS page 25 of the "Norton" draft and is interpolated into the Centenary text (295.14–299.23) as Hawthorne's note prescribes (Morgan).

Ancillary Documents: Associated with the "Septimius" story are eight brief memoranda (here labeled Study 1 through Study 8 for identification) and a précis that we have called a Scenario. It should be stressed that the present ordering of the several Studies carries no authorial sanction but does reflect a progressive development of plot and character, as described in the Historical Commentary.[1]

---

[1] This ordering of "Septimius" Studies differs from that of Edward H. Davidson, *Hawthorne's Last Phase* (New Haven, 1949) as follows:

Centenary	Davidson 1949
1	A
2*	B
3	C
4	D
5	H
6	G
7	F
8	E

* Contains also the closing paragraph of Davidson D.

Study 1: A folio of white laid paper stock used in "Septimius" drafts and Scenario, folded to make two leaves 9¾ by 7¾ inches. The upper left corner of the first recto contains an oval blindstamp of a locomotive and tender above "P & P". Closely written over both sides of each leaf (Berg).

Study 2: A single leaf, 7¼ by 4⅜ inches, of white wove paper, inscribed in black ink on recto and and verso (Morgan).

Although conjectural, it seems strongly possible that this Study continues and concludes with a paragraph on the sheet containing Study 4 (the paragraph is set off from Study 4 by being inverted, and is unrelated to it in content; conversely in its congruity of subject matter with Study 2, especially the close-knit references to the protagonist's beloved, the passage seems to follow naturally and is here transferred to conclude Study 2).

Study 3: A trimmed leaf of white laid paper, 8⅛ by 5⅛ inches, with chain lines approximately 1 inch apart. Inscribed in black ink on recto and verso; damaged by a small hole near foot and a tear at foot affecting two words in final sentence; two horizontal folds and fragments of sealing wax on verso indicate mailing, confirmed by particles of envelope flap glued to verso (Berg).

Study 4: A single leaf, 8 by 5 inches, of white laid paper, torn from a larger sheet, leaving the right edge of the recto rough. Horizontal chain lines are approximately ¾ inch apart. Hawthorne's initial inscription, occupying the top third of the recto, is a paragraph that appears to conclude Study 2 and is discussed above as part of the manuscript description of that Study. One can assume that subsequently Hawthorne picked up the leaf, and inverting it, wrote Study 4, filling the verso and concluding in the available space on the recto, marking it off from the earlier inscription with a row of asterisks. Centered above the opening paragraph is a now cryptic notation "X/X", and immediately to its right is a symbol resembling "N" which is perhaps intended as an insertion sign; it accompanies an adjacent sentence squeezed into the top margin, but no corresponding sign appears further along in the text to indicate an insertion point (Huntington).

An undated pencilled transcript of this entire sheet (except for the squeezed-in sentence just noted), evidently in the hand of Julian Hawthorne, is in a folio diary of his that bears a printed date of 1880; the paragraph we associate with Study 2 is written on a separate page headed "Sept. 2" (University of California, Berkeley).

Study 5: Two leaves of white wove paper, 7$\frac{3}{16}$ by 4$\frac{3}{8}$ inches, inscribed in black ink on rectos and versos, unnumbered except for "2" above the opening paragraph. The leaves may represent an original folio split apart at some time (Morgan).

Study 6: A single leaf of white wove paper, 5$\frac{1}{8}$ by 4$\frac{1}{16}$ inches, inscribed in black ink on recto and verso (Morgan).

Study 7: Two leaves of blue wove paper, the first 7$\frac{3}{4}$ by 4$\frac{15}{16}$ inches and the second 7$\frac{3}{4}$ by 4$\frac{3}{4}$ inches, inscribed in black ink on rectos and versos. The leaves may represent an original folio split apart at some time and subsequently trimmed; the first leaf shows evidence of such a tear. Centered at top of first recto is the marking "X XXXX", which may bear some relation to the symbol that heads Study 4. At the foot of the second verso, inverted, Hawthorne at some time scribbled "Warwick—Redfern—Old Curiosity-shop," referring not to the Septimius story but to details concluding his essay "About Warwick," which he sent off on October 5, 1862, for publication in the December *Atlantic Monthly*. It cannot be determined whether the Study or the scribble came first, and the probable terminal date established for the latter is no help in dating the former (Morgan).

Study 8: A folio now split into two leaves of white laid paper with cubed pattern, the lines three to an inch, originally a letter of November 5, 1861, from James T. Fields on the two rectos, asking Hawthorne's permission to list the forthcoming romance in his *Atlantic* prospectus for 1862. The first three sentences of the Study are written between Fields's paragraphs on the initial recto, the remainder on the two versos. Vertical and horizontal folds indicate mailing form (Morgan).

Scenario: Two leaves, 9¾ by 7¾ inches, from the same white laid stock as that used for "Felton" and "Norton" drafts and similarly blindstamped; inscribed on both rectos and versos; after filling the second verso Hawthorne concluded the Scenario in the top margin of the first recto (Morgan).

The Dolliver Romance Manuscripts

Hawthorne wrote only three segments of this, his last fictional effort. The familiar title, though not found in the manuscript, is validated by the form of his references to the work in two letters. Because he labeled the initial segment as a chapter we have extended the designation to the other two (untitled) parts, conventionalizing Hawthorne's arabic into his usual roman numerals and omitting periods after chapter titles and numbers.

Chapter I: Written in a fairly large, clear hand on both sides of twelve leaves of white laid paper, trimmed to 8⅝ by 7 inches and paginated 1–24. Compositors' marks indicate that this was Hawthorne's fair copy prepared for publication. His heading *"Fragments of a Romance./*Chapter 1./ The Brazen Serpent." has been crossed out and replaced by "A scene from the Dolliver Romance" pencilled in at the top of the page by another hand (Concord Free Public Library).

Ink has faded in substantial parts of the first six pages, but ultraviolet photography has somewhat enhanced the dimmest passages, allowing a reading of all except Centenary 449.5–21, for which copy-text is *Atlantic Monthly*, XIV (July, 1864), 101.

The *Dolliver* draft passages printed among Ancillary Documents (pp. 550 ff. above) include an earlier state of the four final paragraphs of the chapter and a further variant of the close. On the first of these see also the following paragraph.

Chapter II: Written on five leaves, 9¾ by 7¾ inches, of the same white laid stock used for both "Septimius" drafts. The chapter occupies pages 10–18 of a manuscript wanting pages 1–8; page 9 and the top half of 10 represent in rough draft the four closing paragraphs of Chapter I, followed immediately by Chapter II in an equally rough state. Page 18 has been inscribed, inverted, on a sheet paginated "9" and containing a variant version of a passage on Dr. Swinnerton with which the chapter concludes; this latter page number implies that a draft of the entire chapter, otherwise lost, may lie behind the extant manuscript (Morgan).

Chapter III: This fragment was written on eight leaves of the same white laid paper, 9¾ by 7¾ inches, as used for the preceding chapter. The manuscript, also a rough draft, is paginated 11–25, [26] blank, and begins in mid-sentence; the missing pages represent something like a chapter in extent, and one may conjecture that it could logically have ended on MS 14 (Centenary 483.14). What follows could then have been considered a fourth segment of the story except that there is no sign of a break in the manuscript at this point (Morgan).

Ancillary Documents: Associated with the composition of *Dolliver* (whether they preceded or accompanied his chapter drafting cannot be determined) are eleven brief memoranda, here labeled Studies 1–11 for identification. The ordering of the series carries no authorial warrant, but does reflect such sequential development as the evidence offers.[2] The Julian Hawthorne collection contains pencilled transcripts of six *Dolliver* Studies—three by Sophia Hawthorne (Studies 4, 5, and 9) on loose scratch paper, and three evidently by Julian (Studies 7, 10, and 11) in his folio diary bearing a printed date of 1880 (University of California, Berkeley).

Study 1: A single leaf, 7¾ by 4 inches, torn or cut from a sheet of white laid paper used generally for Hawthorne drafts of the 1860s; vertical chain lines approximately 1¾₆ inch apart; right recto edge unevenly cut, left and top edges roughly torn; inscribed on both sides of the leaf. Part of what may be a signature appears along the right edge of the verso (Huntington).

Study 2: A sheet folded along the short axis to form two leaves 6 by 3¹³⁄₁₆ inches. The upper lefthand corner of the first recto contains an embossed seal within which is the

---

[2] This labeling of *Dolliver* Studies differs from that in Davidson, *Hawthorne's Last Phase*, as follows:

Centenary	Davidson *1949*
1	A
2	F
3	
4	B
5	
6	D
7	G
8	E
9	
10	C
11	H

name of the stationer, "DE LA RUE & CO LONDON." The sheet was originally a letter of July 22, 1863, from Fields regarding printer's proof of Hawthorne's *Our Old Home* and the reception of his "Civic Banquets," in the August *Atlantic* just issued. The (unpaginated) letter occupies page 1 and the top quarter of page 3; Hawthorne's notes fill page 2, the available portion of page 3, all of page 4, and conclude with one line at the top of page 1 above Fields's salutation. A line of loose ovals and crosses precedes Hawthorne's opening paragraph (Huntington).

Study 3: A single leaf, 7 by 4⅞ inches, originally a letter from Fields, undated but assignable to July 3, 1863, on the basis of a related note Hawthorne wrote Sophia later the same day (MS, Huntington Library), concerning proof of either "Civic Banquets" or *Our Old Home*. Inverting the leaf, Hawthorne began his inscription on the verso and concluded on the recto interlining Fields's note. The verso retains faint traces of pencillings erased before the inked Study was written; they represent revisions of Hawthorne's prefatory letter dedicating *Our Old Home* to Franklin Pierce, and are to be dated within the fortnight preceding July 18, 1863, the date on which Hawthorne submitted his revised text of the dedicatory preface (Mrs. Phyllis Gordan).

Study 4: A sheet of light blue laid paper watermarked "Whatman 1855" folded to make two leaves, 8¾ by 5⅜ inches. The first recto contains a letter of June 16, 1863, from Ticknor & Fields. Hawthorne's notations fill the other three pages (Berg).

Study 5: This memorandum appears to have survived only in a seven-page transcript, which Sophia Hawthorne pencilled on scratch paper approximately 8¾ by 5½ inches. The first three and one-quarter pages, headed "Grimshawe or Dolliver", are a copy of *Dolliver* Study 4. Study 5, labeled here "Another scrap", is on pages 4–6, and Study 9, "Still another bit", occupies pages 6–7 (University of California, Berkeley).

Study 6: A single leaf, 8 by 5¼ inches, of white laid paper with vertical chain lines an inch apart; the right recto edge has been torn. Inscribed on both sides of the leaf (Huntington).

Study 7: A single leaf, 8 by 5 inches, bearing a blind-stamp oval belt surrounding a shield with "Superfine" around the top curve; originally a note evidently to Sophia Hawthorne signed "Geo. Sumbner & Co., Boston," and dated August 27, 1863, concerning Marseilles fabric the firm could not supply. The signature is obscure and cannot be verified from current Boston directories. Hawthorne's inscription, inverted, fills both sides of the sheet. Centered above the beginning of the Study is "2" in Hawthorne's hand (Berg).

Study 8: A single leaf, 7⅝ by 4¾ inches, of white laid paper, with vertical chain lines 1⅜₆ inch apart; uneven on right recto, as if torn from a larger sheet; inscribed on both sides (Morgan).

Study 9: "Still another bit"; see note for Study 5, above. Sophia Hawthorne transcript (University of California, Berkeley).

Study 10: A sheet folded to make two leaves, 8 by 5 inches, with blindstamp of anchor in shield on the first recto, containing on the rectos a letter of July 6, 1863, from H. P. Ross of Albany, New York, requesting Hawthorne's autograph. The Study fills the available space on all four unnumbered pages, beginning at the foot of 3, proceeding through 4, the top of 1, all of 2, and concluding at the top of 3 (Berg).

Study 11: A single leaf, 7½ by 4¾ inches, originally a note of September 18, 1863, from Hawthorne's Salem friend, David Roberts, acknowledging a presentation copy of *Our Old Home*. The Study, preceded by three crosshatches, begins on the verso, inverted, and concludes on the recto, crossing Roberts's inscription (Berg).

PRINTED COPY-TEXT FOR THE CENTENARY EDITION

A passage near the beginning of *The Dolliver Romance*, Chapter I, represented by Centenary 449.5–21, has faded into invisibility and, being unrecoverable by present technology, is here supplied from the periodical text that Hawthorne saw in proof, *Atlantic Monthly*, XIV (July, 1864), 101.

A NOTE ON EDITORIAL PRACTICES

This edition of the "Septimius Felton" and "Septimius Norton" drafts, together with their loosely related sequel, the three segments of *The Dolliver Romance*, reproduces Hawthorne's working papers (unfinished save for fair copy of the first *Dolliver* chapter) with as close an approach to the ideal of a clear text as is possible. We have, however, used angle brackets to set off his intercalary notes and directions to himself, describing the manuscript position of each in an Alterations entry. Most frequently he inserted such passages between paragraphs and they are usually so placed here; those interlined within paragraphs appear in the Centenary text at the point dictated by the logic of the context. An exception is made of those notes heading the first page of both "Septimius" drafts, where for considerations of Centenary format the bracketed notes follow rather than precede the first paragraph. Hawthorne's verbal directions or graphic signs for rearranging narrative elements we have removed from the text to an Alterations entry that describes the change and cites the authority for it; if reordering cannot be carried out because it would entail rewriting, Hawthorne's directions are retained in the text.

Emendations are made only of inadvertent errors that could create confusion and of misspellings resulting from careless inscription; acceptable variants and inconsistencies in compounding or captalization have been retained. Except for silent elimination of variant spacing in contractions, all Centenary changes are recorded in the list of Editorial Emendations.

Emendation of Substantives. These include (1) additions necessary to sense: "might yielded" becomes Centenary "might have yielded", "to done" becomes "to be done", "there certain" becomes "there were certain", "seemed be" becomes "seemed to be"; (2) elimination of dittography: "with with" becomes "with"; (3) correction of a patently miswritten word, such as "establing", "competetent", "becaused", or carelessly inscribed forms such as "seeed", "whic", "firesdes"; (4) correction of a miswritten construction, such as "as I ever I was", "an madly", "thought I a"; (5) the completion of words divided at MS line-end and left unfinished: "produc-|" emended to "productive", and the normalization of such anomalies as "be-|before", "indel-|ble", "bot-|ttle". All such changes are recorded in the list of Editorial Emendations.

Emendation of Accidentals. The following emendations of punctuation are recorded in the list of Editorial Emendations: the addition of a missing element in pairs of parentheses (as at 209.2); the addition or deletion of punctuation (as at 387.13, 87.20); and the replacement of one mark by another (as at 121.1).

Inconsistencies and Anomalies Preserved. These include personal names which Hawthorne changed within or between drafts: Septimius Felton|Norton|Hilliard Veren; Aunt Kezia(h)|Zezia(h)|Nashoba; Portsoaken|Ormskirk; Robert Hagburn|Hagbourn|Hagdorn; and the several designations of the British soldier; Dolliver|Dorsey; Pansie|Pansy|Posie. Such acceptable variant spellings as "moccoson"|"moccosson", "powwow"|"powow", "vallies", "journies", are retained along with an archaic adverbial use of "abrupt"; also preserved are inconsistencies in compounding, such as "hillside"|"hill-side"| "hill side".

Reordering of Passages. Hawthorne's drafts reflect constant revision of his original inscription. In addition to his usual habit of writing over wiped-out words, he often inserted a change above or following a cancelled passage. Sometimes he interlined substitute readings without cancelling the superseded language. Here except for the fair copy of *Dolliver*, Chapter I, Hawthorne continued to employ additional modes of revision evident in "Etherege" and "Grimshawe": when he wished to transpose passages he might use such rubrics as "(See below about Aunt Nashoba's story.)" and "(Insert before Aunt N's story what is at the end.)", also sometimes marking with arrowhead pointers the beginning and end of affected passages. He used other transpositional signs—vertical lines, diagonal lines, two- or three-tiered carets, occasionally a simple connecting line indicating a revised sequence—with or without verbal rubrics. Revisions thus directed or implied have been made in the Centenary text, and entries in the Alterations list set out the authorial sanction for all such changes; verbal rubrics are then reproduced in the list and not retained in the text. Transpositions are occasional in "Septimius Felton," frequent in "Septimius Norton," and rare in the *Dolliver* draft chapters.

Physical Division within Manuscripts. Hawthorne's "Septimius" Scenario, reflecting the content of the "Septimius Felton" draft, divides the story into fifteen scenes, and thus offers a basis for breaking the narrative in the interest of reader convenience; occasional divisions marked by Hawthorne are duly noted in the Alterations list. The same general principle of scene division has been followed by the editors in determining division points in "Septimius Norton." The problem does not arise with *Dolliver*, where three discrete manuscripts define a pattern of organization.

C. M. S.

EDITORIAL EMENDATIONS
IN THE COPY-TEXT

Every editorial change from copy-text is listed here. For each entry, the Centenary reading is at the left of the bracket and the rejected reading follows the bracket. An asterisk * indicates that an accepted emendation appears in the manuscript but was not made by Hawthorne; the list of Alterations in the Manuscripts contains an entry giving details. A vertical slash | indicates the end of a manuscript line. In recording punctuation emendation, a wavy dash ∼ represents a word before the bracket, and a caret ∧ indicates the absence of a punctuation mark in the manuscript. A crux is reported at 240.11 in 'could make up to the dead youth'; 'make up' is derived from a parallel passage in the Felton draft; copy-text inscription appears to be a non-word, 'erap'.

SEPTIMIUS FELTON

3	MS *page is headed* Begin.
3.5	decay,] ∼;
3.5	called] caled
*3.9	who] whom
4.18	in] in in
4.31	two-story, gabled house] two-story house, gabled house
5.4	well-to-do] ∼∧∼ – ∼

5.6	although] althought
5.6	there] they
5.13	homestead,] ~;
5.18	baccalaureate] baccalaurate
5.21	stead.] ~∧
6.13	speculations] spephelations
6.22	slighter] slighetr
6.25	"Slighter] ∧~
7.3	"For] '~
7.7	existence)] ~,
7.11	sweet.] ~∧
7.16	Yes] Yet
7.17	gloomily] gloomly
7.23	solemnity] solemity
7.24	buoyant] buyoant
8.2	you?"] ~. ∧
8.11	live?] ~.
8.13	know.] ~∧
8.15	many, many] ~∧ ~
8.16	rest."] ~. ∧
8.25	No,] ~∧
8.27	"Oh] '~
9.1	red-lipped,] ~ – ~∧
9.2	gentle.] ~∧
9.4	ugly,] ~∧
9.28	up,] ~∧
10.2–3	scholarship] scolarship
10.3	for which] ~—~
10.14	desk] deask
10.18	you,] ~∧
10.27	within.] ~∧
10.29	so."] ~. ∧
10.30	it?] ~,
11.5	trusted] truted
11.26	contrivance] contrvance
11.27–28	spiritual?] ~.
11.28	day] idea
12.16	"I] ∧~

12.25	us?] ~.
13.17	is] *omit*
13.24	What] "~
14.8	ripening] repining
14.16	thitherward.] ~∧
14.18	housekeeper] houseker
14.20	inattentive] attenti- |tive
14.27	"Nephew] '~
15.1	"and] ∧~
15.9	Septimius.] ~∧
15.13	man,] ~∧
*15.27	of] *omit*
16.7	communities] communites
16.16	soldiers'] ~∧
16.18	it.] ~∧
16.20	Fools] Foos
17.2	King's] King
17.12	ennobling] enobling
17.14	seemed] seemes
17.20	greens,] gre[*blot*]
17.22	heroes] heoes
17.32	studies] students
18.4	"Septimius] ∧~
18.6	heads?] ~.
18.9	man.] ~∧
18.11	are! They] are!", they
18.15	¶ Whether] *no* ¶
18.24	its] it's
18.27	he] the
19.8	too, and] too, [*blot*]
*19.14	been] *omit*
19.18	village?] ~.
19.24	Rose.] ~;
19.27	"Oh] '~
19.27	"Look] ∧~
19.31	approached] approach
20.2	time,] ~∧
20.6	alarum! The redcoats] ~! ~ read coats

20.15	"Hark] ∧⁓
*20.21	deal of courage] deal courage
20.22	redcoats] readcoats
20.31	of] *omit*
21.1	redcoats] red∧ | coats
21.15	"Human] '⁓
21.23	boy,] ⁓∧
21.27	great] ⁓,
21.30	fiercely.] ⁓∧
22.1	get such] get as such
22.3	Septimius] ⁓"
22.22	she.] ⁓∧
22.23	"Perhaps take] '⁓ ⁓
23.8	brevity?] ⁓.
23.19	book; he could] ⁓; ⁓ coud
23.22	was] is was
23.31	in] *blot*
24.2	sound] soud
*24.22	veiled it.] veiled.
24.23	shots,] ⁓∧
24.29	strange it] ⁓, ⁓
25.9	curses] curse
25.12	which] w whic
25.13	much as a] much a
25.18	one] on
25.20	side] aside
26.2	and levelled] and, at levelled
26.8	Septimius's] Septimius
26.11	Ah,] ⁓,"
26.11	you,"] ⁓∧ ∧
26.16	Come;] ⁓∧
26.24	officer.] ⁓∧
26.27	prisoner."] ⁓. ∧
26.33	Come;] ⁓∧
27.2	command] comman
27.2	Fire!] ⁓∧
27.4	antagonist] antagonists
27.5	Septimius] ⁓,

27.5	were] wher
27.22	perhaps] pepaps
27.28	stump,] ∼.
28.3	had ceased] had | had ceased
28.4, 23	young] yung
28.5	home;] ∼∧
28.25	dying,] ∼.
28.27	spoils] spoil
28.27	according] accords
29.7	contemptuous] contempetuous
29.13	"with] ∧∼
29.26	falls.] ∼∧
*30.5	of] omit
30.8	"I] ∧∼
30.11	read] omit
30.12	paper."] ∼.∧
30.13–14	that through] that thrugh
30.15	straight] strait
30.21	side.] ∼∧
*30.25	enough] omit
31.16	praiseworthy] paraiseworthy
31.24	strength] strengh
31.24	among] ammong
31.31	What good could] Whist could
32.3	fail?] ∼.
32.6	an] a
32.11	earthiness] earthness
32.20	imagination] imgination
32.33	as] omit
33.8	afflicted] afficted
33.9	immortality.] ∼∧
33.20–21	toil, . . . him,] ∼∧ . . . ∼∧
*33.22	listen to the] listen the
33.27	shooting] ∼,
33.33	pebbles] pebbbles
34.2	voice] omit
34.3	here?] ∼.
34.4	minister.] ∼∧

34.18	death] dead
34.18	publicly] publikly
34.20	"Yes] '~
34.27	"A] '~
34.30	think, Septimius,] ~ₐ ~ₐ
*35.6	as] *omit*
35.14	Septimius.] ~,
35.19	"though] ₐ~
36.10	himself.] ~ₐ
36.19	in] on
37.17	him,] ~;
38.5	out,] ~ₐ
38.7	thing!] ~?
38.8	so; does] ~?"; ~
38.8	stories?"] ~?'
38.9, 12	Yes, Rose,] ~; ~;
*38.24	did it] did
38.25	with] with	with
38.27	spirit,] ~.
39.31	nature,—] ~, ₐ
40.13–14	devilishness] devlishness
*40.17	not] *omit*
41.4	this] ths
41.15	their] thir
41.27	Hagburn,] ~ₐ
42.4	hurt?] ~!
42.19	purse] purpose
42.30	to] it
*43.29	been] *omit*
43.30	cheerful] cherful
43.31	young] youg
44.11	because] becaused
44.14	by his] by by his
44.17	possessor?] ~.
44.24	was,] ~;
44.29	and] *omit*
44.31–32	thereafter] thereafeter

45.11	pursuits] pursuts
45.15	ministerial] ministrial
45.18	an] a
45.23	Septimius's] Septimius
*45.26	by] *omit*
46.4	Why,] ~∧
46.10	alone.] ~∧
46.16	"that] ∧~
46.19	"so] ∧~
46.22	But, Septimius,] ~∧ ~∧
46.23	path?] ~.
46.30	valleys] vallys
47.3	covered] coverd
47.3–4	valley] vally
47.11	enclosure] enlosure
47.18	he.] ~∧
47.20	"except] ∧~
47.22	mother!"] ~!'
47.26	it,] ~∧
47.27	present."] ~. ∧
47.30	"who] ∧~
48.21	is of] is of	of
49.6	Latin] latin
49.7	interspersed] intespersed
49.9	unintelligible] unintelli-	gble
49.10	erudition] erurdition
49.11	pressing] prressing
49.17	affair,] ~∧
49.30	inherited—] ~—,
49.31	receive] recive
50.3	it?] ~.
50.4	egotism,] ~∧
50.8	him] his him
50.13	were—] ~,
50.17	because] Because
50.19–20	power of a telescope] powers of telescope
50.21	individual] ndivdual

50.21	brilliancies.] ~∧
50.22–23	earnestness of application] earnestness application
50.23	years.] ~∧
52.1	"you] '~
52.5	covering] coving
52.33	that] tha
53.1	prove] proove
*53.2	be] *omit*
53.4	able, to] ~∧ ~
53.14	return] returned
54.1	habiliments] habilments
54.5	battles] batles
54.17	fired] fied
54.27	officer's] officers
55.3	confirmed] confimed
55.14	religion] reliligion
55.18	war?] ~.
55.21	pulpit?] ~.
55.26	use the] use in the
55.29	stretched] streetched
55.32	joining] joiing
56.23	that he] that it
56.28	happy,] ~∧
56.32	secret] scret
57.12	this?] ~,
57.16	frighten] frghten
57.16	Rose?] ~,
57.33	with] with with
58.4	same] *omit*
58.17	blossom;] ~."
58.17	juice.] ~∧
58.29	deep] dep
59.10	life,] ~∧
59.28	society)] ~∧
59.28	"There] ∧~
60.5	Septimius's] Septimius
60.6	be] *omit*

60.12	Septimius,] ~∧
60.21	you] *omit*
60.21	flowers?] ~,
61.22	strange surprise] strange of surprise
61.26	when] which
61.28	exemplification] explemification
62.7	own."] ~.∧
62.10	Septimius's] Septimius
62.11–12	descended] descned
62.26	unsubstantiality] unsubsubstaniality
62.32	her] *omit*
63.9	continually] continally
63.10	by his side] by side
63.23	General] Genal
64.12	-spokenness] -spokeness
64.14	are] *omit*
64.15	Septimius.] ~∧
64.20	see."] ~.∧
66.11	seemed] seemedd
66.20	necessary] neccessary
66.23	ascetic] ascestic
66.28	imperfectly] impefectly
67.9	Septimius's] Septimius
67.32	secret] scret
68.10	spring."] ~.∧
68.24	to-and-fro] ~∧~ – ~
68.24	surprised] surprise
68.26	accustomed] acustomed
69.18	quitted] qutted
70.9	not] *omit*
70.11	suspicion] suspcion
70.23	thoughts?] ~,
70.33	Aunt] aunt
71.2	"Sir] ∧~
71.9	Aunt] aunt
71.18	be] *omit*
71.26	muttering,] ~∧
71.26	curious!] ~?

71.29	what!] ~?
72.5	with] *omit*
72.10	Anything] Any | thing
72.11	receive] recive
72.19–20	least as much] least much
72.28	ushered] usherd
72.33	Portsoaken,] ~ₐ
72.33	himself,] ~ₐ
73.11	roughness] rougness
73.15	Aunt] aunt
73.19–20	examining] examing
74.7	secret] secet
74.8	possession of] possession of it
74.8	therefore] therfore
74.9	subject.] ~ₐ
74.14	one,] ~ₐ
74.14	sitting] "~
74.18	fascination,] ~ₐ
74.21	inquiries] inqui- | ies
74.33–75.2	"I thought . . . down."] (~ ~ . . . ~.ₐ
75.18	continually] continally
75.26	sedulously] sedulouly
76.5	perpetration] perpeptration
76.13	English.] ~ₐ
76.17	purport] puport
76.18	it] *omit*
76.29	potency] poetncy
76.32	Bacon,] ~ₐ
77.8	death?] ~.
77.8	Septimius.] ~ₐ
77.11	at his] at its
77.21	too hard] to hard
78.25	decoction] dedoction
78.30	that?] ~,
78.30	Septimius.] ~ₐ
79.21	great] grat
79.31	perception] percption
80.9	if you ever] if ever

80.10	settle] set- | ttle
80.12	you!"] ~!∧
80.19–20	which was] which he was
80.25	philosopher] phiosophy
81.28	might] *omit*
83.2	it."] ~.'
83.18	it] *omit*
83.25	to] *omit*
83.33	grandfather] granfather
84.3	perfect."] ~.∧
84.4	Aunt] aunt
84.8	admirable),] ~)∧
84.28	nature.] ~;
85.11	weariness of] weariness [*blot*]
85.16	everybody] everbody
85.25	imbibing] imbibeing
85.33	flower.] ~∧
86.6	Septimius's] Septimiuss
86.8	thinking] think- |
86.19	toothsome] tooothsome
86.26	it?] ~.
86.28	"For] ∧~
86.33	agreed] ~,
86.34	recipe] recipee
86.34	manuscript] manscripts
87.6	whereas] wheras
87.16	drinks] dinks
87.19	ingredient?] ~.
87.20	Septimius,] ~,"
88.18	his own] her own
88.18	too,] ~∧
88.22	doubtless] doubless
88.33	to-and-fro] ~ – ~∧~
89.15	possibilities] possibilies
89.23	whereas] wheras
89.33	face.] ~∧
90.2	grave,] ~∧
90.15	answered] answeed

90.19	-beds.] ~ₐ
90.28	bloomed] bloom
90.29	boquet] boqut
91.2	covered] coveed
91.4	"there] ₐ~
91.16	traversing] travesing
91.23	poisonous,] ~;
92.8	more."] ~·ₐ
92.14	incrusted] incruted
92.21	"I] ₐ~
93.10	if to be] if it to be
93.21	if] *omit*
94.2	it] *omit*
94.3	where] wherre
94.7	is] *omit*
94.22	science] silence
95.9	dying] diying
95.20–21	everything,] ~ₐ
95.24	a] *omit*
96.26	offered] offer
97.15	pursued] pursed
98.6	onward] oward
98.15	frame."] ~·ₐ
98.19	elsewhere] elsewere
99.7	potent] poetent
99.15	say] saw
99.22	years] *omit*
100.18	superstition] superstion
100.25	philanthropy] philanthopy
100.32	characteristics] characterstics
101.3	edifice] edefice
101.4	ground] groud
101.12	dispersed] peperd
101.22	script] scipt
101.25	arbitrary] arbitary
101.32	language] Language
102.18	counsel] counsell
102.22	like] like like
102.23	philosopher's] philosophers

102.33	it.] ~∧
103.1	experienced] experience
103.4	happiness] happines
103.9	long—] ~.—
103.14	outline] ouline
104.4	only to itself] only itself
104.13	received] receved
104.15	be] *omit*
104.26	heart.] ~∧
105.7	be] *omit*
105.25	act;] ~,
105.26	habits.] ~∧
106.3	beggars] begars
106.4	ear-shot.] ~ – ~∧
106.12–13	trouble thee,] trouble,
106.14	self-laudation.] ~ – ~∧
106.18	not] ~,
106.21	grow.] ~∧
106.30	arrow,] ~∧
107.7	flowers,] ~∧
107.11	gathered] gatherd
107.20	receive] recive
107.28	too] to
107.30	took it out] took out
108.1	virtue] virture
108.1	incalculable] incalcuble
108.12	there?] ~.
108.14	blossomed] blossomeed
108.32–33	characteristics] charac- | terics
109.11	many] many a
109.11	a great] as great
109.23	seemed] seemd
109.29	fervent] fevent
109.30	rich,] ~∧
110.10	at it with] at with
110.19	health] heath
110.29	whenever] when ever
111.3	acidity,] ~∧
111.13	kitchen.] ~∧

111.15	also] aso
111.17	of] *omit*
111.17	liquor] liqur
111.21	again.)] ~·∧
111.26	of] *omit*
112.6	an] a
112.13	you?] ~.
112.14	neighbor?] ~.
112.15–16	"Damn the Doctor! You can] "Damn the Doctor," can "You can
112.26	quick,] ~∧
112.27	say!"] ~!∧
112.30	well as to] well to
113.5	had for] had fr
113.10	assuage] assauge
113.12	friends?] ~∧
113.17	shredded] shred
114.14	have] have have
114.16	good."] ~·∧
114.18	nostrum.] ~∧
114.19	taint it.] taint.
114.25	lips,] ~.
114.27	but] *omit*
115.3	taste?] ~.
115.4	lose] loose
115.8	don't] dont
115.22	elixir] exlixir
115.22	immortality] mortality
116.22	regular] reg- | ar
116.24	Septimius,] ~∧
116.25	chamber?] ~.
117.11	contrive] contive
117.16	There] Ther
117.22	heroic ecstasy] heoic esctasy
117.24	doubtless] doubless
117.31	and] And
118.27	was] is
118.31	see] she
118.32	No,] ~∧

118.32	doubtless] doubless
119.3	Auntie."] ~·ᴧ
119.7	tomorrow.] ~ᴧ
119.21	for some] for for some
119.25	seemed] semed
119.29	wise] ~,
119.31	behold,] ~ᴧ
119.33	dishevelled] dishelleved
120.10	"That] ᴧ~
120.11	there] there there
120.17	you?"] ~?ᴧ
120.29	Mother] Moter
120.29	witch,] ~ᴧ
120.30	Ai!] ~.
121.1	Kezia?] ~!
121.3	me,] ~ᴧ
121.14	up at] up at up at
121.16	humankind] humanᴧ | kind
121.23	ha!—] ~ᴧ—
121.27	Hearth?] ~.
121.29	times!"] ~!ᴧ
122.3	talk] take
122.19	boughs] bows
122.24	her] his
122.27	from it.] ~ ~ᴧ
122.32	features] featurs
122.33	perceived] percived
123.3	clasped] claped
123.5	trouble] troble
123.13	'twon't] ᴧ~
123.13	worth your] worth while your
123.17	won't] wont
123.19	comes!] ~?
123.19	Septimius.] ~,
123.26	nature.] ~."
123.31	if I should] if should
124.5	Septimius.] ~."
124.22	available] avalable
124.28	dram-] dam-

125.8	meanwhile,] ~∧
125.12	wondered] wondred
126.5	Dacy,] ~∧
126.12	"Do] ∧~
126.12	then?] ~∧
126.13	that,] ~?
126.16	evidently] evdently
126.31	Nature?] ~.
127.1	succeed] suceed
127.10	admit] amit
127.17	off] of
127.26	possibilities] possibiteles
127.26	no] *omit*
127.27	possibilities] possibiteles
128.1	hostility,] ~∧
128.5	humanity] humani-	tity
128.9	individual] invidual
128.11	knew] new
128.12	enlightenment] enlightement
128.20	conglomerated] coglomerated
128.27	bottle] bot-	ttle
128.29	tearful] terarful
129.3	smoke.] ~∧
129.9	was] *omit*
129.20	everyday] every∧	day
130.4	drawn] dawn
130.4	precincts] preincts
130.27	liabilities] liabities
130.29	stubbornness] stubborness
131.9	suffered] suffred
131.15	here] her
131.19	elderly] elde-	ly
131.20	realize] ralize
131.22	there] ther
131.31	a] *omit*
132.1	shouting, "Tory] ~∧ ∧~
132.3	months] month
132.6	everybody] everbody
132.18	may still be] may be still be

132.29	saying,] ~ₐ
132.29	"Come] '~
133.13	doubtless] doubless
133.16	whatever] whihever
133.21	American] Amerian
133.26	same time,] same,
133.31	wondered] *omit*
134.4	web?] ~.
134.5	you,"] ~ₐₐ
134.16	Doubtless] Doubtess
134.27	what brings you] what you brings you
134.28	Boston?] ~.
134.30	production] production
134.32	naturalist] natualit
135.6	locality?] ~.
135.7	know,"] ~,'
135.11	naturalist] natualit
135.11	burning] burig
135.22	else?] ~.
136.8	superstition] superstion
136.15	whether] whither
136.22	practitioner] practioner
136.23	"The] ₐ~
136.29	Portsoaken] Portsoaten
137.2	would] wold
137.3	decidedly] decidely
137.8	scrupulousness.] ~ₐ
137.13	cannot] can
137.16	important] impotant
137.17	'Steep . . . quarter.'] "~ . . . ~."
137.20	given] give
137.21	distil.] ~ₐ
137.23	neglected.] ~ₐ
137.27	through] though
138.19	glows of radiance] glows | radiance
138.23	two pair] four pair
138.24	and] *omit*
139.8	it to be] it be
139.23	see] ~,

139.24	familiar] familar
139.26	intimations.] ~ˎ
139.27	common-sensible] ~ˎ~
139.32	charlatanic] charlaatanic
140.10	but] *omit*
140.19	bottle,] ~ˎ
141.11	race.] ~ˎ
141.17	impenetrable] impentrable
141.26	intermarried] intermried
141.27	succeeded] succeded
142.4	predecessor] predecssor
142.5	for Septimius's] fe Septimius
142.10	found] fond
142.18	succeed] succed
142.31	temporary] temporay
143.13	wonder,"] ~,'
143.13	musingly,) ~ˎ
143.13	are] *omit*
143.25	chest?] ~.
143.27	cabinets?] ~.
143.30	carry] *omit*
143.32	bound] boud
144.3	of] *omit*
144.7	so,] ~ˎ
144.11	records] rcords
144.16	if] of
145.4	not] not not
146.4–5	decoction,] ~ˎ
146.18	he,] ~ˎ
147.5	also,] ~ˎ
147.9	produced] produed
148.5	obscurity] obsurity
148.21	their] he
148.23	collector] colector
148.28	–book.] – ~ˎ
148.29	himself] himsef
149.7	unattainable.] ~ˎ
149.15	owl-like] owlike
149.19	look;] ~,

150.11	unknownness] unknowness
150.16	faces?] ~.
150.24	one] *omit*
151.15	up,] ~⌃
151.16	woman do] woman could do
151.19	ennobling] enobling
151.21	beside] side
151.24	to] *omit*
151.25	away;] ~;"
151.32	now."] ~.⌃
152.14	find out] find it out
152.17	have] *omit*
152.19	fruit] fruiet
152.27	another!"] ~!'
152.30	hereafter] herafter
153.7	"Are] '~
153.12	discovering] Discvering
153.26	–bound] –bund
154.16	found] find
154.24	shrewd] shrew
154.26	forefathers] forefather
155.9	inside] in side
155.9	something] someting
155.13	be.] ~⌃
155.18	been] *omit*
155.21	handling it] handlig in it
155.26	familiarly] familiary
155.30	said,] ~⌃
155.31	"Come] ⌃~
156.5	responsibilities] responsibilites
156.8	you!"] ~!'
156.9	you?] ~?"
156.15	and so] and to
156.20	Robert,] ~;
157.1	undergone] ungdergone
157.4	through] thrugh
157.4	as ever I] as I ever I
157.5	evening] ev- | ning
157.16	thought] though

157.20	discontented] disconted
157.31	soldiers] soldier
158.6	through] thrugh
158.13	Homeric] homeric
158.29	himself,] ~∧
159.6	you?] ~.
159.8	"since] ∧~
159.8	The] "~
159.21	permits] permts
159.27	soon?] ~.
159.28	happinesses?] ~.
159.30	it,] ~∧
160.12	Septimius's] Septimius
160.16	proceeded] proceed
160.23	latter] former
161.5	at all] to all
161.9	connection] conncetion
161.26	murdered] murdred
162.19	incompatible,] ~∧
162.33	of] *omit*
163.2	"Doctor] ∧~
163.3	Juris] Jure
163.11	Elizabeth] Elizabh
163.19	draught] daught
163.23	thereon] therefore
163.27	me] thee
164.1	dependent] depenendent
164.5	this] *omit*
164.14	valley] vally
164.18	if] *omit*
164.22	zenith] zenth
164.31	triumph] trimph
165.2	mad] made
165.12	patriotism] patiotism
165.15	about] abut
165.16	wise] wisely
165.20	as] *omit*
166.3	necessity] necessary
166.4	it] *omit*

166.7	waiting?] ~.
166.9	him.] ~∧
166.14–15	day to day,] day,
166.28	pillion] pinion
166.28	and every] and the every
167.12	pervaded] pevaded
167.23	Museum] museum
167.29	right,] ~∧
168.10	concocted] concoceted
169.14	some] ~,
169.19	thousand years,] thousand,
169.23	goblet?] ~.
169.23	shivered] shiverd
169.27	flushed] fluhed
169.29	Septimius's] Septimius'
170.5	together?] ~∧
170.6	I think] *omit*
170.9	anticipations] anticipiations
170.25	guests] guest
171.20	are] *omit*
171.24	ones."] ~.∧
171.27	that.] ~∧
171.28–29	examining] examing
172.8	dispute] disput
172.15	contrive] contive
172.31	playday?] ~,
172.31	Dacy] Day
173.17	crown] cron
173.31	next?] ~.
174.2	prophecies] phrophesies
174.4	formed] formd
174.5	fingers'] finger's
174.23	once?] ~.
174.26	live] liv
174.27	wickedness."] ~.∧
175.3	me!"] ~!'
175.5	"There] ∧~
175.6	next?] ~.
175.20	do."] ~.'

175.23	steel."] ~·ₐ
176.3	successive] successve
176.10	stale.] ~ₐ
176.14	alarm,] ~;
176.17	matter] mater
176.27	Nature.] nature.
177.11	that?"] ~?ₐ
177.17	conversed] con- | rsed
178.10	"I] ₐ~
178.17	"Bless] ₐ~
178.19	of] *omit*
179.15	anew] ane
179.27	blood.] ~ₐ
179.30	founder] fouder
180.13	Devil] Dvil
180.16	Septimius's] Septimius'
180.23	you] *omit*
180.25	pastor,] ~ₐ
180.31	eyes.] ~."
181.6	looked quiet] looked and quiet
181.16	foot it in] foot in
181.19	travellers] traveller
181.24	Septimius] Sepmius
182.1	"Am] '~
182.1	Septimius?"] ~?'
182.3	"A] ₐ~
182.8	that] *omit*
182.12	poor] ~,
182.18	mysteriousness] mysterious
182.20	light;] ~,
182.23	comparison to] comparison for
182.26	fast!"] ~·ₐ
183.22	fortune,] ~;
183.25	late?] ~,
183.30	by-and-by] ~ – ~ₐ~
184.8	yes;"] ~;ₐ
184.14–15	and a] and in a
184.22	this?] ~.
184.28	halter] hater

184.28	Felton] Feton
184.29	laughed.] ~ᴧ
185.4	reverend] revend
185.5	"I] ᴧ~
185.18	between them;] between;
185.20	in.] ~,
185.22	shiver."] ~.'
185.25	is] *omit*
186.4	Venetians] venetians
186.14–15	choice household] choice hold
186.27	so?] ~.
186.29	pursued] purssued
186.33	offered] offerd
187.11	pity] pretty
187.12	characteristic] characteritic
187.20	remember] rember
187.26	it] they
188.12	an] a
188.13	life?] ~.
188.16	miserable?] miserabl.
189.5	him.] ~."
189.7	drink?] ~.
189.9	moment] momet
189.26	discovered] discoveed
189.29	were the] where the
190.27	loved;] ~;"
190.30	over her] over ther
190.32	No;] ~ᴧ
191.15	kiss.] ~,
191.16	(She] ᴧ~
191.18	But] "~
191.20	be] *omit*
191.21	immortality?] ~!
192.5	rummaged] rumaged
192.11–12	Portsoaken.] ~ᴧ
192.12	amiss."] ~.ᴧ
193.3	Septimius's] Septimius
193.6	bewildered] bewilded
193.20	Septimius,] ~ᴧ

193.25   an] an an
194.3   countryman] county | man
194.10   superstition] superstion

SEPTIMIUS NORTON

195.2   books, ~ₐ
195.7   which] ~,
196.2   thrusting] thruting
196.4   mind,] ~ₐ
196.5   desired,] ~ₐ
196.12   exceptional] exception
196.18   young] youn
196.21   Septimius,] ~ₐ
196.24   objects] object
196.27   intricacies,] ~ₐ
196.28   foliage,] ~ₐ
196.33–197.1 (old conservatives there)] ₐ~ ~ ~ₐ
197.2   steep hill-side] steep side hill-side
197.3   "I] ₐ~
197.3   Septimius] Septimius Septimius
197.14   country] ~)
197.20   rusticity,] ~ₐ
197.21   received] receved
197.26   Norton,"] ~ₐₐ
197.27   salutation] salution
197.27   "—provided] ₐ—~
197.29   faithfully] faithfuly
198.4   are] omit
198.19   possess.] ~ₐ
198.27   as] upon
198.28   it.] ~ₐ
198.30   neglect] neglet
199.7   friend's] friends
199.24   legends] ~)
199.25   for he] for your he
199.27   Poh,] ~;

199.31	they are,] they,
199.32	each] *omit*
199.33	so,] ~∧
200.4	principle] principal
200.5	be] *omit*
200.7	not] *omit*
200.8	"But] ∧~
200.8	upon me,] upon,
200.19	the possibilities] the possibilies
200.29	immortality?"] ~?∧
200.32–33	capabilities] capabites
201.9	individual] individul
201.10	lives."] ~∧∧
201.16	it?] ~∧
201.20	before] be- | before
201.33	how,] ~,"
202.6	friend.] ~∧
202.11	all] al
202.12	by the] by the the
202.21	room] roo
202.22	breathing] brea- | ing
202.27	you.] ~."
203.4	for] *omit*
203.5	sweet enough,] ~ ~∧
203.12–13	and to] and if to
203.26	off,] ~∧
204.9	beliefs] beleifs
204.9	irreverent] irrevent
204.11	man,] ~∧
204.12	sufficient] sufficent
204.21	unexhausted] unexhaused
205.4	him] *omit*
205.5	kettle.] ~ & &.
205.5	After] (after
205.6	(with] ∧~
205.9	Septimius] *omit*
205.11	called it,] called,
205.17	boy. Ask] ~," "~
205.20	it"] ~∧

205.22	him) "and] ~; ∧~
205.24	be a secret] be secret
205.25	Septimius,] ~∧
205.27	decoction] doction
205.32	declining] delcining
206.15	it's made of,] it's,
206.17	himself.] ~∧
206.21	You] "~
206.21	it. You] ~." "~
206.27	Thank] "~
207.2	very] very very
207.9	Nashy,] ~∧
207.14	him, he] him∧ He
207.16	in] of
207.20	time,] ~,"
207.21	moss] *omit*
207.21	epitaphs,] ~∧
207.27	dust.] ~∧
207.30	lion.] ~∧
208.1	as] *omit*
208.16	when the dead] when to the dead
208.20	very,] ~∧
209.1–2	lifetime's] lifetimes
209.2	(Septimius] ∧~
209.8–9	out of some] out some
209.21	streamed] stramed
209.22	old,] ~∧
209.22	see,] ~—
209.26	not have overtopped] not have not overtopped
209.29	felt.] ~∧
210.2	delusions,] ~∧
210.2	sombre] ~,
210.3	results.] ~∧
210.27	Garfield] ~,
211.14	no,] ~.
211.19	Indians?] ~.
211.21	say?] ~.
212.2	be,"] ~,∧
212.3	"that] ∧~

212.9	Phillip's] Phillips
212.13	now?] ∼.
212.28	You,] ∼ˬ
214.4	a] *omit*
214.4	one] *omit*
214.18	were] ∼,
214.24	he] h he
215.12	too.] ∼ˬ
215.21	sight,] ∼ˬ
215.28	"Alarm! Alarm! Alarm!"] ˬ∼! ∼! ∼!ˬ
215.30	them] *omit*
215.32	shouted] should
215.32	"Alarm! Alarm! Alarm!"] "∼! alarm! ∼!"
215.32	—trailing] ˬTrailing
215.33	in] ∼,
216.7	you,] ∼ˬ
216.8	sister.] ∼ˬ
216.10	was the misty] was misty
217.22–23	mother, sister,] ∼ˬ ∼ˬ
218.3	could to keep] could keep
218.7	wakened] wokened
218.13	women.] ∼ˬ
218.21	scouts,] ∼ˬ
218.22	monster,] ∼ˬ
219.2	"and] ˬ∼
219.14	villain] villian
219.16	young man's] young's man
219.26	angel!] ∼!"
220.5	women?"] ∼?ˬ
220.8	make,] ∼ˬ
220.13	sword,] ∼ˬ
220.18	her."] ∼.ˬ
220.19	Norton,] ∼,"
221.6	sword!"] ∼!ˬ
221.19	of] *omit*
221.27	hearty,] ∼ˬ
222.3	"They] ˬ∼
222.9	feeling of a] feeling a
222.16	Seppy,"] ∼,'

222.19	grandfather's] grandfathers
222.21	night?] ~?"
222.21	washerwomen.] ~∧
222.26	meet] met
223.3	nozzle] nuzzle
223.20	are] were
223.28	around] ~,
223.28	is in a] is a
224.7–8	of the] of of the
224.9	thing] *omit*
224.24	sympathies grow] sympathies tend grow
224.31	not?] ~.
225.4	find."] ~∧∧
225.8	as] (~
225.10	establishing] establing
225.12	of] *omit*
225.15	this)] ~))
225.18	deceived] decieved
225.27	is in such] is such
226.9	have] *omit*
226.11	Nashoba,"] ~,'
226.12	pouch,] ~∧
226.23	curiously] curiouly
226.23	with] wit
226.25	&c.] ~∧
227.1	which] which which
227.13	have] *omit*
227.31	barrels,] ~∧
227.32	prophetic,] ~.
228.4	muffled,] ~∧
228.5	ragged,] ~∧
228.6	minute—] ~.—
228.7	mass.] ~∧
228.18	faintly] fainly
228.20	next he] next was he
228.21	was] *omit*
228.22	were] ~,
228.32	Septimius's] Septius's
229.5	poured] bored

229.12	shot."] ~;$_\wedge$
229.23	stagger] stager
229.25	them,] ~.
229.26	track] trak
229.26	road.] ~$_\wedge$
229.28	effect.] ~,
229.33	perceived] peceived
230.1	knees] kneeses
230.15–16	irregularity.] ~$_\wedge$
230.18	great-] ~$_\wedge$
230.24	townspeople.] ~——
230.29–30	temptation,] ~.
230.30	security,] ~$_\wedge$
231.1	young man was] young was
231.2	Satan,] ~$_\wedge$
231.7	were] *omit*
231.17	trunk of a] trunk a
231.18	him,] ~$_\wedge$
231.19	readiness as the] readiness the
231.22	boughs,] ~$_\wedge$
231.23	but] but but
232.1	ground] grund
232.7	Septimius's] Septimius
232.10	he.] ~$_\wedge$
232.13	too] to
232.21	it)] ~$_\wedge$
233.6	"Am] $_\wedge$~
233.14	ground.] ~$_\wedge$
233.20	Now,] ~$_\wedge$
233.24	aim,] ~$_\wedge$
233.27	kick] *omit*
234.3	"Come] '~
234.12	deadly!"] ~! $_\wedge$
234.23	me.] ~."
234.24	Then,] ~;
235.8	up.] ~$_\wedge$
235.9	here,"] ~,'
235.28	me,] ~$_\wedge$
235.29	you,] ~$_\wedge$

235.30	work)] $\sim_\wedge$
236.2	inflicted,] $\sim_\wedge$
236.4	Septimius's] Septimius'
236.24	time.] $\sim_\wedge$
236.32	young] youg
237.4	visible.] $\sim_\wedge$
237.24	intricacies] intracies
237.28	continued.] $\sim_\wedge$
237.30	-place,] - $\sim_\wedge$
238.7	spot."] $\sim._\wedge$
238.17	fellow's] fellows
238.22	penalty] pealty
238.31	grave.] $\sim$."
239.2	was a child] was child
239.5	Amen."] $\sim$.'
239.6	die,] $\sim_\wedge$
239.11	moments] $\sim$,
239.20	he.] $\sim_\wedge$
239.22	dream.] $\sim_\wedge$
240.1	that he] the he
240.3	was] were
240.5	strength] strenght
240.6	probabilities] probabities
240.11	make up] erap
240.19	an] a
240.24	man.] $\sim$;
240.25	It] it
241.16	anticipation] an- | icipation
241.25	-owl's] -owls
241.28	heard in it] heard it
241.28	before.] $\sim_\wedge$
241.31	hill,] $\sim_\wedge$
241.32	her,] $\sim_\wedge$
242.16	Septimius's] Septimius
242.21	instinct] insstinct
242.21	Aunt] aunt
242.22	change] *omit*
242.23	as its] as | as its
242.28	dead?] $\sim$.

243.8	Without a funeral] without a funeral
243.9	Why,] why∧
243.11	it.] ∼∧
243.24	my own] my my own
244.10	owner's] owners
244.16	him."] ∼∧"
244.17	as much] as as much
245.3	surprise.] ∼∧
245.3	was as if] was if
245.19	is] *omit*
245.30	brow?] ∼.
246.10	and the] and the and the
246.14	doubts, . . . idea,] ∼∧ . . . ∼∧
246.27	enough] *omit*
246.27	feet?] ∼,
247.8	know.] ∼∧
247.15	day—] ∼∧
247.17	heard—] ∼∧
247.23	me.] ∼."
247.24	hear it,] ∼ ∼∧
247.27	"It's] ∧∼
247.28	"but] ∧∼
247.29	decorations."] ∼∧∧
247.32	grave,] ∼∧
248.9	visible,] ∼∧
248.18	was] *omit*
248.19	aforesaid,] ∼∧
248.21	in.)] ∼.∧
248.29	rout] route
248.30	All] all
249.2	"You] ∧∼
249.7	rest of] rest of of
249.8	day.] ∼∧
249.9	to do] ∼ - ∼
249.13	Septimius.] ∼∧
249.14	Nashoba?"] ∼?'
249.19	Norton.] ∼,
249.21	staring.] ∼∧
249.28	wax,] ∼∧

249.29	perceived] peceved
250.2	them,] ~ₐ
250.2	had] *omit*
250.14	insensibly] insensably
250.22	"No] '~
250.22	I'll] Ill
250.26	'twill] ₐ~
250.27	you'll take] youll take
250.28	Who] Who's
250.29	be?] ~.
250.30	are] *omit*
250.32	no!"] ~!ₐ
251.21	took the] took to
251.25	mortals;] ~ₐ
252.12	attitude] attude
252.18	to] *omit*
252.23	Nashoba's] Nashobas
252.30	moreover,] ~ₐ
253.3	wizards,] ~ₐ
253.8	origin.] ~ₐ
253.22	evolved] eveovled
253.26	taking] taken
253.33	were] where
254.13	sphere] spere
254.20	receiving] receving
254.24	difficult,] ~ₐ
255.2	manuscript] man- | script
255.5	Septimus.] ~ₐ
255.6	"What] ₐ~
255.6	she.] ~ₐ
255.8	however.] ~ₐ"
255.12	bound] boud
255.17	brother,] ~ₐ
255.19	boy!"] ~!ₐ
255.20	Septimius.] ~ₐ
255.22	neither] neith
255.24	Hagdorn?] ~.
255.31	anxiety] anaxiety
256.1	sober] ~,

256.4	even'g] eveng
256.10	life.] ~∧
256.13	father's] father
256.18	which it sinks] which sinks
256.18	indelible] indel- | ble
257.2	outside.] ~∧
257.19	itself] its
258.1	were] *omit*
258.5	tempests] tempets
258.9	they] thei
258.12	supposed] suppose
258.23	subject] subect
258.25	credited] crdited
258.29	meeting.] ~∧
259.6	annihilate] annilate
259.22	title] tittle
260.23	superstition] superstion
261.8	spoil,] ~∧
261.9	were] *omit*
261.11	have] *omit*
261.33	this] the this
261.33	him] them
262.1	if] if if
262.24	idle,] ~∧
262.25	fishing,] ~∧
263.5	Sparks] sparks
263.6	fits.] ~∧
263.15	the by-word] the the by-word
263.22	himself] *omit*
263.32	produced a] produced a a
264.5	times supplied] times were supplied
264.7	productive] produc- |
264.16	was the] was the was the
265.1	—a ... man—] ∧~ ... ~∧
265.9	into] it
265.12	moments.] ~∧
265.18	other.] ~∧
265.18	brother,] ~∧
265.28	accused,] ~∧

265.29	found guilty, and] foud and guilty and
266.1	do] does
266.10	to] too
266.21	something that] somethat
267.5	Sagamore,] ~ₐ
267.19	store,] ~ₐ
268.2	were] were were
268.17	somehow contracted] somehow had contracted
270.6	ever, inclined] ~ₐ~,
270.7	wished,] ~ₐ
270.28	having] havin
271.21	cause,] ~ₐ
271.31	business-like] ~ₐ~
272.13	young man's] young's man
272.22	in] *omit*
272.22	deposit it there] deposit there
272.32	vanish] vanishing
273.11	irreconcilable] irreconciliable
273.15	dream,] ~;
273.22	mystery;] ~.
273.25	away.] ~ₐ
274.7	wonder,] ~ₐ
276.5	was] *omit*
276.16	be] *omit*
276.27	if] *omit*
276.28	safeguard.] ~ₐ
277.13	air?] ~.
277.18	is, Septimius,"] ~ₐ ~,'
277.23	nature] na- | ure
277.24	yestreday,] Yesterday;
277.24	at] *omit*
277.25	gathering] gatering
278.5	tumultuous] tumultous
278.11	"of] ₐ~
278.16	one,] ~ₐ
278.16	go.] ~ₐ
278.23	Who] Whom
278.25	who] "~
278.32	-balls,] ~ₐ

279.3	firesides] firesdes
279.3	and wither] and with- | and wither
279.5	discontented] disconted
279.13	happily] happiy
279.23	Septimius,] ~;
280.2	yours.] ~."
280.3	minister."] ~ʌʌ
280.13	Septimius,] ~.
280.18	her.] ~ʌ
280.27	that he] that that he
280.29	as] as as
281.23	wonder.] ~ʌ
281.25	"There] '~
281.28	descent] desent
282.19	worn a] a worn a
282.22	quickened] quicked
282.26	as] *omit*
282.30	and even] ~,~
283.2	placid] ~,
283.3	bordered] borderd
283.10	sympathizing] sympathing
283.22	neighbors,] ~ʌ
284.6	than] the
284.6	Septimius's] Septimius
284.19	grave.] ~ʌ
285.4	a war,] a war, a war,
285.13	century,] ~ʌ
285.18	belief] beelief
285.23	by] *omit*
285.24	far] *omit*
285.25	effecting] effected
286.10	dictates.] ~ʌ
286.11	to] *omit*
286.21	moon.] ~ʌ
286.22	foaming] foaing
286.22	fragrance] flagrance
286.28	doing.] ~ʌ
287.1	of yellow] of of yellow
287.5	to] *omit*

288.13	shrill] shill
288.18	to be interested] to interested
289.1	wholly] wholey
289.14	"it] '~
289.16–17	woman at] womat at
289.31	them."] ~.ᴧ
290.15	Septimius,] ~ᴧ
290.16	woodland] wooland
290.30	Septimius's] Septimius
291.3	them] their
291.7	"Your] '~
291.8	You're] Youre
291.23	"Septimius] '~
291.25	afraid] afraiid
291.26	"Dear] '~
292.8	"The use!] '~ ~!
292.14	years?] ~?"
292.22	if it takes] if takes
292.27	It's] Its
292.29	Nashoba] Seppy
292.29	Septimius.] ~ᴧ
293.2	great grandfather's] great grandfathers
293.5	fault."] ~.ᴧ
293.20	principle] principal
293.31	do] to
294.1	almost] almost almost
294.3	no] *omit*
294.12	Septimius's] Septimius
295.3	appalled] apalled
295.17	diseases,] ~.
295.22	I?] ~ᴧ
295.28	child.] ~."
295.30	it] *omit*
295.30	old,] ~ᴧ
295.31	it;] ~ᴧ
296.11	sure,] ~ᴧ
296.21	am] *omit*
297.16	Septimius.] ~ᴧ
297.19	subtle] subte

297.29	strength] strenght
298.8	them.] ~."
298.11	yourselves."] ~.ᴧ
298.15	"my faith] '~ ~
298.18	might?"] ~?ᴧ
298.21	better] "~
298.23	now?] ~,
299.3	weapons.] ~."
299.23	me."] ~.ᴧ
300.3	instructor,] ~ᴧ
300.7	friendly] ~,
300.11–12	had last] had at last
300.19	me.] ~ᴧ
300.27	resemblance.] ~ᴧ
300.30	one.] ~?
301.1	one] *omit*
301.28	advice?] ~.
301.33	quiet] quet
302.6	mind."] ~ᴧᴧ
302.22	country,] ~,"
303.9	this] *omit*
303.28	phosphorescent] phosphoresent
304.7	confusion.] ~ᴧ
304.15	torches,] ~ᴧ
304.25	sprinkled] sprinked
304.25	about,] ~ᴧ
304.29	up";] ~;"
304.30	juice.] ~ᴧ
304.32	it,] *omit*
305.2	bed.] ~ᴧ
305.28	be] bee
306.3	poor] por
306.6	but] but but
306.8	view,] ~ᴧ
306.14	examining] examing
306.20	In] "~
306.29	be] *omit*
306.32	characteristics] characterists
307.20	and] *omit*

307.24	he] her
307.28	not] *omit*
307.29	laughing.] $\sim_\wedge$
308.3	Septimius's] Septimius
308.3	look] looker
308.14	it,] $\sim_\wedge$
308.31	hysterical] hyster- | cal
308.32	it.] $\sim_\wedge$
309.4	of] *omit*
309.14	be] *omit*
309.20	away] way
309.22	with] *omit*
309.29	her] *omit*
310.4	Septimius's] Septimius
310.4	fertile] fertiel
310.9	her;] $\sim_\wedge$
310.10	Home,] $\sim_\wedge$
310.12	nigh] night
311.7	especial] especiall
311.13	somehow] some | how
311.14	him.] her.
312.2	whether] wheth
312.8	her] her her
312.12	"Who] $_\wedge\sim$
312.12	it?] $\sim_\wedge$
312.18	selectmen] select | men
312.18	military] milatry
312.19	mother] motherly
312.22	Septimius.] $\sim_\wedge$
312.23	way] *omit*
312.25	brain-touched] brain | touched
313.8	sympathy"] $\sim_\wedge$
313.10	"She] $(\sim$
313.11	not] *omit*
313.11	it.] $\sim)$
313.26	that,] $\sim_\wedge$
313.26	suppose,] $\sim_\wedge$
313.29	if] *omit*
314.14	sympathies.] $\sim_\wedge$

314.15	Rose,] $\sim_\wedge$
314.16	smiling] "$\sim$
314.22	elements?] $\sim_\wedge$
315.11–12	prospect of] prospect of of
316.7	life.] $\sim_\wedge$
316.22	intelligence,] $\sim_\wedge$
316.24	to] to to
316.28	himself] herself
316.33	blood-stained] blood-stain
317.8	Septimius's] Septimius
317.8	mind,] $\sim_\wedge$
317.25	unrecognized.] $\sim_\wedge$
317.27	likewise,] $\sim_\wedge$
317.30	that she] that it she
318.3	had] *omit*
318.11	him.] $\sim_\wedge$
319.3	neighbor,] $\sim_\wedge$
319.15	medicament,] $\sim_\wedge$
319.26	whatsoever] whatsover
320.2	irregular.] $\sim_\wedge$
320.5	symbolically.] $\sim_\wedge$
320.7	against] again
320.10	Wherefore] Wherefor
320.14	a] an
320.15	great] grat
320.15	lover] love
320.15	country,] $\sim_\wedge$
320.15	a madly] an madly
320.16	whatsoever] whatsover
321.5	unwholesome.] $\sim_\wedge$
321.9	affliction] affiction
321.20	life.] $\sim_\wedge$
321.21	Likewise] likewise
321.27	meat.] $\sim_\wedge$
322.3	increase.] $\sim_\wedge$
322.13	aloft,] $\sim_\wedge$
322.18	things] thing
322.27	moreover] morever
323.7	of] *omit*

323.13	majestic,] ~∧
323.25	contributing] contribting
323.31	writing,] ~∧
324.7	(Insert] ∧~
324.13	winter] winer
325.2	peculiarity] pecliarity
325.4	thought] though
325.10	thought] though
325.17	merriment] mer- | ment
325.29	him] her
325.29	of] *omit*
326.5	came;] ~∧
326.13	or] for
326.19	girl.] ~∧
328.2	ineluctable] ineluctible
328.11	knitting,] ~∧
328.14	harpsichord.] ~∧
328.15	"Do] ∧~
328.33	herbs.] ~∧
329.3	about it,] about,
329.7	possible] posssible
329.7	vents).] ~∧.
329.9	die."] ~.∧
329.15	"I shall] '~ ~
329.15	"I am] '~ ~
329.25	(Like] ∧~
329.28	keep] kep
329.32	with mankind] with a mankind
330.7	pride.] ~∧
330.20	a] an
330.21	sets] set
330.21	athwart] awhart
330.25	great] greath
330.27	before] beefore
330.28	it is so] it so
331.3	the] The
331.4	overcome,] ~."
331.7	at] *omit*
331.14	Nashoba,] ~∧

331.14	pipe,] ~ᴧ
331.15	again;] ~"
331.20	fellow.] ~ᴧ
331.27	dreaming] deaming
331.31	capable] capabable
332.3	certainty] certaintly
332.4	too] to
332.15	Sybil,] ~ᴧ
332.17	words.] ~ᴧ
332.19	creature,] ~ᴧ
332.21	nonsense?"] ~?ᴧ
332.22	"Come] ᴧ~
332.24	tell us of] tell of us of
332.24	an] a
332.25	woods."] ~,ᴧ
332.27	out.] ~ᴧ
332.28	that.] ~ᴧ
332.29	"I] '~
332.29	"there] '~
332.30	say] saw
332.30	unknown] unknow
333.1	"I] ᴧ~
333.5	you?] ~.
333.8	"if] ᴧ~
333.11	so,] ~ᴧ
333.19	for, as you confess,] ~ᴧ~~~ᴧ
333.21	in] and
333.25	Smithills] Smithill's
334.11	handkerchief] handerchief
334.12	what] *omit*
334.14	successive] sucsessive
334.20	plaster.] ~ᴧ
334.27	not] *omit*
334.29	original] orginal
334.33	four sides] foursides
335.3	are] *omit*
335.10	polished,] ~ᴧ
336.17	wherever] ~;
336.18	any] and

336.21	is] are
336.23	dates] date
336.25	persistency] perisistency
336.32	a] *omit*
337.1	known] town
337.13–14	Nature, which] Nature, of which
337.15	the] *omit*
337.21	may] may may
337.25	of] *omit*
337.32	might reach] might to reach
338.6	known] know
338.8	brightened] brigtened
338.14	know] ~,
338.15	an] and
338.17	accomplished] acomplihed
338.18	stunts,] ~∧
338.21	(The] ∧~
338.23	such] ~,
338.30	young,] ~;
339.4	condition] conditions
339.30	hall,] ~∧
340.8	due] ~,
340.15	contemptible] contemptobole
340.22	one of his] one his
341.3	guardian] gardian
341.7	thoughtful] thoughful
341.27	immortality.] ~∧
341.30	you, . . . question,] ~∧ . . . ~∧
342.21	be] *omit*
342.21	hid] *omit*
342.29	confined it;] confined;
343.21	done;] ~,
344.15	him.] ~∧
344.27	do,)] ~∧)
345.12	certain] certaint
345.15	bane)] ~,)
346.16	them] the
346.17	pavement,] ~∧
346.31	upon it,] upon,

346.31	maiden's] maid- | den's
347.1	was] *omit*
347.21	tails] tales
347.23	tail] tale
347.29	blessed] blssed
348.5	stairs.] ~ₐ
348.26	saw] *omit*
349.32	story was] story | he was
349.33	crimson foot] ~ - ~
350.2	returned.] ~ₐ
350.6	coals] colds
350.6	hall, where (as] ~ₐ (~, ₐ~
350.16	lawyers] lawers
350.17	or] ~,
350.19	a] an
351.1	respecting] respeting
351.5	the] the the
351.15	affrighted] affright
351.31	it's] its
352.2	child?] ~ₐ
352.6	drink,] ~,"
352.10	sister-in-law] ~ₐ~ - ~
352.19	purposes.] ~ₐ
352.23	head] heads
353.1	won't] wont
353.3	listen] listened
353.4	tale,] ~ₐ
353.27	fragile] fragil
353.30	substance] sustance
353.31	pipe;] ~,
354.12	questionable,] ~ₐ
354.25	an] a
354.32	(one] ₐ~
355.6	extent] exent
355.10	Nashoba] Nash- | hoba
355.14	traditions,] ~ₐ
355.22	hour),] ~)ₐ
355.31	birches] birchs
356.5	were] *omit*

356.6	knew] *omit*
356.10	thus] this
356.27	who] *omit*
358.23	they] they they
358.24	smoke] smokes
358.25	him] them
359.2	Deity,] ~∧
359.2	the] *omit*
359.16	one,] ~∧
359.28	cremation's] cremations
359.31	with.] ~∧
360.11	build] bulid
360.24	hot.] ~∧
360.28	greatest] gratest
360.33	withheld] witheld
361.23	planting] plant- | ting
361.23	to] *omit*
361.27	the recipe] which recipe
362.7	up,] ~∧
362.10	truth,] ~∧
362.32	too] to
363.19	left out] left it out
363.32	I've] Ive
364.8	cachinnatory] cachinatory
364.9	legend,] ~∧
364.16	the] *omit*
364.24	that] ~,
364.26	'twould] ∧~
364.28	tumultuously] tumultously
365.1	"I] '~
365.5	ingredients."] ~∧∧
365.13	drink.] dink∧
366.14	Nashoba,] ~∧
366.20	Seppy,] ~∧
366.23	lad, I] lad, and I
366.26	of] *omit*
366.27	cousin,] ~∧
367.26	shrouded] shroud
368.4–5	so much dust] so must

368.11	deduced] decuced
368.17	a] a a
368.22	it] omit
369.2	a hill-side] an hill-side
369.7	aside.] ~,
369.24	came,] ~ $_\wedge$
369.27	Septimius] Septimius Septimius
370.3	forty] fty
370.3	Septimius's] Septimius $_\wedge$s
370.8	cryptic] criptic
370.25	(He] $_\wedge$~
370.28	winter,] ~ $_\wedge$
370.31	longer,] ~ $_\wedge$
371.10	new,] ~ $_\wedge$
371.13	sicknesses] siknesses
371.13	even] ~,
372.1	of] omit
372.2	make] omit
372.20	a bristly] an bristly
372.29	brought] broght
372.29	Septimius's] Septimius
373.6	permitted,] ~ $_\wedge$
373.12	Ormskirk,] ~ $_\wedge$
373.14	a] an
373.20	Ormskirk,"] ~ , '
373.21	strangers,] ~ $_\wedge$
373.25	smoke, "I] ~ $_\wedge$ $_\wedge$~
373.27	country] county
373.27	to] at
374.3	spiders."] ~· $_\wedge$
374.33	girls'] girl's
375.5	time."] ~· $_\wedge$
375.6	they] the
375.7	Charles] ~'
375.9	his] its
375.9	short] shot
375.18	choleric] choleic
376.20	friend?] ~!
377.2	at] omit

377.9	which] (~
377.11	over,] ~∧
377.25	although] alhough
378.14	needle] kneedle
378.22	vegetable] vegtabe
378.23	invitation.] ~∧
378.28	"with] ∧~
378.28	and] "~
379.5	Septimius's] Septimius
379.8	too] to
379.11	trunk] truck
379.17	that,] ~∧
379.19	Norton.] ~∧
379.30	fellow,] ~∧
380.8	mixture] *omit*
380.11	and] ~,
380.14	guarding] garding
380.16	back.] ~∧
380.18	-door.] ~∧
380.32	"though] '~
381.2	Indian] Indian's
381.3	-luck."] ~.∧
381.9	and] and and
381.11	weapon's] weapons
381.16	world.] ~∧
381.16	he.] ~,
381.22	"it] ∧~
381.26	which] *omit*
381.31	grandfather] grandmother
382.11	Nashoba's] Nashoba
382.21	keenness] keeness
382.22	it] *omit*
382.24	not,] ~∧
382.26	recourse."] ~.'
382.28	questions] question
382.29–30	flask, . . . on,] ~∧ . . . ~∧
383.7	Garfield,] ~∧
383.19	propounded] prounded
384.1–2	-covered flask] -covered with flask

384.2	Nashoba's] Nashobas
384.29	can't] cant
384.30	"Not] no ¶
385.8	extinct] instinct
385.21	infusion] inffusion
385.26	be] *omit*
386.4	indeed] ideed
386.12	ejaculating,] ~ᴧ
386.13	"Very . . . truth!"] '~ . . . ~!'
386.17	Nashoba's] Nashobas
386.18	laughter] laugher
386.19	a] *omit*
387.5	overtures] overteures
387.8	purpose] purose
387.9	Before] Befor
387.10	dwells] dwell's
387.11	Boston.)] ~.ᴧ
387.12	"Seppy] '~
387.12	as soon] "~ ~
387.13	"that] ᴧ~
387.14	mischief."] ~ᴧᴧ
387.15	mean,] ~ᴧ
387.24	anything."] ~.ᴧ
387.25	that] that that
387.30	and] *omit*
388.17	herself] hersef
388.22	England girl were] England was
389.11	was] *omit*
389.26	murderous,] ~ᴧ
390.3	herself] hersef
390.12–13	poor brain-shattered] ~ – ~ᴧ~
392.5	memory.] ~ᴧ
392.21	at] *omit*
393.5	thought too] thought it too
393.22	business, the interests,] ~ᴧ ~ ~ᴧ
393.33	which, however,] ~ᴧ~ᴧ
394.3	of *omit*
394.5	much?] ~.
394.5	Florist."] ~.ᴧ

394.6	Indian-like] ~∧~
394.13	wonders] wonder
394.22	production?] ~.
395.1	seed] seeed
395.4	Speak,] ~∧
395.11	corpse.] ~∧
395.25	woo it out] woo out
395.33	seemed] *omit*
396.4	might] *omit*
396.5	soil] spoil
396.15	Rose.] ~∧
396.19	back.] ~—
396.28	sprite-like] ~ ~
396.33	but] *omit*
397.3	annihilated] annihlated
397.6	blackness] backness
398.4	an] a
398.6	heavily,] ~∧
398.16	by] to
398.20	and, . . . heart,] ~∧ . . . ~∧
398.27	toad-stool!"] ~ - ~!'
399.9	centre] cetnr
399.11	continue?] ~.
399.12	foeman?] ~!
399.17	applied] appleid
399.24	competent] competetent
400.13	had] has
400.29	were.] ~∧
401.12	days,] ~.
401.16	-step] -sttep
401.20	girded] grided
401.24	breathe.] ~∧
402.9	infirmities.] ~∧
402.17	earthen] earth
402.24	that] *omit*
402.24	been] *omit*
402.26	either] eith
403.10	Ah,] ~∧
403.13	I'll] Ill

403.13	again."] ~.ʌ
403.17	say,] ~.
403.28	cold] coold
404.6	assistance.] ~ʌ
404.11	interruption] interrupption
404.13	manuscript.] ~ʌ
404.14	Seppy,] ~ʌ
404.15	well] unwell
404.17	now,] ~ʌ
405.8	bedside] beside
405.25	soil;] ~.
405.26	leaves,] ~ʌ
405.28	of] *omit*
405.31	an] a
406.8	me."] ~.ʌ
406.11	"I] ʌ~
406.11,20	Sagamore's] Sangamore's
406.31	as] as as
407.15	you,] ~ʌ
407.20	about it,] about,
407.22	it; but] ~ʌ "~
408.6	woods)] ~ʌ
408.10	it] *omit*
408.12	covered] coverd
408.23–24	why should it] why it should
408.26	family,] ~ʌ
408.30	methods. Who] methods who
408.31	from?] ~.
409.3	live)] ~ʌ
409.15	motion] mootion
409.19	roots,] ~ʌ
409.23–24	if somebody had] if had somebody had
410.10–11	sensible of (or . . .) a] sensible (or . . .) of a
410.14	bubbles.] ~ʌ
410.17	which] whic
410.19	where] whence
411.18	to be a] to a be a
411.27	women.] ~ʌ

411.31	before,] ~∧
412.2	you've] you ve
412.12	"Then] '~
412.13	measure."] ~·∧
412.16	her.] ~∧
412.18	"Do] ∧~
412.21	"People] '~
412.22	it's] its
412.30	doctor's] doctors
413.4	it] *omit*
413.22	one,] ~∧
413.25	skin)] ~∧
413.29	an] and
414.1	out] it
414.9	adamant.] ~∧
414.16	to-and-fro] ~ – ~∧~
414.31	stood face] stood to face
415.4	almost be called] almost call
415.14	Potent,] ~∧
415.26	preternaturally] preternatually
415.28	incessant] encesant
415.30	evolved] elvolved
416.9	sunshine] sunshinne
416.24	it be] it to be
416.29	dreamer."] ~?∧
416.30	yourself.] ~?
416.30	end."] ~·∧
416.33	gave] *omit*
417.8	Garfield] ~,
417.13	repetition] repetiition
417.19	with] ~,
417.27	an] a
418.12	Love,] ~∧
418.14	passions, any of them,] ~∧~ ~ ~∧
418.17	But] ~,
418.23	require] requr
418.24	planted—]
418.31	distress] distred

419.3	looking-glass,] looking,
419.10	was] ~,
419.11	pale?] ~.
419.19	conquered] conquer
419.19	Hilliard] Hilliar
420.3	prognostics] prognostices
420.22	hand,] ~ₐ
420.23	work,] ~ₐ
420.25	other).] ~,)
420.30	It] "~
420.31	exclaimed] "~
420.32	nobody] no body
421.1	then,] ~ₐ
421.2	moment] ment
421.4	world!] ~,
421.6	away.] ~ₐ
422.6	me.] ~ₐ
422.7	Hilliard.] ~,
422.8	better,] ~ₐ
422.30	how] thow
422.31	indivisible] indvisible
423.10	inveterate] inverterate
423.16	of] *omit*
423.17	drink?] ~,
423.28	rivalry.] ~,
423.29	-bed?] ~.
423.31	Hilly] hilly
424.4	dear),] ~,)
424.9	grandmothers,] ~ₐ
424.25	commiseration] commisseration
424.28	much?] ~.
425.23	Aunt] *omit*
425.28	good?] ~.
425.33	live] love
426.6	have] *omit*
426.15	sermons.] ~ₐ
426.27	I] and
427.7	Nashoba's] Nashobas

427.15	were.] ~,
428.2	benign.] ~$_\wedge$
428.11	others?] ~.
428.20	Righteousness,] ~$_\wedge$
428.21	face,] ~$_\wedge$
428.25	they'll] theyll
429.2	flight] fligh
429.23	darling] darlg
429.24	mustn't] musn't
429.24	want] *omit*
429.27	well.] ~$_\wedge$
430.1	-off,] ~$_\wedge$
430.3	full breath of] full of breath of
430.6	about] abut
430.8	see her] her see
430.9	bedside] beside
430.11	her?] ~,
430.13	wandering] wadering
430.13	mischief] mishief
430.16	there's] there
430.21	shadow,] ~$_\wedge$
430.22	water,] ~$_\wedge$
430.23	say."] ~.'
430.24	else?] ~,
430.25	were] *omit*
430.27	in] *omit*
430.32	it's] its
431.1	"Can] $_\wedge$~
431.7	Hilly,] ~.
431.8	you,] ~$_\wedge$
431.9	thing.] ~,
431.10	sip.] ~.,
431.10	sprightly] sprigtly
431.13	away."] ~.$_\wedge$
431.17	Tomorrow] Tommorrow
431.22–23	awake, . . . awake,] ~$_\wedge$ . . . ~$_\wedge$
431.25	we] *omit*

431.27	of] *omit*
431.28	as it] at
431.29	if] of
431.30	to] *omit*
432.2	into] into into
432.2	of] *omit*
432.3	bitterness.] ～∧
432.6	occasion] reccasion
432.15	perspicacious] pespicacious
432.18	hastened?] ～.
432.24	statesmen] Statesmen
433.1	there really is] there is really is
433.19	she] *omit*
433.20	himself] him
434.3	is] *omit*
434.7	state."] ～·∧
434.25	maid,] ～∧
434.28	come.] ～∧
434.30	rheumatism;] ～,
434.32	themselves] themselveslves
435.11	hearth.] ∧～
435.12	"There's] '～
435.18	betaken] mistaken
435.20	emotions,] ～∧
435.21	him,] ～∧
436.3	which] whic
436.13	cycle] cicle
436.16	a] as
437.10	address] addess
437.12	wantonness] wantness
437.15	dejected,] ～∧
437.16	Hilliard.] ～∧
437.24	you."] ～·∧
438.5	said] "～
438.5	is,] ～;
438.10	vine.] ～∧
438.21	how—] —～

438.23	speak of,] ~ ~?
438.24	"that] ∧~
438.25	say] *omit*
438.25	things?] ~∧
439.21	it?] ~.
439.29	to] *omit*
439.34	be] *omit*
440.21	and] (~
440.21	(whatever] ∧~
441.8	it;] ~,
441.12	straight] straigt
441.13	dying;] ~.
441.15	so,"] ~∧∧
441.20	"That] ∧~
442.11	herbs] hirbs
442.17	aspect;] ~,
442.22	apple, pear, wormwood,] ~∧~, ~∧
443.3	graves] grave
443.12–13	family; it was] family, was
443.20	herbage.] ~∧
443.30	spicy,] ~∧
444.2	year,] ~;
444.21	foot,] ~∧
445.4	which] *omit*
445.9	is] *omit*
445.10	proportions] pportions
445.11	since he] *omit*
445.13	to] *omit*
445.14	having] having having
445.25	suddenness] suddeness
446.21	palace,] ~;
447.1	themselves] himselvs
447.9	everything] everthing
447.10	atmosphere] attmosphere
447.20	pervaded] pevaded
447.24	Rose,] ~;
447.24	different reason,] different,
447.29	had] ~,
448.2	to] *omit*

The Dolliver Romance

NOTE: For the first chapter the two sources of emendation are *AM*, the *Atlantic Monthly*, XIV (July 1864), 101–9, and CENTENARY. Thereafter the CENTENARY emendation before the bracket and the manuscript reading after the bracket are unlabeled.

450.33	with] *AM*; by MS
454.1	waistcoat] *AM*; westcoat MS
454.33	to her] *AM*; to to her MS
456.15	"Ah] *AM*; ~ MS
458.10	to give] *AM*; to to give MS
458.26	the] *AM*; the the MS
458.30	with] *AM*; with with MS
459.2	to] *AM*; into MS
460.18	grandson's] CENTENARY; son's MS, *AM*
461.4	probably as the] *AM*; probably the MS
462.8	Dr.] *AM*; Doctor MS
465.10	Grandsir] *AM*; Dr. MS
465.22	man] *AM*; mans MS
465.29	years.] *AM*; ~ MS
466.17	before).] ~.
466.18	bread,] ~
466.18	hasty-pudding.] ~ – ~
467.2	love in it] love it
467.2	observe] *omit*
467.7	hearts,] ~
467.8	away,] ~.
467.17	people,] ~
467.24	doctor,] ~
467.28	known] know
467.31	without] *omit*
468.28	had] had had
468.30	something] some- |
468.31	character,] ~

469.5	them.] $\sim_\Lambda$
469.8	succeeded in puzzling] succeeded puzzling
469.20	winter,] $\sim_\Lambda$
469.21	he] omit
469.32	perhaps] perhas
470.7	hope,] $\sim_\Lambda$
*470.8	he] omit
470.10	superficialness] superficalness
470.17	brought] broght
470.18	thriven] thiven
470.25	manuscripts] man- | scripts
471.3	trade,] $\sim_\Lambda$
471.10	imaginative] imag- | tive
471.12	remarkable] remark
471.16	supersede] supesede
471.21	them,] $\sim_\Lambda$
471.31	position] posi- |
472.10	shaken,] $\sim_\Lambda$
472.29	passion,] $\sim_\Lambda$
473.3	doctors] doctor
473.9	them.] $\sim_\Lambda$
*473.9	lost] omit
473.15	youth's] youthe's
*473.16–17	one case,] one,
473.21	honored] hon- | ed
473.23	preparations] prep- | ations
*473.25	had] omit
474.2	public.] $\sim_\Lambda$
474.3	terrible event;] terrible;
474.8	Dolliver's] Dollivers
*474.9	as the oldest] as oldest
474.10	discernible] discernable
474.16	reverential] revertial
*474.29	soul] sould
474.31	nostrils.] $\sim_\Lambda$
475.2	grandpapa's] grandpapas
475.3	garden, resolved] garden, and resolved
475.5	appropriated] appropri- | iated
475.13	shrivelled] shivelled

*475.13	leaf, both] leaf, and both
*475.15	about it,] about,
475.19	little Pansie came] little, came
475.21	Pansie,] ∼∧
475.25	grandson's] son's
476.4	forth] *omit*
476.13	entertain] *omit*
476.14	follies.] ∼;
476.17	And] and
476.20	flower] flow
476.24	the] he
*476.26	apprehensive] apprensive
476.32	grave!"] ∼! '
476.32	kitten] kiten
477.8	onward] ∼,
477.9	running] runing
477.10	Dolliver,] ∼∧
477.12	person's] person
477.14	grandpapa] pgrandpapapa
477.15	wrinkled] wrinked
477.19	and] "∼
477.25	grandpapa,"] ∼∧ "
477.30	in to] into
478.5	it;] ∼.
478.6	grandson] son
478.6	memorial.] ∼∧
478.17	anyone] was
478.20	inscribed] inscibed
478.21	Physitian.] ∼. '
478.28	it."] ∼·∧
479.4	" . . . see] see
479.7	as] *omit*
479.19	"grandpapa] '∼
479.21	Te] te
479.21	hee."] ∼·∧
479.22	"That] ∧∼
480.13	much] *omit*
481.13	theory] thery
481.15	material] mater-	

481.22	quack's] quacks
481.23	thing!] ~!∧
481.25	bottle] bottel
481.33	it] *omit*
482.14	had] ~,
482.19	cut—] ~)
482.22	Dr.] ~∧
483.13	one's] ones
483.19	to] *omit*
484.2	originally near-sighted] originally a near-sighted
484.15	brightness] brigtness
485.16	"a] ∧~
*485.24–25	taking it;] taking;
485.30	Nevertheless] Never- | less
485.32	omit it,] omit
*486.7	two] *omit*
486.14	small.] ~∧
486.25	by! 'The] ~! "~
486.25	Cordial'?] ~∧?
486.26	'Life-drops'?] "~ – ~"?
486.26–27	'Youth in a bottle'] "~ ~ ~ ~"
486.31	'The] ∧~
486.31	cordial'!—] ~!"—
487.6	'Pshaw'!"] "~∧!"
487.7	"Pshaw!"] "~!∧
487.8	know."] ~.∧
487.10	its] its'
487.19	greenness] greeness
488.6	haughty] hauhty
488.20	"It] ∧~
488.24	it.] ~∧
*489.4	itself] himself
489.8	moment] ~,
489.11	softer] softier
489.15	'I'll] '~
489.32	It's] Its
490.23	mistaken] mistake
490.29	sneer.] ~∧
490.29	rogue?] ~.

491.9	"Ah] ∧~
491.12	"I] ∧~
491.12	me,] ~∧
491.16	"I] ∧~
491.19	you] you you
491.24	musty] muty
491.26	an old] (~ ~
492.11	"and] ∧~
492.11	again!"] ~!∧
492.12	Colonel,] ~,"
492.12	correct,"] ~,∧
492.13	startled,] ~∧
492.23	it?"] ~?'
492.24	"I'll] ∧~
493.2	say!"] ~!'
493.17	blazes),] ~)∧
493.18	"I'll] ∧~
493.20	had] omit
494.11	"Fool] ∧~
494.19	if] omit
494.22	drinking-] dringing-
494.24	"For] ∧~
495.5	sate a] sate in a
495.24	frantically,] ~∧
495.26	floor.] ~∧
495.27	apothecary.] ~∧
496.2	one,] ~)
496.11	it.] ~∧
496.13	street,] ~∧
496.14	blew] blow
496.15	through] throgh
496.15	methought] methoght
496.16	now] know
496.29	delicate] delicately
497.2	who] whom
497.9	without] with- |
497.12	Colonel's] Cololonels
497.12	testified] testitified
497.27	them?] ~.

ANCILLARY DOCUMENTS

499.9	which] whih
499.19	this man who] who man who
500.5	which] whihc
500.18	years!"] ~!'
501.10–11	its . . . its] it's . . . it's
502.8	it?] ~.
502.17	"I tell] '~ ~
502.20	Septimius."] ~,'
502.21	confined."] ~._∧
503.2	phantom?] ~.
503.14	fact,] ~;
503.28	pretty,] ~_∧
503.32	bear.] ~_∧
504.6	an] a
505.16	live.] ~_∧
505.26	this.] ~_∧
506.2	expressed] expessed
506.16	secret] secet
506.16	course] couse
506.31	humanity,] ~_∧
507.6	-hilted] -hlted
507.8	perceptible] peceptible
507.10	comes] *tear in* MS: [ ]mes
507.11	sincere] *tear in* MS: s[ ]re
507.20	as to make] as make
508.7	interferes] interferers
508.7	fiercely] feiercely
508.12	Septimius] Septimi- | ius
509.7	receipt] recipt
509.26	end.] ~_∧
509.29	estranging] es- | stranging
509.30	attained.] ~_∧
510.6	discussion] discusssion

510.9		receives] recives
510.14		Septimius] Sep- | *page end*
510.25		benevolent] benevolnt
511.1		indulges] induleges
511.2		Septimius] Sep- | *page end*
511.15		Septimius's] Septimius
511.16		necessary] neceessary
511.22		christening] christing
512.2		was.] ~ᴧ
512.19		man.] ~ᴧ
512.21		cultivation.] ~ᴧ
513.3		addresses] adresses
513.11		descent] des[*ink blot*]t
513.12		anywise] awise
513.13		these] this
513.18		he to] to he
513.18		marry,] ~ᴧ
513.23		whither] whiher
514.24		concerned] concerne
515.2		blood.] ~ᴧ
515.7		elixir] exlixir
515.13,	19	himself] himsef
516.3		the talent] the the talent
516.14		Septimius's] Septimius
516.19		leaves.] ~ᴧ
516.29		secret] secet
517.13		alchymist] aclchymist
517.15		finding by] finding that by
517.31		round] roud
518.7		title] tittle
518.9		if] of
519.9		Arcadian] Acardian
519.18		excitement,] ~ᴧ
519.21		ideas.] ~ᴧ
519.23		father's] fathers
520.5		be] *omit*
520.25		&c.] ~ᴧ
521.26		from] *omit*
522.8		&c.] ~ᴧ

523.14	also] aso
524.13	crisis,] ~;
525.17	receipt] reciept
525.18	before.] ~∧
526.11	yield] yeild
527.3	Sybil;] ~∧
527.10	*Scene.*] ~∧
527.15	herself] himself
527.25	Septimius,] ~∧
527.30	&c.] ~∧
528.10	Revolution.] ~∧
529.6	Septimius's] Septimius
529.20	introduced] intoduced
530.11	impracticability] impractably
531.6	agitation] agi- | tion
531.15	might last] might at last
533.9	¶ He] *no* ¶
533.19	prolonging] prolong
533.20	incalculable] incalcu- | able
533.23	incurred] incurried
534.6	were] was
534.10	at] *omit*
534.14	70—10] ~∧~
534.15	door-step.] ~∧
535.5	morning?] ~.
535.7	dances,] ~∧
535.30	whereupon] wherupon
535.32	neighborhood] neighbrhood
536.3	so.] ~∧
536.5	minister.] ~∧
536.11	whom] who
536.11	had] has
536.32	does he,] does,
537.12	sister] brother
537.16	who,] ~∧
537.17	in] *omit*
537.22	beginning.] ~∧
540.7	again.] ~∧

540.16	besides] besieds
540.28	are] *omit*
541.26	ingredient] ingred-|ent
542.3	cheerfulness] cherfulness
542.4	child,] ~ₐ
542.13	receipt] recipt
542.32	man] *omit*
543.6	knows] know
543.11	it] *omit*
543.18–19	to be] to to be
544.13	sees] seees
544.13	prophetically] prohetically
544.15	thinks] thinkes
544.22	wholly] wholy
544.25	ends.] ~ₐ
547.4	do] *omit*
547.10	to] *omit*
547.21	&c.] ~ₐ
547.29	chemist] chemist's
549.9	latter] former
549.14	an] and
549.19, 24	&c.] ~ₐ
550.6	wild,] ~ₐ
550.13	magnanimity] magnamity
550.25	not] *omit*
550.25	it,] ~ₐ
551.4	things,] ~ₐ
551.4	inability] inabity
551.9	He] he
551.15	we really] we we really
551.17	torpor,] ~ₐ
551.20	it] *omit*
551.30	against him,] against—shook him by the hand,
551.31	touch.] touch ‖ or when they jostled against him.
552.3	children] chiden
552.11	of a] of a of a
552.18	all,] ~ₐ

552.22	whom] which
552.23	pilgrimage,] ~$_\wedge$
552.24	opening,] ~$_\wedge$
553.1	ground,] ~$_\wedge$
553.3	remembered] remmembered
553.7	liked."] ~$_{\wedge\wedge}$

REJECTED FIRST-EDITION
SUBSTANTIVE VARIANTS

NOTE: The first chapter of *The Dolliver Romance* is unique in being the only portion of Hawthorne's unfinished works to have been prepared for the printer and presumably proofread by the author. Departures from manuscript readings may or may not represent Hawthorne's alterations; substantive variants not accepted are listed here. *AM* refers to "A Scene from the Dolliver Romance," Atlantic Monthly, XIV (July 1864), 101–9.

449.0	Fragments . . . Serpent.] MS; A SCENE FROM THE DOLLIVER ROMANCE. *AM*
450.10	duly] MS; daily *AM*
451.9	dusty] MS; dirty *AM*
451.17	glimmered] MS; gleamed *AM*
454.19	would] MS; could *AM*
454.21	this] MS; his *AM*
455.25	women-folks] MS; women-folk *AM*
458.25	nor] MS; and *AM*
458.25	latter] MS; later *AM*
464.11	wrinkles] MS; the wrinkles *AM*
464.19	brow] MS; brows *AM*
465.27	Thence] MS; Hence *AM*
466.1	dawn] MS; draw *AM*
466.10–12	But . . . story.] MS; *omit AM*

WORD-DIVISION

1. End-of-the-Line Hyphenation in the Centenary Edition

Possible compounds hyphenated at the end of a line in the Centenary text are listed here if they are hyphenated within the line in the copy-text. Exclusion from this list means that a possible compound appears as one unhyphenated word in the copy-text. Also excluded are hyphenated compounds in which both elements are capitalized.

5.17	school-keeping	148.17	iron-clasped
18.21	spring-like	151.20	hill-top
19.32	shirt-sleeves	159.10	school-house
24.30	fellow-creatures	163.22	hill-top
29.28	burial-grounds	169.31	self-denying
36.7	death-moments	178.4	ill-fortune
43.23	half-chopt	186.13	village-meeting-|
61.9	abiding-place		house
64.11	free-spokenness	196.29	hill-top
66.32	hill-top	196.32	pitch-pines
83.31	pow-wows	203.1	Witch-blood
87.34	chimney-corner	203.23	great-grandfather
116.28	sub-conscious	226.9	match-lock
119.28	five-|and-seventy	227.30	cross-belts
124.28	cross-grained	238.3	hill-top
141.19	common-place	241.12	life-tenacity
146.24	beef-eaters	243.27	pick-axe

245.10	death-radiance	435.4	chimney-corner
248.19	bed-clothes	442.15	burial-ground
249.10	great-grandfather	453.19	looking-glass
249.11	communion-bread	453.29	baby-fingers
252.11	chimney-corner	455.13	great-grandfather's
279.18	ill-fate	455.24	summer-morning
282.28	pitch-pines	456.21	great-grandpapa
283.15	often-trodden	457.15	dimly-remembered
303.18	life-blood	458.4	poverty-stricken
303.25	blood-stained	460.14	breaking-up
309.17	cast-aways	485.29	well-considered
311.3	to-and-|fro	507.4	hill-side
341.5	lofty-purposed	516.18	forest-leaves
355.29	arrow-heads	524.17	iron-bound
363.4	poor-house	538.2,9	herb-woman
367.24	hill-top	539.1	apple-tree
376.1	fore-finger	540.14	herb-woman
390.12	brain-shattered	541.30	to-and-|fro
403.15	fire-place	543.5	herb-woman
423.28	herb-woman	550.13	re-awakened
434.24	cross-grained	551.26	old-fashioned

2. *End-of-the-Line Hyphenation in the Copy-Text*

The following possible compounds are hyphenated at the ends of lines in the copy-text. The form adopted in the Centenary Edition, as listed below, represents Hawthorne's predominant usage as ascertained by other appearances or by parallels within the copy-text.

16.9	farm-house	44.28	hill-top
18.7	broomstick	51.3	woodshed
18.30	door-step	79.31	keen-eyed
29.23	grave-yards	81.4	war-disturbed
32.25	death-contorted	88.8	commonplaceness

99.20	footstep	364.15	herb-drinks
108.10	hill-top	427.8	death-bed
122.32	pain-distorted	436.21	to-day
128.31	skunk-cabbage	444.12	death-bed
148.25	firesides	449.15	criss-crossed
152.19	world-fruit	450.15	grandson
153.29	great-|great-	451.5	stiff-backed
	grandfather	452.18	small-clothes
162.26	age-long	453.9	bedtime
176.26	co-effort	453.17	faint-heartedness
178.23	wedding-cake	454.16	large-eyed
203.1	herb-drink	455.26	grand-aunts
203.15	orchard-house	456.7	grandfather
210.31	powder-horn	457.9	sunrise
212.24	countrymen	459.30	grandson
243.29	grave-digger	463.17	life-long
258.27	pine-trees	464.33	townspeople
262.14	byestanders	485.8	outdid
271.7	pooh-pooh	486.28	lifetime
272.23	hill-side	493.10	net-work
275.5	hill-top	521.6	long-lived
359.21	war-clubs		

3. *Special Cases*

The following possible compounds are hyphenated at the ends of lines in both copy-text and Centenary Edition. Words appear here in the adopted Centenary form, which is obscured by line-end hyphenation: 334.11 finger-tips 397.24 hill-top

ALTERATIONS IN THE MANUSCRIPTS

This listing takes account of all alterations in Hawthorne's manuscripts except for undeciphered deletions and the simple mending of letters or words without alteration. Hawthorne's practice in deletion was to wipe out wet ink with a finger and to cancel dried inscription with pen strokes. In the Alterations list, *over* means "in the same space" and *above* and *above caret* mean "interlined"; the presence of a caret is always noted.

In addition to the revisions he carried out, Hawthorne left evidence of further intended changes. He resorted to any blank space on inscribed leaves to add notes which by their position may not seem immediately pertinent. These notes are inserted in the Centenary text at the point dictated by the logic of the context. Hawthorne usually wrote out directions to indicate repositioning of paragraphs; for smaller units he marked the limits of affected passages with arrowhead pointers, diagonal or vertical lines, or carets—often two- or three-tiered. Wherever possible the Centenary text carries out his intention and an Alterations entry describes his directions or signs.

Empty square brackets signify one or more undeciphered letters; letters within square brackets are conjectural on some evidence although not wholly certain. Alterations not in Hawthorne's hand are indicated by an asterisk before the page-line reference of the entry; "SH" stands for Sophia Hawthorne.

SEPTIMIUS FELTON

*3.9   who] 'm' of original 'whom' cancelled with vertical strokes typical of SH

3.9	two] over wiped-out 'thr'
3.9	years] above 'younger'
3.14–15	Septimius . . . up.] added at left top margin of MS page
3.16	Septimius . . . house.] added at right top margin of MS page
3.19	ridge] above uncancelled 'hill'
3.20	one] 'o' over 's'
3.21	the heart] over wiped-out 'the village'
4.20–21	cloven . . . place] above caret
4.31	gabled house] over wiped-out 'but with only'
4.32	crowded] 'c' over wiped-out 'at'
5.12	rich] above caret
5.16	Cambridge] 'C' over 'c'
5.23	hill] above caret; preceded by cancelled 'which'
5.25	The] over 'She'
5.27	quick] 'q' over wiped-out 'pr'
5.33	would have] 'wou' over 'was'
6.4	mature] above caret
6.6	let] over wiped-out 'leave'
6.8	chip] over wiped-out 'pl'
6.12	wild] 'w' over wiped-out 'a'
6.18	grandfather] preceded by cancelled 'father thinks'
6.28	old] over 'wi'
7.24	laughing—] dash cancels period
8.14	and shivering] above 'doubtfully'
8.18	You] 'Y' over double quotation mark
8.20	go—] dash cancels period and double quotation mark
8.30	assenting] above 'an'
9.1	so golden haired] above caret
9.3	I] preceded by wiped-out 'am'
9.6	gone.] period cancels comma
9.6	But] over 'and'
10.4	like] over wiped-out 'one'
10.5	homely] 'h' over 'c'
12.15	sadly—] dash cancels comma
12.18	your] over 'own'

12.32–33 fireplace stood] originally 'fire stood'; 'place' squeezed in

13.4 dusty] 'du' over wiped-out 'clo'

13.17 an] over 'is'

14.18 was] over 'hou'

14.22 of her] 'of' over 'for'

14.26 leave] over 'rise'

14.31 by way of blessing,] above caret

15.10 his aunt] staff of 'h' crossed in error

*15.27 portion of his] 'of' added in hand of SH

15.29 as possible] 'as' above 'possible'

16.9 Horsemen] 'Ho' over possible 'Ri'

16.17 last] 'st' over 'p'

18.6 the house] 'the' over 'up'

18.9 Well . . . man] added in space after preceding paragraph

18.10 Keziah] 'K' mended from 'Z'

18.21 morning] above 'beautiful'

*19.14 been] above caret, in hand of SH

*19.15 of ordinary] 'the' added above 'ordinary' in hand of SH

19.24 "He was running] over wiped-out 'and his fam'; preceded by inadvertently uncancelled semi-colon

19.27 gracious] 'gra' over 'hea'

19.32 hatless] 'ha' over 'coa'

20.2–3 glaring . . . Septimius] above caret

20.8 And] 'A' over 'O'; preceded by wiped-out double quotation mark

20.12 and] over exclamation mark and double quotation mark

20.17 hide] 'h' over 'g'

*20.21 deal of] 'of' above caret, in hand of SH

21.6 beer] above cancelled 'ale'

21.18 better] preceded by cancelled 'little'

21.21 the well] 'the' squeezed in over 'a'

21.23 a petulant boy] above 'young officer'

22.8 glance] 'e' mended over original wiped-out 'ing'

22.20 Rose] 'R' over double quotation mark

24.4	kind of] above caret
24.17	almost simultaneously] above caret
*24.22	it] above caret, in hand of SH
24.23	what] 'w' over 'ef'
25.12	which] MS 'w whic'; second 'w' over 'th' of poorly wiped-out 'with'
25.15–16	One . . . stood.] preceded and followed by two-tiered caret, the sentence originally followed 25.13 'village.'; its transposition point marked before 'He looked' by a cluster of lines above a caret
25.27–29	Describe . . . seemed.] added in space at end of paragraph
26.1	towards] 'to' over 'the'
26.4	because] 'bec' over 'his'
26.8–10	Septimius's . . . incitements.] added in space at end of paragraph; MS reading 'Septimius'; 'bl' of 'bloody' over wiped-out possible 'Ind'
26.17	officer] 'off' over 'man'
26.20	—that] dash cancels comma
26.22	to a] 'a' over 'f'
26.24	are] over 'you'
26.25	among] over partially wiped-out 'on the'
26.28	As prisoner] 'As' over '[ ]h'
26.29	arousing] 'arou' over 'awak'
27.3	spoke] 'sp' over 'ga'
27.13	It is] over 'You are'
27.16	look so—] dash cancels exclamation mark
27.25	been] 'b' over 'h'
27.27	then] preceded by comma intended to cancel period, and wiped-out double quotation mark; over wiped-out 'It'
27.28	decayed] preceded by cancelled 'fallen and'
27.28	If] mended from 'It'; followed by cancelled 'would [be too much]' and wiped-out comma
27.30	You] preceded by cancelled 'We are at war', the 'We' over wiped-out 'You'; 'You' inscribed over cancelled exclamation point

28.4–5	with . . . home] added in space after preceding paragraph
28.6	but] 'b' over 'y'
28.14	that was] 'that' above caret
28.16	give] mended from 'gives'
28.17–18	mysterious] 'm' over 'wo'
28.24	though my] over wiped-out 'yet your blood'
28.26	You] 'Y' altered from 'I'; 'ou' over 'am'
*28.32	direction] cancelled, and 'address' added above in hand of SH
29.4	a woman's] above cancelled 'the'
*29.9	direction] cancelled, and 'address' added above in hand of SH
29.12	England.] followed by wiped-out double quotation mark
29.14	Elizabethan] above caret
29.19	little] above caret
29.24	distaste for] over wiped-out 'preternaturally []f'
30.2	pocket] over wiped-out 'book'
*30.5	of] above caret, in the hand of SH
30.9	Uncle] marked above and below by horizontal lines and followed by an interlined question mark, in realization that ascription to the soldier's "Uncle" of what was to be revealed as an ancient manuscript, was unsatisfactory
30.15	bullet—] dash cancels comma
30.23	if there were] over wiped-out 'had there been'
*30.25	enough] above caret, in the hand of SH
30.27	this] over 'a'
30.28	There; let me] over partially wiped-out 'Ah; there is a br'
30.29	did as] over 'was a'
31.8	the body] above 'him down'
*31.17	see] preceded by 'could' above caret, in hand of SH
31.24	energy] above uncancelled 'courage'
31.28	Septimius] 'Sep' cancelled by line but then completed

32.6   fate had] 'had' above cancelled 'was'
32.10   some] above caret
32.34   let the] 'the' over 'it'
33.20–21   while . . . him] above caret
*33.22   to the] 'to' added in left margin in hand of SH
33.33   among difficult pebbles] above 'into its depths, levelling'; MS 'pebbbles'
34.20   scores] over wiped-out 'hundre'
*35.6   as] added in right margin in the hand of SH
35.17   you."] originally 'you. Does it'; 'Does it' wiped out and quotation marks added
35.26   putting] followed by cancelled 'to'
36.21   now] 'k' of original 'know' cancelled
36.31   and fusil] above caret
37.13   by] over 'to'
38.7   if] over 'yo'
*38.24   did it] 'it' added in the hand of SH
38.27–28   feeling . . . murderer.] added in space after 'spirit.' but leaving that period uncancelled
39.18   be fierce] 'b' over 'fi'
39.29   half-] 'l' over 'f'
*40.17   not] above caret, in hand of SH
40.29   in] 'to' of original 'into' cancelled
41.24   came] 'c' over 'g'
41.28   left] above cancelled 'right'
42.7–8   Rose— . . . it—] originally '~; . . . ~."'; first dash cancels semicolon and second is over wiped-out period and double quotation mark
42.9   Robert] 'R' over wiped-out double quotation mark
42.11   a] over 'his'
42.15   given] 'g' over 'i'
42.19   also] over 'and'
43.21   recess] 'rece' over wiped-out 'val'
*43.29   been] above caret, in hand of SH
44.18   edge] above cancelled 'ridge'
44.20   and] 'a' over 'in'

44.20   him] 'h' over 'it'

*44.23   Garfield] cancelled, and 'Hagburn' added above
        by SH

45.22   hill-] 'h' over 'p'

*45.26   by] above 'post', in hand of SH

45.33   (and] parenthesis cancels comma

46.4   what] over 'wat'

46.30   long, tame ridges] above caret and uncancelled
        'hills'

46.31   life.] period cancels comma

47.21   He] over 'Has'

*47.31   Garfield] cancelled, and "Hagburn' added
        above, in hand of SH

47.33   and] over 'or'

47.33   down] preceded by cancelled 'or'

48.3   wither,] followed by cancelled 'and grow yellow'

48.8   single] 's' over 'a'

*48.9   Garfield's] cancelled, and 'Hagburn's' added
        above, in hand of SH

48.29   He . . . day.] added in bottom margin of MS
        page

49.6   words] 'w' over 'fo'

49.21   was his] 'his' over 'its'

50.18   as he] 'h' over 'w'

*50.18   bring it] 'to' added above 'it' in hand of SH

50.24   (He . . . sentence)] added in space at end of
        paragraph

51.11   into] 'in' over wiped-out 'lik'

52.3   in] over 'this'

52.5   Well] 'W' over 'B'

52.6   with] over 'in'

52.14   exaggerated] initial 'e' over 'h'

52.31   undying] 'un' above caret

*53.1–2   to be] 'be' above caret, in hand of SH

54.5   battles] 'b' of MS 'batles' over 'th'

54.11–21   In this. . . . end.] preceded by hatch sign
        added to indicate, along with hatch sign and
        curved brace before 'Then came . . . way.'

	(54.22–28), transposition of the passage to include more matter about the "old codger" before the change of subject to the soldier
54.22	Then came . . .] originally followed 'gunpowder.' (54.11); see Alterations 54.11–21
54.24	sought] 'g' over 't'
54.26	though] followed by wiped-out terminal 't'
55.8–15	So . . . design.] followed by asterisk; see Alterations 55.23–25
55.12	by and] 'a' over wiped-out 'by'
55.23–25	Go . . . vanished.] an asterisk added in right margin to call NH's attention to this paraphrase of the sentence at 55.8–15, for future revision
55.28	at] 'a' over 'i'
56.8	strife] above cancelled 'struggle'
56.15	opposition] initial 'o' over 'a'
56.17	had come] 'h' over 'c'
56.24	everything] 'y' over 't'
56.32	in] 'i' over 's'
57.9	Birth] 'B' over 'b'
57.16	I] over wiped-out 'you'
57.32	sweet] over wiped-out 'lips'
58.3–4	undefinable] 'd' over 'f'
58.12	its individual] 'its in' over wiped-out 'the stars'
58.17	it . . . juice] above original 'blossom. This . . . now'
58.32	levelled] 'v' over 'ev'
59.13–14	Perhaps there . . . girl.] added in space after paragraph; 'there' mended from 'they'
59.21	vigorous] 'v' over 'sl'
59.22	drooping] 'd' over 'g'
59.24	looked] followed by wiped-out 'a'
59.24	met] 'm' over 'b'
60.3	and yellow pine-spikes] above caret placed in error after semicolon
60.10	laid] over wiped-out 'threw'
60.12	spoke] over wiped-out 'said, at'
60.18	be] over 'her'

60.24	find] 'f' over 'th'
60.27	top] over 'side'
60.28	strewn] 'st' over wiped-out 'over'
61.2	for] 'f' over wiped-out 'it'
61.3	live] above cancelled 'dwell'
61.10	who] 'w' over 's'
62.26	unsubstantiality] MS 'unsubsubstaniality' with 'un' over 'in'
63.7	witchcraft] 'tc' over wiped-out 'ch'
63.31	but she] 'sh' over 'is'
64.16	almost] 'alm' over wiped-out 'lov'
64.23	insists] initial 'i' over 'o'
65.2	on which] 'on' over wiped-out 'of w'
65.19	away, and] 'aw' over 'wa', 'and' over wiped-out 'th'
65.23	with] 'w' over 'of'
65.28	compel] above uncancelled 'alter'
66.4	had] 'd' mended from 's'
66.16	during] 'd' over 'a'
66.25	reference] 'ref' over wiped-out 'reli'
66.28	(or] parenthesis cancels comma
67.2	it—] dash intended to cancel comma
67.23	was] followed by wiped-out comma
67.30	brood] 'br' over 'ov'
68.9	looked] 'loo' over wiped-out 'wat'
68.11–12	Septimius . . . studies.] added in space after paragraph, separated from text by large curved line
68.23	effort.] period mended from semicolon
68.28–29	(He . . . minutely)] added in space after paragraph
68.31	dressed] 'd' over wiped-out 'in'
68.31	had] above caret
69.6	excellent] 'exc' over wiped-out 'pi'
69.10	memorable] over wiped-out 'little hillo'
69.17	late] terminal 'ly' wiped out
69.17–18	surgeon] above 'of his'
69.21	practise] over wiped-out 'try'
69.29	Sir?] question mark over double quotation mark

69.31   me!] exclamation mark over double quotation
      mark
69.32   niece] above cancelled 'daughter'
70.3   uncle] above 'father' which is inscribed over
      'uncle'
70.5   being] over wiped-out 'I take'
70.5   (the] parenthesis over 'to'
70.8   young] above 'be a'
71.19   which] over wiped-out 'of'
71.22   to] over wiped-out 'abo'
71.25   At] over 'He'
72.19   sharply] 'h' mended from 'p'
72.21   Keziah] 'K' mended from 'Z'
73.6   Nothing!—] dash over wiped-out double quota-
      tion mark
73.19   over] above caret
73.26   him?"] question mark cancels comma and
      double quotation mark
73.31   who] 'w' over 'o'
73.32   again?"] question mark cancels comma and
      double quotation mark
74.14   sitting] 's' over wiped-out 'p'; preceding double
      quotation mark not wiped out
74.15   pouch] 'ou' over 'ip'
74.23   Keziah] 'K' mended from 'Z'
74.29   Devil's] 'De' over wiped-out 'very'
74.30   (for] parenthesis cancels comma
74.33–75.2 "I . . . "I . . . down."] added within paren-
      theses, without the quotation marks, in avail-
      able space at foot of MS page, after paragraph
      ending 'English' (76.13), evidently to replace
      tentative ' "I thought," quoth the Doctor, "I
      could drink anything, but—" ', interlined
      above 'But the valiant Doctor sipped,'; initial
      and interior quotation marks before 'I' sup-
      plied from superseded passage, and final one
      a CENTENARY emendation
75.6   silver] over wiped-out 't[   ]ess'

75.6	cup] 'c' over wiped-out 'f'
75.8	decoction] first 'c' over wiped-out 'd'
75.17	apposition] 'a' over 'o'
75.19	long] 'l' over 'a'
75.30	all] over wiped-out 'we'
75.32	virtues] 'v' mended from 'b'
76.11	apposite] 'a' over 'o'
76.26	in] over wiped-out 'among'
77.3	he] over 'one'
77.11	had] 'd' over 've'
77.12	it.] period cancels semicolon
77.14	strict] 'st' over 'ce'
77.14	be kept] 'be' over 'to'
77.18	decay] 'de' over wiped-out 'yo'
77.25	D'Aubignys] 'y' over 'e'
77.32	effect.] followed by wiped-out double quotation mark
78.11	put them] over wiped-out 'making a fire'
78.13	Whereas] over wiped-out 'Sometimes'
78.19	some] 'so' over 'th'
78.28	elixir] 'l' over 'x'
78.29	a] mended from 'an'
79.9	young] over wiped-out 'Doctor'
79.12	if] over 'al'
79.15	our] over 'her'
79.32	openly] 'op' over 'av'
80.18	what] above caret
81.8	character.] period supersedes comma
81.8	upon] 'up' over wiped-out 'of'
81.20	fantastic] above caret
81.21	Kezia] 'K' mended from 'Z'
82.4	So] preceded by wiped-out double quotation mark
82.17	witch] 'tc' over wiped-out 'ch'
83.3	Keziah] 'K' mended from 'Z'
83.15–17	The . . . blood-root.] added in space after paragraph
83.18	love] 'l' over 'v'

83.32   were] over wiped-out 'your a'
84.19   had] 'h' over 'th'; preceded by wiped-out comma
84.27   so] 's' over 'd'
84.28   nature. So . . .] 'nature' was originally fol-
          lowed by a semicolon and 'and they thought
          it time that so good a man and so great a
          warrior and wizard should be gone to the
          happy hunting-grounds, and that so wise a
          counsellor should go and tell his experience
          of life to the great Father, and give him an
          account of matters here, and perhaps lead
          him to make some changes in the conduct of
          matters here;—and so, all these things duly
          considered, they very reverently assassinated
          the great, never-dying Sachem; for though
          safe against disease, and undecayable by age,
          he was capable of being killed by violence,
          though the hardness of his skull broke to
          fragments the stone tomahawk with which
          they at first tried to kill him'; NH then inter-
          lined two hatch marks before 'and they', and
          after 'kill him' inscribed a left brace and two
          hatch marks before the revision to follow
          'nature'; he added a note '(See below)' in top
          margin of MS page to call attention to the
          troublesome spot, and in the Norton draft
          (pages 357-62) recovered many details; the
          period after 'nature' is a CENTENARY emenda-
          tion
84.28   a] over 'the'
85.1   ever] altered from 'them'
85.8   last)] parenthesis cancels comma
85.9   of his] 's' over 'm'
85.9   breast] over wiped-out 'and his'
85.10–18 Make . . . him.] preceded by two and fol-
          lowed by four vertical lines, added in space
          at end of paragraph before the next was
          begun; the top margin note '(See below)'
          remarked upon in Alterations entry 84.28

	may refer also to this direction for future revision
85.12	Undying] 'U' over 'u'
85.15	—his intolerable wisdom—] above 'and . . . command'
85.19–20	Describe . . . &c] added in space after 'him.' after the next paragraph had been inscribed
85.21–22	Perhaps . . . which] interlined between 'Describe . . . &c' and first line of next paragraph
85.32–33	They . . . flower] 'They . . . beautiful' above the line, and 'purple flower' below, before 'But . . .'
86.6	great-] above 'grandfather'
86.10	his] over 'the'
86.16	her mother] 'her' above cancelled 'and grand', the 'and' cancelled inadvertently
86.27	Yes] over 'No'
86.33	most] over wiped-out 'in all'
87.6	concoction] 'co' over 'br'
87.13	salutary] 'salu' over wiped-out 'salub'
87.21	and] 'an' over wiped-out 'po'
87.27	knee] over 'arm'
87.34	chimney-] 'chim' over wiped-out 'kitch'
89.4	in] over wiped-out 'his'
89.4	was] preceded by wiped-out double quotation mark
89.14	uncertain] 'uncer' over wiped-out 'certain'
89.21	deeds] over 'more'
90.1	ascribe] mended from 'ascribes'
90.4	me] 'm' over 'b'
90.18	also] 'l' over 'r'
90.21	laughable,] comma cancels dash
91.4	Dacy—] dash cancels semicolon
91.12	where] 'w' over 'th'
92.11	shall] 'all' over 'ould'
92.11	the] over 'a'
92.14	humanity] comma cancels period
92.15	another.] period cancels comma

92.19   Nobody] 'N' over 'A'

92.29   mark] 'm' over 's'

92.31   handkerchief?—] question mark added after inscription of dash

93.6   men] over cancelled 'once' which is over undeciphered letters

93.12   of—] dash cancels comma

93.14   It is] over 'how' and a preceding comma cancelled by period

94.4–5   purpose—] dash cancels comma

94.10   object in] 'o' over wiped-out 'of'

95.4   control,] comma cancels dash

96.3   in] followed by uncancelled 'o' and downstroke of possible 'n' at right edge of MS page, seemingly in erroneous start of 'one' which was inscribed after 'was' on next MS line

96.8   in] 't' of original 'int' cancelled

96.14–15   He . . . her.] added in space after paragraph

96.17   he carried her into] over wiped-out 'then [   ] to'

96.21   he] over wiped-out 'the'

97.3   lord] followed by cancelled 'took a portion of her virgin blood, in'

97.3   buried her] over partially wiped-out and inked over 'a goblet, and [   ]'

97.4   to] over 'in'

97.8   all along] over wiped-out 'and right to the'

97.11   them as death.] above 'them', 'He' was added as if to begin an alteration but was then wiped out

97.13   could] 'co' over 'to'

97.24   there it] 're' added to original 'the'; 'it' over wiped-out 'rushes'

97.32   place] 'pl' over 'wh'

98.1   track] 'ck' over possible 'il'

98.15   Sir] over wiped-out 'The'

98.28–29   and . . . door-step] added above 'up . . . a bloody track' preceded by the clue word

	'home;' to indicate insertion after original 'and so home he came,'
98.29	into] over wiped-out 'to'
99.4	Sir] over 'the'
100.4	(See other sheet)] added in top margin of MS page above 'marvellous legend'; reference is to the preceding narrative
100.26	at] over 'int'
101.12	smooth pond] 'sm' over wiped-out 'pon'
101.18	Applying . . .] above the first line of the paragraph are four marks suggesting asterisks to indicate a space break
101.32	that language] 'at' over 'e'; 'l' mended from 'L'
101.32	in] above caret
102.17	at] over wiped-out 'for'
103.6	perished] 'per' over wiped-out 'exp'
103.25	his] 'h' over 't'
103.33	astray, partly] 'par' over wiped-out 'by its'
104.13	its] above caret
104.15	moral] above caret
104.26	Bask . . . heart] added in space after paragraph at the top margin of MS page
104.30	thy mental] over wiped-out 'thine eyes st'
105.5	intercourse] above uncancelled 'friendship'
105.23–24	Do not . . . years. Do not . . . habits] added in confined space following paragraph, the second sentence following directly after the first
106.3–4	If beggars haunt . . . ear-shot] for want of space, MS 'If begars haunt' was interlined above 'elsewhere.' of preceding sentence, and the rest of the sentence interlined above the next sentence following here
106.12–14	If . . . self-laudation] for want of clear space, interlined within the preceding paragraph, above 'and drink . . . Also, the breath' (106.6–8)
106.22	fervently] above uncancelled 'much'

106.22	keep] over wiped-out 'hold'
106.30	nor be . . . arrow] above 'horse, nor confront a'
107.7	& . . . it] above caret
107.9	is apt] 'is' over wiped-out 'gi'
108.6	He . . . some time.] added in space after paragraph, separated from body of text by curved brace
108.16	dew] a final 'y' wiped out
108.16	upon] 'up' over wiped-out 'of'
110.7	an undefined] 'an un' over wiped-out 'aver'
110.15–16	Describe . . . illness.] added in space beside two previous short paragraphs of dialogue
110.21–22	She . . . sunshine] added above 'and was . . . upon;'
111.10	in] over wiped-out 'that'
111.15	and . . . tea-cup] above cancelled 'carefully measured out'
111.16	and . . . old] over wiped-out 'three teaspoonsfuls of her'
111.21	(She . . . again.] added in space after paragraph
111.27	bed] above caret
111.29	or] over 'ab'
111.31	trying] over wiped-out 'attempt'
112.2	in] above caret
112.15–16	"Damn the Doctor! You can] ' "Damn the Doctor," can' added above 'You . . . ' ; see corresponding Emends entry
112.17	kitchen] 'kitch' over wiped-out 'fire'
113.19	when] 'w' mended from 'it'
113.24	on] over 'f'
113.28	and] over wiped-out 'as if'
114.29	not] 'n' over wiped-out 't'
114.30	upon] 'up' over wiped-out 'it'
114.31	right, Seppy] 'right' followed by wiped-out double quotation mark; 'Se' over wiped-out 'sa'
115.17	bed] above caret
116.5	at it] 'at' over 'it'

116.8	brow] above uncancelled 'forehead'
116.13	could] 'c' over 'it'
116.21	own] over wiped-out 'pulse'
116.23	ghastly] 'g' over 'p'
116.27	put] over wiped-out 'list'
117.19	for his] over 'in this'
117.31	to] over 'he'
118.5	have] 'ha' over wiped-out 'bee'
118.9–17	Each . . . it.] preceded and followed by three vertical lines to mark passage for future reference or revision
118.11	above all] 'ab' over wiped-out 'the' and 'all' over 'ev'
118.23	vacant] above cancelled 'cold'
119.29	to] over 'tha'
119.32	you] over 'he'
120.5	well,] followed by wiped-out single quotation mark
120.18	calm] 'm' over 'l'
120.18–19	Doctor—] dash cancels comma
120.19	for] mended from 'of'
120.32	and . . . sky] added above 'could . . . blaspheme' with '&c' to indicate inclusion in the speech
121.3	Seppy] preceded by cancelled double quotation mark
121.22	known] over wiped-out 'and'
122.2	goodness.] period cancels comma
122.16	the pines] 't' mended from 'p'
122.25–27	Oh. . . . from it.] after NH wrote these sentences following 'roof.' (122.20), he marked the passage with two-tiered carets before and after, to signal repositioning in order to continue the description of Indian life; the insertion point is not marked, but CENTENARY placement is determined by the cue of 'dull!' to which the passage relates
123.9–10	and a . . . Heaven] above 'there . . . trees to'
123.12	darling] 'dar' over wiped-out 'boy'

123.13   while] 'whi' over 'wi[   ]'
123.15   and] 'a' over 'b'
124.5   herbs] 'h' over partial 'S'
124.29   old maid] 'old m' over wiped-out 'witch'
125.3   West] 'W' over 'w'
125.3   tasted] followed by cancelled 'it'
125.3   Mrs Hagburn] above 'one of the old women',
          uncancelled except for 'women'
125.5   now] 'n' over 'I'
125.14   himself] 'h' mended from 'p'; 'se' over 'f'
126.2   others] 'ot' over wiped-out 'w'
127.8-9   (put . . . hinders)] added in bottom margin of
          MS page, below the clause following here
127.16   cold] above cancelled 'hot'
127.19   but] mended from 'and'
127.20   in] over wiped-out 'the'
127.21   placed] altered from 'persons'
127.28   bring . . . finally] added above 'upon . . . of'
127.33   Enemy] 'E' over 'e'
128.8   to] over 'his'
128.15   committed] 'com' over 'perm'; second 'm' added
          above line
128.20   so that] over wiped-out 'as thou'
129.3-5   (One . . . way)] added at end of paragraph,
          before inscription of following paragraph
129.7   Lexington] 'x' over 'g'
129.10   almost] 'a' over 'as'
129.11   What] 'W' over 'It'
129.30   that] initial 't' over 'w'
130.8-9   (Put . . . person)] added in space at end of
          paragraph
130.13   of] above caret
131.1   Insert . . . town] interlined between paragraphs
131.13   wooden] 'w' over 'h'
131.17   maimed] mended from 'married'
131.18   many] 'm' over 'th'
131.28   people] 'pl' over 'le'
131.33   of] over wiped-out 'upon'

132.26	and] 'a' over 'w'
132.32	night-cap] 'n' over 'k'
132.32	German] 'G' over 'g'
133.13	spider] 'd' over 'p'
134.3	typified] 'ty' over wiped-out 'th'
134.12	head] 'a' over 'd'
134.18	and] followed by wiped-out comma
134.19	enemies] 'ies' over wiped-out 'y'
134.20	come] 'c' over 's'
134.31	to] over wiped-out 'tell'
134.32	hand] terminal 's' wiped out
135.5	it—] dash cancels period and double quotation mark
135.11	The] preceded by cancelled double quotation mark
135.11	red] over wiped-out 'great'
135.19	reproduction] over wiped-out 'propagation'
136.3	answered] 'ans' over wiped-out 'been'
136.6	the bed] 't' over 'it'
136.8	kill] 'k' over 's'
136.21	be a] originally 'become'; 'a' over wiped-out 'come'
136.24	no private] 'no priv' over wiped-out 'except [me]'
137.6	Aunt] 'A' over 'a'
137.17	moonlight] 'light' above uncancelled 'shine' of MS 'moonshine'
137.27–28	and . . . make] over wiped-out 'though for my part I have'
138.6	you] preceded by wiped-out comma
138.23	upon] 'up' over 'on'
139.24	My] 'M' over wiped-out double quotation mark
139.32	singular] 'u' over 'l'
139.32	charlatanic] 'la' above caret after 'r' of 'charatanic', resulting in MS 'charlaatanic'
141.29	It was] 'It w' over wiped-out 'though'; preceded by comma mended to period
141.31	(a grandson, not a son)] added in margin at

	foot of MS page, below 'one son . . . arrival'
142.1	prominent] 'pro' over wiped-out 'chi'
142.3	man] 'm' over wiped-out 'p'
142.3	slightly] 's' over wiped-out 'a'
142.20	half] 'h' over 'I'
142.28	remember . . . wizard] added above 'melon . . . enough'
142.30	maiden] over 'woman'
143.4	The] over wiped-out 'He'
143.5–6	and had intermarried] 'and had interma' over wiped-out '[ ] of a'
143.15	he] 'e' over 'is'
143.31	childhood] 'chi' over 'you'
144.3	her] 'h' over 't'
144.25	yourself] above caret
144.25	aristocracy] preceded by cancelled 'titled'
145.3	me] 'e' over 'y'
145.8	do] over 'not'
145.30	My] 'M' over 'Yo'
145.32	in] over 'it'
146.9	home. He] period and 'H' over wiped-out comma and 'h'
146.28	on] over 'air'
147.18	the science] 'the s' over wiped-out 'through'
148.15	an] 'a' over 't'
150.2	yet . . . same] above 'ways . . . the'
150.12–13	Sometimes . . . him.] added in space after paragraph
150.14	Could he] over wiped-out 'Septimius'
151.17	friendship] 'frie' over 'love'
151.18	lonely] 'e' over 'y'
151.21	beside] MS 'side'; 's' over 'h'
151.25	away;] semicolon cancels period; followed by uncancelled double quotation mark
151.27	live] 'v' over 'f'
151.32	Dacy—] dash cancels colon
152.7	brow] 'b' over 'f'
152.9	a] over 'for'

152.22	you] 'y' over 's'
152.23	it is—] dash cancels comma
153.12	mingled;] semicolon cancels period
153.32	family] above caret
154.12	or garret] 'or' mended from 'of'
154.21	an] over wiped-out 'the'
154.25	beadle] above uncancelled 'warden'
155.12	sea] 'a' over 'p'
156.28	its] over wiped-out 'the'
157.2	toil] over 'life'
157.15	and though] over wiped-out 'when the'
157.32	priest] 'pr' over wiped-out 'cha'
158.30	the war] 'the' added above 'war'
159.28	one sword] over wiped-out 'whatever'
159.30	how] 'h' over wiped-out 'wh'
160.1	tame. So] period cancels comma; 'So' over wiped-out 'if'
160.14	strange] 's' over wiped-out 'p'
161.11	records] over wiped-out 'infor'
162.4	fulfilled] 'll' over 'ff'
162.27	above] 'a' over wiped-out 'be'
162.27	whom] 'w' over 'hi'
162.29–30	a resting] over wiped-out 'an [ ]p'
162.33	one of the persons] originally 'the first person'; 'first' cancelled, 'one' interlined with a caret, and terminal 's' added to 'person'; 'of' is a CENTENARY emendation
163.2	to] over 'of'
163.10	my] 'm' over 'f'
163.20	he could] 'c' over 's'
165.15	as sane] 'as' above caret
165.15–16	as he . . . past] above caret
165.22	itself] 'it' over wiped-out 'up'
166.14	it.] period cancels comma
166.31	it] over 'he'
167.8	covering] over wiped-out 'day by day'
167.11	hue] 'h' over 'w'
167.17	of life] 'o' over 'li'

167.19	nights] over wiped-out 'days'
167.26–27	The . . . part] above 'whom . . . modes'
167.30	Aunt . . . death-bed] above 'through . . . Sybil'
167.30–31	and . . . footstep] above 'from . . . some'
168.2	a] over 'dre'
168.11	his] over 'wat'
169.14	deep] 'd' over 'm'
170.19	much] 'm' over 'h'
170.28	to] above caret
170.28	mission] 'm' over 'p'
171.1	boundaries—] dash cancels comma
171.5	and converse] 'a' over comma
171.15	after] over wiped-out 'all th'
171.24	contemptible] 'i' over 'l'
171.29	mankind] 'man' over wiped-out 'peo'
172.17	rotten] 'rot' over 'evil'
172.26	we will] 'e' over wiped-out 'il'
172.32	answered] 'a' over wiped-out 'S'
173.19	behind,] comma over wiped-out period; double quotation mark imperfectly wiped-out
173.27–28	have gained] 'h' over 'g'
174.8	prayers] followed by cancelled 'through me'
174.12–13	(He . . . one.)] added in space at end of paragraph
174.20	hundred] 'hund' over wiped-out 'cent'
174.26–27	The rampant . . . wickedness.] 'T' over double quotation mark; the passage was added to original paragraph after the following sentence had been inscribed
175.21	The virtues of plants &c &c &c] added in space after paragraph
175.25	of] over wiped-out 'as'
175.33	always] 'w' over 'l'
176.1	the] over wiped-out 'act'
176.4	may] 'm' over wiped-out 'f'
176.7	and] 'a' over 't'
176.28	heretofore] 't' over 'f'

177.1–3	(He . . . posterity)] added in space after paragraph
178.1–18	It . . . marriage."] added after the paragraph ending 'dream upon.' (181.23); enclosed by curved braces, an earlier closing brace after 'wedding.' having been previously added and then wiped out; transposed by direction of a note 'Rose asks Sybil to be her bridesmaid)' added above 'And now . . . Hagburn's' (178.19–20) in the top margin of the MS page
179.5	trouble] 'u' over 'b'
180.16	this] above caret
180.26	would] 'wou' over wiped-out 'some'
181.26	into] over wiped-out 'over'
181.31	may set] over 'now I'
182.1	Am] 'A' over 'a'
182.3	—nothing] dash over wiped-out 'her'
182.16	to] over 'into'
182.23	for] above cancelled 'of'
183.13	brandy] 'b' over wiped-out 'w'
183.24	learned] 'learn' over wiped-out 'good'
183.31	of] over 'for'
184.2	squaw] 'sq' over 'Ind'
184.5	if] above caret
184.15	tall-] over wiped-out 'bed'
184.15	ready] 'ad' over wiped-out 'dy'
184.19	his] over wiped-out 'the'
184.26	if I had] 'if' over 'I'; 'I had' over wiped-out 'had for'
184.27	time] final 's' wiped out
184.29	Some . . . laughed] added below 'old Felton was hung with."' in space after the next sentence
184.31	the minister] below uncancelled 'Robert Hagburn'
184.33	I] over double quotation mark
185.11	gifts] over wiped-out 'power'

185.20	in.] period cancels comma; followed by wiped-out 'she'
186.18	Do] over wiped-out 'But'
186.20	pallid] over wiped-out 'fingers'
186.32	fear] over wiped-out 'death'
187.20	Do] over wiped-out 'I'
187.21	would] 'w' over 'do'
187.28	Septimius.] followed by wiped-out 'looking like'; period mended from comma
187.31	no one] 'no' over 'to' and 'one' over 'no'
188.7	life] over wiped-out 'man p'
188.15	inmost] 'in' over wiped-out 'he' or 'sec'
188.18	to] over wiped-out 'its'
188.30	young,] comma cancels dash
189.5	mockingly] 'ly' over 'he'
189.17	quaff] 'q' over 'dr'
189.26	discovered] MS 'discoveed'; 'dis' over wiped-out 'est'
189.27	said] 's' over 'th'
190.6–7	which . . . grave] above caret
190.26	shifting.] followed by wiped-out double quotation mark
190.28	Forgive] preceded by wiped-out double quotation mark
190.29	bending] above cancelled 'turning'
190.32	live] over wiped-out 'die'
191.9	well—yes] dash cancels comma
191.14	it.] followed by wiped-out double quotation mark
191.16–17	She . . . way)] added in space at end of paragraph
191.29	among] over wiped-out 'all s'
191.33	Portsoaken.] period cancels semicolon
192.13	This] over 'His'
192.20	niece] over wiped-out possible 'dau'
192.25	consented to] 'to' above caret
192.25	or instigated] above caret
192.33	even a suspicion] over wiped-out 'a fantastic'
193.11	vanished] 'va' over 'pro'

193.13	greatly] 'gr' over 'm'
193.29	Septimius] 'S' over 'o'

Septimius Norton

195.1–2	as . . . books] above caret
195.2	towards] over wiped-out 'at sunset'
195.4	West] 'W' over 'w'
195.5	affording] preceded by cancelled 'overlooking'
195.6–7	his native neighborhood below] 'his native' added above uncancelled 'the' and 'below' added above 'neighborhood'
195.7–8	once seemed] over wiped-out 'with its bays'
195.8	the] above cancelled 'a'
195.9	reaped] above cancelled 'had'
195.10	harvests] preceded by cancelled 'fields'
195.11	were] followed by wiped-out comma
195.12	who] over wiped-out 'that'
195.15	and had] 'had' above 'as'
195.17–18	some . . . puritanism] above 'meditations . . . instructed'
195.19	indulge—] dash cancels comma
195.20	pursuit] above cancelled 'object'
195.21	ever] over wiped-out 'for'
195.21	Pilgrims] 'Pi' over wiped-out 'ea'
195.22	object] 'b' over 'j'
196.1	destined. But] period mended from comma; 'B' over 'b'
196.1	there were] above caret
196.3	trim] above caret
196.3–4	which the narrow] above cancelled 'of his mind, on'
196.5	hardly] 'ha' over 'no'
196.5–6	save . . . weeds] above 'nor. . . . and'
196.15	It . . . sunset.] added in top margin of MS page
196.16–17	(Dr. Ormskirk . . . visionary.)] interlined be-

	tween 'as . . . books' (see 195.1–2) and the first sentence of the following narrative
196.18	It . . . divinity] added in space after first paragraph (197.2), near the right margin
196.19–20	The . . . character] added above 'It . . . divinity' in space at end of paragraph, set off from context by small vertical lines
196.28–29	the foliage . . . thoughts] above caret and uncancelled 'of his thoughts' and 'at the swelling buds'
196.28	the exceeding] preceded by wiped-out 'the'
196.30	at] over wiped-out 'and'
196.31	bring . . . it] above 'other things and . . . which'
196.32	—allude to Rose—] below 'and the dusky hues'
196.33– 197.1	old conservatives there] preceded by two-tiered caret, added after paragraph; insertion point marked by a caret; 'there' mended from 'them'
197.3	"I . . . Septimius] added after paragraph, above two cancelled starts of new paragraph: 'It was was unmistakeably a clerical personage,' and ' "In your customary place, Septimius, which', whereof 'Septimius' was left uncancelled; 'timius' of final inscription 'Sep- | timius' over 'which'
197.5	or it might be three] above caret; an earlier inscribed 'or three' below 'Two' was wiped out
197.6	nine] above 'eight'
197.6	in] 'i' over 'o'
197.7	what] 'at' over 'ic'
197.8	It is always good] 'so he' inscribed and wiped out; replaced by 'I always have found it good', with 'I al' over the deletion; 'I' mended to 'It', 'is' added above 'always' and 'found' cancelled but 'have' and 'it' left, in error
197.11–12	There . . . student] added in space at end of paragraph

197.13–14	Some . . . in . . . country] added in cramped space after 'There . . . student' with 'in . . . country' enclosed by parentheses for separation from the earlier note and from the previously inscribed first line of the next paragraph
197.16	manner] 'm' over wiped-out 'exp'
197.17	probably] above 'possibly'
197.20	stipend] 'sti' over wiped-out 'sal'
197.21	was] followed by cancelled 'contradicted by the ex'
197.21	or] over wiped-out 'by'
197.24	the country] 'the' over 'a'; 'country' above uncancelled 'village'
197.26	Mr. Norton] above 'replied'
197.27	—provided] dash cancels comma; second terminal 'd' cancelled
197.29	faithfully] MS 'faithfuly'; second 'f' over 'l'
197.31	your] 'y' over 'm'
197.31	my] 'm' over 'y'
198.4	am] over wiped-out 'fear'
198.5	from seeds] over wiped-out 'and of [ ]'
198.8	Papists] above cancelled 'monks'
198.10	(that] parenthesis cancels comma
198.15	the Rev.] above 'Mʳ'
198.17	allude to it] preceded by cancelled 'avow it'
198.20	and beside] above caret
198.27	as if] above was added 'upon', but the following construction requires retention of 'as if'
198.27	had] lines added above and below, perhaps to mark for emendation
198.27	and] over wiped-out comma and 'fi'
198.27	come,—] followed by cancelled 'or rather will [ ] itself already strong'
198.27	you . . . it] above 'a faith . . . come'
198.32–33	The . . . wits.] added in space at end of paragraph
199.2	to] above caret
199.4	won.] period cancels comma

199.5	dark] over wiped-out 'forehe' followed by cancelled 'brooding'
199.17	have] above 'maintained'
199.18	throughout] over wiped-out 'through life'
199.18–19	in . . . house] over wiped-out 'sometimes it had bette'
199.21–22	away. They . . . it.] a two-tiered caret after 'away.' marks insertion point for the alteration 'They . . . it.' which was added in space above the paragraph
199.23–24	as . . . legends] above caret
199.24	legends—] dash cancels comma
199.27	with a] over wiped-out 'impatiently'
199.28	not] over wiped-out 'my'
199.33	what] over wiped-out 'I find'
200.1	mental] 'men' over wiped-out 'intell'
200.2	prejudiced] above 'impression'
200.5	the true] 'the t' over wiped-out 'my B'
200.12	its] 'i' over 'a'
200.32	with all its] over wiped-out 'to be something for'
201.4	one] 'e' over 'ce'
201.14–15	some degree] 'some' over wiped-out 'justice'; 'd' over 'of'
201.19–20	understood; snatch] semicolon over wiped-out dash; 'snatch' over wiped-out 'only'
201.21	make] 'm' over wiped-out 'to'
201.25	duration.] period cancels semicolon
201.27	decrepit] 'd' over 's'
201.28	It is my] over wiped-out '[ ] only'
201.29	scheme] 'h' over 'ie'
201.32	step] 't' over 'p'
202.2	to you] 'to' over 'y'
202.4	live] over wiped-out 'linger'
202.9	a European] 'a' over 'an'
202.9	Another] over wiped-out 'No, and'
202.13	all] over 'is'
202.17	further;] semicolon cancels period
202.21	dark room] 'dark r' over wiped-out 'dark ho'
202.28	with] 'w' over wiped-out 'wh'

203.1	queerness] over wiped-out 'own Indian [ ]f[ ]'
203.4–5	being . . . sister] interlined with a caret
203.8–11	Aunt Nashoba. . . . feathers)] the first sentence added in clear space above paragraph beginning "I have my own ways . . .", filling the space completely; the rest of the note added below the paragraph in clear space
203.14	to] above 'if I may', cancelled except for 'if'
203.15	-house.] period cancels comma
203.18– 205.5	So the young men parted; and Septimius retired . . . kettle] as the scene was originally written, Septimius's meditation took place after the meal, but Hawthorne decided that it should come before the pre-dinner chores; we may assume that the notes about Aunt Nashoba (203.8–11) were already inscribed, and that Hawthorne was obliged to move up the page to clear space before the minister's last speech: there he inscribed 'Septimius goes from the hill-top to his study, instead of being summoned to split wood & to supper by Aunt Nashoba.'; the matter which is here transposed, 'Septimius retired . . . kettle', was originally preceded by '¶ After their frugal meal' which he cancelled by circling, and the remainder of the passage, which had followed 'himself.' (206.17) now precedes 'After doing . . . (205.5)
203.18	a] above 'room' which is over wiped-out 'the'
203.23	great] above 'his'
203.24	grandfather] 'an' over 'eat'
203.24	These books] over wiped-out 'Some of these'
203.26–27	having . . . generations] above caret
203.30	for] over wiped-out 'which'
204.2	To confess] over wiped-out 'In truth'
204.4	lurid] above caret
204.6	(it] parenthesis cancels comma
204.11–12	that . . . rest] above caret
204.13	so] 's' over 'f'

204.13	that, for] 'for' over wiped-out 'at'
204.15	And] followed by cancelled 'with this perfection of'
204.15	being so perfect] above caret
204.16	man's] over wiped-out 'his'
204.16	was it possible] over wiped-out 'it was not'
204.16	purpose] 'r' over-wiped-out 'p'
204.17	he] over 'his'
204.22	strength] 'gth' over 'ght'
204.23–24	bewildered him] over wiped-out 'its spiritual fr'; preceded by cancelled 'transferred'
204.26	sense] 's' over wiped-out 'f'
205.3–5	Out of . . . kettle] this bridge passage, followed in MS by '& &.', connects the end of the transposed passage with the previously written account of pre-dinner chores
205.3	summoned] 's' over 'a'
205.5	to boil] 't' over 'f'
205.5	After] MS '(after'; the parenthesis cancels 'b'
205.6	with] 'w' over 'as'
205.8	lawless] above cancelled 'thoughts'
205.8	speculations] 'sp' over 'an'
205.9	did] over wiped-out 'lit'
205.10	came at] 'at' over 'to'
205.11	as she called it,] MS 'as she called,' over wiped-out 'made from some'
205.12	shrub] above uncancelled 'weed'
205.16	(Here . . . Christianity)] added above the passage that follows here
205.17–18	Ask . . . it," said she.] MS ' "Ask . . . '; this sentence added above '(Here . . . Christianity)' after the latter had been inscribed, as the squeezed-in placement of 'she' to the left of both additions implies; the passage inserted by indication of a two-tiered caret after 'boy," ' of MS 'boy," said Aunt Nashoba.', the insertion requiring elimination of superfluous punctuation; MS 'said she' supersedes original 'said Aunt Nashoba'

205.21	large spoonful] above cancelled 'lump'
205.26–27	and . . . convulsion] above caret
205.27	decoction,] comma cancels period
205.30	a] over 'an'
205.32	declining] MS 'delcin-' above cancelled 'rejec' of original 'rejecting'
206.9–10	out of her] over wiped-out 'as human'
206.24	food] above 'meat'
206.24	putting] 'put' over wiped-out 'with'
206.25	the] above 'tincture'
206.27	may] 'm' over 'it'
207.2	made the] over wiped-out '[ ] yet'
207.2	and] over wiped-out 'with'
207.6	could] 'c' over 'w'
207.10	of this] 'of' above caret
207.12–14	Yes . . . too.] added after inscription of the following sentence, with 'Yes . . . helped' interlined below 'A great . . . Aunt' but 'and the noble . . . too.' continued in space above the first sentence, emphasizing the addition's position before 'It was said . . . '
207.13	helped him] 'hel' over 'aid'
207.14	It was said of him] added above original beginning 'He took up'
207.15	all the] originally 'a Chris'; 'Chris' wiped out, 'll' added after 'a', and 'the' inscribed at a slant over 'is'
207.16	somehow] 'so' over 'w'
207.19–22	and . . . him."] added in space after paragraph
207.21	yellow] 'y' over 'g'
207.27	dust] over wiped-out 'remains'
207.27	Every living] 'l' over wiped-out 'b' of original 'Everyb'
207.32	of the] 'the' over 'this'
208.1	Nature] 'N' over 'an'
208.6	only] 'on' over 'a p'
208.10	and green beauty] above 'gloss which perhaps'
208.20	the mysterious] 'the' above caret
208.20	characteristic] initial 'c' over wiped-out 'th'

208.25   a perpetual] the article over 'p'; second 'p' over 'f'

208.28   lovely] 'lo' over 'bl'

208.32– 209.2   And . . . death.] preceded and followed by three diagonal slashes; in the absence of any sign for transposition, it may be conjectured that the marks call attention to a proposed change of scene associated with the addition 'Septimius . . . disturbed)' following 'death.'

209.2–3   Septimius . . . disturbed)] added in space at end of paragraph

209.2   goes] over wiped-out 'looks'

209.4–6   In . . . night, there . . . dwelt.] between 'night,' and 'there' was originally inscribed 'which was', followed by 'the eve . . . felt.', now transposed to 209.27–29 by direction of the note added above the paragraph, 'Put first sentence at the end'; a heavy parenthesis was added before the paragraph to call attention, and another was added after 'felt' at the end of the passage to be transposed; 'which was' is superseded by the later phrasing: see note for 209.26–27

209.10–11   once . . . woods—] above 'strong . . . again'

209.12   set off it] over wiped-out 'fired it'

209.13   besides] over wiped-out 'this'

209.18–19   The air . . . made.] with a wavery vertical line before and after, added in space after the paragraph; here transposed without authorial sign to follow the sentence in which the topic of the air is introduced

209.19   The] over wiped-out 'And'

209.20   with unusual] over wiped-out 'behind the hill'

209.22   of] over 'old'

209.23   really prophetic] above cancelled 'ghastly'

209.24   armies] preceded by cancelled 'shadowy'

209.25   shadow] above 'the rout'

209.26   have] 'h' over wiped-out 'n'

209.26–27   for . . . great] in MS followed by '&c' to indi-

	cate overlap with 'the eve . . . felt.' of original first sentence of paragraph, transposed by NH's direction; see note for 209.4–6
209.30	story] followed by cancelled 'is intended'
209.30	to record] above 'object, the'
209.30	the] 't' over wiped-out 'to'
209.32	strange] enclosed by pen strokes, perhaps for future alteration to avoid repetition by 'strange' later in the sentence
209.32– 210.2	pursuit in which . . . delusions] a two-tiered caret after 'pursuit,' marks the insertion point for 'in which . . . delusions' which, preceded by a similar sign, was inscribed following 'results' (210.3)
210.1	strange] 'st' over wiped-out 'many'
210.3	of the] above 'course'
210.4	running . . . vine] above 'sometimes leads us'
210.5	its tendrils] preceded by wiped-out 'its effusions'
210.5	them,] followed by cancelled 'the necessity of alluding to such'
210.6	accept the] 'ac' over possible 'c'; 'the' over 'a'
210.9	develope] preceded by cancelled 'illustrate'
210.11	a] above cancelled 'the'
210.14–15	Describe . . . to)] added in space at end of paragraph
210.16	was yet] over wiped-out 'yet sho'
210.18	man] above caret
210.18	in the neighborhood] over partially wiped-out 'the neighborhood'
210.18	had met] over 'were assem'
210.19	of a] over wiped-out 'that'
210.21	muster] above cancelled 'band'
210.22	several] 's' covers comma
210.27	Queen] over wiped-out 'King's'
210.30	militia] 'mi' over wiped-out 'sol'
211.4–6	told, as men . . . enveloped] the paragraph originally ended 'told.'; 'as men . . . enveloped' was interlined with a caret inserted between 'told' and period; the addition began

	in error with 'men' at left edge of the page; NH added 'as' in the right margin following 'enveloped,' from which it was separated by a comma rather than a period, in error
211.7	said] over wiped-out 'sho'
211.9	slaying and] 'nd' over 'll'
211.11	trembling.] period cancels comma; followed by wiped-out 'and'
211.12	dear] 'd' over 'l'
211.17	to] over wiped-out 'do'
211.18	came] over 'wa'
211.19	Satan] 'S' over 'th'
211.20	that the barrel] 'that' followed by cancelled 'it was forged in'; 'the' over 'a'
211.20	in] 'i' over 'o'
211.24	"I know not . . .] double arrows added before the paragraph would seem to indicate a transposition point, but there is no evidence of what the change would be
211.25	coolly, for] comma replaces wiped-out period and quotation mark; 'f' over possible 'E'
211.26	still] 's' over wiped-out 'of'
211.27	almost] 'alm' over wiped-out 'bec'
212.1	incalculably] 'in' over wiped-out 'the'
212.2–3	added . . . shudder—] above caret
212.3	hold] 'h' over 't'
212.5	as if] above caret
212.6	what] 'at' over 'ich'
212.11	a] over 'his'
212.17	Englishmen] above uncancelled 'one of'
212.19	life—] dash cancels comma and double quotation mark
212.28	man's life—] dash cancels comma
212.30	There] preceded by wiped-out double quotation mark
212.31	by the] 'b' over wiped-out 'the'; 'the' over wiped-out 'st'
213.5	by] over wiped-out 'all'
213.8	Hagburn] above uncancelled 'Garfied'

213.10	conscious] 'con' over wiped-out 'kno'
213.11	whether] above 'that' which is underlined by penstroke probably intended as cancellation
213.11	looking on] above 'there'
213.12	in his arm] over wiped-out 'in the [ ]'
213.18	be hugged] 'hug' over wiped-out 'kiss'
213.22	freshest] over wiped-out 'own days'
213.27	tenderer] 'tend' over 'love l'
213.28	whom] preceded by cancelled 'in'
213.32	as if that] over wiped-out 'and [ ]'
214.3	muttered] above uncancelled 'said'
214.24	for he] MS 'h' followed by cancelled 'is an old Yorkshire ['York' over 'English'] man, you know'
214.25	those he] over wiped-out 'our fore[ ]'
214.30	grandfather] 'gran' over wiped-out 'as he'
214.33	tried—] dash cancels semicolon
214.33	and to-day as well] over wiped-out 'for if we Americans'
215.1	if] above 'we'
215.6	rough, coarse] above caret and uncancelled 'brutal'
215.7	great, or] 'great' above cancelled 'high'; 'or' over wiped-out 'an'
215.12	and . . . too] above caret
215.14	that are] 'that' followed by cancelled 'find their kind of exercise', 'kind' over 'sort'
215.17	dirt] over wiped-out 'road'
215.20–21	looking as if he had seen some ghastly sight] 'looking . . . seen' in space between the first and second lines above, 'some ghastly sight' in space above 'at a headlong gallop.'
215.21	headlong] 'he' over 'ga'
215.21–22	gallop. He was in] period cancels comma; 'He was in' over wiped-out 'in his shirt'
215.22	shirt-] 'r' over 't'
215.22	and had the] over wiped-out '[ ] appearance'
215.23	his] 'h' over 'th'

215.28–29	—and] dash cancels comma
215.31	out of his cloud of] over wiped-out 'out of the cloud of dust'
215.32	he] over wiped-out 'He'
215.32–33	—trailing . . .pennon.] MS 'Trailing . . .pennon.' added in space above the paragraph; inserted by reference to the similar passage in the "Felton" draft (20.8–9)
216.3–4	It . . . dread.] added above 'itself . . . fainter.'
216.7	you, Rose!] 'Rose' is squeezed in; the comma is a CENTENARY emendation
216.7–8	Septimius . . . sister] above 'there . . . bless'
216.10	such was] above cancelled 'in' and inadvertently cancelled 'the'
216.10	misty] over wiped-out 'haste'
216.10	quite] over wiped-out 'she quite'
216.11	precise] above caret
216.13	hasty] above caret
216.13	rung as for] above uncancelled 'as'
216.17	The whole . . .] double arrows added before the paragraph propose a transposition, but further signs are lacking; conjecturally, NH may have intended moving the paragraph to follow the added 'It seemed as if wars must follow helter-skelter after this messenger of dread.' (216.3–4), consolidating passages dealing with general description, and moving the short scene between Robert and Rose to join that involving Septimius, at 218.3
216.17	now] above caret
216.17–19	Pale-faced . . . heads] added above 'Young men . . . '
216.23	King's] 'K' over 'k'
216.24	on the] over wiped-out 'ramparts'
216.31	as] over 'and'
216.33	richer and] over wiped-out 'dearer than'
217.4	the] over wiped-out 'food'
217.7	country.] period cancels semicolon
217.10	while] over wiped-out possible 'which'

217.13–14	strange, nervous rapture] 'nervous' above 'tremulous'; 'strange, tremulous rapture' over wiped-out 'high, heroic, tremendous crisis'
217.17	angel] 'n' over 'g'
217.22–23	mother, sister] 'mother' over wiped-out 'another'; 'sister' interlined with a caret; the comma is a CENTENARY emendation
217.23	watched] preceded by cancelled 'and'
217.25	the] over 'into'
217.30	a great] 'a gre' over wiped-out 'great'
217.31	up] over 'him'
217.31	people,] comma cancels dash
218.3	did what he could] above 'tried to keep his cold'; 'tried to' cancelled, the 'to' in error
218.6	be observant] 'be ob' over wiped-out 'observe'
218.8	acts] above cancelled possible 'whirl'
218.10	irregular] 'irr' over wiped-out 'deep'
218.13	Join . . . women] added above 'I can't go.'
218.18	they . . . officers] added in space at end of paragraph
218.21–22	or . . . monster] above caret
218.22	advancing at] over wiped-out 'coming forward'
218.23	spy out] above uncancelled 'avoid any'
218.25	temporary] above caret
218.31	make . . . fascinating] added in space at end of paragraph
219.4	and] above 'incensed'
219.6	confronted] over wiped-out 'in contact with'
219.9	at] over wiped-out 'while'
219.9	very] over wiped-out 'respe'
219.11	dear,"] quotation mark over wiped-out 'he'
219.12	tell a] over wiped-out 'show t'
219.13	him while] 'him' is squeezed in; 'while' above caret
219.17	by] above 'come'
219.18	red] above 'have'
219.18–20	My . . . head.] added in space at end of paragraph
219.31	pretty] 'pre' over 'dea'

220.2   person of shy habits] above caret and uncancelled 'shy, retired ['retired' underlined] person'; the alteration was made after the inscription of 'But . . . rage.' at 220.3–4

220.3   propensity] above cancelled 'readiness'

220.3   readily] above cancelled 'quite'

220.3–4   But . . . rage.] inserted two MS lines above original 'do. "Coward . . . make' for want of space immediately above

220.6   irascible enough, but] above caret

220.7–8   being . . . then] above caret

220.11   keep] above cancelled 'have'

220.11   physical] above uncancelled 'bodily'

220.12–13   escaped . . . sword] above uncancelled 'eluded his attempt'

220.19   cried] over wiped-out 'said'

220.21   forward,] comma supersedes uncancelled dash

220.23   The] 'e' over 'en'

220.27   snatch] 'sn' over 'k'

220.27–28   laughing merrily] above 'with his'

220.32   Rose . . . annoyed] above 'nonsense." said Rose'

221.1   him for a boy's] over wiped-out 'him" said Rose'

221.2   do . . . shoulder—] above 'a comely young man, and'

221.3   and sister] 'a' over 's'

221.5   nor] over 'and'

221.6   any] above cancelled 'nor'

221.7   that] over wiped-out 'had'

221.9   a] over 'qu'

221.9   step] above cancelled 'march'

221.9–10   passed in] 'in' above cancelled 'along the road disclosing', followed by inadvertently repeated 'in'

221.10   and disclosed] above 'spectators, and the'

221.16   advance] at line end, 'ad' over 'ap'; 'vance' over 'proach'

221.17	wearied] originally 'weary'; 'ie' over wiped-out 'y'
221.17–18	bemuddied] 'muddied' above cancelled 'smeared'
221.19	each] above 'their'
221.24	man] 'm' over 'h'
221.27	hearty] above caret
221.28	made] 'm' over 'yo'
222.1	homely] lines added above and below, perhaps for emendation
222.6	Somehow] over possible 'It makes a body'
222.19	these] 'ese' over 'em'
222.22	(Rose . . . somewhere)] added in top margin of MS page above 'rudeness . . . in'
222.23	In spite] over wiped-out 'The awe'
223.2	taking] over wiped-out 'drinking'
223.6	fiery] over wiped-out 'ardor'
223.7	herself] second 'e' over 'l'
223.14	this early] above 'bore the woman's'
223.16–17	(remarks . . . -time)] above 'Aunt . . . whirlwind'
223.19	and another] 'd' over 'y'
223.20	of the contents] 'of the con' over wiped-out 'of which'
223.20	(and they] over wiped-out 'we shall be'
223.25	outside] 'o' over 's'
223.29–30	wholly to] above caret
223.32	stirred] above cancelled 'moved'
223.32	motives] above cancelled 'motives impulses'
224.2	blind] above caret
224.4	stream] followed by cancelled 'of passions'
224.4	flecked] over wiped-out 'tawny'
224.9–10	signalizing] 'sig-' over wiped-out possible 'thus'
224.13	dark matters] 'dark ma' over wiped-out 'matters that'
224.14	gone] over wiped-out 'reigned'
224.16	paths] above 'he'
224.17–18	of . . . faith] above 'gloomy . . . intel- | '
224.18	are apt] above 'depth'

224.22	were] over 'was'
224.24	grow] above 'tend'
224.26	left . . . fermentation] above caret and cancelled 'have managed'
224.28	Would] over wiped-out ' "I am'
224.31	not?] MS period over comma; question mark is CENTENARY emendation
224.31	It is] over wiped-out 'Am I'
224.32	ordinary] above caret
224.33	common] above caret
225.1	free] 'ee' over 'from'
225.5	absurd] 'a' over wiped-out 'id'
225.6	immortality] over wiped-out 'continuance,'
225.8	meditations] 'm' over 's'
225.8	as] 'a' over 'f'
225.9	existence] 'ex' over 'li'
225.10	for the vain] over wiped-out 'with the hope'
225.10	establishing] 'es' over 'sa'
225.13–15	If . . . to-day.] above 'we might . . . up; otherwise, we rise'
225.15	(Let Septimius say this)] added in space after the paragraph; a note referring not only to the interlined 'If . . . to-day.' (225.13–15) but to the latter half of the paragraph beginning with 'as' (225.8), by indication of large parentheses added before 'as' and after 'this)'—i.e., a second parenthesis after 'this)'
225.23	love] 'lo' over 'ha'
225.25	semblance] preceded by cancelled 'quiet'; 's' cancels comma
225.26	slumbering] above cancelled 'sleeping'
225.30	an] over 'un'
226.5	the old gun] over wiped-out 'your grandfath'
226.9–10	The . . . wheel-lock.] added in space at end of paragraph
226.12	a great bullet-pouch] above 'as . . . in'
226.13	roam] inscribed over 'ro' is a figure looking like '9', of uncertain import; it appears six lines from the foot of MS page 9

226.13   do] over 'act'

226.22–25   He . . . &c] added in space at end of previous paragraph above 'Septimius . . . back.' which is at the foot of the MS page

226.26   The abrupt ascent] 'The' over 'His'; 'abrupt' lined above and below in dissatisfaction of repeated use in the sentence; 'ascent' followed by cancelled 'of which'

226.27   abrupt] above caret

226.31   through entwining] 'entwining' above caret which cancels original 'the' after 'through'

226.32   his] over wiped-out 'the'

226.33   west] above cancelled 'village'

227.1   which] followed by cancelled 'deviating slightly from' with a second 'which' added above cancel, in error

227.3   anxiously] above cancelled 'eagerly'

227.4   and] followed by cancelled ', as it were'

227.15–17   and windless . . . eastward] above original 'was . . . sunny, and moreover . . . Septimius'

227.18   a] over 'as'

227.18   more especially] over wiped-out 'and indeed'

227.19   stretch] 'c' over 'h'

227.21   time,] followed by cancelled 'had'

227.28   the people] above 'of all, anticipating'

227.28   anticipating] mended for clarity, preceded by wiped-out badly placed 'an'

227.30–31   finishing . . . -barrels] above 'and made . . . audible, without . . . although'

227.32   prophetic, and in the] the paragraph originally ended with 'prophetic.' at MS line-end; NH began a new paragraph, 'But,' and then continued the previous sentence with 'and' in the indention and 'in the' inscribed over 'But,'

228.1   suddenly] lines are drawn above and below; 'su' over wiped-out 'in t'

228.2–3   so . . . quiet] added in space above the paragraph, above the beginning of 'a long ['a long' over wiped-out 'far off'] way off, so that the

	sound scarcely smote upon the stillness', which 'so . . . quiet' is clearly intended to supplant, avoiding the repeated sibilants
228.3	immediately] above 'what'
228.4	once;] semicolon cancels period
228.4	then soon afterwards] above caret
228.5	ragged] above 'and'
228.5	report] 'r' over wiped-out 'f'
228.5	many discharges] underlined, perhaps for future emendation
228.6–7	—producing . . . mass] above 'scattered . . . minute'
228.12	hundred] 'hu' over 'thou'
228.14–15	The . . . sounds] added in space at end of paragraph
228.17	but] followed by cancelled comma
228.18	drums] preceded by cancelled 'a'
228.19	beat] over wiped-out 'roll'
228.20	next] above cancelled 'then'
228.20	he perceived] MS 'was he perceived' over cancelled 'down the path fr'
228.22–23	galloped] over 'rode'
228.23	messenger] 'me' over possible 'one rider'; 'n' over 'g'
228.24	with] 'w' over 'by'
228.25	shriek] above cancelled 'cry'
228.28	or . . . fences] above 'scattered . . . and'
228.32	foes.] followed by cancelled 'There was something'
228.32	They seemed other, & the same.] interlined below 'sudden foes.' and cancelled 'There was something'
228.33	spectacle] 'spec' over wiped-out 'thing'
229.1	well] 'w' over 's'
229.6	almost a handful] 'almost' above caret inadvertently placed after 'a'
229.12	deadly] initial 'd' over 's'
229.18	defiant] lines drawn above and below; 'de' over wiped-out 'beat'

229.18	rattle] 'ra' over wiped-out 'bea'
229.18	seemed] over wiped-out 'forbid'
229.19–20	considerable] above 'in great'
229.23	drop] 'd' over wiped-out 'an'
229.23	under] over wiped-out 'in the a'
229.25	the wounded] 'the' inserted after inscription of 'wounded'
229.26	leaving . . . road.] above 'along . . . two'
229.28–30	Thereupon . . . shouts] preceded by three vertical lines, and followed by '&c &c', the passage was added after the paragraph; its placement is indicated by a two-tiered caret below 'shouts' of original 'effect, and then there were shouts'; the period following 'effect' in placing the alteration is a CENTENARY emendation
229.29	, crossed] over wiped-out 'and cros'
229.30	were shouts, shrieks, and] underlined, in dissatisfaction or in aid for insertion of 'Thereupon . . . shouts'
229.32–33	foe; although . . . not] semicolon cancels period; 'although . . . not' above cancelled 'Septimius shuddered'
229.33– 230.1	any . . . purpose] lines drawn above and below, probably for future revision
230.3	thing] 'g' over 'k'
230.7	march] over wiped-out 'an'
230.8	abreast] 'ab' over wiped-out 'of'
230.10	subalterns] over wiped-out possible 'platoon'; followed by uncancelled period which was intended to be replaced by comma which follows
230.12	there] over wiped-out 'there had'
230.13	it] over wiped-out 'as'
230.14–16	In . . . irregularity] added above 'commander . . . horseback'
230.16	commander] 'com' over 'man'
230.17	horseback;] semicolon cancels period
230.21–22	bleeding . . . more—] added after 'townspeo-

	ple—' with placement indicated by a line drawn from 'dust' down to 'bleeding'; the period after 'townspeople' is a CENTENARY emendation
230.22	he himself] over wiped-out 'then [ ]'
230.23	Cain] 'C' over 'c'
230.26	at] over 'on'
230.30–31	and for . . . murder!] added above 'only . . . temptation' and in the clear space following
231.1	was] above caret
231.2	or . . . angel,] above caret which covers a comma after 'Satan' preceded by a vertical line for separation from 'murder!'
231.2	some] over 'his'
231.5	and blaspheming] 'and' above cancelled 'swearing'
231.8–9	straggling foemen] over wiped-out 'foemen enemies'
231.10	side] above uncancelled 'slope'
231.10	gorge] above uncancelled 'gap'
231.12	as their] over 'would'
231.17–18	or dwarf . . . hide him] above caret, inscribed between the first and second lines above 'pine' because space immediately above was blocked by the earlier alteration 'treeing himself'
231.18–19	treeing himself] added above 'pine', wiped out, and again inscribed, above 'the canny Indian'
231.21–22	rustling . . . boughs] above 'keeping shoulder'
231.23–24	but protruding their bayonets] 'but' near end of MS line above 'and' of 'and staring', evidently as conjunction for 'protruding their bayonets', interlined above first words of following line, 'round apprehensively,' to take precedence in the sentence; 'but' was then also added in the left margin before 'protruding'
231.25–26	As . . . face] above 'shoved aside'; an unintegrated addition for possible future revision of the sentence

232.1 bracken] over wiped-out 'ground oak'
232.2 The] mended from 'They'
232.2 party] above caret
232.3 was] 'w' over 's'
232.5 impress] terminal 's' over 'sion'
232.6 piercingly] 'p' over 'on'
232.9 make . . . possible] added in space at end of paragraph
232.10 fire] above uncancelled 'shoot'; 'shoot' followed by cancelled ascender of an incomplete letter
232.12–13 because] above caret
232.13–14 impulses] followed by cancelled comma
232.18 though] above caret and cancelled 'but'
232.21 (This . . . it] added in space at end of paragraph
232.24 seemed] above caret and cancelled 'was'
232.25 take] above 'your'
232.25 sweetheart] 'swee' over wiped-out 'charming'
232.27 in] above 'have'
232.29 account] above wiped-out 'the score'
232.33 buoyancy] 'c' over 't'; preceded by wiped-out comma
233.3 feeling] 'f' over 'g'
233.4 moment.] period cancels comma
233.14 Never!] followed by cancelled 'This is my own ground, and if you would take me from it' below which was added 'This is my own ground', and the phrase, for clarity, was added again above 'Assault . . . peril'
233.17–18 between us] above caret
233.20 kindle your firelock] above caret
233.22 The young Englishman] MS 'The young officer' over wiped-out 'As the young of'; 'Englishman' above uncancelled 'officer'
233.23 he and] 'a' over 'S'
233.26 officer's] over wiped-out 'bullet'
233.27 sent into] above caret
233.27 kick] cancelled, then enclosed by horizontal

	lines for future reconsideration
233.28	heavily loaded] 'heavily lo' over wiped-out 'of heavi'
233.32	young] 'yo' over 'of'
234.5	vanquished] 'i' over 'h'
234.6	rusty] above 'of ordnance'
234.7	your] 'y' over 'a'
234.12	—and] dash cancels exclamation point; 'and' over wiped-out double quotation mark
234.23	I] over 'sa'
234.25	in the] over 'for his'
234.29	forget] 'e' over 'o'
234.31	remorse] 'm' over 'g'
235.3	surge] above cancelled 'mass'
235.6	were] above cancelled 'had'
235.10	homesick] above caret
235.11	save] over wiped-out 'but'
235.14	Septimius, in a] 'in a' over wiped-out 'rushed'; comma added after 'Septimius'
235.14–15	precipitated himself] above 'rushed down'
235.17	an] over wiped-out 'ear'
235.19–20	from . . . lips] above cancelled 'some of the cool water,'
235.21	when his] MS 'when' followed by cancelled 'Septim- |' and uncancelled 'ius' before 'his'
235.23	the hollow] above caret
235.23	own] above caret
235.26	him] above 'us'
235.26	one's] above uncancelled 'one'
235.27	him] above uncancelled 'us'
235.27	My] over wiped-out 'Our'
235.28	me to] 'me' above uncancelled 'us'
235.28	my] over 'our'
235.29–30	but . . . work] above 'fired . . . mysterious'
235.30–31	state of existence] above caret placed after uncancelled 'world'
235.31	to] over 'of'
236.1–2	vainly . . . inflicted] above caret
236.3	know] above cancelled 'see'

236.4	that] 'th' over 'br'
236.6	erase] above uncancelled 'wash'
236.7	stain . . . blood] over wiped-out 'blood stain [ ]'
236.7	and] interlined with a caret; preceded by cancelled 'which I see on your hand. So let that pass! I am dying'; the penstroke inadvertently did not cross 'which'
236.8	nobody—] dash cancels semicolon
236.9	poor] above caret
236.9	mother] over wiped-out 'father'
236.13	reflections] above 'thoughts'
236.13	poor] above 'dying'
236.13	youth's] 'you' over 'm'
236.14	recall] 'ca' over 'm'
236.17	in] over wiped-out 'to'
236.19	victor.] followed by wiped out double quotation mark
236.19	them—] dash cancels colon
236.20	yet . . . life] above 'which I shot amiss'
236.21	battle—] dash cancels semicolon
236.23–24	My watch . . . time] above 'long . . . they'
236.24	purse—] dash cancels exclamation mark
236.25	inherited . . . ancestral] over wiped-out 'am officially only [ ] estate'
236.25	great] above caret
236.27	more] above caret
236.27	a picture] above cancelled 'something'
236.29	that] above uncancelled 'which'
236.29–30	address] over wiped-out 'direction'
236.31	once] over wiped-out 'again'
236.32	his] above cancelled 'the young man's'
237.9	May] over wiped-out 'Pray'
237.10	but] above caret
237.15–16	gave . . . of] over wiped-out 'dictated an address'
237.28	As . . . continued] added above the paragraph
237.29–30	my . . . burial-place] above caret
237.31	square] above 'low'

237.31   hollow ancient] above caret
237.32   in front] 'in fr' over wiped-out 'of [   ]'
237.32   cottages] 'co' over 'ho'
238.8   Here, and] over wiped-out '[   ] in'
238.20   shall] above 'will' which has lines drawn above
          and below
238.27   voice, remembering that his] 'remembering that
          his' above cancelled 'I am a student of divin-
          ity almost a clergyman.'; original period after
          'voice' and double quotation mark inadver-
          tently left; the comma after 'voice' is a CEN-
          TENARY emendation
238.27–28 and . . . profession] above caret
239.1   words] above caret
239.5   God] 'G' over 'g'
239.6   die] added below 'Francis'
239.9   whether] 'ther' over 'm'
239.10   not already] above caret
239.10   drawn.] period cancels comma; followed by
          cancelled 'Life had entirely departed, how-
          ever, when'
239.10–11 Septimius . . . tree.] note for future alteration,
          added in bottom margin of MS page below
          'breath . . . drawn.'
239.11   a few] over wiped-out 'after that,'
239.12   uttering] above uncancelled 'murmuring'
239.12   words,] followed by cancelled 'if it might not
          rather be, indeed'
239.13   intermingled] over wiped-out 'with a slight'
239.16   quite] over wiped-out 'perfectl'
239.17   started] followed by 'and met | the eyes of
          Septimius with a wild, troubled gaze,' can-
          celled except for 'and met'
239.20   thought] followed by uncancelled (in error) 'I'
          and cancelled 'felt'
239.20   was] above caret
239.21–22 And . . . dream] interlined below first two
          sentences of the paragraph after the first line
          of next paragraph had been inscribed

239.26	What was it?] above 'and gave himself'
239.28	act] over 'ho'
240.2	flesh] 'sh' mended over 'sh' and wiped-out 'fle'
240.3	a fly] above caret; followed by cancelled 'the flies' and unchanged 'were'
240.13	of feature] lined above, below, and to the right, perhaps for future reconsideration
240.14	some mode] over wiped-out 'p[ ] in'
240.17	to be] over wiped-out 'exchan'
240.24–25	There . . . preserving.] above 'there could . . . man'
240.26	and] a question mark added above
240.31	serving] over wiped-out 'p[ ]ing it'
241.2	centuries] 'cent' over wiped-out 'hund'
241.3	of earth] above 'spot would'
241.7	when] over wiped-out 'at the'
241.16	any] 'a' over 'I'
241.23	he heard] originally 'he was struck'; 'heard' over wiped-out 'struck' but 'was' not cancelled
241.24	voice] above uncancelled 'tone'
241.25	fierce] lines drawn above and below for later reconsideration, since 'fierceness' appears shortly after
241.26	it;] over partially wiped-out 'and'
241.30–31	just . . . hill] above caret
241.31–32	with . . . her] added above uncancelled 'with all the Indian Squaw alive in her,'
242.7	or . . . carrion] above 'things . . . attraction'
242.10	shot] 'o' over 'oo'
242.14	he had a mother] marked by lines above and below
242.18	capable] over wiped-out 'that was'
242.19–20	awoke the . . . influences] above 'overcame . . . whose'
242.21	Aunt] 'N' of original 'Na' wiped out and 'unt' added; 'A' is a CENTENARY emendation
242.25	a beauty] 'a' over 'be'
242.25	his mother's] 'his mo' over wiped-out 'mother'
242.29	raise] above uncancelled 'revive'

242.30–31 Your . . . it."] above 'referred . . . herself'

242.33 to] over 'of'

243.8–9 Without a coffin?] added above 'a funeral?' so close to top edge of MS page that the hook of the question mark is absent

243.9–11 "Why . . . heathenish! I shall . . . it."] added after first line of following paragraph was inscribed, 'enish!' in space of paragraph indention and 'I shall . . . it." ' interlined; final period is CENTENARY emendation

243.11 to] over 'it'

243.19 Nashoba.] period cancels comma

243.20 be a] 'a' over 'p'

243.22 deacons] 'd' over 'g'

243.24 fat earth] above 'have clinging'

243.26 as long] 'as lo' over wiped-out 'with'

243.29 office of] over wiped-out 'task of grave'

244.2 crimson silk] above 'off his'

244.2 (which] parenthesis cancels comma

244.3 and might have] over wiped-out '[   ] that'

244.8 did] followed by cancelled 'more than half'

244.9 on the dry] over wiped-out 'ticking as busil'

244.11 pause] over wiped-out 'stop'

244.11 the] over wiped-out 'Septi'

244.12 -sided] above caret

244.17–18 (Septimius . . . it)] added in space at end of paragraph

244.20 last] 'l' over 'h'

244.21 and it] 'a' over 'n'

244.23 marble] above 'pale'

244.24 to a] 'a' above caret

244.25 the very] 't' over wiped-out 'v'

244.26 His] over wiped-out 'The ex'

244.28 angelic.] followed by cancelled 'The expression'

244.29 as if] above 'seemed' followed by cancelled 'like'

244.29 were] above caret

245.1 great] above caret

245.3–7	It . . . rapture.] originally inscribed after 'face.' (245.11) and preceded by a three-tiered caret; insertion point for repositioning marked by a two-tiered caret after 'surprise'
245.6	and kindled] 'and' over wiped-out 'kind-'
245.9	beheld] above uncancelled 'seen'
245.9	lingering] 'lin' over wiped-out 'light'
245.12–13	has been] over partially wiped-out 'was decreed'
245.21	firm] over wiped-out 'faith in'
245.21	immortality] horizontal lines drawn above and below
245.24	claim] 'c' over 'h'
245.25	man] 'n' over wiped-out 'de'
246.5	never] 'n' over 'gi'
246.11	piece] 'ie' over 'ea'
246.12	unending] above 'meditations'
246.14	an . . . idea] above 'chiefly . . . doubts had'
246.22	and] over wiped-out 'though'
246.22	of] over 'so'
246.28	Aunt] 'A' over 'a'
246.29	but] over 'and'
246.30	with] 'w' over 'th'
246.31	blood] 'blo' over 'wo'
247.4	rheumatic] 'r' over 'A'
247.10	holding] over wiped-out 'showing them'
247.10	eyes] 'e' over 'fa'
247.12	They . . . breast.] added in space at end of paragraph
247.14	great] over wiped-out 'grand'
247.15	one] over wiped-out 'when a'
247.15–17	she . . .heard] above caret
247.19	for it.] caret added before period, but no words
247.19–23	Now . . . me.] preceded by a two-tiered caret, added after 'worse for it.' (247.25), the insertion point marked by a similar sign added before 'So . . . ' (247.23)
247.20	drink] over wiped-out 'bottle'
247.21	what] 'at' over wiped-out 'ether'

247.21–22   would happen] 'would' followed by cancelled
             'be the re' and 'hap' over wiped-out 'sult'
247.24   lest . . . hear it] above caret
247.27–29   It's . . . decorations] interlined below the pre-
             ceding sentence
247.30–31   The . . . it] added in space after 'Septimius.'
             (247.26)
247.32   youth] 'y' over 'the'
248.4–8   Then taking hold . . . coffin,] originally, the
             first sentence of the paragraph was 'Taking
             hold . . . coffin.' it was followed by two
             vertical lines and 'Before . . . him.' (247.32–
             248.4), which was indicated to be inserted
             as the first sentence by two vertical lines
             placed before the paragraph; the alteration
             continued 'Then taking hold &c—a sort of
             green coffin,' and the new passage continued
             with 'through . . . earth.'
248.9–10   on . . . earth.] above caret placed in error be-
             fore comma following 'visible'
248.12–13   and pebbles] 'a' over wiped-out 'in'
248.19   aforesaid] above 'mother'
248.20–21   (The . . . in.] added in space at end of para-
             graph
248.22–32   All this whole . . . him.] preceded by double
             arrowhead pointers, added after the para-
             graph ' "Let them wonder . . . ' (249.5)
             which originally ended 'minister to do!'
             (249.9); transposition directed by double
             arrows at left margin below paragraph ending
             'bed-clothes.' (248.20)
248.25   and more] above caret
248.29   enemy's] 'y' over 'ies'
248.29   a] over 'th'
248.31   for the young] over wiped-out 'as the vol'
249.1–4   "Let it . . . be."] supersedes ' "It looks too
             much ['too much' above cancelled 'wonder-
             fully'] like a grave," observed Septimius.',

which was inscribed after the paragraph ending 'bed-clothes.' (248.20) but then scored
by horizontal lines above and below in indication of abandonment, with a note '(see
below)' added above the line

249.9–12   Bloody fingers should not . . . and yet I don't
know . . . Indian."] added after the altera-
tion at 249.1–4 had been made; proceded by
an ampersand after MS 'to-do!', 'Bloody
fingers should not ['should not' interlined
with a caret] . . . and yet' fills out the MS
line; above 'and yet' a note '(see below)'
directs to the continuation 'I don't know . . .
Indian." ' added in an unindented line below
the paragraph ending 'be." ' (249.4)

249.12   too] above caret

249.15   it—] dash cancels comma

249.19   Norton. Let us] 'Let us' over ', and me'; the
period is a CENTENARY emendation

249.20   Aunt] 'a' over 'th'

249.21   staring] above 'Nashoba'

249.21   Dear . . . strangely.] above caret

249.23   we] above uncancelled 'you'

249.24   him.] followed by cancelled 'But I have heard
that there was an old'

249.27   his] above uncancelled 'Septimius's'

249.28   and sealed with black wax] above 'and appar-
ently con- | '; 'black' is above 'with wax'

249.31   besmeared] underlined as if for reconsideration

249.32   arranging] 'arr' over wiped-out 'bur'

249.33   hand] 'n' over wiped-out 'd'

249.33   this] 'h' over 'p'

250.1   package] above cancelled 'bundle of papers, and
having'

250.1   documents] 'd' over 'th'

250.5   had] 'h' over 'p'

250.5   which] over wiped-out 'that'

250.7   some] above caret and uncancelled 'a'

250.10	bones] 'bo' over 'ash'
250.14	insensibly] 'ins' of MS 'insensably' over wiped-out 'took'
250.15	youth's] 'th' over wiped-out 'ng'
250.20	bored] above 'ated' of uncancelled 'perfor|ated'
250.23	witchcraft] terminal 's' wiped out
250.24	if you] 'you' over wiped-out 'ch'
250.27	package] 'pa' over 'bu'
251.23	Septimius] 'S' over 'it'
251.24–25	prolonged] 'e' over 'd'
252.1	executor] 'c' over wiped-out 'u'
252.12	squatted] above is uncancelled 'an' of conjectured 'an attitude' not completed but superseded by '(a favorite attitude'
252.12	(a] parenthesis cancels comma
252.12–13	derived . . . Indians] above 'favorite . . . hers)'
252.14	first of] over wiped-out 'taking a'
252.23	demons] over wiped-out 'phantoms'
252.24	scandal] 'sc' over wiped-out 'the'
252.33	and] over wiped-out 'with'
253.1	infernal] 'in' over 'h'
253.11	lock] 'l' over 't'
253.14	were not any more than] original 'could not keep his spirit within their circuit any more than' was cancelled through 'more' ['more' crossed inadvertently] and 'were not any' was added above the cancel
253.14–15	the slight trammel of] above caret
253.15	a book] preceded by 'a broken', the participle cancelled but not the article
253.17	feel] second 'e' over 'a'
253.21	beginning] over wiped-out 'coming'
253.22	moral] above caret
253.23	intoxicant] 'in' over 'be'
253.23	tend to] above caret
253.24	life] 'l' over 'f'
253.26	taking] MS 'taken' over wiped-out 'killin'
253.27	often] 'of' over 'be'
254.5	and mixed] above 'anomalous brood'

254.11	natural] above caret
254.11	the boundaries 'the bound' over wiped-out 'which in the'
254.11	and capabilities] above 'boundaries of which'
254.21–22	—a . . . hide—] above 'very . . . course'
254.24	it appears to us] above caret
254.32	these] 'es' over 'em'
254.33	which might] 'which m' over wiped-out 'suggested'
255.12	mine—arm] dash cancels semicolon over wiped-out probable comma; 'a' over wiped-out 'as'
255.12	bound] 'bo' of MS 'boud' over 'and'
255.23	say.] over wiped-out period and 'Let'
255.28	had not yet] over wiped-out 'and had not y'
255.32	that] 'th' over wiped-out 'of'
256.2	had often] 'd' over 's'
256.9	and a bayonet] the article added beneath 'and'
256.21–22	The . . . pernicious.] added above two dashes centered after the preceding paragraph to indicate a space break; the note refers to the paragraphs which follow
256.23	to] over 'the'
256.29	it] 'i' over 'a'
257.4	ocean] over wiped-out 'water'
257.6	objects] 'obj' over 'thi'
257.9–10	obscurity of the] originally 'obscure annals of'; 'annals of' wiped out, 'obscure' mended to 'obscurity', and 'of the' added
257.13	claim] 'c' over wiped-out 'it'
257.23	improve] over wiped-out 'make this'
257.32	in after] 'in a' over wiped-out 'after'
258.6	emigrants] 'e' over 'i'
258.30	And . . . &c] added in space at end of paragraph
258.31	dark] 'd' over wiped-out 'S'
258.31	Puritan] above uncancelled 'and hideous'
258.31	portrait] above uncancelled 'character'
258.32	drawn] 'draw' over wiped-out 'show'
259.19	it] 'i' over 's'

259.32	means] 'e' over 'whi'
260.7	changing] 'ch' over wiped-out 'dy'
260.11	of] above caret
260.20	saw] over wiped-out 'see'
260.28	kind] 'ki' over wiped-out 'cont'
261.2	by over a score] over wiped-out 'slightly [ ] dis[ ]t'
261.2	cut and] over wiped-out 'pierced'
261.5	plundered] above caret and uncancelled 'burnt'
261.7	noble] 'nob' over wiped-out 'feat'
261.10	at] over wiped-out 'have'; preceding comma then added
261.15–30	In . . . fracture.] in MS page 18, this paragraph follows 'The boy . . . fit.' (262.23–263.23) with additional details of a topic of the paragraph ending 'conjecture.' (261.14); it is preceded by a double arrowhead pointer and followed by three diagonal strokes to mark it for transposition, but NH in error placed a double arrow for insertion before 'The boy . . .' instead of before the preceding paragraph 'We have said . . .' (261.32) which followed 'grounds for conjecture.'; the mechanical nature of the error justifies the order of the CENTENARY text
261.20	steel. Some of] period cancels semicolon; 'Some of' over wiped-out 'One of t'
261.25	impossible] 'im' over 'p'
261.29	cup] over wiped-out 'ves'
261.31	Vague . . . ancestors] for lack of open space, added interlined above last line of paragraph
261.33	him—] dash cancels semicolon
262.13	unsinged] second 'n' over 'g'
262.17	or] over 'and'
262.27–28	beneath . . . stood] above 'comprising . . . township'
262.29–30	produced] preceded by cancelled 'looked'
262.33	swallow] 'swa' over 'ho'

263.4	frame] over wiped-out 'house'
263.5–6	Sparks . . . fits] MS 'Sparks . . . ' above 'neighbors . . . inefficiency'
263.11	together.] period cancels comma
263.19	sometimes a devillish rage] above 'melted . . . early'
263.20	after the great] over wiped-out 'and after being sou'
263.23	in a] over wiped-out 'and'
263.28	her] above 'off'
264.2	he took to] over wiped-out 'which was instin'
264.6	Prophets] 'p' mended from 'p'
264.14–15	in savage fashion] above caret
264.16	the most] above caret
264.22	overheard] above uncancelled 'known'
264.27	diabolical] 'dia' over 'hid'
264.30	and scalped] over wiped-out 'an Indian with'
264.31–32	In . . . excommunicated] added in top margin of MS page above 'there were stories . . . '
265.1	a sly, crafty man] above 'sermons under its'
265.1	most] 'm' over wiped-out 'p'
265.3	them;] semicolon cancels period
265.5	and] 'an' over wiped-out 'fu'
265.6–7	who was] over wiped-out 'a pretty'
265.13	bears] 'be' over wiped-out 'po'
265.16	subsisted] third 's' over 't'
265.18–20	His . . . both.] added in space at end of paragraph
265.21	there] over 'his'
266.3–4	her blood] 'her blo' over wiped-out 'she was'
266.9	and generally] 'and gen' over wiped-out 'a cast of'
266.13–14	Aunt . . . several.] added in space at end of paragraph
266.28	rebellious] 'b' over wiped-out 'll'
266.32	had] over 'was'
266.32	been] 'b' over comma
267.1	in] 'i' over comma

267.16   woman] above uncancelled 'female'

267.19   a propensity . . . store] above 'wayward . . . uncouthness'

267.32   One] over wiped-out 'Our'

268.16   an] over wiped-out 'ed'

268.30   of which] 'w' over 'th'

269.1-2   (Aunt . . . medicines.)] added in space at end of paragraph

269.27-29   Rose . . . girl.] added in top margin of MS page above 'One thing more . . .'

270.18   (contrary] parenthesis cancels comma

270.21   towards] over wiped-out 'from her'

271.12   also] 'a' over wiped-out 'if'

271.20-21   not . . . cause] added in space above the paragraph, the insertion point indicated by a caret

271.29   for] over wiped-out 'to'

271.30   agents.] period over wiped-out comma, followed by wiped-out 'if'

272.1-2   that to] 'th' over wiped-out 'it'

272.3   in his untimely] over wiped-out 'always with him'

272.7   conscience to] followed by cancelled 'commit them to the guardianship'; ' commit' inadvertently crossed out

272.7-8   them to the keeping] over wiped-out '[   ] there in the g'

272.27   flame] above uncancelled 'fire'

272.30   into] 'i' over 'h'

272.31   dusky] 'k' over 't'

272.31   be withdrawn] above 'and vanish'; MS reads 'vanishing', 'ing' added at a slant below the line

272.33   either] initial 'e' over 'of'

273.11   so] 's' over 'to'

273.15   the sweet] 'the sw' over wiped-out 'the huckle'

273.17   an] over wiped-out 'a life'

273.18-22   the grave, so . . . mystery] three vertical lines added after 'the grave,' mark the insertion point for 'so . . . mystery', which, preceded

	by three vertical lines, was inscribed after away.' (273.25);
273.25	of heaven] 'of h' over wiped-out 'had'
273.26	wondered] 'on' over wiped-out 'he'
274.4	many] over 'men'
274.5	slain] 'sl' over wiped-out 'kill'
274.6	of] 'o' over 'm'
274.7	searching . . . him] above caret
274.10	It seems] over wiped-out 'The [ ], I f'
274.14	a] above uncancelled 'the'
274.27	the] over wiped-out 'mere'
274.31	interposed] 't' over 'p'
275.9	by and] over wiped-out 'adopt'
275.12–13	common-place judgments] above uncancelled 'opinions'
275.13–14	like . . . herbs] above caret
275.21	rose] 'r' over 'R'
275.22	that] over wiped-out 'which'
275.24	skirting] 'ski' over wiped-out 'alon'
275.24	the foot] 'the' over wiped-out 'at the'
275.26	helping] 'l' over wiped-out 'p'
276.4	unity] 'un' over wiped-out 'clo'
276.5	intimate] followed by wiped-out comma
276.6	have] 'h' over 'b'
276.8	more] 'm' over wiped-out 'g'
276.11	latter] above caret
276.12	had] 'd' over 's'
276.12	being brought] over wiped-out '[ ] a little'
276.17	and] over 'into'
276.33	want] above cancelled 'need'
277.2	lamentable] first 'a' over 'e'
277.17	his arm . . . grace.] added in space at end of paragraph
277.22	have any] over wiped-out 'do what'
277.23–24	Till yesterday] 'Till' above MS 'Yesterday'
277.27	And] 'A' over 'R'
278.11	of a] preceded by cancelled 'a'; 'a' over 'wo'
278.13	continued] 'con' over wiped-out 'sa'
278.15	take] above caret

278.16	though . . . hardest] above 'womanly . . . bid'
278.19–20	all . . . country] above caret
278.24	thousands] 'thou' over wiped-out 'good'
278.31	with bullets] above 'down, shattered'
279.3	yearn] above underlined 'pine'
279.6	tasting] over wiped-out 'the taste'
279.7	and grief] above caret
279.8	men."] followed by wiped out 'Rose will have esca'
279.9	escape] above cancelled 'have escaped'
279.11	we] above caret
279.12	hope] 'h' over 'in'
279.12	come] 'c' over 's'
279.17	poor] 'po' over wiped-out 'da'
279.25	as such natures] over wiped-out 'and it intensified'
279.27	do] 'o' over 'e'
279.30	you—] dash cancels comma
280.2–3	Besides . . . minister] horizontal lines added above and below, perhaps in dissatisfaction with the phrasing
280.13–14	looking . . . smile] above 'Septimius . . . something'
280.15	precious] above caret
280.16	season."] quotation mark over wiped-out 'It'
280.17	robbing] 'r' over 's'
280.24	yours—nay] over wiped-out 'yours is as old'
280.27	tell us] above cancelled 'say'
280.28	—that the] dash over wiped-out comma; 'that the' over 'the dan'
281.1	manly] above caret
281.6–7	because . . . murder] above caret
281.14	men] over wiped-out 'people'
281.15	were] over wiped-out 'till yes'
281.19	qualities,] comma cancels dash
281.20	—such] 'such' over wiped-out 'and pene'
281.20–21	and feeling] above caret
281.22–23	Who . . . wonder] above caret

281.23	all] 'a' over 'hi'
281.25	wrong] above 'something'
281.26	fermented] 'ferm' over wiped-out 'always'
282.2	(if] parenthesis cancels comma
282.5	brother] 'br' over wiped-out 'f'
282.9	planted] 'n' over 'c'
282.10	out] over wiped-out 'of'
282.12–13	amid . . . birch] above 'road . . . there, and their ideas'
282.14	wondered] 'on' over 'hen'
282.18	intensest] 'int' over wiped-out 'high'
282.22–23	quickened] MS 'quicked'; 'c' over 'k'
282.23	moving] 'm' over 's'
282.30	even] over wiped-out 'the'
283.2	view] 'vi' over wiped-out 'of'
283.3	ridges] 'd' over 'll'
283.3	bordered] 'bor' over 'over'
283.4	anywhere] 'any' over wiped-out 'that'
283.21	said, and half-] above 'believed by'
283.29	and] over wiped-out 'on th'
283.30	long] above caret
283.30	brown] 'br' over 'de'
284.3	ground.] period cancels comma
284.13–19	Many . . . grave.] in MS 23, NH began a discussion of Septimius's deciphering with ' "I know not . . . packet.' (284.23–285.31) and then added a short introduction 'Many . . . grave.' with a double arrow before it marking it for transposition; the insertion point is marked by a double arrow before 'I know not . . . ' (284.23) and above that line a note '(See further down the page)'; the rearrangement is also marked by three vertical lines at the end of the original first paragraph, after 'packet', and three lines before 'Another . . . ' (285.32), which in MS follows 'Many . . . grave.', to emphasize their connection

284.20–22	Old . . . portraits &c] added above 'But . . . story.' (284.12), relating to the passage that here follows
284.30	brought] 'bro' over wiped-out 'bef'
285.8–9	(his . . . moments)] above 'had . . . so'
285.10	stray] below cancelled 'go'
285.14	with] 'w' over wiped-out 'f'
285.15	egotism] above caret
285.16	own] above caret
285.23	or] squeezed in below the line, over comma
285.27–28	there] 'er' over 'is'
286.2	perhaps] above caret
286.3	out a] 'o' over 'a', 'ut a' over wiped-out 'case'
286.4	apt to be] above 'is a stubborn'
286.4	entity] followed by comma over wiped-out semicolon
286.11–12	Aunt . . . &c] added in space at end of paragraph
286.15	he] over wiped-out 'it'
286.20–21	with . . . moon] above 'herself . . . light'
286.21	a light] 'a l' over wiped-out 'foa'
286.24	Aunt] over wiped-out 'the old'
286.29	steeping] 's' over wiped-out 'of'
286.32	veteran-like] preceded by cancelled 'composure'
287.6	curiously] 'curi' over wiped-out 'wit'
287.9	letters.] period cancels comma
287.15	chiefly] 'chi' over wiped-out 'or s'
287.17	more] 'm' over 's'
287.18	but] over wiped-out 'and'
287.23–24	property] over wiped-out 'estates'
287.24	with] over 'whi'
287.24–25	or pedigrees] 'or p' over 'to pe'
287.29	exceeding] 'ex' over 'an'
288.3	sentence,] followed by cancelled 'to something like the following purport'
288.11	(Make . . . strongly)] interlined above 'He had but . . . '
288.22	Rose . . . botany.] added in top margin of MS, there being no space in minutely written

	passage to place the note above 'They went over the hill . . . '
289.6–13	A strange . . . witches.] inscribed after 'Delicate . . . inheritance'' (289.32–290.13), preceded by a double arrow to mark it for transposition; a double arrow before ' "Ah, Seppy' marks the insertion point
289.7	possible] 'ble' over wiped-out 'lity'
289.33	account?] question mark cancels dash
290.5	leafy] 'fy' over 'ves'
290.5	it—] dash cancels comma
290.11	you;] semicolon cancels dash
290.19	witch] 'c' over a second 't'
291.2	the spikes] 't' over 's'
291.3	soil,] over wiped-out 'fertility'
291.5	let] 'e' over 'i'
291.16	still] 'st' over wiped-out 'had'
291.22	afraid] 'fr' over 'w'
291.28	conscience?] question mark cancels comma
291.28	Seppy!] followed by wiped-out double quotation mark
291.30	D'ye] 'D'y' over 'Do', 'e' over 'y' of wiped-out 'you'
292.6	"Where would] 'Where w' over wiped-out '[ ], Au'
292.14	years?] followed by wiped-out double quotation mark
292.27	It's kept me alive] above cancelled 'Come, dear Seppy'; MS 'Its', the apostrophe a CENTENARY emendation
293.14	life] 'l' over 'f'
293.16	and fate] 'and' over wiped-out 'seem'
293.16–17	to hinder] over wiped-out 'to prevent'
293.18	original] above caret
293.25	heard,] comma cancels semicolon
294.6–7	(This . . . it.)] added in space at end of paragraph
294.12	Septimius's] 'Septimius' over wiped-out 'his study to'

295.14– 299.23	Septimius. . . . me."] in MS 25, the line 'obtained a lift to the village.' (295.12–13) is followed by the paragraph 'The legendary patriarch . . . ' (299.24); the dialogue here interposed appears on a MS leaf marked by NH '25 (additional)'
295.17	as valetudinarians do their diseases] inscribed following 'concerned.' (295.19); preceded by a caret from which a wavering line leads up to a caret erroneously placed between 'conversation' and the associated comma; 'vale' over wiped-out 'sick'
295.23	he had] over wiped-out 'his visitor'
295.30–31	old, & . . . it] comma partly covered by caret for placement of '& . . . it', added above the paragraph
296.11	then] followed by cancelled comma
296.17	yet] above caret
296.20	old] above caret
296.28	I think] 'I' over wiped-out 'If'
296.32	see] above cancelled 'take'
297.4–9	help. And . . . seventy-nine.] a two-tiered caret after 'help.' and the note 'see below' above it, mark the insertion point for 'And . . . seventy-nine.', which, preceded by a similar caret, was inscribed after 'nervous.' (297.27)
297.9	seventy-nine] 'nin' over 'six'
297.9	always frost-nipt] added above 'church-yard nap' (297.4)
297.9	always frost-nipt] added above 'church-yard nap'
297.12–14	Dear . . . south'ard] interlined, beginning above the final sentence and continuing in space at end of paragraph, and following short sentence ' "Yes," said Septimius.'; 'south'ard' is over 'sort of' of wiped-out ', "a sort of'
297.14	first] above caret

297.19	quite] above 'declare'
297.28	'tis] over 'I'
297.33	there] 't' over wiped-out 'if'
298.5	one] over wiped-out 'but'
298.8–11	I . . . yourselves.] preceded and followed by three vertical lines, inscribed in MS following 'Longer . . . weapons,' (298.32–299.3); transposed by indication of four vertical lines added after 'them.'
298.21	and sounder] above caret
298.26	on] over 'in'
299.13	like] 'l' over 't'
299.14–15	all over me] above caret
300.3	near] 'n' over 'to'
300.7	earnestness] 'ea' over wiped-out ', f'
300.10	had] above 'thought'
300.10–17	himself. He spoke . . . spoke.] 'himself,' was originally the end of the paragraph, followed by ¶ ' "Septimius . . . me." ' (300.18–19), the MS line of which was then marked at left margin by pairs of horizontal dashes above and below, to isolate it; 'He' was added after 'himself.' at MS line-end, and 'spoke . . . spoke,' continued the paragraph beneath ' "Septimius . . . me." ', which is here transposed to follow the insertion point indicated by three horizontal dashes at left margin under the final line of the paragraph
300.21	It is] over wiped-out 'You'
300.26–27	nearly] over wiped-out 'thirt'
300.29	Sir?] question mark cancels comma
301.4	I] over wiped-out 'S'
301.22	here] over wiped-out 'would'
301.28	a great] 'a g' over possible 'muc'
302.17	live a] over wiped-out 'life a life'
302.22	country,—] comma cancels period; dash beneath uncancelled double quotation mark

302.30	he] over wiped-out 'his'
302.32	very) 'v' and 's'
303.30	grew so] over wiped-out 'was quite'
304.4	often] over 'serv'
304.7	having] over wiped-out 'without'
304.8–9	with flint and steel] badly inscribed above 'of a heap of pitch-'; then 'flint and steel' repeated above 'deemed him' two lines up, in the previous sentence
304.13	cannot] 'can' over wiped-out 'will'
304.29	and then] 'and' preceded by cancelled 'and'
305.3	step by step] above 'trace Septimius's'
305.4	made,] followed by cancelled 'into the mysteries of the old manuscript,'
305.5	himself] 'him' over 'som'
305.9–11	Septimius . . . askance] added in available space at end of paragraph concluding 'bed.' but referring to passage which follows here
305.12–13	(The . . . happened)] added in space after paragraph ending 'scene.'
305.16	breathe] above cancelled 'as it were, blow'
305.24	meditations] preceded by cancelled 'thought'
305.27	buds and] above cancelled 'foliage of'
305.28	It would] over wiped-out 'As the'
306.5	it vacant] 'it v' over wiped-out 'him'
306.6	that] over wiped-out 'girl'
306.8	on a nearer view] above caret
306.17	seem] above cancelled 'appear'
307.4	should] over wiped-out 'loved'
307.13	answered] 'a' over 's'
307.17	wood] above 'anemones'
307.18	or even] over wiped-out 'butter'
307.20	looked up] above 'laughed'
307.24	and lacking fullness] above caret
307.27	her whole] 'her' over 'the'
307.29	still laughing] above caret
307.30	place.] followed by wiped-out double quotation mark

308.8   whether it will] over wiped-out 'when it will sprin'

308.9–10   (She . . . malignancy) added in space at end of paragraph

308.14   the flower, so beautiful] 'the flower, beau' over wiped-out 'a beautiful flower'; 'so' above 'beautiful'

308.21   were] over wiped-out 'had'

308.22   Then there] over wiped-out 'And sud'

308.26   very] 'v' over 'fa'

309.5   flower] 'r' over 'rs'

309.11   seemed preparing] 'seemed p' over wiped-out 'was turning'

309.24   —break] dash cancels comma

309.26   and] 'a' over 'p'

310.1–7   him. If . . . uncertain seemed . . . it.] 'him.' was originally the end of the paragraph, followed by ¶ ' "Are . . . her' (310.8–9); three slant lines were put after 'her' and five lines in caret-like form placed after 'him.' and followed by 'If . . . uncertain', the new sentence continuing with 'seemed . . . it.' below ' "Are . . . her', which is here transposed by the sign of two horizontal dashes at left margin beneath final line of the paragraph; see also note for 310.9

310.9   but . . . shudder.] above 'to detain her' and in space at the end of the sentence; an addition after arrangement for amplifying the previous paragraph had been made; see note for 310.1–7

310.10   Far?—] dash cancels semicolon; question mark then added

310.19–20   till . . . your friends] horizontal lines drawn above and below; 'your' over wiped-out 'friends'

310.28–29   (Perhaps . . . goes)] added in the only space available, after ' "Will . . . Septimius.'; ap-

	plies to the paragraph which follows here
311.21	death] followed by caret for insertion of wiped-out interlineation 'or a memory th'
311.34	phantom] over wiped-out 'unear'
312.13	daughter] followed by cancelled 'or connection of some slain British officer'
312.14	English] above 'gentleman'
312.17	a] over 'it'
312.17	the camp to] over wiped-out 'the selectmen'
312.18	about] over 'had it'
312.23	I . . . school] above 'and . . . pleasant'
313.10–11	She . . . it] added within separation marks resembling parentheses, in space at end of previous paragraph, three MS lines above 'And then . . . '
313.16	we] over 'she'
313.18	(which] parenthesis cancels comma
313.25	I saw that] above cancelled 'told me'
313.26	do] over 'tha'
313.28	Yet] 'Y' cancels double quotation mark
315.13	except] 'ex' over wiped-out 'th'
315.15	the young] over wiped-out 'Septim'
315.17–26	recipient. As . . . light.] a two-tiered caret was added after 'recipient.' to mark the insertion point for 'As . . . light.' which, preceded by a two-tiered caret, was inscribed after 'life' (316.7)
315.24	dim] 'd' over wiped-out 's'
315.24	dust] over 'light' and crowding 'in'
315.26	vast globes] 'vast g' over 'globes'
316.1	whether . . . original] over wiped-out 'made a constant patchwork with'
316.3	in that language] above 'expression for any'
316.7	purposes] over wiped-out 'thoughts'
316.13	an interval] 'an in' over wiped-out 'the cr'
316.20	truths . . . intelligence] bracketed between horizontal lines
316.21	natural] above cancelled 'art,'

316.23	sought, should] 'shoul' over 'had'
316.25–26	(He . . . flower)] added in space at end of paragraph
316.30	stiff] 's' over 'f'
317.8	mind] above caret
317.10	made] over wiped-out 'shad'
317.20	even the] 'even' above 'the' which is over wiped-out 'they'
317.24–25	Madmen . . . unrecognized] above 'Heroic . . . us'
317.27	and] over wiped-out 'fling'
317.28	virtues] 'v' over 'f'
317.32	at losing] 'at l' over wiped-out ', and'
317.32	laws] 'l' over 'r'
318.8	pursuit] over wiped-out 'absurd'
318.9	young] above 'wild'
318.10	ridiculous] preceded by cancelled 'unpardonable'; 'ri' over wiped-out ', in'
318.16	in] over wiped-out 'his'
319.5	for . . . time] above caret
319.9	shut] 't' over 'p'
319.13	nor] 'h' added above 'or'
319.13–14	or thy dog] above 'horse'
319.14	it be that] above caret
319.14–15	whit cold and torpid] 'cold and' above caret; another caret after 'torpid', either incorrectly placed for 'cold and' or meant for another alteration not completed
319.15	medicament] above uncancelled 'medicine'
319.15–16	a little dose thereof] over wiped-out words; 'dose' written again, for clarity, above the line
319.17	rankle] followed by wiped-out caret and wiped-out interlineation, possibly 'within'
319.18	poison] preceded by cancelled 'deadly'
319.18	moreover,] above 'work'
319.23	thy enemy] 'thy' over 'he'; 'enemy' above caret
319.23	nevertheless] above 'yet the'
319.26	thee in whatsoever case that] MS 'in whatso-

	ever case' interlined with a heavy caret after 'thee' meant to supersede uncancelled smaller caret placed in error after 'that'
319.27	for the advancement of] above 'live one man in peace', 'in' over 'at'
319.28	strife] followed by a caret but no interlineation added
319.28	sore] over wiped-out 'trouble'
319.30	the remembrance thereof] above 'sweep it out from mind' with 'it' uncancelled and a second 'from' written over 'out' before uncancelled 'from', in error
319.32	five and] above 'some'
319.33	speedily] above uncancelled 'quickly'
320.4	rule] above 'this'
320.4–5	is worthy in itself, and worthiest taken symbolically] originally 'is worthiest symbolically'; caret placed after 'is' for insertion of 'is worthy in itself, and worthiest' which, preceded by a caret, was inscribed following 'symbolically'; 'taken' above caret; original 'is worthiest' uncancelled
320.7	thine] above MS 'again'
320.8	hers. If] period over wiped-out semicolon; 'If' over wiped-out 'and'
320.14	melancholy] above cancelled 'imperfect'
320.15	a great . . . country] above caret; MS 'grat'
320.15–16	madly benevolent] 'madly bene' over wiped-out 'over benevolent'
320.16	who] over wiped-out 'that'
320.19	find] followed by cancelled 'on one side or the other'
320.24	as joyously] 'as j' over wiped-out 'with'
320.30	wholesomely] above caret
320.32	concentrates] over wiped-out 'brings th'
321.1	whereof] 'w' over 'of'
321.4	are apt to] above caret
321.5	good] 'g' over 'b'
321.7	so cover the] above cancelled 'destroy the whole'

321.8   sick people] 'and afflicted' was interlined with a caret after 'sick'; 'afflicted' was cancelled but 'and' was left, inadvertently

321.9   persons] 'pers' over wiped-out 'peop'

321.15   in] above caret

321.20–21   life. Howbeit . . . rate.] a two-tiered caret added after MS 'life' marks the insertion point for 'Howbeit . . . rate.' which, preceded by a two-tiered caret, was inscribed after 'take.' (321.26); period after 'life' is a CENTENARY emendation

321.22   buxom] 'bu' over 'ma'

321.24   drug] above cancelled 'medicine'

321.28–29   outward] followed by cancelled 'ben'

321.29   entire] 'en' over wiped-out 'wh'

322.4   keep] 'k' over 't'

322.5   the possession of life] above 'upon it mightily'; 'it' cancelled

322.8   toil and torment] over wiped-out 'a [　]ing life'; preceded by cancelled 'trouble of'

322.10   be] over 'as'

322.13   great] above caret

322.13   approach] preceded by cancelled 'climb a precipice, nor'

322.14   at] over 'on'

322.15   an] mended from 'a' and over wiped-out 'ste'

322.16   nor] over wiped-out 'and'

322.21   so] over wiped-out 'if'

322.22   sleep] over wiped-out 'slumber'

322.23   superfluous] above uncancelled 'needless'

322.31   golden rules] above caret and cancelled possible 'regulations'

322.32   manuscript. He] period mended from comma; 'He' above cancelled 'and'

324.8–10   Insert . . . &c)] added in space at end of paragraph above three dashes indicating a break in the narrative; the note refers to the passage beginning 'So absorbed . . . '

325.10   the] over wiped-out 'his'

325.11	a pleasure] above 'felt that'
325.19–20	and wild] over 'and so wild'
325.30	little] over wiped-out 'had though'
326.6	long] over wiped-out 'other'
326.11	nerves] 'ner' over wiped-out 'mind'
326.17	things] 'th' over 'cir'
326.21–22	to make] 'to' over 'her'
326.31	heart] followed by wiped-out comma
327.2	degree] above cancelled 'sort'
327.5	Doctor . . . relative,] above caret erroneously placed before the preceding comma
327.7	shortly before] 'shortly bef' over wiped-out 'at the outbreak'
327.12–13	communication] initial 'c' over wiped-out 't'
327.14	she knows music] above 'desultory education'
327.15	more] over wiped-out 'some'
327.18	sunnier] originally 'sunny cl'; 'ier' over wiped-out 'y cl'
327.19	something] above cancelled 'marks'
327.25–27	(Sometimes . . . them.)] added in space at end of paragraph
327.28	naturally] above caret
327.31	at] over 'her'
328.11	and knitting] above caret
328.11–12	and holding . . . hand,] a caret after 'and' marks the insertion point for 'holding . . . hand,' which, preceded by a caret, was inscribed after 'harpsichord' (328.14)
328.14	keys] over wiped-out 'strings'
328.18–19	This . . . herb."] added in space at end of paragraph; 'T' over quotation mark
328.20	a large] over wiped-out 'the ea'
328.20	jug] 'j' over wiped-out 'p'
328.21	covered] over wiped-out 'with'
328.22	beneath] over wiped-out 'which'
328.31–33	He . . . herbs] added above 'He knows' in space at end of previous paragraph
329.5	nose] above cancelled 'mouth'
329.8	to] over wiped-out 'and'

329.20   about] above caret and cancelled 'in'

329.25–26   Like . . . acquaintance] added in space at end of paragraph; refers to passage that follows here

329.29   was] over wiped-out 'heard'

329.30   war] over 'rumor'

330.14   trembling] preceded by cancelled 'composedly'

330.16   rewarded] above underlined 'well ended'

330.20   vile] mended from 'wile'; above cancelled 'ugly' before which 'an' was left unchanged

330.21   sets] 's' of MS 'set' over 'it'

330.21   engulphing] above 'catching all'

330.23   for] above caret

330.24   had the] 't' over 'a'

330.25   deeds] above uncancelled 'things'

330.26   of his fore finger] above caret

330.26   turning] 'tu' over wiped-out 'of'

330.27   before] MS 'bee' over wiped-out 'at b'

330.29   which seems] over wiped-out 'is made a jest'; the preceding comma then inserted

330.30   delusion] 'de' over wiped-out 'del'

330.31   waits] over wiped-out 'await'

331.3   weakness] preceded by cancelled 'human'

331.3–4   the . . . mistake] MS 'The . . . mistake' interlined with a caret below 'weakness'

331.7–8   "Then . . . further."] preceded by cancelled ' "If you tremble it so dreadfully," said Rose', of which 'If you tremble' is over 'Do you forget' and 'dreadfully' is above cancelled 'completely'; for the MS transposition of the sentence, see note for 331.9–12

331.7   tremble] 't' over possible 'fe'

331.7–8   but rise] over wiped-out 'as if you'

331.8   go] 'g' over 'f'

331.9–12   They . . . evading it.] in MS, this sentence followed the paragraph ending 'above it." ' (331.6) and preceded ' "Then . . . further." ' (331.7–8), but a note was added after it, '(put this after Rose's speech)'

331.10	and passion] above caret
331.14	knocking . . . again] above caret; followed by superfluous double quotation mark
331.19	poor] above caret
331.19	skeleton] above caret
331.19–20	death, this meagre . . . fellow] a line drawn under 'death' turns and goes up to 'this meagre . . . fellow' added in space at end of the paragraph concluding 'further.' (331.8)
331.20	As to] above uncancelled 'Of'
331.26	vanish] over wiped-out 'e[ ]'
332.2	wreath] above 'deed'
332.3	certainty] 'y' over partially wiped 'I'
332.3	the utter] 'the' over 'and'
332.4	too] over 'so'
332.5	to doubt] 'to do' over wiped-out 'that the'
332.7	And . . . realize it.] above the sentence which follows here
332.8	but were] over wiped-out 'and had'
332.11	Death] above cancelled 'a grave'
332.13	comes from it] above cancelled 'there'
332.18–19	changing . . . creature] above caret
332.24	You . . . but] followed by '&c" ', inscribed after 'woods'; transposed by logic of the sentences and Sybil's reply
332.27	pipe,] comma cancels period; 'knocking . . . out' added
332.29	the] over wiped-out 'Au'
332.30	they say] MS 'they saw' above caret
332.31	imp . . . her] above caret; the sentence was perhaps meant for review, and the superfluous alteration is therefore kept
333.2	pleasant] above caret
333.2	raise] above cancelled 'plant'
333.5	would you] 'would y' over wiped-out 'was born'; preceded by cancelled 'for it is the manorhouse of the village where I'
333.11–12	so . . . mind] over wiped-out 'has got a lot of truth that it'

333.17   then," said] comma and quotation mark added; 'said' over wiped-out 'the'

333.19   as you confess] above cancelled 'I suppose'

333.21   has] over wiped-out 'I hear'

333.21   in] over wiped-out 'and'

333.22   corner] above 'chimney'

333.24   a door] 'a' above cancelled 'one of the'; 'door' mended from 'doors'

333.25   into] over wiped-out 'from'

333.26   is] above 'there'

333.28   trodden] first 'd' over 'f'

334.1   that] above uncancelled 'so'

334.2   and] 'a' over 's'

334.3   the] over wiped-out 'wh'

334.8   might] 'mi' over wiped-out 'you'

334.9   rain] preceded by cancelled 'drizzling'

334.18   houses] above cancelled 'residences'

334.18   England.] period cancels comma

334.18–20   It . . . plaster] added in space above the paragraph to replace a cancelled passage: 'some portions of it being older than the Norman Conquest, and having been the residence of a Saxon Thane; and there is still this fact, you may still see the timbers of oak, that was hewn above a thousand years ago, and still looks as stalwart as ever, hard as iron, although it is thought, so aged are they, that [MS 'that that'] the gigantic old skeleton, preposterously ponderous as it is', with 'its dusty skeleton, cut of red' interlined above 'see the timbers of oak'

334.19   houses,] followed by cancelled 'nor yet of brick'

334.22   and the] over wiped-out 'for all f'

334.32   now] preceded by cancelled 'is'

334.32   seems] above caret

335.3   been] over wiped-out 'fallen'

335.4   looking] over 'ever'

335.6   side] preceded by cancelled 'the thir'

335.10   highly polished] above 'oak, carved'

335.11	foliage] 'a' over 'g'
335.12	family] 'f' over wiped-out 'th'
335.24	coal] altered from 'cold'
335.30	for] 'f' over 'to'
335.32	lives. But] period cancels comma; 'But' over wiped-out possible 'least'
336.2	think] 'k' over wiped-out 'l'
336.7	Ghosts . . . images.)] added in space at end of paragraph
336.17	deep] 'd' over 'cr'
336.19	from century] 'c' over 'h'
336.23	several] over wiped-out 'many'
336.23	assigning] 'assi' over wiped-out 'all of'
336.30	Baron, then the] above caret
336.30	Smithills] 'S' over 's'
336.32	Some] over wiped-out 'that'
337.4	fame; the more especially] semicolon cancels period; 'the more espec' over wiped-out possible 'But he did not h'
337.9	hiding] 'h' over 'p'
337.9	as] over wiped-out 'or'
337.14	are] over wiped-out 'there'
337.15	to be] 'to' over 'ac'
337.19	Baron] 'B' over 'po'
337.20–21	contrive or win] above cancelled 'wrest from Nature'
337.22	have] 'h' over 'con'
337.24	when] 'w' over wiped-out 'f'
338.4	a man] over wiped-out 'a loving'
338.7	bear fruit] over wiped-out 'be the fruit', the 'b', however, dry and visible, was used for 'bear'
338.14	the] over wiped-out 'my'
338.17	accomplished] 'a' over wiped-out 'f'; followed by cancelled 'but ends all things.'
338.18	heroic] 'her' over wiped-out 'high'
338.18	stunts] above 'ends'
338.21–22	The . . . subjects)] added in space at end of paragraph

338.26	dim] above 'wilderness'
338.27	known] followed by cancelled 'the dangers in one of your forests, there were wild and horrid creatures'
338.28	until] over wiped-out 'and'
338.30	spell] over wiped-out 'secret'
338.32	decree] over wiped-out 'choice'
338.33–339.1	as children] over wiped-out 'by way of for'
339.1	by] over wiped-out 'he'
339.3	on] followed by cancelled 'fearful conditions'
339.4	was the] above caret and uncancelled 'were these'
339.5	man] 'm' over a left parenthesis
339.5	zeal] preceded by cancelled 'too'
339.6	had] over 'was'
339.9	be] over 'by'
339.16	his own] over wiped-out 'that which'
339.19	he] over 'the'
339.22	once in] above cancelled 'during those'
339.32	each] 'ea' over 'ye'
339.33	potent] horizontal lines drawn above and below
340.5	comforts] 'com' over wiped-out possible 'an'
340.6	by] over 'de'
340.19	out] above caret
340.20	moreover] above caret
340.21	such] over wiped-out 'just'
340.22	one] above 'his'
340.28	The poor Baron] 'The poor B' over wiped-out 'He looked a'
340.32	averting] 'a' over 's'
341.1	orphan] over wiped-out 'awful'
341.6	kindness] above cancelled 'affection'
341.7	thoughtful] MS 'thoughful' over wiped-out 'depths of'
341.8	bestow] 'b' over 'f'
341.10	broad] above cancelled 'Gothic'
341.12	the folio] 'the' over 'a', 'folio' over wiped-out 'vol'

341.12	green] over wiped-out 'bloom'
341.18	existed,] followed by cancelled 'neither had confessed it, or was conscious of it'
341.19	at] over wiped-out 'ha'
341.21	rubbing] 'r' over wiped-out 'g'
341.29	this] above caret
341.29	hideous] above uncancelled 'ugly'
341.30	beyond a question] above caret
342.4	am] over 'ha'
342.5	the scholar] above blot and 'to'
342.6	up to] 'up' over 'it', 'to' over wiped-out 'a'
342.10	Mind] 'M' over 'H'
342.16	I will] over wiped-out 'It was'
342.16	matter] mended from 'murder'
342.18	thought] 'th' over wiped-out 'ar'
342.19	necessary] preceded by cancelled 'absolutely'
342.22	mighty] 'm' over wiped-out 'a'
342.31	the] over wiped-out 'a'
342.33	in cold] 'in co' over wiped-out 'bring'
343.1	bringing] 'b' over 'f'
343.8	texture] above cancelled 'life'
343.9	that it] 'th' over 'of'
343.15	difficult] 'd' over 'f'
343.20	touching] over wiped-out 'about'
343.22	buried] over wiped-out 'medit'
343.23	throwing] 'th' over wiped-out 'st'
343.25	glancing] 'g' over wiped-out 's'
343.29	strength] over wiped-out 'courage'
344.2	having] 'h' over wiped-out 'an'
344.7	sweet] above caret
344.10	gone] over wiped-out 'been'
344.16–18	(He . . . gained.)] added in space at end of paragraph
344.18	thinks] 'k' over 'g'
344.19	several hours] above 'with the' which is preceded by 'till midnight' cancelled by a bracket of lines

344.20	manuscript] 'm' over wiped-out 'de'
344.29	more ancient] 'more an' over wiped-out 'where the'
344.32	left] over 'buried'
345.3	ear] 'e' over 'h'
345.3	heart. And] period cancels comma; 'A' over 'a'
345.4	maid's] above uncancelled 'child's'
345.5	and nothing] 'and n' over wiped-out 'and it'
345.6	set his left foot] above caret and cancelled 'tramp'
345.7	(which] parenthesis cancels comma
345.11	wood] above cancelled 'coal'
345.13	hotter] 'h' over 'c'
345.14	strongest] 'stro' over 'win'
345.14–15	some say] originally 'sometimes'; 'say' over wiped-out 'times'
345.16	earnestly] above caret and cancelled 'quietly'
345.19	beef] 'b' over 'f'
345.19	a venison] 'a v' over wiped-out 'a gr'
345.19	an] over 'om'
345.20	the Baron's] over wiped-out 'his breakfast'
345.25	the] over wiped-out 'that'
345.26	rushes that strewed] above 'floor of the hall'; 'floor' over wiped-out 'pavement' and followed by cancelled 'pavement'; 'the rushes' also added below the line
346.7	—one] dash cancels comma
346.8	rain] above cancelled 'scrubbing'
346.8–9	no scrubbing] 'no' over wiped-out 'nor'
346.9	efface] mended from 'effacing'
346.11	Intersperse ludicrous things] referring to the following narrative paragraph; added in printed form in top margin of MS page above 'one crimson foot mark' (346.7–8)
346.12	(Read . . . beginning.] added in top margin of MS page above 'could wash . . . efface' (346.8–9) but referring to the paragraph

which follows here, in which orderly organization had not been effected in composition
or in signs for revision

346.13   But] over 'You'

346.14   washed] 'was' over 'clean'

346.16–17   the man . . . pavement] above 'chambermaid
     . . . called'

346.18   or whatever] 'or wh' over wiped-out possible
     'whose'

346.20   blood! Wherever] exclamation point cancels
     semicolon; 'W' over 'e'

346.23   threw up] above 'held up'

346.25   reddened] over wiped-out 'and thus reddened'

346.25–29   At last . . . again.] preceded by three vertical
     lines as if signaling an insertion of a subse-
     quently written passage, but no such plan
     seems to have been developed further and
     similar signals later in the paragraph bear an
     independent interpretation, as indicated in the
     entry for 346.32–347.1

346.29   the dreadful] 'the' over 'his'

346.32–
347.1   The foot print . . . afresh.] preceded by three
     vertical lines, added in space at end of para-
     graph (348.5) after the first line of the fol-
     lowing paragraph had been inscribed; its in-
     sertion point was marked by three vertical
     lines following 'forth.'

346.32   threshold] 'thr' over 'door'

346.33   struck] 's' over 'i'

346.33   but] over wiped-out 'and'

347.2–3   made . . . holiest] over wiped-out 'knelt at the
     confessional in [   ]'

347.5   royal] 'ro' over 'King'

347.11   our] above uncancelled 'my'

347.16   there would] over wiped-out 'the constables'

347.22   looking] 'l' over 'co'; preceded by wiped-out 'a'

347.22–23   snuffing along] 'snuffing al' over wiped-out 'as
     if they f'

347.23   tail] MS 'tale'; 'ta' over 'ba'

347.26	shuddering] 'shud' over wiped-out 'pityi'
347.29– 348.2	After . . . behind him.] the sentence originally read 'After . . . menials &c &c', an evident rewriting of the beginning of an earlier sentence, the continuation of which following 'menials' is indicated by ampersands; the original sentence inscribed following 'forth.' (346.32) is here spliced into the revised text; it began 'The menials received the Baron with low reverence,' but the first five words are superseded by the expanded revision
348.3	several] MS 'sev- | eral'; 'eral' over wiped-out possible 'few'
348.6	day] over 'morn'
348.10	shedding] over wiped-out 'a fragrant'
348.10–11	up the turret] over wiped-out 'along the'
348.16	foretaste] first 'e' over wiped-out 'f'
348.28	bleeding] 'bl' over 'po'
349.2	but] over wiped-out 'and'
349.10–12	(Some . . . family)] added in space at end of paragraph; reference is to paragraph which follows here
349.15	earth] 'ear' over 'lan'
349.18–19	and under] 'and' over wiped-out 'un'
349.24	dark] over wiped-out 'melanch'
349.26	like] over wiped-out 'the'
349.28	vault] 'v' over 'f'
349.31– 350.2	stories. Another . . . returned] five vertical lines added after 'stories.' mark the insertion point for 'Another . . . returned', which was added after 'Hall.' (350.20), preceded by four vertical lines and followed by three
350.3	came] 'c' over 'e' of 're'
350.3	his ancient] over partially wiped-out 'Smithills'
350.4	kept] 'k' over wiped-out 'st'
350.5	brands] over wiped-out 'coals'
350.13	two] over wiped-out 'a hun'
350.16	Old Bloody Foot] over wiped-out 'any descendants of'

350.16	by] over wiped-out 'th'
350.19	Baron's] 'b' over 'es'
350.21	crimson] above 'flowers'
350.28–29	when, in the improvements] 'when,' followed by wiped-out 'a'; 'in the impr' over wiped-out 'hot house'
350.30	Smithills] second 'i' mended over 'l'
351.8	without] 'wi' over wiped-out 'a fl'
351.11–13	—telling . . . flights—] added in space at end of paragraph
351.14	(which the girl] over wiped-out 'was concluded'
351.16	of] 'f' over 'r'
351.17	time] above caret
351.17	tragic] followed by cancelled 'passages of it'
351.18	concluded] 'conc' over wiped-out 'end'
351.30–31	get me some seed] above uncancelled 'tell me the name'
351.31	crimson] over wiped-out 'pretty'
351.31	I reckon] 'I reck' over wiped-out 'that mig'
352.3	might] over wiped-out 'could'
352.3	if] over wiped-out 'its'
352.6	mighty curious] 'mighty cur' over wiped-out 'very curious'
352.7	taught] over wiped-out 'had'
352.12	more] 'm' over wiped-out 'fo'
352.16	people] 'ple' over 'for'
352.17	upon it, too] preceded by cancelled 'it'; 'it' above 'upon'
352.17–19	(I . . . purposes.)] added in clear space, addressing the reader rather than himself; period is CENTENARY emendation
352.24	like] followed by cancelled 'an obstreperous giant'
352.25	up] over 'its'
352.30	I've] over wiped-out 'She'
353.3	All prepared to] above caret and uncancelled 'So she began, and all'
353.4	truth, Sybil's] comma over wiped-out punctuation: 'Sybil's' over wiped-out 'the old'

353.4–5	perhaps . . . fancy] above caret
353.10	His . . . England] over wiped-out 'He felt for the moment'
353.11–12	frightfully] above cancelled 'long'
353.12	to superstition] 'to' over 's'
353.12	at best] above caret
353.13	early] 'ea' over wiped-out 'sc'
353.13	to which all] over wiped-out 'where all exploit'
353.19	godlike] followed by cancelled 'when wealth is to be had for the gathering, and found'; 'when wealth' over wiped-out 'and when they'
353.27	seemed] over wiped-out 'c[ ]h'
353.32	not] 'n' over 'd'
354.6	and did] 'and' over wiped-out 'hold'
354.8	If] over 'Since'
354.9	in short] horizontal lines drawn above and below
354.10	with Septimius] above caret
354.10	many] above uncancelled 'most'
354.13	mingled] 'm' over 'co'
354.18	doubt] 'u' over 'f'
354.21	And] 'A' over 'S'
354.22	answer one way or the other] preceded by cancelled 'stedfastly'; 'one . . . other' above caret
354.23–24	and . . . No!"] preceded by comma that cancels period added to the original sentence above '(Insert . . . end.)' (see Alterations entry 354.31–355.16)
354.31–355.16	Now, touching the legend. . . . legend.] beginning 'Now, touching the above legend,' the paragraph follows 'But . . . &c.' (367.4) on MS page 39; double arrows in the indention, a note in the top margin, '(See below about Aunt Nashoba's story.)', and the note '(Insert before Aunt N's story what is at the end.)' added in available space before the beginning of her narrative on MS 37, direct transposition, in which 'above' is necessarily discarded
355.4–11	believed. As . . . benefit.] 'believed.' followed

by two-tiered caret at insertion point for 'As
. . . benefit', which, preceded by a two-tiered
caret, was inscribed following a sentence now
superseded, 'She . . . familiar.' (see note
for 355.11–16)

355.11–16   But . . . legend.] introduced by the preceding
'and so, perhaps, Aunt Nashoba fabled chiefly
for Sybil's benefit', this sentence supersedes
that which originally followed 355.4 'believed.': 'She was a very queer and inscrutable old woman; and she may have had a
notion, possibly, of capping Sybil's tradition
with one as strange, and made more grotesque by the unaccustomed imagery with
she herself was familiar.'

355.13   at least] above caret

355.14–15   a part . . . superstition—] indicated by caret;
added after the sentence, separated from it
by a vertical line

355.14   Indian] over wiped-out 'super'

355.15   superstition] MS 'super-|stition', 'st' over wiped-
out 'sup'

355.17–18   He . . . races] added interlined between paragraphs

355.21   habit] above cancelled 'way'

355.22   hour] above caret

355.26   too] over wiped-out 'was'

355.31   birches] 'birc' over 'pines'

356.3   red race] 're' over wiped-out 'R'

356.5   their] above caret

356.6   Nobody] followed by cancelled 'whence he
came, though'

356.7   said] over wiped-out 'with'

356.11   the] altered from 'their'

356.13   (knowing] parenthesis cancels comma; 'knowing' over wiped-out 'knew all'

356.20   qualities] above uncancelled 'endowments'

356.23   perplexed] 'perpl' over wiped-out 'troubl'

356.27   might] 'mi' over 'cou'

357.4   seemed] over wiped-out 'was an eld'

357.6–12   one. It . . . use.] 'one.' is in the second line of the MS page, but is not followed by a mark for the insertion of an alteration; in the narrow top margin is the note '(see below)'; 'It . . . use.', preceded by three vertical lines, was inscribed after "deathless.' (357.31) and is transposed by judgment of the consonance of a series of related sentences

357.8   man] over wiped-out 'ruler'

357.13   counsellors) above cancelled 'men'

357.20   soaked] over wiped-out '[]pt'

357.21   If there were] over wiped-out 'If there was a'

357.22   —say] dash cancels comma

357.23   wait] 'w' over 'p'

357.24   their great-] 'ir gre' over wiped-out 'grandchil'

358.22   gruffly] above caret

358.23   And] followed by 'they laid the whole case before him', cancelled except for 'they', which was left in error; 'him' over wiped-out 'the'

358.29   depart] above caret and cancelled 'be gone'

358.29   or] above cancelled 'and'

358.31   giving] over wiped-out 'having'

358.33   or] above cancelled 'and'

359.2   their other Deity] 'ir' added to 'the'; 'other Deity' above caret

359.2   evidently] 'ev' over wiped-out 'be'

359.14   distance] 'd' over 't'

359.14   flint] above caret

359.15   because] 'be' over 'and'

359.16   if . . . one] above caret

359.22   stone] above caret

359.26   an] over wiped-out 'so'

359.28   in . . . smoke] added above 'danced about it and . . . rejoiced'

359.31–   The white ashes . . . fire. But . . . sat] added
360.6   after 'longer.' (360.15), 'sat' followed by '&c'; the insertion point is marked by four vertical lines after 'with.', where 'But . . . sat' super-

	sedes the beginning of the original sentence 'And when the fire began to subside, there they beheld the Great Sagamore,'
359.33	glow] over wiped-out 'play'
360.1	thought] 'th' over wiped-out 'w'
360.5	fury] 'u' over wiped-out 'l'
360.5	saw] over partially wiped-out 'could'
360.6	in the] over wiped-out 'smoking'
360.6	most] over wiped-out 'embers', followed by un-wiped comma
360.11	of] 'o' cancels comma
360.13	the] over wiped-out 'him'
360.16–17	A . . . was] inscribed along left margin of MS page
360.19	his throne] 'his t' over wiped-out 'the th'
360.20	garments,] followed by cancelled 'and the vapor of the heat'
360.22	furnace] 'urnac' over wiped-out 'ires'
360.23–24	He . . . hot] above 'And out of that realm . . . ,'
360.29	should] 'sh' over 'wo'
361.13	out] 'o' over wiped-out 'of'
361.14	that] over 'now'
361.15	away] initial 'a' over 'h'
361.16	forever] 'fore' over wiped-out 'bequ'
361.23	peace,] followed by cancelled 'and'
361.23	build] 'bui' over 'wi'
361.27	recipe of] over wiped-out 'was preserved'
361.28	you] over wiped-out 'shall'
361.32	great grandson] 'great' above caret
362.1	ago] 'a' over 's'
362.5	bloody] over wiped-out 'his'
362.6	still] 'st' over 'as'
362.6	should] over wiped-out 'seemed'
362.24	catechisms] 'cate' over 'chat'
362.24	scenes . . . Concord] above 'and took . . . planting'
362.25	land] mended from 'lands'
362.25	are] 'a' over 'p'

362.26	it—] over wiped-out 'them'
362.30	and went] 'and' over 'wen'
363.5	finally] above caret
363.13	I] over 'if'
363.16	really] over wiped-out 'valuab'
363.25	should] 'sho' over 'wer'
363.26	Cape] over wiped-out 'Squ'
363.27	When] 'W' over 'I'
363.29	on] over wiped-out 'with'
363.30	it seemed] over wiped-out 'Abner Garfield'
364.4	holding] 'ho' over wiped-out 'li'
364.8	cachinnatory] MS 'cachinatory'; 'ca' over wiped-out 'ch'; second 'c' over 'ch'
364.19–20	it from . . . twisted.] 'it' followed by caret cancelling period and marking insertion for 'from . . . twisted.', which, preceded by a caret, was inscribed after 'for it.' (364.23); a double caret after 'twisted.' marks end of the alteration, and the final sentence of the paragraph begins on the same line
364.21	yourself] 'r' over 's'
364.24	(and] parenthesis cancels comma
364.24	I've] 'I' over 'if'
364.31–33	(Perhaps . . . it.)] added in space at end of paragraph
365.1	the] over 'it'
365.4	garden] 'gar' over wiped-out 'soil'
365.6	half-opaque] above caret and cancelled 'turbid'
365.12	contributing] 'con' over wiped-out 'af'
365.13–14	smelt delicately] over wiped-out 'applied his nose'
365.18–19	miraculously] 'm' over wiped-out 'p'
365.19	an] mended from 'a'
365.27	fabled] over wiped-out 'told of'
365.29	scorching] 'or' over wiped-out 'h'
365.33	came] over wiped-out 'a sen'
365.33	hideous] above caret
366.3	ugly] over wiped-out 'bad'
366.6	However] over wiped-out 'Knowing'

366.7–8	hereditary] over wiped-out 'sanctity in which'
366.8	furthermore] 'fu' over wiped-out 'the'; 't' over wiped-out 'h'
366.16	Aunt Nashoba] above 'potency'
366.20	and] 'a' over 'A'; preceded by comma mended from period
366.24	to be an] above caret
366.24	woman] above 'and'
366.26	one] 'o' over wiped-out 'of'
366.26	it] above cancelled 'there'
366.27	some fourteenth cousin] above cancelled 'one'
367.2–3	with . . . go] added below the paragraph with insertion indicated by a caret
367.5	apply . . . alone] added in top margin of MS page immediately above 'It has often . . .', indicating intention of revision; see also note for 367.6–7
367.6–7	Begin . . . visitor] interlined below first line of paragraph 'It has often . . .', because there was no space above after the addition of 'apply . . . alone' (see 367.5) but intended to set future revision in motion; a double arrow in the indention at left directs attention to the spot
367.18	is] over wiped-out 'in'
367.24–25	on the hill-top] above 'life and courage'
367.25	for] 'f' over 'o'
368.1	bricks] 'b' over 'c'
368.8	(or] parenthesis cancels comma
368.12–13	stubbornly resisting] over wiped-out 'substance in the focus of a lens'
368.17	weaving] above cancelled 'making'
368.30	with] over wiped-out 'perhap'
369.2	wild] 'ld' over wiped-out 'ldly'
369.3	life and] over wiped-out 'the ques-'
369.6–7	I find . . . aside] added in space at end of paragraph
369.7	but] over 'part'

369.21   cryptic] 'cr' over 'ch'
369.26   to find . . . it,] interlined (for want of space
              directly above original 'to turn in the mys-
              terious lock this cryptic key.') between the
              first and second lines above; the alteration
              requires rejection of uncancelled 'to turn'
              and 'this cryptic key'
369.27   find] over wiped-out 'whic'
369.30   of subtle ingenuity] over wiped-out 'that would
              have been his'
369.31   due.] period cancels comma
370.4   bringing] first 'i' over 'l'
370.7   such] over 'the'
370.25–26   he . . . flower.)] added in space at end of
              paragraph
370.30–31   when . . . longer] above 'cold . . . death, is
              . . . to the'
370.32   and of] over wipe-out 'of the'
370.33   endless life] 'end' over wiped-out 'life'
371.1   they] 'th' over 'co'
371.3   earth] 'e' over 'w'
371.15   There should] over wiped-out '[   ] they'
371.20   were] 'w' over 'h'
371.23   any] over wiped-out 'mor'
371.31   white] 'w' over 'sh'
372.5   first] 'ir' over 'o'
372.11   apparent] above 'figure'
372.11   is true] 'is t' over wiped-out 'was'
372.11   in the least] 'in the l' over wiped-out 'precisely'
372.14   whom] above 'a young'
372.18   elderly] first 'l' over 'd'
372.19   on which] over wiped-out 'that with'
372.23   green] 'en' over 'at'
372.28   applying] over wiped-out 'and applying'
372.29   smoke] over wiped-out 'breath'
372.30   of a] over wiped-out 'that a'
372.31   on short legs, a] over wiped-out 'walking on
              short'

373.1   making] above cancelled 'making'

373.2   hill-top,] followed by cancelled 'like a man who had seen the world.'

373.5–6   as well . . . permitted] above 'himself . . . blew'; caret erroneously inserted after 'astride'

373.6   nodded] above cancelled 'held out his hand'

373.6   gracious] followed by cancelled 'kind of way'

373.11   Speak . . . decidedly.] added after the phrase of Alterations entry 373.13–14, in space after paragraph ending 'said he.' (373.8)

373.13–14   connected with the chemical department] added in space after paragraph ending 'said he.' (373.8), above 'of the medical corps'; 'the chemical department' above and to the right of 'connected with'

373.14   chemist or] above caret

373.16   (on the gentle suggestion] over wiped-out 'quitted Boston on'

373.20   civilly] lines drawn above and below

373.20–21   still . . . strangers] above 'that . . . favorably'

373.23   your] over 'ow'

373.24–25   with . . . smoke] above caret

373.27   sincerely] 'sin' over wiped-out 'des'

374.2   more] over wiped-out 'espec'

374.9   principally] 'princip' over wiped-out 'partly to'

374.13   you.] followed by cancelled 'I am sure my sister and myself'

374.32   science. And] period over wiped-out comma and 'A' over wiped-out 'a'

375.9   in] over wiped-out 'he'

375.11   boy!] exclamation mark cancels comma and double quotation mark

375.12   his companion] above cancelled 'Septimius'

375.15   on his] over wiped-out 'as th'

375.26   had] over wiped-out 'made'

376.5   by which time] over wiped-out 'where Septimius'

376.13   some] above cancelled 'a' which is over wiped-out 'a cur'

376.13	wild] over wiped-out 'garden f'
376.19	of] above caret
376.21	"My sister] preceded by period which cancels comma; 'My s' over wiped-out 'though'
376.22	interest] 'in' over wiped-out 'acqu'
377.6	But] over wiped-out 'My s'
377.8	to] over 'and'
377.33	or] over wiped-out 'and'
378.1	endowment] 'en' over wiped-out 'g'
378.5–6	(Septimius . . . men)] added in the top margin of MS page; insertion of the proposed addition is marked by an arrowhead pointer before Doctor's speech which follows here
378.8	most] above cancelled 'many'
378.29	would] above cancelled 'will'
379.12	and] 'a' over wiped-out 'h'
379.14	to] over 'it'
379.15	That] 'a' over wiped-out 'is'
379.20	said] 's' over 'a'
379.22	A] over wiped-out 'I'
379.23	I think] 'I th' over wiped-out 'it d'
379.23	as] over wiped-out 'br'
380.5	and bowed] 'and b' over wiped-out 'greeted'
380.5	surprised] initial 's' over wiped-out 't'
380.9	dry] followed by cancelled 'yellow'
380.10–11	whole, and a skin] comma replaces wiped-out comma; 'and, a skin' over wiped-out 'a strange s'; deletion of comma after 'and' is a CENTENARY emendation
380.12	intermixed] 'inter' over wiped-out 'blood'
380.19	the] over wiped-out 'Sep'
380.25	hedge-growths] 'grow' over wiped-out 'matt'
381.5	standing] 'stand' over wiped-out 'gazing'
381.8	A spider] over wiped-out 'He [　] at it'
381.12	again.] period over wiped-out comma
381.28	wrought] followed by cancelled 'in open work, with some bands with'
381.29	a] mended from 'an'
382.1–2	(Herbs . . . goes.)] added in top margin of

	MS page above ¶ 'Septimius replied . . . '
382.12	weeds] over wiped-out 'herbs'
382.13–14	scattered . . . everywhere] originally 'scattered every-where'; the alteration, preceded by a caret, was inscribed below the line and placed by a caret between uncancelled 'scattered' and 'every-where'
382.15	barn-door,] comma cancels period
382.17	so for] followed by cancelled 'tasting poison'
382.18	beast] 'be' over wiped-out 'an'
382.21	him] over wiped-out 'with'
382.22	and finally] 'a' of 'and' over wiped-out 's'
382.24	he.] period cancels comma
382.24	It . . . not] interlined below 'Excuse . . . said'
382.27–28	During . . . embarrassed] added in space at end of paragraph
382.29	leathern] altered from 'bottle'
382.29–30	with . . . on] added above 'encourage much intercourse' (383.10–11) without sign for insertion; although somewhat nearer 'his own flask' at 383.3–4, it would be awkward there, and is here arbitrarily placed at the first mention, when the Doctor offered the flask to his companions
382.32	bumper] 'bum' over wiped-out 'brim'
383.8	homage] 'hom' over wiped-out 'aff[]'
383.16	destruction] 'des' over wiped-out 'Ind'
383.18	half] 'l' over 'f'
383.24	blunted] 'blun' over wiped-out 'f[ ]t'
383.25	his feet] 's' over wiped-out 'm'
384.1	from] over 'his'
384.8	to crush] 'to' over 'ch'
384.8	squat] 'sq' over 'Do'
384.17	share] 'sha' over wiped-out 'acc'
384.24	Rose] over wiped-out 'Aunt'
384.31–32	He . . . &c] added in space at end of paragraph
385.6	offshoots] 'off' over wiped-out 'other'
385.9	cottages] over wiped-out 'English'

385.13	vastly] 'va' over wiped-out 'a f'
385.22	sources. For] period over wiped-out comma; 'For' over wiped-out 'with'
385.23	was] over 'had'
386.2	from.] period cancels comma
386.4	indeed] MS 'ideed'; terminal 'd' over 'th'
386.10	characteristicalness,] comma cancels period
386.23–25	(The . . . possession.)] added in space at end of paragraph
387.2	German] 'Ger' over wiped-out 'pipe'
387.9	again.] followed by wiped-out 'This meeting, however, did not'
387.9–11	(Before . . . Boston.] MS 'Befor'; added in space at end of paragraph, the parenthesis over wiped-out 'not'; see preceding note
387.20	in his] over wiped-out ',' said'
387.27–28	(Look . . . sketch)] not MS page 43 but page 45 of the Felton draft has a paraphrase of the passage (80.13)
387.29	tobacco] lines drawn above and below
388.2–3	(Something . . . disturbed)] added above final word of paragraph and in space after paragraph
388.4	an] mended from 'a'
388.5	intimacy] over wiped-out 'friendship'
388.17–18	common to] 'c' over wiped-out 'to'; 't' over 'o'
388.18	to cheer] 'to' over wiped-out 'c'
388.21	for] mended from 'of'
388.31	connected] initial 'c' over wiped-out 'of'
389.16	Sybil] 'S' over 'R'
389.24	after] over wiped-out 'in t'
389.27	poison to] 'nous' of original 'poisonous' wiped out and 'n' added more broadly; 't' over the wiped-out 's'
389.33	acquaintance] initial 'a' over wiped-out 'f'
390.2	where] 'w' over wiped-out 'of'
390.9	tears] followed by cancelled semicolon
390.32	inevitable] altered from partly wiped-out 'miser'
391.1	thought] initial 't' over 'f'

391.1	as] over wiped-out 'to'
391.2	his] 'h' over 'in'
391.12	fell] 'f' over 'a'
391.14	about] 'ab' over wiped-out 'for'
391.17	and] over 'or'
391.27	slow] over wiped-out 'dark st'
391.32	meagre] above cancelled 'barren'
391.32	clearing] over wiped-out 'cultivating'
392.1–5	promise. This . . . memory] a two-tiered caret after 'promise.' marks the insertion point for 'This . . . memory' which was added in space at end of paragraph, preceded and followed by two-tiered carets
392.9	laid] over wiped-out 'caught'
392.13	laugh.] period over 'w' of wiped-out ', which'
392.16	and] 'a' over 's'
392.20	puck-] over wiped-out 'wild'
392.23	she.] period over wiped-out comma, followed by wiped-out 'gl'
392.24	exclaimed] 'exc' over 'cried'
392.25	nothing] over wiped-out 'an access'
392.27	it!" repeated] 'it!" re' over wiped-out 'what I'
392.29	by] over 'no'
392.33–393.1	appeared] 'app' over 'clos'
393.9	arm] 'a' over wiped-out 'h'
393.17	in] over 'th'
393.31	they] 't' over 's'
394.8	or] over wiped-out 'mul-'
394.12	flowers] over wiped-out 'blos'
394.16	A . . . stool] added in space at end of paragraph
394.21	not] above caret
394.28	it;] semicolon cancels period
395.6	It must be heart-shaped.] added in top margin of MS page just above the paragraph that follows here
395.10	which it] over wiped-out 'it might'

395.11	right . . . corpse] added in top margin just above the sentence; inserted without authorial sign
395.18	all crimson. It] over wiped-out 'as crimson as blood'
395.23	open to] over wiped-out 'have its'
395.28	closed] over wiped-out 'folde'
396.11	not] above 'rather'
396.14	sort of fascination] over wiped-out 'certain [ ]ation'
396.16–17	(There . . . flower)] added in space at end of paragraph
396.23–24	Pah . . . it."] 'Pah' over closing double quotation mark
396.25	With] preceded by cancelled 'She drew Rose away, and they descended the hill together.' after which was inscribed 'Then, as with', 'as' above caret; 'Then' cancelled, 'as' inadvertently left, 'with' altered to 'With'
396.26	she plucked] 's' over 'a'; 'plucked' over wiped-out 'tore the'
396.26	from] over wiped-out 'into'
396.33	suppose) initial 's' over wiped-out 'h'
397.1	had] over 'an'
397.21	from] over wiped-out 'to Syb-'
397.32	power] 'r' over wiped-out 'rs'
398.3	dull] 'd' over wiped-out 'e'
398.5	now] above 'flashing'
398.6	ascending] 'asc' over wiped-out 'risi'
398.20	tearing open the heart] above 'flowers and pulled'
398.22	abruptly] 'abru' over wiped-out 'easi'
398.24–25	There . . .heart.] added above 'knew not why.', continuing in space at end of paragraph
398.27	scarlet] over wiped-out 'red toa'
398.29	hillock] over wiped-out 'grave'
398.31	and] over wiped-out 'a sort'
399.6	it] 'i' over wiped-out 'a'

399.7	and] over wiped-out 'the'
399.10	every] initial 'e' over 'g'
399.11	rich] over wiped-out 'wild'
399.16	yesterday.] followed by wiped-out ', g'
399.18	evolving] 'ev' over wiped-out 'th'
399.33	(in] parenthesis cancels comma
400.2	nation] 'nat' over wiped-out 'being'
400.2	an] altered from 'a in'
400.7	how] over 'to'
400.10	the] 't' over 'T'
400.24	be] 'b' over 't'
400.27	an unworthy] 'an' mended from 'a'; 'unworthy' above caret
400.31–32	(binds . . . it)] added above the paragraph
401.2	her acquaintance] 'her acq' over wiped-out 'and her ac'
401.3	and her] 'h' over 'c'
401.4	health.] period cancels comma
401.7	or] over 'an'
401.8	uglier] over wiped-out 'aspec'
401.9	acquaintances] initial 'a' over 're'
401.10	dull] over wiped-out 'face'
401.10	from] 'f' over wiped-out 'i'
401.12–14	days, spreading . . . flue.] a caret, erroneously inserted before the comma after 'days', marks the insertion point for 'spreading . . . flue.', which, preceded by a caret and followed by two vertical lines, was inscribed after 'inwardly' and the caret for 'or . . . breathe' (see Alterations 401.24)
401.15	torrid] above 'burning'
401.18	her handkerchief] above cancelled 'the [ ] flapped'
401.24	or . . . breathe] above caret after 'inwardly' which precedes the caret before 'spreading . . . flue.' (see Alterations 401.12–14)
401.24	a] over 's'
401.26	somewhat] 'w' over 'thi'
401.27	unwholesome] 'un' over 'wh'

401.32	disposition] 'd' over 'li'
402.1–10	extenuate. She . . . infirmities] a two-tiered caret after 'extenuate.' marks insertion point for 'She . . . infirmities', which, preceded and followed by three vertical lines, was added after 'Nashoba.' (402.23)
402.10	own] 'ow' over 'in'
402.10	from] 'f' over 'a'
402.11	it] over 'wa'
402.11	henlike] 'h' over 'he'
402.15	would] 'wou' over 'and re'
402.24	might have] above uncancelled 'was'
402.26–27	chilled frame] 'ed' added; 'ed fr' over wiped-out 'body'
402.28	nurse] over 'make'
402.28	her,] a terminal 's' wiped out
402.29	alive, and light her pipe] a second comma added after 'alive'; 'light her pipe' over wiped-out 'but Aunt Nashoba'
402.31	demeaned] 'de' over 'Ro'
403.13	again.] period cancels comma
403.22	as] over right parenthesis
403.28	and] over wiped-out 'exteri'
403.30	morning] 'mo' over wiped-out 'day'
403.31	effort] above uncancelled 'attempt'
404.1	taken] 'tak' over wiped-out 'left'
404.5	her dry] 'her' above cancelled 'that'
404.10	feeling] followed by cancelled 'himself'
404.14	croaked] over partly wiped-out 'said the'
404.15	not very] above uncancelled 'a little'
404.17	I can] over wiped-out 'I'll squa'
404.20	poor] 'po' over 'Au'
404.24	half] above 'wild'
404.25	human's] over wiped-out 'door'
404.26	(wondering] parenthesis cancels comma
404.31	on] over 'in a'
405.4	I've] 've' over 'fel'
405.7	and sit] 'a' over 's'
405.7	by] 'b' over 'm'

405.8	tell] over wiped-out 'you'
405.10	Hilliard] 'H' over wiped-out 'Sep'
405.10	she] 's' over 't'
405.11	wasted] 'was' over wiped-out 'lost'
405.14	I've wondered if you] over wiped-out 'You wondered if I'
405.16	it's a] over wiped-out 'after I'
405.17	to] over 'th'
405.18	wonderful] 'won' over wiped-out 'bitte'
405.18	Hilly.] period cancels comma
405.19	hand,] comma cancels period
405.20	dictated] 'dic' over wiped-out 'lis'
405.21	rare] above 'occurrence'
405.24	of] above 'or'
405.25–27	roots . . . leaves, twigs . . . knowledge.] 'roots . . . leaves' added in limited space above paragraph and 'twigs . . . knowledge.' continued below the paragraph in space after the next two speeches; comma after 'leaves' is a CENTENARY emendation; insertion is without authorial sign, but rounds out 'his tincture of botanical science' with 'practical knowledge'
405.28	the name] above caret
405.29	lips] over wiped-out 'm'
405.30	inscribed] over wiped-out 'for the'
406.12	said Aunt] over wiped-out 'for this was'
406.23	Hilly] above cancelled 'Seppy'
406.23	And] over wiped-out 'The'
406.27	Aunt] 'A' over 'N'
406.31	of] 'o' over 's'
406.33	steaming] originally 'steam had'; 'ing' over wiped-out 'had'
407.3	his] 'hi' over 'po'
407.8–9	She . . . takes.] added in space at end of paragraph
407.10	he . . . stern;] above caret inadvertently placed before the preceding comma
407.11	being so unusual] above caret
407.19	lease of] over wiped-out 'begin'

407.19	life.] period cancels comma
407.21–22	"my . . . it] added above original 'quietly and wearily; "but . . . sake'
407.26–27	and the . . . right] above caret
407.28	put] above cancelled 'set'
407.31	there's] 's' over 'is'
407.33	gather] 'g' 'over 'f'
407.33	another] over wiped-out 'a harvest'
408.4	consummated] mended from 'consummation'
408.7	hastening] mended from 'hastened'
408.12	covered . . . lid] MS 'covered'; over wiped-out 'sat down to watch the slow process'
408.13	Aunt] over wiped-out 'the old'
408.19	mixture] above underlined 'recipe'
408.26–27	hand, in . . . family] five vertical lines after 'hand,' mark insertion point for 'in . . . family', which, preceded and followed by a cluster of vertical lines, was inscribed after 'methods' (408.30)
409.4	decrepitude] first 'e' over 'is'
409.11	wretched] 'wre' over 'ste'
409.18	Hilliard] over wiped-out 'Septimius'
409.33	instinctively] over wiped-out 'anxious to'
410.9	Hilliard] 'Hi' over 'Sep'
410.11	heavy] above caret
410.12–14	concoction. He . . . bubbles] in top margin of MS page a note '(See below)' and a line drawn diagonally to a cluster of vertical lines after 'concoction.' mark the insertion point for 'He . . . bubbles' which was inscribed below 'Then . . . measure.' (412.12–13), set off by a bracket in the left margin, preceded by a cluster of vertical lines, and followed by three vertical lines, a note '(see above)', and a closing bracket
410.13	studded] 'stud' over wiped-out 'cov'
410.14	The process] over wiped-out 'The vegetable'
410.17	herb-woman] 'herb' over wiped-out 'woman'
410.17	been] over wiped-out 'wished'

410.20	kept] 'k' over wiped-out 'ob'
410.21	measuring] 'mea' over wiped-out 'pouring'
410.23	was] over wiped-out 'caught'
410.23	contiguity] 'con' over wiped-out 'fire'
410.25	flame,] comma cancels period
410.26–27	expired. It . . . (It.] the paragraph originally ended with 'expired.', but after the next paragraph had been written to 'secret.' (410.32), 'It . . . it.' was interlined above 'expired.' and below it, between paragraphs in such a constricted hand that NH prudently repeated the passage after 'secret.', preceded by two vertical lines and enclosed in parentheses for separation from the direct quotation of Septimius; three vertical lines were added after 'expired' to mark the insertion point
410.30	weakening] over wiped-out 'and the strength'
411.1	unless] 'un' over wiped-out 'with'
411.5	refrained] over wiped-out 'forfeited his'
411.6–8	At . . . bitterness.] added above the paragraph in space at end of previous paragraph; inserted without authorial sign by sequent thought of 'He was not yet ready . . . '
411.15	new] above caret
411.28	treading] over wiped-out 'and spil'
411.29	yet] over wiped-out 'every'
411.30	on] over 'at'
411.32	much] above caret
412.1	though . . . weary] above caret
412.5–6	in . . . tone] above 'replied . . . virtues'
412.14	dear] 'd' over period and quotation mark
412.15	by the] 'the' over 'kin'
412.24	these] over 'that'
412.30	doctor's] 'd' over 's'
412.31	all] above caret
412.31	is] over 'it'
413.1	screwing] over wiped-out '[ ]ldly'
413.2	you to make] over wiped-out 'out of you'
413.5	time.] period cancels comma

413.14	she] 'h' over 'ai'
413.19	herb-drinks] over wiped-out 'infernal brews'
413.21	As with] over wiped-out 'No, but'
413.23	feel] over 'am'
413.25	(Perhaps . . . skin] added in space at end of paragraph
413.26	He . . . with] added in available space after 'still." ' (413.10), the note pertains to the paragraph that follows here
413.27	being] over 'her co'
413.28	withdrew] above 'after'
413.31	summon] over wiped-out 'the floor'; preceded by cancelled 'knock upon'
413.32	need] over 'want'
414.6	on] mended from 'one'
414.11	feverishly] lines drawn above and below
414.12	sphere] over wiped-out 'world of'
414.19	room. In] period over wiped-out comma; 'In' over wiped-out 'as'
414.19	brief] over wiped-out 'rapid'
414.20	cast his eyes] above cancelled 'look'
414.20	looking-glass] initial 'l' over wiped-out 'm'
414.21	two] above 'front'
414.22	face] above 'people'
414.23	Hilliard] 'H' over 'Sep'
414.25	possess] 'pos-' over wiped-out 'have'
415.4	called] 'c' of MS 'call' covers comma after original, cancelled 'termed'
415.5	between his eyebrows] over wiped-out 'from the centre of the'
415.6	his nose] 'his' over 'the'
415.9	bloom] above cancelled 'youth'
415.10	He] over 'As'
415.16	that] over wiped-out 'bro'
415.20	recurring] preceded by cancelled 'settling down'
415.25	adopted] 'do' over 'ss'
415.26	fast;] semicolon cancels period
416.1	craftier] 'craf' over wiped-out 'wiser'
416.4	of] 'o' over 'in'

416.8   its] over wiped-out 'in'

416.10–15   delight. Was . . . possession.] 'delight.' followed by five vertical lines to mark insertion point for 'Was . . . possession.' which, preceded by four vertical lines, was inscribed after 'held it!' (416.18)

416.18   often] over 'once'

416.21   its] over wiped-out 'the'

416.23   most] above uncancelled 'all'

416.23   out of] above uncancelled 'remote from'

416.24–25   or subvert an] over wiped-out 'an empire, or sub'

416.26   make] 'm' over 'kno'

416.29–30   "You are a dreamer."—that is what it says. "You are deluding yourself. You are toiling] originally phrased interrogatively; the first 'You are' added above uncancelled 'Are you Not', 'You are deluding' above uncancelled 'Are you not making a fool of', final 'You are' over wiped-out 'Are you not'; question marks after 'dreamer' and 'yourself'. unchanged in MS, are made periods by CENTENARY emendations

416.31   waste] above uncancelled 'wreck'

416.32   that] over wiped-out 'all th'

417.4   Battle] 'B' over 'b'

417.5   for valor] over wiped-out 'for his valor'

417.5–6   In his] over 'The re'

417.9   had found, without] 'had found, wi' over wiped-out 'without even se'

417.12   high] above cancelled 'heroic'

417.17   Love . . . nature] lines drawn above and below as a mark of dissatisfaction with the passage

417.17   was to be] 'w' over 'h', 'b' over 'to'

417.19   with] over wiped-out 'or else,'

417.21   dying . . . republics] below 'gliding things . . . '

417.26   should] over wiped-out 'might last'

417.26	endure] above uncancelled 'last'
417.27	an hour] 'hour' above 'a day'; 'an' is CENTENARY emendation
417.28	one hour] 'h' over 'p'
417.30	mortal] 'mo' over wiped-out 'man'
418.5	advices] above cancelled 'rules'
418.5	advices] above cancelled 'rules'
418.5	you] over wiped-out 'were'
418.6	Golden] 'G' over 'g'
418.7	Rules] 'R' over 'r'
418.8	great] 'g' over 'e'
418.10	Fling] 'F' over 'r' of wiped-out 'Or'
418.10	aside] 'a' over 's'
418.10	toss] above uncancelled 'fling'
418.11	in] above uncancelled 'with'
418.14	any of them] above caret
418.18	ethereal] followed by cancelled 'immortality'
418.21	passion] preceded by cancelled 'very divinest'
418.23	fully] above caret
418.25	to make] 'to' over wiped-out 'th'
418.25	Old] 'O' over 'o'
418.26	feeling] 'feel' over 'idea'
418.32	so that he should] over wiped-out ', or because the path of the'
418.33	after] over 'of his'
419.4	in his forehead] above 'and measuring'
419.12	Hilliard would have] over wiped-out 'he would have supposed'
419.13	or scene] above caret
419.15	chamber] above cancelled 'room'
419.24	fairly] 'f' over 'w'
419.32	when he had] over wiped-out 'he rose, and'
420.1	on tiptoe] above caret
420.4	as to be] over wiped-out 'that she sh'
420.10	one] over 'a man'
420.11	an . . . student,] above 'Hillard was'
420.12	with her] above caret
420.16–20	Finding . . . dead, Aunt Nashoba missing, and even . . . contents)] original reading 'dead,

	and even . . . . contents)' was followed by 'Aunt Nashoba missing, and even the brown jug &c', in a clumsy revision to have 'Aunt Nashoba missing' follow 'dead'
420.17	dead] over wiped-out 'out'
420.18	even] above 'the'
420.22–23	bending . . . work] above caret; 'work' above cancelled 'and'; the phrase supersedes un-cancelled 'bending down his head.', inscribed after MS 'other.)' (420.25)
420.23–24	(beneath] parenthesis cancels comma
420.28	at home] over wiped-out 'in the kit'
420.30	Ill] preceded by cancelled 'Poor Auntie'; 'I' over double quotation mark and 'i'
420.30–31	It . . . that!] above caret; preceded by super-fluous double quotation mark
420.31–32	And . . . you] originally 'And no better nurse than yourself'; 'better . . . yourself' cancelled and 'body . . . you' added above
420.32– 421.1	My . . . have] over wiped-out 'I will creep up stairs'
421.4	cried] 'c' over 's'
421.5–6	and . . . away] above caret
421.5	and] over 'as she'
421.6	Aunt] over wiped-out 'She'
421.9	she—] above 'Rose'
421.13	Aunt] preceded by cancelled 'poor'
421.13	lonely] 'l' over wiped-out 'th'
421.15	ask] over wiped-out 'get her'
421.17	Hagburn] 'Hag' over wiped-out 'Garfi'
421.18	the old wretch] above caret
421.26	sad] 's' over 'b'
421.27	ever] above caret
421.31	that] over wiped-out 'whic'
421.32	Aunt] over wiped-out 'you'
422.1	answered] 'an' over 'sa'
422.3	That is all my] over wiped-out 'Begone, you f'
422.4	teach] preceded by cancelled 'attend to your own matters'

422.6	You . . . me] added above 'about . . . comprehend.'
422.7–8	We . . . better] added above 'not . . . Hilliard'
422.8	submissively] horizontal lines drawn above and below
422.8	and sadly] above caret
422.11	this] over 'wa'
422.11–12	far from] 'far f' over 'not th'
422.17	adjacent] above caret
422.19	because] followed by cancelled 'immediately'
422.29	hurried] preceded by cancelled 'heavy knocks'
422.31	snatched] 's' over 't'
423.6	or an earlier one] above caret
423.13	but an] over wiped-out 'despite'
423.27	cried] 'c' over 'A'
423.27	Aunt] 'A' over 'a'
423.27	the] above 'intense'
423.27–28	bitterness] 'bitter' over 'scorn'
423.28	Do] over wiped-out 'I'm'
424.1	bitter] over wiped-out 'veno'
424.7	Christian] 'Chris' over wiped-out 'Indian'
424.8	happy] over wiped-out 'Indian'
424.13	This] over ' "Do not', wiped out except for already dried double quotation mark
424.16–17	idiosyncrasy] second 'i' over 'y'
424.24	hide his] over wiped-out 'conceal'
424.25	commiseration] MS 'commisseration'; 'com' over wiped-out 'yet'
424.27	the poor] 'the' over wiped-out 'me'
424.28	me] over 'so'
424.28	Be] 'B' over 'I'
425.5	strange] above 'new'
425.11	instead.] period cancels comma
425.12	steeped . . . and] above caret; 'in that' over wiped-out 'enough'
425.14	I used] preceded by cancelled 'We foolish mortals long'; 'long' over wiped-out 'have'
425.14	won] above cancelled 'almost'

425.17	it,] 'it' over 'al'
425.20	then] above caret
425.20	and pleasant to] above caret
425.22	alive] over wiped-out 'sensitive'
425.23	that] over wiped-out 'Aunt N'
425.23	and] over wiped-out 'of p'
425.25	for] 'f' over 'I'
425.26–27	old Bloody] over 'the great'
426.7–8	Christion] 'C' over 'c'
426.12	and all . . . people] above caret
426.14	the Lord] 'the' over wiped-out 'God'
426.14	that] over wiped-out 'when'
426.15	myself.] 'my' over 'in'; period cancels comma
426.15	And . . . sermons] above 'soon . . . his'
426.16	And I] 'And' over wiped-out 'and', which originally followed 'myself,' (see note above); 'And . . . sermons' (426.15) is now placed between the two original sentences
426.17	straight gravel-walks] 'gravel' over wiped-out '-walks' of 'straight-walks'
426.19	forest] over wiped-out 'wood'
426.21	pale] over wiped-out 'frigh'
426.24	no] over 'use'
426.27	by the time] over wiped-out 'when you die'
427.2	seemed] 'se' over wiped-out 'to'
427.3	guessed] preceded by cancelled 'than'
427.8	rites] above uncancelled 'exercises' which is followed by cancelled 'and words of holy comfort,'
427.10	which] over wiped-out 'such'
427.11	in] over 'on'
427.11	(having] parenthesis cancels comma
427.15	as] over wiped-out 'and'
427.15–23	were. And yet . . . back, still . . . soil.] after 'were' the period cancels a comma and a two-tiered caret marks transposition point for 'And yet . . . back' which was inscribed after 'soil.' and is preceded by a two-tiered caret

and followed '&c' to indicate a replacement joining 'still' of original 'were, and her bundle of forest-products on her back, still'

427.22	had] over wiped-out 'w'
427.24	might] over wiped-out 'was'
427.26	hold it above] 'hold it a' over wiped-out 'put it into h'
427.32	the many] 'many' above 'the'
428.3	She howls too] added in space at end of paragraph
428.4	think] 't' over 'y'
428.9–10	or any] 'or' over 'm'
428.11	keeps] above cancelled 'makes'
428.12	but] over wiped-out 'and'
428.13	till they] over wiped-out 'and turn'
428.16	to] over 'the'
428.17	ear for] over 'for mu'
428.18	harping forever, and] over wiped-out 'singing and harping forever'
428.18	psalm] 's' over 'a'
428.20–21	his . . . face] originally 'him Hilly'; 'stern' added above 'Hilly', then 'his dark, stern face &c' added below the line
428.32	I've] over wiped-out 'I have'
429.1	on the very] over wiped-out 'and shoo'
429.2	flight] MS 'fligh' above uncancelled 'flock'
429.2	and wizards] above caret
429.11	bow.] period followed by wiped-out exclamation point
429.13	itself] 'its' over wiped-out 'aw'
429.15	ease] 'e' over 'a'
429.15	awake] 'aw' over wiped-out 'wh'
429.30	I shall] 'I' over 'it'
429.31	next.] followed by cancelled 'But the life is fluttering in me'
429.32	and] above caret
430.1	Hilly. It . . . contented.] a caret below 'Hilly' marks the insertion point for 'It . . . con-

	tented.' which, preceded by a two-tiered caret and followed by two vertical lines, was inscribed after 'them.' (430.6)
430.2	breeze] above uncancelled 'wind'
430.6	One] 'O' over 'H'
430.13	But] 'B' over double quotation mark
430.15	were] above caret
430.16	If there's] MS 'If there' over partially wiped-out 'Was there'
430.18	was] over 'is'
430.21	like a shadow] above caret
430.21–22	like the . . . water] added below 'dreamy . . . shifts' as a continuation after 'like a shadow'
430.23	It's no great] over wiped-out 'I dare say'
430.24	asked] over 'said'
430.30	something] altered from 'somewhere'
430.30	dreamily] above 'Aunt'
430.32	comes] 'com' over partly wiped-out 'has'
430.33	out] over wiped-out 'now'
431.1	nothing] 'no' over wiped-out 'for'
431.2	passionately grasping her hand] 'passionately' above 'forgetting', and 'grasping her hand' for lack of interline space, inscribed farther along, above 'for . . . except'
431.4	affection] 'a' over possible 'g'
431.8	and for . . . you] above 'Nothing . . . love'
431.10	sip.] preceded by cancelled 'last'; originally followed by comma and 'though, somehow, as ['as' above 'somehow'] there was a queer taste in that last cup.', which was cancelled by two horizontal lines that failed to cover 'that last cup'; period added after 'sip'
431.11–12	next, . . . strangers."] comma after 'next' cancels period; 'and not be downcast' added in line; 'at going among strangers."' interlined above the next sentence
431.12	going] initial 'g' over 'b'
431.13	all] above caret
431.15	Well] 'W' over wiped-out 'G'

431.17   Tomorrow] 'To' of MS 'Tommorrow' over wiped-out 'H'; preceded by cancelled 'Good-night'

431.22   or . . . awake] above caret

431.27   waking] over wiped-out 'consciousness'

432.1   We] over wiped-out 'I k'

432.2–3   into the hot tide of Hilliard . . . bitterness] after original 'into Hillard . . . bitterness' was added a two-tiered caret and 'into the hot tide' at the end of the line; inserted without authorial sign; 'of' is a CENTENARY emendation

432.3   venom] followed by cancelled 'and bitterness'

432.4   we] 'w' over wiped-out 'for'

432.5   quite] 'q' over 's'

432.7   of those] over wiped-out 'mysterious'

432.7   sensuous] above uncancelled 'mysterious'

432.10   Hilliard] altered from 'Had'

432.13   results] above cancelled 'deeds'

432.15   perspicacious] MS 'pespicacious' above uncancelled 'harmless' in which the 'l' is over 'f'

432.17   which] above is wiped-out 'with'

432.18   not] over 'rem'

432.23–28   Not . . . but statesmen . . . immorality. Even . . . fratricide.] originally 'Even . . . fratricide. Statesmen . . . immorality. Not . . . but &c.'; NH's 'Not . . . but' is intended as a new beginning of the 'Statesmen . . . ' sentence and the '&c.' serves as a bridge to 'Statesmen'; in addition to this reversal of parts, a further transposition in the order of the revised sentence and of 'Even . . . fratricide' is indicated by two-tiered carets preceding 'Statesmen' and 'Even'

432.28   fratricide] preceded by cancelled 'homicide'

432.30–33   suffer. And. . . . it?] a two-tiered caret after 'suffer.' marks the insertion point for 'And. . . . it?' which, preceded by a similar sign, had been inscribed after 'this.' (433.11)

432.33	entirely] above uncancelled 'most'
433.1	really] over wiped-out 'is such'
433.3	breast] over wiped-out 'mind'
433.3–4	constituted] third 't' over 'd'
433.5	part of it,] followed by cancelled 'rankling in the guilty breast'
433.19	along] over wiped-out 'after'
433.29	do] over 'ar'
434.2	corpse] 'c' over 'ol'
434.11	how to] over wiped-out 'what it'
434.16	hastily] 'has' over wiped-out 'forth'
434.16–17	Robert Hagburn's] over wiped-out 'the nearest neighbor'
434.19	discussing] 'd' over wiped-out 't'
434.19–20	among themselves] above caret
434.21	character] above uncancelled 'life'
434.25	no . . . Christian,] above 'too . . . witch-blood'
434.26	and too much Indian] over wiped-out 'with Indian blood'
434.27–28	or the . . . world,] above caret
434.28	or, . . . come] a continuation of the addition noted above, inscribed in line after 'rheumatism' (434.30), preceded by four vertical lines and followed by three, separating the passage from 'but the Doctor'
434.33	day.] followed by cancelled 'On the whole, however, it would seem throughout to her' of which 'On the' was over wiped-out 'And it would'
435.3	and the house] originally 'and they hoped that now the house'; 'they hoped that' cancelled and 'the house' written over wiped-out 'now the house'
435.5	they were glad] above caret erroneously placed after 'that'
435.8	half-blooded] over wiped-out 'would stu'
435.13	off, and] 'off' over 'out'; 'and' over wiped-out ' "She's'

435.18–22	Meanwhile . . . doors.] below this sentence in MS are two dashes marking a break; they originally were below a MS space; afterward, "Meanwhile . . . doors.' was inscribed above the dashes, but obviously serves as the beginning of the following scene; the break is placed before the alteration
435.19	troubled with] above caret and cancelled 'he had'
435.20–21	or when . . . him] above caret
435.28	Aunt] 'A' over wiped-out 'th'
435.29	he] mended from 'the'
436.3	sprang;] semicolon cancels period
436.4	could tread] 'could' over 'was'; 'tread' over wiped-out 'treat'
436.9	astringency] 'astrin' over wiped-out '[ ]ness'
436.11	calm;] semicolon cancels dash
436.12	the] over 'tu', followed by cancelled 'rbuent'
436.12	of emotion] above caret
436.15	tears] preceded by cancelled 'outward expression'
436.24	his mode] 'his' above caret
436.25	of the] over wiped-out 'of his'
436.27	therefore] 'there' over wiped-out 'very'
436.30	presently] over wiped-out 'partly'
436.31	alone;] followed by cancelled 'an object, it might be seen, not difficult to be obtained'
437.2	in which] 'in w' over wiped-out 'out of'
437.3	root] above cancelled 'tale'
437.3–4	(see below)] above 'and out of'; reference is to Sybil's speech, 438.4–13
437.7	her hand] over wiped-out 'her arm'
437.11–12	She . . . ground.] added in space at end of paragraph
437.15	weary] above caret
437.18	playthings;] semicolon cancels period
437.24	I would speak] over wiped-out 'I wish to speak'
437.29	oddly] over wiped-out 'int'

438.2	We] over closing quotation mark
438.6	off] altered from 'out'
438.9–10	This. . . . vine] followed by '&c', above caret after 'mischievous.' (438.13); transposed without insertion mark
438.11	here—] dash over period and closing quotation mark
438.14	could] 'co' over wiped-out 'saw'
438.31	true,"] comma and quotation mark over wiped-out 'sa'
439.2	had] above 'could have'
439.17	what] 'w' over 'th'
439.20	How] 'H' over 'A'
440.14	her equable] 'her' over 'an'
440.20	put down] over wiped-out 'made her'
440.22	and his] over wiped-out 'but soon'
440.30	Nothing—] dash cancels exclamation mark
441.17	heard] above caret
442.15	committed] 'c' over 'p'
442.15–16	burial-ground] preceded by cancelled 'old'
442.16	that] over wiped-out 'top'
442.22	wormwood] above 'pear'
442.32	that, in] over wiped-out 'in the co'
443.27	stairs] over wiped-out 'gar'
443.30	pungent] above 'virtues'
443.31	like] over wiped-out 'that she'
444.3	old] preceded by cancelled 'the'
444.3	laid] over wiped-out 'put it'
444.6	shivering] 's' over 'a'
444.14	Saints] 'S' over 'the'
444.21	afterwards] 'w' over 'h'
444.24	promising] 'pro' over 'wa'
444.26	hoar] over wiped-out 'fro'
444.32	naturally] above caret
444.32	autumn] 'au' over wiped-out 'fall'
444.33	begin to] over wiped-out 'soon cover'
445.3	show of] 'show' above cancelled 'petty arts'; 'of' over wiped-out 'cha'
445.6	follies] 'fol' over 'del'

445.8	and indeed] over wiped-out 'the atmosp'
445.13–14	burial ground] above 'grave'
445.20	position] over wiped-out 'stand-point'
445.31	out] and wiped-out 'from that'
446.1	fearing] over wiped-out 'a stran'
446.10	whether . . . saw] above caret
446.10–11	wreath of] above 'vapor'
446.17	have] over wiped-out 'men'
446.20	marble] over wiped-out '[ ] pillars'
446.24	material] above 'substance'
446.29	would] above caret
446.30	plowed] over wiped-out 'will'
446.30	homes] over wiped-out 'who'
447.1	themselves] MS 'himselvs'; 'v' over 'f'
447.1	characters] initial 'c' over 's'
447.6	than that] altered from partly wiped-out 'that they'
447.9	and beautiful] 'and bea' over wiped-out 'in its pro'
447.10	atmosphere] 'a' over 'at'
447.19	the] 't' over 'p'
447.19	a subtle] 'a' over 'so'; 's' over wiped-out 'm'
447.23	something] 'thi' over wiped-out 'wh'
447.32	to] over wiped-out 'the'
448.6	all] altered from 'alo'

THE DOLLIVER ROMANCE

*449.0	Fragments of a Romance.] cancelled in pencil; added above in pencil, probably not NH's hand, is 'A Scene from the Dolliver Romance'
*449.4–21	Old . . . Doctor,] MS faded to the point of invisibility; text from *Atlantic Monthly*
450.4	rusty] above cancelled 'aged'
450.14	experimental] above caret; the preceding 'a' then mended to 'an'

450.15	long ago] above caret
450.16	reposited] above caret
450.31	twinge] followed by cancelled 'was'
*451.3	himself] followed by a second 'himself' cancelled in pencil, perhaps not by NH
451.8	multitudinous] 'tu' above caret
451.16	that] over wiped-out 'which'
451.17	between the bed-curtains] above caret
451.27	seemed to have] above caret and cancelled 'had'
451.28	in the] 'in' above caret
451.32	men—] dash cancels comma
452.4	Christian] above caret following cancelled 'man'
452.8–9	in the earlier days] above cancelled 'among the Puritans days'
452.9	or] above caret
452.10	would] 'wou' over wiped-out 'only'
452.10	as] followed by cancelled 'as'
452.11	dispenser] 'dis-	' over wiped-out 'phys-'
452.12–13	followed his business] above caret and cancelled 'practised'
452.16	the symbolic snake] above caret and cancelled 'this'
452.23	only] above caret
452.31	it was] above caret
452.32	doomed] above caret
453.2	might scarcely] above caret and cancelled 'would hardly'
453.9	taste] above caret and cancelled 'drop'
453.9	taken] above caret and cancelled 'tasted'
453.28	poor] above caret
453.32	fashion.] followed by cancelled 'It was said to have been originally'
454.3–4	the beloved . . . youth,] above caret
454.5–6	as . . . ragged,] above caret
454.9	(as] parenthesis cancels comma
454.9–10	and their attire . . . hue] above caret
454.12	him] above caret
454.29	a] above caret

456.5	Dr.] over wiped-out 'the'
456.5	cheerily] above caret
456.11	poor] over 'more'
456.14	mouth] above caret
456.18	the kiss] above caret and cancelled 'it'
456.20	grandpapa] above caret and cancelled 'me'
456.21	the table] above caret and cancelled 'breakfast'
456.24	delicately] 'd' over wiped-out 's'
456.27	his] over wiped-out 'the'
456.32	these] 'se' over wiped-out 'y'
456.33	companions] above caret
457.13	The] over wiped-out 'for'; preceding period mended from semicolon
457.13	doctor's] above caret after cancelled 'old man's'
457.13–14	poor Bessy's offspring,] above caret
457.17	their] above caret
457.20	dead] above caret
457.31	features] above cancelled 'faces'
457.32	great-grandchild] 'ea' over 'an'
458.1	Dr. Dolliver] 'Dr. Do' over wiped-out 'the doct'
458.32	pretty] above caret
459.15	from] above caret before cancelled 'out of'
459.16	her widowed husband,] above caret after cancelled 'him'
459.23	brass] above caret after cancelled 'elf' of original 'itself'
459.23	have seen,] followed by cancelled 'it lost the greater'; above is cancelled 'the inauspi'
459.26	deposited] above caret after cancelled 'buried'
459.32	so] 's' over wiped-out 'b'
459.33	then—] dash cancels comma
460.1	good—] dash cancels comma
460.4	all] above caret
460.12	doctor] 'd' over 'D'
460.24	throughout his] 'throughout' mended from 'throught'; 'his' above caret
460.24	personally] above caret
461.1	cure.] followed by cancelled '; and it was prob-

	ably the result of the same scrupulosity that Dr. Dolliver always declined to enter the medical profession'
461.28	rustic] above caret and cancelled 'rough'
461.29	humble] above caret and cancelled 'rustic'
461.33	marble] above caret
462.1	and] over wiped-out ', cons'
462.20	their] mended from 'the'
462.20	fellow-citizen.] above caret and cancelled 'inhabitant'
462.21	that had] 'that' above caret
462.25	patriarchal] 'patriar' over wiped-out 'venerable'
462.31	Doctorate] 'Do' over wiped-out 'title'
463.4	public] over wiped-out 'people's'; followed by cancelled 'memory'
463.13	indurated] 'ind' over wiped-out 'yea'
463.16	bring] mended from 'be'
463.17	Grandsir Dolliver] above caret and cancelled 'him'
463.17	as] followed by cancelled 'being'
463.23	that] mended from 'these'
464.1	smiles] above caret and cancelled 'is'
464.1	whom] above caret
464.12	Age] 'A' over 'a'
464.19	be smoothed] 'be' above caret
464.20	laid] terminal 'ly' wiped out
464.31	with the] over wiped-out 'in some'
465.3	cheery] 'y' over wiped-out 'ing'
465.8	bring him] 'him' above caret
465.10	old Grandsir] in MS, 'old' followed by 'Dr.' above caret
465.13	the] above caret
465.15	Pansie] 'P' over 'p'
465.16	as if] above caret after cancelled 'that'
465.21	and chiming] above caret
465.30	stole] above caret after cancelled 'came'
466.8	just now] above caret
466.13	Dolliver] 'D' over 'to'

466.14	pleasanter] above underlined uncancelled 'sharper'
466.17	or] followed by cancelled 'his own'
466.17	Pansie] preceded by cancelled 'Little'
466.18	hasty-pudding] above caret
466.20	odd] above caret
466.22	ascertained] 'as' over wiped-out possible 'lea'
466.24–25	an . . . revelation] above 'or . . . parents'
466.26	as . . . seem] above 'them, in some instances'
467.3	in] over wiped-out 'the'
467.5	indelibly] above 'plaister'
467.5	font] followed by four short vertical lines, usually a signal for rearrangement of elements; a line leads to a caret following 'know it'
467.8–9	leaving . . . house.] above 'called it away. If . . . Pansie's'
467.10	often] above uncancelled 'sometimes'
467.12	having been] above 'mother of Acadian'
467.14	a] over wiped-out 'the'
467.16–17	no sympathy . . . people] above caret placed in error before comma following 'it'
467.18	man.] period mended from comma; followed by cancelled 'to which'
467.19	If] above cancelled 'When'
467.26	accustomed] above uncancelled 'wont to'
467.27	a variety of] above cancelled 'some'
467.28	had] above cancelled 'were'
467.29	days] above cancelled 'settlement'
467.30	adopted] followed by cancelled ', not with'
468.4–5	doubted . . . quite to] followed by cancelled 'decide', the whole above caret
468.6	considerably] above uncancelled 'much'
468.7	singularly] 'si' over wiped-out 'gl'
468.13	in terms] over wiped-out 'anath'
468.13	most] over wiped-out 'highest'
468.14–15	by . . . lived] above is cancelled 'knowledge to which he was'

468.15–16	and to . . . ornament] above 'affirmed . . . fellow-men. Our old'
468.18	fully] above caret
468.20	far] above cancelled 'much shaken in his'
468.25	(he . . . plants)] in top margin of MS page
468.26	little] above caret
468.28	or] over wiped-out ', the'
468.30–31	were . . . character] above caret after uncancelled 'had'
468.31	learned] over wiped-out 'famous'
469.3–5	They . . . them] above 'and told . . . hundred fold.'
469.9	perhaps,] followed by cancelled 'in consequence'
469.14	unless . . . secret] above caret
469.15	imagine the] followed by cancelled 'solemn and'
469.20	putting . . . winter] above 'nurtured . . .possible'
469.23–24	(Here . . . flowers)] in space at end of paragraph
469.27	shrubs] above uncancelled 'plants'
469.28	vegetables] above caret
469.30	thus early] above caret
470.4	were employed] above original 'talents lay in', 'lay' uncancelled
470.5	analysis] above caret and uncancelled 'research'
470.7	him] followed by cancelled 'to wonder and even'
*470.8	he] above caret; not hand of NH
470.10	mock-mystery] above obliteration, apparently of the same word
470.14–15	into extensive] lined through as if a cancellation, but integral with sentence
470.19	luxuriance] 'l' over 'b'
470.25	Grandfather] 'G' over 'g'
470.31	manuscript] 'man' over wiped-out 'writ'
471.3	Edward] horizontal lines above and below may indicate that space was originally left for inserting a name
471.3–4	the conduct of] above caret
471.8	simple-minded] above caret

471.12	abilities] above caret
471.18	world—] dash cancels comma
471.20–21	and whether . . . them] above 'real . . . nostrums, is more'
471.23	Brazen Serpent] above cancelled 'Galen's Head'
471.32	sad and] 'and' above caret
472.5–6	wronging . . . what] horizontal lines above and below, beginning with ' | -ing' of 'wronging'
472.7	eye] terminal 'e' over 'es'
472.7	might] followed by cancelled 'by'
472.10	as if . . . shaken] above caret
427.13–16	Is not . . . ill?] above 'and delusive . . . disastrous'
472.19	One] 'after a' added above but not integrated into sentence
472.19	awoke and] above original 'wife, seeing'
472.19	seeing] 's' over wiped-out 'f'
472.21	arose in] preceding comma cancels parenthesis; 'in' over wiped-out 'of'
472.24	sunk] 'su' over wiped-out 'his'
472.24	out] 'ou' over wiped-out 'of'
472.27–29	and it . . . passion] above original 'legacy . . . beside it. Doctors were called'
472.30–33	It may . . . survive it.] above original 'jury . . . contrivances with'
473.9	selling them.] followed by a large caret extending through 5 MS lines and the direction 'see other side' indicating a transposition of paragraph elements which CENTENARY carries out; see also alteration entry at 474.6
*473.9	lost] above caret; not hand of NH
*473.17	case] above caret placed in error after comma following 'for'; not in hand of NH
*473.21	honored] MS 'hon- | ed'; 'hon- | ' followed by marginal asterisk in an ink not NH's
473.22	iniquity] second 'i' mended from possible 'ie'
473.25	bleached] 'c' over partial 'h'
*473.25	had] above caret; not in hand of NH
*473.32	Pansie] MS 'Posy' mended in hand not NH's

474.1	perhaps] above caret
474.2	lived] 'live' over wiped-out 'died'
474.6	man.] followed by a two-tiered caret and the direction '(look before)' related to NH's instruction described in alteration entry at 473.9
474.7	and piety] above caret
*474.9	the oldest] 'the' above caret, perhaps not in hand of NH
474.10	inevitably] above caret
474.11	all his] over wiped-out 'the old'
474.13	suspicion] initial 's' over 'p'
474.14–15	careless and] circled as if signalling revision; 'l' over 'f'
474.16	world] followed by cancelled 'tosses carelessly'
474.21	though] above caret
474.23	peculiarly] above caret
474.28	either] initial 'e' cancels comma
*474.29	soul] terminal letter, probably 'd', obliterated in an ink not NH's
474.31	scent] above uncancelled 'smell'
475.3	plants] over wiped-out 'flowers'
475.4–5	shingle . . . roof] above caret and uncancelled 'trowell'
475.9	vast] over wiped-out 'great'
475.10	This] over wiped-out 'which'; the preceding period mended from comma
475.10	much] 'm' over wiped-out 'f'
475.13	shrivelled, cankered] MS 'shivelled, can' over wiped-out 'Pansie and the'
*475.13	leaf,] followed by 'and' cancelled in different ink, probably not by NH
*475.15	it] squeezed in above comma following 'about'; probably not NH's hand
475.17	vigorous] 'v' over 'p'
475.18	plant] 'p' over vertical stroke
475.21	comically] 'com' over wiped-out 'oddly'
475.22	his] mended from 'the'
475.22	naughty] 'na' over wiped-out 'ugl'
475.30	wear] followed by cancelled 'one of'

475.31	and one] above uncancelled 'where they'
475.32	and] followed by cancelled 'made'
476.1	the] over 'her'
476.3	death,] comma over semicolon
476.7	beauty,] followed by cancelled 'and, at the same time,'
476.14–17	And with . . . of it.] above MS 'follies; and therefore . . . exclamation'
476.24	dropping] 'd' over wiped-out 'fl'
476.24	old gentleman] above caret and uncancelled 'he'
*476.26	apprehensive] MS 'apprensive' mended with insertion of 'hen' above 'en', not by NH
476.28	and] over 'an a'
476.29	open] over 'ajar'
476.30	great-] above 'by'
476.31	our] 'o' over 'D'
476.32– 477.2	The kitten . . . back.] added in space at end of paragraph
477.5	swinging] underlined as if to signal possible revision
477.8–10	with outstretched . . . Dolliver] above 'fled onward, plying . . . ominous'
477.12	a] over 'him'
477.15	suddenly] above caret
477.19	Grandpapa] final 'a' over 'p'
477.20	recollecting her remedy] above caret
477.21	murmured to himself] underlined as if to signal possible revision
477.29	sensibilities] above underscored but uncancelled 'fitful sympathies'
478.5–6	and . . . memorial] above original 'so . . . it. He . . . repugnance'
478.7	to] over wiped-out 'at'
478.23	of his] preceded by cancelled 'of his'
478.29	(Here . . . window)] inserted between paragraphs
479.1	a flickering] 'a' above caret
479.24–25	Sight . . . &c] added in space at end of paragraph

479.26	(He . . . time.)] inserted between paragraphs
480.5	(if] parenthesis cancels comma
480.16	save] over wiped-out 'but one'
480.20	It] over wiped-out 'And'
480.31–32	It dropped into it with] over wiped-out 'It diffused itself [sparkl]'
481.3	at] over wiped-out 'it'
481.33	he was] 'w' over 'ha'
482.2	time] over wiped-out 'toil'
482.7	trifle] followed by cancelled 'to an antiquarian'
482.13	so] above caret
482.13	one night] over wiped-out 'he thought'
482.14	suddenly] above 'had be- |'
482.14	bethought] 'b' over 'd'
482.15	said,] followed by wiped-out closing parenthesis
*482.27	want] followed by 'only' cancelled in different ink, perhaps not by NH
483.22–23	the sleepers] 'e' of 'the' over 'em'
483.29	were] 'er' over 'it'
484.6–7	in the glass] above caret
484.7	to] above 'but'
484.8	gleaming brightness] horizontal lines above and below
484.12	had] 'h' over 's'
484.18	knee] 'ee' over 'ees'
484.21	he held] above caret
484.21	that] above caret
*484.23	would] followed by 'would', cancelled in different ink, perhaps not by NH
484.24–25	He . . . possible.] added in space at end of paragraph
484.31	nervous] 'r' over 'v'
485.10	towards] followed by cancelled possible 'of'
485.13	lately] above 'was in'
485.18	(I] parenthesis cancels comma
485.23	dose] 'd' over possible 'so'
485.24	on] over wiped-out 'after'
*485.25	it;] 'it' squeezed in before previously inscribed semicolon, in hand not NH's

485.29	was] 'w' over partial 'h'
485.29	already] initial 'a' over 'h'
*485.30	Nevertheless] 'the' above caret, in hand not NH's
*485.32	omit it] 'it' above caret, in hand not NH's
486.6–7	Another . . . feverish.] above caret
*486.7	two] squeezed in before 'or' in hand not NH's
486.20	such] over 'a com'
486.27	my fair] 'my' over wiped-out 'the'
486.28	my neighbors] 'my' over wiped-out 'the pu'
487.3	matter,] followed by wiped-out quotation mark
487.26	meeting] above 'church'
488.2	by] above caret
488.12	half] 'h' over wiped-out 'f'
488.23	and . . . it] above caret
489.2	be . . . pall-bearers] above uncancelled 'walk to his funeral yet'
*489.4	itself] above cancelled 'himself', in hand not NH's
489.28	To my] over wiped-out 'Do you'
489.32	cursed] above caret
490.20	who survived] above 'fairly beyond'
490.26	they] 'th' over 'w'
491.7–8	(The . . . it)] added at end of paragraph
491.22	dullness] above cancelled 'brightness'
491.30	interpreted] 'i' over 'h'
491.32	still] 't' over 'k'
492.13	however,] above caret
492.28	long?"] followed by wiped out 'Seven'
492.29	ago] over 'since'
493.4	convinced] 'co' over 'he'
493.14	hour] 'ho' over 'ol'
493.18	right!] exclamation cancels comma
495.11	with] 'w' over wiped-out 'that'
495.20–21	The . . . himself.] above 'frightened . . . bottle'
495.24	frantically,] followed by cancelled 'clasped both hands across his forehead,'
495.24–25	as if . . . him,] above partial caret
495.28–29	(He . . . look.)] above 'There . . . over'

495.31	and] 'a' over wiped-out 'of' and the preceding comma subsequently added
496.2	his] above caret
496.3	dark] above caret
496.19	with] 'w' over 'b'
496.20	seemed] 'se' over 'ha'
497.1	am] 'a' over 'h'
497.2	glad] 'gl' over 'has'

ANCILLARY DOCUMENTS

499.14	close] 'l' over 'e'
500.22	it] over wiped-out 'li'
501.17	—and] dash over 'a'
504.6	idea] 'i' over 'n'
504.21	decypherable] after 'y', a letter 'f' cancelled
505.7	frown] over 'groove'
507.12–13	Express . . . humbug.] added squeezed into top margin of MS page
507.14	Septimius] 'e' over 't'
508.4	theological] 'h' over 'o'
508.10	morn^g—] dash cancels comma
508.14	into] 'in' over 'co'
508.17	Briton] 'B' over 'y'
508.19	buries the] over wiped-out 'is charged by'
508.23	immortality] 'im' over wiped-out 'the'
509.8	a supervision] 'a' over wiped-out 'as'
509.18	not] over 'with'
509.26	The . . . end] interlined between paragraphs
510.9	receives] MS 'reci' over wiped-out 'takes'
510.12	sometimes] 'some-	' above 'often', followed on next line by cancelled 'turns' preceding 'times'
510.15	Uncle] over wiped-out 'who'
513.15	in] above caret
513.23	grimy] 'gr' over wiped-out 'pr'
513.29	From] 'ro' over 'or'

515.17	him. He leaves] 'He leav' over wiped-out '; he leaves' and the preceding period inserted
516.4	mother] 'mo' over wiped-out 'father'
516.13	Bloody footstep.] added in space at end of paragraph
516.27	his wife] 'his' over 'the'
517.11	heir] 'h' over 'w'
517.13	alchymist] MS 'achhymist' mended to 'aclchymist'
517.15	by] over 'the'
517.19	The other member] 'The other m' over wiped-out 'After generation'
518.13	at] 'a' over 'l'
518.19	fell] over 'was'
518.29	hereditary] 'h' over wiped-out 'ch'
519.10–11	Allusions . . . seen.] added at end of paragraph
519.11	Kezia] 'K' over 'Z'
519.21	On] over wiped-out 'The'
519.26	excitement.] period mended from comma
519.28	witnesses] 'w' over 's'
520.2	here will be] over wiped-out 'Third Scene:—'
520.9	relative] 'rela' over wiped-out 'descen'
520.14	should] 'sho' over wiped-out 'not'
520.22	Aunt Keziah comes] over wiped-out 'The minister comes'
521.3–4	used . . . sacraments.] above 'the . . . goblet'
521.4–5	once . . . out] above 'iron-bound box, that . . . great'
521.15	to give an account] over wiped-out 'Fifth scene'
521.18	couched] 'co' over wiped-out 'gr'
522.24	those] 'ose' over 'at'
522.27	transitory] over wiped-out 'he[ ]'
523.11–12	The . . . it.] added in space at end of paragraph
523.28–29	Iron-box. . . . untold.] added in space at end of paragraph
524.7	behaves] 'be' over 'an'
524.8	suspicious] 'spici' over wiped-out 'perstit'
524.12	at] over 'of'

524.22	The Doctor] 'The Doc' over wiped-out 'Septimius'
524.29–30	Before . . . fails.] added in space at end of paragraph
525.1–2	There . . . box.] inserted at top of MS page
525.6	being] over wiped-out 'p[ ]g'
525.7	estate] initial 'e' over 'h'
525.23	stage] over wiped-out 'as[ ]e'
525.26	The old English] over wiped-out 'At another stage'
526.10	ridicule] 'rid' over wiped-out 'g[ ]'
526.31	because] 'be' over wiped-out 'as'
527.11	vase] above cancelled 'goblet'
527.26	dies.] followed by wiped-out 'and'; the period over wiped-out comma
527.29	cinders] 'cind' over wiped-out 'the c'
528.18	Do] over 'do'
530.14–17	(It. . . . woods.)] evidently inscribed last in the only available space, at top of first MS page of scenario
531.11	younger] 'yo' over 'le'
531.22	wishes] 'w' over uncrossed 't'
532.18	war—] dash cancels comma
532.21	agency] 'ag' over 'an'
534.16	an] 'a' over 'in'
535.27	witches] 'c' over 'h'
541.4	ridiculously] 'd' over 'lo'
541.12	(for] parenthesis cancels comma
541.22	in] above caret
541.29	tend] preceded by cancelled 'in'
542.19	that] initial 't' over question mark
543.4	happy] 'h' over 'rep'
543.26	makes] followed by cancelled 'him'
544.21	lead] terminal 'ing' wiped out
547.12	receipt] preceded by cancelled 'bottle'
548.13	longer—] dash cancels comma
551.1	feeling . . . torment] above caret
551.1	fret] over 'fire'; also written at top of MS page
551.3–4	this confused . . . things] above caret

551.9	hobbled hastily] above 'stole to the', 'stole' uncancelled
551.9	half-hoping] above 'looking-glass'
551.9–10	He was . . . by the] MS 'he was . . . by the' above cancelled 'with almost a hope that he should'
551.11	form,] followed by cancelled 'which'
551.15	that we] MS 'that we are' followed by cancelled 'never believe it'
551.15	really] above caret
551.17	chill] above caret
551.17	torpor] followed by cancelled 'that strangely muffles us in its chill garment'
551.18	which] above uncancelled 'that'
551.20–21	might now be] above caret
551.21	his form] 'his' over 'bent'
551.28–29	the cheery . . . they] above caret placed in error before a comma following 'him'
552.1	seemed] followed by cancelled 'ready'
552.3	the] over 'a'
552.6–8	Somehow . . . quaint] above 'own . . . kiss her'
552.8	great-grandpapa] second 'g' over 'd'
552.11	an] above 'evening'
552.11	evening] followed by cancelled 'even as late'; above the cancel is interlined cancelled 'and in'
552.11	of a] MS 'of a of a' in error, one 'of a' added above caret
552.13	moments] 'mo' over wiped-out 'brigh'
552.15	kissed] 'ki' over wiped-out 'ga'
552.17–18	mingled . . . all] above caret
552.19	ruddy] above caret
552.20	hearth] 'he' over 'ca'
552.20	I hope, the] over wiped-out 'passes it in [ ]tes'
552.21	consolatory] above 'a glimpse'
552.22	woman] above uncancelled 'spirit'
552.23	her] 'h' over 'a'
552.23	brief] 'br' over 'ea'

552.23	earthly pilgrimage] 'earthly pilgrim- | ' under-scored
552.24	stole . . . opening] above caret
552.24	permitted to] followed by cancelled 'do all but'
552.25	dimly] over wiped-out 'faintly'
552.26	meditations] 'ions' over 'ed'
552.27	call] over wiped-out 'would'
552.31	of] above caret
553.1	lying . . . ground] above caret
553.3, 6	Grandsir] 'G' over 'g'
553.3	remembered] 'mem' above caret after 'm' of 'rembered'

COMPOSITORIAL STINTS IN
THE DOLLIVER ROMANCE, CHAPTER I

At the upper left on MS page 1 is the name of Leary. The page 3 bracket "al[most" (Centenary 451.1) begins *Atlantic Monthly*, XIV (July, 1864) 102ª.28 and the page 6 bracket "being [haunted" (Centenary 453.5) begins *Atlantic* 103ª.28; they are apparently not stint markings. Leary's take of almost eight pages ends after 270 *Atlantic* lines at 104ª.8 "pur-]port" (Centenary 454.29), and Phillips's name is signed at the first opening on page 9 (Centenary 455.5). The page 12 bracket "in [the" (Centenary 457.20) begins *Atlantic* 105ª.42 and "197 Phillips" is entered immediately below. Phillips's second stint of 192 *Atlantic* lines ends on page 17, where Cormack takes over at the first opening (Centenary 461.15) and sets 148 *Atlantic* lines until Phillips resumes at a paragraph break eleven lines from the foot of page 21 (Centenary 464.15) and sets 91 *Atlantic* lines to the end of the chapter.

Two of these compositors are known to us from other *Atlantic* settings of Hawthorne: Cormack did two stints of "Chiefly about War-matters" in 1862 and John Leary a short take of "A London Suburb" in early 1863.